The Bloomsbury Companion to  ـᴜphy

Other volumes in the series of Bloomsbury Companions:

Forthcoming in Philosophy:

The Bloomsbury Companion to Continental Philosophy

Edited by

John Mullarkey

and

Beth Lord

B L O O M S B U R Y
LONDON · NEW DELHI · NEW YORK · SYDNEY

Bloomsbury Academic
An imprint of Bloomsbury Publishing Plc

50 Bedford Square	175 Fifth Avenue
London	New York
WC1B 3DP	NY 10010
UK	USA

www.bloomsbury.com

First published in 2009 by Continuum

British Library Cataloguing-in-Publication Data
A catalogue record for this book is available from the British Library.

ISBN: HB: 978-0-8264-9830-4
PB: 978-1-4411-3199-7

Library of Congress Cataloging-in-Publication Data
Continuum companion to continental philosophy
The Bloomsbury companion to continental philosophy / edited by John Mullarkey and
Beth Lord. – First [edition].
pages cm. – (Bloomsbury companions)
"First published in 2009 by Continuum."
Includes bibliographical references and index.
ISBN 978-1-4411-3199-7 (pbk.) – ISBN (invalid) 978-1-4411-9788-7 (epub) –
ISBN 978-0-8264-9830-4 (hardcover) – ISBN (invalid) 978-1-4411-2890-4 (ebook pdf)
1. Continental philosophy. 2. Philosophy, Modern–21st century. I. Mullarkey, John,
editor of compilation. II. Lord, Beth, editor of compilation. III. Title.
B805.C66 2013
190'.9051–dc23
2012037246

Typeset by Newgen Imaging Systems Pvt Ltd, Chennai, India
Printed and bound in Great Britain

Contents

Contents

Contributors

Andrew Aitken completed his PhD at Goldsmiths College, University of London, on Gaston Bachelard's Historical Epistemology contra Bergson and Husserl. His research concerns the interaction between positivist attitudes to science within continental philosophy and those of ontological critique, bearing largely upon the problem of technology.

Gary Banham is Reader in Transcendental Philosophy at Manchester Metropolitan University. He is the author of *Kant's Transcendental Imagination* (2006) and co-editor (with Diane Morgan) of *Cosmopolitics and the Emergence of a Future* (2007). He is also the general editor of the Palgrave Macmillan series Renewing Philosophy.

Rosi Braidotti is Distinguished Professor in the Humanities at Utrecht University, founding director of the Centre for Humanities and Honorary Visiting Professor in the Law School at Birkbeck College, University of London. Her books include: *Patterns of Dissonance* (1991), *Nomadic Subjects* (1994), *Metamorphoses: Towards a Materialist Theory of Becoming* (2002) and *Transpositions: On Nomadic Ethics* (2006).

Douglas Burnham is a Professor of Philosophy at Staffordshire University. He has written extensively on Kant and Nietzsche, and less extensively on Heidegger, Derrida and hermeneutics. Current projects include work on Nietzsche and literature, on wine and sensibility, and on art and space.

James Burton researches and teaches on a range of topics in continental philosophy and cultural theory, with particular interests in the philosophy of memory, Henri Bergson, poststructuralism, and philosophical and cultural theories of fiction. He teaches cultural theory at Goldsmiths College, University of London, where he completed his PhD on Bergson, Saint Paul and Philip K. Dick in 2008.

Jonathan Lahey Dronsfield is a Reader in Theory and Philosophy of Art at the University of Reading, and sits on the Executive Committee of the Forum for European Philosophy, London School of Economics. Currently he is working on a book on Derrida and visual art.

Melanie Ebdon is a lecturer in English Literature at Staffordshire University. Her teaching and research specialism is primarily in ecocriticism, with further interests in postcolonial criticism, magical realism and Gothic literature.

Hector Kollias is a lecturer in French at King's College, London. He is currently working on two projects: on the relation between queer theory and queer writing in contemporary France; and on the inception and development of the notion of literature from the 18th century to the present. He has published articles on philosophy, literature and literary theory.

Bill Martin is a philosophy professor at DePaul University in Chicago. He is the author of nine books, most recently *Ethical Marxism: The Categorical Imperative of Liberation* (2008). He is also a musician, as well as an avid bicyclist and chess player. At present he is working on a book on Alain Badiou and the renewal of the communist hypothesis.

Todd May is Kathryn and Calhoun Lemon Professor of Philosophy at Clemson University. He is the author of nine books of philosophy, including *The Political Thought of Jacques Rancière* (2008) and *Death* (2009). His area of specialization is recent French thought, especially Foucault, Deleuze and Rancière.

Dorothea Olkowski is a Professor of Philosophy at the University of Colorado at Colorado Springs. She is the author of *The Universal (In the Realm of the Sensible)* (2007) and *Gilles Deleuze and The Ruin of Representation* (1999). She has co-edited a number of books including *Feminist Interpretations of Maurice Merleau-Ponty* (2006) and *The Other – Feminist Reflections in Ethics* (2007). She is currently working on a book entitled *Nature, Ethics, Love*.

John Protevi is an Associate Professor of French Studies at Louisiana State University. He is the author of *Time and Exteriority: Aristotle, Heidegger, Derrida* (1994) and *Political Physics: Deleuze, Derrida and the Body Politic* (2001). His current research is at the intersection of dynamical systems theory, affective cognition and politics. His latest book is *Political Affect: Connecting the Social and the Somatic* (2009).

Daniel W. Smith teaches in the Department of Philosophy at Purdue University. He has translated Gilles Deleuze's *Francis Bacon: logique de la sensation* and *Critique et clinique* (with Michael A. Greco), as well as Pierre Klossowski's *Nietzsche et le cercle vicieux* and Isabelle Stengers' *Invention des sciences modernes*. He has published widely on topics in contemporary philosophy, and is currently completing a book on Gilles Deleuze.

Caroline Williams teaches political theory at Queen Mary, University of London. She is the author of *Contemporary French Philosophy: Modernity and the Persistence of the Subject* (2007) and is currently completing a book manuscript *Spinoza and Political Critique: Thinking the Political in the Wake of Althusser*.

Introduction

Beth Lord

The Bloomsbury Companion to Continental Philosophy (or *BCCP*) is a snapshot of continental philosophy as it is practised now. Through fourteen essays by leading researchers in the field and key resources for study and reference, it presents continental philosophy in a new way: as a dynamic and multi-faceted subject contributing to, and gaining from, the many other disciplines with which it continually intersects.

There are several companions, encyclopaedias and dictionaries to continental philosophy already on the market. What makes the *BCCP* innovative and different? First, it is organized according to thematic areas of continental philosophy, and not according to proper names or schools of thought. Second, each essay focuses on what continental philosophy is today and how it is practised now.

Most of the other guides on the market have a familiar format: they are organized chronologically to mirror university survey courses, their chapters categorized according to well-defined philosophical movements. Starting with Kant and the German idealists, they move chapter by chapter through Hegel, Marx, Kierkegaard and Nietzsche before considering each of the major philosophical movements of the twentieth century, from phenomenology and existentialism to critical theory and poststructuralism. These books are often excellent: they are valuable in providing an overview of a historical movement of thought and in marking the development of continental philosophy through the twentieth century. But their drawbacks are many. Those published to date tend to finish on the high note of poststructuralism, the latest philosophical movement amenable to treatment as a complete and distinct whole. Current post- or non-poststructuralist thinkers cannot, it seems (or cannot *yet*) be grouped together to form the next 'chapter' in continental philosophy. There is a certain set of ideas and methods thought to be common to Jean-François Lyotard, Jacques Derrida, Julia Kristeva, et al., but after that, things start to get messy. How should a 'companion' categorize the work of Alain Badiou, for instance, which may be considered 'poststructuralist' in some of its central concerns, but uses methods and arrives at conclusions which are opposed to poststructuralism in every conceivable way? The problem of fitting the varied experiments and outputs of a philosopher into one neat chapter-category is not restricted to current thinkers, of course: while the early Merleau-Ponty, for example, undoubtedly belongs in a 'Phenomenology' chapter, some aspects of his later work fit him more comfortably among the poststructuralists, other aspects amongst a more recent grouping of continental naturalists. The problem of categorizing a thinker becomes still more acute when his or her place in 'the tradition' has not yet been decided.

Furthermore, without being able to appraise his or her entire career, it is often uncertain whether and when a current thinker should be counted a 'continental philosopher'. Is Slavoj Žižek a philosopher, a cultural theorist, a psychoanalyst or something else entirely? And when does a thinker *become* a philosopher, discussable on a par with Kant, Husserl and Derrida? In the past, the publication and translation of a 'magnum opus' has been taken to be necessary for recognition as a continental philosopher, but today's philosophers – Jacques Rancière, Giorgio Agamben and even Derrida himself are good examples – are as likely to distinguish themselves through articles and short works as through big, career-defining books. The lack of a single canonical text adds to the difficulty of placing contemporary figures in the historical narrative of continental philosophy. Lacking clear categories for philosophers practising today, and uncertain of their ultimate place in the historical narrative, the standard anthologies tend to leave them out. This has the unfortunate (if unintentional) effect of suggesting that continental philosophy comes to an end with the Derridean legacy, with continental philosophy dissolved into deconstructivist 'theory' at the end of the twentieth century.

The *BCCP* is not organized in this way. Not to be too millenarian about it, this is a book whose outlook is not from the end of the twentieth century, but from the beginning of the twenty-first. Our aim is decidedly not to add the next 'chapter' to the narrative of continental philosophy from Kant to poststructuralism. Perhaps in fifty years' time, the shape, structure and commonalities of such a 'chapter' will have become clear. Here, we focus on the mess of philosophical thought going on around us – uncategorizable (in terms of fixed historical epochs) and ill-defined (in terms of coherent bodies of thought) *now*. Indeed, if poststructuralism teaches us anything, it is to be suspicious of fixed categories and definitions such as those through which 'continental philosophy' is often presented. This book is 'post-poststructural' in that it is compiled 'after' the poststructuralist injunction to renounce such fixity (though we do not pretend to have succeeded in doing so altogether). If there is a chronological starting-point for this book, poststructuralism is it, because continental philosophers today are in most cases working 'after' – i.e. within, through or in response to – that very influential set of methods and ideas from the latter half of the twentieth century.

Philosophers 'after poststructuralism', therefore, play an important role in this book. Gilles Deleuze, Alain Badiou, Jacques Rancière, Judith Butler,

Michel Henry, Isabelle Stengers and Slavoj Žižek are some of the philosophers you will encounter most frequently here (along with many and various less well-known philosophers working in specific fields). But the chapters of this book are not dedicated to the 'names' of twentieth- or twenty-first-century continental philosophy. Instead, they are divided according to some of the thematic areas continental philosophers are working on now: difference, life, consciousness and the body, science, art, literature, psychoanalysis, sex and gender, metaphysics, politics, and ethics. In addition, the book features two meta-philosophical essays, one on the question of research methods in continental philosophy, the other on continental philosophy's future. These two essays open and close the collection by considering many of the same questions: What is continental philosophy? How do we characterize it now, and how will we recognize it in the future? How do we, as philosophers, theorists, practitioners and students, *do* continental philosophy, and how do we make it what it will become?

This book presents a synchronic look at the practice of continental philosophy today, rather than a diachronic look at its history and development. That is not to say that the history and development of ideas are ignored; all the essays commissioned for this book deal with problems and questions with long genealogies in ancient philosophy, the Enlightenment and the philosophical movements of the twentieth century. This is particularly relevant to those chapters concerned with 'traditional' philosophical topics (Daniel W. Smith's essay on metaphysics and ontology looks back to Plato, Aristotle and the Presocratics to explore the transformations achieved by Heidegger, Deleuze and Badiou), and to those closely bound up with developments initiated in the twentieth century (Todd May's chapter, 'Philosophies of Difference', focuses on Derrida, Levinas and Deleuze, three of the most influential thinkers of difference since 1960). But none of the essays featured here presents its area of continental philosophy solely through the history of its development. Partly, that is because we deem a retelling of that history to be unnecessary. We believe that a basic familiarity with 'continental philosophy' from the early modern period through to the mid-twentieth century can be assumed of readers of this book. Since that familiarity is bound to be selective (for students, general readers and academics alike), an A to Z glossary of thinkers and movements follows the main essays, as a reference guide to the major names and movements of continental philosophy from Kant to poststructuralism. Also included is a timeline (1750–2008) that charts the development of continental philosophy in political, scientific and artistic contexts, while the 'Resources' section directs readers to online sources for further research.

Freed up from summarizing the historical lineage of the field, the writers of the twelve main essays were asked to focus on the *very latest* work in their

own area of continental philosophy. The result is twelve core essays exploring what 'continental philosophy' is today. John Protevi's 'Philosophies of
Consciousness and the Body', for instance, shows how phenomenological
treatments of perception, affection and intersubjectivity have been transformed since the early 1990s, not only by 'pure' philosophers such as Michel
Henry, but especially by those considering philosophy alongside the biological
and cognitive sciences, such as Dan Zahavi, Francisco Varela and Natalie
Depraz. Protevi presents today's philosophies of consciousness and the body
both in reference to the phenomenology of Husserl, Heidegger and Merleau-
Ponty, and in dialogue with contemporary science and analytic philosophy of
mind. Hector Kollias's chapter, 'Psychoanalysis and Philosophy', explores the
work of contemporary philosophers – including Jacques Rancière, Slavoj
Žižek and Judith Butler – in relation to the classical psychoanalytical positions of Freud and Lacan. He looks at the philosophical questions that
are now emerging from the productive convergence of philosophy and
psychoanalysis: questions of sexuality, ideology and radical ethics, for
instance. In her strongly contemporary chapter, 'Feminist Philosophy', Rosi
Braidotti calls poststructuralism and deconstruction the 'classical' positions
to which current feminist philosophy responds and seeks to move
beyond. When the once-subversive has become mainstream, she argues, the
challenge for feminist philosophy is to find the 'conceptual creativity' to
produce new forms of radicalism. Braidotti identifies new paths in
'post-anthropocentric' vitalist philosophies of embodiment, ecology and
biotechnology that have the potential to transform theories of sexuality and
the sex/gender distinction.

The turn to naturalism is prominent across the essays in this collection: so
much so that one could venture to say that the future of continental philosophy is naturalism, the point at which the gulf with analytic philosophy
may finally be bridged. Naturalism emerges in different forms through this
volume: materialism, vitalism, and eco-philosophy among them. Not only
Braidotti, but also Bill Martin ('Continental Marxist Thought'), Caroline
Williams ('Politics and Ethics'), and Douglas Burnham and Melanie Ebdon
('Philosophy, Literature, and Interpretation'), show that the embodied *ecological* environment is already a key theme for continental philosophy in the
early twenty-first century. Braidotti, Williams and Martin discuss how political positions have embraced the new naturalism: the ecological Marxism of
James O'Connor, the matter-realism of Donna Haraway, and the radical
immanentism of Elizabeth Grosz and William Connolly, for instance. Burnham
and Ebdon discuss a new field of literary analysis, 'ecocriticism', that makes
environmental thought a critical practice; it is a mode of *reading* texts that
causes us to reconsider the boundaries between 'natural' and 'human', the
'lived environment' and 'lived experience', both literarily and philosophically.

From this perspective, continental philosophy's connection to the sciences is potentially of more significance than its (historically, supposedly stronger) connection to the arts. The often fraught nature of the relationship between continental philosophy and science in the twentieth century – as experienced by Bergson, Bachelard, Husserl, Heidegger and others – is presented by Dorothea Olkowski ('Philosophies of Life') and Andrew Aitken ('Philosophies of Science'). These essays stress that, with the recent turn 'back' to life, matter and – in the case of Badiou – mathematics, continental philosophy finds a new and central place in contemporary culture, reflecting on the developments of biotechnology alongside variants of analytic naturalism and materialism. The philosophies of technology of Gilbert Simondon, Don Ihde and Bruno Latour, and the process philosophy of Isabelle Stengers, are important in this regard, as Aitken shows. Could this scientific priority threaten to open another gulf – this time between the natural sciences and the arts, *within* continental philosophy? Burnham and Ebdon suggest the contrary: that a scientific grounding is crucial to a philosophical understanding of art and literature. Along similar lines, Olkowski argues that the 'harmony between the natural and human sciences' is possible through the Bergsonian tradition of continental philosophy. Through this reconciliation, she stresses, continental philosophy finds a new way to address what Hannah Arendt calls 'the human condition' – in concrete connection to the earth.

The contemporary focus of the *BCCP* does not mean that continental philosophy is cut off from historical foundations. Our aim is to present continental philosophy as a dynamic set of practices occurring now, shaped by, but not wholly defined within, historical movements. This is nicely illustrated by Gary Banham's chapter, 'The Continental Tradition: Kant, Hegel, Nietzsche'. Beyond describing these thinkers as historical reference points (or mere sparring partners) for contemporary continental philosophy, Banham presents them in terms of notions of time in connection with language, representation and expression. He offers an interpretation of the texts of Kant, Hegel and Nietzsche as unfolding differently in time, and therefore as distinctively 'futural'. Banham considers the 'past' of continental philosophy as revealing the question of its future, and the 'future' of continental philosophy as necessarily involving its past expressions. Current and future philosophies, in being discussed and unfolded throughout this book, involve and reveal the genealogies of the problems and concepts they use. John Mullarkey's essay on 'The Future of Continental Philosophy' closes the collection by outlining some of the current themes that promise to become central in future work. However, he also problematizes the possibility of such a forecast, given continental philosophy's persistent ability to subvert the notions of its own predictability and of what counts as proper to philosophy (or even what counts as philosophy at all).

Notwithstanding this problematic of the future (and occasionally even exacerbating it), the essays collected in the *BCCP* reveal historical lineages that are sometimes ignored in narratives of the history of continental thought. If continental philosophy does not 'end' with Derrida, nor does it necessarily 'begin' with Kant. Thinkers like Etienne Balibar, Gilles Deleuze and Genevieve Lloyd find resources in the texts of Spinoza for addressing contemporary problems in politics, ethics and metaphysics. This collection reveals the extent to which contemporary thought increasingly sees Spinoza as foundational for the problems, questions and methods of continental philosophy. The chapters by Daniel W. Smith ('Metaphysics and Ontology'), Caroline Williams ('Politics and Ethics'), Bill Martin ('Continental Marxist Thought') and Rosi Braidotti ('Feminist Philosophy') draw attention to Spinoza's monism, materialism, naturalism and radicalism as grounding principles for much contemporary metaphysics, ethics and politics. It becomes clear that continental political philosophy today is practised far more in the Spinozistic tradition than in the Kantian one. The rise of philosophies of immanence over those of transcendence is a prominent theme. Williams stresses the importance of the distinction between ethics and morality in continental philosophy, leading to *immanent* conceptions of subjectivity, affect and political community that are very different from those assumed in the 'transcendent' Kantian tradition. Whether reconceived in terms of power, the relation to the other, or the event, contemporary continental ethico-political thought is strongly linked to the 'critique of metaphysical and political humanism' initiated by Spinoza and continued by Nietzsche, Foucault and Deleuze. Bill Martin, however, argues that the Kantian contribution is as fruitful as the Spinozistic for contemporary politics, when considered in conjunction with Marx. Martin discusses what has become of Marxism 'after' Sartre, Adorno and Althusser, and retrieves a 'Philosophical Marxism' that is both theoretically profound and pragmatically engaged, making the resources of critique also resources for activism.

The sources and influences of continental philosophy have always carried across disciplines. Today, continental philosophy is increasingly practised outside of philosophy departments, 'just down the corridor or in the next building', as Douglas Burnham and Melanie Ebdon put it. Relations to literature and art, which have historically been at the heart of continental philosophy, are treated by Burnham and Ebdon ('Philosophy, Literature, and Interpretation') and by Jonathan Lahey Dronsfield ('Philosophies of Art'). Burnham and Ebdon's chapter looks specifically at ecocriticism as a contemporary mode of literary analysis, one that is intertwined with both aesthetics and philosophy of nature. They show that ecocriticism has a lineage in Kant's theories of beauty, sublimity and natural organization, in Nietzsche's vitalist critique of Kant's teleology and 'ecosystemic' connection of life and art, and in Heideggerian and Merleau-Pontian 'ecophenomenology'.

Dronsfield's chapter, by contrast, considers how current continental philosophy of art has attempted to overcome 'aesthetics'. Philosophy of art is no
longer the science of the sensible; instead, art must be thought as 'the expression of sensation, the exposition of sense, or the partition of the sensible'. The
new terms of the relationship between art and sensation – as conceived by
Jean-Luc Nancy, Rancière, Deleuze and Derrida – leads Dronsfield to consider
how we are to think the relation between art and truth 'after' aesthetics. Badiou's 'inaesthetics' is but one way this traditional pairing is being overturned.

Continental philosophy is interdisciplinary by its very nature. Psychology,
cognitive science, film theory, literary criticism, politics and gender studies are
not simply domains for the 'practical application' of continental philosophy.
Increasingly – as Dronsfield stresses with respect to contemporary art theory
and practice – they are where continental philosophy is practised and *made*.
The chapters of this book have been chosen according to these different ways of
doing continental philosophy, with different practitionary audiences in mind.
For example, in commissioning two separate chapters on literature and art
(which many standard anthologies would group together under 'aesthetics'),
we reflect the ways in which *practices* in these two fields are markedly different.
Of course, we could have subdivided further, reflecting differences among
those who work specifically on painting, architecture, music or film. We have
been unable to include so many chapters here, but we believe theorists and
practitioners in these fields will find much of value in this book nonetheless.

As will now be evident, each chapter takes in the work of a number of
thinkers. There is, intentionally, considerable overlap. Alain Badiou, one of
the most widely discussed contemporary philosophers today, is treated in a
number of chapters here according to different aspects of his work: 'Metaphysics and Ontology', 'Politics and Ethics', 'Continental Marxist Thought',
'Philosophy, Literature, and Interpretation', 'Philosophies of Science' and
'Philosophies of Art'. This dividing-up of Badiou's work does not imply that
Badiou's philosophy of art is unrelated to his political theory, or that Badiou
himself treats them as distinct domains. But rather than provide a chapter on
'Badiou' that attempts to pin down and summarize the totality of his work to
date, we treat strands of his work as they arise in relation to their context.
After all, a philosopher does not produce a body of work ready-formed in
his or her own name. Each work arises in a critical context and in relation to
questions posed and answered by others as well as themselves. The essays in
this book introduce philosophical works as arising in contexts and amidst
questions, not as fixed bodies grouped under a proper name. In this way we
introduce philosophers as practitioners, and encourage the reader to enter
into contexts of practice. This *practitionary* approach is most strikingly taken up
in Burnham and Ebdon's chapter, 'Philosophy, Literature, and Interpretation'.
While the major contemporary thinkers in this area are cited and related to

key historical contexts, the essay is primarily an example of the *practice* of ecocriticism as a new and emerging branch of philosophy of literature. Similarly, Bill Martin, in 'Continental Marxist Thought', reveals a way of practising philosophy that is tied to specific political commitments.

This book is, as we said at the outset, a companion to continental philosophy as it is practised now. The *practice* and *use* of continental philosophy contribute to the book's aim: to present continental philosophy as the varied ways of thinking and writing undertaken by those who use continental philosophy in the arts, the sciences and the social sciences. This book is not a companion to reading about philosophy, but to *doing* philosophy, and perhaps even to 'making' philosophy – in the sense of creating new philosophical disciplines and inter-disciplines. In considering philosophers as practitioners, do we reduce them to being masters of a particular craft or skill – people who have the know-how to think in a certain way? Or – alternatively – do we make the mistake of splitting the practice of philosophy into a million sub-disciplines, so that anyone who is thinking about their own practice (whatever that practice may be) is 'philosophical', an art anyone can master? (We are all familiar with the abuses of the term 'philosophy' in history.) What, after all, are the 'research methods' of continental philosophy, the common set of practices that joins all these chapters as engaging in 'the practice of continental philosophy'? James Burton's opening meta-philosophical essay, 'Research Problems and Methodology: Three Paradigms and a Thousand Exceptions', discusses some of the problems with the notion of 'the practice of continental philosophy' and, indeed, with the notion that there is 'continental philosophy' as one discipline. Readers who are disappointed that this introduction has not answered – has not even asked – the fraught question 'what is continental philosophy?', should turn first to Burton, who reviews the many attempted solutions to the problem of defining the field.

As editors, we gracefully decline to provide an answer to this question at the outset. The answer to this question is this book as a whole. Continental philosophy is all these topics, all these themes, all these practices and more.

2 Research Problems and Methodology
Three Paradigms and a Thousand Exceptions

James Burton

Introduction

An outline of the central research problems in contemporary continental philosophy could easily end up turning into a partial (in both senses) summary of the major problems in contemporary culture. This is something I want to avoid here. It is nevertheless worth noting at the outset that continental philosophy has always addressed, and continues to address, what its most influential thinkers have taken to be the most pressing concerns facing humanity in the modern era. The research problems of continental philosophy thus connect and overlap with the central issues – whether understood in academic or more everyday cultural terms – in politics, art, literature, science, history, cultural studies, psychology, and virtually any discipline or sphere of modern experience that one can name.

The question of the methodology of continental philosophy is no more manageable or straightforward. The chapters of this volume on 'Current Research' present at least twelve distinct areas, within each of which the reader is likely to find quite divergent methodologies even among thinkers dealing with the same broad themes and issues. Indeed, it may well be that the only common factor shared by the most influential thinkers generally referred to as continental philosophers has been the invention of new methodologies – which in itself could be said to give the major strands of continental philosophy a hyper-methodological character, one that would simultaneously constitute a radically anti-methodological approach to the history of philosophy. Such might be a general characterization of poststructuralist thought, for instance.

Given the broad (if not limitless) range of continental philosophy's interests and its array of heterogeneous methodologies, some reduction and simplification will be necessary here. My aim is to be reductive in a useful rather than a misleading way. Instead of drawing a partial theoretical sketch of contemporary culture, or presenting in compressed form the philosophical methods covered elsewhere in this book, I will attempt to outline some of the broad approaches emerging from the work of recent and contemporary philosophers that have been most influential in shaping continental philosophy – remembering that, strictly speaking, this term has a relatively short history and refers to a particularly Anglophone categorization of certain areas of modern thought.[1]

The first three sections of this chapter describe three 'paradigms' that I suggest delimit much of the field of current research in continental philosophy. Each of these is exemplified by a key figure – respectively, Jacques Derrida, Alain Badiou and Gilles Deleuze. (Though chronologically these three thinkers had their periods of greatest influence in the order Derrida–Deleuze–Badiou, for thematic reasons I will deal with Badiou before Deleuze here.) This is not intended as an overview of the philosophies of these three figures, but rather an indication of the broad *methodological* characteristics associated with their work that have most contributed to shaping the Anglophone study of continental philosophy, and especially those which distinguish them from one another, making it possible to conceive of them as representing alternative paradigms. Since the deconstructive approach associated with Derrida (but also finding close associations in the work of a number of previous and contemporaneous thinkers) has had the longest-running and most pervasive effects, it can be said to have had a more-or-less formative influence on Anglophone continental philosophy as it is today. For this reason my discussion of the first paradigm will be conducted partially with reference to several of the existing introductions to continental philosophy in English, where such influence is reflected. In contrast, in discussing Badiou, whose influence has been much more recent, but proportionately extensive, it will be necessary to focus more on summarizing his particular philosophical approach; in doing so I will emphasize its deliberate self-dissociation from approaches associated with the first paradigm, in order to try to point towards some of the possible reasons for its increasing appeal. In the third section, I consider Deleuze and his work with Guattari as representing a third paradigm that is again significantly different in terms of methodology and guiding principles to the other two, while having some common ground with both. Since it is Deleuze whose approach might be considered the most hyper-methodological of these three figures, producing the most open-ended and connectible set of philosophical concepts and relations, I will have opportunity in this third section to consider the three paradigms alongside and with respect to one another.

A necessary danger of this approach is that the description I will give may appear to marginalize the several areas of contemporary research in continental philosophy that do not correspond to one of these three paradigms. I will attempt to rectify this somewhat in the final section of this chapter by considering some other important strands of contemporary research: some of these bear no necessary or direct relationship to the thinkers mentioned above (e.g. research around the philosophy of science, including the work of thinkers such as Isabelle Stengers and Michel Serres); some are influenced by poststructuralist and associated thinkers yet retain a critical distance from them (e.g. feminist philosophy, under the influence of figures such as Luce Irigaray, Hélène Cixous and Julia Kristeva); and some where a philosopher's greatest influence on methodology can be said to have been in disciplines other than philosophy (Michel Foucault, and his role in the development of genealogical and social constructionist approaches being the most notable example) – even as these transdisciplinary effects may be said to cast such disciplinary boundaries into doubt. Indeed, the latter constitutes the same paradoxical problem referred to in my opening paragraph: philosophy has a constitutive relationship to non-philosophy which I have had to partially suppress in order to avoid simply providing an account of modern culture or the broad problems addressed by today's humanities and social sciences; indeed, it may well be the case that philosophy has itself repeatedly found it necessary to suppress this relation in order to best address itself to wider culture and translate non-philosophical problems into philosophical ones.

One more complication worth mentioning at the outset concerns the fact that the term 'continental philosophy' has a double referent – designating both a field of post-war Anglophone academia, and a collection of post-Kantian works in other languages (primarily German and French) arising initially from the philosophical critique of the Enlightenment. This in itself is not necessarily unusual. To some extent, it is simply a reflection of the convention operative in any naming of an academic discipline, whereby an object of study is combined with the mode or method of its study. In everyday usage, for example, it is generally unnecessary to distinguish between 'history' as the events of the past and 'history' as the record and academic study of such events; students of Classics do not ordinarily find it necessary to note that Aeschylus' work only became 'classical drama' centuries after it was written. Nevertheless, it may be argued that the conflation of object and mode of study in continental philosophy *is* more problematic than in such cases. For here the terminological conflation seems to reflect an actual conflation or subsumption, whereby it becomes difficult or impossible for those within certain groups, designated by linguistic, national or other forms of cultural boundaries, to produce works of continental philosophy having an equivalent status to those that they study. Simon Glendinning, for example, suggests that the division places the Anglophone discipline of continental philosophy in a secondary or parasitic role with regard to the philosophical texts produced in other languages that are its central focus. (2006, p. 15) On the other hand, it would also be necessary to recognize that the designation is likely to be largely irrelevant for thinkers working in academic cultures that have not been marked by an analytic/continental division – and indeed, that indifference can also be found on the part of Anglophone philosophers.

The three 'paradigms' I present below attempt to mediate these two referents of 'continental philosophy': the primary aim is not to identify the most important developments in recent and contemporary French philosophy, but those which have been most influential on Anglophone continental philosophy – even though, as one might expect, the two largely coincide.

First Paradigm: The Possibility of Impossibility

> On occasions when I have to be quick, like now, I often define deconstructions by saying, 'It's what comes along [*arrive*: happens],' but also, 'It is the possibility of the impossible.' (Derrida, 2005, p. 114)

It is only following the Second World War that 'continental philosophy' begins to be used self-descriptively by philosophers; indeed, as Critchley notes, academic departments in the United Kingdom do not begin to employ the term officially until the 1970s (2001, p. 38). A recurrent motif in post-war continental philosophy has been the sense that philosophy, at least in the recognizable form of a tradition descending from Plato via Descartes and Kant (but also the continental tradition itself) is coming to an end.[2] This sense, expressed variously in the works of a diverse range of (especially French) post-war philosophers, thus forms the climate in which continental philosophy as an Anglophone discipline emerges. Its widespread effects may be discerned in the proliferation of the prefix 'post-' to describe several of the major philosophical and related academic trends of this period (poststructuralism, postmodernism, posthumanism, etc.).

It is difficult to determine a direct origin or cause of this sense of the closure of philosophy. However, certain factors can be identified: the ethical inconceivability of the events of the Second World War, including the rise of Nazism and the extermination of European Jews; the seeming inability of philosophers to explain these events, or the asserted impropriety of attempting to provide a rational explanation for them; and influential arguments (most prominently on the part of Heidegger, but prefigured by Hegel and Nietzsche and taken up subsequently by Derrida and others) that metaphysics has reached its concluding phase, its inadequacy manifested either in its inability to counter the deleterious effects of industrial modernity on life, or in the limitations imposed upon it by the discourse in which it must be presented.

This sense of the ending or closure of philosophy or metaphysics – at least where it is taken to be in some sense productive rather than stultifying for modern thought (whether or not a given thinker equates such thought with philosophy) – is frequently associated with some figure or notion of impossibility. This impossibility is found in Heidegger in the inability of philosophy to think – or save humanity from – technology (to think Being in a way that shelters it from technology), and the need for poetry to take over this task (1977a, 1977b). For Lyotard, the absence of any universal rule of judgement for determining disputes (in heterogeneous discourses or 'genres') renders absolute consensus (and therefore total satisfaction of all sides) impossible, resulting in what he calls 'the differend' (1988, p. xi). Nancy takes the impossibility of any pre-existing 'single, substantial essence of Being' (2000, p. 29) as the basis for his re-thinking of community and sociality (e.g. 1991; 2000). With Levinas's 'ethics as first philosophy', philosophy based on questions of Being as its first principle likewise becomes impossible: '[t]he ontological condition undoes itself, or is undone, in the human condition or uncondition' (Levinas, 1985, p. 100).[3]

It should be noted that none of these positions sets itself up as though philosophy were *literally* coming to an end (whatever that would mean); nor are these figures of impossibility calls for the surrender or abandonment of the lines of enquiry in which they are found. Rather, they point towards the ending of a former approach to, or understanding of, philosophy and philosophizing that has become ethically untenable, politically suspect, or insufficient on some theoretical grounds (often its own) requiring the calling into question of previously central philosophical concepts or concerns (e.g. Being, the subject, reason). In each of the cases mentioned above, the discovery or exploration of impossibility is treated as the site of a new philosophical productivity. Heidegger's 'destruction' – the 'critical process' of 'de-constructing' traditional concepts is the only means by which ontology can be assured of 'the genuine character of its concepts' (Heidegger, 1982, p. 23). Lyotard calls us to 'attest to the unpresentable' and to 'activate the differends' (1992, p. 25), explaining that the tiresome state of modern theory '(new this, new that, post-this, post-that, etc.)' means that '[t]he time has come to philosophize' (1988, p. xiii). Levinas forms a new ethics on the basis of the impossibility of knowledge of the Other and the shortcomings of ontology. These are challenges to the primacy of Being: they not only suggest the impossibility of both metaphysics and ontology traditionally conceived, but, importantly, seek to explore that impossibility, to seek out its constitutive role in human culture and thought. An alternative way of stating this would be to say that 'ontology', when taken to designate access to Being through language and reason, becomes an impossibility which then forms the basis for the possibility of 'ontology' as the (never absolute or complete) discussion *of* and reasoning *about* Being. Derrida's *différance* would be the epitome of such founding impossibility – the impossibility of meaning, of access to the real beyond *logos*, that is the precondition for every discursive and linguistic engagement with the question of Being: 'the play of the trace, or *différance*, which has no meaning and is not . . . this bottomless chessboard on which Being is put into play' (Derrida, 1982, p. 22).

Derrida's dominance of the Anglophone continental philosophical scene through much of its lifespan (and especially through the 1980s and early 1990s) is reflected in the various introductions to the subject that have appeared in English over the last two decades, in which notions of the impossible, the unsayable, the un(re)presentable, are all offered as defining aspects of continental philosophy *per se*. Figures of impossibility are often deployed in such introductions in the context of attempts to identify what it is that most differentiates the field from the tradition of analytic philosophy. Richard Kearney, for example, describes analytic philosophy as a set of investigative practices attempting (in the wake of Kant's pure reason and the transcendental analytic) to establish the known and the conditions of the knowable, in clear, logical and unambiguous statements; to this he contrasts continental philosophy as a series of attempts to 'say the unsayable' (to approach the noumenal of Kantian experience) through the use of 'extraordinary language' (Kearney, 1994, p. 3).

According to this kind of perspective, analytic and continental philosophy are fundamentally separated by their divergent responses to the experience of impossibility. Such a (stereotypical) characterization presents analytic philosophy as dealing wherever it can with problems that are solvable in the logical terms in which they are stated, almost like mathematical equations. The implication is that there is no room in analytic philosophy for impossibility: if a problem appears insoluble, either it is insufficiently stated, insufficiently analysed or it is a false problem – the nonsensical presenting itself as though meaningful. In contrast, continental philosophy is characterized as particularly concerned with problems that cannot be elaborated in such language, and which are ultimately, in a logical sense, insoluble. In other words, continental philosophy attempts to inhabit and explore, rather than dismissing or removing irresolvability.

In a more recent introduction to continental philosophy, Andrew Cutrofello (2005) uses this motif of the differing responses to impossibility to differentiate between the two sides, taking Bertrand Russell and Derrida as exemplary representatives of analytic and continental philosophy respectively. Cutrofello compares Russell's approach to his paradoxes with Derrida's response to the aporia (each taken to represent a subsequent form of what Kant referred to as 'antinomies'). Where for Russell the apparent contradiction (for example, of his Barber paradox) must be resolved through reasoned dispute (unless one is to give up in despair), for Derrida there is 'an obscure ethical duty' to 'endure the shock of the antinomical, succumbing neither to despair nor to a triumphalist solution' (Cutrofello, 2005, p. 406).[4] The analytic representative refuses impossibility while the continental embraces it. It is easy to see why, among some thinkers, this leads to what Critchley calls 'the tempting twilight zone of the *X-Files* complex' (2001, p. 121), where science and metaphysics respectively accuse one another of obscurantism and scientism. (For Critchley, philosophy is at its best when it polices itself against such excesses, and at its worst when it succumbs to them.) With respect to Cutrofello's example, however, such accusations would be mistaken (and misleading): both obscurantist and scientistic discourse seek to convince us that the impossible is in fact possible – whereas in Cutrofello's account, both Russell and Derrida want to maintain the difference between the possible and the impossible, the solvable and the insoluble; the difference between their approaches is that one is interested in identifying and dealing with only the possible, while the other wants us to bear witness to the experience of impossibility.

Although what Cutrofello calls Derrida's 'obscure ethical duty' may for some become an end in itself (the shock experienced by facing the aporetic in abstract thought or expression may be enough to call one to this duty), we can also relate it to the diverse and often troubling experiences of impossibility in everyday life: the impossibility of knowing how the content of my dreams relates to my waking life; the impossibility of resolving two nations' claims to the same territory in a way that will satisfy both; the impossibility of accepting the death of a loved one, or death in general; the impossibility of adequately defining justice, or freedom, or love, in general and for a given circumstance. The ethical dimension of reflecting on such impossibilities is then perhaps not so obscure, and it is possible to see how the kind of continental philosophical approach that wants to dwell in and do its best to understand or come to terms with the experience of impossibility (a task that is presumably itself impossible, or at least, interminable, though no less worthwhile for this reason) may form the broad methodological basis for a wide range of philosophical investigations into different cultural phenomena.

I noted above that a potential difficulty in addressing the methodology of continental philosophy is that one may find it necessary to understand many of its central thinkers as effectively *anti*-methodological with regard to previous philosophy. In the following section I discuss Badiou as probably the foremost example of a contemporary thinker attempting to reintroduce a systematic methodology into continental philosophy (though perhaps at the same time to render meaningless the delineation of 'continental' philosophy as a separate category from analytic philosophy). Yet Badiou remains something of an exception, even if his growing reception is suggestive of an increasing general desire for systemacity among philosophers and students of philosophy. Those thinkers conventionally labelled as poststructuralists, such as Derrida, Deleuze, Foucault, Kristeva, may indeed be understood, in the wake of Nietzsche, as taking an anti-systematic approach to philosophy – which constitutes an anti-methodological approach in the context of those large philosophical systems that dominated the first century of continental philosophy, starting with that of Hegel. However, poststructuralism need not for this reason be understood as attempting to bring about the end of philosophy. In that such systems were themselves attempts to escape the Enlightenment's placing of reason as the absolute foundation for subsequent human endeavour, they may also already be considered part of this same anti-methodological tradition. The whole of continental philosophy would in this sense consist of 'a number of novel intellectual approaches' to the critique of Enlightenment, shaped by responses to Hegel. (West, 1996, p. 2)

One might still argue that such anti-systemacity reaches such a pronounced intensity in the diverse approaches of poststructuralist thinkers that something like an ending of (recognizable) philosophy, or a period of philosophy (possibly continental philosophy itself) appears to be coming to an end; hence rumours are beginning to circulate of the onset of 'post-continental philosophy' (Maldonado-Torres, 2006; Mullarkey, 2006). Yet an asserted impossibility of access to Being, the breaking down of traditional understandings of Truth, Reason, the subject, etc., need not in itself constitute such an ending. Indeed, the heightened concern with impossibility or irresolvability constitutes just as much a return – especially in the case of Derrida – to the origins of the Western philosophical tradition, in the aporias of Plato's dialogues and at the foundation of Aristotle's *Metaphysics*. In a sense that establishes a certain continuity with the foundations of Western philosophy, then, according to the 'impossibility' paradigm I have been discussing, continental philosophy could be summarized as a series of attempts to cope with the acceptance of supposed noncompossibles (without becoming *non compos mentis*): its activity is the invention of techniques for situations in which there can be no technique – the know-how of no-how.

Second Paradigm: The Possibility of Philosophy

Even if the various experiences of impossibility or the aporetic are productive for the kind of work in continental philosophy that valourizes them, there are nevertheless those for whom all talk of impossibility in regard to philosophy, and of the end of philosophy, is pretentious and debilitating. One such thinker is Alain Badiou, whose own philosophical project, and that which for him constitutes *the* legitimate approach to philosophy, is to understand the general conditions of its *possibility*.

For Badiou the concern with the 'end' or contemporary 'impossibility' of philosophy is both a conceit and a 'dangerous deficiency', a 'prophetic posture' (1999, pp. 30–1) that keeps philosophers from doing what they should be doing. For example, if philosophy finds it impossible to address the extermination of European Jews by the Nazis, this is because 'it is neither its duty nor within its power to conceptualize it' (Badiou, 1999, p. 30). In his view, allowing impossibility to reign in this area of contemporary history and thought would be akin to 'making the Jews die a second time', allowing Nazism a late act of vengeance through bringing to an end areas of philosophy and politics in which Jewish thinkers have historically played a decisive role (Badiou, 1999, p. 31) There is (as there often is) some polemicism here on Badiou's part: as I noted above, those influenced by and/or working on the thinkers Badiou names in relation to this talk of impossibility (e.g. Heidegger, Derrida, Lacoue-Labarthe, Nancy) may be expected to see such work as rich with possibility for philosophy, even while such possibility tends to circulate around figures of the impossible, the unknowable, the inexpressible, etc. Nevertheless, Badiou's disregard for these obsessions reflects a sense found to varying degrees among many working in continental philosophy today (including Anglophone thinkers) that the success of poststructuralism in questioning, deconstructing and subverting the central concerns and approaches of previously dominant philosophical traditions has left continental philosophy adrift, lacking direction or programme.

Schroeder's recent 'critical introduction' to continental philosophy is based on an assessment along these lines: for him, the subject is in a state of malaise or crisis following poststructuralism's effective 'silencing' or 'paralysing' of the other major continental traditions (2005, pp. x–xviii). In his Preface, Schroeder briefly summarizes how this point applies to various past traditions and their contemporary legacies, noting that this effect of poststructuralist and postmodernist critiques was in each case due to their targeting weaknesses of which the adherents to or heirs of a given tradition (e.g. Hegelianism, Freudianism, phenomenology, structuralism) had already become at least partially aware. When someone else voices one's own self-criticisms, the attempt to mount a defence can seem as futile as continuing as if the criticisms did not apply. Thus, even given the productive or positive side of poststructuralist, postmodernist, and other discussions of the impossibility of philosophy, the end of metaphysics, there remains a sense for many that continental philosophy has indeed reached something like a closing phase, of a chapter at least, with the apparent waning of poststructuralism in the absence of its central figures. As Critchley writes, 'it is at least arguable that the present state of philosophy is interestingly marked by the exhaustion of a whole series of theoretical paradigms' (2001, p. 123).

This would be one reason why a thinker like Badiou has become increasingly widely read among continental philosophers, with the past decade seeing most of his major philosophical work to date appearing in English translation. In contrast to the 'aporetic' mode discussed in the previous section, Badiou wants to establish the general conditions that make philosophy possible, in order that it may take (and, presumably, subsequently take again, indefinitely) *'one more step'* in the course it has been following since Descartes, whereby Being, truth and subjectivity – probably the three concepts most called into question by poststructuralism – may remain its central concerns (1999, p. 32). Badiou's appeal could be said to consist in his 'undoing' of the poststructuralists' 'undoing' of such concepts: that is, in his defence of the possibility and importance of philosophy continuing to focus on something like a traditional notion of Being without perpetually deconstructing it; on an understanding of subjectivity that does not necessitate its radical dispersal; and on an idea of truth that is neither produced by philosophy nor wholly constructed by the political and economic forces of a given society or era.

Badiou's philosophical system is most fully developed in his 1988 work, *Being and Event* (appearing in English in 2005) and succinctly stated in his *Manifesto for Philosophy* (1989; English translation, 1999). Rejecting any account of philosophy that sees it as contingent on particular social structures or religious contexts, Badiou asserts that its conditions are procedural and 'transversal': that is, they may take place in different socio-political, historico-cultural contexts – *across* different contexts. They are 'uniform procedures . . . whose relation to thought is relatively invariant' (Badiou, 1999, p. 33). Such are what Badiou calls *truth procedures*. If they have something like a characteristic of universality, this is because they recur, and have recurred, in this transversal manner, escaping each particular set of circumstances in which they may be found to operate. Thus they attain to something closer to objective truth than Foucault's conception of truths as socially and historically produced, or Derrida's revealing of the instability of any signification – yet without appealing to any transcendental principle or form of absolute judgement. The four 'truth procedures' (or 'generic procedures') that Badiou identifies have not existed always or everywhere, but have been repeatedly brought (or thought) together by (Western) philosophy, starting with Plato. In this way Badiou is able to introduce a rigorous systemacity into his philosophy while avoiding the danger of falling back into some form of structuralism or what Kearney calls 'metaphysical foundationationalism' (1994, p. 2).

Badiou's four conditions of philosophy – each corresponding to a kind of truth procedure – are 'the matheme, the poem, political invention and love' (1999, p. 35) (More generally, Badiou refers to science, art, politics and love).

The task of philosophy for Badiou is (that is, has been, and should continue to be) the thinking of the compossibility of these conditions and the truths that emerge in them: not the production of truths, but the offering of 'a mode of access to the unity of a moment of truths, a conceptual site in which the generic procedures are thought of as compossible' (1999, p. 38). If one or more of the four conditions is lacking, then philosophy, for Badiou, is in a state of dissipation. This system thus takes into account philosophy's historical relation to other discourses, to 'non-philosophy' (which as I noted at the beginning of this chapter is virtually a defining relation for continental philosophy) – while at the same time setting up a basis for the criticism of any philosophy which ties itself too closely or exclusively to any one of these philosophical others.

Badiou uses the term 'suture' to describe the procedure by which philosophy ties itself to one or two conditions at the expense of others, arguing that philosophy since Hegel has been dominated by such suturing – first to its scientific and political conditions in the nineteenth century, and then, from Nietzsche to Heidegger, to the poetic, a situation that is 'extended in Germany by the philosophic cult of poets, in France by the fetishism of literature' (1999, p. 66). In response to the various claims or suggestions concerning the ending and impossibility of philosophy (and more specifically the impossibility of its being systematic), Badiou argues that 'it is not impossible at all, but *hindered* by the historic network of sutures' (1999, p. 65). A crucial philosophical task, for Badiou, is thus 'de-suturation' – and at present the most pressing issue is philosophy's de-suturation from its poetic condition (1999, p. 67).

Crucial to all this is Badiou's approach to the question of ontology. Where Derrida and others had identified the inadequacy of language to allow absolute access to Being, Badiou is broadly in agreement. Where he differs is in the assumption that there is no alternative mode than the linguistic through which to think ontology. His alternative, developed at length in *Being and Event* (Badiou, 2006) is that mathematics provides a tool for understanding and reasoning with the fundamentals of Being, in the form of set theory. This turn away from verbal language to mathematics as a (the) means of pronouncing 'what is expressible of being qua being' (Badiou, 2005, p. 17), allows Badiou to escape the Heideggerean-Derridean hegemony of 'questioning' in the contemporary (continental) philosophical scene, in the direction of *answering* the problems of ontology.

Thus Badiou's work can be seen as one particularly systematic and increasingly influential example of an attempt to address a general research problem for current continental philosophy – the question of its renewal following the effects of poststructuralism. In Anglophone continental philosophy, this is connected to a sense that the task of establishing the significance of post-Kantian non-analytic philosophers for modern thought – through interpreting, translating and commenting on their work – has largely been achieved, even if the institutional space that has been carved out for such work remains relatively small (but with a proportionately large field of overlapping interest in other disciplines). Coupled with the suspicion among some that such commentary and interpretation is really all (Anglophone) continental philosophy can do (or at least, what it has largely tended to do) – as expressed for example by Glendinning (2006) and Osborne (cited in Glendinning, 2006, p. 123) – this can seem to give the contemporary face of continental philosophy a quizzical expression of 'what next?'. This might lead to the kind of response represented by Critchley's call to Anglophone philosophers to stop 'worshipping a series of proper names' and start using continental traditions for 'doing creative, inventive thematic work and not restricting oneself to translation and commentary' (2001, p. 125). Or, as with Schroeder (2005), it may fuel critical re-examinations of the major traditions of continental philosophy in order to restore a sense of their continued significance for contemporary concerns. For others it may be a case of waiting (or searching) for the next thinker or paradigm capable of exerting a Derridean level of influence to emerge from French philosophy.

In any case, such aspects of the contemporary continental scene go some way to explaining the increasing appeal of Badiou's work, as an original and highly systematic attempt to establish new foundations for a continuation of the Platonic philosophical tradition that circumvent its poststructuralist dis-assembling. Badiou's radical gestures, through which he attempts to re-open – or rather, open (again) in a fresh manner – traditional lines of philosophical enquiry, are: to assert that it *is* possible to address the true nature of Being, using set theory to avoid falling into the endless play of signifiers that Derrida reveals as keeping language at a distance from the real; to assert that it *is* possible to have a notion of truth, based on a new concept of the Event and the recurrence of the truth procedures it effects, that transversally cuts across different socio-historical contexts, contrary to the assumptions of the Nietzschean-Foucauldian genealogical approach; and to assert that there are subjects that partake of universality and singularity, and which may have a political-revolutionary impact that does not depend upon their radical dissolution or dispersal into something like Deleuze and Guattari's 'Body without Organs' (see below).

Badiou also identifies a more specific set of 'research questions' which, for him, should come to occupy the space of compossibility that his philosophical system aims to develop. Briefly, these are centred on 'a thinking of the Two' beyond dialectics and class struggle, in relation to the Event; on the thought of 'the object and objectivity' and its implications for subjectivity, or 'the problem of the *subject without object*'; and on what he refers to as 'a thinking of the indiscernible' that would link together the other two questions in an identification of 'Truth with the nondescript, the nameless, the generic' (Badiou, 1999, pp. 91–6). Whether or not these questions, in the way Badiou formulates them, will come to occupy a dominant place in future philosophical research remains to be seen, and to some extent depends on the testing of his philosophical system that is just getting underway. Yet the significance of this system, and its apparent opening of a way of returning to 'the constitutive triad of modern philosophy . . . Being, subject and truth' (Badiou, 1999, p. 108), are already having significant effects on continental philosophy and the discussion of its methods (see, e.g., Hallward, 2003; Riera, 2005; Mullarkey, 2006, especially pp. 83–124 and 157–86).

One possible consequence of a philosophy as systematic as Badiou's is that it may deter partial engagements. That is, one may find that if one does not embrace the system in its entirety, it becomes difficult to engage with it at all. This is not to say that we are obliged to read or react to Badiou in certain ways, but that his project – as with any project presented in the form of a manifesto – does demand a certain commitment. This should mean that research in continental philosophy following directly from Badiou's approach will adhere quite carefully to the conditions he has laid down – leading, one might expect, to a certain testing of the capacity of his system to allow 'one more step' (and one more, and one more, etc.) to be taken, with the results of this testing determining the extent of his continued influence on continental philosophy.

On the other hand, there is a possibility that Badiou's philosophical approach may end up suffering from the systemacity that appears to be its strength. Though the combination of his four truth procedures with the call for de-suturing would seem to allow philosophy to maintain its openness to non-philosophy even while re-instating itself as independent of such spheres, the net effect could be simply the shrinking of the boundaries or narrowing of the definition of 'philosophy proper', and the labelling of, for example, works of philosophy of science, aesthetics and so on as something other than philosophy. Such an attempt to re-draw the boundaries of philosophy would then presumably meet with either contention or disinterest on the part of the producers of such works – depending on the degree of importance they attach to having their work understood as philosophy 'proper'.

Regardless of such potential difficulties, it can be said that engagement with Badiou's philosophy is currently increasing among Anglophone continental philosophers, and may be expected to inspire or fuel a number of further developments in terms of research and method – whether this means rigorous adherence to his system and the continued development of its implications, or more loosely related attempts to develop new philosophical systems, to find other ways to re-found traditional conceptions of Being, subjectivity, etc., or to attempt in other ways to 'do' philosophy without the limitations imposed by language.[5]

I now want to turn to Deleuze as an exemplary representative of an alternative means of escaping the seeming *impasse* constituted by philosophy's dependence on the language it uses to pursue its crucial concerns, one which seemingly refuses the binary choice between the Derridean thrall to the experience of impossibility and the Badiouian rejection of language as the mode of ontological thought altogether, establishing an alternative path (or multiplicity of paths) through the sheer creativity of thought.

Third Paradigm: Concept Creation

As with most philosophers, there are many contenders for the 'main principle' or 'key theme' in Deleuze's work – among them, in this case, are multiplicity, life, difference, intensity, flux, affect, immanence, creativity and the virtual. Some of these could be used to link him thematically with one of the two thinkers I have treated as exemplary of the first two paradigms I have described, starting perhaps with his ontological concerns with difference (Derrida) and multiplicity (Badiou).[6] The question to be considered here is: what are the characteristics of the Deleuzian approach that would allow us to talk of a third paradigm, a different *general* method or approach, rather than simply a complementary project revolving around the same themes as those of his contemporaries? This would partly be determined by the complex of Deleuzian themes/principles – the fact that he deals with difference and multiplicity in a vitalistic and intensive mode, for example: such are the characteristics of the productive, creative approach he takes to philosophy, which he defines in the last of his collaborations with Félix Guattari as 'the discipline that involves *creating* concepts' (Deleuze and Guattari, 1994, pp. 1–12). The fact that there are clear grounds for comparison between his work and that of Derrida on the one hand and Badiou on the other, while this is not (at least not obviously) true of Derrida and Badiou together, is perhaps indicative of the open and affirming qualities that distinguish the Deleuzian approach.

There is a strong performative dimension to each of the two 'paradigms' discussed so far. Declarations of the end or ruination of philosophy (or metaphysics) contribute to bringing about a sense of its coming-to-an-end. Badiou, reacting against these performative statements of 'the closure of an entire epoch of thought and its concerns' (which he also attributes, in its own way, to the analytic tradition) (2005, p. 14), declares the continued possibility of philosophy, and through doing so attempts to bring about a return of what he sees as the Platonic tradition of 'philosophy *itself*', in the form that he understands it and which he sees as necessary (1999, pp. 136–7). Deleuze's approach throughout his work – and especially in the texts he produced in collaboration with Félix Guattari – could be said to be performative in a different way: his texts, words, phrases are already *doing* in a multiplicity of heterogeneous ways what he wants us to understand as connecting directly, immanently – rather than at a distance, by representation, signification – to other modes of doing, acting, becoming, of all varieties and registers. If this kind of performativity may also be found in places in Derrida and Badiou, their overall projects nevertheless maintain this distance between language and Being, whereas Deleuze's ignoring (or refusal) of such a distance, justified or not, allows him to address the most serious topics of philosophy, as Derrida put it, 'the most gaily, the most innocently' (cited in Patton and Protevi, 2003, p. 6), with a philosophical freedom not often found among his contemporaries.

This is reflected in Deleuze's attitude to the talk of the end of philosophy, which, as we have seen, is so important (in quite different ways) for Derrida and Badiou. Deleuze and Guattari write: 'the death of metaphysics, or the overcoming of philosophy has never been a problem for us: it is just tiresome, idle chatter' (1994, p. 9). If Deleuze shares with Foucault and Derrida a concern with revealing and challenging the hegemony, in both philosophy and cultural and everyday existence, of former conceptions of the subject, of Being and truth, he is also interested in giving a positive and productive account of alternatives to such dominant totalities. If he shares with Badiou a distaste for the One, the Absolute, the Whole, the multiplicities he deploys in opposition to such figures are grounded in a very different ontology from that made possible for Badiou by set theory. Deleuze's ontology is one in which difference (as opposed to identity) is constitutive, and takes the form of movements rather than things, elements or indeed conceptual operators for distinguishing between elements. Deleuze's understanding of difference, as most extensively elaborated in *Difference and Repetition* (Deleuze, 1994), heavily influenced by his early reading of Nietzsche as a philosopher of difference (see Deleuze, 2006)[7] and his engagements with Bergson's philosophy of duration and movement,[8] is to be understood not as the product of reflection, but as an integral aspect of existence, a process which 'makes itself' (Deleuze, 1994, p. 28). Repetition, likewise, is 'real movement, in opposition to . . . a false movement of the abstract' (Deleuze, 1994, p. 23) and bears difference within it. Where this focus on the originary and origin-displacing role of difference may seem to align Deleuze philosophically with Derrida, and where the replacing of identity with difference as the fundamental ontological principle seems to lead towards Badiou's thought of multiplicity, it is this emphasis on 'real movement' that most discernibly takes him away from both and into quite different territory.

This is not to say that there is not something like 'movement' in Derrida's and Badiou's responses to the difficulties surrounding key philosophical concepts such as Being, truth and subjectivity in the poststructuralist era – that is, in the context in which all talk of pure origins, universal structure, absolute foundations and the primacy of the One and the Same is being radically undermined. In fact, it could be argued that something like a turn to movement, to process and event, is what all such challenges almost necessarily demand (and this would be one possible way of explaining why temporality remains such a large theme, almost a meta-theme or horizon across or around twentieth century philosophy). Yet the very different *kinds* of movement, or the different ways movement is 'mobilized' in these different thinkers, determine the divergent paths which their responses to such challenges take.

In our first paradigm ontology becomes, as we saw, effectively impossible: there is no access to an underlying Being through *logos* – merely statements, arguments, discourses in which different onto*logies* are presented, implied, accepted, challenged, defended, etc., and which may be examined (or deconstructed) to reveal both the social and political effects in which they are inscribed and the impossible conditions of *différance* on which they depend. In *Speech and Phenomena*, Derrida frequently writes of 'the movement of différance' (1973, pp. 67, 82, 137, e.g.). The relatively atemporal, eternal or Ideal structure and contents of the world in traditional ontological formations give way to movement in the form of the underlying play of difference that renders such conceptions possible – the impossibility of the absolute knowledge of Being constituting their possibility. Badiou likewise starts from the limitations of philosophical language with regard to Being, but instead of regarding this as signifying the impossibility of ontology *per se*, instead reads it as a sign of the need to separate philosophy and ontology – '[n]ot, as a vain, "critical" knowledge would have us believe, because ontology does not exist, but rather because it exists fully, to the degree that what is sayable – and said – of being qua being does not in any manner arise from the discourse of philosophy' (Badiou, 2005, p. 19). Where Derrida might be said to take up the significance of philosophy's inadequacy for ontology in light of its long-running, shaping concern with ontology – to explore this as one among other aporias structuring philosophy and indeed thought – Badiou turns elsewhere in search of an adequate means of ontology, finding it in mathematics and set theory: 'we must *take on* the multiple and rather mark the radical limits of what language can constitute. Whence the crucial nature of the question of the indiscernible' (Badiou, 1999, p. 104). Here, something like movement or process is found in the form of logical operations ('there is no one, only the count-as-one'; Badiou, 2005, p. 24), and of truth procedures ('truth is a type of being'; Badiou, 2005, p. 236). The focus then becomes the relationship between mathematics, as ontology, and philosophy, dealing with 'events' – or rather opening and articulating a space for the convergence and recognized compossibility of truth-making events in other discourses (in science, art, politics and love).

In contrast, Deleuze places movement at the very heart of things. His movement is vitalist, processual and creative, in a sense closer to the ontological perspectives of thinkers like Bergson and Whitehead, and to the philosophical approach (in Deleuze's reading, at least) of Nietzsche.[9] From such a viewpoint, the incapacity of language to address Being renders ontology neither fundamentally impossible nor beyond philosophy, but signifies the inadequacy of traditional or conventional language for facilitating the proper thought of movement and process (and for allowing thought to realize itself *as* movement). This is a point made frequently, and influentially for Deleuze, by Bergson, for whom 'language . . . always translates movement and duration in terms of space' (Bergson, 1988, p. 191).[10] Consequentially, for Deleuze, philosophy must be ceaselessly *creative* with both thought and its expression, inventing or fabricating new concepts through the unconventional and unexpected use of language: 'some concepts must be indicated by an extraordinary and sometimes even barbarous or shocking word . . . Some concepts call for archaisms, and others for neologisms, shot through with almost crazy etymological exercises' (Deleuze and Guattari, 1994, pp. 7–8).

Thus, thought, language and Being are not, for Deleuze, to be conceived as belonging to distinct realms. If thought consists in movement, this is movement in the same sense that is inherent to matter, life, and indeed everything – from flows of desire to the organization of social institutions, from geological formations to taxation. This is a correlate of Deleuze's fundamental commitment to a philosophy of immanence: '[a]lthough it is always possible to invoke a transcendent that falls outside the plane of immanence . . . all transcendence is constituted solely in the flow of immanent consciousness that belongs to this plane' (Deleuze, 2001, p. 31). This ontology based on flux or becoming means that, in the face of the inadequacy of traditional conceptions of Being, truth, subject, etc., a key aspect of the philosophical task for Deleuze becomes the elaboration of what there is *instead* – a task which in Derrida and Badiou, for very different reasons, is found to be more-or-less beyond philosophy.

Many of the concepts Deleuze creates, which appear perhaps most creatively and with the greatest proliferation in the *Capitalism and Schizophrenia* volumes written with Guattari, are elaborations of this 'instead'. If not Being, then what? If there is no subject, then what is it that 'we' have been thinking about all these years, and who has been doing this thinking? If art and language do not signify or represent, then what is it that we mistake for representation – and how does this 'represent' itself to us as representation? Thus in place of the subject, for example, Deleuze and Guattari talk of a heterogeneous set of flows of desire, which may intersect, affect or block one another, become diverted or re-directed – of which certain sets may be specific to what we think of as a certain individual – not a subject, but a 'body without organs', a dimensionless surface itself determined by these flows of intensity (Deleuze and Guattari, 1983, pp. 9–16; 1980, pp. 149–66). Deleuze's commitment to immanence means that these flows of desire must be able to connect with all other types of flow, even in (or indeed, as a necessary effect of) their heterogeneous multiplicity. Hence, with Guattari he develops a new terminology of the machinic, which has nothing to do with the menacing themes of Heideggerian technology or Bergsonian mechanization, but operates as a neutral designation of 'things that do' or what we might call 'doings': desiring-machines may connect with social machines, abstract machines, war machines, with any other site of 'effect-production' or 'flow-redirection'. A further aspect of the 'machine' terminology is, again, this emphasis on 'doing' or 'happening' – on the production of effects as opposed to signification or representation: books, words, discourses, conscious and unconscious images *do* or *produce*, like any other machines: they connect with other kinds of machines, such as desiring-machines, producing the kind of effects that we have tended to associate with a human subject, but which might rather be understood in terms of an affect that now indicates the indiscernibility (and therefore consistency or continuity) of human and non-human.

My purpose here is not to summarize the panoply of Deleuzian (and Deleuze-Guattarian) concepts, especially given the large and growing number of introductions to his and their work (e.g. Massumi, 1992; Goodchild, 1996; Marks, 1998; Colebrook, 2002; Khalfa, 2003) My aim is simply to give a sense of what renders the Deleuzian approach or method different enough to the work of the other thinkers I have discussed to be considered another paradigm. The effects of Deleuze and his work with Guattari have been great within philosophy and beyond, and connect with a range of current research areas underpinned by notions of affect, intensity and various forms of vitalist or process ontology. What such research may be said to have in common is a commitment to the multiplicitous heterogeneity of existence, and the immanent interaction between processes and elements elsewhere taken to belong to different orders of reality.

I have identified three broad paradigms, all corresponding to a response to the breakdown, challenging or de(con)struction of traditional philosophical concepts in the poststructuralist context: one either explores the breakdown of these categories, and considers the apparently founding impossibilities that seem to be revealed by this breakdown; or one focuses on what there is instead of such categories (if not subjectivity, Being, then what?); or one attempts to re-found them in something like their traditional sense, yet in a 'new' way that would be adequate to the events or developments that had cast them into doubt. Derrida, Deleuze and Badiou each represent an exemplary and influential attempt to follow one of these three paths. However, having begun this chapter by expressing my concern at the imposing diversity and heterogeneity of contemporary continental philosophy and its research problems and methods, I have risked arriving at a depiction that would all too neatly divide the field into three parts. In the final section I would like to turn to some areas of ongoing research that do not fit comfortably into any of these three paradigms, including several which might have a claim to constituting an equivalent paradigm in their own right (and indeed, for which this claim would constitute one of their principal concerns).

A Thousand Exceptions

Given the political and critical dimensions of much continental philosophy, it necessarily deals frequently (and often constitutively) with Otherness in a variety of forms – with the excluded, the forgotten, the repressed or oppressed subjects, elements, themes, groups and voices within both academic philosophy and culture at large. A well-known example is Derrida's concern with the subjugation of writing to speech as the guarantor, indicator and signifier of presence, truth and identity in Western culture and metaphysics – and his attempt to reverse the hierarchy to reveal the way such notions are already dependent on writing as a technique of difference, of differing and deferral. Such concerns are at work from the beginning of Derrida's career. As his work develops and as attentive readings of his work start to appear it becomes clear that this reversal is (or is intended to be) applicable to multiple such hierarchies or binaries, e.g. masculine/feminine, reason/madness, colonizer/colonized, norm/Other, etc. Any of the suppressed elements in such pairings can theoretically be revealed through deconstruction as having a relation to the dominant element that is equivalent to (if not exactly the same as) that of the relation of writing to audible speech, i.e. as both the enabling and repressed element: '[t]he difference that brings out phonemes and lets them be heard and understood [*entendue*] is itself inaudible' (Derrida, 1973, p. 133). The aptness of deconstruction for addressing a range of sites of the suppression of Otherness is reflected in its influence on a wide range of thinkers concerned first of all with one or other such instance – even if some of these thinkers will also seek to highlight certain limitations of deconstruction along with other philosophical traditions. At the same time, the apparent hegemony of deconstruction, and various other aspects of poststructuralist thought within certain fields – as reflected for example in my discussion of the 'aporetic' paradigm above – then becomes an issue.

Feminist philosophy is one major area of research in contemporary philosophy in which one finds characteristically poststructuralist approaches alongside attempts to point to the limitations of these approaches (at least as they have been employed by their most influential [male] thinkers). Under the influence of thinkers such as Luce Irigaray, Hélène Cixous and Julia Kristeva, this can be identified as a major area of contemporary research in continental philosophy that would not fit easily within any of the above paradigms. Where some such research takes an explicitly critical approach to the repression of the feminine in particular within Western culture and thought (e.g. Cixous, Irigaray), others address this as part of a broader ethical and critical concern with the suffering or repression of any 'othered' or silenced subject (e.g. Kristeva, Spivak, Le Doeuff). The fact that I am referring to such thinkers here under the sub-heading of 'exceptions' is both an indicator that the 'exception' (firstly, in these cases, the 'feminine', and its status *as* exception) is their central concern – and a justification of the continued necessity and importance of their projects. Even if the thinkers around whom I have centred my discussion of three paradigms above can be said in their different ways to share such ethical and/or political concerns with exclusion and social/cultural inequality – and even if two of them were born in north African countries – they nevertheless effectively speak and write with the status and/or from the position of white European males.

Much of the hitherto most influential feminist philosophy arose from a combination of a psychoanalytic approach (whether Freudian, Lacanian, or departing from both) with aspects of various poststructuralist approaches, deconstruction in particular. The result is that aspects of the work of a philosopher such as Irigaray can be considered at once a continuation or development of such traditions, and simultaneously a critique: where Freud claims to have uncovered the repressed origins of human culture in the primal act of patricide (in *Totem and Taboo*), Irigaray looks for what is repressed within this account itself – namely, the feminine, and the matricidal scene that precedes the supposedly foundational killing of the father (Irigaray, 1991, p. 36 and *passim*). Using a reading style inspired by Derrida, she is able to trace the exclusion and suppression of the feminine within the history of philosophy as well as Western culture – yet to do so in relation even to poststructuralist thought itself. Irigaray draws from the tools Derrida's approach offers for uncovering the suppressed element in the hierarchies that have structured Western culture, demonstrating the dependence of the dominant element upon its excluded-included other. Yet at the same time, deconstruction's apparent equation of writing with the feminine (or with any subdominant category) can be said to re-assign a metaphoric or tropic status to the feminine in a way that it does not do for the masculine (or for speech, essence, truth, etc., all of which are now seen to have a masculine character). In the terms of this kind of critique, there is an undermining (deconstruction) of the masculine (the subject, Being, etc.), but no attempt (or need) for a reconstruction or restoration of the feminine (which remains the silent deconstructive tool), while the masculine, deconstructed but never destroyed, continues to speak, to construct and deconstruct using its rhetorical tools.

For this reason it would have been problematic to suggest that Irigaray, along with other philosophers who approach (or reproach) influential representatives of poststructuralism from a critical perspective, feminist, anti-colonialist or otherwise (e.g. Spivak's criticisms of Deleuze and Foucault in her seminal 1988 essay 'Can the Subaltern Speak?'), is covered by the first of the paradigms discussed above. Yet placing Irigaray and other feminist philosophers in the category of 'exception' is equally risky. As Margaret Whitford writes, Irigaray 'does not simply want to be relegated to another space, outside culture, on the margins. She wants to *think* sexual difference, to bring the maternal genealogy into *thought*' (1991, p. 134). This is therefore not a question of one or several strands of philosophical research among others, but one which calls for a recovery of a founding and constitutive dimension of philosophy (beyond those emphasized by various poststructuralist approaches) that it has itself forgotten; an attempt at a renewal of philosophy that would seek to regain something far older than the Platonic–Cartesian tradition of philosophy that Badiou (in his own, 'new' way) wants to reinstate. It is what the latter tradition had itself already suppressed, along with the memory of that suppression: '*Forgetting that we have forgotten* is sealed over at the dawning of the photological metaphor-system of the West' (Irigaray, 1985, p. 345).

In this sense, Irigaray can be said to be calling for a philosophical and cultural engagement with the forgotten, repressed feminine that would parallel Heidegger's call at the beginning of *Being and Time* (Heidegger, 1962) for a return to the question of Being (which is a questioning, he suggests, that Western philosophy and culture have forgotten that they have not been properly undertaking). Whether Badiou's injunction to 'forget the forgetting of the forgetting' (1999, p. 115), directed at Heidegger and his influence upon subsequent French philosophy, would also apply to feminist philosophy and/or to Irigaray is not certain; similarly, we might expect, but cannot be sure, that Irigaray would take issue with the supposed gender-neutrality of Badiou's universalism. What these comments on forgetting from quite different camps do highlight, however, is the difficulty concerning both the idea of including *and* the idea of excluding Irigaray or Spivak or a number of other philosophers concerned with Otherness, subalternity, etc., from one of the paradigms in the first three sections of this chapter. Though Irigaray, along with some other feminist philosophers, shares both Badiou's will to break with the dominant philosophical genealogies of the post-Kantian era, and the call for a renewal of philosophy in an older form, what is intended by this renewal – the hoped-for results in each case – would be widely divergent. It would make no more sense to include Irigaray in my second (Badiouian) paradigm than in the first, even though she could methodologically be said to have much in common with each.[11]

The fact that feminist philosophy retains the status of one among other strands of philosophical research (which, in some empirical sense, one must accept that it is), is a sign of its continued importance and necessity – which, for a thinker such as Irigaray perhaps, will not diminish until the 'paradigms' which attempt to submerge their masculine or male conditions beneath an air or mask of gender-neutrality, have themselves taken on the status of exceptions.

The representative of poststructuralism who is perhaps most explicitly concerned with, or at least, who pays attention in the greatest social and historical detail to the exclusion or subjugation – the exception – of the Other, is Foucault. A strong case could be made for a Foucauldian paradigm alongside the three discussed above, given the enormous influence of his Nietzsche-inspired genealogical approach to social history and epistemology (that is, to both the philosophy and the different possible histories of the relations between power and knowledge). If there is a partial justification for not dealing with the (various) Foucauldian approach(es) in this chapter, it is that his methodological influence has been felt most strongly beyond philosophy, in subjects such as cultural studies, sociology, history, media studies, etc. – subjects that tend to refer to their key thinkers as 'theorists' at least as often as 'philosophers'. In this sense Foucault, though undoubtedly a writer of important works of philosophy, has been taken up more as 'cultural theorist' than continental philosopher (though admittedly, the distinction is ultimately somewhat arbitrary, and meaningful only in limited contexts). A similar argument could be made regarding the work of Walter Benjamin, another thinker whose work has been of great importance for Anglophone continental philosophy, yet whose greatest *methodological* influence has been in other (though related) areas of contemporary research – in cultural studies, literary studies, the sociology and history of art, etc. As with Foucault, the lack of references to Benjamin in the first three sections of this chapter is not intended to minimize his importance for continental philosophy, but only to reflect the fact that it would be hard to identify a Benjaminian 'paradigm' of current philosophical research in the manner that I have suggested organizes large parts of the field.

Another area (again, if it can be described as a single area) that would not fit easily into any of my three paradigms is the philosophy of science. Some of the research in this area is directly influenced by Foucault – in particular where elements of what has come to be called social constructionism are involved. Again, it may be argued that much of this work would be better described as something other than philosophy – for example, as sociology, cultural studies, anthropology or historical research. Nevertheless, the pioneers of new methods of studying the cultural influences on science and technological research, such as the use of ethnography in laboratory settings (Latour, Woolgar, Rabinow) or actor-network theory (Callon, Latour) necessarily make philosophical statements about the nature of the reality (material, ontological, social, semiological) they study. Various areas of cultural research into science and technology can be said to be not only applying, but also developing the implications of work by past philosophers such as Bachelard, Canguilhem, Deleuze and Foucault; while other thinkers, such as Ian Hacking, develop the implications of questions around social construction and the nature of scientific and historical knowledge in an explicitly philosophical mode.

Meanwhile, there are other philosophers who address issues and themes related to science in ways that retain the broadly critical or questioning approach of poststructuralism with regard to traditional conceptions of truth, knowledge and ontology, without fully subscribing to a view of reality as socially constructed (as indeed, many of the thinkers just mentioned no longer do). Isabelle Stengers is one of the most prominent thinkers who addresses scientific concepts, practice and knowledge within a critical philosophical frame. In works such as *The Invention of Modern Science* (2000) and *Power and Invention* (1997) Stengers examines such aspects of the history of science, not to undermine the 'truths' it produces, but to call into question its claims for the universality of these truths, and its claim to exclusive rights over truth and objective knowledge. Elsewhere, notably in collaboration with the chemist Ilya Prigogine (1984), Stengers draws on both scientific research *and* philosophy to address the metaphysical or ontological assumptions that underpin such supposed objectivity, demonstrating the significance of alternative ontologies to the atomistic or Being/beings-based conceptions, such as the processual or vitalist ontologies of thinkers like Bergson and Whitehead.

Another philosopher who deals extensively with scientific concepts in an unconventional manner and who belongs to the same generation of French poststructuralists as Derrida, Foucault and Deleuze (while to some extent working independently of it) is Michel Serres. The approach Serres takes to the history of thought has something in common with Deleuze's nonlinearity and eclecticism, while going further in the degree to which he links scientific concepts and ideas to other philosophical and cultural phenomena. Where Deleuze was able to escape the burden of the history of philosophy by producing subversive re-readings of previous philosophers, making them fit his own concerns at least as much as they determined them, Serres refuses alignment with particular philosophical traditions in order to (re)invent his own 'freedom of thought' (Serres and Latour, 1995, p. 43). Serres's method, if it can be called a method, is developed around the figure of Hermes – the cunning, shape-shifting trickster of Greek mythology – both the 'messenger of the gods', and the roguish thief and bringer to light of hidden meaning (the hermetic). Serres attempts to embody these characteristics in his philosophical work, much of which consists in a series of reflections on the relations he discerns between seemingly unconnected scientific and other socio-cultural phenomena, as in *The Parasite* (1980), in which he relates information theory, fables about exchange-relations and table manners, and parasitology.

If the Nazi genocide constitutes the horizon and impossible condition for other thinkers of Serres's generation (especially those corresponding to the first paradigm above), for Serres the determining event is Hiroshima: 'Hiroshima remains the sole object of my philosophy' (Serres and Latour, 1995, p. 15). Hence, the need to think science in a way that is not always scientific – and indeed, to 'out-think' it – to be fast enough to trace and think through the significance of multiple connections between scientific and cultural phenomena without getting bogged down in any one area: 'One must travel quickly when the thing to be thought about is complex' (Serres and Latour, 1995, p. 70). Though Serres' approach is unique and protean (while also having influenced the methods of other theorists and philosophers engaging with science, including both Latour and Stengers), it could for these very reasons be taken as paradigmatic of an eclectic approach that refuses to be slowed down by the history of philosophy (as found for example in the works of Virilio or Baudrillard, even as such figures' approaches are quite different in other respects).

On the other hand, every thinker mentioned in this chapter, indeed every philosopher, and therefore every philosophical method, is unique. Hence, the list of philosophers and approaches that do not fit into my three paradigms could be extended, perhaps indefinitely (and could even, perversely, be made to include those I centred the paradigms around). Part of the problem here, which is also the strength of continental philosophy, and which was crucial in each of my paradigms, is the constitutive role of non-philosophy (or, simply, 'culture'). As I implied at the outset of this chapter, this can make the list of 'research problems' of continental philosophy virtually endless – while the extent to which continental philosophy develops its approach in relation to such non-philosophical phenomena (objects, processes, concerns) likewise renders unmanageable the range of possible methodologies. Thus there would be a thousand, a million exceptions to any set of paradigms advanced as a rough delineation of the field of contemporary continental philosophy. Perhaps this in itself accounts for philosophy's historical need to suppress certain non-philosophical elements on which it constitutively depends (literature, art, science, the feminine, the animal) – not only so that it remains possible to conceive of philosophy, always temporarily, but repeatedly, as in some sense independent of its others, but also so that it may continue to engage in the quintessentially (continental) philosophical practice of uncovering, championing and re-imagining them.

3 The Continental Tradition
Kant, Hegel, Nietzsche

Gary Banham

The discussion of the tradition of continental philosophy is not a discussion of something that is past, as when analytic philosophers speak of the history of philosophy. Rather, the tradition of continental philosophy is something that is futural, for it is not a recounting of something that we are now done with. The possibility of continental philosophy as a continuous mode of philosophy is bound up with an invention of its history. It is to attempt a way of explicating and defending this contention that the present piece is written. So I am not just going to present an account of three famous thinkers with a rendition of some of their most salient points. Rather, what I wish to do is bring out how a relation to the three thinkers named in the title of this piece is part of the formation of a temporal *practice* of philosophy, a practice that is part of a relation to futurity within thinking. It is this relation to futurity within contestation and reproduction of a tradition that is specific to the historical character of continental philosophy. The thinkers we will reprise here will be visited through a demonstration of the way in which this relation to futurity has been found within their texts.

The Future of Kant

The first point to make concerning the reception of Kant within continental philosophy is that this reception has been constantly marked as a site of philosophical invention, not just an occasion for scholarly attention. Hence, for example, the generation of philosophers immediately after Kant, the so-called 'German Idealists' already considered the future of philosophy as bound up with the reading of his work. This conception was consistently thought of as part of the transformative inheritance of Kant's *system*. Such an investigation was part of a unification of the disparate elements of Kant's enquiry after the manner signalled by Kant himself but that was disputed by those thinkers who precisely wished to think futurity in a manner that is not bound to systems.

The systematic reading of Kant has three possible locations in the formulations of his work: in relation to the unity of self-consciousness, the emphasis on freedom as the keystone of the whole and the description, prominent in the First Introduction to the *Critique of Judgment*, of the faculties and their relation. Intriguingly these systematic possibilities of unification have correlates in metaphysical illusions as specified by Kant. Emphasis on the unity of self-consciousness understood in the illusory way leads to paralogisms. The account of freedom as something demonstrable by means of positive argument is central to the structure of the antinomical nature of reason and attempts to think philosophy itself systematically involve the temptation of dogmatic totalization with concomitant scepticism following. This parallelism is not meant to completely forestall the systematic response to Kant but to warn of the temptation that is involved in following it through.

Such a comprehension of the temptation towards a recuperative dogmatic reading of Kant's system is one of the bases of an anti-systematic reading of Kant, such as is found, paradigmatically, in the work of Jean-François Lyotard. While the history of Lyotard's reception of Kant is multi-layered, it is the case that in this reception there is an insistent attempt to separate the distinct layers of Kant's works in order to present their specificity so that we should not work to systematically unify them. Hence, on this account Kant's work should be seen as one that un-works.[1] If the systematic reading that took shape in the period of German Idealism has the possible consequence of a recuperative dogmatism, does not the anti-systematic reading bear the converse chance of recuperative scepticism? The distinctive rupture that will be found within the Critical system on its account will be one that will rupture the subject, thus preventing transcendental psychology; dissolve the world, thus negating its distinction from nature; and make the completion of critique impossible, thereby disbarring doctrine. The parallel here, as with that given with regard to the Idealist reading, is not sufficient to simply dispel this reading but is again of a weight to render it questionable.

Rather than track the paths and possibilities of these two readings – readings both far from and close to each other in both letter and spirit – I will instead focus only on the question that seems evident to anyone who works on trying to understand the basic movement of Kant's thought: What is the way in which time is here pictured and how, if at all, does Kant account for both its passing and its relation to the transcendental unity of apperception? This double question touches on one of the possible areas of unification of the system in terms of a transcendental unity that might be the ground of a metaphysics of subjectivity and the image of motion that is given in terms of temporality and that might be thought to require, in its capturing of diversity, a resistance to unification.

The question of the manner of presentation of temporality is addressed in the A-Deduction by means of a threefold examination of synthesis which begins with a discussion of the importance of distinguishing 'the time in the sequence of one impression' from that of another (Kant, 2007, A99). The distinction between the sequence in distinct impressions is here one that requires each particular impression to be grasped as unity as this is required, states Kant, 'in the representation of space' (2007, A99).[2] There needs to be a unity for a given impression to be seen as such and this unity is the product of synthesis. This basic doctrine of the *Critique* is presented prior to both the transcendental synthesis of imagination and the transcendental unity of apperception. Nor is this point only made in the A-Deduction, as there is a precisely parallel passage in the B-Deduction where Kant writes: 'Only in so far . . . as I can unite a manifold of given representations in *one consciousness*, is it possible for me to represent to myself the *identity of the consciousness in [i.e. throughout] these representations*' (2007, B133). As with the A-Deduction passage so here we see a clear statement to the effect that the capacity of synthesis of given representations is required in order for the recognition of the action of synthesis that is given in the notion of transcendental apperception to be possible. This synthetic process, described at A99, as running through and holding together, involves capturing a sense of temporality that involves both flux and stability or, more strongly, the ability to present a stable image of movement.

Motion is described as being that which 'first produces the concept of succession' (Kant, 2007, B155) and is hence the source of all that will later be examined in the Second Analogy. While the ability of capturing motion in a stable presentation is hence essential to the possibility of transcendental synthesis as such, it is rarely directly thematized, either by Kant or his commentators. What has received attention, and which I will now attempt to relate to the point concerning the relation of motion to an image, is the doctrine of schematism in Kant. One of the problems of connecting these questions concerns the manner in which Kant presents the procedure of schematism in the *Critique of Pure Reason*. The point of the schematism is to provide a condition for pure concepts to relate to pure intuitions, but the basis of this connection requires a distinction between schemas and images with the example of the distinction between them that Kant gives concerning numbers and geometrical objects. However, the fundamental place in which Kant draws the distinction between images and schemata is one that is of particular interest:

The pure image of all magnitudes (*quantorum*) for outer sense is space; that of all objects of the senses in general is time. But the pure *schema* of magnitude (*quantitas*), as a concept of the understanding, is *number*, a representation which comprises the successive addition of homogeneous units. Number is therefore simply the unity of the synthesis of the manifold of a homogeneous intuition in general, a unity due to my generating time itself in the apprehension of the intuition. (Kant, 2007, A142–3/B182)

Here time is clarified as being the image of all objects of the senses with space being that which allows the possible presentation of all magnitudes. So space and time differ in that only with the former added to the latter can we arrive at measurement in the sense of having determinable magnitudes. If time presents an image of sensible objects in some general sense then we may wonder how this is possible. Schematization, as distinct from images, provides the means of giving enumeration. This schematization is further here described as 'generating time itself'.

Despite the thrust of this passage Martin Heidegger has popularized a view according to which Kant's notion of transcendental schematism is described as an image after the pattern of the presentation of the schema of pure sensible concepts that is involved in presenting a multiplicity by a number.[3] Effectively Heidegger's conception of the possibility of presenting an image of movement by means of schematism is one of movement that is separated from force.[4] However, while Heidegger's means of presenting the conception of schema-image does have problems, there is a point in the notion since Kant clearly states that time itself cannot be represented except through the drawing of a line (2007, B154). So, while the schematization of magnitude is what Kant states 'generates' time itself, the image of time is given in a form that requires spatialization of it. Even so, we may still wonder how all of this accounts for the ability to present an image of motion.

In the citation given above, Kant speaks of successive addition but also traces this possibility of successive addition back to the synthesis of the manifold of a homogeneous intuition. So, for the synthesis that generates the succession (and hence time itself) to take place it is requisite that intuition itself be homogeneous in character. With regard to time, however, there is a basic rationale for this homogeneity as without it the relations between distinct times (such as 'earlier' and 'later') would be impossible.[5] So the unity of time that is produced by transcendental synthesis is one that has to be seen *as* a unity, as without such a precondition to the representation of time being given, we could not arrive at a way of relating elements of time to each other.

If time is a medium of representation and this medium is one whose elements (moments) are each homogeneous to each other, then what can be represented within its structure must partake of the nature of this representing apparatus. So the elements of motion would then be only enumerable as being units of a structurally similar sort. However, this point concerning the representability of motion relates to the ability of what gives to itself the representation of motion to be able to so give the representation. This possibility of being able, that is, to represent time has only thus far been explicated in formal terms without being related to what undertakes this representation or how it does so. That movement of representation is what is termed 'auto-affection' and is one with the transcendental synthesis of imagination: 'the understanding, under the title of a *transcendental synthesis of the imagination*, performs this act upon the *passive* subject, whose *faculty* it is' (Kant, 2007, B153). The subject thus is necessarily in process and its nature is expressed through formation. Not only is this the case but there is an essential relation to futurity expressed in the formation in question.

The sense of this futurity is expressed in the necessity not just of self-affection as the ground of the unity of temporality but of this temporality having in its structure the expectation of a time to come. While this time to come is foreshadowed in each present it is also contained within understanding's operation as something finite in nature. One reading of these claims is that given by Heidegger: 'If the transcendental power of imagination, as the pure, forming faculty, in itself forms time – i.e., allows time to spring forth – then we cannot avoid the thesis . . .: the transcendental power of imagination is original time' (1990, p. 131).[6] This view would allow the image of motion to be determinative for Kant and shut down in the process any true futurity for it. But alongside the theoretical image of motion there are other forms of schematization that allow for differential forms of futurity.[7] Within the *Critique* itself there is a distinctly different notion of schema, the one I would term a final end schema where Kant speaks about the schema of an Idea as expressed in the development of a science: 'in the working out of the science the schema, nay even the definition which, at the start, he first gave of the science, is very seldom adequate to his idea. For this idea lies hidden in reason' (2007, A834/ B862). Kant goes on to make clear here that with an Idea there is a necessary development, which could not be foreseen in those who began the science, and yet which is the presupposition of its development. The schema of the Idea hence expresses teleology but the purpose that is found within the development is over and above the aims of anyone working within the province of the science. So here an image of futurity is clearly given as open and precisely as open *due to* its teleological nature.

In the *Critique of Practical Reason* there is a different sense of schema again expressed, what is there termed a 'typic' which involves not the schema of a case according to laws but rather 'the schema of the law itself' where the law 'is what the understanding can put under an idea of reason on behalf of judgment' (Kant, 1996a, Ak. 5:68–9). What is produced in this way is what is described in the *Groundwork* as the formula of the law of nature whereby '*the nature of the sensible world*' is used as the type of an intelligible nature (Kant, 1996b, p. 196). By means of this procedure it becomes possible to imagine the intelligible world as governed by a form of causality in which the determination of the will is formed by something other than natural connections. In setting out the nature of such thinking by using the schema of the law itself Kant formulates the conception of a pure law and then thinks of this law in terms of its possible motivational force for the will. In treating the latter he is led to the notion of *respect* and its connection to the *example* provided for us by the character of another person.

The example of the other person provides a basis for the humiliation of my self-esteem while simultaneously raising me to the standard of practical reason. However, as Kant was subsequently to discuss in *Religion within the Limits of Reason Alone*, the receptivity to the example of the other requires the adoption of a moral standard that is integral to a *moral rebirth* and this rebirth is here not presented as once and for all but rather as continuous. The continuous opening that is required for moral awakening to be possible and for its effects to be actual is summarized also in the *Religion* in terms of the discussion of human history given there. There is then a form of practical futurity that can be classified as a moral eschatology. Within the limits of this practical vision there is a different account of futurity to that given in the schema of theoretical understanding but one that has many points of connection to the final end schema discussed towards the close of the *Critique of Pure Reason*.[8]

So there are thus far at least two distinct images of futurity in Kant: the one provided in terms of the homogeneous sense of temporality that emerges from the schema of understanding, and the one that emerges in practical reason if this latter is taken to be extensively connected to the final end schema. In addition to these two there is also set out a distinctively aesthetic sense of temporality in the *Critique of Aesthetic Judgment* as Kant there speaks of both a kind of 'lingering' that halts the passage of time in relation to the beautiful and an infinity of reflection with regard to the sublime that overcomes the schema of homogeneity that we found in the first *Critique*.[9] These aesthetic temporalities involve a purposive disruption of the homogeneous accumulation that is given to theoretical understanding. The sublime is, however, double-edged in its relation to temporality since while the mathematical sublime augurs a way of presenting that does not permit totalization of time, the dynamical sublime relates us to force in such a way that we are reminded again of our vocation and reawakens a sense of practical temporality. The possibility of relation between the aesthetic sense of temporality and practical temporality is also given in a different way to the beautiful when Kant speaks of it as the symbol of the good. The possibility of this symbolization is what connects the deepest sense of the aesthetic to that of the practical.

Kant's overall system can be summarized on the reading given here as requiring a consistent procedure of reference to an image of temporality where the nature of this image is formed each time by a kind of schema. The procedure of schema differs in theoretical philosophy from that in practical as while the former is given via a primary reference to quantitative synthesis, the latter requires by contradistinction a form of dynamical image that transcends sensibility. The ability of aesthetic presentation to partake of the sensible while transcending it permits a third form of futural image, but this third form links the other two while also maintaining a tension between them. Unless the three elements of temporality here pictured are retained in a unitary image that also maintains difference, the future of Kant will remain dirempted between systematic and anti-systematic readings.

The Future of Hegel

Both the reception of Hegel and the possibility of the futurity of Hegel stand in marked contrast to those of Kant. The reception of Hegel was initially the scene of division with the formation of philosophical parties who split on the question of the potential radicality or conservatism of his System. Unlike with the case of Kant, the split does not concern systematicity, as the existence of a Hegelian system has never been cast in doubt: Hegel's thought has, in fact, been cast as the very image of philosophical systematicity. The split between conservative and revolutionary readings of Hegel – the split that enabled the emergence of both the thought of Marx and of the further systems of Marxism – has however concerned *at its root* the question as to whether there is even the possibility of a future *in the wake* of Hegel. This question of whether Hegel has left a future for philosophy or history to open into marked in a decisive fashion the twentieth-century reading of his work, not least in France. Within this tradition of reading Hegel – in a manner at once extremely paradoxical and radically inventive – stands the work of Alexandre Kojève. On Kojève's account Hegel's thought only makes sense if we see it as announcing the end of history where this end is one in which man has come to himself after the closure of the era of alienation. Such an account would appear to leave us without any serious futurity with a play opening up that cannot be the source of anything truly meaningful.[10] Response to this account of the 'end of history' reading of Hegel was key to twentieth century assessments of his philosophy, and it recently re-emerged as an important issue with the apparent revival of this conception in the work of Francis Fukuyama.[11]

The focus on this 'end of history' reading of Hegel has produced a decided impression that, *in the wake of Hegel*, there is no future for philosophy or, indeed, for anything much else. Such an account of Hegel's System is the basis of a set of creative resistances to it that marked much twentieth-century thought.[12] With this resistance has come a reaction in particular to something that is surely essential to this System, namely its thought of the Absolute. As Heidegger, for example, writes: 'time is what is *alienated* from the absolute and from the essence of being itself' (1988, p. 145).[13] Heidegger and those who follow his reading of the Hegelian understanding of time take it to be indicative of a failure on Hegel's part not merely to provide room for futurity but also for any originary comprehension of temporality in general.

To open out anew the possibility of a future of and for Hegel has been the mission of Catherine Malabou who has written a book entirely with this purpose. In order to begin to give a chance to this other type of response to Hegel let us not begin by citing Malabou herself but instead look directly at how Hegel uses the term 'schema'. Hegel argues in the *Phenomenology* that it should be seen in relation to the singular individual: 'The singular individual is the transition of the category from its Notion to an *external* reality, the pure *schema* which is both consciousness, and, since it is a singular individual and an exclusive unit, the pointing to an "other"' (1977, para. 236).[14] Malabou understands the import of the discussion of the schema here without referring to the presence of the singular individual, merely summarizing Hegel's statement as requiring us to think that being schematizes itself. This summary is startling enough since it requires an immersion of being into time that is both exorbitant in requiring temporality to be co-terminous with being and in its exorbitance at war with the apparent absence of time from Absolute Knowledge. The latter discussion in the *Phenomenology* appears to require a jettisoning of time from the essential along the lines suggested by Heidegger when Hegel states that time 'appears as the destiny and necessity of Spirit that is not yet complete within itself' (Hegel, 1977, para. 801). If being is that which, on Malabou's reading, 'schematizes itself', and yet the standpoint of the Absolute would appear as one in which time is departed from it as something incomplete, how do we think the relation between these propositions which seem to contradict each other's basic intent?

The response to this question will guide the account I am going to suggest of the future of Hegel as, in a sense, it also guides Malabou's attempted recovery of this future. The citation concerning the apparent departure of Absolute Knowledge from temporality is in fact given at the very opening of Malabou's book with the intent of describing by means of it the essential logic of Heidegger's account of Hegelian temporality. Before describing the means in which Malabou attempts to bring together these two statements from the *Phenomenology*, it is first worth examining the serious question of what it means to read the statements in Hegel's works. This is by no means simple since the appearance of contradiction that we have picked out between these paragraphs could be replicated with any number of others, and this for an essential reason: that statements in Hegel are not to be read in the way they would be in other works. Hegel himself is explicit concerning the importance of a different way of reading being required if his philosophy – speculative philosophy – is to be read:

> The philosophical proposition, since it *is* a proposition, leads one to believe that the usual subject-predicate relation obtains, as well as the usual attitude towards knowing. But the philosophical content destroys this attitude and this opinion. We learn by experience that we meant something other than we meant to mean; and this correction of our meaning compels our knowing to go back to the proposition, and understand it in some other way. (Hegel, 1977, para. 63)

Experience is described in this statement in a way that is consonant with the general thrust of Hegel's thinking. When something is experienced we engage with meanings and happenings that we did not expect, that take us by surprise, that operate in a manner that takes us off our feet or leads us to think that we are ourselves off our heads. The possibility of surprise would be something like the structure of experience in general. One of the ways this is revealed is through the structure of language, which contains meanings we did not expect when we expressed ourselves. We thus find that expression is something independent of 'intentions', if the latter are understood as pure thought processes. Not only is this picture of experience suggested by Hegel in a general way but he also makes clear in this statement from the Preface to the *Phenomenology* that his own thinking *in* its philosophical way of being stated is a thinking that is expressed in a manner that is that of experience itself. Thinking is not here given in a way that can be captured by mere summary and expounded according to a fixed manner: it is itself mobile, it is part of the self-schematization of being and as such our experience of it will alter as we experience generally so that we learn what is here at issue not in one encounter but through many. All of which is as much as to say that Hegel *will take us by surprise.* 'The *proposition* should express *what* the True is; but essentially the True is Subject. As such it is merely the dialectical movement, this course that generates itself, going forth from, and returning to, itself' (Hegel, 1977, para. 65).

So to begin to comprehend the relationship between statements that appear at odds with each other we first need to learn how to read Hegel in a general sense. This reading, we have already learned, is related to experience and to the way that experience constantly gives us lessons, not least about ourselves. It is not just that things are not what we take them to be, or others who we assume they are, but also we ourselves are not what we first, second or third, imagine we are. So to learn to read Hegel is simultaneously to comprehend something about ourselves. 'Because of this necessity, the way to Science is itself already *Science*, and hence, in virtue of its content, is the Science of the *experience of consciousness*' (Hegel, 1977, para. 88). If it is right then to relate to Hegel as an experience of self-discovery where we accept an original occlusion of our nature from ourselves then it follows that we must be constantly in need of awakening from a slumber concerning our situation, and it is this fact of being steeped initially in unconsciousness that makes the relation that would emerge from immersion in Hegelian thinking such a strange one. The point of Malabou's reading of Hegel emerges precisely from understanding this strangeness as one of being related to plasticity on the grounds of Hegel's statement that 'only a philosophical exposition that rigidly excludes the usual way of relating the parts of a proposition could achieve the goal of plasticity' (1977, para. 64).

This 'goal of plasticity' would be one of the identification of subject and substance at which 'Notion corresponds to object and object to Notion' (Hegel, 1977, para. 80). Now we can return to the reference to the singular individual that we found in Hegel's discussion of the schema and which Malabou's summary interpretation seemed to leave behind. The manner in which the reader of Hegel becomes able to read the work is the moment at which the isolated particularity of their reading is left behind to become immersed in a singularity of experience or, as Malabou puts this: 'Singularity is the ostensive, open portion of subjectivity, and particularity its occulting and concealing side: enclosed within itself, it reveals nothing but its own solipsistic being' (2005, p. 181). In focusing on reading in a way that requires the connection of the reader to the nature of the content we practice a reading that treats the text as if it were an experience that we are having trouble digesting. Experience is difficult in the nature of its surprise, and philosophy on Hegel's exposition is surprising also in its difficulty. The connection between difficulty and surprise is effectively the root of the problem of experience. We can take these points further by following a striking analogy Hegel uses:

> Spirit is indeed never at rest but always engaged in moving forward. But just as the first breath drawn by a child after its long, quiet nourishment breaks the gradualness of merely quantitative growth – there is a qualitative leap, and the child is born – so likewise the Spirit in its formation matures slowly and quietly into its new shape, dissolving bit by bit the structure of the previous world, whose tottering state is only hinted at by isolated symptoms. . . . The gradual crumbling that left unaltered the face of the whole is cut short by a sunburst which, in one flash, illuminates the features of the new world. (Hegel, 1977, para. 11)

Just as Kant spoke of rebirth in terms of the conversion required for morality to be practised and in that way woke us from the sense of homogeneous time we had derived from the abstract presentation of theoretical schematization, so here Hegel in his reference to the process of being born requires a sense of how there are breaks or ruptures in the formation of subjectivity that cannot be assimilated to mere forms of continuance. There is something like an event, the event of birth, and this event shapes suddenly a new world even if it is initially so only in a simple way. The re-working of the world is what emerges from the rupturing beginning of something from within that world. This re-working opens the world to a future that was present within it but which must still surprise it.

How can this surprise manifest itself, however, if Hegel's account of the externality of temporality to the standpoint of the Absolute is given as suggested earlier? Malabou suggests one answer to this when she relates the time that is determined in the *Phenomenology* chapter on Absolute Knowledge to a linear homogeneous conception (2005, pp. 128–9).[15] This account would view time itself on the level of modernity and suggest a temporality as emergent beyond modernity.[16] The question that emerges in relation to this account, however, since Malabou relates temporal modernity both to the philosophy of subjectivity and the emergence of Protestantism, concerns the nature of post-Christian temporality and how it is experienced temporally.[17] The problem with this reading would be that while it presents a way of freeing Hegel from the conception of the futureless 'end of history', it gives only a general image of the future which, in its connection of philosophy to religion, still suggests an engagement to come without enabling any sense of the shape of the future that is, as it were, shadowed in Absolute Knowledge.

The mention of a temporality that is left behind in the discussion of Absolute Knowledge should rather be read in a speculative manner: the standpoint of the Absolute is one in which temporality is essentially interiorized and it is this *essential* interiorization that requires departure from time as merely given externally. The standpoint of the Absolute is thus not one that should be set out merely in the form of departure from the past in order for the newness of birth to be given in a complete form. Rather, the birth in question has to summarize as its responsibility the past that it has been given. This summary is at each point of birth complete and also fragmentary.[18] The nature of the maturation required thus constantly changes form, but while engaged in this movement continues to be haunted by a past that cannot be done with. Recognition of this essential engagement with the past is what sharpens the comedy of history on Hegel's account.[19]

Between the recognition of essential temporality as interior to self-formation and the continued failure to complete the relation to the past comes the surprise that is futurity. The future thus always takes us in a way that we did not expect, though we could always have seen it coming. The necessity to recognize the surprise of the future as its inevitability: that is the nature of the speculative movement. This movement is open to the future essentially but this 'open' would be one that requires an unending engagement with the past. Rather than accept the melancholy conservatism of some of Hegel's adherents or the completeness of break suggested by his revolutionary readers, it is the necessity of an engagement that will always surprise in its chance of a necessary encounter that will open the reading of Hegel up to a future that cannot be totally captured.

The Future of Nietzsche

Of the three thinkers discussed here, the one who has had perhaps the stormiest of receptions is Nietzsche. Associated for a long time with some of the worst elements of the twentieth century, he has subsequently become a sign of a form of philosophy that resists assimilation to conventional canons and procedures of investigation. Nothing around the reception of Nietzsche has been simple: the editions of his works have been sites of contestation, as have the status of fragments and passages that, for a variety of reasons, he never published himself. The fact of Nietzsche's breakdown into madness has also been taken to reveal the impossibility of his thinking. Despite the controversy surrounding his work, Nietzsche has been one of the most frequently referenced philosophers in contemporary Continental works and, indeed, in contemporary art and literature. This wide nature of his felt affect has itself both caused suspicion and been an occasion for celebration. What is certain is that virtually every major thinker in Europe has felt a need to respond to his work at some time or other.

Since Nietzsche is the site of such wide and multifaceted controversy, it is particularly difficult to summarize the main contours of his reception. A central question that has recurred, however, concerns the nature of Nietzsche's relationship to philosophy itself. This question has been on occasion linked to the nature of Nietzsche's relation to metaphysics, with Heidegger for example claiming that Nietzsche is the 'last' metaphysician.[20] Subsequent readers of Nietzsche have disputed this claim, but the argument concerning metaphysics has tended to become subsumed into a general discussion of Nietzsche's relationship to philosophy itself. Those readers who think of Nietzsche as distinct from metaphysics often accompany this argument with one that distinguishes him from the institution of philosophy itself, or at the very least as someone who requires us to undertake the enquiry that is philosophy in quite a different way than hitherto. The division in the reception of Nietzsche thus in a sense is related to the question of what type of future Nietzsche provides an image of: Is it a future in which repetition of *the same* will take place or is it one that will require *selection*? I have deliberately phrased the question in a manner that indicates that the question of the reception of Nietzsche is intimately related to the understanding of Nietzsche's view of temporality, particularly in his teaching of the eternal return.

In taking the reception of Nietzsche to be related to readings of the eternal return I do not wish to minimize a number of other key questions in the

interpretation of his work. Alongside the eternal return Nietzsche places discussion of the will to power, and the relationship between these two thoughts
has been a vexed question in Nietzsche studies.[21] Further, Nietzsche's inquiries into aesthetics are both the starting point of his philosophical work and the
subject of some of his last pieces (such as *The Case of Wagner*). Understanding
how and why Nietzsche re-draws the philosophical enquiry into aesthetics
is clearly of real interest. So also would be the use Nietzsche makes of natural
science, not merely in his so-called 'free spirit' trilogy but throughout his
work. Finally, there is obvious reason to be concerned with the nature of
Nietzsche's responses to Christianity and to the history of morality. However,
important as all these topics are in the understanding of Nietzsche's philosophical work, none of them gives such a decided key to the nature of his
view of futurity as does examination of his teaching concerning the eternal
return.

The examination of the teaching that Nietzsche offers under this title is,
however, inseparably bound up not merely with the nature of his image of
futurity but also with the philosophical question of what it is that makes
Nietzsche such a truly singular thinker. The reason for saying this is that
Nietzsche, in presenting this teaching, also says something singular about the
meaning of being the one who can present it, as when he writes in *Ecce Homo*:

> I shall now tell the story of Zarathustra. The basic conception of the work,
> the *idea of eternal recurrence*, the highest formula of affirmation that can
> possibly be attained – belongs to the August of the year 1881: it was jotted
> down on a piece of paper with the inscription: '6,000 feet beyond man and
> time'. (Nietzsche, 1979, p. 99)

Here we see Nietzsche's remembrance of the insight that motivated *Thus
Spoke Zarathustra* as being one that lifted him into a rare state of ecstasy.[22] The
ecstasy in question is due to having attained such a high formula of affirmation, as the idea of eternal return represents. The connection of the idea to the
ecstasy is reiterated in a number of places by Nietzsche, but unquestionably
forms part of the reason why, in this work, Nietzsche makes such drastic and
dramatic claims about himself and the nature of his works.

The communication of the ecstasy in question led Nietzsche to invent new
genres of philosophical writing. I do not here refer to the celebrated use of
aphorisms but more to the use of writing to attempt to engage in a kind of communication that is at war with its own ability to communicate, as it appears
to be dealing with something essentially non-communicable. Alongside the
ecstasy that accompanies the teaching of the idea of eternal return came a
kind of disgust that is stated in a repeated fashion in Nietzsche's writings and
not least in *Zarathustra* which opens with a contrast between the Overman

and the 'last man'. The last man is described as the one 'who makes everything small' and is clearly intended as an image of the summation of everything that leads to resistance to the very idea of the eternal return: 'The greatest all too small! – that was my disgust at man! And eternal recurrence even for the smallest! that was my disgust at all existence!' (Nietzsche, 1969b, p. 236).

The experience of the insight into eternal return occurs to one who fears what the rest of the age seemed to welcome: namely, the equality of humanity. The reactions of disgust at this in Nietzsche's texts concern the problem that such equality could merely be an equal mediocrity. The levelled achievement of such equality is what is symbolized in the figure of the last man and Nietzsche's image of this figure is as one with his diagnosis concerning Christianity. However, this rancorous image of Christianity and morality is one that itself runs against the deepest sense of the teaching of return as indicated again in *Ecce Homo* where Nietzsche speaks of 'redeeming the entire past' (Nietzsche, 1979, p. 75). There are two basic questions concerning the eternal return: first, how does it enable us to deal with the disgust aroused by the image of the past, and secondly, how can it be assumed as an idea without destroying the one who would embrace it? The first problem seriously runs through Nietzsche's texts creating an immense problem concerning the stability of his contrasts, a question of stability that Nietzsche often explicitly indicates he understands:

> To *communicate* a state, an inner tension of pathos through signs, including the tempo of these signs – that is the meaning of every style; and considering that the multiplicity of inner states is in my case extraordinary, there exists in my case the possibility of many styles – altogether the most manifold art of style any man has ever had at his disposal. (Nietzsche, 1979, 'Why I Write Such Excellent Books', §4)

This multiplicity of states and styles includes the crossing of the central contrasts sketched within the work. So would Nietzsche then be one who could not bear the consequence of return since he would both be the one to announce it and the one to announce the reasons for repelling it?

The images of the past in Nietzsche are persistently ambiguous. In the *Genealogy of Morals*, for example, the discussions of *ressentiment*, the ascetic ideal and 'bad conscience' all involve the same forms of ambiguity. The discussion of the origin of 'bad conscience' in the second essay of the work, for example, traces it back to the awakening of consciousness and the setting of consciousness against instinct, declaring that 'the existence on earth of an animal soul turned against itself, taking sides against itself, was something so new, profound, unheard of, enigmatic, contradictory, *and pregnant with a future* that the aspect of the earth was essentially altered' (Nietzsche, 1969a,

II §6). Here futurity itself as *a possibility* is shown to come from bad conscience, and, furthermore, with 'bad conscience' consciousness emerges, in order to make 'all ideal and imaginative phenomena' (Nietzsche, 1969a, II §18) available to us at all. Similarly, while the bad conscience is described as an illness it is so, says Nietzsche, in the same manner that pregnancy is (1969a, II §19). So it is bad conscience that brings the future into being, and with it the possibility of art itself, about which Nietzsche reveals the same kind of ambivalence as he does about 'bad conscience' (and not merely in his complex dealings with the question of Wagner). The ascetic priest is described as 'among the greatest *conserving* and yes-creating forces of life' (Nietzsche, 1969a, III §14) and the ascetic ideal itself 'is so universal that all the other interests of human existence seem, when compared with it, petty and narrow' (III §23).

The answer to the question concerning the past thus is double-edged: while Nietzsche may think: 'Too long, the earth has been a madhouse!' (1969a, II §23), this madhouse is also what has produced all that is valuable in addition to all that is crazed. The separation of one from the other would thus be an immense task, and while the archetypes of Overman and 'last man' seem to emerge as indications of distinctly different futures, may they not cross each other? The question of the past in its double-edged character, in other words, creates a question of the future as similarly double-edged, and indicates how even a future thought through the prism of eternal return is as capable of producing disgust as affirmation. Since the past is the product of the manner in which consciousness has been forced to come forth under emergency conditions of living, and such consciousness has produced the tremendous pressure of humanity upon itself that we term the history of morals, and that a selective sense of return has to select that which is creative, does this not *mandate* the return of that history *once more*?

> To look from a morbid perspective towards *healthier* concepts and values, and again conversely to look down from the abundance of *rich* life into the secret labour of the instinct of *décadence* – that is what I have practiced most, it has been my own particular field of experience, in this if in anything I am a master. (Nietzsche, 1979, 'Why I Am So Wise', §1)

If the earth is all too long a madhouse and yet the madhouse is the condition of everything of value having value at all, then what else can be the result of this thought than a journey to the madhouse? Think here of Nietzsche's description of Jesus:

> an instinctive hatred of *every* reality, as flight into the 'ungraspable', into the 'inconceivable', as antipathy towards every form, every spatial and temporal concept, towards everything firm, all that is custom, institution,

> Church, as being at home in a world undisturbed by reality of any kind,
> a merely 'inner' world, a 'real' world, an 'eternal' world. (Nietzsche,
> 1968, §29)

Then think of the state indicated in the final letters when Nietzsche signs himself 'Dionysus', 'the Crucified', and declares himself to be 'all the names in history'. The former state of Jesus is described in *The Anti-Christ* by Nietzsche as the state of an idiot: the idiot being the one who is impossibly sensitive and hence can no longer touch anything. The latter state indicated in the last letters is one in which everything in history, all the fateful names and the signs of divinity, are assumed. These states are apparent antipodes and yet effective equivalents, since in neither are actions any longer possible.

The state of experience of the eternal return is a state of dissolution: no one is the subject of eternal return, the points of history are equivalent and the future is a repetition that requires infinite affirmation. As Pierre Klossowski puts this: 'We are other than what we are now: *others* that are not elsewhere, but *always* in this *same life*' (1997, p. 41). The division of life into the forces that fight against each other through and by means of consciousness creates a set of physiological types that engage in severe and cruel combat. Nietzsche is the victim of this combat, one crucified by the struggle in question and tortured into a silence that mirrors the incommunicable communication that the multiplicity of his styles represents.

> Every profound thinker is more afraid of being understood than of being
> misunderstood. The latter may perhaps wound his vanity; but the former
> will wound his heart, his sympathy, which says always: 'alas, why do *you*
> want to have as hard a time of it as I had'? (Nietzsche, 1972, §290)

Nietzsche's relation to philosophy is problematic because his work marks the crisis of *experiences* which are rare in their intensity and yet symptomatic of something essential in the era after the intensity of Christianity has passed but in which its legacy is still undigested.[23] The difficulty of a relation to temporality that will enable an overcoming of the disgust created by the repeated need for torture and cruelty for the formation of anything imaginative and ideal: this relation that requires an affirmative of the terrible since it is so bound up with the beautiful, it is this that is at the heart of Nietzsche's teaching of eternal return and it is on this rock that he breaks. His teaching is bound up with his illness and yet his illness is borne in the future of culture.

The basic question of Nietzsche's thinking is hence bound up with the experience of the singular individual that is named 'Nietzsche'. This name, 'all the names of history' is what is inherited as a task and set of intensities. The inheritance of Nietzsche necessarily is marked by the same ambivalences, ecstasies and disgusts that formed the thought itself. There is a specular relation between Nietzsche and his readers. 'Every profound spirit needs a mask: more, around every profound spirit a mask is continually growing, thanks to the constantly false, that is to say *shallow* interpretation of every word he speaks, every step he takes, every sign of life he gives' (Nietzsche, 1972, §40). Nietzsche had to move between each state described, each symptom diagnosed; he could not keep still in one or rest secure in a given evaluation as the activity of the evaluations was one he understood to emerge from contracts that required binding of forces. These actions of binding manifest symptoms and the valuations we normally give are ways of expression of the physiologies that are active in the bindings in question. Nietzsche lucidly states this and tracks the manifestations of covering over involved in the masking of spirit by its double, the constant manifestation of *döppleganger* at work in the appearance of Zarathustra's 'ape' and the possibility of utilization of Zarathustra by Nietzsche himself as a sign opposite to the one that historically was given him.

So the future of Nietzsche must effectively remain 'to come' in the further recourse of forces to the use of his texts in manners that oppose some of their tendencies in the furtherance of others. The possibility of a reading of Nietzsche that could freeze him into doctrinal statements that one could finally and decisively say yes or no to is alien not merely to the atmosphere of his thought, but to the very possibility of it as an expression of experiences that are beyond the reader. The requirement of reading Nietzsche is thus that one does not expect to master his texts but rather to be borne by them towards futures one can anticipate only in the sense of a monstrosity yet to manifest its figure for this time. There is hence plenty of future yet in the works of Nietzsche, between Apollo and Dionysus, between Dionysus and the Crucified, between Schopenhauer, Wagner and Spinoza, for a temporality yet to be given any determinate shape. But these futures will unsettle: it is the nature of the works signed 'Nietzsche' to so unsettle as the experience of eternal return must lead to the acceptance that not only must one become what one is, but that one is it already, and yet that what one is cannot be of the order of knowledge.

In Nietzsche's case it is not an attitude that responds to his thought that attempts to overcome the divisions between his interpreters or the division between the elements of the texts signed in his name. The experience of the division between temporality and morality is the one that Nietzsche sets before us so that a responsible attitude towards him neither leaves him in the past nor thinks of itself as being what can guide the legacy of this thought in future. Nietzsche's fate is thus one that will manifest itself further in forms beyond comprehension and yet which will be all the more fierce in arrival the more the time enacts an attitude of resistance to it. The nature of relation to this philosophical body of thought is hence one in which its statement is integral to its possibility of comprehension and yet in which this statement cannot be recuperatively possessed (as some have imagined is possible for Hegel). It is this inability to assimilate Nietzsche's thinking to a stable image which is at heart the reason for his work continuing to vex. If we could fix it and determine its sense through a full description of the meaning of will to power and its relation to eternal return, we would then have done with it and return to painting grey in grey. But just as the plasticity of Hegel reveals the futurity of his work, so the mania gripping Nietzsche's work creates in the reader a mimetic need to return to reading that which is essentially incomplete. The writings that accumulate around Nietzsche's name and which show no sign of diminishing are the signs of a continued problem with the legacy of *ressentiment*. Jumping over this legacy is not possible, so that Nietzsche's work will remain a schooling that involves as much melancholy as joy.

The Future of Continental Philosophy

The three figures examined here have been taken to be thinkers who are not merely past, and not least because each gives images of temporality that do not permit the satisfactions of a linear completion of assimilation of a thinker. Continental philosophy is distinctively related to its tradition precisely in its acceptance of legacies that are understood to decisively mark the present and the possibilities of futurity. The three figures examined here are distinct examples of the manner in which the pressure of inheritance can be manifested, and I have given in my exposition certain summary simplifications of their images. The necessity of simplification was indeed part of what we expounded here as one of the lessons of Hegel, but the danger of all such simplification was similarly seen to be part of the plasticity of his message. With each simplification there is a danger that the image presented, an image necessarily partial, will be taken for the whole and used as sufficient for engagement with the thought rather than a first base on which to build. To avoid that possibility I have insisted in each case on the multiple possibilities each of the thinkers examined offers to thought. The futurity at work in Kant's work, for example, was shown to involve at least three elements with the distinctions between theoretical reason, practical reason and reflective judgment required to be held in productive tension with each other. Hegel was shown to still offer images of futurity despite the common reading of his work as closing off all possible engagement with novelty on the grounds of an end of temporality in the Absolute. The Absolute was suggested to be unified in division, an image that does not permit the closure some have wished to assume in Hegel and the speculative proposition was thus the expression of an experience that could not be one of closure. Nietzsche's work, by contrast, sometimes taken to be a fresh exposition of futurity and innocence, is here suggested instead to be marked by the burden of inheritance in an unusually decisive way. The burden of this inheritance indeed is suggested by the account given here to be what is essential to the possibility of understanding the teaching of eternal return.

Each of the thinkers examined is a thinker whose work is marked by divisions, ruptures and ambivalences. The nature of the interpretive task is thus one that requires a movement between unification and division and this, while most prominent in Hegel, is also pronounced in Nietzsche and Kant. The nature of the movement in question is not the same between the thinkers, as the questions engaged with and the nature of the way they are treated is different in each case. Singularity is essential to the experiences of each but it is a different singularity in each case. Inheritance of singularity is similarly different with each one who inherits so that the future of continental philosophy can no more be given in any particular way of thought than it can in its relation to any one of its illustrious ancestors. The inheritance of continental philosophy must be multiple and its possible futures plural: only in this way will it continue to be able to be thought that traces the nature of *experience*.

Part I

Contemporary Continental Philosophy

Metaphysics and Ontology

Daniel W. Smith

In the popular mind, metaphysics is often characterized as the philosophical theory of everything that pertains to the Beyond, to what is beyond experience – God, the soul, the spiritual, belief in the afterlife (Adorno, 2000, p. 6). No doubt this is what led F. H. Bradley to quip that metaphysics is simply an attempt to find bad reasons for what one is going to believe anyway (cited in van Inwagen, 2002, p. 14). Translated into philosophical terms, this would imply that metaphysics is a philosophy of the transcendent as opposed to the immanent. Nietzsche famously ridiculed metaphysics as a doctrine that assumes the existence of a world behind or beyond the world that we know and can know (the 'two worlds'). In *Zarathustra*, he dubbed this other world the *Hinterwelt*, the 'back-world', and he called those metaphysicians who concerned themselves with this other world *Hinterwelter*, 'backworldsmen' (an allusion to the word 'backwoodsmen', *Hinterwälder*) (Nietzsche, 1954, p. 142).[1] Nietzsche's target was primarily Platonism: behind the world of phenomena or appearances, there was supposed to be concealed a truly real, permanent and unchanging world of essences, existing in itself, and the task of metaphysics was to unravel and reveal this other transcendent world. In this regard, metaphysics can be seen to be the result of a secularization of mythical and magical thinking – Plato's Ideas have been called gods turned into concepts (Adorno, 2000, pp. 5, 18).

Yet it would be simplistic to identify metaphysics with transcendence *tout court*. In its most general sense, metaphysics is an attempt to determine the constitutive structures of Being on the basis of thought alone, and thus it is a form of philosophy that takes *concepts* (or Ideas or Forms) as its object. This is why, from the start, metaphysics has been intertwined with problems of logic and epistemology, culminating in Hegel's teaching that logic and metaphysics were really one and the same, immanent to each other. It is true that in Plato, the most transcendent of metaphysicians, these concepts were deemed to be of a higher order of being than existing things; yet even in Plato's late period, one can already find the phenomenal world asserting itself increasingly against the Idea, perhaps under Aristotle's growing influence. The primary object of metaphysics, in other words, is not transcendence *per se* but rather the *relation* between transcendence and immanence, between essence and existence, between universal and particular – or, in Heidegger's parlance, the *difference* between Being and beings.[2]

The fact is, however, that the terms 'metaphysics' and 'ontology', like many other terms in philosophy, are highly over-determined, and their meaning and use vary with different philosophers and in different traditions. Moreover, in European philosophy, especially since Hegel and Heidegger, the development of metaphysics and ontology has been intimately linked to the rereading and retrieval of various figures in the history of philosophy. In Hegel, these figures tended to be taken up as moments in the dialectic, whereas Heidegger tended to read previous thinkers as his own contemporaries, rather than as representatives of a particular period or 'position'. Most contemporary European philosophers follow Heidegger in this regard, and often develop their own thought in the context of their readings of past thinkers. We have used these two rubrics as our guiding thread in the discussion that follows. On the one hand, we will attempt to elucidate the sense that is ascribed to the terms metaphysics and ontology (and their interaction) in several recent thinkers whose work has focused on these issues (Jacques Derrida, Emmanuel Levinas, Gilles Deleuze, Alain Badiou). On the other hand, we will contextualize the trajectories of these thinkers by examining the positions some of their primary historical interlocutors – notably Kant and Heidegger. The result will be a partial but hopefully perspicuous overview of the complex issues involved in contemporary debates in continental metaphysics and ontology.

Ontology in the European tradition is resolutely post-Kantian and post-Heideggerian: it was Heidegger who renewed interest in ontology in European philosophy, following Kant's attempt to determine the legitimacy and scope of traditional metaphysics. In Kant, the difference between ontology and metaphysics can be summarized in the difference between two types of concepts: categories and Ideas. 'The proud name of an Ontology', Kant famously wrote, 'must give place to the modest title of a mere Analytic of pure understanding' (which has sometimes been called a 'metaphysics of experience') (Kant, 1929, A247/B303, p. 264). Kant defined a category as a concept of the understanding that can be said of *every* object of possible experience. The concepts 'red' and 'rose' are not categories, since not all objects are roses, and not all roses are red; but 'causality' is a category because we know, prior to experience, that it is a universal predicate that can be said of *every* object of experience (every object has a cause and is itself the cause of other things). More precisely, a category is more than a predicate. It is a *condition*, a condition of possible experience: it is the categories that define the domain of possible experience; they tell us what it means for any object whatsoever to *be*. In Aristotle's language, the categories are the different senses in which Being is said of beings, *they are the different senses of the word 'Being'*. In Heidegger's formulation, the categories are the fundamental 'determinations of the Being of beings' (Heidegger, 1988, p. 102; cf. p. 117). Numerous philosophers have proposed tables of categories: Aristotle proposed a list of ten categories; Kant proposed an alternative list of twelve, derived from the model of judgment.[3] An *Idea*, by contrast, is the concept of an object that goes *beyond* or *transcends* any possible experience.[4] In the 'Transcendental Dialectic', the longest section of the *Critique of Pure Reason*, Kant sets out to expose the three great terminal points of traditional metaphysics – the Soul, the World and God – as *illusions* internal to reason itself. We can know *a priori* that there is no object that could correspond to such Ideas; we can never have a 'possible experience' of them. The aim of Kant's transcendental philosophy, in the *Critique of Pure Reason*, is to distinguish between the illegitimate (transcendent) Ideas of traditional metaphysics, and the legitimate (immanent) categories that determine the domain of possible experience, or ontology.[5]

The greatness of Kant's critical project, however, lies less in simply having demarcated the domains of ontology and metaphysics than in tracing out their complex interactions. Kant himself assigned to transcendent Ideas a positive and legitimate use as ideal *focal points* or *horizons* outside experience that posit the unity of our conceptual knowledge as a problem; as such, they can help regulate the systematization of our scientific knowledge, and serve as the postulates of practical reason (we act morally *as if* there were a God and a soul). Heidegger, in his influential *Kant and the Problem of Metaphysics*, emphasized the foundational role played in Kant by the temporal powers of the productive imagination – *schematizing* and *synthesizing* – without which the categories could never determine the spatio-temporal dynamisms of experience (Heidegger, 1962b). In the *Critique of Judgment*, one of the most remarkable texts in the history of philosophy, Kant pushed his earlier analyses in a new and surprising direction: when *synthesis* breaks down, it produces the sentiment of the *sublime*; and a schema, when freed from the legislation of the understanding, is capable of becoming a *symbol* (a white lily is an analogue of the Idea of Innocence). In both these cases, Kant attempted to show that there is *a presentation of Ideas that is immanent within experience itself*, even if this presentation is negative, indirect or 'analogical'. The *Critique of Judgment* thus configured the relation between ontology and metaphysics in a more complex manner than the *Critique of Pure Reason*, setting the agenda for Romanticism and German Idealism, and their current revival (for instance, in the debates concerning the metaphysical and non-metaphysical readings of Hegel; for a perspicuous analysis see Lumsden, 2008).

Post-war French philosophy was similarly engaged in the problems surrounding Kant's critique of metaphysics. Jean-François Lyotard, for instance, wrote extensively on the concept of the sublime (the presentation of the unpresentable) in his effort to think the distinction between the modern and the 'post-modern' (see Lyotard, 1984 and 1994). More importantly, perhaps,

Jacques Derrida's later work, which focuses on pure Ideas such as the gift, hospitality, forgiveness, justice, democracy and so forth, was presented by Derrida himself as a practical variant of Kant's 'Transcendental Dialectic'.[6] Kant had already shown that, whenever we speak of something 'pure' we are outside the realm of possible experience, which always presents us with impure mixtures.[7] Similarly, Derrida shows that a pure gift is an impossibility, since when I accept the gift and say 'Thank you', I am in effect proposing, in a movement of re-appropriation, a kind of equivalence between the giving and my gratitude, thereby incorporating the transcendent logic of the pure gift into an immanent economy of exchange and debt. We can *think* the pure gift, we can even *desire* it, but we never encounter it in experience. When Derrida was looking for a term to describe the formal status of concepts (or rather, 'quasi-concepts') such as the gift, he initially thought of adopting the Kantian term 'antinomy', but decided to use the Greek term 'aporia' instead, in order to distance himself from Kant (the fundamental difference between Kantian Ideas and Derridean quasi-concepts is their temporal status) (Derrida, 1993, p. 16).[8] The fundamental aporia of the pure Ideas analyzed by Derrida is that the condition of their possibility is their very impossibility – which is why he describes his list of quasi-concepts as 'so many aporetic places or dislocations' with Being (Derrida, 1993, p. 15). In general, one might say that, after Kant, there remained two ways of doing metaphysics: either (1) by returning to pre-critical metaphysics (whether or not one remains preoccupied with the traditional metaphysical problems of the existence of God, the immortality of the soul, or the freedom of the will); or (2) by attempting to develop a rigorously post-Kantian metaphysics that jettisons the Idea of the Self, the World, and God (even if this meant returning to pre-Kantian thinkers such as Hume, Spinoza and Leibniz from a post-Kantian viewpoint). Most subsequent metaphysics in the European tradition has followed this latter route, taking Kant's critique as a *fait accompli*. If there is to be a post-Kantian metaphysics, it must be a metaphysics that, in Deleuze's words, 'excludes the coherence of the thinking subject, of the thought world, and of a guarantor God' (1994, p. 58, translation modified). Deleuze's development of a purely immanent theory of Ideas in *Difference and Repetition* is perhaps the most radical attempt to reconcile metaphysics and ontology in the post-Kantian context.

Martin Heidegger's *Being and Time* inaugurated the renewal of interest in ontology in European philosophy, and took it in a new direction.[9] Heidegger emphasized the importance of what he called the 'ontological difference' between Being (*das Sein*) and beings (*das Seiende*). For Heidegger, metaphysics is the domain of thought that concerns itself with *beings* (the ontic). Utilizing a medieval distinction, special metaphysics (*metaphysica specialis*) concerns the 'regional ontologies' of the various sciences (biology examines the being of living organisms; theology examines the nature of God as the highest being etc.) whereas general metaphysics (*metaphysica generalis*) examines the most general concepts that can be predicated of *any* possible being, or all beings as a whole (such as Kant's categories). But if metaphysics constitutes the root of philosophy, the soil from which it draws its nourishment is *ontology*.[10] Rather than examining specific beings, or the nature of beings in general, ontology asks the question of Being itself (the ontological), and in this sense, every metaphysics can be said to presuppose an ontology (Heidegger, 1975). For Kant, the problem with metaphysics is that it is the locus of transcendent illusions, whereas for Heidegger, the problem with metaphysics is that it has forgotten and concealed the question of Being.[11]

Heidegger wrote *Being and Time* as a propaedeutic to his investigation into this question of Being.[12] The book poses the preliminary question: What are the conditions under which the question of Being can even be asked? To do this Heidegger undertakes an existential analytic of '*Dasein*' as a parallel to the transcendental analytic undertaken by Kant in the *Critique of Pure Reason*. Whereas Kant's analytic provided a deduction of the *categories* as the conditions of possibility for objects and our knowledge of objects (a metaphysics of experience), Heidegger's analytic attempts to deduce the fundamental categories of *Dasein*'s existence, which he thus calls *existentialia* rather than categories. If categories concern the being of objects (What?), *existentialia* concern the being of Dasein (Who?), starting with the fundamental *existentialia* of Being-in-the-world. But as Kierkegaard had shown, the uniqueness of *Dasein* is that it is confronted with two basic existential possibilities: it can either flee from its own being, which is what takes place in our 'average everydayness' (inauthenticity), or it can choose its own being and disclose new possibilities for itself (authenticity). This is why it is the fundamental problems of *temporality* and *truth* that come to the fore in *Being and Time*. The being of *Dasein* turns out to be revealed, not in an essence or in a pre-existing 'human nature', but in what Heidegger calls the three 'ex-stases' of time: in its authentic existence, *Dasein* is always outside itself, transcending itself, open to new possibilities of Being. But if this temporal structure constitutes the 'truth' of *Dasein*'s being, it remains concealed in its everyday existence, which is why Heidegger argued, famously, that the traditional concept of truth as *adequatio* (the correspondence between a proposition and a state of affairs) found its primordial existential ground in the notion of truth as *unconcealedness* (*aletheia*). For there to be a science, a 'region' of being must have already been *disclosed*. But this process of disclosure requires a type of thinking that is not merely representational: attaining the 'truth' of Being requires a thought that is not merely directed towards beings as they are already given to us, but that is capable of disclosing *new* possibilities of Being.[13]

For Heidegger, this propaedeutic examination of the being of *Dasein* serves as the guiding thread for his interpretation of the concept of Being itself, which has a similar structure. If Heidegger calls for an 'overcoming (*Überwindung*) of metaphysics' or a 'destruction' of the history of ontology, it is because the history of metaphysics itself has consisted of a 'forgetting' of the question of Being, concealing the question itself under various determinations. These determinations of Being have included the *Idea* in Plato, *substantia* and *actualitas* in Medieval philosophy, *objectivity* in modern philosophy, *technology* in modern science, and the *will to power* in Nietzsche (the last metaphysician).[14] In his own attempt to think and disclose the question of Being, the later Heidegger turned to the Presocratics, to language, to poetry (Hölderlin, Rilke). But just as Kant had shown that the true object of an Idea was a *problem*, and was grasped in a *problematic* mode, Heidegger showed that ultimately the concept of Being is itself a *question*, that it is grasped in the mode of *questioning*. In Plato, famously, the question of Being appears primarily in the form, 'What is . . .?' [*ti estin*?]. Plato wanted to oppose this to all other forms of questioning – such as Who? Which one? How many? How? Where? When? In which case? From what point of view? – which he criticized as minor and vulgar questions of opinion that expressed confused ways of thinking (see Robinson, 1953, pp. 49–60). Heidegger's fundamental insight, in short, was that *Being always presents itself to us in a problematic form*: it constantly discloses new possibilities, it is the production of the new, the creation of difference. Once Being is disclosed in a particular manner, metaphysics can indeed articulate the categorical truths of both Being *qua* being as well as existing beings, and it can conceive of truth 'in the already derivative form of the truth of cognitive knowledge and the truth of propositions that formulate such knowledge' (Heidegger, 1998, p. 280). But in doing so, metaphysics 'drives out every other possibility of revealing', it blocks access to Being's self-disclosure (*es gibt*), its character as the 'origin' of the new (Heidegger, 1977, p. 27).

We find in Heidegger, then, a new distribution of metaphysics and ontology. For Kant, ontology determines the domain of possible experience (the categories of the Transcendental Analytic), whereas what traditional metaphysics thinks transcends possible experience (the illusory Ideas of the Transcendental Dialectic). For Heidegger, ontology is the exploration of the question of Being, whereas metaphysics is what conceals the question of Being, just as 'average everydayness' separates *Dasein* from its own being (the Existential Analytic). To some degree, every subsequent philosopher in Europe has worked in Heidegger's shadow, whether positively and negatively, and in the remainder of this essay, we will briefly chart out the four Heideggerian paths taken by Levinas, Derrida, Deleuze and Badiou.

Emmanuel Levinas offered a critique of Heidegger that separated ontology and metaphysics in a new manner: the two central claims of his *Totality and Infinity* are that 'metaphysics precedes ontology' and that 'metaphysics is an ethics' (Levinas, 1969, pp. 42–3, 78–9). Levinas offers a strong critique of ontology, which he defines as that movement of thought that can only comprehend the singularity of things through the mediation of a neutral middle term, which alone renders being intelligible – such as the generic concept of category in Aristotle, or even the 'Being of beings' in Heidegger. But in this movement – whatever form it takes – the singularity of the existent, its *alterity*, is neutralized; the other is reduced to the same and thematized, possessed. Levinas's metaphysical project has a twofold aim. First, in general terms, it attempts to reverse this movement, to 'escape from being', to assert the primacy of the other over the same, and to recover a primordial relationship with alterity (Levinas, 1985, p. 59). Guided by the formal structures of the 'idea of the infinite' in Descartes' *Meditations* and the 'Good beyond Being' (*agathon epekeina tes ousias*) in Plato's *Republic*, Levinas argues that what he calls the 'metaphysical relation', which is prior to ontology, is a relation with *a radically absolute and transcendent Other* (the infinite, the Good) that cannot be thought, and is not a concept, a representation or a thematization (Levinas, 1969, p. 211). What then is it? This is the second pole of Levinas's thought. For Levinas, the relation with the Other is an *ethical* relation, and not a relation of knowledge. Much of Levinas' work is devoted to exploring the structures through which the metaphysical relation is concretized in the ethical relation: (1) the alterity of the *face* of the other, which signifies the other's transcendence; (2) the *command* of the other ('Thou shalt!'), which is not convertible into a content of consciousness; (3) the fundamental *passivity* of the I in relation to the command of the other and (4) the infinite *responsibility* of the I for the other, which for Levinas is 'the essential, primary, and fundamental structure of subjectivity' (and not, as for Heidegger, transcendence) (Levinas, 1985, p. 95). Heidegger himself had written little on ethics, and Levinas' double revolution, against both Aristotle and Heidegger, is to have posited ethics as 'first philosophy', and not ontology; and, in a post-Kantian vein, to have re-linked ethics and metaphysics (transcendence).

In a not dissimilar vein, Jacques Derrida's early work took over the Heideggerian task of 'overcoming metaphysics' or 'destroying ontology'. For Derrida, metaphysics is determined by its structural 'closure', and deconstruction is a means of disturbing this closure, creating an opening or an interruption. The notion of metaphysical closure itself depends on a movement of transcendence, that is, an 'excess over the totality, without which no totality would appear' (Derrida, 1980, p. 117). Since one cannot transcend metaphysics as such – there is no 'outside' to the metaphysical tradition – one can only destructure or deconstruct metaphysics from within. The project of 'overcoming metaphysics', in other words, is an impossibility, but it is this very impossibility that conditions the possibility of 'deconstruction'. Rather than trying to get outside metaphysics, one can submit 'the regulated play of philosophemes' in the history of philosophy to a certain slippage or sliding that would allow them to be read as 'symptoms of something that *could not be presented*' in metaphysics (Derrida, 1981, pp. 6–7).[15] Immanent within metaphysics, there lies a formal structure of transcendence that can *never* be made present as such, but that nonetheless functions as the 'quasi-transcendental' condition of metaphysics itself. Derrida thus situates his work, he says, at 'the *limit* of philosophical discourse', at its margins, its borders or boundary lines (Derrida, 1981, p. 6). Derrida attempts to *think* this formal structure of transcendence-within-immanence through concepts such as *différance* (which is at best a 'quasi-concept', since the notion of a concept is itself metaphysical). If metaphysics is defined in terms of presence, then *différance* is that which marks 'the disappearance of any originary presence' (Derrida, 1983, p. 168), that which thereby exceeds or transcends metaphysics, and thereby, at the same time, constantly disrupts and 'destabilizes' metaphysics.[16] Commenting on Heidegger's notion of the 'ontological difference', Derrida writes that

> there may be a difference still more unthought than the difference between Being and beings. . . . Beyond Being and beings, this difference, ceaselessly differing from and deferring (itself), would trace (itself) (by itself) – this *différance* would be the first or last trace if one still could speak, here, of origin and end. (Derrida, 1984, p. 67)

The long series of notions developed in Derrida's work – *différance*, text, writing, the hymen, the supplement, the pharmakon, the parergon, justice, messianicity, justice and so on – are all traces of this formal structure of transcendence, marked by their aporetic status. For Derrida, *différance* is a relation that transcends ontology, that differs from ontology, that goes beyond or is more 'originary' than the ontological difference between Being and beings. In this sense, Derrida's work can be seen as an effort to overcome *both* metaphysics and ontology.

Deleuze is one of the few European philosophers who explicitly pursued a post-Heideggerian metaphysical project. 'I was the most naïve philosopher of my generation, the one who felt the least guilt about "doing philosophy"', he once said in an interview. 'I never worried about overcoming metaphysics' (Deleuze, 1995, p. 88). In Deleuze, metaphysics and ontology are combined: ontology is a metaphysics of difference (Being = difference). Heidegger had himself pointed to such a possibility, despite his separation of metaphysics and ontology:

> When we think the truth of Being, metaphysics is overcome. We can no longer accept the claim of metaphysics to preside over our fundamental relation to 'Being' or to decisively determine every relation to beings as

such. But this 'overcoming of metaphysics' does not abolish metaphysics. . . . If our thinking would succeed in its efforts to go back to the ground of metaphysics, it might well help to bring about a change in the human essence, a change accompanied by a *transformation of metaphysics.* (Heidegger, 1998, p. 279, emphasis added)

What would be the nature of this transformation? Such a transformed metaphysics would necessarily take as its object the disclosure of Being itself – that is, the production of the new, the creation of difference – thereby reuniting what Heidegger had separated. This is the path taken by Deleuze, who referred to himself as a 'pure metaphysician', and whose magnum opus, *Difference and Repetition,* can in part be read as a rethinking of *Being and Time* (Being is difference, and time is repetition).[17]

In developing his philosophy of difference, Deleuze's *Difference and Repetition,* like Heidegger's *Being and Time,* begins with a discussion of Aristotle, since it was Aristotle who bequeathed to later thinkers the fundamental problem of metaphysics. To modify a famous phrase of Whitehead's, metaphysics can be seen as a series of footnotes to Aristotle (cf. Whitehead, 1979, p. 39). Aristotle had a solution to Heidegger's question of the 'ontological difference' that he summarized in a well-known thesis: *different things differentiate themselves only through what they have in common.* Two terms are said to differ when they are other, not by themselves, but by belonging to some other definable thing (the One becomes two). Aristotle had distinguished between three types of difference – specific, generic and individual difference – but what is 'common' for each of these three types of difference is not the same: the relation of species to their common genus is not the same as the relation of individuals to their common species, or the relation of categories to each other and to 'Being'. In Deleuze's reading, though, Aristotle's metaphysics subordinates difference to four interrelated principles: *identity* in the concept and the *opposition* of predicates (specific difference), *resemblance* in perception (individual difference), and the *analogy* of judgment (generic difference). Deleuze's philosophy of difference can be seen as a kind of systematic rethinking of the problems generated by Aristotle's metaphysics.

What is wrong with Aristotle's metaphysics? Put simply, it provides an inadequate solution to the Heideggerian problematic of ontological difference. On the one hand, *it cannot posit Being as a common genus* without destroying the very reason one posits it as such, that is, the possibility of *being* for specific differences; it can therefore conceive of the supposed 'universality' of the concept of Being only as a quasi-identity. On the other hand, it has to relate Being to particular beings, but *it cannot say what constitutes their individuality*: it retains in the particular (the individual) only what conforms to the general (the concept). An equivocal or analogical concept of Being, in other words, can only grasp that which is univocal in beings. *A true universal is lacking, no less than a true singular*: Being has only a distributive common sense, and the individual has no difference except a general and reflexive one in the concept.[18] To overcome these limitations of Aristotle's metaphysics, Deleuze proposes two fundamental theses. On the one hand, he systematically contrasts the 'analogy of Being' (Being is said in several senses) with the doctrine of the '*univocity* of being' (Being is said in a single sense). There are indeed *forms* of Being, but unlike the categories, these forms introduce no division into Being and do not imply a plurality of ontological senses. On the other hand, the single sense of Being is *difference*, which constitutes a field of individuation that *precedes* generic, specific and even individual differences. In this manner, the universal (univocal Being) is said immediately of the most singular (difference), independent of any mediation. If Deleuze considers himself to be a Spinozist, it is because this is precisely the ontological programme laid out in the opening of Spinoza's *Ethics*: the *attributes* are irreducible to genera or categories because while they are *formally* distinct they remain equal and *ontologically* one; and the modes are irreducible to species because they are distributed in the attributes as individuating differences or degrees of power, which relate them immediately to a univocal being (substance). Perhaps no one has gone further than Deleuze in exploring the consequences of this metaphysical realignment of ontology.

On the one hand, Spinoza carried the univocity of Being to its highest point through a profound re-conceptualization of the notion of substance. From Aristotle through Descartes, philosophy defined the individual as a substance, even if the comprehension and definition of substance varied. Descartes' concept of substance, for instance, remains *equivocal* since it is said in at least three senses (body, soul and God), and these three types of substance are substances only by analogy, each being defined by a different 'essential' attribute (extension, thought and infinite perfection). Spinoza's revolution was to make substance equivalent to Being *qua* Being: Being is itself an absolutely infinite, unique and univocal substance (*Deus sive natura*), whose constitutive elements are the attributes (thought and extension).[19] There is no other substance apart from Being, and the concept of substance thus has a univocal sense. Unlike Aristotle's categories, the attributes do not introduce a plurality of ontological senses into Being, nor is there any hierarchical superiority of one attribute over the other (parallelism). In his own writings, Deleuze will simply take the final step and eliminate the notion of substance entirely. 'All Spinozism needed to do for the univocal to become an object of pure affirmation', he writes, 'was to make substance turn around the modes' (Deleuze, 1994, p. 304).

One the other hand, Spinoza's conception of 'beings' is even more revolutionary. Beings are not substances, nor do they have attributes or properties (since substance is Being itself, and the attributes are the elements of Being). What then are beings? Beings are *modes*, that is, they are *manners* of Being, *modifications* of substance – they are *degrees of power*. Beings that are distinguished by their degree of power realize *one and the same* univocal being, except for the difference in their degree of power. Aristotle sought the principle of individuation (1) in the particular attributes or properties (specific differences) (2) of *fully constituted individuals*, and Spinoza shows the untenability of Aristotle's position on both these points.[20] First, what is it that determines the relevant property that makes individuals part of the species 'human'? The human can be defined as a rational animal, a featherless biped, an animal of erect stature, an animal who laughs or who uses language and so on. The choice of any one of these traits, however, is accidental and variable: abstractions such as 'genus' or 'species', 'classes' or 'kinds', depend as much on the needs and motivations of classifier as on the nature of the objects being classified. Natural history had its foundation in Aristotle: it defined an animal by what it *is*, it sought its qualitative *essence* (analogy of Being). Modern ethology, by contrast, under a Spinozistic inspiration, defines an animal by what it *can do*, it seeks its quantitative *power*, that is, its *capacity to be affected* (univocity of Being): what affects is a being capable of sustaining? What excitations does it react to? What are its nutrients and poisons? What affects threaten a being's cohesion, diminishing its power, or even destroying it? What affects enhance its power? From this viewpoint, a workhorse does not have the same capacity to be affected as a race horse, but rather has affects in common with the ox. The same criteria can be applied to inanimate physical objects: what are the affects of a slab of granite? What forces can it tolerate – for example, the forces of heat or pressure? What are its maximal and minimal thresholds? In this way, we arrive at immanent 'types' of modes of existence that are more or less general, but which do not have the same criteria as the abstract ideas of species and kind. (When Nietzsche later spoke of will to power, he meant something very similar: power is not something the will wants; rather, power is something that every being *has*: beings are defined by the power they have, that is, their capacities and capabilities.)

Second, and more importantly, whereas Aristotle sought the principle of individuation in the properties of fully constituted individuals, Deleuze finds it in the processes that account for the *genesis* of individuals. When Deleuze says that Being is related immediately to individuating differences, he says:

> we certainly do not mean by this latter individuals constituted in
> experience, but that which acts in them as a transcendental principle: as
> a plastic, anarchic and nomadic principle, contemporaneous with the
> process of individuation, no less capable of dissolving and destroying
> individuals than of constituting them temporally; intrinsic modalities of

65

being, passing from one 'individual' to another, circulating and communicating underneath matters and forms. (Deleuze, 1994, p. 38)

The list of notions that Deleuze develops in *Difference and Repetition* – difference, repetition, singularity, virtuality, problematic etc. – are all differential notions that describe the composition of this field of individuation (though they do not describe a list of categories).[21] If Deleuze, following Simondon, critiques Aristotle's hylomorphic schema, it is because this field of individuation precedes *both* matter and form. Matter is never completely inert – it always contains incipient structures, potentials for being formed in particular directions or ways (clay is more or less porous, wood is more or less resistant); and form is never simply imposed from the outside, since it can only work by translating or 'transducing' itself into a material by a series of transformations that transmit energy, and thereby 'inform' matter (iron melts at high temperature, marble or wood split along their veins and fibres). In other words, there is an individuating process of *modulation* at work behind both form and matter.

Deleuze's entire ontology entails a practical conversion in philosophy, which Deleuze describes as a shift away from *morality* to *ethics*. Morality is fundamentally linked to the notion of essence and the analogical vision of the world. In Aristotle, the essence of the human is to be a rational animal. If we nonetheless act in irrational ways, it is because there are *accidents* that turn us away from our essential nature: our essence is a *potentiality* that is not necessarily realized. Morality can therefore be defined as the effort to rejoin man's essence, to realize one's essence. In an ethics, by contrast, beings are related to Being, not at the level of essence, but at the level of existence. Ethics defines a man not by what he *is* in principle (his essence), but by what he *can do*, what he is *capable* of (his power). Since power is always effectuated – it is never a potentiality, but always in act – the question is no longer 'what *must* you do in order to realize your essence?' but rather 'what are you *capable* of doing by virtue of your power?' The political problem, in turn, concerns the effectuation of this power. What conditions allow one's power to be effectuated in the best fashion? Conversely, under what conditions can one actually desire to be separated from one's power? One can see clearly how these ontological questions form the basis for the ethico-political philosophy (and corresponding 'existential' notions) developed by Deleuze and Guattari in *Capitalism and Schizophrenia*, and how Deleuze's philosophy forms a systematic whole.[22]

The philosophy of Alain Badiou – which is organized around the three poles of Being, the event, and the subject – once again separates metaphysics and ontology. Badiou's magnum opus, *Being and Event*, opens with a consideration of Parmenides' problem of the One and the Multiple: whereas beings are plural, and are thought in terms of multiplicity, Being itself is thought to be singular; it is thought in terms of the One (Badiou, 2005, pp. 23–4). Badiou resolves this problem with an axiomatic decision: the One *is not*. The discourse of *ontology* (the science of Being qua being), Badiou will argue, is given to us in mathematics, and more precisely, in axiomatic set theory (Zermelo-Frankl), precisely because the latter provides us with a pure theory of the multiple. Metaphysics, by contrast, is always a metaphysics of the One: 'We can define metaphysics as the commandeering of being by the one' (Badiou, 2006, p. 42). By the 'One', Badiou means two things. On the one hand, the One implies any attempt to totalize Being qua being, or to think multiplicity as a whole. Many thinkers before Badiou have claimed that the Whole is neither given nor givable: Kant argued that the Idea of the Whole is a transcendent illusion; Bergson argued that the Whole is equivalent to the Open, since it is the constant production of the new. Badiou arrives at the same de-totalizing conclusion through the path of formalization: there can be no set of all sets without falling into contradiction (Russell's paradox). Consequently, Being qua being always presents itself as a non-totalizable multiplicity – a pure and inconsistent multiplicity ('the multiple is radically without-oneness, in that it itself comprises multiples alone') (Badiou, 2006, p. 47). But from this point of view, on the other hand, the 'one' exists only as an operation (the 'count-as-one') that renders a multiplicity consistent.[23] Thus, the 'one' also implies that beings – entities, quiddities – are themselves unities. On this score, Badiou likes to cite Leibniz's maxim as the central tenet of metaphysics: 'That which is not *one* being is not a *being*' (Badiou, 2006, p. 42). Badiou thus accepts the problem bequeathed to philosophy by Heidegger, but without accepting Heidegger's solution: 'Can one undo this bond between Being [ontology] and the One [metaphysics], break with the metaphysical domination of Being by the One, without ensnaring oneself in Heidegger's destinal apparatus?' (Badiou, 2006, p. 42). Badiou frees himself from the 'metaphysical temptation' of the One through his appeal to axiomatic set theory: Being qua being is the thought of the pure multiple, and beings themselves are multiples of multiples.

If the *event* constitutes the second pole of Badiou's philosophy, it is because set theory itself comes up against its own internal impasses, such as Russell's paradox or the problem of the continuum.[24] In Lacanian terms, if set theory provides Badiou with a formalization of the 'symbolic', then the 'real' is the impasse or internal gap that axiomatic formalization confronts internally. These impasses constitute the site of what Badiou calls 'events'. As such, events appear in Badiou's work under a double characterization. Negatively, so to speak, an event is undecidable or indiscernible from the ontological viewpoint of axiomatics: it is not presentable in the situation, but exists (if it can even be said to exist) on the 'edge of the void' as a mark of the infinite excess of the inconsistent multiplicity over the consistent sets of the situation.

Put simply, an event is that which cannot be discerned within ontology; it is the 'impossible' of a situation, even if it is immanent to the situation. Positively, then, it is only through a purely subjective 'decision' that the hitherto indiscernible event can be affirmed, and made to intervene in a situation. Lacking any ontological status, the event in Badiou is instead linked to a rigorous conception of *subjectivity*, the subject being the sole instance capable of 'naming' the event and maintaining a fidelity to it through the declaration of an axiom (such as 'all men are equal', in politics; or 'I love you', in love). In this sense, Badiou's philosophy of the event is, at its core, a philosophy of the 'activist subject': it is the subject that names the indiscernible, the generic set, and thus nominates the event that recasts ontology in a new light.

As in Heidegger, the concept of truth likewise receives a new determination in Badiou's work. If Badiou holds that 'philosophy is originally separated from ontology' (Badiou, 2005, p. 13), it is because philosophy itself is conditioned by events. And if Badiou distinguishes truth from knowledge, it is because knowledge is what is transmitted, what is repeated, whereas truth is something new, it is a break from accepted knowledge. A truth process appears because an event has interrupted the transmission and repetition of knowledge. Badiou identifies four domains in which the production of truth operates, and which serve as the condition of philosophy: *art* (e.g. the appearance of theatrical tragedy with Aeschylus), *science* (e.g. the eruption of mathematical physics in Galileo), *politics* (e.g. the French Revolution of 1792), and *love* (an amorous encounter that changes one's life). These four domains mark out the instances of individual or collective subjectivity. Badiou distinguishes between the *construction* of a truth from an event, and its *forcing*, which implies the fiction of a completed truth. To say 'I love you' is a finite declaration, a subjective choice; but to say 'I will always love you' is a forcing, the anticipation of an infinite love. Galileo's claim that 'all nature can be written in mathematical language' is the forced hypothesis of a complete physics. 'In a finite choice there is only the construction of a truth, while in infinite anticipation of complete truth there is something like power' (Badiou, 2002). This potency of truth goes beyond the subject of truth, but also contains the possibility of a 'disaster', that is, a total knowledge that destroys the condition of truth itself (the event, the point of the 'real' in a situation). As in Heidegger, one finds in Badiou a reconfiguration of the relations between ontology, metaphysics, and truth that makes it one of the most original and radical of contemporary philosophies.

Philosophies of Consciousness and the Body

John Protevi

Introduction

Defining the Limits of the Field

Because 'consciousness and the body' is central to so many philosophical endeavours, I cannot provide a comprehensive survey of recent work. So we must begin by limiting the scope of our inquiry. First, we will concentrate on work done in English or translated into English, simply to ensure ease of access to the texts under examination. Second, we will concentrate on work done in the last fifteen years or so, since the early 1990s. Third, we will concentrate on those philosophers who treat both consciousness and the body together. Thus we will not treat philosophers who look at body representations in culture, nor philosophers who examine socio-political bodily practices with minimal or no reference to consciousness. Finally, even with the philosophers we choose to treat, we cannot be comprehensive and will instead make representative choices among their works.

With that being said, we will have a fairly liberal definition of continental philosophy, operationally defined as that which makes (non-exclusive) reference to the classic phenomenology of Husserl, Heidegger and Merleau-Ponty. Thus we will include the radical phenomenology of Michel Henry and Jacques Derrida, who refer to the phenomenological classics from within a 'purely' philosophical perspective, that is, one with little or no reference to the biological and cognitive sciences. We will also treat other thinkers who seek to use phenomenology in conjunction with the biological and cognitive sciences; in doing so we will examine the use of phenomenology to contest certain claims in analytic philosophy of mind, namely the representationalist interpretation of cognition in terms of computationalism and connectionism, as well as the cognitivist or 'mind-reading' treatment of intersubjectivity in 'Theory of Mind' debates.

Guiding Threads and Forecast

In Part I, we will first examine two forms of radical phenomenology: pure immanence (Henry) vs transcendence in immanence (Derrida). In the phenomenological tradition, the concepts of 'consciousness' and 'the body' are part of a network that includes those of 'self', 'self-consciousness', 'self- or auto-affection' and 'subject or subjectivity'. We will concentrate on three key notions in the radical phenomenology of Henry and Derrida: life as auto-affection, temporality and intersubjectivity. In Part II, we treat three types of recent work at the intersection of cognitive science and phenomenology: (a) that done in the Husserlian tradition (Maxine Sheets-Johnstone, Dan Zahavi, Francisco Varela and Natalie Depraz); (b) that done in the Heideggerian tradition (Hubert Dreyfus, Mike Wheeler) and (c) that done in the 'enactive' school (Varela, Evan Thompson, Alva Noë and Shaun Gallagher).

Due to space limitations, we will unfortunately not be able to address some interesting work in 'somaesthetics', that is, the body as the site of reflective self-knowledge, including its involvement in social and political contexts (Manning, 2006; Schusterman, 2008); nor can we treat Deleuze-inspired work on perception (Smith, 1996, 2007), movement and affect (Massumi, 2002) and 'political physiology' (Protevi, 2009).

I: Radical Phenomenology

Henry

Michel Henry's work is gaining more attention in the Anglophone world (Bernet, 1999; Calcagno, 2008; Mullarkey, 2006; Sheets-Johnstone, 2007; Zahavi, 1999a, 1999b, 2007). Two recently translated works display his phenomenological mastery (*Material Phenomenology*, 2008) and his religious philosophy (*I Am the Truth: Toward a Philosophy of Christianity*, 2003). We will concentrate on the first of these works, but will refer to the latter at times.

Henry insists that *classical* phenomenology aims at the transcendental conditions of possibility of manifestation or appearance, that is, *how* things appear (not *what* appears). For Henry, 'classical' or 'historical' phenomenology is based in the claim that things appear as constituted by intentional acts, what he will call being 'thrown into the light of the world'. Intentionality is thus a condition of possibility of appearance; in other words, intentionality is a transcendental feature of subjectivity. But is intentional, constituting, subjectivity – transcendental subjectivity – itself such an object? We risk an infinite regress with a positive answer: it seems that making intentional subjectivity into an object requires another subjectivity to whom that objectified subjectivity appears (Zahavi, 1999a, 1999b, 2003, 2007). Zahavi points out that Kant solved this problem by means of the paralogism: only constituted or empirical subjectivity appears as a phenomenon; constituting subjectivity does not in fact appear as a phenomenon; it is purely a transcendental condition. But to deny that transcendental subjectivity appears at all is to deny the possibility of a phenomenology of constituting subjectivity. How then does transcendental subjectivity appear, if not as an explicit object? Is there a 'pre-reflective self-awareness' in which subjectivity is given, that is, a way subjectivity appears to itself that would not be an intentional object-constitution? In *Material Phenomenology* (Henry 2008), Henry subjects Husserl's treatment of self-awareness to a careful reading, concluding that Husserl fails to isolate the 'auto-affection' of life as the true way in which subjectivity manifests itself; this failure necessitates a new, 'radical' phenomenology. (For Henry, 'auto-affection' is the purely immanent feeling that living beings have of the concrete modes of their life. One of Henry's prime examples is pain: pain is revealed in and through its very passive givenness: there is no intentional object constitution in the experience of pain, just pain as a purely immanent experience of life revealing itself to itself: a self-manifestation or self-appearance.) *Material Phenomenology* takes its title from his treatment of *hyle* in Husserl's published works, notably the *Lectures on the Internal Consciousness of Time* (hereafter, the *Lectures*) and *Ideas I*; it also includes an examination of Husserl's methodology in *The Idea of Phenomenology* (along with an examination of Heidegger's notion of phenomenology as laid out in *Being and Time*), and concludes with an analysis of Husserl's treatment of intersubjectivity in *Cartesian Meditations*. Throughout the book the emphasis is on the way the auto-affection of life is the self-manifestation of subjectivity; intersubjectivity, in turn, is rooted in a 'shared pathos' of life.

Henry has all along insisted that phenomenology's breakthrough was to concentrate on the mode of givenness of phenomena: not what appears, but 'how' it appears. However, phenomenology remains tied to the traditional philosophies it sought to surpass by its adherence to a certain 'ontological monism', that is, the equation of being with being seen, with being exposed in an Outside, with being made visible in the 'light of the world' (Henry, 2008, pp. 2, 55, 58, 91). A radical phenomenology would, however, concentrate on an 'originary manifestation' as the mode in which phenomena are 'phenomenalized', prior to this ecstatic exposure. The discovery of this originary manifestation is Henry's claim to innovation; he is, in his eyes, the first to have thematized this originary manifestation as 'auto-affection', or 'the pathetic immediacy in which life experiences itself' (Henry, 2008, p. 3). This originary manifestation is not object-constitution via intentionality (again, what Henry calls 'appearance in the light of the world'), but self-appearance, which is to be distinguished from all manner of constitution, even the 'self-constitution' via 'longitudinal intentionality' Husserl proposes in the *Lectures* (we will return to this point below). Insofar as phenomenology's adherence to 'ontological monism' leads it to define being as appearance in the 'light of the world' shed by intentional consciousness, life is not a being, but prior to being qua phenomenon. Thus life is not subject to study by biology (Henry, 2003, pp. 33–52), nor indeed to study by phenomenology, when that is defined as the study of appearance in light of the world, that is, illumination by intentionality, even longitudinal intentionality. Life is not an intentional object, even a 'self-constituted' one.

To see how phenomenology misses life, Henry tells us we have to examine how Husserl treats *hyle* and *morphe*, matter and form, material impression and intentionality. We should emphasize that in *Material Phenomenology* Henry treats Husserl's notion of *hyle* as it appears in so-called static phenomenology, that is, as the objective or non-intentional aspect of *noesis*. Even though it is the non-intentional part of subjectivity, *hyle* as 'purely sensuous lived experiences' is animated by intentionality (Henry, 2008, p. 7; commenting on #85 of *Ideas I*). If one were to fulfil the promise of a material phenomenology, one would bracket intentionality to yield 'the hyletic or impressional component as the underlying essence of subjectivity' (Henry, 2008, p. 9). At this point, in a reading that betrays certain formal similarities with Derridean deconstruction, Henry diagnoses a 'slippage' (2008, p. 10) in Husserl that takes what would have been material or hyletic phenomenology and interprets it from the point of view of the intentionality animating it. In other words, rather than focus on sensuous impressions in their own right, Husserl sees them as matter *for* intentionality, that is to say, as 'adumbrations through which the sense qualities or the noematic moments of the object are grasped intentionally' (Henry, 2008, p. 10). Matter qua pure sensuous impression is thus no longer self-given, but given *to* form, or better, 'it gives itself to form in order to be informed, constituted, and apprehended by it' (Henry, 2008, p. 11). This means phenomenological matter is thrown into the exteriority of the light of the world. But in itself, if it could be grasped in itself, we would experience it in its radical immanence; as Henry will claim, this self-manifestation of the hyletic content is the auto-affection of life.

Henry would insist that his isolation of pure phenomenological matter is not a betrayal of transcendental phenomenology. On the contrary, it is for him the truth of the transcendental. The intentional, as constituting the irreal and transcendent thing, rests upon the material sensuous impression as something 'purely subjective and radically immanent' (Henry, 2008, p. 17). This is a 'first givenness', which is 'always already given and presupposed' before being 'given a second time in and through intentionality, as a transcendent and irreal thing' (Henry, 2008, p. 17). Now Husserl would say that to understand the manifestation of material sensuous impression, we have to turn to the 'archi-constitution' we find in internal time-consciousness, which is proposed to us as the basis for all appearance. As Henry puts it, Husserl holds that 'temporality is the archi-ek-stasis that constitutes the archi-phenomenality'

(2008, p. 20). But here we find an 'aporia', Henry claims, which gives us 'the philosophical death of life' (2008, pp. 20–1). Phenomenology is unable to properly isolate the impression because it conforms to the ontological monism of philosophy in which manifestation is exposure in light, that is, intentional object-constitution. So in its analyses of internal time-consciousness, phenomenology will suffer its 'most spectacular, significant, and decisive setback' (Henry, 2008, p. 22).

Now if there is one thing Husserl's *Lectures* are known for, it is the focus on primal impression. Henry can then ask 'why doesn't the thesis of impressional consciousness open onto a material phenomenology in the radical sense?' (2008, p. 24). The negative answer can be blamed on the same old villain, intentionality: 'the auto-impression in each impression, which is the reality of absolute subjectivity as the essence of all reality and as the flesh of life, is reduced to a pure ideality in the intentional presentation of the now' (2008, p. 26). To understand Henry's distinction between self-manifestation or self-appearance and self-constitution, we should recall the standard reading (for a résumé, see Zahavi, 2003), in which Husserl, echoing Kant, attempts to demonstrate that time-consciousness is the most primordial and fundamental of all structures of consciousness. Unlike Kant's search for universal and necessary conditions to which objects must conform, however, Husserl begins his reflection with the concrete ego and through the reductions isolates the transcendental structures of intentionality and time-consciousness that result in the temporal constitution of objects and of the flow of conscious states. In the *Lectures* Husserl describes the form of all acts as the 'living present', which has the structure of primal impression-retention-protention. Husserl distinguishes recollection and retention, so that what appears in the concrete living present, including the contents of retention (which is said to be continuous with primal impression) is perceived, while it is this whole living present that is re-presented in recollection. The primal impression of the living present springs up again new, and the whole of perceived time slides along, as the former impressions are retained along with former retentions, which tail off and sink away. Thus we can describe a 'double intentionality' at work in time-consciousness. A 'transverse' intentionality constitutes temporal objects, while a 'longitudinal' intentionality allows time-constitution to appear to itself in a 'primordial consciousness'. In Zahavi's reading, Husserl maintains that constituting subjectivity does indeed appear to itself in internal time-consciousness; it is not the constituted object of another ego, but it is self-constituting thanks to its 'longitudinal' intentionality (Zahavi, 2003). The process by which new primal impressions are generated, however, the ultimate level of time-generation, is described by Husserl, bowing to the fear of an infinite regress, as atemporal. About this 'absolute subjectivity', Husserl says, 'all names are lacking', although we do seem able to say something of its paradoxical nature, both mobile and immobile.

Regarding the ever-renewed primal impression and the anonymity of absolute subjectivity, Henry harshly criticizes the 'incoherence and absurdity' of Husserl's phenomenology, its 'failure', its resorting to 'subterfuge', 'ontological mystification' and 'sophisms' (2008, pp. 26–48). The problem is neglecting the self-givenness of impression ('first givenness') in favour of constituted givenness ('second givenness'). Henry writes: 'to this crucial question about the most original phenomenality, which is the phenomenality of constituting as such, Husserl offers no other response than a restatement of the phenomenality of the constituted' (2008, p. 31). In other words, Henry cannot accept that longitudinal intentionality as the self-constitution of subjectivity is adequate to the demands for a self-manifestation of subjectivity. He continues: 'as such, the act of constituting never becomes a phenomenon and the ultimate constitutor thus remains "anonymous". This anonymity epitomizes the phenomenological failure of Husserlian phenomenology' (2008, p. 31). The key failure, in Henry's eyes, is Husserl's positing of retention as internal to the living present (2008, pp. 27–8; cf. Zahavi, 1999b, 2007). This internality of retention destroys the primacy of impression for Henry, as it does for Derrida. They draw opposite conclusions, however. In contrast to Derrida, who thinks that impression presupposes retention, Henry insists that retention (which is part of the 'now' or living present) presupposes impression: 'it is the reality of the impression in its original subjective reality – as an *Ur-impression* – that enables the now to exist' (2008, p. 32). Although he acknowledges that Husserl is 'aware of the internal difficulties of his thought' (2008, p. 37), for Henry, Husserl's assumption that manifestation is intentional object-constitution – even (or perhaps especially) when subjectivity is said to be self-constituting via longitudinal intentionality – ultimately ties him to ontological monism and forbids him access to material phenomenology as the focus on the self-manifestation of subjectivity as auto-affectivity.

When he turns to his own positive description of the primal impression, Henry writes that the living present is unchanging Life, a stable form for changing content. 'Like the Euripus Strait, life is changing, but yet through its variations it does not cease to be Life in an absolute sense. It is the same Life, the same experience of the self that does not cease to experience itself, to be absolutely the same, one single and same Self' (Henry, 2008, p. 38). Life is thus Henry's key term. Its auto-affection is non-ecstatic, pure self-immanence (Henry, 2008, p. 2). It is self-manifestation without intentional constitution, even self-constitution (Henry, 2008, p. 3). Now Zahavi (1999b, 2003, 2007) reminds us that in Heidegger's reading of Kant, the structure of auto-affection has been interpreted in terms of time as subjectivity. Zahavi identifies this as the key point, and points us to passages in *I Am the Truth* where auto-affection is said to be dynamic: 'life, as we know, is a movement, a process' (Henry, 2003, p. 159; cf. Sheets-Johnstone, 2007). However, and this is undoubtedly a paradoxical, or at least provocative, formulation, Henry insists that the temporality of life has no ecstases: 'The movement of coming into itself that is never separated from itself is life's own temporality, its radically immanent, inex-static, and pathētik temporality' (Henry, 2003, p. 159). Although these formulations come from Henry's religious philosophy, and so strictly speaking lie outside the scope of this article, we might say that here Henry is trying to come to grips with two demands of his radical phenomenology: (1) he has to take account of the changing content of the primal impression, while (2) insisting on the complete immanence of auto-affection. We feel different things, but the experience of feeling has always the same, completely immanent, structure of auto-affection: our feeling reveals itself in itself, as pure passive givenness. Thus any temporalization of Life can only be an 'eternal movement, an eternal flux in which life continuously experiences itself' (Henry, 2003, pp. 159–60). No doubt much more can be said about this 'Ipseity' of life, this 'Self that life eternally generates, and which is never separated from itself' (Henry, 2003, p. 160), but we will have to move on to our third topic, intersubjectivity.

The basic structure of Henry's argument is the same, so we can be brief in our treatment. In Henry's reading of the *Cartesian Meditations* in his *Material Phenomenology*, the constituted ego, which is used as the basis for the 'apperceptive transfer' with the alter ego, misses the 'original' ego self-given in auto-affection (Henry, 2008, pp. 108–9). Rather than a 'phenomenology of perception applied to the other' (Henry, 2008, p. 114) we should recognize our 'real experience' of the other in terms of 'a feeling of presence or absence, solitude, love, hate, resentment, boredom, forgiveness, exaltation, sorrow, joy, or wonder' (2008, p. 104). The problem comes with the famous reduction to the sphere of ownness in *Cartesian Mediations* 5. Here Henry will oppose the ('true') transcendental Ego with the 'constituted ego' that is the basis for Husserl's analysis (2008, p. 108). Here we see a 'demotion of the original Ego to the rank of a psychophysical ego appearing in an objective form in the world of my sphere of belonging' (Henry, 2008, p. 110). Now we must be careful to remember that for Henry 'the light of the world' is his term for intentional constitution: the originality of self-manifestation is 'deposed' in the reduction to the sphere of ownness. The elements of the sphere of ownness 'are deposed in the sense that appearing, which is the basis of their being ... is their appearing in this first world of ownness' (Henry, 2008, p. 106). Following the thesis of ontological monism, this 'first world of ownness' is still a world for Henry; it presupposes yet forgets the non-worldly, non-appearing auto-affection of life. As a result of this demotion, 'the worldly ego in the primordial sphere of ownness functions as the pivot of the pairing association with the body of the other' (Henry, 2008, p. 110). In focusing on the constituted ego, Husserl also enacts a 'demotion of the body' in which 'the body is no longer the radically subjective and immanent "I can" that I am and that is identical to my ego' (Henry, 2008, p. 110). The key thesis, again, is that constitution is not primary self-manifestation: '*It* [the constituted body] *is shown in ownness but not in itself*' (Henry, 2008, p. 110; italics in original). The fundamental problem for Henry is that Husserl does not examine the true reason why the other can never be presented, but only appresented. From the fact that 'every subjectivity understood in its original way . . . escapes from every perceptual presentation' (Henry, 2008, p. 112) we should not conclude, as do Levinas and Derrida, that the other is too much an other to be presented. Rather, Henry will insist, 'it is not because the alter ego is an alter [that it escapes perception]; it is because the other is an ego that I cannot perceive the other in itself' (2008, pp. 112–3; cf. Zahavi, 2007). That is because the true ego, the transcendental Ego that is the 'Ipseity' of transcendental Life, can never 'appear' in the 'light of the world', but only self-manifest in auto-affection.

At this point we can move to consider Derrida's recent work. In one sense, everything Derrida has ever done concerns auto-affection, temporality and intersubjectivity, so the points of comparison and contrast with Henry will be our focus.

Derrida

As Derrida's work on the phenomenology of life as auto-affection, temporality and intersubjectivity is so well known, we can move quite quickly. We will concentrate on *On Touching – Jean-Luc Nancy* (Derrida, 2005; see Lawlor, 2006 for an excellent analysis). In this last of his major works, Derrida uses a reading of Nancy's writings on touching to take us on a tour of the history of philosophy, encompassing extended readings of Aristotle, Maine de Biran, Ravaisson, Husserl, Levinas, Merleau-Ponty and others. As Derrida (curiously? meaningfully?) never mentions Henry in *On Touching*, we will focus on Derrida's reading of Husserl therein to enable a confrontation with Henry's *Material Phenomenology*.

Part II of *On Touching* is comprised of five 'exemplary histories' of touch, focusing on how a certain privilege of the human and the hand as sites of auto-affection, which Derrida names, with typical insouciance, 'humanualism' (2005, p. 214). The second chapter of Part II is entitled 'Tangent II'; it treats Husserl's analysis in *Ideas II* of the two hands touching as a privileged site of auto-affection for Husserl. At stake is the constitution of the 'body proper' [*corps propre; Leib*]; in Derrida's reading of Husserl, the body 'becomes body proper only through touch' (Derrida, 2005, pp. 160, 169). In Husserl's analysis of the auto-affection of the two hands touching, Derrida finds 'a very familiar landscape ... freedom, spontaneity, the will of an ego, the Ego-subject as will, its can-will [*pouvoir-vouloir*], the motor activity of a free, spontaneous, immediate, and so forth, movement' (2005, p. 160).

Now we should note that Derrida agrees with Henry about the centrality of vision in the history of philosophy, but instead of decrying this as leaving behind the truth of life as auto-affection, Derrida disengages a curious relation between vision and touch, the latter supposedly bypassing mediation and allowing auto-affection. Thus we see a certain 'optical intuitionism [that] as paradoxical as this may appear – always and necessarily fulfills itself ... in an intuition tactually filled-in and in the hyperbole of continuistic haptocenteredness' (Derrida, 2005, p. 161). Lawlor points to the way any such 'hyperbolic' auto-affection is always contested by Derrida: 'For Derrida, there is no pure intuition, not even in my own lived-experience. Even in my solipsistic sphere of ownness, there is only ever a *Vergegenwärtigung* [re-presentation], and therefore some sort of nonpresence and nonbeing' (Lawlor, 2006, p. 16). Thus instead of assuring vital self-presence, the auto-affection of the two hands touching relies on re-presentation; lived experience, the lived body, life itself, is thus never pure for Derrida, so that vital auto-affection plunges us into 'the abyssal problem of life, phenomenology as thinking of the living, transcendentality of the living present, and so forth' (Derrida, 2005, p. 164). Auto-affective life is an 'abyssal problem' for Derrida, whereas for Henry, it is the truth that philosophy should have established for itself.

We are now in a position to recap how Derrida's well-known theses on temporality and intersubjectivity inform his reading of Husserl and provide a contrast with Henry. Derrida shows how in *Ideas II* Husserl wants to establish that 'the self-relation of touch ... acts without empathy or analogical appresentation' (2005, p. 171). This immediacy is what sight is missing; vision lacks the 'possibility of ... a double sensation fully intuitive, direct, and synchronous' (Derrida, 2005, p. 171). Thus Husserl would have it that the 'touching-touched pair is grounded in a temporal coincidence meant to give it its intuitive plenitude' (Derrida, 2005, p. 172). This is exactly what Derrida cannot accept; from his earliest work to his latest, he insists on space at the heart of time and exteriority at the heart of the interiority. Thus with regard to the touching-touched experience he writes: 'this detour by way of the foreign outside ... is at the same time what allows us to speak of a "double apprehension" (otherwise there would be one thing only: only some touching or only some touched)' (2005, p. 175). Here we can see that Derrida follows Husserl's text past the point where Henry says Husserl fails by not keeping to the immanent auto-affection of life revealed in pure hyletic content prior to intentionality's 'second givenness'. For Henry, of course there is foreignness in the two hands touching; that is exactly why it is a bad model of auto-affection, for it is already entangled in too much transcendence just by being an intentional object. Henry is happy to say there is 'only some touching' without a constituted ego – or better, to emphasize the passivity of auto-affective life, 'only some touched' – but he would insist that this 'some touched' self-manifests in its hyletic content as the auto-affection of life, without and before having a constituted object or a subject. We are thus faced with a difference in levels of analysis between Derrida and Henry. Derrida traces how Husserl isolates the body proper as I vs not-I in the sphere of ownness. But the I of phenomenology as constituted ego is already transcendent for Henry, when compared to the Ipseity of the auto-affection of life. But Derrida will not admit any access to such full self-presence prior to intentionality, or at least not any *phenomenological* access. He thus refuses what Zahavi calls Henry's 'phenomenology of the invisible' (Zahavi, 1999b). Thus Derrida writes: 'in the experience termed "solipsistic" of the manual touching-touched ... the touching-touched cannot be accessible for an originary, immediate, and full intuition, any more than the alter ego' (2005, p. 176).

Derrida insists that auto-affection for the subject constituted in the sphere of ownness (and ultimately in internal time-consciousness) involves hetero-affection. Derrida renders his question precise:

> I ask whether there is any pure auto-affection of the touching or the touched, and therefore any pure, immediate experience of the purely proper body, the body proper that is living, purely living. Or if, on the contrary, this experience is at least not already haunted, but constitutively haunted, by some hetero-affection related to spacing and then to visible spatiality. (Derrida, 2005, p. 179)

With the term 'spacing' Derrida refers back to the analyses of *Voice and Phenomenon*, where we can find a certain 'economy of exteriority' relating 'spacing' to real space and to the space of vision, even the 'interior' space of intuition (Protevi, 1993, 1994). In such economies, there is never purity, only an economy of mixtures, as Derrida makes clear: 'Where Husserl seems to draw a line between, on the one hand, pure auto-affection of the body proper in the "double apprehension" of the touching-touched, and, on the other hand, the hetero-affection of sight or the eye ... shouldn't one rather distinguish between several types of auto-hetero-affection without any pure, properly pure, immediate, intuitive, living, and psychical auto-affection at all?' (Derrida, 2005, p. 180). This economy of exteriority 'would presuppose interruption in general, and a *spacing* from before any distinction between ... psychical "spreading out" ... and extension of the real [reell] thing' (Derrida, 2005, p. 180). On the basis of this 'spacing' prior to the distinction of inner and outer and ultimately internal to time, Derrida proposes that 'the constitution of the body proper thus described would already presuppose a passage outside and through the other, as well as through absence, death, and mourning' (2005, p. 180).

Here we see an exact chiasm: for Derrida, hetero-affection renders auto-affection possible; Henry would say the exact opposite. The key point on which to focus is that they place auto-affection on different levels, Henry in a basic reality of life, Derrida in phenomenological constitution. We can thus say that while both demonstrate the 'failure' of Husserl's phenomenology to isolate a pure constituted auto-affection, they differ in their next moves. While Henry produces a radical phenomenology of the invisible, Derrida produces a radical phenomenology of mixture. (Of course, one can question whether these radical 'phenomenologies' deserve the name, but that's a story for another time.) Again, Henry would completely agree that Derrida has demonstrated the failure of Husserl's phenomenology to square the principle of principles of intuitionism with the economy of exteriority revealed in Husserl's text on the supposedly pure auto-affection of the two hands touching (as well as with the 'voice that keeps silent' of *Voice and Phenomenon*). But Henry thinks he has gone beyond Husserl; he claims to have produced a radical phenomenology, a material rather than intentional phenomenology, a phenomenology of 'invisible' self-manifestation without intentional constitution. It is this radicality of pure self-manifestation that Derrida refuses; if there is to be a phenomenology for Derrida, it is an intentional phenomenology; if there is to be appearance or manifestation, it is on the basis of intentional constitution, so that there is no self-manifestation that is not a self-constitution. Thus any auto-affection is (self-) constituted for Derrida; as (self-) constituted, it implies intentionality; and as intentional, it implies spacing and hetero-affection.

As this is the crucial point, a restatement is in order. The basis for all manifestation for Derrida, following Husserl, is internal time-consciousness, where the living present is self-constituted in longitudinal intentionality. Of course there is no already constituted ego that is the basis for this; it's an ongoing process of auto-affection. But the auto-affection is the process of self-constitution by longitudinal intentionality. That's where Henry objects, since it's still intentional constitution. Henry says that intentionality relies on *hyle*, that is, on the impression, which for him is not constituted, even self-constituted, but purely given ('first givenness'). Another way to put it: Henry objects to the way longitudinal intentionality puts impression together with retention and protention to form the living present or now. He thinks Husserl should have stayed with the impression by itself. So he agrees with Derrida as to what the *Lectures* text says (that impression goes together with retention and protention). It is just that Henry thinks that is a mistake, whereas Derrida thinks it is the moment of truth in Husserl, the moment where his fidelity to description leads him to describe things as they really are, even if that true description eviscerates the principle of all principles of intuitionism by inscribing absence at the heart of presence.

We can conclude by going back to Henry's phrase 'the philosophical death of life' (Henry, 2008, p. 21), where we see very interesting connections with Derrida. For Derrida, life and death are intertwined, so that we have death at the heart of life. Literally, as in the heart transplant, where technology is put inside the natural body in the logic of the supplement, so that what is denigrated as inferior or posterior (technology), becomes instead the constituting essence of the supposedly superior and prior (nature) (Derrida, 2005, p. 179; cf. Lawlor, 2006, p. 29 and Varela, 2001). But for Henry, life is a pure self-manifesting essence that philosophy qua theoretical study, that is, intentional object-constitution, kills. So what he does is not 'philosophy' or 'historical' phenomenology, but radical phenomenology. For Henry, the history of philosophy is ontological monism, which means holding at a distance for vision in the light of the world. For Derrida, however, as we know, the history of philosophy is the metaphysics of presence, that is, the holding close to self in 'haptic' intuition. So for Henry there is a closeness that philosophical distance betrays, while for Derrida, there is a distance that philosophical closeness covers up. Henry thus agrees with Derrida that Husserl's text betrays the way intentionality destroys immanent self-manifestation; he just wants to affirm that immanence. But desire for pure immanence is what Derrida cannot accept. It may be that the ultimate reasons, the reasons 'in the last instance' shall we say, are political: Henry sees the non-natural outside – science and technology – as alienating, as barbarism, as destroying the pure immanence of 'life' that must be preserved from its grasp (Henry, 2003). But Derrida sees the desire for pure immanence as tied into the history of injustice, the pure being the good and the impure being the bad that needs correction. The best we can do – the only just thing we can do – is to live in the impurities of our economies of exteriority.

II: The Engagement with Cognitive Science

Husserl

As a transition to our examination of works that use Husserl to engage with problems in cognitive science, let us examine two works on the question of temporality and auto-affection, or, as it is also known, 'pre-reflective self-awareness'. Such a notion of pre-reflective self-awareness, Zahavi explains in two books (1999, 2005), is needed to avoid the infinite regress of 'reflection theory' whereby subjectivity is made the intentional object of yet another subjectivity. So to avoid such a regress, Zahavi (2003) provides a reading of internal time-consciousness in Husserl's *Lectures* as pre-reflective self-awareness. Zahavi defends Husserl from Henry and Derrida by making two key points relative to our previous discussion. First, he will attempt to demonstrate that self-constitution via longitudinal intentionality is fully self-manifestation. Thus, contra Henry, there is no deeper layer of auto-affection; contra Derrida, there is no ineradicable absence at the heart of presence because there is no after-effect in which consciousness becomes self-aware only after the delay of retention brings the just-past into the present. Second, Zahavi claims that the structure of the living present, impression-retention-protention, is an 'ecstatic unity'. Thus, contra Henry, primal impression is ecstatic, that is, it has a temporal articulation as opposed to fully in-ecstatic auto-affective Life; contra Derrida, it is a unity, as it is not riven by the alterity supposedly carried by retention.

Sheets-Johnstone (2007) provides a powerful counter-argument to the preceding treatments of auto-affection; for her, auto-affection is not 'ontological' but is founded in feelings of a phenomenologically accessible 'qualitative kinetic dynamic' (2007, p. 370). Sheets-Johnstone begins by criticizing the failure to reference Husserl's concept of kinesthesia (awareness of bodily motion) in the treatment of the two hands touching by Henry, Derrida and Zahavi: 'the omission makes the act – "one hand *touching* the other" – a wholly pointil-list, static phenomenon' (Sheets-Johnstone, 2007, pp. 363, 371). Sheets-Johnstone finds a 'transcendental clue' for a way out of this impasse in Husserl's notion of a 'foundational dynamic', that is, the way we are ceaselessly active, even though our activity is based in the passivity of affection (2007, pp. 364–5). To get to the truth of the position she advocates – that 'temporality and movement are inextricably linked, and that animation is at the heart of self-affection' – we have to criticize the notion of kinesthetic 'sensation', Sheets-Johnstone claims (2007, pp. 365, 367). Rather than the 'temporally punctual and spatially pointillist notion of sensation', we have to remember that kinesthesia occurs in the linkage of sensation and motion (Sheets-Johnstone, 2007, pp. 366–7), a notion we will see reprised in Alva Noë's 'enactive' work (Noë, 2004). The problem with Henry's notion of the auto-affection of Life, Sheets-Johnstone feels, is that it is ontological rather than phenomenological; it is 'oddly devoid of experiential moorings', so that 'Henry's ontology is not girded in substantive descriptions of "the feeling of movement", descriptions that would *show concretely how subjective movement is not a matter of sensation but of dynamics*' (2007, pp. 369–70; italics in original). At the heart of Sheets-Johnstone's philosophy, developed at length in her important book *The Primacy of Movement* (1999), is the notion of 'animate form'; this is cashed out here in terms of 'movement [that] . . . creates its own particular temporal quality in the process' (2007, p. 371). This entails that 'we are pre-reflectively aware not of a self but of a qualitatively felt familiar dynamics' (Sheets-Johnstone, 2007, p. 372); thus, for Sheets-Johnstone, we have thereby de-ontologized or de-reified the implication of 'self' in 'self-affection'.

While there is much more that could be said about Sheets-Johnstone's work, especially her interesting reading of emotion and movement – 'emotions are dynamically patterned forms contoured by the very shifting bodily tensions, contradictions, rushes, attenuations, spatialities, and rhythms that create them' (2007, 379) – we will have to let this suffice and move on to a consideration of 'neurophenomenology'.

The provocative term 'neurophenomenology' (seemingly designed to elicit opposition from both classical phenomenologists and hard-core cognitive scientists) comes from an article by Francisco Varela (1996). Varela explains that neuroscience works from a 'third-person' perspective, while phenomenology works from a 'first-person perspective'. The 'explanatory gap' then opens up between third-person accounts of conscious experience – which rely on accounts of unconscious neural processes – and first-person accounts. To address the explanatory gap, Varela's neurophenomenology proposes that neuroscience and phenomenology should create a mutually enlightening, reinforcing and constraining relation. As we would expect, neurophenomenology faces two challenges. A first challenge to neurophenomenology comes from the cognitive sciences, concerning the status of first-person perspectives, which were kicked out of psychology in the twentieth century as unreliable 'introspection'. But Varela pointed out that phenomenologists were not just people picked up off the streets; they had undergone years of training to sharpen their ability to report on their experience. Second, Husserl thought phenomenology could never be naturalized; many phenomenologists follow him in discounting the utility of third-person perspectives for phenomenology. In response, Varela, along with the other editors of the essay collection *Naturalizing Phenomenology* (Petitot et al., 1999), tries to overcome such antinaturalism by claiming it stems from Husserl's 'having mistaken certain contingent limitations of the mathematical and material sciences of his time for absolute ones' (Petitot et al., 1999, p. 42). To naturalize phenomenology, for these thinkers, is to attempt a 'qualitative physics of phenomenological morphologies'; should such a 'pheno-physics' be successful, they claim, it would demonstrate that 'what Husserl called "inexact morphological essences", essences foreign to fundamental classical physics, are indeed amenable to a physical account, provided that we rely upon the qualitative macrophysics of complex systems (and no longer on the microphysics of elementary systems)' (Petitot et al., 1999, p. 55).

We will return to the use of dynamical systems theory lying behind the notion of a 'qualitative macrophysics of complex systems' when we consider the enactivist school below. But first, let us ask what it is that neurophenomenology does. As Varela's long-time collaborator Evan Thompson (2007) explains, neurophenomenology does not really address the 'hard problem' of consciousness (the relation of mental and physical; see Chalmers, 1995). The hard problem is badly formed; it is impossible, because it is based on the insoluble Cartesian mind–body problem. Instead of accepting dualism or trying a reductionism or looking for a mysterious extra element, we need to reformulate the mind-body problem as a 'body-body' problem (lived body vs living body or *Leib* vs *Körper*). The ultimate goal is an integration of first and third person perspectives, that is, an integration of phenomenology and biology (Thompson, 2007, p. 237; cf. Jonas, 2000).

Let us now look at an example of neurophenomenology in action. While Zahavi (2003) makes no explicit reference to brain science in his reading of internal time-consciousness in Husserl's *Lectures*, Varela (1999) reads the 'temporal density' of the living present in terms of neurodynamics. The key to this exemplification of neurophenomenology is therefore Varela's use of dynamical systems theory to bridge the gap between phenomenology and brain science. Thompson (2007) provides a very useful overview of Varela (1999). First, Thompson notes that Varela proposes three temporal scales of neurological events. They are the 1/10 scale of fast neural events (10–100 milliseconds), the 1 scale of large-scale integration of distributed brain waves (250–500 milliseconds) and the 10 scale for reporting events using short-term memory (1–3 seconds). Along with his three temporal scales, Varela has three hypotheses:

1. For every cognitive act, there is a singular, specific neural assembly that underlies its emergence and operation.
2. A specific neural assembly is selected through the fast, transient phase-locking of activated neurons belonging to subthreshold, competing neural assemblies.
3. The integration-relaxation processes at the 1 scale are strict correlates of present-time consciousness. (Thompson, 2007, pp. 329–34)

We need to recall two things at this point. First, Varela is not after the qualia of first-person experience, but its structure, that is, the temporal 'density' of the living present. Second, we should recall that brain science has been divided between localists and globalists throughout its history. Recently, neurody-namics has assumed the globalist mantle, studying neural events in terms of the large-scale integration of distributed brain waves. A leading concept here for such integration is 'phase synchrony' (Thompson, 2007, pp. 332–3). Putting these two together, we see that the upshot of Varela (1999) is that neuroscience confirms the phenomenological finding of the living present by showing that there is a minimal time within which conscious acts can occur. Now this confirmation is not merely a correlation between two separate realms, but an example of the mutual illumination of neuroscience and phe-nomenology proposed by 'neurophenomenology'. As Thompson explains, 'the term *strict correlates* in Hypothesis 3 is thus misleading because this hypothesis is meant to be causal, nor merely correlative. The aim is to explain how the temporal structure of experience is caused by and realized in the dynamic structure of biological processes' (Thompson, 2007, p. 334). While there are important ontological and epistemological points about 'emergence' to consider in the phrase 'caused by and realized in', we can at least see why Thompson will say that 'cognitive time . . . arises from an endogenous and self-organizing neurodynamics. According to Varela, this dynamics can be described as having a retentional-protentional structure' (2007, p. 335). In an important preview of what we will discuss in the 'enaction' section below, Thompson reminds us that such cognitive dynamics is not brain-bound, but embedded in a larger system: 'neural assemblies and large-scale integration are thus always embedded in and modulated by particular bodily and environmental contexts' (2007, p. 336).

Let us now move to discuss time and emotion, with a focus on protention. While an extended comparison with Sheets-Johnstone (2007) would prove very interesting, let us concentrate on Varela and Depraz (2005). Once again, Thompson has a good recap (2007, pp. 375–8). To understand the neo-Husserlian/neurophenomenological take on emotion, the distinction of receptivity vs affectivity must be understood. Receptivity is the active orienting to something, and so it is founded on affectivity as being affected by something, as the 'allure' or 'pull' on attention. Affectivity is thus our basic 'openness' to the world. By careful reflection we can see the stages of an emotional episode, which involves the shift from affectivity to receptivity. In his original synthesis, Thompson puts Varela and Depraz (2003) together with Lewis (2000 and 2005) on the neurodynamics of emotion. (See also Colombetti and Thompson, 2007, for a nuanced critique of Lewis.) In Thompson's reconstruction, the structure of an emotional episode has five stages: (1) a precipitating event or trigger; (2) the emergence of affective salience, that is, the sense of the event's meaning; (3) a feeling tone, which possesses a pleasant/unpleasant polarity; (4) a motor embodiment and (5) a visceral-interoceptive embodiment. In sum, 'affective allure amounts to a parameter that at a certain critical threshold induces a bifurcation from passive affection ("passivity") to an active and motivated orienting ("receptivity") towards something emerging as affectively salient or prominent' (Thompson, 2007, pp. 377–8). Thompson concludes that 'valence needs to be understood not as a simple behavioral or affective plus/minus sign, but rather as a complex space of polarities and possible combinations (as in the chemical sense of valence)' (2007, p. 378). (We will address the biological basis for such 'valence' in the discussion of 'sense-making' below in the enaction section.)

In the neo-Husserlian approach, then, consciousness is fundamentally based in our affective openness to the world; one of its aspects is pre-reflective self-awareness; and the body is (at least) our organ of sensibility and action. I say 'at least', for in Sheets-Johnstone's conception, the body is the very the basis of consciousness in its feeling of qualitative kinetic dynamics. As with all our recaps (especially when they are recaps of recaps), we have only indicated the bare outlines of rich and provocative analyses. In the hope that these will entice readers to further exploration, let us move to the next section.

Heidegger

In considering the use of Heidegger to consider questions of cognitive science, Hubert Dreyfus is undoubtedly the historically most important figure here, as he is in the entire relation of phenomenology and cognitive science. In the epochal *What Computers Can't Do* (which first appeared in 1972), Dreyfus launched a critique of Artificial Intelligence as representational and disembodied, predicting its failure due to its inability to solve, among other issues, the 'frame problem' (Dreyfus, 1992). The frame problem is ontological and epistemological at the same time. The world is assumed to be made up of discrete facts (states of affairs) that are arranged in arbitrary situations. The states of affairs have no meaning in themselves, so that the meaning is created by the knowing agent. Now computers are representational systems working on a linear input-processing-output model. They are physical symbol systems in which meaningless input is encoded in meaningless representations arranged in a certain syntactic order. Changes to the syntax of meaningless symbols are supposed to generate semantics, so that cognition is this change to the syntax; it is the middle step supposed to generate meaningful output from meaningless input. In computationalist work, which is based in classical computer architecture (i.e., computers with a central processing unit), then, cognition is the rule-bound manipulation of discrete symbols. In connectionism, which arose with advances in neural nets or 'parallel distributed processing', the network weights (the strength of the connections at any one node) are supposed to do the representational work, and changes in the network weights precisely *are* the processing, that is, the cognition itself. For both approaches, the frame problem arises when the input changes, and the computer has to update its reading of the situation: to which set of its stored facts does the changed environment now correspond? The system cannot find the right interpretation rule for a changing environment simply by searching through a database of facts and interpretive rules, for it would have to have rules for picking the right rules, and so forth. Thus Dreyfus concludes that changes in syntax cannot generate semantics insofar as they are incapable of choosing the appropriate frame for the interpretation of the input. Dreyfus showed that AI got around the problem by restricting the world of the AI agent. But when they moved from such restricted 'micro-worlds' (clean environments with only a few objects and restricted tasks) to anything approaching a realistically complex world, the frame problem reappeared. The basic problem with AI for Dreyfus is that its proponents failed to see that 'world' is a set of meaningful relations, not a set of meaningless facts. For Dreyfus, then, Heidegger's analysis of world as a set of meaningful relations and *Dasein* as in-the-(meaningful)-world shows the ultimately Cartesian presuppositions of AI. Far from being purely empirical engineering, AI was instead chock-full of unexamined and problematic philosophical assumptions. If they had read Heidegger, Dreyfus claims, instead of having unconsciously absorbed Descartes, the AI workers would have realized that for human beings, there is no 'frame problem', or better, that solving frame problems is just what we do every day as massively, fundamentally, interpretive agents.

Michael Wheeler's *Reconstructing the Cognitive World* (2005) picks up on Dreyfus's pioneering work and proposes that Heidegger is useful not just in defeating Cartesian representational AI but also in illuminating the presuppositions of successful embodied-embedded cognitive science, especially some forms of robotics. Wheeler proposes four key points of this 'third wave' of cognitive science (following classical computationalism and connectionism): (1) 'online' intelligence is primary (online intelligence produces 'a suite of fluid and flexible real-time adaptive responses to incoming sensory stimuli'); (2) such online intelligence 'is generated through complex causal interactions in an extended brain-body-environment system'; (3) the third wave requires 'an increased level of biological sensitivity'; (4) the third wave adopts a dynamical systems perspective (Wheeler, 2005, pp. 11–14). But while the most radical of the dynamical systems proponents, such as the enactive school we examine below – and, in a late turn, Dreyfus himself, as we will soon see – think themselves able to dispense with representations entirely, Wheeler will defend a notion of 'action-oriented representations' at work even in online intelligence. (No one denies human beings are capable of 'offline' representations: we can do logic, after all. The controversy is whether representations are used in everyday 'smooth coping' as Dreyfus calls it.) In Wheeler's account, action-oriented representations, echoing Andy Clark (1997), are 'poised between mirroring and control' (Wheeler, 2005, p. 197). Thus they mirror the world, but in an 'ego-centric', 'situation-specific' and 'transient' manner dedicated to the action of the agent (Wheeler, 2005, p. 197), not to what one might call the true or accurate picturing of an independent world. The world is mirrored in action-oriented representations, Wheeler says, but 'the world . . . *is itself encoded in terms of* possibilities for action' (2005, p. 197; italics in original). (Here one would have expected Wheeler to turn to J. J. Gibson's notion of 'affordances', as have many others, but Wheeler keeps his distance (2005, p. 301); another avenue for interesting connections might have been with Bergson's idea in *Matter and Memory* of perception as virtual action, but we can't fault Wheeler for keeping his focus on Heidegger!).

It is precisely on the notion of action-oriented representations that Dreyfus criticizes Wheeler in his review of the latter's book (Dreyfus, 2007). Supplementing his Heideggerian and Merleau-Pontian base with dynamical systems theory (in the form of Walter J. Freeman's work in neurodynamics (2000)), Dreyfus upholds a strong anti-representationalist position on the basis of an ultimately ontological argument. Criticizing Wheeler's adherence both to action-oriented representations and to the 'extended mind thesis' (that cognitive processes can be said to include extra-somatic ingredients, such as notebooks and computers), Dreyfus writes:

> Heidegger's crucial insight is that being-in-the-world is more basic
> than thinking and solving problems; it is not representational at all. That
> is, when we are coping at our best, we are drawn in by solicitations
> and respond directly to them, so that the distinction between us and
> our equipment vanishes. (Dreyfus, 2007, p. 254)

He continues, striking at the heart of the extended mind thesis: 'Heidegger's and Merleau-Ponty's understanding of embedded-embodied coping, therefore, is not that the *mind* is sometimes *extended into the world* but rather that, in our most basic way of being – i.e, as skillful copers – we are not minds at all but *one with the world*' (Dreyfus, 2007, pp. 254–5; italics in original).

For the most part, then, in Dreyfus's appropriation of Heidegger and Merleau-Ponty, consciousness is interpretation not representation, and the body is not the processor of representational information, but the site of interpretive skills enabling our everyday 'smooth coping'. Once again, we cannot follow all the details of these issues here. But we can use Dreyfus's late turn to dynamical systems theory as our bridge to the enaction school.

Enaction

The founding work in this school of thought is *The Embodied Mind* (Varela et al., 1991); a major reformulation, updating and extension is Evan Thompson's *Mind in Life* (2007). For the enactivists, cognition is the direction of an organism's action. Enaction thus harkens back to Varela's work with Humberto Maturana on 'autonomous systems', that is, those systems that have sufficient internal complexity and feedback so that 'coupling' with their environment 'triggers' internally directed action. This means that only those environmental differences capable of being sensed and made sense of by an autonomous system can be said to exist for that system, can be said to make up the world of that system (Maturana and Varela, 1980, p. 119). In the terms Varela later developed, then, such a world is not represented but 'enacted'. The positing of a causal relation between external and internal events is only possible from the perspective of an 'observer', a system that itself must be capable of sensing and making sense of such events in *its* environment (Maturana and Varela, 1980, p. 81). While Maturana thought it possible to extend the notion of autopoiesis beyond the cellular level (an extension picked up by Niklas Luhmann for his sociology), Varela thought it best to speak only of autonomous systems rather than autopoiesis once past the cellular level. Now as we have seen, the basic notion in Varela's version of neurophenomenology is to use dynamic systems theory at both the neural and the (phenomenological) organism level. For Varela, nervous system activity is a dynamic system with massive internal feedback phenomena, thus constituting an 'autonomous system' whose action 'enacts' a world. But 'autonomy' in this sense does not indicate some realist notion of 'independence'; after all, organisms are not just nervous systems! An organism arises as a 'meshwork of selfless selves' when the 'autonomous' nervous system works together with the immune system (itself an 'autonomous' system with cognitive properties), digestive system, endocrine system and so on (Varela, 1991). In other words, the organism is emergent for Varela; it arises from, and mutually constrains, its component systems. But even at the brain level, we find a certain form of emergence: neural firing patterns, blending sensory input with internal system messages, emerge from a chaotic background in which subliminal patterns 'compete' with each other for dominance. Once it has emerged victorious from this chaotic competition and established itself, what Varela 1995 calls a 'resonant cell assembly' (RCA) forms a determinate pattern of brain activity. Over time, the repetition of a number of such patterns provides a virtually available response repertoire for the system.

The enactivist notion of a complex organism emergent from the interplay of multiple autonomous systems helps explain why they insist on positing a biological basis of the judgements 'good' and 'bad'. This value polarity is grounded in basic organic capacities for affective cognition. Witness the single-celled organism's ability to make sense. 'Sense' has, perhaps fittingly, a threefold sense: sensibility, signification and direction.[1] A single-celled organism can sense food gradients (it possesses sensibility as openness to the environment), can make sense of this difference in terms of its own needs (it can establish the signification 'good' or 'bad') and can turn itself in the right sense for addressing its needs (it orients itself in the right direction of movement). Varela points to what he calls the 'surplus of signification' opened by the sense-making of the bacterium: 'There is no food significance in sucrose except when a bacterium swims upgradient' (1991, p. 87). This fundamental biological property of sense-making or affective cognition is one reason why the Cartesian distinction of mental and material has no purchase in the enactive approach. There is no 'mental' property (in the sense of full-blown reflective consciousness) attributable to the single-celled organism, but since there is spontaneous and autonomous sense-making, there is no purely 'material' realm either. Affective cognition in humans is simply a development of this basic biological capacity of sense-making. Jonas notes that 'the organic even in its lowest forms prefigures mind, and ... mind even on its highest reaches remains part of the organic' (2000, p. 1). Thompson (2007) thus harkens back to Jonas in upholding the 'strong continuity' thesis of life and cognition (see Wheeler, 1997).

For the enactivists, then, sense-making is a biological capacity inherent in living bodies, but it seems too much of a stretch to link the sense-making of basic organisms with the consciousness qua sentience or pre-reflective self-awareness that a lived body enjoys (or 'suffers' as Henry would have it!) (Thompson, 2007, pp. 161–2).

With this background in the basic concepts of the enactive approach, we can now turn to Alva Noë's notion of the virtual content of perception (Noë, 2004). Noë posits a differential relation between movement and perception so that the content of perceptual experience is 'virtual'. Thus some content is 'present *as available*' (Noë, 2004, pp. 66–7). In other words, you experience an object as something whose appearance would vary in precise ways as you move in relation to it (Noë, 2004, p. 117). This means that some perceptual detail is present *as accessible*; furthermore, 'experiential presence is virtual *all the way in*. Experience is fractal and dense' (Noë, 2004, p. 216). Noë continues in this vein: 'Qualities are available in experience as possibilities, as potentialities, but not as completed givens. Experience is a dynamic process of navigating the pathways of these possibilities. Experience depends on the skills needed to make one's way' (Noë, 2004, p. 217). The ground of perceptual experience is embodied sensorimotor skills; because of this embodied ground, 'what we experience outstrips what is represented in consciousness' (Noë, 2004, p. 217). Borrowing Gibson's term, Noë claims that objects in the world are perceived as 'affordances': 'to perceive is (among other things) to learn how the environment structures one's possibilities for movement and so it is, thereby, to experience possibilities of movement and action afforded by the environment' (Noë, 2004, p. 105). As I hope this brief sketch shows, Noë's work offers very interesting possibilities for crossing the 'analytic-continental divide', as the 'virtual' connection of perception and movement suggests possible articulations with Bergson (Robbins, 2006), with Husserl and Merleau-Ponty (Sheets-Johnstone, 2007) and with Deleuze and Whitehead (Massumi, 2002).

We can now move to the conclusion of our review with a look at Shaun Gallagher's *How the Body Shapes the Mind* (2005), which is a noteworthy achievement in several respects germane to our purposes here. First, we can note how Gallagher distinguishes the body schema as 'a system of sensory-motor capacities that function without awareness or the necessity of perceptual monitoring' from the body image as 'a system of perceptions, attitudes, and beliefs pertaining to one's own body' (Gallagher, 2005, p. 24).

This distinction enables him to intervene in debates in child development. Against the notion that the infant is a pure 'blooming, buzzing confusion' with no way to register somatic boundaries, Gallagher, relying on Meltzoff and Moore's (1977) classic work on neonatal imitation, proposes that the infant has 'innate' body schema enabling self-other differentiation. For neonates to be able to imitate, they must have some 'primitive' body schema and 'some degree of proprioceptive performative awareness' (Gallagher, 2005, p. 74). Together these work with an 'intermodal' neural system so that 'proprioception and vision are already in communication'; this enables infants to 'translate' visual information about the other's body into awareness of the analogous body parts of its own body (Gallagher, 2005, p. 75). Gallagher goes on to propose 'mirror neurons' as part of the neural base for neonate imitation (2005, p. 77). With this notion of 'mirror neurons' we can move to our last topic, empathy, which ties together consciousness, the body and intersubjectivity.

After many years of comparative neglect following intense scrutiny in the early phenomenological movement, empathy has gotten a good bit of attention lately (see Steuber, 2006, for a survey of both historical and contemporary work). The most basic component of empathy is what is known as 'emotional contagion' or a shared affective state: that is, you feel what another person is feeling. We will refer to this as 'proto-empathic identification'. In recent philosophy, empathy is involved in the controversies surrounding 'Theory of Mind', that is, our ability to attribute mental states to others. As explanations for the widely shared capacity for empathy, we first find simulation theory, which in its most rigorous formulation posits the idea that perception of others triggers a separate internal modelling that enables the attribution of affective cognitive states to them (Ratcliffe, 2007). Simulation theories are thus a 'first-person' standpoint; the discovery of human 'mirror neurons' (which fire when we observe a goal-oriented action) gave a great boost to simulation theory (Gallese and Goldman, 1998). The most current scholarship (Decety and Lamm, 2006) here does not rely on action-oriented mirror neurons (as Gallese thought in his 'shared manifold' article of 2001), but on what Gallese, Keysers and Rizzolatti (2004) call 'viscero-motor centers'. An important set of confirmation findings are those of Singer et al. (2004), in which 'empathy for pain' is correlated with increased activity of the anterior insula and the anterior cingulate cortex, which map the viscera.

A second approach to empathy comes from phenomenological accounts, which find the simulation theory approach still too representational and appeal to a field of directly felt corporeal expressivity or 'primary embodied intersubjectivity' grounding our 'pragmatic interaction' with others (Gallagher, 2005, p. 223; see also Thompson, 2001 and Ratcliffe, 2007). These phenomenological accounts are thus a 'second-person' standpoint, as opposed to the first-person simulationists and the third-person 'Theory Theory' proponents (in 'Theory Theory', the perception of others leads to inferences as to the affective cognitive states to be attributed to them). For Gallagher, simulation theories align with fully cognitive 'Theory Theory' inferences as special cases 'unable to capture the full range of second-person interactions' (Gallagher, 2005, p. 224). Empathy for the second-person phenomenologists is grounded in a primary corporeal intersubjectivity in which body expressions of the other are immediately felt as meaningful: 'in most intersubjective situations we have a direct understanding of another person's intentions because their intentions are explicitly expressed in their embodied actions, and mirrored in our own capabilities for action' (p. 224).

Let us end with a brief consideration of the political consequences of the new research on empathy. First, and most importantly, we can say that the right wing view of human nature is false insofar as it focuses exclusively on the individualist/competitive content of human nature, whether that comes in the mode of the rueful paleo-conservative acknowledgement of the fallen nature of mankind or the neo-liberal celebration of competitive entrepreneurship (the domestic face of the neo-conservative equation of 'freedom' with capital mobility). In the face of all this, we have to find the courage to insist that human nature is equally, nay predominately, prosocial. Now of course there are sociopaths. But this only defeats the claim that human nature includes a wide-spread prosocial tendency if you have an essentialist view of 'nature': as if in identifying human nature we were isolating a finite set of necessary and sufficient characteristics for belonging to the human species and claiming that prosociality belongs on that list. So the counter-example of sociopaths would defeat such a claim – if it were advanced in an essentialist manner. But we have to see 'nature' as statistical, as the dominant cluster of the distribution of traits in a population, as we are taught by Darwin and population thinking. We might even think of nature as that which occurs 'for the most part', as Aristotle puts it (*Physics* 2.8.198b35, in Barnes, 1984), if we can remove the teleology and just retain the truth of the observation: at any one time, species traits clump together.

We have to insist on the following: the prosocial character of human nature is revealed by the widespread capacity for proto-empathic identification. Based in mother–child primate relations, proto-empathic identification has been extended in human evolution to kin and then to in-group and finally to all other humans, and, often, to other animals. We see here an occasion for the rehabilitation of the theory of moral sentiments proposed by Adam Smith and David Hume (de Waal, 2006), not to mention the need to recognize the role of cooperation in evolution (Kropotkin, 2007; Gould, 1988). The primate basis of prosociality, Frans de Waal argues, is extended to include a sense of fairness, reciprocity and harmonizing: 'In stressing kindness, our moral systems are enforcing what is already part of our heritage. They are not turning human behavior around, only underlining preexisting capacities' (de Waal, 2006, p. 181). The challenge we face is to extend the range of prosocial impulses from the in-group, protect them from the negative emotions of rage and fear and build on them to genuine altruism, that is, acting for the sake of the other, not just feeling what the other feels (Joyce, 2007). All this is not to deny the selfish nature of the basic emotions of rage and fear. The key to a progressive politics of human nature is studying how such selfish, negative emotions are manipulated, or, more positively, how a social order is constructed to minimize them and to maximize positive affects (Singer, 1999; Gatens and Lloyd, 1999).

So in the recent work on empathy, we see a final take on consciousness and the body. Consciousness must be seen in its affective (open and emotional) mode, not simply as the site of cool and calculating cognition, and the body cannot be seen merely as the source of behaviours which form the sensory input for our simulations or inferences of the inner mental life of others, but is the site in which shared emotion or 'proto-empathic identification' enables a recognition of our widely distributed prosocial nature.

Philosophies of Difference

Todd May

One way to interpret much of recent French philosophy would be to see in it a common rejection of philosophies of identity in favour of various philosophies of difference. We will canvass several of the most important recent philosophies of difference here. However, in order to understand what is at stake, it is necessary first to understand what is meant by a philosophy of identity and a philosophy of difference.

The idea of a philosophy of identity is tied to the traditional philosophical project of constructing a foundational philosophy. A foundational philosophy is one that gives thought an absolute ground, one that cannot be doubted. A foundational philosophy is like the foundation of a house. If the foundation is strong, then the house built upon it will be stable. Similarly, if a foundational philosophy is strong, then the beliefs built upon it – whether by philosophy or science or religion – will be stable as well. What makes a belief stable is that it cannot reasonably be doubted. But in order for a belief to be immune to reasonable doubt, it must be built upon other beliefs that are themselves immune to doubt. This requires that, at bottom, there must lie a set of beliefs of which we can be entirely certain. A foundational philosophy tries to offer those bottom-line or bedrock beliefs.

In the history of philosophy, the most famous example of a foundational philosophy is probably that of Descartes. His methodological doubt consists in doubting everything of which he cannot be certain, until he arrives at that which cannot be doubted, the doubting subject. From there, he builds back those beliefs of which he can be certain, using proofs of the existence of God and the principle of clarity and distinctness along the way.

For the purposes of our investigation, however, perhaps the most important foundational philosopher is Edmund Husserl, who writes near the end of the nineteenth century and into the 1930s. Husserl, like Descartes, seeks to found philosophy on a bedrock of certainty. However, in contrast to Descartes, he appeals not to *reason* but to *description*. He grounds his certainty in what cannot be doubted, but what cannot be doubted are the appearances of what is in front of him. The things of which they are appearances can be doubted, but that he is having an experience of particular appearances cannot. You, for instance, can doubt that the experience you are having is of a book in front of you. But you cannot doubt that you are experiencing particular book-like appearances.

Husserl seeks to take those appearances, called phenomena, and describe them in order to understand their structure and what must be true in order for them to appear as they do. Thus, his method is called phenomenological. Where Descartes tries to reason his way back from the doubting subject to the richness of the world, Husserl seeks to describe his way from the appearances to their structure. In both cases, however, the project is to construct a bedrock of philosophical certainty that will ground our further beliefs (at least the right ones among those further beliefs).

In this short discussion, the term *identity* has not yet arisen. What is the relationship between foundational philosophy and a philosophy of identity? The identity is the bedrock out of which the philosophical foundation is constructed. For Descartes, the bedrock is the doubting subject; for Husserl, it is the appearances in the certainty of their appearing. In all foundational philosophies, the identity is the *something* that lies at the bottom: the material, one might say, out of which the foundation is constructed.

However, why might we want to call this something an identity? There are two reasons. First, it can be identified. That is to say, the founding something, whatever it is, can be picked out from our experience and given an identification, a label. This picking out and labelling itself involves two elements: the perceptual (Husserl) or rational (Descartes) moment of picking out and the linguistic moment of labelling. What these two elements offer in their convergence is a particular identity, one that can be located and/or isolated in thought and therefore become the object of philosophical reflection. The second reason for calling this something an identity follows from the first. The reason something can be identified is that it possesses a certain sameness or uniformity. We need to elucidate this sameness a bit, since it will prove important for understanding recent philosophies of difference.

For Husserl, the sameness attaching to appearances (or, in Husserl's terms, appearances *as* appearances) is that they are all the same thing. They are all appearances. These appearances may be of different types. There are visual appearances, sonorous appearances, tactile appearances, even imaginary appearances. But in order for them to be appearances, they must have something in common. This something is what makes them the same thing. What they all have in common is that they appear.

A foundational philosophy, in order to succeed, must have some kind of identity as its bedrock. The reason for this is logical. If there were more than one thing at the bedrock, the question would arise of the relation between these two things. If the doubting subject *and* appearance were at the bedrock of a philosophical foundation, one would have to confront the question of what the relation is between reason and appearance. How do they relate?

Which is more important? If one is more important, does not it become the real bedrock? If not, then how exactly do they relate? In answering these questions, one will have to appeal to a further bedrock, one that brings everything together into a particular identity. And this new identity will then be the real bedrock of the philosophical foundation.

For most of its history philosophy has been foundational. It was not really until the dawn of the twentieth century that the possibility arose that philosophy was not concerned with the ultimate foundation for our beliefs. There are, of course, different paths one might take in order to move away from foundationalism, and several of these have been taken over the past hundred or so years. One could, for instance, as happened in the early twentieth-century analytic philosophy, tie the philosophical project to the scientific one. In taking this route, one can see philosophy as a matter of clarifying scientific terms or explaining what science does. Alternatively, one could seek to understand our world much as traditional philosophy has, and yet recognize the barriers to foundationalism, whether they be language or history or something else.

Yet another way to move away from foundationalism would be to create philosophy that, like traditional philosophy, delves into the depth of our experience, but instead of finding an identity there that would found our beliefs, discovers a difference or differences that resist being incorporated into any kind of foundational project. A project like this would, in one sense, mimic traditional foundationalist philosophy. It would seek to think the bedrock of our beliefs. What would distinguish it from foundational philosophy would be the discovery or recognition that that bedrock is not one of identity, that it cannot serve as an epistemic foundation, a foundation for knowledge. This would be because, in one way or another, that bedrock does not consist in an identity upon which other beliefs can be founded. Instead of an identity, there would be difference. Such a philosophical project, or set of philosophical projects, would be called philosophies of difference.

In the last half of the twentieth century, and continuing on into the twenty-first, philosophies of difference have held an important place in continental philosophy. Not all non-foundationalist or anti-foundationalist philosophies are, properly speaking, philosophies of difference. For instance, I will argue near the end of this essay that Michel Foucault's work is not a philosophy of difference, although it has affinities with them. However, three of the most important continental philosophies of the last fifty years are philosophies of difference in this sense. The work of Jacques Derrida, Emmanuel Levinas and Gilles Deleuze constitute powerful philosophies of difference. These three, to be sure, are not the only philosophies of difference that are current in continental philosophy. Many strands of contemporary feminist philosophy, for instance, are philosophies of difference, and draw on a variety of philosophical approaches to difference (see Braidotti's chapter on Feminist Philosophy in this volume). However, in order to keep this essay manageable, we will remain focused on the three central thinkers named above.

We cannot, however, turn directly to these philosophies. In continental philosophy, much more so than in the analytic tradition, philosophy is done with an eye to one's predecessors. Philosophy is seen as an ongoing dialogue with those who came before. Before turning to the work of Derrida, Levinas and Deleuze, then, it would be worth pausing over two important predecessors who loom large in the philosophies of difference these thinkers construct: Friedrich Nietzsche and Martin Heidegger. To call either of them philosophers of difference in anything like the sense that we will with the thinkers we focus on would be a stretch. However, there are elements in each which have proven important for the philosophers who follow them.

Nietzsche, as those who are familiar with his work will readily testify, is an unclassifiable philosopher. That is perhaps why he has been appropriated to so many conflicting philosophical views: elitist and democratic, right-wing and left-wing, existentialist and anti-existentialist. The element of his thought most influential on philosophies of difference, though, has to do with a book written in 1962 by Gilles Deleuze, *Nietzsche and Philosophy* (Deleuze, 1983). In this book, Deleuze focuses the issue of philosophical difference on Nietzsche's distinction in *The Genealogy of Morals* between the master and the slave. In particular, Deleuze wants to distinguish Nietzsche's master/slave view from Hegel's dialectic of master and slave in the *Phenomenology of Spirit*. For Hegel, the dialectic of master and slave starts with a fight to the death between the two. The slave, unlike the master, is unwilling to die. Therefore, he submits himself to the master, labouring for him. But because the slave labours and the master does not, the slave develops while the master does not. In the end, then, the slave becomes dominant and sets the stage for the next dialectical move.

In this dialectic, there is always a recovery by the dialectic of what might seem to escape it. The slave and the master are different, but then come together in a dialectical unity. That dialectical unity, for Deleuze, is the moment of identity that Nietzsche resists. For Hegel, even if there is no identity of the Cartesian type, no bedrock upon which one can found one's beliefs, there is instead always a dialectical recuperation of what seems outside identity. To put the point a bit too simply, if for Descartes there is an identity at the beginning of the epistemic process, for Hegel (at least in Deleuze's view) there is an identity at the end of the dialectical process.

Nietzsche's master and slave contrast with the dialectical view, precisely because there is no recuperation of the difference between them. The slave is reactive; he defines himself by reference to the master. More precisely, the slave is resentful of the master, and inverts that resentment by claiming superiority.

The master, by contrast, defines himself without relation to the slave. The master is active. He does what he does, acting through the expression of his own most powerful or creative forces without regard to what the slave does or how the slave sees him. As Deleuze puts it, the slave 'needs others to be evil in order to be able to consider himself good. *You are evil, therefore I am good*; this is the slave's fundamental formula . . . This formula must be compared with that of the master: *I am good, therefore you are evil*' (Deleuze, 1983, p. 119). Even this might be a little misleading. It is perhaps more accurate to emphasize the dissymmetry between the two even further by saying that for the master the formula is simply, 'I am good'.

By removing any symmetrical or dialectical relation between slave and master, Nietzsche introduces difference into his philosophical view. Since there is nothing to mediate between slave and master, there is no common identity they would be able to share. This leaves the hope for any Cartesian or Husserlian project bereft, and lays the groundwork for later developments, particularly in Deleuze's thought. Elements of it can also be seen, however, in the work of Heidegger.

Heidegger's contribution to a philosophy of difference revolves largely around what has come to be called the *ontological difference*. This is the difference between Being and beings. For Heidegger, the project of philosophy (or, in his later work, the project of thought as opposed to philosophy) is that of thinking Being or the meaning of Being. 'The Being of beings "is" not itself a being. The first philosophical step in understanding the problem of Being consists in . . . not determining beings as beings by tracing them back in their origins to another being – as if Being had the character of a possible being' (Heidegger, 1992, p. 46). For him, the question of Being is the forgotten question of philosophy, and he takes it as his task to recover that question. In seeking to recover the question of Being, the fundamental obstacle to be faced is that we have come to think Being in terms of beings. That is, we think of Being as a particular, if special, type of being. An analogy here would be that of how people often think of God as a particular type of being rather than as something utterly removed from the kinds of concepts that are applicable to the beings we encounter in our lives. In fact, even using the word *something* seems to encourage this approach.

For Heidegger, as for the later thinkers of difference, the reduction of Being to beings is inseparable from the project – or hubris – of a philosophical mastery of Being. If Being can be reduced to the status of beings, then it can be understood, placed in our categories and ultimately tamed. This attempt at mastery is inseparable from philosophical foundationalism and the privileging of philosophies of identity. One way to read a foundationalist philosophy of identity is as an attempt to master the world epistemically, by finding the categories within which ultimately to bring it under the sway of one's comprehension. This, in turn, privileges the thinking subject and threatens to see the world simply as the object of one's thought and action. As his career evolves, Heidegger becomes particularly critical of this attitude, which he begins to associate with philosophy as a whole.

At the heart of the foundationalist project, which in Heidegger's view is the thinking of Being in terms of beings, is the privileging of presence. One can see how this would work. If Being is thought simply in terms of what can become present to one, then, since it is beings that become present to one, Being is conceived on the model of beings. Further, in keeping with the hubris of this philosophical orientation, Being is conceived as *that which presents itself to me*. I privilege myself as the thinking subject, the subject to which Being becomes present, rather than seeing myself as subject to or involved with Being. For Heidegger, the way to escape the fate of such a philosophical orientation, which has been the orientation of philosophy since Plato, is to respect the ontological difference and to think Being from within the terms of that respect: to think Being as Being rather than as a being.

Derrida, Levinas and Deleuze carry on the trajectory instituted by Nietzsche and Heidegger. In fact, one might say that, without them, there would be no trajectory. That there is a group of philosophies called philosophies of difference is not a result so much of the writings of Nietzsche and Heidegger as it is the work of these later thinkers that fold their predecessors into a particular philosophical framework or orientation. Nietzsche and Heidegger, as philosophers of difference, are retrospective products of the views of Derrida, Levinas and Deleuze.

Turning first to Derrida, we might want to elucidate his famous 'concept' of *différance* at the outset. Although he famously states that *différance* is 'neither a *word* nor a *concept*' (Derrida, 1973, p. 130), it is certainly the central moment of his philosophical view. In different works, he uses different terms to capture this moment. However, there is a structural similarity among these terms, and we will retain the term *différance* as a coverall term.

In Derrida's view, *différance* involves a particular economy that underlies the movement of all of Western philosophical thought. In that sense, it seems on the surface to be similar to philosophical foundationalism. Is not philosophy a search for the foundations at the bottom of our thought? However, the difference here is that *différance* cannot serve as a foundation. On the contrary, it is that which resists being utilized as a foundation. And that is because it cannot serve as an identity. *Différance* is precisely that which prohibits there being an identity that can serve as a philosophical foundation.

In order to see how this is, we can turn to Derrida's treatment of Husserl in his 1967 essay *Speech and Phenomena* (Derrida, 1973). Although our treatment will be a bit cursory, it should capture in broad terms the operation of *différance*. Husserl, as we have seen, seeks to offer a foundationalist philosophy grounded in a phenomenological approach. What he can be certain of, what forms the foundation for his philosophy, are appearances as appearances. He can doubt the things that seem to appear to him. But he cannot doubt the appearances themselves. Appearance is the identity upon which his philosophy rests.

Derrida approaches Husserl's philosophy by way of the question of time, and then the question of space. He turns first to the question of time in Husserl's philosophy. Husserl's treatment of time is, of course, phenomenological. He is not interested in time as an abstract concept, but rather time as it is lived. Husserl recognizes lived time cannot be a series of present instants. Each instant, in order to be an instant, would have to narrow its parameters until it is only an abstract instant, like a Euclidean point. Every instant of lived time must carry a bit of the past along with it, in order to have any 'thickness' at all. He calls this past *retention*. And since lived time is also oriented toward the future, it must also have a *protention* of the future embedded in it. The living present, then, is composed of an instant 'surrounded' by a retention and a protention.

As Derrida points out, this creates a particular problem for Husserl. What makes appearances the foundation of Husserl's philosophy is that they cannot be denied. What makes them undeniable? Their sheer presence. That I have this appearance, right here in front of me, at this moment, cannot be denied. As Derrida points out, however, on Husserl's analysis of time, that appearance that is right here and right now in front of me is not entirely present to me. In order for there to be a living present, it has to comprise not only the here-and-now but the no-longer-quite-now and the not-quite-yet-now. To put the point another way, the present is partially constituted by what is not present.

Derrida makes the same move with Husserl's philosophy regarding space as well as time. This space is that between the signifier and the signified. If the signified is the immediacy of one's thought, then in order for it to be represented in its pure identity, it would have to be able to be translated without remainder into that which signifies it. To put the point simply, thought would have to be wholly represented in language, and language would have to be the complete and faithful translation of thought. Otherwise, the philosophical rendering of appearances, which must happen in language, would betray the appearances as they appear to the subject to whom they appear, the subject who encounters them.

However, this representation without remainder is impossible. There is no pure presence of the signified within the signifier, just as there is no pure presence of time. This is because signifiers are repetitive; the same signifier is used in different situations. Therefore, the signifiers of language cannot capture the uniqueness of any particular appearance. Signifiers must generalize. (Elsewhere, Derrida argues also that signifiers help structure particular appearances, so that, in the end, there are no such things as uniquely particular appearances.) Therefore, Husserl's attempt to capture philosophically appearance-as-appearance cannot succeed in offering a foundation for philosophy.

From this summary of Derrida's treatment of Husserl, we can begin to build an understanding of *différance*. *Différance* is both a temporalizing and spatializing movement that prevents things from becoming entirely present to themselves or to others. It is a movement that undercuts identity, not by replacing it with something else, but by showing how a particular identity, in order to be the identity it is, must be partially constituted by that which is not identical. If this sounds paradoxical, it should. If it were not paradoxical, then it would perhaps be possible to re-constitute a foundationalist philosophy based upon an identity. But *différance* is not an identity. That is why Derrida insists that it is neither a word nor a concept. *Différance* does not function in the way words or concepts function. Rather, it is a movement that lies beneath the operation of words and concepts, preventing them from becoming entirely present to themselves.

In Derrida's view, this movement is characteristic of the entirety of Western philosophy, although Western philosophy has sought to keep it at bay. The strategy of keeping this movement at bay has taken different forms, but always through the same movement. There is an exclusion of what seems opposed to a particular identity, but which in fact is partially constitutive of that identity. '[M]etaphysics has always consisted in attempting to uproot the presence of meaning, in whatever guise, from *différance*' (Derrida, 1981, p. 32). The central exclusion, however, is that of absence in the name of presence.

This is where Derrida's debt to Heidegger becomes manifest. It is Heidegger, as we have seen, that first articulates the domination of presence in the history of Western philosophy. Derrida's approach to the privileging of presence is distinct from Heidegger's. For Heidegger, the privileging of presence elevates human subjectivity and prevents us from adequately approaching the question of Being. For Derrida, by contrast, it is the failure to recognize the operation of *différance* that characterizes Western philosophy, or, in the term used by both Heidegger and Derrida, western metaphysics.[1] Nevertheless, as Derrida recognizes, his thought derives from that of Heidegger in several ways. First, he sees the history of Western philosophy as a history of *metaphysics*, a history that ties thought to the privileging of presence. Second, this privileging of presence is related to a privileging of the subject. After all, it is the subject to which presence is present. Third, a new type of thought, one that would escape at least somewhat the grip of metaphysics, must assume a different form from that of the logic of traditional metaphysics. Derrida writes, in what might be an echo of Heidegger, 'The history of presence is closed, for "history" has never meant anything but the presentation of Being, the production and recollection of beings in presence, as knowledge and mastery' (Derrida, 1973, p. 102). Finally, this new type of thought cannot entirely escape metaphysics, since we cannot step outside of our history, and our historical legacy is a metaphysical one. One of the main tasks, then, of this new type of thought is to engage with its own historical legacy in a movement of what Derrida calls *deconstruction* and Heidegger *destruction*, in order to see the operation of privileging presence at work.

Derrida's philosophical critique of identity has echoes in that of the thought of Emmanuel Levinas. Although Levinas works on the ethical plane rather than, as Derrida mostly does, on the plane of language, his thought became increasingly influential on Derrida over the course of the latter's career. Although Derrida offers a critique of Levinas in an early article (Derrida, 1978), by the late 1980s Derrida is in tighter conversation with both the ethical and religious themes that animate Levinas' work.

Levinas, like Derrida, is in conversation with Heidegger, and through him with the history of Western philosophy. His view of Heidegger, however, is more critical than that of Derrida. This is, in part, because of his interpretation of Heidegger's concept of Being. (Levinas's second major work, after *Totality and Infinity*, is entitled *Otherwise than Being*.) The problem with the concept of Being, and indeed with all concepts utilized by the Western philosophical tradition, is that they constitute a form of violence against the Other. Levinas does not specify what this Other is, and it is at times unclear whether he means other people or God or an intersection of the two. For our purposes, it will be enough to refer to other people.

Others are, in Levinas's view, infinitely other to us. By this he means that their experience is entirely distinct from ours, and that it cannot be reduced to any categories from our experience within which to place it. How could I possibly understand what it is like to be another person, to inhabit his or her world? But to think of the other as somehow something I can understand or comprehend, is not only to make an epistemic mistake. It is not only to be intellectually wrong. It is also an ethical wrong. To reduce the other to my own categories or way of taking up the world is to do violence to him or her. It is to betray the uniqueness, the specificity of their experience, a specificity that will ever elude me.

This wrong is one that has been perpetrated, however, throughout the history of Western philosophy. 'Western philosophy has most often been an ontology: a reduction of the other to the same by the interposition of a middle and neutral term that ensures the comprehension of being' (Levinas, 1969, p. 43). In Levinas's eyes, the thinking of Being, ontology, has been a betrayal of the other through the imposition of categories that reduce it to the same. That imposition happens by means of identity: of a 'middle and neutral term' that acts as the foundation for a reduction of other to same. Whether that term be God, or appearances, or something else, the history of Western philosophy (what Levinas calls *ontology*) operates through a series of identities whose function is, among other things, to eliminate that which is infinitely other.

If this is all there was to Levinas's view, then there would be little more there than a call to respect the differences of others from myself. But there is more. For Levinas, not only is the other irreducible to my categories, that very irreducibility of the other is partially constitutive of who I am. At the very core of my being, I am constituted by a call to recognize the other who is always infinitely other to me.

> Vulnerability, exposure to outrage, to wounding, passivity more passive
> than all patience, passivity of the accusative form, trauma of accusation
> suffered by a hostage to the point of persecution, implicating the identity
> of the hostage who substitutes himself for the others: all this is the self,
> a defecting or defeating of the ego's identity. (Levinas, 1981, p. 13)

This is a paradox that is not unlike the Derridean paradoxical character of *différance*. There is something outside of me, something that I cannot bring under the sway of my own categories or phenomenological experience or way of being or seeing, whose call to me for recognition is part of who I am. To put the point in Derridean terms, my presence to myself is partially constituted by an irreducible absence. Where for Derrida the absence is embedded in the history of Western philosophy, for Levinas it is embedded in the subject of experience itself. While Western philosophy, for both Derrida and Levinas, seeks to suppress this absence, the location of the absence (or other) resides in different places for each.

For Levinas, the other who constitutes me lies at the basis of all ethical experience. It is at once an ethical grounding and a partial constitution of who I am. Where, if anywhere, in my experience do I confront this grounding? It happens in the face of the other. The face of the other reveals at once my own vulnerability and the vulnerability of the other. In fact, it is through the vulnerability of the face of the other – its vulnerability to my violence – that my own vulnerability to the other can be recognized. 'The face in which the other – the absolutely other – presents himself does not negate the same, does not do violence to it ... This presentation is preeminently nonviolent, for instead of offending my freedom it calls it to responsibility and founds it' (Levinas, 1969, p. 203).

We must be clear here. For Levinas, the grounding of my responsibility to the other does not occur through some sort of analogy with my own experience. It is not because I recognize in the face of the other someone else just like me that I become responsible. If that were the case, then Levinas's philosophy would be one of identity rather than difference. It would be founded on a sameness or identity between my experience and that of the other. However, for Levinas, matters are quite the opposite. It is not that I see myself in the face of the other that I become responsible to him or her; it is precisely because I see the infinite otherness of the other. What calls me to responsibility, what founds me as a responsible being, is precisely my inability to incorporate the other in its vulnerability to my categories or way of seeing. To seek to incorporate the other is precisely to do violence to him or her. It is to fail to respect the vulnerability of the other as other. Therefore, the founding of my own ethical experience occurs on the basis of something that lies outside me, something I cannot master but that nevertheless constitutes me: it is an exterior that partially founds my very interiority.

When Levinas announces, then, that ethics precedes ontology, he is not merely proclaiming the relative importance of ethics in relation to ontology. He is making a statement about ontology itself. Ontology, Being as Being, is founded on ethics. It is founded on a constitutive experience that cannot itself be appropriated by ontology. Whereas for Heidegger, it is ontology – the study of Being as Being – that must be opposed to the history of Western philosophy, in Levinas's eyes the overcoming of that history – or at least some of the ill effects of its legacy – must take place outside of or before ontology. Ethics performs the function that Heidegger sought in ontology.

Although differently oriented, Levinas's thought remains one of difference. It refuses the reduction of thought to any categories of sameness or identity. What must be thought, in his view, is the other in its irreducibility to the same. At the ground of experience is not a foundation of identity on which philosophy can be built, but rather a dislocation in the relation of oneself to oneself, a dislocation that is nothing other than one's responsibility to another that one cannot assimilate. And thus, like Derrida, Levinas does not seek to offer an account that will complete or fulfil the foundationalist project of Western philosophy; he seeks instead to offer an account of why that project must always founder. And, like Derrida, it founders on the irreducibility of difference to identity.

If we turn our attention to Gilles Deleuze's philosophy of difference, we find not only a distinct approach to difference. We find an entirely divergent approach. To put this divergence baldly, if for Derrida and Levinas it is an irreducible movement of presence and absence or other and same that founds a philosophy of difference, for Deleuze it is difference itself. For Derrida and Levinas, philosophy is not to be founded on identity because identity is always intertwined with what-is-not-identity. For Deleuze, by contrast, philosophy is not to be founded on identity because it is instead to be founded on difference. In this sense – and perhaps in this sense only – Deleuze's philosophical approach mirrors that of traditional foundationalist philosophy. There is something at the bottom of thought, something that lies beneath and grounds it. Only this something, for Deleuze, is not any form of identity. It is instead difference, difference itself. And the project of philosophy is nothing other than the thinking of this difference.

Before we begin to unpack what Deleuze means when he says that 'Being is said in a single and same sense of everything of which it is said, but that of which it is said differs: it is said of difference itself' (1994, p. 36), we should note that there are at least two directions in which one might take his thought of difference. We might call these directions ontological and normative. If we take Deleuze ontologically, then we take him to be making claims about being, offering us an ontology that he believes to be the correct ontology. Alternatively, if we interpret him normatively, then we take him to be setting up an ontology, not for the sake of making claims about being, but instead for the sake of creating a picture of things that opens up new possibilities for living. In other words, if we think of being as difference, then we are more likely to experiment with our world and our lives than if we do not. This latter interpretation is more in line with Nietzsche's question, 'Suppose we want truth: *why not rather* untruth?' (1966, p. 9). For the record, I tend towards the second interpretation, but there is also good evidence in Deleuze's writings to support the first.

To take being as difference is to say that the identities we encounter in our everyday lives are not all there is to being. These entities are the expression of something deeper, and that something deeper is difference. Deleuze is emphatic that difference, the deeper thing subtending identities, is not outside or beneath those identities, but rather within them. The reason for this is that, again like Nietzsche, he wants to reject a picture of things that has any form of transcendence. For Nietzsche, transcendence implies that there is something outside this world, better than it, and by means of which our world is to be judged. The traditional transcendence would be God. But it could also be, for example, Plato's forms. Thought that relies on transcendence always denigrates our world in favour of another one. That is a form of slavery in the Nietzschean sense we discussed earlier. Think here of the traditional Christian view that we are all sinners and that we need to deny ourselves in order to become closer to the transcendent God. Deleuze finds this type of thought abhorrent. He wants to celebrate and experiment in our world, not deny it for the sake of another.

The question for him, then, is how to think a difference subtending or inhabiting the identities we encounter in the world that is not something transcendent but rather immanent to those identities. In order to do so, he introduces a pair of terms – the actual and the virtual. These can perhaps be best understood by contrast to the possible and the real. The real is what exists; the possible is what does not exist but can. In Deleuze's contrast, the possible is a model and the real an instantiation of that model. In other words, the real is the same thing as the possible, with the added characteristic that it is real, that it exists.

The virtual contrasts with the possible in two ways. First, the virtual is not a mirror of the actual. The actual is different from the virtual. Second, the virtual is real. *'The virtual is fully real in so far as it is virtual'* (Deleuze, 1994, p. 208). Although the actual is close to the real in the possible/real distinction, the virtual is not analogous to the possible. The actual is that which exists in such a way that we can have phenomenological experience of it. The actual consists of identities as we experience them. The virtual, by contrast, is that which expresses itself by means of these identities. The virtual is expressed in identities, and yet remains in the identities that express it.

To begin to get a picture of this, we can imagine the Japanese art of origami: the folding of paper into particular shapes. If the shapes are the actual, then the paper is the virtual. The shapes, in this sense, are particular expressions of the paper. Extending this analogy a bit further, the paper can express itself in different ways. It can become a variety of different figures: bird, dog, kite, etc. That is to say that the paper is not any particular identity, but rather that which expresses itself in particular identities. Furthermore, it is capable of a variety of expressions, even when it is expressing itself in a particular one. Finally, the paper remains *within* any given expression. The paper does not transcend its expressions, but instead inhabits them.

The virtual, the paper, is difference. It is what inhabits various identities but cannot be reduced to any of them and can express itself in different identities. This means, among other things, that no given state of identities is a necessary state. Things could always be otherwise, very much otherwise, than they are. If we think of being as difference, then, we think of identities as radically contingent. This reveals the normative aspect of Deleuze's thought. Thinking of being as difference is an invitation to experimentation, to see what else could come to actualization aside from what is already there. As Deleuze says in his major book on Spinoza, *'We do not even know of what a body is capable'* (1990, p. 226).

We need to go a bit deeper into his thought in order to grasp more clearly the character of difference as he conceives it. If we stay with the origami analogy, we think of difference too much in the way of an identity. The paper, after all, is an identity: it is paper. For Deleuze, however, difference – that is to say, being as difference, or difference-in-itself – cannot be captured by any identity. Identities are actual, difference is virtual. Indeed, difference is virtuality itself. One way Deleuze characterizes difference is to say that difference involves relations without positive terms. Positive terms would be identities. So if there are relations without positive terms, then there is a virtuality that can express itself in particular positive terms, but does not consist in those positive terms themselves.

To grasp this idea, we might think of how genes express themselves in human development. It has been shown that, biologically, there is no particular determinism to how genes create the human organism. There is, instead, a lot of possible variation, depending on the physical and environmental conditions under which the foetus develops. We might see the genetic field, then, as a virtual field of difference that expresses itself in a particular human being depending on the conditions it finds itself under. However, we can go further. The conditions in which a foetus develops may themselves be influenced by the genetic field of the foetus. It is not as though there is an evolving genetic organism on one side and a set of physical and environmental conditions on the other. The two are intertwined. So instead of saying that the genetic field evolves into a particular human, depending on the conditions, it would be more accurate to say that there is an entire field of relations that expresses itself in a particular way depending on how those relations unfold. And, in keeping with the analogy with origami we saw earlier, however this expression goes, the field will remain within whatever particular expression does emerge, within the actualization of a particular human being.

This gets us closer to Deleuze's concept of being as difference, difference as a field of relations without positive terms, one that actualizes into positive terms without losing the differential field. The differential field continues to inhabit those terms. Experiential reality – reality as we experience it – is richer, fuller than what presents itself to us. There is always more than appears to us. This is why Deleuze is dismissive of phenomenology. Phenomenology limits itself to an investigation of the actual, when the deep possibilities of our world are recognized only when we investigate the virtual field of difference that is coiled within it.

Deleuze's view of difference occupies an interesting place between traditional foundationalist philosophy and the work of Derrida and Levinas. Like the former, it reserves a place for a particular something – difference – that forms the basis for our experiential world. '[D]ifference is behind everything, but behind difference there is nothing' (Deleuze, 1994, p. 57). However, like Derrida and Levinas, this something that is behind everything cannot act as a foundation in the sense traditional philosophy seeks. Since what is behind everything is difference, rather than some form of identity, there is no possibility of using it as a basis for the traditional philosophical project of grounding knowledge. Difference is precisely that which resists acting as an epistemic grounding. It is not stable enough. It cannot be known in language. It cannot be confronted directly. It appears not in itself but only through its effects, through its actualization.

There is a figure we have not discussed here that some people would want to see as a philosopher or at least a thinker of difference: Michel Foucault. It is probably worth pausing over why, at least in my view, Foucault is not a philosopher of difference in anything like the sense that Derrida, Levinas and Deleuze are. The reason he is not a philosopher of difference is not, of course, that he is a philosopher of identity. Like the philosophers of difference that we have discussed here, Foucault's views do indeed seek to undercut philosophies of identity. They attempt to show historically that many of the identities that have been used to found philosophical thought – reason, soul, knowledge – are in fact historically constituted. The distinction between Foucault and the philosophers of difference is that Foucault does not appeal to anything that has the structure of difference in order to undercut identity. We might say that his approach is historical and bound to contingency rather than philosophical and bound to difference.

For Foucault, the problem with the identities that have founded thought is twofold. First, and of less concern to us here, these identities often act in politically oppressive ways. Received concepts of reason and the soul, for instance, are nodal points of practices that serve to bind people to oppressive social arrangements by getting them to think of themselves and their world in certain, constricted ways. Second, of more moment, the problem with these identities is that they are historically constituted and therefore cannot be the kinds of absolutes necessary to serve as philosophical foundations. For something to be able to stand as a philosophical foundation, it must be certain, unshakeable. Historical contingencies, however, are precisely that: contingent. They arise under certain conditions and pass away when the conditions that support them no longer exist. They do not make for the kinds of foundations upon which one can build knowledge.

Take, for instance, the concept of reason. If reason, at least in some of its current manifestations, is the product of an engagement with (and an exclusion of) madness that arose during the seventeenth and eighteenth centuries – as Foucault argues in his early *History of Madness* (Foucault, 1972) – then we cannot appeal to some sort of absolute and indubitable Reason in order to found philosophy or to serve as an unchangeable methodological principle. We must ask what kinds of reason we are talking about, where it comes from, what purposes it might serve. And, if we use a form of reason to ask these questions (which, of course, we must), that form of reason cannot, in its turn, be immune from questions. Therefore, we cannot even take our own approach as a sort of foundation.

This approach to subverting identities is distinct from the approaches of Derrida, Levinas and Deleuze. It does not posit a philosophical conception of difference – either as an alterity in interplay with identity or as difference itself – that resists being conceptualized in terms of identity. Instead, it historicizes particular identities that are proposed as philosophical foundations. In this sense, the philosophies of difference embraced by Derrida, Levinas and Deleuze remain with the same philosophical field that characterizes philosophies of identity. They are recognizably philosophical projects. That is why I call them philosophies of difference. Foucault's approach, by contrast, steps outside the philosophical arena to that of history. Nevertheless, his histories, while not philosophical in the sense that characterizes the work of Derrida, Levinas and Deleuze, has important philosophical implications and effects.

We see, then, that the philosophies of difference that have arisen over the course of the latter part of the twentieth century do not abandon philosophy. They raise questions about its traditional approaches and assumptions, but they continue its conceptual work. They represent one of the most important challenges to traditional philosophy, but they do not encourage us to jettison the kind of thought the history of philosophy has bequeathed to us. If one or another of the approaches canvassed here is compelling, then our task is that of asking not only how to conceive the world adequately, but also, and perhaps more so, how we might think of the world otherwise than we currently do.

7 Politics and Ethics

Caroline Williams

Introduction

[I]n the broad sense, every philosophy is practical and political: an Ethics.
(Althusser, 2003, p. 12)

From Hegel to Heidegger, continental philosophy has always had a strong
ethical dimension, but an important aspect of much contemporary continental philosophy is its powerful effort to conjoin ethical with political thinking. It is the nature and form of this relationship *between* politics and ethics,
and the power of its philosophico-political effects, that has generated some of
the most interesting and insistent questions in continental philosophy today.
There is, however, very little agreement about precisely how to constitute this
relation between politics and ethics. Are we to conceive of ethics as a distinctive mode of thinking *about* politics, or should we rather think of politics as
a distinctly *ethical practice*? Is politics subordinated to ethics as a form of first
philosophy, as Levinas argues, such that the turn to ethics is, necessarily, a
turn away from politics? Or might we best speak, after Derrida and Foucault,
of a co-belonging or an inhering of both within the domain of the *ethico-
political*? What, moreover, is the *difference* arising within, and between, the
various approaches to the study of politics and ethics, and what might be
the consequence(s) of this difference?

Such questions are not merely rhetorical, beckoning one to reflect upon the
nature of the relation between politics and ethics; they are also deeply political, setting out the parameters, ontological frameworks and initial (political)
questions that guide the philosophical approach to this relation. In addition to
thinking about the *kind* of ethics, and the *conception* of politics and the political
embraced here, we need then to think about the kinds of questions asked *of*
politics and the nature of the relationship established between the realms of
the ethical and the political. Contemporary continental philosophers from
Levinas, Derrida and Habermas, to Badiou, Foucault and Deleuze, to name
only some of the most prominent and best recognized within this field, each
pose the question of a certain kind of ethics within the context of a distinctive
conception of politics and the political. It is the aim of this chapter to explore

the terms of this relation within a selection of key philosophical figures within contemporary continental thought.

We need, at this introductory stage, to underscore the essential, operative difference between *ethics* and *morality* (initially posed by Hegel in terms of *Sittlichkeit* and *Moralität*). For the purposes of this chapter, ethics and morality will not be used interchangeably as they are by some philosophers and political theorists. Indeed, I would argue that the distinction here opens up a deeper set of preoccupations around both the question of subjectivity (specifically, the ethical construction of the subject), and the nature of the political as a site of opening to difference and contingency, both of which are key aspects of contemporary continental philosophy (Critchley, 2007; Marchart, 2007). Discourses of morality, often presented in a Kantian form, commence with the principle of moral autonomy and presuppose some concept of human nature or principle of moral subjectivity which acts in accordance with a rule or law. A moral subject thus acts according to a pre-existing law, usually a prescriptive and universal maxim, to which it is both obligated to conform its conduct, and indeed, is supposed to will, in a disinterested way, that it does so conform. An ethical subject, by contrast, requires no such constitution according to an *a priori* moral law, and there is no moral law that precedes and produces a certain form of ethical conduct. On this reading, ethics is concerned with the kinds of relations and practices that may ground, frame, or, to use Foucault's words here, fashion a subject of ethical conduct. Ethics arises, one might argue, only with the *suspension* of the question of moral foundations. For Derrida, as we shall see below, ethics always takes place within such a space of uncertainty, when there are no clear parameters of a moral kind, where no law is fitting to the situation; instead, it is this very *undecidability* that inaugurates a decision to act, to respond, to address the situation. It might be that both politics and ethics are reduced to formalities or repressed within philosophical discourse when we assume some principle of moral autonomy, stable identity and unencumbered moral agency for the subject, or some prescriptive moral rule or law to guide us. According to Butler (2005), for example, it is the destruction of a common ethos, the loss of ground of moral agency and the very opacity of the self, that has opened up the possibility of new shapes of ethical relation and responsibility.

Ethics, then, delineates a quite different field of questions and mode of thinking about politics than that of morality, and a different web of concepts and concerns. We must underscore that every conception of ethics that we consider here, takes place in the wake of the critique of metaphysical and political humanism, and the undoing of every principle and foundation. If an appeal to ethical 'subjectivity' is often central to the question of ethics, it is, as we shall see below, a subject undone and pluralized by the philosophical work of continental thought. This critique of humanism must also be tied to the presence of Marxism – in both its Sartrean and Althusserian forms – in continental philosophy, with which many of the thinkers discussed here have an inescapable relation, thinking differently but nonetheless with a Marx for our times (see Bensaïd, 2002). Ethics is often also deeply ontological and builds its practice upon some notion of being and relation, but again, the ontological shape of this ethics is fissured, interrupted, marked, by the very critiques of ontology present in continental thought. Politics, too, must be understood in this ontological sense, undergoing a kind of retreat and retracing from which the philosophical exigency of the political as a question arises (see Lacoue-Labarthe and Nancy, 1997). It is this broad milieu of questions and preoccupations which establishes the continental approach to ethics and politics as a quite different kind of animal to that pursued by the combination of morality and politics.

This does not, of course, imply any kind of *unity* of approach to these questions within contemporary continental philosophy. For some thinkers, it is the *ethical motivation* of the subject that is critical: the sensibilities, affective comportment, the attunement to the Other and otherness, which fills out the content of ethical subjectivity. For others, ethics is tied to an account of *power*, affect and bodies (human and non-human). For others still, ethics is always derived from the opening up of an *event*, which induces an ethical relation to truth. In every approach, each of which remains nameless at present, a certain attentiveness to politics produces a distinct mode of ethical thinking.

Defining the Limits

Having considered some of the terms of debate critical to the discussion here, it is necessary to establish some limits and boundaries to this wide-ranging topic. One extremely helpful tool can be found in Giorgio Agamben's genealogical map of continental philosophy, which establishes two intersecting paths sign-posted 'transcendence' and 'immanence' respectively (Agamben, 1999). Along the former path, Agamben places Levinas and Derrida, and he traces the genealogy of their thought to Husserl and Kant, via Heidegger. Along the latter path of immanence, he locates the philosophy of Deleuze and Foucault, and he elicits the form of their thought in Nietzsche and Spinoza, also via an engagement with Heidegger. While it is clear that there are no watertight divisions (genealogy itself is, after all, an open, tree-like series of connections), Agamben's map has, for us, a certain heuristic value, allowing us to speak of a *politics and ethics of transcendence* where what is political about a particular mode of thinking arises only out of an experience of something which is formally impossible, discernable only through a certain attentiveness to its *conditions* of (im)possibility, and is in some way 'beyond' or lacking in that thing. Here, we may locate not only Levinas and Derrida but also certain forms of psychoanalytic politics of the Lacanian real. On the other hand, we can associate a *politics and ethics of immanence* with a range of approaches that understand the conditions of politics to be found in a reflection upon the ontological conditions of being and life as a field of forces, affects and intensities, a generative and abundant form of existence that produces matrices of power, truth and knowledge (Foucault). Politics and ethics here become associated with affirming a body's power and persistence (Deleuze), creating the political conditions for flourishing and nurturing an ethics of generosity and abundance (Connolly). In introducing some of the most prominent efforts to configure a politics and an ethics within continental philosophy, we will utilize Agamben's framework to locate positions, and to mark out some of the consequences of thinking ethics via transcendence or immanence. We will also have to supplement and transform the map where necessary. In the case of Badiou, for example, politics is a condition of philosophy and there is no *distinctive* account of ethics, yet nonetheless an important ethical and political structure is given to the event of truth in philosophy. We turn first to consider the most dominant model of the ethics of transcendence before considering the critique and counter-position presented by Badiou.

Towards an Ethics and Politics of Transcendence

For both Agamben (1999) and Smith (2003), deconstruction operates within the interval between the closed totality of metaphysics and the formal transcendence of *difference*, as that which disrupts and destabilizes any 'metaphysics of presence'. It is the thinking of this interval, or aporetic space, where every determinate opening, problem, or question, interrupts and exceeds metaphysical closure, which inaugurates the ethico-political moment of deconstruction. Certainly, there cannot simply be a politics of deconstruction, just as there can be no theory or method of deconstruction (aside from one that reifies its activity). However, evidenced by the sheer number of political and ethical questions explored by Derrida in the last fifteen years at least (and also recognizing that many of his earlier works broached such themes too, albeit, for some, obliquely), it is clear that deconstruction has powerful political consequences. These discussions range from questions of friendship, justice and responsibility, to democracy, hospitality and forgiveness (see, for example, Derrida 2000, 2005, 2006). We can only intimate the enormous value of these interventions here, and via one or two examples from Derrida's more recent reflections, limit ourselves to excavating the ethico-political *sense* or *moment* of deconstruction, and thinking about the political effects produced by its wake.

Derrida has always held a certain complex debt to Levinas and it is this debt that is, for some, central to his later writings, establishing deconstruction as above all *an ethics* (for example, Critchley, 1999; Beardsworth, 1996). It is Levinas's rethinking of being and essence according to an *a priori* ethical structure of relation to the Other that undoes every principle of subjectivity, and makes this unravelling the inescapable condition of every possible social and ethical relation. This 'gestation of the other in the same', to use Levinas's words, expels the 'I' outside of being, entailing a radical *subjection* of the subject; a state of being hostage to the other that precedes every choice, responsibility, freedom. Thus,

> I am assigned without recourse, without fatherland, already sent back to myself, but without being able to stay there, compelled before commencing ... [T]o be oneself, the state of being a hostage, is always to have one degree of responsibility more, the responsibility for the responsibility of the other. (Levinas, 1991, pp. 103, 117)

While remaining critical of Levinas's attempt to both escape the phenomenology – and indeed the anthropocentrism – of the subject (to which, Derrida argues, his work will always remain indebted and dependent), and to prioritize an ethics *beyond* and prior to politics (for example, Derrida, 1999), some of the most insistent political discussions found in Derrida's own writings nonetheless take from Levinas this attentiveness to the ethical relation to the other, and particularly to the state of being hostage. With this articulation of 'an underivable interpellation' that comes from the other, Derrida deconstructs the Kantian idea of moral autonomy, prefixing it with a radical heteronomy. For example, in *Adieu* (1999) and later texts (2000, 2006), Derrida explores the problematic of hospitality, and the relation between guest and host, as the very principle of ethics. Without imperative or duty, hospitality is unconditional and absolute; following Levinas, it calls upon the host to substitute him or herself for the guest, to be invited *by the other* into his home, to receive the hospitality that is given to the other, to be welcomed by he who is welcomed, to interrupt the *ipseity* of the subject. And yet, for Derrida, hospitality is a self-contradictory concept marked, at one and the same time, by a series of risks: (i) that the other be folded into the internal laws of the host (based on nationality, language, family, culture, etc) such that 'hospitality limits itself at its very beginning . . ., [and] remains forever on the threshold of itself' (Derrida, 2006, p. 225); (ii) that the other be determined as stranger, rather than remaining the undetermined, infinite, 'not-knowing' otherness that is essential to a hospitality always to come (Derrida, 2006, pp. 216, 226); (iii) that the troubling opposition, deconstructed on several occasions (for example, in *The Politics of Friendship*), between friend and enemy, guest and stranger, hospitality and hostility, introduces a violence and a limit into the heart of hospitality, which is often authorized by law and restricted by some legal imperative. In this way, the gift of hospitality is framed by a series of ethico-political possibilities that challenge and move beyond its particular normative conditions of existence.

Derrida takes the structure of this ethical relation much further than Levinas is able to do, given the latter's resistance to thinking the political itself as a form of ethical relation. His interventions within international politics and constitutional law, read alongside his engagement with Kantian themes, illustrate how he similarly goes beyond Kant's own effort to separate – and give priority – to the ethical (or rather moral law, right) over politics: the authority of moral law is grounded in the faculty of reason, in what Kant understands as the limits of the possible (and politics). In contrast, deconstruction inscribes the political *in* the ethical, and political and ethical imperatives become indissociable and unconditional (Derrida, 2002, p. 305).

To return momentarily to hospitality: Derrida points out many of the tensions he finds in this ethical concept through his reading of Kant's 'Perpetual Peace', where the *possibility* of hospitality is delimited according to juridically regulated right. As we have seen, it is here, in the interval between the law of conditioned hospitality and its transgression (and *transcendence*), that deconstruction as ethics, as justice, as hospitality itself becomes (im)possible. Deconstruction inheres in this ethico-political space, defined by Kant as a *perpetual* peace towards which we must strive, and by Derrida as a threshold or opening, an undecidability, and as a future without horizon or messianism. Crucially, this does not leave deconstruction without a politics, oscillating (negatively) between the possibility and impossibility of hospitality (or justice/law, democracy/authority, etc), since politics *is* this moment of transcendence when an action, a strategic decision which appears impossible, is demanded by the 'here and now' of a situation. In this way, deconstruction is a form of infinite and interminable negotiation and critique, an always contested process without resolution; it is also a strategic way of inventing and instituting new norms and of contesting again and again the dominant forms of law and politics and their legitimizing practices.

In terms of the political effect of this ethics of transcendence, Derrida claims a certain militancy for his interventions, arguing that the aporetic structure of democracy (always undoing and critiquing its own substantial forms) makes it the only political paradigm that is *universalizable* since its singular enactments provoke 'universal' norms (Derrida, 1992, 2006). Democracy also means something more than its state form, for Derrida, and he hopes for the creation of an innovative, post-international form of democratic space that never ceases to invent new accommodations and divisions of sovereignty (2006, pp. 86–8). We will take the opportunity to think about the scope of this ethico-political engagement by contrasting it later with that emerging from Deleuzian politics, as well as the recent thought of Alain Badiou. At this juncture, however, we must point out that it is the (Kantian) aspect of Derrida's work that has most recently placed deconstruction in close proximity to Habermasian discourse-ethics (see Critchley, 2000; Matuštik, 2006). While we do not have the space here to identify the range of positions common to their seemingly diverse philosophico-political perspectives (see Thomassen, 2006 for a valuable collection of these), it is clear that some kind of *rapprochement* had occurred in the years prior to Derrida's death, presenting the opportunity to think the ethical injunction of democracy-to-come with the model of democratic deliberation.

There was certainly something strategic in the discussions and political interventions Derrida and Habermas shared (see Barrodori, 2003, and Thomassen, 2006) and in their alliance against what Matuštik calls 'the new political onto-theology of sovereignty' (2006, p. 287). However, Habermas's account of the construction of moral norms through intersubjective communication and ethical deliberation offers an arguably limited form of procedural justice for testing norms and resolving political conflict, one that tends, I would argue, to retreat from, and hence *depoliticize*, both politics and ethics. If moral norms are the result of deliberative processes premised on autonomy and equality, symmetry and reciprocity, and the inclusion of all subjects, then, for Habermas, they necessarily transcend all contingent and arbitrary factors and form a legitimate basis for (the universal form of) law. It is only constitutional law, grounded upon the legal authority of a democratic system and deliberative practices that can build peace and stability and ensure the validity of moral norms. Nevertheless, if there is a relationship between ethics and politics here, it is one between constitutionalism and democracy, that is, between *law* and politics, rather than the kind of ethical attentiveness to law and justice demanded by deconstruction (which, for Habermas, itself risks a kind of ethical overload in the public sphere). It is also a relationship sewn together by a certain privileging of a socio-historical *telos* of modernity. Thus, it is those states with embedded practices of constitutionalism and deliberation, operating according to the Kantian principle of practical reason, that are more likely to move towards the kind of cosmopolitanism and 'global' justice imagined by Kant and Habermas (see, most recently, Habermas, 2006). Arguably, the limit of Habermas's position here is that it fails to accord significant value to that which cannot be accommodated or easily recognized by rational communication or constitutional law, and which may be supplemented by an ethical sensibility of forgiveness (Matuštik, 2006). There are also contingent aspects of constitutional democracy (its particular manifestations, practical limits and exclusions) that reveal the limits and the aporia inhering in both constitutionalism and democracy (see Derrida, 2006, and Thomassen (ed.), 2006 for a discussion). As we have argued above, it is a kind of institutionalization of undecidability as *interminable negotiation* that is sought by the ethico-political practice of deconstruction.

To some extent, Derrida and Habermas are conducting quite different kinds of politics, despite their strategic comments on Europe, etc. However, both thinkers risk, for Badiou, the *depoliticization* of politics because they end up either substituting ethics for politics, or merging the two together. Both remain part of the ethical ideology criticized by Badiou in *Ethics: An Understanding of Evil* (2001) where he claims the contemporary focus on ethics is both synonymous with a Kantian form of ethics (which always restricts ethics from thinking the singularity of a situation) and is nihilistic in form (introducing a paralysing moral responsibility into political life). Does this require an inversion of the Levinasian position, such that politics must keep its distance from ethics in order to remain political? Let us briefly turn to the prescient philosophy of Alain Badiou to think through this question.

The Ethics of a Truth-Event

For Badiou, ethics must have a more specific and derived effect than that encapsulated by an ethics of transcendence; there exists an *ethics of truth* only in relation to the singularity of an *event* and the conflict produced in its relation to what has gone before. Ethics is associated neither with a kind of ethical decisionism (and its opposite), or with a relation to alterity, and to a transcendent beyond. If ethics is attached to the immediate (political) scene of an event, the same must be said of the subject, which is given no ontological function, status or condition outside of the rupture with the given that constitutes the event. In this way, the 'subject' of politics, science, art and love (the four key domains considered by Badiou), is induced by the process of truth itself, and arises as a truth-effect *only* insofar as a fidelity to the event persists. The continued usage of the term 'subject' here is perhaps a loaded one, given its myriad conceptual contortions in contemporary continental philosophy, and Badiou clearly wants to separate subjectivity from its many metaphysical functions. Subjectivization is both what makes truth happen and yet the subject is unable to persist without the faithful attachment to the future consequences of the event. Thus, when Badiou, paraphrasing Beckett, emphasizes the maxim to 'keep going', this refers to neither the agency nor the ethical deliberations of a subject but solely to the insistence to 'persevere in that which exceeds your perseverance' (2001, p. 47). What is the *political shape* of the event and this peculiar, *non-subjective* ethics of commitment?

The ontological basis of this position is one that gives rise to a very clear practice of politics. Politics usurps the prominent place usually given to philosophy, which becomes tied, in *Metapolitics*, to the *sui generis* activity of thought thinking new distinctions and partitions, which help to understand the shifting *political* condition (Badiou, 2005, p. 62). For Badiou's ontology of pure multiplicity where, contra Levinas, infinite alterity (differences) *is all there is*, everything is initially underdetermined and unfixed. It is from this ontology of immanence that the chance-like, aleatory event emerges, out of step with the historical, and removed from all relation to transcendence, but wholly tied to a specific situation. This ontology is best expressed in the domain of politics (rather than the domains of love, aesthetics or science), where the multiple as the greatest number, the infinite, has the strongest force (as mass, multitude, etc.), and where the axioms that guide the singular situation can also be universalizable, most clearly in equality, which is *indifferent to differences*, and is thus the *sine qua non* of political axioms for Badiou (as it is for Rancière, 1999).

Badiou proposes a 'subtractive politics', one generated at a distance from the institutional ground of the state and liberal democratic processes; the truth-event is born in situations other than democratic politics where the discourses of multiculturalism and group solidarity reign. But we can still question the kind of critical relation that remains here between the occasion of singular situations and the political state itself. Might the *rarity* of events be delimited by the power of this other, more organized politics, in the form of global capital? This is not the place to discuss Badiou's relation to Marxism in general, or Althusser and Sartre in particular (see Hallward, 2001, 2004), but the connection between the aleatory nature of the event and the wider frame of power relations deserves attention. Before turning to explore this problem in the context of other ethico-political frameworks of immanence, notably those of Deleuze and Foucault, we will draw attention, albeit briefly, to the current work of Simon Critchley (2007) and Judith Butler (2004, 2005). Both develop quite novel readings of Levinas, and, like Derrida too, seek to utilize Levinasian ethics to advance a theory of politics and relationality. To what extent can their more recent writings respond to the lack of politics present, for Badiou, in an ethics of alterity?

The Precarious Politics of Alterity

In his book *Infinitely Demanding: Ethics of Commitment, Politics of Resistance*, Critchley argues that radical politics today requires a *meta-political* ethical moment in order to generate the motivational content for political agency and subjectivity: 'If ethics without politics is empty, then politics without ethics is blind' (2007, p. 13). Politics thus becomes a kind of ethical practice built upon a particular conception of ethical experience and subjectivity. Critchley's argument here, which shares several points worthy of comparison with

Butler's, endeavours to make Levinas truly political. He agrees with Levinas that the subject is *hetero-affectively* constituted, dislocated by an experience of infinite responsibility to the other, and further agrees that such ethical responsibility issues in an infinite demand that always exceeds the subject. His concern, however, is that the 'absolute passivity of the self' (Levinas, 1973, p. 110) introduced by the structure of this ethical demand (persecution, obsession, etc), might induce in the subject an experience of traumatic neurosis. Without a transformative psychoanalytic practice of sublimation, this results in a destructive vision of a divided subject, paralysed and unable to act. Lacan's recourse to the experience of the tragic and the beautiful as forms of ethical sublimation offers Critchley no solution here since it evokes, for him, a certain authenticity and heroism that distorts our experience of ethical finitude. Critchley draws instead on Freud's short essay on humour in order to suggest that we need to evoke a sense of humour and laughter at the super-ego: 'a maturity that comes from learning to laugh at oneself, from finding oneself ridiculous' (2007, p. 83).

It remains unclear how this quasi-Nietzschean tool relates precisely to our experience of ethical responsibility to the other. Indeed, Žižek has suggested that Critchley leaves out the brutally sadistic, denigrating and mocking aspect of humour: 'the humorous super-ego is the cruel and insatiable agency which bombards me with impossible demands and which mocks my failed attempts to meet them . . .' (Žižek, 2008, p. 342). For Žižek, whose position here (like Badiou's above) directly opposes the kind of politics that issues from an ethics of transcendence, the subject is an anti-ethical agency. Indeed, every ethical demand, for both Žižek and Lacan, is a necessary (imaginary) act of covering over and protecting, to varying degrees, the subject from irruptions from the deathly real; from a primordial experience of deathly negativity at the heart of the (split) subject that cannot be transcended (see Žižek, 2008, pp. 342–5). However, it is perhaps the kind of politics embraced by Critchley that produces Žižek's strongest consternation, being untied from any ontological conception of the emergence of the political and the subject; there is, for Critchley, no transitivity between politics and ontology, and we should not pin our hopes on any such conception of 'weak ontology' (Critchley 2007, p. 105; White, 2000).

Critchley develops his political theory out of a longstanding engagement with the work of Ernesto Laclau. Laclau's 'post-Marxist' reconfiguration of the concept of hegemony as the articulation of different elements of 'society' (through economic, political and ideological struggles), recognizes the contingency of this process and its responsiveness to re-articulations and dislocations within it, calling this political form 'radical democracy'. Critchley takes from Laclau the idea of hegemonic articulation and ties this to Badiou's quite different focus upon a *fidelity to the event* in order to cultivate an anarchic multiplicity in the fabric of the political (for Laclau's difference from Badiou, see Laclau, 2004). It is this latter aspect that assists Critchley's conception of ethics as *commitment*. While he questions both the possible circularity of the double genesis of event and subject in Badiou's philosophy, and the relation of ethics to (axiomatic) truths (preferring to talk about truth as the procedure through which the justification – and critique – of norms takes place), Critchley wants to hold on to the idea of ethics as a *subjective process*. No doubt there are aspects of this utilization that Badiou would find questionable, but these two positions have certainly generated a fascinating dialogue regarding the relation between contemporary radical politics and ethics (see the 2008 volume of *Symposium* for Badiou's response to Critchley's book (Badiou, 2008), and further discussion).

Butler's recent work is also to be situated within the heterodox continental space of the ethico-political, and once again, as part of her argument, she takes up and reconfigures the Levinasian injunction of the Other discussed above. However, rather than viewing her recent books as marking a shift into new territory, it could instead be suggested that Butler's entire corpus to date has been broadly concerned with the ethico-political question of identity and its contingent articulation (See Lloyd, 2007; Loizidou, 2007). Indeed, in keeping with the claim in this introduction, namely that politics and ethics are inextricably bound, Butler would likely argue that ethics cannot be separated from the production of norms, and therefore from the problem of normativity and the practice of critique (see Butler 2002, 2000). This makes it necessary to consider the complex process of formation of the subject and its effect upon ethical responsibility.

In *Giving an Account of Oneself* (2005), Butler enriches the Foucauldian sense of ethics as a practice of self-relation, arguing, as she did in the *Psychic Life of Power* (1997), that Foucault's lacklustre relation to psychoanalysis prevents him from theorising adequately the ethical relation to the other (for example, Butler 1997, p. 18; 2005, pp. 16, 127). In addition, she traces the philosophical complexities engendered by poststructuralist conceptions of the subject, arguing that the resulting loss of ground for the transparent ethical subject should be embraced. Not only might this counter the ethical violence entailed by the quest for self-identity, but it may also allow one to recast the subject as a problem *for* ethics:

> This is not the death of the subject . . . but an inquiry into the modes by
> which the subject is instituted and maintains itself, and how the norms
> that govern ethical principles must be understood as operating not only
> to guide conduct but to decide the question of who and what will be
> a human subject. (Butler, 2005, p. 110)

Rather than mourning the destruction of a common ethos and its often exclusionary norms of moral accountability, we might better explore the new forms of ethical relationship available in its wake. After all, Butler notes, 'it may well follow that it is precisely by virtue of the subject's opacity to itself that it incurs and sustains some of its most important ethical bonds' (2005, p. 20).

In many ways, this is a truly Foucauldian enterprise. Butler is one of Foucault's most creative readers today, researching in the spirit of Foucault's thought, but also taking him beyond and outside the zones of his own engagement. Here is not the place to offer a detailed assessment of Foucault's growing interest, during his latter years, in the ethics and aesthetics of the Greek and ancient worlds and their usefulness for thinking ethics today (see Deleuze, 1988a; Macherey, 1998; and O'Leary, 2002). We must, however, indicate the centrality of this interest to the discussion of politics and ethics in this chapter, more generally, and to Butler's current project, in particular.

If Foucault's writings of the 1960s and 70s evinced a concern with the other of reason and madness, his later failure to think the other in the context of ethics is decisive, for Butler, given that the very being of the self is dependent upon the existence of the other. According to Butler, it is because we seek to respond, to give an account, to search for recognition from the other (even though the satisfaction of this incessant desire will always fall short in an experience of *méconnaissance* or misrecognition), that the dyadic scene of self and other becomes so important. There is, nonetheless, enormous value in the attention Foucault gives to the different ways in which the history of norms has shaped the ethical conduct of the subject; ethical practices produce the subject and delimit its conditions of existence. Ethics creates the subject, or better, creates modes of subjectivation wherein the subject takes form. At the same time, and as part of this process of subjectivation and subjection, Foucault underscores the importance of a self-delimitation and self-stylization whereby a singular practice of the self upon the self takes place. There is no form of power without the complement of a retroactive freedom. This is why Deleuze associates the emergence of the Foucauldian subject with 'folded force', which is itself a figure of immanence (Deleuze, 1988a, p. 84). It is in the margins or folds of this power/freedom, forever attached to the moral norms that engender its very being, that the subject may create new practices of self-formation. Thus, new ethics and political practices in contemporary societies cannot come about via the *transcendence* of the norm, as if the social normativity shaping ethical relations could be discarded, but only by creating new forms of individualization and new practices of ethical formation designed to reshape the contours of contemporary politico-ethical relations. It is this attention to the transformatory potential present in the iterability of norms that has been central to Butler's work to date.

Butler takes this sketch of Foucault's position on ethics and subjectivity as her starting point in *Giving an Account of Oneself* but she gives greater emphasis to the ways in which norms also frame the scene of recognition, arguing *with* Foucault that the reflexive critique that is part of ethical self-questioning 'involves putting oneself at risk, imperilling the very possibility of being recognized by others' (Butler, 2005, p. 23). It follows that 'certain practices of recognition or, indeed, certain breakdowns in the practice of rec-ognition mark a site of rupture within the horizon of normativity and impli-citly call for the institution of new norms' (2005, p. 25). In fact, the ethical address to the other depends on this social dimension of normativity, which may occlude the other and render opaque their singular identity. It is for this reason that Butler turns to Levinas, but also to psychoanalytic efforts to theorize the primary relations that feed the desire for recognition (see Butler, 2005, chapter 2).

Butler's preoccupation with the horizon of our ethical relation to the other is tied to the *failure* of all our efforts to give an account of ourselves. This is because the structural conditions that frame that account decentre and unravel the subject in ways that make the attribution of responsibility seem impossible. Nevertheless, it is the deconstruction of ethical agency and the apparent dilution of responsibility that instead becomes 'an indispensable source of ethics' (2005, pp. 36–40). In her examination of the deeper patterns of relationality that accompany the subject's decomposition, Butler discusses, among other aspects, the otherness that is constitutive of the self, the immense difficulty of authorship or linguistic agency, and our attachments to a psychic history that precedes self-formation and is beyond full recovery – even through psychoanalytic technique. Reading Levinas via the French psycho-analyst Jean Laplanche, she enriches our understanding of the scope of rela-tionality, pointing to the ways in which seduction, as well as persecution, inform the ethical demand and contribute to its normativity. Laplanche iden-tifies the ways through which objects 'seduce' the subject, creating as they do so, a residual zone of interiority and a series of dynamic psychic processes. Kafka's tale 'Cares of a Family Man' becomes, on Butler's reading, a fascinating point of entry into this landscape of alterity and responsibility, where agency becomes a complex process, 'and the "I" finds itself to be foreign to itself in its most elemental impulses' (Butler, 2005, p. 71).

The introduction of psychoanalysis into the discussion here is unavoidable given the necessary relationship between subject formation and ethical com-mitment, but it does raise all sorts of questions that are beyond the scope of this chapter (see Zupančič, 2000, Harasym, 1998, and Kollias's chapter on Psychoanalysis and Philosophy in this volume, for an indication of this scope). Butler, like Critchley above, worries that the infinite responsibility proffered by Levinas may result in a kind of ethical masochism where the primary persistence of life itself, identified by Spinoza as *conatus*, may itself become threatened and destroyed (Butler, 2004, p. 140, and 2005, p. 44). In a related essay (2006), Butler joins Deleuze and others in querying the view that Spinoza is an ethical optimist, as she also implicates him in the themes raised here. Discussing once again 'the desire to live' via Spinoza's image of a conative striving for persistence, she suggests that an *ek-stasis* is produced by the mobility of desire, 'a dependency on an externalization, something that is palpably not-me, without which no perseverance is possible' (Butler, 2006, p. 112). It is for such reasons that Butler talks of a 'precarious life' in the sense that the ethical failure of recognition can render the subject without a 'right' to life, as somehow inhuman, as merely 'bare life' to draw upon Agamben's term in *Homo Sacer*. But it is also 'precarious life' which makes ethics both difficult and necessary since its agency has now become differentiated and more tenuous; our reminder of a 'common vulnerability, a common physicality and risk, . . . which can provide a way to understand that none of us is fully bounded, utterly separate, but rather we are in our skins, given over, in each other's hands, at each other's mercy' (Butler, 2005, pp. 100, 101).

We have now strayed a considerable distance from an ethics of transcendence, although there are clearly many common themes developed in the perspectives considered above. It is apparent also that the shadows advancing over the present discussions are those of Spinoza and Nietzsche rather than Kant. This observation is supported by Agamben's genealogy or map, presented in the introduction above. Let us, then, trace some of the more interesting ethical pathways in this adventure with immanence, and also advance some of the more suggestive remarks around the relationship between subjectivity and ethics raised thus far in the chapter.

Thinking Ethics and Politics as Immanence

In a chapter on Spinoza entitled 'On the Difference between the *Ethics* and a Morality', Gilles Deleuze describes Spinoza's *Ethics* as an *ethology*, the primary task of which is to consider the capacities of bodies to affect and be affected (Deleuze, 1988b, p. 27). The focus of the *Ethics*, then, is upon a physics and an *ethos* of bodies – not just the corporeal composition of bodies and the multiple relations constituting them, but also the patterns of agreement and disagreement which compose their practical encounters. The question guiding Spinoza's practical philosophy is not the one that orients the subject in relation to morality: what *ought* I to do? It is rather the question that must always be, at least for Spinoza and Deleuze, of a different ontological order to this one, namely, what can a body do? Of what *affects* is a body capable, and how can it be moved to experience joyful affects?

Now, this ontology, and these ontological questions about the *potentia* of bodies, must be situated within a thinking of immanence which is not without its own complexities. (For example, can immanence, as that which has no outside, generate any kind of ethics? Will the attribution of value always require a form of transcendence?) At the same time, it seems critical to at least attempt to flesh out the *kind* of ethico-political practice engendered by this commitment to thinking immanence, and how this might differ from a thinking of transcendence. As Daniel Smith notes,

> The ethical themes one finds in transcendent philosophies such as those of Levinas and Derrida – an absolute responsibility for the other that I can never assume, or an infinite call to justice that I can never satisfy – are, from the point of view of immanence, imperatives whose effect is to separate me from my capacity to act. (Smith, 2003, p. 62)

There might be quite different ethical and political consequences emerging from these philosophical discourses, and we need now to mark out the stakes of this latter philosophical position.

In 'Immanence: A Life', Deleuze attempts a formulation: 'Absolute immanence is in itself: it is not in something, *to* something; it does not depend on an object, or belong to a subject' (2001, p. 26). Here, and elsewhere with Guattari, he describes immanence as a kind of *pre-philosophical* or non-philosophical plane of pure, infinite variation, of fractal multiple curves, each of which depends upon 'which infinite movements are retained and selected, succeed and contest each other in history' (Deleuze and Guattari, 1994, p. 39). In this way, philosophy performs a kind of political and historical *institution*, at times (perhaps more often) bringing into being concepts, modes and forms of life that rest upon a necessary principle of transcendence, and at other times (perhaps more rarely), creating forms of life that express and enhance the infinite power (*potentia*) of nature and thought. It is for this reason that Spinoza, Nietzsche and Bergson remain so close to Deleuze's thinking of an ethics resting upon immanence, as each recognizes the intensive, infinite movements of an image of thought expressing a possible (ethical) world.

Spinoza's ontology, in particular, is singled out by Deleuze and Guattari, precisely because his image of the infinite grounds of thought and world endeavours to ward off every form of religious, moral and political transcendence of life. For Spinoza, every finite expression of substance is thus in a state of perpetual becoming and transformation; the finite world is not simply a mirror of a primordial nature. All individual things express unique compositions and dispositions, degrees of compatibility with other bodies that, in turn, may augment or diminish their affective structure. These will also be inseparable from certain habits, norms and forms of existence (that is, an ethics) that fold and delimit the body. It is here, between Spinoza's ontology of becoming and Nietzsche's more overt concern with ethical experimentation, that we can place the later Foucault's interest in an aesthetics of existence and an ethics of freedom, as well as William Connolly's recent work on modes of ethical responsiveness and democratic engagement. Both of these projects, one might argue, also stand in close proximity to Butler's preoccupation with politics and ethics discussed above (see Connolly, 2000).

Returning briefly to Spinoza: this ontology of life as becoming leads Spinoza in the *Ethics* to replace morality with a focus upon 'a typology of immanent modes of existence' (Deleuze, 1988b, p. 23). The task of this practical philosophy is to map out a passage to a form of ethico-political freedom, a passage that is rooted in our knowledge and understanding of affective life, and of the affective *density* of the political. Here, Spinoza advances in leaps and bounds, and a number of contemporary thinkers, in addition to Deleuze, have developed his analyses here (see, for example, Balibar, 1997, 1998; Massumi, 2002; Montag, 2005; Negri, 1991, 2004). Spinoza describes a number of primary affects that present this state of passage for bodies, and their virtual movements and regroupings will involve increases and decreases of bodily *potentia*. There is no subject of ethics for Spinoza; no transcendent moral values to act as our guide. It is instead a question of *what can be done* within a given set of inter-relations and the congealing of a particular political body. It is a question of how the affects can be harnessed and enhanced so as to generate a kind of eternity of thought (outside of the dominant symbols of theological transcendence), and a city able to express this joyful knowledge in the form of political virtues: Epicurean friendship, equality and ethical recognition as forms of reciprocal interdependencies where no singularity is lost within an all-pervasive universalism (see Balibar, 1998).

As John Rajchman notes, for both Spinoza and Deleuze, what commences as a problem of logic becomes a practical problem of life, and also a political problem of the city (see Rajchman, 2000, p. 81). To think an ethics of life, one must begin by thinking politics outside the logic of transcendence presupposed by ideas of a social contract. This is where the plane of immanence described by Deleuze is most useful since it allows for a theorization of composite multiplicities rather than discrete subjectivities. As a series of multiplicities, political composites are forever evolving and mutating in accordance with their diverse affective encounters. In this way, they *exceed* or overflow their containment within any identity or political grouping. Nonetheless, affective relations also become passional political forces that, *at the same time*, attempt to create and delimit norms of interaction and social control. In *Anti-Oedipus*, described by Foucault as 'a handbook of ethics', Deleuze and Guattari identify the affects as immanent to politics. They are bound tightly to the political infrastructure, helping to conduct the mechanisms for their own repression, as well as creating the conditions for their expression. Spinoza also presents the affects in a similar way through his description of the ineliminable problem of *affective ambivalence* which draws the affects towards vacillation and manipulation, and renders the political body passive and moralistic. Here, politico-ethical life becomes fragile and subject to the violence of exclusion. However, a political system that continues to exclude the multitude (which must be understood in its Deleuzian formulation and not as an already-constituted political identity), Spinoza argued, will tend to provoke their indignation and rebellion.

It may be the case that the ontological weight of this formulation of immanence is too much to bear for many continental theories of politics and ethics (see, for example, the critique of Deleuze by Badiou, 2000; White, 2000). Certainly, life, in all its forms, cannot flourish without an ethos of generosity, responsiveness, commitment or fidelity (*whatever* their ontological sources may be); and this requires, in turn, a coming to terms with the visceral attachments existing between bodies. It is such an ethos of pluralization and responsiveness that underscores the political formulation of this position, represented most emphatically by William Connolly (1999, 2005). Connolly describes himself as an immanent naturalist, and his research remains close to the perspective on immanence sketched out here. Like Butler and Deleuze, he argues that a politics that underestimates the power of affect upon the constitution of ethical life will remain impoverished, unable to enhance life, or to create a mode of living ethically. And, in response to the differing political effects of transcendence and immanence, Connolly suggests a form of agonistic respect, a dwelling 'inside the subtle points of convergence between one image bound to the fugitive forces of immanence and another attuned to the mystical whispers of transcendence' (Connolly, 2005, p. 106).

Conclusion

It has not been possible to do more than indicate one perspective on the breadth of attention to ethical and political questions within contemporary continental philosophy. Many names have gone unmentioned, whose contributions to this discussion must nonetheless be noted (for example, Agamben, Nancy, Rancière). It is clear that the map or diagram of immanence and transcendence presented by Agamben has done much work by framing the quite different kinds of political and ethical questions asked through each perspective. However, it is also apparent that, despite multiple ontological divergences, there remain numerous points of convergence and interaction between the two. Two common issues in particular stand out. First, an awareness of the importance of theorizing a form of ethical 'subjectivity' that is always beyond the reach of the agency of the subject. This deconstruction of the subject has been rethought in various ways (i.e. as a form of radical alterity, as composite bodies, or as a form of 'subjectivity' without the subject, etc.) In every case, however, ethics commences when the subject is *decomposed* and rendered opaque; it is this unravelling of the subject that *makes room* for ethical thinking. Second, there is a shared understanding of the undecidable and contingent nature of the political. It is this thinking of politics as always inscribed in the domain of ethics, which prevents thought from occupying a position of groundless indeterminacy. Certainly, both positions (broadly conceived) avoid the risk of the moralization of politics that could be produced by such a turn to ethics. In contemporary continental philosophy, the opposite is the case: just as ethical thinking about the fragility of existence inspires a form of political thinking, so the provisional or conditional state of the political world, and our philosophical recognition of this fact, demands that political thinking become ethical too.

Continental Marxist Thought

Bill Martin

A discussion of the place of Marxism in continental philosophy has to run along at least two major paths, which are not exactly axes, but which instead connect at various points. The first of these paths has to do with a historical irony, namely that Marxism is everywhere or almost everywhere in twentieth-century continental philosophy, even in some seemingly unlikely places, but, on the other hand, this tradition is in danger of being lost altogether, set aside or somehow forgotten even by those who ought to know better. The second path has to do with defining this subject itself, in terms of a tradition or set of traditions, a subject that has many internal fractures.

The irony of the seeming eclipse of Marxist theory in our postmodern capitalist world, an eclipse that is not mainly about the exhaustion of a theoretical paradigm or approach, is that 'continental Marxist thought' provides us with an embarrassment of riches. A list of all of the figures who either were Marxist (in whatever sense) or who had some serious engagement with Marx or Marxism, and who were also in some sense 'continental' philosophers, is a very long list. On the first point we might mention figures who are relatively obscure even among most continental philosophers, from Kostas Axelos and Nicos Poulantzas (Greek refugees from fascism who did most of their work in Paris), and Trân Duc Thao (who wrote in Paris on Marxism and phenomenology before he disappeared back into Vietnam), to Enzo Paci and Karel Kosík (who were interested in relating Husserl and Heidegger to Marxism). There is much to be said for a scholarship of retrieval in the case of these figures, a scholarship that will further attest to the power of a Marxist approach to philosophy. On the second point, we might mention even figures such as Heidegger, Arendt and Derrida. In other words, Marxian questions and impulses are everywhere in continental philosophy.

And yet there does seem to be a real danger that this work will be lost. Fredric Jameson argues that the more direct engagement with Marx on the part of Derrida, Deleuze and de Man (unfortunately, the latter pair passed away before this engagement came to fruition) has to do with the withering of intellectual life and philosophy in general, again in our postmodern capitalist world (see 'Marx's Purloined Letter'). It seems likely, in a dialectical Marxist spirit, that this work of retrieval can really only be accomplished as an integral part of a transformation that is not only backward looking – and, again, what goes for Marxism would seem to go for philosophy and humanistic learning in general. Much more needs to be said on this question, but let us leave it for now that the history and fate of scholarship and theory in Marxism is a more significant question than some may at first understand.

A second theme that will prove useful as a point of departure is recognition of the conflicted relationship that runs through Marxism in the twentieth century. Put simplistically, we have Marxisms that are more focused on activism and practice, and we have Marxisms that are more focused on developing theory within and working from Marx's ideas. In my book, *Ethical Marxism: The Categorical Imperative of Liberation* (which aims at an intermotivation of Kantian and Marxist themes), I propose a distinction between 'Philosophical Marxism' (PM) and 'Revolutionary Movement Theory' (RMT). The distinction needs to be developed and enriched, I think, and it is not proposed as an impermeable barrier. To put it simply, the distinction is between what Lenin was doing, as a 'leader-theorist' (or even 'activist-theorist'), on the one side, and what Adorno was doing, as an activity approaching 'pure theory', on the other. We might say the same thing for Mao and Althusser, or other pairings. Significantly, Lenin had already proposed a similar distinction between himself and Marx, the latter as a 'revolutionary philosopher' and Lenin as a 'philosophical revolutionary'.

Unfortunately, and I say this as an admirer of Lenin, the latter's formulation of the distinction was meant to cut off conversation, or at any rate it had that effect as the distinction was 'applied' through the channels of 'official' Soviet Marxism. The effect was on the whole intellectually stifling, though it also led to some interesting dichotomies. One might base an entire theory on the way the dichotomy between 'official' and 'unofficial' Marxisms played out in Paris alone (it can be mentioned here that the Stalingrad Station is in Paris, not Russia). On the one side was some of the most wretchedly dogmatic nonthought ever to be found, while on the other was some of the most creative Marxist thought ever cooked up, from figures as diverse as Bataille, Lefebvre, Sartre, Debord, Vaneigem and the Situationists. An interesting comparison might be made with official church theology, as there were indeed creative figures who somehow remained within orthodoxy (or at least they were not burned at the stake), and who indeed reshaped orthodoxy. But then, one of the most important figures we could discuss in continental Marxism in his final years sometimes wandered the streets in his bathrobe, in his neighbourhood near a convent, announcing to the nuns, 'Je suis le grand Althusser!'

Let us mark, apart from the complexities and nuances of the situation, only hinted at now, that Marxism as a theoretical enterprise in the context of continental philosophy always had that rather difficult to deal with 'elephant in the room', Soviet Marxism.

From this point on the main focus will be on Philosophical Marxism, but with an awareness of the 'elephant'. We are interested here in this work in the context of continental philosophy, so this is the place to point out that one aim of putting forward the term 'Philosophical Marxism' is to go beyond and replace the idea of 'Western Marxism'. The origins and development of continental Marxism itself were very much caught up with the institutional embodiments of power/knowledge complexes (as with everything else, but then the point is to trace the actual history). We want to bring two subjects together: the distinction between Revolutionary Movement Theory and Philosophical Marxism, on the one side, and philosophy as critique of culture, on the other. The founding act of philosophical retrieval that gave rise to continental Marxism was the recovery of Hegel, especially as a response to Engels's interpretation of Marx's philosophy. Two ironies must be mentioned here. First, despite his own valourization of Hegel, Lenin contributed to this 'Engelsism' with his formulation, 'Marx plus Engels equals Marxism'. Second, this return to Hegel was given further impetus by work done in the Soviet Union itself, by the Marx-Engels Institute, where many of Marx's early works were published for the first time – works such as the *1844 Manuscripts* and *The German Ideology*. And, of course, this publishing and translation effort also made possible a retrieval of the early Marx, even as instrumental reason was taking over the official organs of the International Communist Movement. Even before all of this, before the consolidation of Stalinism in the Soviet Union, a crucial line was crossed, when the 'Central European Hegelian Marxists [Karl] Korsch and [Georg] Lukács [were] denounced by Zinoviev at the 1924 Comintern Congress' (Anderson, 1996, p. 119).

One result of this condemnation was that the closer a philosopher was to the Soviet Union – either geographically or ideologically – the more likely he or she was to practise Marxism as cultural critique, aesthetics, and literary theory. Lukács is a prime example: after the condemnation he renounced his masterwork, *History and Class Consciousness*, and entered into a long period where he was mainly engaged with the development of the theory of literary realism and the criticism of non-realist trends. (Later, after the 1956 Soviet invasion of Hungary, Lukács remarked that he had come to realize that Kafka was in fact a realist.) Ironically, or perhaps not, *History and Class Consciousness* became the cornerstone of the emerging continental Marxism, and there ensued several decades where continental Marxist philosophers sought solace in Hegel and the early Marx. While the official channels of Soviet Marxism also attempted to lay claim to the legacy of humanism, this claim sounded hollow against the background of the actualities of the Stalin period. At the same time, at least some philosophers were not unaware of a kind of bifurcating process at work in the world, and we might wonder even today at the sense of a historical turning point, and

The Bloomsbury Companion to Continental Philosophy

a real 'event', in the siege of Stalingrad and the decisive turning-back of the Nazi *Wehrmacht*.

Clearly, now, the question of the *event*, of its definition and even its possibility, has become crucial for Marxist thought, because it is unclear what could count as a historical turning point in 'our time', if indeed there even is such a thing. We will return to this question in discussing more recent figures.

Against this violent bifurcation of 'East' and 'West', it is difficult to speak up for the vitality of philosophical pluralism and even a Marxist philosophical pluralism – and an argument could be made for the idea that Revolutionary Movement Theory always hinges around some sense of a bifurcation. This goes back, undoubtedly, to Marx's argument about the 'two great camps', the capitalist classes of different countries and the single, international proletarian class. I think it is possible to retain and develop the political economy of the mode of production and class struggle without making philosophy a matter of mere 'correspondence' to some bifurcated schema.

Within continental Marxism itself, figures such as Adorno and Sartre seem worlds apart, and yet they share themes of incarnation and redemption, and they remind us that there is a good argument to be made that the very possibility of Marx's thought is enabled and underwritten by the background of Judaism and Christianity, as refracted through German Idealism.

Understood this way, Althusser appears to be worlds away from both Adorno and Sartre, and the comparison here can tell us a good deal about some of the trends in Marxism that emerged in what we might call the 'post-1968 period'. In other words, in the period since what is arguably the last time that there was a general sense that world-historical events were taking place: the Tet Offensive in Vietnam (in which the tide was turned against the most powerful nation on the planet), the 'Events of May' (not only in Paris, though crucially there, but also in Prague, Chicago, Mexico City and elsewhere), and the Cultural Revolution in China (the experimental attempt at 'revolution within the revolution'). Subsequent Marxist philosophy can be understood in this 'post-evental' frame. Significantly, post-1968 Marxist thought also has to be understood as occurring in the context of the end of the first wave of socialist revolutions. Indeed, we might divide this thought into three categories: (i) that which mainly looks back towards some previous 'model' (Paris Commune, Soviet, Chinese or perhaps even Albanian) and argues that we need to 'get back to where we once belonged' (to borrow a phrase from Paul McCartney); (ii) that which understands the socialist experience to be completely exhausted or even fundamentally misguided to begin with, and which therefore turns away from politics and towards the project of some sort of ethics (some argue that this also occurs when politics is rendered into 'the political'); and (iii) that which is hopeful and anticipatory towards future openings, but where these are understood as something radically new, 'revolutions that as yet have no model' (as Gayatri Spivak once put it) (Spivak, 1980).

Mapping these categories further, we might say that there is one fundamental continuity here (represented also by some of those continental figures who related or continue to relate to Trotskyism), one field that is in some sense discontinuous but perhaps is not, and one that aims towards a fundamental discontinuity.

It is mainly the latter group upon which we should focus now. In some sense the first group takes care of itself, as they are most interested in a kind of 'restatement', while the second group, represented perhaps best by Jürgen Habermas, is no longer concerned primarily with contributing to the philosophical or political projects of Marxism.

The third group seeks to reinvent Marxism, revolution and communism. This does not mean that there are not continuities and historical retrievals involved in this work. In fact, one of the things that distinguishes this group is that it departs from the retrievals that characterized earlier generations of continental Marxists, or it departs from the forms that these previous retrievals took. A key instance here is that of Habermas and Derrida. Both can be said to develop a certain Kantian perspective, though a major difference is that Derrida provides a 'dangerous supplement' to Kantian intersubjectivity, namely intertextuality. In Habermas, however, Kantian intersubjectivity becomes a discourse ethics that will, he hopes, help to reinvigorate liberalism, whereas Derrida is more interested in the infinite responsibility that at least operates on the terrain of what he calls the 'ethical-political', and that must issue in new, responsible forms of organization.

In general, there are different 'returns to Kant', many of them merely reformist and liberal. These can be seen at the point where Habermas and John Rawls come together, mediated to some extent by ideas from Hannah Arendt and perhaps leading ultimately to the 'postmodern bourgeois liberalism' of Richard Rorty. My intention here is not to be merely dismissive of this path of thinking – as a matter of fact I find it sometimes fruitful and in any case instructive. And, on one level, if these figures are doing something interesting and insightful, and helping us to understand political possibilities (most obviously, concerning the unfinished project of modernity, whether this project is capable of being finished, and whether we ought to try to finish it), then it should not matter whether their thought can be called 'Marxist' or what-have-you. After all, there are key figures within the most recent wave of continental Marxism who do affirm Marxism in some sense, but who say little or nothing about modes of production (and relations and forces of production and so on) or classes and class struggle. Derrida and Badiou would be chief among these. On another level it is worth taking stock of those figures who still align themselves with some version of the Marxist project, however this project is conceived. Slavoj Žižek, for instance, has also contributed to a valuable retrieval of Kant (and he is very helpful in pointing out the 'hidden Kantian premises' at work in some figures who take their work to be antithetical to a Kantian perspective, Badiou again being a chief example). Žižek does in fact interrogate the mode of production and argue that we need to find a way to reinsert the economic dimension into the work of some recent theorists of 'pure politics'.

Speaking even as someone who is working towards revolutionary intermotivations of Kant and Marx, however, there is no question that the retrieval that has most lit up the sky of recent continental Marxist thought is that of Spinoza. For this we can most thank Althusser, who said that, even more than his affirmation of a certain structuralism he wanted to proclaim allegiance to a certain Spinozism. As Andrew Cutrofello explains:

> For Althusser, empiricism is the presumption that there is an equivalence between 'the true' and 'the given.' Knowledge is then conceived on the model of the 'mirror' relation between the knower and the known; to read a phenomenon is to attend to it in the manner in which it is given (Althusser and Balibar, 1977, p. 19). But givenness is an imaginary lure, as Lacan shows in his account of the mirror stage (Althusser and Balibar, 1977, p. 35). Such a lure is ideological in the sense that it is produced by something that disappears behind it: 'there can never be a given on the fore-stage of obviousness, except by means of a giving ideology which stays behind. . . . If we do not go and look behind the curtain we shall not see its act of "giving": it disappears into the given as all workmanship does into its works' (Althusser and Balibar, 1977, p. 163). Thus empiricism is an *essentially* ideological doctrine because it bars the way to a structural analysis of that by which the given is given. (Cutrofello, 2005, p. 180)

Badiou cites both Spinoza and the apostle Paul against arguments that centre on concerns with mortality and mourning (for example in the Introduction to his *Meta-Politics*). Undoubtedly he is responding to Derrida, though Badiou exercised tact in not mentioning the target of his criticisms by name. In an interview, Badiou averred that 'in the end, I'm opposed to the totality of Derrida's conceptions' (Badiou, 2006a, p. 248) but there is a bit of ambiguity in this statement, depending on how one reads the positioning of 'the totality'. To be sure, both were much concerned with understanding the concept of an event, and both were concerned with the possibility of the new. However, for Derrida this is a matter of invention, and his framework remains in some sense hermeneutic (the problematics of language and meaning that Badiou also rejects *tout court*), while for Badiou the new is discovered, and this is a matter of Plato and mathematics and Cantor and set theory.

Badiou also retains a fidelity to Sartre, and this takes us back to the question of the subject. For the other proponents of the new Spinoza, part of the attraction is precisely this Althusserian break with what is considered a remainder of Cartesianism in Kant and Sartre. Badiou understands, I think, that the Cartesian moment is first and foremost a kind of militancy, that it need have nothing to do with individualism or a self that provides its own metaphysical foundation.

Before saying more about the ideas of this new generation of post-Althusserian Marxists, let us set out very quickly the thematics that define this trend. In every case it is a matter of elements that shake up a Marxism that had become sedimented into orthodoxies and even 'establishment' (to use a good sixties term) habits of thought, and elements that reinvigorate a Marxism that had become tired with these very orthodoxies and establishment habits. Again, first there are what might be called the 'new retrievals'.

While not everyone in the group I am going to discuss is a 'new Spinozan', certainly Spinoza plays a central role in this new wave. Perhaps now the way is open to do some Marxism with Leibniz or Plotinus? Seriously, though, this work of retrieval is an important corrective to the general line in Revolutionary Movement Theory, which tends to view the canonical figures of Western philosophy with dismissive contempt. One might instead imagine an approach that views the legacy of all philosophical traditions, including figures unjustly excluded from the canon, as part of the intellectual and historical inheritance of humankind. One of my own projects is to find a way to work with the 'animal question' in Marxism, so surely I would want to make a place for Pythagoras and Porphyry. Or we could simply say: What is going on with a 'Marxism' that wants to deny itself philosophical resources?

Second, one way to look at this new wave is not only in terms of developments coming out of Althusser, but even in terms of a trajectory that runs 'Sartre, Althusser, . . .', or even 'Sartre, Althusser, Derrida, . . .'. In other words, what's next? To be sure, and third, the trajectories of Nietzsche, Freud and Lacan figure into this as well. But also, and fourth, the unorthodox political trends of the 1960s: the Black Panther Party, *'Tiers Mondialism'*, Maoism, new trends in anarchism (and what Badiou calls the 'anarcho-desirers', which then brings Deleuze and Guattari into the discussion), the Italian Autonomist movement and the Situationists, are a crucial background to the work of this new wave. Fifth and finally, there are continuing and newly-formulated engagements with Judaism and Christianity in the new wave of Marxism.

This is to leave aside fruitful interactions between Marxist thinking, activism and ecological concerns, and even what has been called the 'new agrarianism', and it may be worth considering why these concerns are not much a part of the new wave of Marxism in continental Europe. There is more to this question than simply the fact that these concerns have intermingled with Marxism more in North America (for instance, in the work of James O'Connor; see *Natural Causes: Essays in Ecological Marxism*, 1997) and in other parts of the English-speaking world (in the UK, for instance, see Ted Benton, *Natural Relations*, 1993; Benton concentrated his earlier efforts on Althusser, and it would be worthwhile to explore further his shift in focus). The fact remains that, some elements of Third Worldism and fascinations with guerilla strategies aside, continental Marxism remains too Eurocentric. It might be argued that much Marxism in the United States, by the same token, remains too economistic, and that Eurocentrism is simply a species of economism as found in the work of Europeans. Certainly, it is worth investigating how Negri can combine a sort of wild and woolly autonomism with a fairly sedate workerism, and how, on the other hand, Badiou breaks with any framework of 'material interests' by formulating what Žižek calls a theory of 'pure politics' with no place for an event to occur on the plane of the economic.

Within these broad and yet in some ways constrained parameters, there remain many figures deserving of attention, for instance Etienne Balibar and Jacques Rancière. I am acutely aware that the construction of the 'Sartre, Althusser, . . .' trajectory cannot do justice to these and many other worthy figures, in an essay that has not even mentioned such key thinkers as Max Horkheimer, Herbert Marcuse and Cornelius Castoriadis, to say nothing of the most glaring omission, Antonio Gramsci. I could go on, but then the honour roll could go on and on – all of the names remain a testimony to the vibrancy of Marxism. On the other hand, there is something to be said for synoptic intellectual history that develops themes and their interrelation, and then one has to go off and study particular figures in detail – and in Marxism this has to do with the motivation of understanding that is connected to changing the world.

Coinciding nicely with the turn into the new millennium, *Empire*, by Antonio Negri and Michael Hardt (2000), was the biggest publishing event in Marxism in some years. In *The Resources of Critique*, Alex Callinicos provides a good description of how a Marxism that turns again to ontology faces two possibilities: 'one [ontology] for which transcendence is routine, a product of the constant overflowing of Being, the other for which events and the subjects constituted through fidelity to them are rare' (2006, p. 120). The first of these is associated by Callinicos with Deleuze, the second with Badiou. Callinicos goes on to say that 'Antonio Negri is the most important contemporary figure to take Deleuze's side in this political debate' (2006, p. 121), and it might be added that this is a debate within the terms of Spinozism and an attempt to understand 'pure immanence'. It is worth noting, additionally, the way that Badiou, in his book on Deleuze (*The Clamor of Being*, 1999), characterizes this debate as being about grace – the grace that permeates reality, on the one hand, and the grace that instead *'occur*[s], by interruption or by supplement, and however rare or transitory it may be, we are forced to be *lastingly* faithful to it' (Callinicos, 2006, p. 120, quoting Badiou). If Badiou seems one-sided at times, we might wonder if these two sides of grace and ontology are mutually exclusive, or if they might instead need each other. It is hard to not be reminded of the two sides of freedom in Sartre's philosophy, the one an ontological condition (to which we humans are *condemned*), the other a more practical matter – and from there, of course, we are pointing back towards Rousseau.

In Negri's collaborative works with Michael Hardt, *Empire* can be seen as part of a trilogy (perhaps its centrepiece), beginning with *Labor of Dionysus: A Critique of the State-Form* (1994) and culminating (for now, at least) with *Multitude: War and Democracy in the Age of Empire* (2005). The whole series is evidence of a vitalism that springs from Nietzsche and works its way towards the biological preoccupations of Deleuze and Guattari. What in Badiou is episodic is, in Negri and Hardt, a permanent resource set against sovereignty (always understood as inherently tyrannical), a creative collectivity that demands a democratic insurgency. Both thinkers have their own separate intellectual careers, but Negri was already a major figure in European radical politics when Hardt appeared on the scene; even the collaborative works oscillate between the two poles of Negri's activism, *'operaismo'* (workerism), and autonomism. Whereas in Badiou 'the figure of the worker' is the 'void' of capitalism (and Badiou has focused especially on the *sans papiers* of France, those 'illegal' workers who are more in the position of a real proletariat – though Badiou somehow also rejects the language of class, or perhaps it is the political economy of forces and relations of production), in Negri and Hardt the workers, increasingly networked through the new means of communication, are the *overflow*. This overflow itself is conditioned by the development of cyber-capital, especially in the field of what Negri and Hardt call 'immaterial production'. Against this updating of political economy in the age of what might be called postmodern capitalism, Badiou and Deleuze look a good deal like traditional metaphysicians – and neither did either of them deny this. However, Lenin and Mao, being 'state philosophers' for Negri and Hardt, and therefore at best representing new configurations of sovereignty, do not figure in the political economy of the new age of Empire. Neither, therefore, do the themes of colonialism and imperialism (in Lenin's sense of capitalism as a mode of production that operates on a global scale, creating divisions among countries and divisions within the working class) or, concomitantly, anti-colonialist and anti-imperialist struggle, play a role in their framework. On the other hand, even as a Sartrean and/or an Althusserian, and even as a supporter of the *sans papiers*, Badiou never ran with the currents of *Tiers Mondialism* either.

These themes will play a role in what follows. To return to the opening of this essay, while the 'elephant' of Soviet Marxism tended on the whole to inhibit and warp creativity in the continental Marxists, there remains the question of the significance of actual anti-capitalist, anti-colonialist and anti-imperialist struggle in the formation of Marxist theory. Apart from the question of Third Worldism, another way of putting the point is that internationalism, along with the question of its philosophical and material underpinnings, is often lacking. After the Second World War, it was easier to take up this question in France than in some other European countries geographically closer to the Soviet bloc, especially given the emergence of what amounted to a Soviet 'Third Worldist' program of neo-colonialist expansion at the end of the 1950s. The one major figure who stood head and shoulders above the rest on this question was Sartre, and it would be very unfortunate, not only in terms of a revolutionary inspiration that we still need, but also in terms of the philosophical underpinnings of internationalism, if we were to lose sight of Sartre's work.

Despite Badiou's claims of ongoing fidelity to Sartre, and despite the warmth that Deleuze clearly felt towards his philosophy, one reason we must seemingly go out on a limb to ask for the restitution of Sartre to discussions of more recent philosophical Marxisms is that many of the Badioueans and Deleuzeans (to say nothing of the structuralists) more or less ignore Sartre, in particular the *Critique of Dialectical Reason* (1982 and 1991). Hence, perhaps the biggest project that remains to be done in Sartre's later philosophy is to bring together the framework of the *Critique of Dialectical Reason* with the writings and activism against colonialism. I have tried to contribute to this project (for instance, in some of the essays in *The Radical Project: Sartrean Investigations*, 2000), but it needs to be the subject of a comprehensive book. It still remains to get a complete picture of the whole of Sartre's project with the *Critique*, with an integration of the two volumes and the book-length 'introduction' to the *Critique* proper, *Search for a Method* (Sartre, 1968). The debate still continues, of course, over whether the second volume by itself is capable of integration. Why should anyone other than scholars of Sartre care about these projects, however? We have come full circle to the scholar/theorist distinction, for it is not the job of the scholar to do this sort of integration (if anything, the job is to demonstrate the *lack* of integration, though this is not an unrelated task). We need the 'Sartrean theorist', or at least the Sartrean voice in the discussions of the new philosophical Marxisms precisely because Sartre always tried to ally himself, in both practice and *theory*, with the oppressed, the alienated, the colonized, the tortured and murdered, the wretched of the earth, with internationalism, and with a large sense of the human project.

Even if many particulars are not entirely captured by this formulation, it might be said that the two main currents of Maoism in the early 1970s in France were on the one side Sartrean and on the other structuralist or Althusserian – even while it might also be argued, on either side, that neither was Sartrean or Althusserian enough! With the appearance of *The Humanist Controversy* (2003) and *Philosophy of the Encounter* (2006) we have a much better sense of where Althusser was going in his later work. Most of this work appeared in French in the period 1993–95, and in English in 2003 and 2006, respectively. However, the work collected in *The Humanist Controversy* was actually completed in the period 1966–67, which puts it in a very interesting context, especially given that Althusser himself declared that the Events of May were thoroughly 'Sartrean'. Surely there was some envy mixed with disapproval in this judgment, as Althusser had to watch the Communist Party of France play the role of the primary negotiating partner with Charles de Gaulle in stifling the rebellion as the summer of 1968 wore on. For some of us Satreans, it is very difficult not to let this history overdetermine the inter- pretation of Althusser's work, a question that Badiou also addresses in his essay on Althusser in *Meta-Politics*. And yet Badiou also helps here with the idea that philosophy should not be collapsed into its 'conditions', one of which is politics, a question to which we will return.

With his concept of 'aleatory materialism', Althusser was not so far removed from Badiou's concern with contingent multiplicity. The essay, 'The Underground Current of the Materialism of the Encounter', begun in October 1982, 'at the end of a terrible, three-year-long ordeal', opens with the dramatic words:

> It is raining.
> Let this book therefore be, before all else, a book about ordinary rain.
> (Althusser, 2006, p. 167)

What follows, it could be said, takes us back to the very early Marx, the Marx of the dissertation on Democritus and Epicurus.

> [T]his book is about another kind of rain, about a profound theme which runs through the whole history of philosophy, and was contested and repressed there as soon as it was stated: the 'rain' (Lucretius) of Epicurus' atoms that fall parallel to each other in the void; the 'rain' of the parallelism of the infinite attributes in Spinoza and many others: Machiavelli, Hobbes, Rousseau, Marx, Heidegger too, and Derrida.
> That is the first point which . . . I would like to bring out: *the existence of an almost completely unknown materialist tradition in the history of philosophy: the 'materialism'* (we shall have to have some word to distinguish it as a tendency) *of the rain, the swerve, the encounter, the take* [prise]. . . . Let us say, for now, a *materialism of the encounter*, and therefore of the aleatory and of

contingency. This materialism is opposed, as a wholly different mode of thought, to the various materialisms on record, including that widely ascribed to Marx, Engels, and Lenin, which, like every other materialism in the rationalist tradition, is a materialism of necessity and teleology, that is to say, a transformed, disguised form of idealism. (Althusser, 2006, pp. 167–8)

Two themes that were common in twentieth-century French philosophy as a whole can be identified here: the need to take full stock of the idea of contingency (a theme also animating the work of Sartre and Derrida, with the former identifying contingency with the need to find a 'consistently atheistic position') and the problem of rationalism, which in France always goes back to Descartes and of course then rebounds upon Sartre. Althusser identified his scientific program with a kind of empiricism, and of course we also see this loyalty in Deleuze, even towards a 'radical empiricism'. Meanwhile, significantly, Badiou avows a new kind of rationalism, one that reverses the priority of logic over mathematics that was endorsed by Russell and Whitehead in *Principia Mathematica*, as well as by Carnap and Quine. What will be interesting in terms of Marxism is how Badiou gets from rain and rhizomes and atoms and the void to Number and number and again the void, but defined as the empty set, or, it could be said, from math to Mao and back again.

Fredric Jameson is not only an important 'summarizer' of continental traditions, he has made many significant philosophical contributions in his own right. Even in the field of 'summarization', part of what is helpful about Jameson's work is that he is able to bring disparate threads of Marxist thought together, as with his reading of dialectical theories of literature in *Marxism and Form*. Furthermore, he achieves dramatic synthesis, with the idea of a Marxist hermeneutics and a hermeneutical Marxism, and perhaps most strikingly in the long opening chapter of *The Political Unconscious*, titled 'On Interpretation', where Jameson creates an interweaving of themes from Sartre and Althusser. This work should still serve as a model for the discussion in contemporary Marxism, though of course the Althusserians are not entirely pleased with how it works out. I recall a snarky article about Jameson from back in the 1980s that opened with the claim that Habermas and Jameson are 'two sides of the same bad coin'. The coin is not so bad to begin with, I think, but it is also the case that Jameson has never rendered Marxism into a reformist liberalism. Furthermore, Jameson makes a very important distinction between 'postmodernism' and 'postmodernism theory' (and it is in the latter category that he places thinkers such as Derrida and Foucault, but without collapsing them into the 'postmodern' mush that many other mere surveyors of this scene do), and therefore he opens the way towards the analysis of a capitalism turned postmodern. This is seen in a remarkable series of books, beginning with the massive *Postmodernism, or, The Cultural Logic of Late Capitalism* (1991), and leading through *The Seeds of Time* (1994) and *The Cultural Turn* (1998). Undoubtedly, Jameson is extending the style of cultural critique especially well-practised by Adorno, but it is not correct to say that his is simply the happier or at least less cranky version. Certainly the latter is true, but it is also the case that *if* Jameson is crucially aware of writing after the exhaustion of the avant-garde (an exhaustion that Adorno recognized), it might be said that he is crucial for recognizing an element that is non-existent in Adorno beyond a certain point: that in addition to the 'bad new things' that need to be addressed before taking solace in the 'good old things' (this comes from Brecht), there might even be some good new things that deserve attention.

In the extraordinary concluding chapter of *Postmodernism*, Jameson takes up Sartre's discovery that there are other people in the world, and he sets this against what might be called a mere 'demographic materialism', where we are liable to experience a kind of 'difference burnout'. Clearly, Jameson is extending the framework of seriality from *Critique of Dialectical Reason* into our present-day society of the politics of speed; famously, the result is a 'loss of affect' that leaves us alienated from alienation itself. While Jameson never leaves Sartre behind in this postmodern scene, in *The Seeds of Time* he is concerned that an existentialist anti-essentialism of the person may leave us completely defenceless against the hyperserializing effects of a commodity logic that knows no bounds. Clearly there is an Adornian theme here as well, and Jameson's analysis is at its most profound when he speaks of a society that is so whipped up that it paradoxically partakes of a 'Parmenidean stasis' that renders death itself meaningless, 'since any historical framework that would serve to interpret and position individual deaths (at least for their survivors) has been destroyed'. Jameson calls this state of affairs 'this world without time or history' (1994, p.19).

Now, again, a hermeneutic perspective such as this may appear to be decidedly rear-guard, and we might compare it to Badiou's own more recent view, in which he argues that humanity is presently 'without a world'. This argument is developed in *Logiques des mondes* (2006, English translation 2008), but Badiou gives a succinct description of it in an interview with Oliver Feltham: 'the "contemporary world" as a world formatted by the totality of capitalism does not form a world for the women and men from which it is composed'. Badiou's path to a world 'which is constituted such that all those who live within it, as fraternal inhabitants, can recognize each other', a notion that 'should guide the politics of emancipation today' (Feltham, 2008, p. 136), does not work through the machinery of meaning and interpretation, but instead mathematics and category theory. On the other hand, that these concepts might motivate an emancipatory politics (struggle for meaning and recognition) does not mean that they have to be taken directly into philosophy – again, this is a benefit of Badiou's notion of philosophy's 'conditions'. What might be more interesting is whether the recognition of this separation might also open up a more meaningful conversation between Badiou's mathemes and arguments on the hermeneutic side. For starters, I would propose a re-reading of Derrida's seminal essay, 'Différance', but starting with a number, perhaps the number one, instead of the letter 'a'.

Another theorist who has done a good job of bringing forward what he calls the 'resources of critique' is Alex Callinicos. I mention him here not only for the fact that he is able to put the work of many thinkers into a certain kind of Marxist relief, but also because he is one of the more rigorous formulators, along with Daniel Bensaïd, of a contemporary neo-Trotskyism. However (and I realize that it is unfair only to bring Callinicos into this discussion for this purpose), he is also typical of that trend in that, no matter how far out he goes with thinkers such as Badiou and Negri, in the end he attempts to reinstate 'classical Marxism'.

In contrast, it seems to me that most of the thinkers we have discussed in this essay, and especially this final group, place a greater stress on discontinuity – and certainly it can be said that Badiou's sense of discontinuity is not only absolute, but perhaps more so than can be sustained. For Badiou, the event is neither temporal nor historical, it is a break – indeed, it breaks the world in two.

Jacques Derrida also studied with Althusser, and worked alongside him for many years at the École normale supérieure, but he was certainly not a 'new Spinozan'. And while Derrida was sceptical of many aspects of Sartre's humanism, he could be said to have engaged with this language far more than his contemporaries, and to have forged a kind of humanism that is on the other side of the anti-humanisms of Heidegger and Althusser and indeed of deconstruction itself. It is fascinating to see the numerous ways that Derrida seemed to be engaging with Sartre without mentioning the latter by name, for instance in his discussions of the 'oath' and the idea of reciprocity in *The Politics of Friendship*. Certainly Derrida can be called humanistic in his prioritization of justice over conceptions of truth, though neither does he reject truth.[1] Here is where Badiou's rejection of 'the totality of Derrida's conceptions' might be discussed in a more dialectical light. Derrida opens many projects within Marxism in his *Specters of Marx*, and I hope these projects are not forgotten in the coming years – but these projects are also present in many of Derrida's texts, from *Of Grammatology* (which I think is almost a kind of *Capital* on the question of language) and the essays collected in *Margins of Philosophy*, to *Politics of Friendship* and *Rogues*.

Rather than pretend to open any of these projects further here, allow me simply to quote a fascinating passage from *Of Grammatology*. This is a passage where Derrida is quoting from Lévi-Strauss's *Tristes Tropiques*, where the latter argues that Buddhism and Marxism both aim at a kind of liberation:

> Our question is therefore no longer only 'how to reconcile Rousseau and Marx' but also: 'Is it sufficient to speak of superstructure and to denounce in an hypothesis an exploitation of man by man in order to confer a Marxian pertinence upon this hypothesis?' A question that has meaning only through implying an original rigor in Marxist criticism and distinguishing it from all other criticism of suffering, of violence, of exploitation, etc.; for example, from Buddhist criticism. Our question clearly has no meaning at the point where one can say 'between Marxist criticism and Buddhist criticism . . . there is neither opposition nor contradiction'. (Derrida, 1974, p. 120)

We need saving from ourselves, it might be said, precisely because we are temporal and historical creatures, and the recognition of this would seem to set off Marxist theorizing from Buddhist criticism.[2]

In many ways Derrida and Badiou seem 'so near, so far', as the saying goes. To tie this up in a too-neat little bundle, twenty-first century Marxism could do with more discussion on the relative priorities of historical and dialectical materialism.

Anyone who has heard Slavoj Žižek speak can hardly read his work without feeling the resonance of his manic energy, which can be dizzying, and yet he has to be commended for bringing a new energy and life to Marxism, and a real radical edge. Perhaps at times Žižek is a little heavy on the provocations, especially the Stalinist ones, but this can be refreshing in that it helps to break through so much merely liberal or 'leftist' claptrap. Žižek has revived the crucial Marxist project of ideology-critique, under the dazzling, paired influence of Hegel and Lacan (where Hegel was always already reading Lacan), even while also crediting the Kantian influence on his understanding of the imagination. As Alex Callinicos writes in *Resources of Critique*, there is a 'certain repetitive quality' to the writing in Žižek's veritable 'torrent' of texts, where, 'after all the fun of reading him, we are left with the eternal recurrence, not of the same, but of the Real' (2006, p. 115). There is indeed sometimes more heat than light. On the other hand, part of Žižek's move, in recent years, to 'a much harder edged Marxist political definition' has been due both to a greater appreciation of the project of Badiou, especially its alternative to 'postmodern relativism', and to an attempt to formulate 'the Lacanian Real [as] an alternative to Badiou's ontology' (Callinicos, 2006, p. 112). One result of this modification is seen in *The Parallax View*, where Žižek argues that Badiou needs to admit into his scheme a fifth domain where an event might occur (which would then constitute a fifth condition for philosophy), namely the domain of the economic.

Certainly there are those who question whether Žižek and Badiou are really on the terrain of Marxism, and this has been the case with Derrida as well. But it might be said that it is precisely in the fact that this question is raised that we might allow that they are making contributions to the Marxist project.

Indeed, what might make this thought still recognizably Marxist (if sometimes barely, or 'at a stretch', as it were) is that it applies creativity towards making manifest the discontinuities in the world, or, it might even be said, in multiplicitous 'being' itself.[3] For both Derrida and Badiou, there is a creative element in searching out the places of possibility, but the difference is that between 'invention' on the one side (Derrida), and 'discovery' on the other. This difference has many ramifications for the question of subjectivity and agency, and again these questions take us back into the ways that materialism might be understood, historically, intertextually, dialectically, even mathematically.

Turning, finally, more directly to Badiou, we might even thematize his problematic as one where it somehow matters to Marxism whether logic comes before mathematics, or the other way around. Perhaps such a discussion makes Badiou more an interlocutor with Frege, Russell, the Vienna Circle and Quine (and Gödel, Tarski, Turing, Cohen and so on), than with most of the trends of twentieth-century continental philosophy, including trends in Marxist thought. Indeed, part of the excitement with Badiou, especially as he is received in the English-speaking world, is that he allows us to think in terms of parallel trajectories of analytic and continental philosophy. Badiou sees a line of thought that runs from Kant to Derrida and Davidson that needs to be overturned, a line of thinking where questions of language, meaning and interpretation are central. Where, in the twin trajectories, the predominant strains (not without significant exceptions) have been the priority of logic over mathematics (analytic philosophy) and the priority of interpretation over (or on a par with) truth, Badiou gives us mathematics over logic and truth quite radically over interpretation.

With mathematics, all we really need are zero and one, or, better, the empty set and the set with one member. And again, the remarkable thing is the idea that this could somehow matter to Marxism, Marx's own interest in working out the differential calculus (which Badiou alludes to from time to time) notwithstanding. Therefore we seemingly do not need the troublesome *interpretive* questions of identity and contradiction (to say nothing of modalities) first of all, but rather Number and numbers, based in set theory and more recently in category theory. To be sure, for much of the vulgar materialism that holds sway in Revolutionary Movement Theory, either intertextual or mathematical materialism is 'idealism', but perhaps this is the place where we might back off from quoting the eleventh thesis on Feuerbach and start over again at the first thesis.

Thus we move from the deconstruction of metaphysics to its recomposition, which again gives Badiou an affinity with Deleuze. But what about actual political movements and the sort of theory that might be a guide to practice? For me, part of the excitement of Badiou's work is that is intertwined with his loyalty to the experience of Maoism. This is, Badiou has said, something of a 'double' loyalty, as it is both the Maoism of the Chinese Revolution and the Cultural Revolution, on the one hand, and the experience in France in the wake of the Events of May, on the other, that he is referring to – and he acknowledges that he may have a conflicted loyalty. This is not a loyalty that is cancelled by the transition to what Bruno Bosteels calls 'Post-Maoism'. However, a key element of Badiou's philosophy is the idea that a 'truth event', and its truth-conditions, its 'sequence', can become 'saturated'. The event is exhausted, played out, it has given us all that it can give us. Beyond a certain point, perhaps not entirely determinable, to 'keep going!' (the fundamental 'ethical' injunction that Badiou takes from Lacan) with a saturated sequence is the very definition of what Badiou calls 'disaster'. For my part, as a Marxist philosopher but also as someone who came through the experience of Maoism (though in conditions and with directions quite different from those in France, and perhaps already too far beyond the point where Badiou would have declared the whole thing disastrous), there is much in Badiou's work that remains to be filled out. There are ways in which it seems one-sided, and yet, on that one side, it also seems deeply insightful and *helpful*.

We might look backward for one more moment before attempting to look forward again, back to the debate over what was the dominant trend in May 1968: existential Marxism, structuralism, anarchism and the 'anarcho-desirers', situationism, etc. Much in these trends can still be brought forward, and indeed this ought to happen, but under a general heading which Badiou sums up nicely under the term 'the communist hypothesis'.

What is the communist hypothesis? In its generic sense, given in its canonic Manifesto, 'communist' means, first, that the logic of class – the fundamental subordination of labour to a dominant class, the arrangement that has persisted since Antiquity – is not inevitable; it can be overcome. The communist hypothesis is that a different collective organization is practicable, one that will eliminate the inequality of wealth and even the division of labour. The private appropriation of massive fortunes and their transmission by inheritance will disappear. The existence of a coercive state, separate from civil society, will no longer appear a necessity: a long process of reorganization based on a free association of producers will see it withering away.

'Communism' as such denotes only this very general set of intellectual representations. It is what Kant called an Idea, with a regulatory function, rather than a programme. It is foolish to call such communist principles utopian; in the sense that I have defined them here they are intellectual patterns, always actualized in a different fashion.

. . . In many respects we are closer today to the questions of the nineteenth century than to the revolutionary history of the twentieth. A wide variety of nineteenth-century phenomena are reappearing: vast zones of poverty, widening inequalities, politics dissolved into the 'service of wealth', the nihilism of large sections of the young, the servility of much of the intelligentsia; the cramped, besieged experimentalism of a few groups seeking ways to express the communist hypothesis . . . Which is no doubt why, as in the nineteenth century, it is not the victory of the hypothesis which is at stake today, but the conditions of its existence. This is our task, during the reactionary interlude that now prevails: through the combination of thought processes – always global, or universal, in character – and political experience, always local or singular, yet transmissible, to renew the existence of the communist hypothesis, in our consciousness and on the ground. (Badiou, 2008a)

As mentioned before, parenthetically, the Stalingrad Station is in Paris, where it is now surrounded by neighbourhoods largely populated by immigrants from the Muslim cultures of North Africa, many without papers.

9 Psychoanalysis and Philosophy

Hector Kollias

Introduction

The relationship between philosophy and psychoanalysis has always been fraught, due, at least in parts, to a reciprocal resistance within both disciplines to assimilate or confront each other, a resistance which dates from Freud's ironic remarks about the superiority of philosophy over his discipline (see Freud, 1916). At the same time, both Freud and most of his disciples, notably Lacan, insist that psychoanalysis is not possible without a certain degree of engagement with the philosophical tradition, and indeed Lacan in particular has offered controversial and radical readings of Descartes, Kant, Hegel and Heidegger among others, while some of Freud's (and also Lacan's) more theoretical or 'speculative' writings are for all intents and purposes very near in both form and content to the philosophical tradition. For its part, this tradition has vacillated, for more than a century now, between open hostility towards psychoanalysis and an engagement with psychoanalytic thoughts and processes that often amounts to a wholesale appropriation of them.

My aim here is to examine work that sits in between the extremes of hostility and appropriation, in order to seek out the many different ways in which the psychoanalytic discipline has been reworked in the hands of contemporary *philosophical* thinkers. For this purpose, I have had to delimit, perhaps quite drastically, the scope of my investigation. I shall only be discussing work that has appeared roughly in the last twenty years, which means leaving out important writings by philosophers such as Jacques Derrida and Stanley Cavell published earlier than my arbitrary cut-off point. I also have to admit to a certain bias towards the French philosophical tradition, which regrettably leaves out whatever contributions to the meeting between the two disciplines have arisen from the German or indeed other traditions, the inclusion of which would have made the goal of conciseness impossible. I offer the same excuse for treating material that has appeared only in book form, rather than journal articles, and also for treating works that have appeared in English or in English translation (with one major exception which I believe to be warranted). I am attempting both to be inclusive and to offer the space for a more in-depth discussion of certain works, an approach that necessitates a combination of brief referencing and more detailed analysis.

In Part I, I shall be looking at the ways in which some philosophers have made psychoanalysis a theme or a concern in their own work. This 'thematic' appropriation of an entire system of thought can lend itself to compelling exegeses for psychoanalysis, for how it came to be, how it differs from or fits in with, the philosophical tradition. In this sense, we are dealing with philosophy attempting to explicate, appropriate, even police psychoanalysis, as we shall see in the discussion of Michel Henry and Jacques Rancière that follows. Part II changes direction and aims to look at the ways in which psychoanalytic teachings (from Freud, but mostly, it has to be said, from Lacan) affect philosophical debates on a variety of crucial issues, from ethics and politics to gender and sexuality. Here I shall no longer divide my examination by name, but proceed thematically, moving in between several important thinkers (Slavoj Žižek, Joan Copjec, Charles Shepherdson, Alenka Zupančič, Judith Butler and others) most of whom share a grounding in some form of psychoanalytic training while at the same time addressing philosophical concerns, and steering a course through debates in which many or all of them contribute. I am hoping that this will give the reader a feeling for both the immensity and range of the field, and for the heated nature of the debates within it.

I Philosophy/Psychoanalysis: How does Psychoanalysis 'fit' in the Tradition?

If the sixties were seen, principally in France perhaps, as the time when philosophy was engaged in a multi-faceted synthesis of Marx and Freud, the time when every French philosopher worth his salt seemingly attended Lacan's seminars and wrote enthusiastically for or against his teachings, it would seem plausible to assume that this engagement with psychoanalysis in philosophical circles waned somewhat in the two decades that followed, only to pick up again in the nineties and until the present time, with a significant revival of interest in Lacan in particular. Philosophers as diverse as Guy Lardreau (Lardreau, 1993), Philippe Lacoue-Labarthe and Jean-Luc Nancy have sought to situate their positions with regard to particular Lacanian ideas. Alain Badiou is one of the most prominent philosophers to engage with Lacan, whom he even calls 'my master' (quoted in Hallward, 2003, p. 11), and his engagement is indeed rich and fruitful, even if Lacan is for him a proponent of what he calls 'anti-philosophy'. I have chosen to look at two philosophers whose engagement is with psychoanalysis as a whole, with psychoanalysis *as such*, and who also attempt to situate psychoanalysis in the western philosophical tradition, to understand how it *fits in* with that tradition: Michel Henry and Jacques Rancière.

Michel Henry – The Genealogy of Psychoanalysis

Michel Henry's *The Genealogy of Psychoanalysis* (Henry, 1993) is an original and daring attempt to situate Freudianism (conflated throughout the work with psychoanalysis itself) at 'the end of the long history of Western thought, of its inability to grasp the only important thing'. Already Henry's polemical intention can be clearly seen, but his philosophical interpretation of psychoanalysis, as well as its positioning in the history of Western thought is very interesting. Following a tradition that begins with Descartes – or at least a Descartes ingeniously reconfigured by Henry – and culminates in Schopenhauer and Nietzsche, Henry's Freud is not so much an innovator as a thinker who continues to think of the unconscious as the complement of consciousness, as that which appears '*simultaneously and as the exact consequence of the concept of consciousness*' (Henry, 1993, p. 2). This doubling of consciousness and the unconscious maps onto the concepts of *representation* (that which allows consciousness to exhibit its conscious components) and *life*, as that which escapes representation. In his analyses of Descartes, Kant, Schopenhauer, and Nietzsche that precede his reading of Freud in the book, Henry tries to show how this dualistic rift is untenable from the monist perspective of what he calls 'material phenomenology' (see Henry, 2008). I cannot go into a detailed discussion of Henry's philosophical positions in general, but shall try to sketch what his reading of psychoanalysis is, as well as comment on the project of a genealogy.

In the language of phenomenology, Henry claims that 'just like the concept of consciousness, the concept of the unconscious is equivocal, simultaneously ontic and ontological' (1993, p. 283). But Henry charges Freud with abandoning 'the ontological concept of the unconscious [. . .] in favour of the diverse empirical contents that take its place and serve to define it: childhood experiences, repressed representations, drives, and so on', describing what he calls 'the fall of the ontological into the ontic', which, 'removing its implicit philosophical significance, turns [psychoanalysis] into a crude psychology trapped in facticity and naturalism' (1993, p. 285). For Henry, the ontological status of the unconscious is equated with life: '*the unconscious is the name of life*' (1993, p. 286). Freud, however, in Henry's reading, seeks to situate the unconscious on its ontic plane, as the domain of representations, by taking in the world of dreams as precisely the world of unconscious representations, the dream as 'the prototype of representation' (1993, p. 293). Henry charges that this conflation with the domain of representation in effect excludes the dream itself from psychoanalytic practice and replaces it with the text of the dream narration, 'a group of significations constitutive of language and arising from thought in the strict sense [. . .] from a sense-giving conscious- ness, a *Sinngebung*, as Husserl says' (1993, p. 292). It is because psychoanalysis substitutes the narrative representation of the dream for the dream itself as imaginative process, unconscious representations for the unconscious as such, that there now appears what Henry describes as a 'gap between imaginal life in general [. . .] and meaning in the linguistic sense', that psychoanalytic theory ends up as a readily-ridiculed collection of 'far-fetched' Freudian 'explanations' (1993, p. 293), or that Henry can mockingly nod to Lacan in saying 'in all seriousness, people can now say that the unconscious is structured like a language' (1993, p. 292). The concept of the unconscious as initially seized by Freud becomes, in its philosophical elaboration by Henry, a weak or even 'bastard' notion that ultimately fails to escape the grip of the all-pervasive philosophy of representation. What properly, according to Henry, belongs to the order of consciousness, namely representations and the general activity of conscious *Sinngebung*, is now improperly smuggled into the domain of the unconscious: 'Thus, representation reclaims what originally stands beyond it. The unconscious, originally representation's other, now contains representation. The aberrant concept of an "unconscious representation" is born' (1993, p. 298). This concept, fundamental to the way Freud understands the unconscious as 'container' both of the drives and of memories and other representations, is for Henry the Achilles' heel of psy- choanalysis, containing 'the two major errors of Freudianism' (1993, p. 298). The first error is the very assumption of such unconscious representations, 'latent' or repressed – an error since for Henry this smuggles the operations of consciousness and 'thought as such' into the realm of what is meant to be their opposite. The second, and probably more important error is that with this smuggling of representation into the realm of the unconscious 'nonrepre- sentability exists only in the form of representability' (1993, p. 299); in other words, the essential character of unconscious processes, the 'ontological unconscious' if you like, is now contaminated by what it is meant to exclude.

The philosophical attack launched by Henry on the Freudian concept of the unconscious is extended to the equally problematic concept of the drive. Despite the obvious efforts by Freud throughout the entire development of his metapsychology to wrest the notion of the drive away from both physio- logical or biological origins and from metaphysical speculation, Henry both disparages the attempts at 'scientificity' and ultimately finds fault with the drive's proper psychic identity, offering itself a wholesale equation of the drive with the phenomenological notion of auto-affection: 'In the final analysis, Freud's "drive" does not mean a particular psychical motion but the weight and charge of actual, inescapable self-impression' (1993, p. 307). The dual status of the drive in Freud's theories, as both affect and representation, allows Henry to counter 'but *affect is not, cannot be, and consequently cannot become unconscious'*, resulting in the damning formulation: *'Thus the basis of the unconscious, as affect, is anything but unconscious'* (1993, p. 303). The drive has the same aporetic fate in Henry's reading as did the concept of the unconscious itself: it is envisaged as the opposite to consciousness and representation, but it is shown to be affect, thus consciousness, and to be representational. If the drive is to retain any conceptual power, Henry argues, these Freudian knots must be disentangled and the drive associated with its true (phenomenological) status: as 'self-excitation – life itself' (1993, p. 311). This is Henry's final answer to the ambiguities and problems posed by Freud's metapsychological theorizing: what Freud designates as unconscious drives, or as endogenous excitations in the psychic apparatus are to be seen as indices for the phenomenological category of 'life' as the category subtending representational consciousness and, at one with it, forms the auto-affection of Being. Anxiety itself, which Henry identifies as the principal affective form of the drive in Freud's theories, 'is the feeling of being, as life. It is the feeling of Self' (1993, p. 312). The unconscious, and the drives it contains, are therefore not essentially separated from the phenomenal realm of consciousness, affect and subjectivity (what Henry has called ek-stasis), as elaborated by the philosophical tradition Henry interrogates, from Descartes to Freud, but are only seen as the original appearance of 'life' as inextricable part of a monist being: 'Freud unintentionally recognizes the fact that the unconscious does not escape every form of phenomenality but within ek-stasis is the site of the first appearance, of its self-appearing as life and affectivity' (Henry, 1993, p. 316).

The rigours of phenomenological interrogation to which Henry exposes the intricate constructions of Freudian metapsychology amount to a radical critique of psychoanalysis. The import and the potential success of this critique must be balanced with an appreciation of Henry's own idiosyncratic version of phenomenology, appended by notions such as an 'original hyper-power' which subtends all powers of the body as ontological potentiality, as well as an 'Archi-body' which is its correlate (Henry, 1993, p. 325). Such an evaluation is not in the scope of the current investigation. What can be said with some certainty though is that Henry's enterprise seeks both to situate psychoanalysis in a long philosophical tradition which it problematizes as a whole, and also, more critically, that in order to do so Henry must insist on a reading of psychoanalysis which, at the very least, goes against the grain of Freudian thought itself. For, if Henry's monist standpoint is hard to miss, Freud's equally staunch declaration (which Henry curiously fails to comment on) that 'our views have from the very first been *dualistic*, and today they are even more definitely dualistic than before' (Freud, 1920, p. 51) may also be allowed to speak for itself.

Jacques Rancière – The Aesthetic Unconscious

Jacques Rancière, in his not yet translated book *L'inconscient esthétique* (*The Aesthetic Unconscious*, 2001), also begins with a philosophical–historical investigation into the Freudian notion of the unconscious, in effect denying the Freudian claim for the 'discovery' of the unconscious: 'if the psycho-analytic theory of the unconscious is formulatable, this is because there already exists, outside the properly clinical realm, a certain identification of an unconscious mode of thought, and because the realm of works of art and literature is defined as the domain of privileged effectivity of that "unconscious"' (Rancière, 2001, p. 11).[1] In a sense, Rancière is thus perform-ing an operation similar to Henry's, that is to say a genealogical approach to the entire discipline of psychoanalysis, with Freud as its anchor. Freud is therefore not a radical innovator so much as he is a representative of a historical moment, the moment Rancière identifies with the change from a 'regime of representation' to an 'aesthetic regime' of understanding thought and art: 'My hypothesis is that the Freudian thought of the unconscious is only possible on the basis of this regime of the thought of art and of the idea of thought which is immanent to it' (2001, p. 14).[2] Freud is, again, contextual-ized, and psychoanalysis finds its conditions of possibility in a more general, philosophically defined domain. Before I discuss in more detail what this contextualization rests on, and how it colours Rancière's view of psycho-analysis, the historical horizon of Rancière's position must be noted, alongside the prominent idea of a type of paradigm shift operating at the change between the two realms of thought that he identifies. A particular consequence of this notion of paradigm shift for psychoanalysis that Rancière brilliantly brings out is the effect of the historical change on the adoption by Freud of psychoanalysis's foundational myth, the Oedipus complex, 'borrowed' from Sophocles. According to Rancière, the fact that, before the advent of the aesthetic regime, authors such Corneille and Voltaire had iden-tifiable difficulties in adapting the Oedipus myth for their own time, puts in doubt 'the universality of Oedipal "psychoanalysis", of the Sophoclean scenario of the revelation of the secret' (2001, pp. 20–1). This is not to say that Freud's own recourse to Sophoclean myth is itself thrown into doubt – on the contrary:

> for Oedipus to be the hero of the psychoanalytic revolution, there must be a new Oedipus, repealing those of Corneille and Voltaire, and attempting to reconnect, beyond French versions of tragedy, and also beyond the Aristotelian rationalization of tragic action, with the tragic thought of Sophocles. There must be a new Oedipus and a new idea of tragedy, that of Hölderlin, of Hegel, or of Nietzsche. (Rancière, 2001, p. 25)

Freud's thought is then, as with Henry's genealogy, placed in a continuum starting with German Idealism, but, unlike Henry, Rancière thinks of this not as a philosophical continuum in the strict sense, but as one formed under the general terms of the 'aesthetic regime'.

So what is the foundational trait, pertinent to psychoanalysis, of this new regime? Rancière is clear:

> the silent revolution called aesthetic opens the space for the elaboration of an idea of thought and a corresponding idea of writing. This idea of thought rests on a fundamental affirmation: there is thought that does not think, thought at work not only in the alien element of non-thought, but in the very form of non-thought. (Rancière, 2001, p. 33)

As opposed to the Platonic/Aristotelian (and also neo-classical: hence the references to Corneille and Voltaire) regime of the presence of *logos*, this aesthetic regime identified by Rancière as roughly concomitant to the paradigm shift brought about by romanticism, offers a type of writing Rancière has identified as 'errant' (see Rancière, 1998, 2004):

> To this living speech normalizing the representative order, the aesthetic revolution opposes the mode of speech that corresponds to it, the contradictory mode of a speech that speaks and stays silent at the same time, that knows and does not know what it is saying. It offers writing, then. But it does this according to two great figures corresponding to two opposed forms of the relation between thought and non-thought. And the polarity of these figures outlines the space of the same domain, the domain of literary speech as speech of the symptom. (Rancière, 2001, p. 35)

Already the pertinence to psychoanalysis is obvious: for the concept of the unconscious to be 'discovered', and for the hermeneutic procedures of Freudian dream-analysis to take hold, a reconfiguration of thought as relating to its 'un-thought' opposite, a thinking of writing as 'mute' or as symptomatic of an un-thought and unwritten domain must first be in place. Rancière continues by identifying those 'two great figures' of mute writing that allow Freud's conception of the unconscious, as well as the psychoanalytic hermeneutic to take off. In its first manifestation, this mute writing is 'the speech that mute things carry with them' (Rancière, 2001, p. 35) – the domain which leads to Freud's symptomatology, the notion that the mute bodily parts of the hysteric, for example, speak of an unconscious truth. In its second manifestation, mute speech is 'the speech of soliloquy, which speaks to no-one and says nothing other than the impersonal, unconscious conditions of speech itself' (Rancière, 2001, pp. 39–40) – leading to the more speculative or metaphysical moments in Freudian metapsychology, grappling with the silent but effective domain of the drives. Thus, the aesthetic unconscious is revealed as an analogue of the Freudian one, as well as posited as the latter's historical/philosophical condition of possibility:

> The aesthetic unconscious, which is consubstantial to the aesthetic regime of art, manifests itself in the polarity of this double scene of mute speech: on the one hand, the speech written on bodies, which must be restored to its linguistic signification by the work of a deciphering and a rewriting; on the other hand, the deaf speech of a nameless power lying behind all consciousness and all signification, to which a voice and a body must be given. (Rancière, 2001, p. 41)

Psychoanalytic theory capitalizes on the advent of the aesthetic unconscious, and an entire discipline is built on the foundations of a far grander and all-encompassing historical paradigm shift.

If the genealogical approach, as well as the overarching concern to put psychoanalysis in some kind of philosophical perspective is shared by Henry and Rancière, their conclusions as to the evaluation of the psychoanalytic enterprise, as well as their interpretations and privileges accorded to one or another facet of Freudianism differ in many ways. Where Henry privileges the ontological/phenomenological import of concepts like the drive and the unconscious to the detriment of the hermeneutics of psychoanalysis found to be too empirical, or too much associated with the level of the 'ontic', Rancière's different point of view and divergent philosophical standpoint allows him to favour the hermeneutic of psychoanalysis (at least where the hermeneutics and analysis of art are concerned) over the ontological configuration of the unconscious which he designates as inherently nihilist: Freud 'wants to see a hermeneutic and elucidatory vocation of art triumph over a nihilistic entropy inherent to the aesthetic configuration of art' (Rancière, 2001, p. 52). Rancière's reading of Freud, in its own terms and in comparison with that of Henry's, is inescapably more partisan: Freud 'privileges the first form of mute speech, that of the symptom that is a trace of history. He emphasizes it over its other form, that of the anonymous voice of unconscious life' (2001, p. 57). Rancière clearly valourizes the Freud who interprets dreams as symptomatic of unconscious psychic phenomena, or the Freud who offers exegeses of texts and art works from a specific hermeneutic model, to the speculative Freud of the metapsychological papers, the Freud of *Beyond the Pleasure Principle* whom Rancière relates to 'the great theme obsessing the time when psychoanalysis is formed: the theme of the unconscious as Schopenhauerian thing in itself' (2001, p. 73). Rancière berates later developments in thought indebted to Freud (he names Lyotard, but one can think also of Lacan and Derrida) for abandoning the hermeneutic principles and staying attached to the nihilistic entropy of the ontologized unconscious, and in particular to the death drive. What this attitude shows, it seems to me, is that the 'wrong' or 'right' Freud is still at stake even in philosophical interpretations of psychoanalysis that explicitly seek to subsume it under a genealogical vision aligning it with other moments in the history of thought. Even when Freud is seen as an exemplar of this or that more general tendency in the course of western metaphysics, the multifaceted ambiguity of his thought – berated or exalted – remains disconcertingly unmalleable.

II Psychoanalysis/Philosophy: How Does Psychoanalysis Affect Philosophy?

Apart from individual philosophers' dealings with Freud and the psychoanalytic discipline in an effort to see where it fits with, or how it deviates from, the Western philosophical tradition, the most exciting developments utilizing the theoretical resources of psychoanalysis within a philosophical context are those associated with the undisputed renewal of interest in the work of Jacques Lacan. There can be little doubt that the name most closely linked with this renewal of interest is that of Slavoj Žižek, and his often brilliant and provocative contributions in the fields of political and moral philosophy will receive due attention here. Of course, the 'Lacan renaissance' has been the work of many different thinkers working in a variety of fields, often in dialogue, sometimes in confrontation with Žižek, and this will also be reflected. Another area in which Lacanian (and also Freudian) psychoanalysis has influenced many debates is that of sexuality, and I shall be discussing developments in queer theory that bear the mark of engagement with Freud and/or Lacan, particularly since such developments (witness the work of Judith Butler or Lee Edelman) unmistakably relate to philosophical issues such as subjectivity.

Ethics

Freud himself attempted to grapple with ethical issues towards the end of his career, and, as Lacan points out, sought to identify the origin of ethical sense, of the moral law, in *Civilization and its Discontents* (Freud, 1930): 'Freud brought to the question of the *source* of morality the invaluable significance implied in the phrase: *Civilization and its Discontents*' (Lacan, 1992, p. 143). This source of morality is none other than the psychic agency of the superego, understood by Freud to make endless demands upon the subject, demands that correspond with the adoption of, or interpellation by, the moral law. In Lacan, the superego is also seen as the site of the demand for *jouissance*, or enjoyment. This is what Lacan introduces to the Freudian ethical considerations, an addition, or a conversion to the (moral) law of the father, which Charles Shepherdson glosses as follows:

> The symbolic law which was said to eliminate incest and institute desire is now supplemented by a perverse and punishing underside – not the return to a natural state, libidinal urge, or biological 'id', which refuses to abide by the law, but another face *of the law itself*, which Freud develops through the concept of the death drive. (Shepherdson, 2000, p. 118)

This, in turn, is read by Lacanians such as Slavoj Žižek and Alenka Zupančič, in conjunction with the elaboration of the 'ethics of psychoanalysis' in Lacan's seminar VII as a basis for a formulation of an ethical theory that is often coined (see Zupančič, 2000) 'ethics of the real'.

Lacan's seminar VII, as well as his seminal paper 'Kant with Sade' (in Lacan, 2007), propose a scandalous identification of the Kantian moral law with the radical 'evil' of the Marquis de Sade. Kantian ethics, often described as contentless or formalistic, is read by Lacan and his followers as leading to an expression of moral duty that, due to its very absence of content (what Kant describes as the demand to act out of duty to the law *regardless of any 'pathological' content*), is identical to radical evil: 'the sublime Law is *the same as* the Monstrous' (Žižek, 1997, p. 219). There are, in effect, two aspects of the moral law: one symbolic, expressed in particular commandments with a symbolic content and import, and the other aligned with the Lacanian domain of the real, that which escapes representation and offers up only the contentless 'universal maxim' that Kant seeks to impose as the sole basis for any moral law that is no longer dependent on pre-determined content. The realm of ethics is therefore already the result of a fundamental ontological split, both in Kant (the split between the phenomenal and the noumenal world), and in Lacan (the rift between the dimensions of the symbolic and the real). As Žižek puts it: 'There is ethics – that is to say, an injunction which cannot be grounded in ontology – in so far as there is a crack in the ontological edifice of the universe: at its most elementary, ethics designates fidelity to this crack' (Žižek, 1997, p. 214). Kant's fundamental notion of following the law solely out of duty to the law, disregarding personal interest (in Lacan's words: 'pathological content') thus maps onto the Sadean scheme where the sadist executioner does not act out of personal interest or concern, but out of sheer fidelity to the obverse of the moral law, or the law of *jouissance*, signalling 'the affinity between the perverted sadist's attitude and the basic Kantian attitude itself – that is to say the attitude of accomplishing one's duty for the sake of duty alone' (Žižek, 1997, p. 232). This shocking version of ethics permits Lacan to conceive of ethics as pertaining to the domain of the real, 'where notions of good and evil become indistinguishable, giving way instead to the forces of destruction and creativity' (Kay, 2003, p. 109).

From this basis, Žižek and Zupančič, leaning on Lacan's reading of Sophocles's *Antigone* in seminar VII, and his reading of Claudel's heroine Sygne de Coufontaine in Seminar VIII, formulate a theory of the ethical act which aligns it not only to the creation of a moral law *ex nihilo*, but to terror and to the death drive. Alenka Zupančič writes of 'the strange structural homology between *terror* and *ethics*' (Zupančič, 2000, p. 216). The ethical act is the act that goes entirely against the dictates of the symbolic law, by repeating the 'primordial' forced choice signifying obedience to the symbolic law of castration, but repeating it 'in reverse', effectively cancelling out the symbolic dimension of the law, with catastrophic but at the same time liberating consequences: 'Therein consists the Lacanian definition of the authentic ethical act: an act which reaches the utter limit of the primordial forced choice and repeats it in the reverse sense. Such an act presents the only moment when we are effectively "free" ' (Žižek, 1992, p. 77). Lacan's examples of such an ethical act are those of Antigone who refuses to submit to the commands of the symbolic law in order to 'realize her desire' (Lacan, 1992, p. 280), and of Sygne de Coufontaine who is forced to make a choice which follows her sense of duty, thus sacrificing the very thing that sustained her sense of duty, what she calls her soul. In both cases the ethical act ends in real or symbolic death: in Antigone's case in her suicide, in Sygne's in her having a sinister, terrifying nervous tic and remaining speechless. Zupančič offers these two different Lacanian readings of tragic plays as two ways in which the psychoanalytic concept of the drive actually lies in the heart of the Lacanian conception of ethics. The drive, in particular the death drive (but, for Lacan, 'every drive is virtually a death drive' (Lacan, 1995, p. 275)), despite its common misreading as a wish *for* death, is strictly speaking *indifferent* to either life or death, belonging to a dimension outside the phenomenal finitude of the human subject, a dimension of the infinite which parasitizes the phenomenal human world of finitude. Zupančič writes: 'there are two modes of this parasitism, each of them resulting in a different figure of the infinite: first, there is the infinite of desire [. . .]; then there is the infinite of *jouissance* [. . .]. Ethics itself can be situated in the passage from one to the other' (Zupančič, 2000, p. 250).

Desire, in Lacanian terms, is a mode of infinity inasmuch as it is maintained by the infinite deferral of its goal. The realization of desire, as is the case in the Lacanian reading of Antigone, allows the subject to escape this infinite deferral and drown herself instead in the infinite of *jouissance*, where it is the drive that is now infinitely satisfied, indifferent to the finite condition of the subject, indifferent to whether the subject lives or dies. This terrifying state is the moment of the ethical act, and it is a moment which connects the subject not to her desire, but to the monstrous measure of infinity that is the drive, the infinity aligned to the Kantian formal ethical law. The ethical act is disastrous for the subject, but it is the only impossible yet also inescapable way in which the subject can go beyond symbolic law and connect itself with the real of the law, or with the law as real.

The ethics of psychoanalysis are thus a terrifying, radical vision of ethics aligned with the ontological split in the subject admitted by both Kant and Lacan, ushering in the monstrous infinity of the drive, such that, in Joan Copjec's words: 'the psychoanalytic subject, being subject to a principle *beyond* pleasure, *is not driven to seek his own good'* (Copjec, 1994, p. 87).

If this appears as a rather doom-laden exploration of ethics, readers may be relieved to encounter a different ethical position that is equally indebted to the ethics of psychoanalysis in the work of Simon Critchley. Critchley admits the grounding of ethics in an ontological split of the subject: 'The ethical subject is [. . .] a *split subject*, divided between itself and a demand it cannot meet, a demand that makes it the subject that it is but which it cannot entirely fulfil' (Critchley, 2007, p. 10). He discusses Lacan's ethics, reading it in relation with the notion of the drive's sublimation, already posited by Freud as the way in which the pressures of drive and superego that form the core of ethical subjectivity for psychoanalysis may be fruitfully transformed into aesthetic production, and judges that 'if the relation to the real is the realm of the ethical, and the work of sublimation is the realm of the aesthetic, then we might say that *the aesthetic intimates the excess of the ethical over the aesthetic'* (Critchley, 2007, p. 73). What this relation between ethics and aesthetics, between infinite demand and the productive work of sublimation allows for is a salutary 'reparation' of the rift brought about by the ethical real: 'we can achieve aesthetic reparation for ethical separation without either losing the radicality of ethical demand, or transforming that demand into a form of oppression' (Critchley, 2007, p. 74). Moving away from the tragic-heroic paradigms of Antigone and Sygne, Critchley latches on to humour and the comic (see also Critchley 2002 for a discussion on humour leaning on Freudian concepts) to come up with a version of the ethical/psychoanalytic split subject that is refreshingly different from those of Žižek or Zupančič: 'the split at the heart of the ethical subject is not some form of masochistic self-flagellation, but rather *the experience of an ever-divided humorous self-relation'* (Critchley, 2007, p. 85). The ethics of psychoanalysis are then, after all, not necessarily tragic, terrifying, or suicidal; but the radical conception of the psychoanalytic split subject, and the cardinal notion of the real that Lacan introduces to the field, will continue to play an important role in the multifarious influences of psychoanalytic thought in the area of political philosophy.

Politics

Lacan's most famous political intervention came in the turmoil of the May 1968 revolution in Paris when he told the students who asked him to take a position on their uprising: 'As hysterics, you demand a new master. You will get it!' (see Žižek, 2001a, p. 30). From this, it would be fair to surmise that Lacan does not easily make a political ally. And yet, recent years have seen a remarkable production of writings utilizing Lacanian theory with the purpose of explaining or criticizing political phenomena, and, even more surprisingly perhaps, an emergence of what is nearly habitually referred to as 'the Lacanian Left' (see Stavrakakis, 1999, 2007). Without a doubt, this is primarily due to the formidable influence of Slavoj Žižek who has probably contributed more than any other thinker to the resurgence of interest in Lacan. Consequently, I shall try to follow Žižek's development of political theory (or rather, theories, as it is becoming clear that in the course of his thought, Žižek often retracts previous positions, changes his attitude and develops his political affiliations – for a more thorough elaboration of such issues, see Kay, 2003, Dean, 2006, and Bowman and Stamp, 2007) emanating from his reworking of Lacanian concepts.

Following the expositions offered by Kay (2003) and Dean (2006), it is useful to begin with Žižek's elaboration of a critique of ideology from a Lacanian standpoint. In this view, the Althusserian notion that ideology involves the unconscious interpellation of subjects is reconfigured to suggest that ideology in fact involves the *failure* of interpellation (see Althusser, 2008). More specifically, in an analysis that Žižek will undertake several times with only minor tunings and reconfigurations, starting with *For They Know Not What they Do* and *The Sublime Object of Ideology* (see Žižek 1991 and 1989), the ideology of totalitarianism involves, in psychoanalytic terms, the adoption of the demands of the superego over and above those of the symbolic law. Žižek explains: 'Therein consists the opposition between Law and superego: law is the agency of prohibition which regulates the distribution of enjoyment on the basis of a common, shared renunciation (the "symbolic castration"), whereas superego marks a point at which *permitted* enjoyment, freedom-to-enjoy, is reversed into *obligation* to enjoy – which, one must add, is the most effective way to block access to enjoyment' (Žižek, 1991, p. 237). This will allow Žižek to think of totalitarian regimes such as Stalin's USSR or Hitler's Germany as aligned with the Lacanian structure of perversion, but it also extends into an impressively wide-reaching analysis of political organizations as relating to the factor of enjoyment (*jouissance*): 'the element which holds together a given community [. . .] always implies a shared relationship towards a Thing, towards Enjoyment incarnated' (Žižek, 1993, p. 201). Racism in all its permutations can thus be explained as the paranoid fear of what Žižek calls 'the theft of enjoyment': 'We always impute to the "other" an excessive enjoyment: he wants to steal our enjoyment (by ruining our way of life) and/or he has access to some secret, perverse enjoyment' (Žižek, 1993, p. 203). In totalitarian regimes this is manipulated by the rulers who express all the hallmarks of what Lacan identifies as perversion, in that they know their attribution of all society's ills to the other's theft of 'our' enjoyment is but a ruse, but they believe it and act on it all the same:

> Hitler [. . .] knows that the image of the Jew as enemy who takes 'all the threads into his hands' is only a means by which to channel the aggressive energy of the masses, to frustrate its radicalization in the direction of the class struggle, and so on, yet at the same time he '*really believes*' that the Jews are the primordial enemy. (Žižek, 1991, p. 245)

This analysis is not only reserved for totalitarianism; it also encompasses what Žižek sees as the fundamental flaw in Western liberal 'politically correct' ideology. In Sarah Kay's words: 'White liberal intellectuals are no more comfortable than racists with other people's enjoyment. They may be "tolerant" of black community politics, but not of white rednecks' (Kay, 2003, p. 138; see also Žižek, 1993). Žižek thus emerges not solely as a formidable critic of totalitarian ideology, but as a wide-ranging polemicist against liberalism as well. In the final analysis, Žižek's engagement brings him to an understanding of capitalism itself as the problematic context in which all these ideological struggles are fought.

Žižek's critique of capitalism is as wide ranging as his critique of ideology, and it too relies upon a thoroughly psychoanalytic understanding of political identifications. His diagnosis of late capitalist society is indebted to Lacan's theme of the 'decline of the father', itself a reworking of Freud's seminal cultural interventions from *Totem and Taboo* to *Moses and Monotheism* (see Freud, 1913 and 1939). In phenomena as varied as cyberspace, UFOs and the modern financial markets, Žižek sees the decline not only of the Oedipal father aligned with the prohibition of incest, submission to the law and (in Lacanian terms) the onset of the symbolic order, but of the father of *Moses and Monotheism*, a father whose function is to represent an inscrutable and wilful God: 'So when, today, one speaks of the decline of paternal authority, it is *this* father, the father of the uncompromising "No!" who is effectively in retreat' (Žižek, 1999, p. 322). The decline of the prohibitory father brings with it the creation of 'new forms of the phantasmic harmony between the symbolic order and *jouissance*' (Žižek, 1999, p. 322), and this, in turn, entails our late capitalist free-for-all obsession with 'life style' as something that needs no account or legitimation – late capitalism in symbolic/social/economic freefall (see also Žižek's polemical analysis of the 'meaning' of '9/11' in Žižek, 2002). But the most trenchant, and possibly most controversial aspect of Žižek's critique of capitalism is his development of the view of capital itself as the real of contemporary social/political formations: 'the Real is the inexorable "abstract" spectral logic of Capital' (Žižek, 1999, p. 276), or: 'today's real which sets a limit to resignification is Capital' (Butler et al., 2000, p. 223). Capital is thus seen as the absolute limit of our thought and our political interactions, such as that all possible movements of resistance *within* its sphere are not in themselves capable of creating a way out of it, and what Žižek calls 'post-modern' political strategies are effectively futile. This view of the real as aligned to capital (as well as being aligned to issues such as sexual difference, see below) is perhaps the crux of the majority of debates surrounding Žižek's thought, not least those he engaged with himself with Judith Butler and Ernesto Laclau (See Butler et al., 2000). Before attempting to restage these debates into the function of the Lacanian real, let's try to see where Žižek's critique of capitalism leads him.

In a few words, it leads him to a reconfiguration of what Hegel, a thinker who is second only to Lacan in Žižek's influences, calls 'concrete universality'. This notion is of cardinal importance to Žižek for a variety of reasons and finds its application in a variety of spheres; it would be fair to say that universality, together with the real, are the two key avatars of his thought, employed in almost every case under his consideration. In political terms, his notion of the universal finds its most sustained elaboration in his contributions to the book he wrote in dialogue with Butler and Laclau, *Contingency, Hegemony, Universality* (Butler et al., 2000), but his most pertinent definition of universality comes much earlier, in a discussion of Lacan's formulas of sexuation: 'the leap from the *general* set of "all men" into the *universal* "man" is possible only through an exception: the universal (in its difference to the empirical generality) is constituted through the exception' (Žižek, 1991, p. 123). What this means is that the notion of the universal Žižek synthesizes from those of Hegel and Lacan is one that does not equate to the sum of particulars, but is in fact 'attached' to an exceptional particularity, what he also calls 'the paradoxical fact that the dimension of universality is always sustained by the fixation on some particular point' (Žižek, 1997, p. 104). In turn, this allows him to see that the way universality is anchored (or *quilted*, to use Žižek's preferred terminology of the Lacanian *point de capiton*) onto a specific particularity results in wholly different universalities, from which a hegemonic struggle can begin: 'the very political opposition between Left and Right appears in a different view perceived from the Left or from the Right' (Butler et al., 2000, p. 316). In his dialogues with Laclau and Butler, he never ceases to point out that individual perceptions of this hegemonic struggle are organized around entirely different conceptions of universality – which prompts the question: what is Žižek's own 'preferred' universality? One could argue, with Sarah Kay, that this is a tricky question to answer as 'a valid universality for him is one that will unite groups of whom he approves in a struggle of which he approves' (Kay, 2003, p. 152). There is, however, as Kay demonstrates, a recurrent 'theme' emerging with progressively greater force in his political writings: the notion of the universality that aligns itself with the 'forced choice' of the ethical act, the notion that assumes that the sacrifice of a positive (such as a liberal concept of freedom or rights) and the self-abandonment into negativity or even terror is the only way of effecting a political transformation of the real of capitalism. At the end of *Tarrying with the Negative* he comes to precisely such a conclusion, when, having rejected the 'new age' solutions of supplanting the absence of the 'big other', he writes: 'Perhaps, however, our very physical survival hinges on our ability to consummate the act of fully assuming the "nonexistence of the other", of *tarrying with the negative*' (Žižek, 1993, p. 237). And this assumption of the negative, reflecting the borrowing of the phrase in italics from Hegel's *Phenomenology of Spirit*, is tantamount to the assumption of what Žižek also calls 'good terror'. He provocatively, and with progressively greater emphasis, associates the salutary form of universality with one that 'should search even more stringently for the "good terror"' (Žižek, 1999, p. 378). Thus, in a curious, but not at all uncharacteristic, opposition to his earlier critique of totalitarian ideology, Žižek will come to extol certain versions of totalitarian terror, and mount a critique on the 'misuses' of the term totalitarianism (see Žižek 2001b). Whatever one may make of his proclamations, the consistency with which the political notion of the 'good terror' maps on to the notion of the impossible ethical act, as discussed above, is unmistakable.

The notion of universality, in conjunction with the functions and uses of the Lacanian real, which play such a remarkable role in the applications of psychoanalytic theory in the realm of political thought, also bring us to consider one last field in which psychoanalysis has galvanized debates, namely that of sexual politics and sexuality in general.

Sexuality

It should come as no surprise that psychoanalysis comes to the fore in discussions of sexuality. From its inception, Freud's discipline saw itself as explaining the phenomenon of human sexuality, and also as treating it more prominently than any previous modes of thought – sexuality is the bread and butter of psychoanalysis. Nevertheless, it must also be noted that the last twenty or so years have seen both a marked decline in Freudian clinical practice, at least in the Anglo-American context, and a sustained effort to think about sexuality in contexts that are explicitly non-psychoanalytic or even anti-psychoanalytic, stemming chiefly from the work of Michel Foucault and giving birth to the critical approaches of queer theory. Thinkers still 'loyal' to the psychoanalytic framework have more often than not acted as polemicists against what is variously called 'historicism' (see Copjec, 1994), 'deconstructionism' (Žižek, 1999 and Butler et al., 2000) or 'rhetoricalism' (Dean, 2000). It is these debates around sexuality that, alongside the newly found interest in the ethics and politics of Lacanianism, have made psychoanalysis a mode of thought that is still relevant and hotly contested today.

The main charge against psychoanalysis from its detractors is that it fails to recognize sexual identifications as historically contingent, and is thus obliged to view sexual difference as given *a priori* and, as a consequence, sexual orientations as normative or pathological. The most important critique of psychoanalysis in this vein has undoubtedly come from Judith Butler, whose continuous engagement with Freud and Lacan (as well as Žižek) cannot be overlooked. Her seminal *Gender Trouble* (Butler, 1990) is often credited with kick-starting queer theory, and while it is undoubtedly critical of Freud and Lacan, it also brilliantly utilizes their concepts in an elaboration of a performative theory of gender – witness her ingenious mobilization of the Freudian theory of melancholia (see Freud, 1917) to suggest that homosexuality represents an originary repressed state which normatively gendered subjects then need to mourn:

> If feminine and masculine dispositions are the result of the effective
> internalization of that taboo [against homosexuality], and of the
> melancholic answer to the loss of the same-sexed object is to incorporate
> and, indeed, to *become* that object through the construction of the ego ideal,
> then gender identity appears primarily to be the internalization of
> a prohibition that proves to be formative of identity. (Butler, 1990, p. 63)

Similarly, some years later, Butler is able to use the Lacanian concept of the imaginary in order to subvert the stability of heteronormative conceptions: 'if to identify as a woman is not necessarily to desire a man, and if to desire a woman does not necessarily signal the constituting presence of masculine identification, whatever that is, then the heterosexual matrix proves to be an *imaginary* logic that insistently issues forth its own unmanageability' (Butler, 1997, p. 239). Butler is clearly an inventive and intelligent reader of psychoanalysis but at the same time her project departs both from Freudian ideas about the formation of sexuality and from what she sees as the intransigent structuralism of Lacan's thought. Her principal effort, from *Gender Trouble* onwards, has been to destabilize substantive conceptions of gender and sexuality, and replace them with a theory of the performativity and continuous rhetorical resignification of gender and sexual identities, in line with the Foucauldian programme of contingent symbolic power and resistance to power. Thus, she writes:

> No longer believable as an interior 'truth' of dispositions and identity, sex
> will be shown to be a performatively enacted signification (and hence not
> 'to be'), one that, released from its naturalized interiority and surface, can
> occasion the parodic proliferation and subversive play of gendered
> meanings. (Butler, 1990, p. 33)

This project is political through and through, and its stake is the possibility of
resisting heteronormative assumptions of gender and sexuality from *within*
the symbolic matrix of signification that produces normative assignations in
the first place:

> If the rules governing signification not only restrict, but enable the assertion
> of alternative domains of cultural intelligibility, i.e., new possibilities for
> gender that contest the rigid codes of hierarchical binarisms, then it is only
> *within* the practices of repetitive signifying that a subversion of identity
> becomes possible. (Butler, 1990, p. 145)

From a Lacanian standpoint, this view is charged with a misunderstanding of
what constitutes sex and sexual identification, namely that it is *not* simply a
matter of discursive significations: 'while sex, for psychoanalysis, is never
simply a natural fact, it is also never reducible to any discursive construction'
(Copjec, 1994, p. 204). Joan Copjec was among the first to object to Butler's
project from such Lacanian grounds, and also to mount an attack on the
discursive, Foucault-inspired historicism underpinning it. The crux of the
matter is the already controversial notion expressed in Lacan's *Seminar XX:
Encore* (see Lacan, 1998) that sex, and sexual difference in particular, is
situated not at the level of the symbolic but at the level of the *real*.[3] This means
that it is not susceptible to resignification, for as Lacan famously suggests 'the
real is always in its place' (Lacan, 1972, p. 55), it lies beyond representation
and signification, seemingly rigid and fixed. For Lacanians like Copjec, the
positioning of sexual difference as real and immovable does not preclude the
politics of resistance inherent in Butler's strategies: 'Sex does not budge, and it
is not heterosexist to say so. In fact the opposite may be true. For it is by
making it conform to the signifier that you oblige sex to conform to social
dictates, to take on social content' (Copjec, 1994, p. 211). In Žižek's words,
sexuality 'points towards the supreme ontological scandal' (Žižek, 1993,
p. 83). This is because the real, and the real of sexual difference in particular,
designates an *impossibility* or an *impasse* of signification: 'in the domain of
sexuality, *it is not possible to formulate any norm which should guide us with a
legitimate claim to universal validity*: every attempt to formulate such a norm
is a secondary endeavour to mend an "original" impasse' (Žižek, 1993,
p. 265). The argument here, one played out in numerous debates between

Žižek, Butler and others, is over the relationship between the real (as 'hard kernel' resisting symbolization, and as 'lack' in the symbolic order itself) and the symbolic as both social normalization or Law, and as the possible site of anti-normative resignification. Žižek is adamant: 'yes, the Real *is* in fact internal/inherent to the Symbolic, not its external limit, but *for that very reason*, it cannot be symbolized' (Butler et al., 2000, p. 121). Consequently: 'precisely as real, sexual difference is *absolutely internal* to the Symbolic – it is its point of inherent failure' (Butler et al., 2000, p. 120). Butler objects to what she sees as an inherent contradiction in the idea of the real being both immovable and at the same time figuring an impossibility and a lack within the symbolic: 'the "real" that is a "rock" or a "kernel" or sometimes a "substance" is also, and sometimes within the same sentence [of Žižek's *The Sublime Object of Ideology*], "a loss", a "negativity"; as a figure it appears to slide from substance to dissolution' (Butler, 1994, p. 198). Charles Shepherdson possibly shows us a solution to this argumentative aporia by pointing out two different conceptions of the real in Lacan, a 'pre-symbolic' and a 'post-symbolic' one, while insisting that, in the logic of the Lacanian *après coup*, 'the real designates something that only exists as a result of symbolization' (Shepherdson 2007, p. 38).[4] Shepherdson thus suggests that 'we might see this sliding from substance to dissolution not as confusion or self-contradiction, but as the simultaneous articulation of two forms of the real' (2007, p. 39).

Ultimately, the Lacanian conception of sexual difference as real has far-reaching implications for feminism, sexual politics, even politics in general. If sexual difference is an impasse, which symbolic (normative or not) significations and imaginary identifications desperately try to 'fix' but necessarily fail, then the world of men and women, homosexual and heterosexual, is always a desperate attempt to cover up the fundamental and unshakeable deficiency of symbolic/representational identifications of sex, gender, and sexuality. As Joan Copjec points out, this is now a very different version of universality: 'Rather than defining a universe of men that is complemented by a universe of women, Lacan defines man as the prohibition against constructing a universe and woman as the impossibility of doing so' (Copjec, 1994, p. 235 – the reference is to Lacan's sexuation diagrams in Lacan, 1998). It is possibly surprising, then, to see that this conception of the real, alongside the equally disconcerting use Lacan makes of the Freudian death drive, has resulted, in recent years, in galvanizing the intellectual energies of thinkers in the field of usually anti-Lacanian queer theory. I am thinking here of two influential and controversial books: Tim Dean's *Beyond Sexuality* (2000) and Lee Edelman's *No Future* (2004 – but see also the essays collected in Dean and Lane, 2001). Dean positions himself against Butler's 'rhetoricalist' project in favour of assuming the psychoanalytic category of desire, anathema to many Foucauldian queer theorists: 'rhetoricalist theories of sexuality effectively evacuate the category of desire from their accounts' (Dean, 2000, p. 178). Adapting not only the category of desire, but the Lacanian conception of the register of the real, Dean is able to defend psychoanalysis from charges of heterosexism, and to claim it for a queer politics:

> Lacan theorizes the real as a variable limit to the speakable and the thinkable. This distinction is politically significant because, although a homophobic culture may figure gay sex, for example, as unspeakable, the figuration is culturally and historically produced rather than necessary. (Dean, 2000, p. 210)

While remaining critical of identity politics, thus adopting the stance most common among queer theorists, Dean aligns this anti-essentialism not to Foucault's constructionism but to psychoanalysis, offering the remarkable provocation that 'psychoanalysis *is* a queer theory' (Dean, 2000, p. 215), a gesture he repeats in his article on 'Lacan and Queer Theory' (Dean, 2003). Ultimately then, it is not the valourization of a homosexual position that matters to Dean, but the (queer) ways in which psychoanalytic categories such as desire can *queer* identity itself:

> as an orientation or an identity, homosexuality is normalizing though not socially normative [. . .] as a sign of desire's perverse *resistance* to orientation or identity, homosexuality may remind us of how desire itself remains potentially antinormative, incompletely assimilable to the ego, and hence inimical to the model of the person, fundamentally impersonal. (Dean, 2000, p. 238)

Lee Edelman also duly suggests that 'queerness can never define an identity; it can only ever disturb one' (Edelman, 2004, p. 17; see also Edelman's previously more rhetorical assumption of similar positions in Edelman, 1994). But Edelman's purpose is the undeniably polemical one of signalling out an *ethical* 'hopeless wager', namely to align the figure of the queer with the death drive: 'the death drive names what the queer, in the order of the social, is called forth to figure: the negativity opposed to every form of social viability' (Edelman, 2004, p. 9). This brilliantly confrontational argument is developed in complex ways that cannot easily be summarized, but what is remarkable is Edelman's sustained and intricate use of Lacanian theory to configure the 'place' of the queer within a symbolic normativity which, in a manner remin-iscent of Žižek, he diagnoses as saturated by the attempt to avoid the 'excess *jouissance*', the 'touch of the real': 'the capacity of queer sexualities to figure the radical dissolution of the contract, in every sense social and Symbolic, on which the future as putative assurance against the jouissance of the Real depends' (Edelman, 2004, p. 16). Not only this, but Edelman also associates this positioning of the queer with the liminal figure of Lacan's ethics – Antigone: 'perhaps, as Lacan's engagement with Antigone in Seminar 7 suggests, political self-destruction inheres in the only act that counts as one: the act of resisting enslavement to the future in the name of having a life' (Edelman, 2004, p. 30). In such provocative alignments of psychoanalytic theory and queer politics it would not be excessive to suggest we find a triumphant return of Freudian and Lacanian thought, worthy of the philosophical consideration given to any of its other (ethical, political) forms.

In the *Introductory Lectures to Psychoanalysis*, Freud stakes a claim for his newly 'discovered' discipline, over and against others, including philosophy, a claim that might strike one as arrogant: 'Neither speculative philosophy, nor descriptive psychology, nor what is called experimental psychology [. . .] are in a position to tell you anything serviceable of the relation between body and mind' (Freud, 1916, p. 45). Philosophers have, since then, often sought to prove him wrong, especially by attempting to contextualize psychoanalysis, and whatever novelties it has had to offer, in the generalized history or genealogy of philosophy. Such attempts are valuable, ingenious, laborious, infuriating – as the case may be. Yet the suspicion remains that the door that Freud opened, the same door that Lacan after him also came through, leads to vivid pastures that the philosophical animal hasn't always been keen to tread on, and which, consequently, remain new and challenging. Psychoanalysis has had the contestations that it has had, has had the *élan*, the reach that it has had, because it *does* offer a complex and rewarding way of configuring the age-old mind/body dualism. It may not be philosophy 'as we know it' – but it most certainly deserves the philosophical consideration it has received, and more.

10 Feminist Philosophy

Rosi Braidotti

In spite of regular reports about the end of feminism as a social movement, at the start of the third millennium feminist philosophy is going through an astonishing period of renewal and growth. The diversification and expansion of feminist philosophies, fuelled by a brand new generation of post-postfeminists, is both supported by and productive of a significant growth of institutional practices, some of which happen outside the strict confines of academic philosophy, mostly in new trans-disciplinary areas like gender, race and postcolonial studies, social theories of globalization and migration, and philosophies of new media and biotechnology. This theoretical vitality raises a range of methodological questions about the uses and the limitations of interdisciplinarity in feminist philosophy and more specifically about the criteria of classification, the use of analytic categories and the canonization processes. As a result, the need for a systematic meta-discursive approach to the inter-disciplinary methods of feminist philosophy is among the top priorities for philosophy today (Alcoff, 2000) as well as women's, gender and feminist studies as an established discipline (Wiegman, 2002). If it is the case that what was once subversive is now mainstream, it follows that the challenge for feminist philosophers today is how to achieve more conceptual creativity (Deleuze and Guattari, 1991).

In a globally connected and technologically mediated world that is marked by fast changes, structural inequalities and increased militarization, feminist scholarship has intensified theoretical and methodological efforts to come to grips with the complexities of the present, while resisting the moral and cognitive panic that marks so much of contemporary social theories of globalization (Fukuyama, 2002; Habermas, 2003). With the demise of postmodernism, which has gone down in history as a form of radical scepticism and moral and cognitive relativism, feminist philosophers tend to move beyond the linguistic mediation paradigm of deconstructive theory and to work instead towards the production of robust alternatives. Issues of embodiment and accountability, positionality and location have become both more relevant and more diverse. My main argument in this essay is that feminist philosophy is currently finding a new course between post-humanism on the one hand and post-anthropocentric theories on the other. The convergence between these two approaches, multiplied across the many interdisciplinary lines that structure feminist theory, ends up radicalizing the very premises of feminist philosophy. It especially results in a reconsideration of the priority of sexuality and the relevance of the sex/gender distinction. I will analyze the different aspects of this convergence and attempt to work out some of its implications.

The Legacy of Feminist Post-Humanism

As starting premises, let me add a few remarks: feminist philosophy builds on the embodied and embedded brand of materialism that was pioneered in the last century by Simone de Beauvoir. It combines, in a complex and ground-breaking manner, phenomenological theory of embodiment with Marxist – and later on poststructuralist – re-elaborations of the intersection between bodies and power. This rich legacy has two long-lasting theoretical consequences. The first is that feminist philosophy goes even further than mainstream continental philosophy in rejecting dualistic partitions of minds from bodies or nature from culture. Whereas the chasm between the binary oppositions is bridged by Anglo-American gender theorists through dynamic schemes of social constructivism (Butler and Scott, 1992), continental feminist perspectives move towards either theories of sexual difference or a monistic political ontology that makes the sex/gender distinction redundant. I shall return later to this crucial aspect of my argument.

The second consequence of this specific brand of materialism is that oppositional consciousness combines critique with creativity, in a 'double-edged vision' (Kelly, 1979) that does not stop at critical deconstruction but moves on to the active production of alternatives. Thus, feminist philosophers have introduced a new brand of materialism, of the embodied and embedded kind. The cornerstone of this theoretical innovation is a specific brand of situated epistemology (Haraway, 1988), which evolves from the practice of 'the politics of locations' (Rich, 1985) and infuses standpoint feminist theory and the debates with postmodern feminism (Harding, 1991) throughout the 1990s.

As a meta-methodological innovation, the embodied and embedded brand of feminist materialist philosophy of the subject introduces a break with both universalism and dualism. As to the former, universalist claims to a subject position that allegedly transcends spatiotemporal and geopolitical specificities are criticized as being disembodied and disembedded, i.e., abstract. Universalism, best exemplified in the notion of 'abstract masculinity' (Hartsock, 1987) and triumphant whiteness (Ware, 1992) is objectionable not only on epistemological, but also on ethical grounds. Situated perspectives lay the pre-conditions for ethical accountability for one's own implications with the very structures one is analyzing and opposing politically. The key

167

concept in feminist materialism is the sexualized nature and the radical immanence of power relations and their effects upon the world. In this Foucauldian perspective, power is not only negative or confining (*potestas*), but also affirmative (*potentia*) or productive of alternative subject positions and social relations.

Feminist anti-humanism, also known as postmodernist feminism, critiqued from within the unitary identities indexed on phallocentric, Eurocentric and normative standardized views of what constitutes the humanist ideal of 'Man'. Feminist anti-humanism resonates with analogous but other(wise) situated postcolonial and race perspectives, which critique humanism or its racist connotations and racialized bias, and oppose to the biased Western brand many other cultural and ethnic traditions of non-Western humanism (Hill Collins, 1991; Shiva, 1997; Gilroy, 2000). This alliance between Western post-humanist and non-Western anti-humanist positions converges on the impossibility of speaking in one unified voice about women and other marginal subjects, thus stressing issues of diversity and differences among them. The pivotal notion in poststructuralist thought is the relationship between self and other. The notion of 'otherness' functions through dualistic oppositions that confirm the dominant vision of 'sameness' by positing sub-categories of difference and distributing them along asymmetrical power relations. In other words, the dominant apparatus of subjectivity is organized along a hierarchical scale that rewards the sovereign subject as the zero-degree of difference. Deleuze calls it 'the Majority subject' or the Molar centre of being (Deleuze and Guattari, 1980). Irigaray calls it 'the Same', or the hyper-inflated, falsely universal 'He' (Irigaray, 1974; 1977), whereas Hill Collins calls to account the white and Eurocentric bias of the subject of humanistic knowledge.

Furthermore, in European philosophy, this 'difference' has been predicated on relations of domination and exclusion: to be 'different from' came to mean to be 'less than'. In the dialectical scheme of thought, difference or otherness is a constitutive axis which marks off the sexualized other (woman), the racialized other (the native) and the naturalized other (animals, the environment or earth). These others, however, are constitutive in that they are expected to confirm the same in His superior position and thus they are crucial to the assertion of the power of sameness.

The fact that the dominant axes of definition of the humanistic subject of knowledge contribute to defining the axes of difference or of otherness has another important implication. They engender simultaneously the processes of sexualization, racialization and naturalization of those who are marginalized or excluded but also the active production of half-truths or forms of partial knowledge about these others. Dialectical and pejorative otherness induces structural ignorance about the others who, by being others, are posited as the outside of major categorical divides in the attribution of subjectivity.

Power produces through exclusion: the others are included in this script as the necessary outside of the dominant vision of what it means to be human. Their reduction to sub-human status is a constitutive source of ignorance and falsity and bad consciousness for the dominant subject who is responsible for their de-humanization.

Post-humanist feminist epistemologies proposed radical new ways to look at the 'human' from a more inclusive and diverse angle. As a result, the dominant vision of the subject in politics, law and science is abandoned in favour of renewed attention to complexities and inner contradictions. Feminist anti-humanist philosophies are committed both to a radical politics of resistance and to the critique of the simultaneity of potentially contradictory social and textual effects (Braidotti, 1994). This simultaneity is not to be confused with easy parallels or arguments by analogy. That gender, race, class and sexual choice may be equally effective power variables does not amount to flattening out any differences between them (Crenshaw, 1995). By extension, the claim to universality by scientific rationality is challenged on both epistemological and political grounds (Spivak, 1988), all knowledge claims being expressions of Western culture and of its drive to mastery.

Throughout the 1990s, the recognition of the normative structure of science and of the partiality of scientific statements, as well as the rejection of universalism and the recognition of the necessarily contingent nature of all utterances, involved two polemics which retrospectively appear symptomatic of great anxiety. One concerned essentialism and the other, relativism. One of the worst lasting effects of the politically conservative backlash of that period was that the affirmative and progressive potential of feminist critiques of the dominant subject position were reduced to and dismissed as being merely relativistic. What I value in those radical feminist positions is precisely the extent to which they allow for a productive critique of falsely universal pretensions. As a consequence, they enact the desire to pluralize the options, paradigms and practices of subjectivity within Western philosophical reason. The recognition of the necessarily situated and hence partial and contingent nature of our utterances and discursive practices has nothing to do with relativism and all to do with accountability, or situated perspectives.

For example, whereas the deconstruction of masculinity and whiteness is an end in itself, the non-essentialist reconstruction of black perspectives, as well as the feminist reconstruction of multiple ways of being women, also has new alternatives to offer. In other words, some notions need to be deconstructed so as to be laid to rest once and for all: masculinity, whiteness, heterosexism, classism, ageism. Others need to be deconstructed only as a prelude to offering positive new values and effective ways of asserting the political presence of newly empowered subjects: feminism, diversity, multiculturalism, environmentalism. All claims to authenticity need to be subjected to serious critical enquiry, but not left hanging in some sort of theoretical undecidability, as Butler would have it (Butler, 2004b). The affirmation of robust alternatives is what feminist philosophies of the subject are all about.

Matter-Realist Feminism

The legacy of this classical but neglected philosophical tradition of high post-structuralist anti-humanism sets the backdrop for the shifts currently taking place in the work of a new generation of feminist scholars (Fraser, 2002). A range of positions has emerged that bridge the gap between the classical opposition 'materialism/idealism' and move towards a non-essentialist brand of contemporary vitalism or thought on 'life itself' (Rose, 2001).

This movement of thought gathers the remains of poststructuralist anti-humanism and joins them with feminist reappraisals of contemporary techno-culture in a non-deterministic frame (Haraway, 1997; 2003; Hayles, 1999). They converge on discourses about 'life' and living matter/bodies: be it under the guise of political reflections on 'bio-power', or in the form of analyses of science and technology, they bring us back to the organic reality of 'real bodies'. After so much emphasis on the linguistic and cultural turn, an ontology of presence replaces textual deconstruction. This return of a neo-realist practice of bodily materialism is also known as: 'matter-realism', radical neo-materialism or post-human feminism. One of the main reasons to explain these shifts concerns the changing conceptual structure of materialism itself, under the impact of contemporary bio-genetics and information technologies. Feminist scholarship here falls neatly in two interconnected areas: new feminist science studies and epistemology on the one hand and political critiques of globalization and its economic and military violence on the other. They converge on the notion that what matters about materialism today is the concept of 'matter' itself (Delanda, 2002). The switch to a monistic political ontology stresses processes, vital politics and non-deterministic evolutionary theories (Grosz, 2004; Irigaray, 1992).

For instance, Karen Barad's work on 'agential realism' (Barad, 2003; 2007) stresses the onto-epistemological aspect of feminist knowledge claims today. Barad's agential realism not only builds on but also radically expands the redefinitions of objectivity and embodiment that took place in high feminist poststructuralism and thus also reshapes the forms of ethical and political accountability that rest upon them. By choosing to privilege neither the material nor the cultural, agential realism focuses instead on the process of their interaction. It accordingly redefines the apparatus of bodily production as material-cultural in order to foster the interrogation of the boundaries between them. This results in specifically feminist formulations of critical reflexivity and a renewed call for the necessity of an ethics of knowing that reflects and respects complexity.

One of Karen Barad's most astute commentators, Iris van der Tuin (2008), claims that this materialistic reconfiguration of the process of inter-action between the material and the semiotic, also known as the onto-epistemological shift, constitutes a new paradigm that ends up displacing both its poles of reference. What gets redefined in the process is the process-oriented, relational and fundamentally affective structure of subjectivity and knowledge production. According to van der Tuin, this approach encourages the constitution of a transdisciplinary perspective that combines feminist science studies, postcolonial studies and Deleuzian feminism in a new brand of third-wave feminist materialism.

Luciana Parisi emphasizes (Parisi, 2004) that the great advantage of Spinozist monism is that it defines nature/culture as a continuum that evolves through variations or differentiations. Deleuze and Guattari theorize them in terms of transversal assemblages or transversal lines of interconnec-tion. At the core of the 'chaosmosis' proposed by Guattari lies a mixed semiot-ics that combines the virtual (indeterminate) and the actual domains. The non-semiotic codes (the DNA or all genetic material) intersect with complex assemblages of affects, embodied practices and other performances that include but are not confined to the linguistic realm. Parisi strengthens this case by cross-referring to the new epistemology of Margulis and Sagan (1995), through the concept of endosymbiosis, which, like autopoiesis, indicates a creative form of evolution. It defines the vitality of matter as an ecology of differentiation, which means that the genetic material is exposed to processes of becoming. This questions any ontological foundation for difference while avoiding social constructivism.

The implications of this argument are twofold: the first point is that difference emerges as pure production of becoming-molecular and that the transitions or stratifications are internal to the single process of formation or of assemblage. They are intensive or affective variations that produce semiotic and a-semiotic practices. This is not just about dismissing semiotics or the linguistic turn, but rather an attempt at using it more rigorously, within the domains of its strict application (Massumi, 2002). It is also important to connect it transversally to other discourses. The second key point is that pri-macy is given to the relation over the terms. Parisi expresses this in Guattari's language as 'schizogenesis' – or the affective being of the middle, the inter-connection, the relation. This is the space-time where the differentiation occurs and with it the modifications. The emphasis falls accordingly on the micropolitics of relations, as a post-humanist ethics that traces transversal connections among material and symbolic, concrete and discursive, lines or forces. Transversality actualizes an ethics based on the primacy of the relation, of interdependence, which values non-human or a-personal life. This is what I call Zoe itself (Braidotti, 2006).

Feminist theory looks carefully at the dislocation of the dialectical relationships between the traditional axes of difference: sexualization/racialization/ naturalization and attempts to come to terms with this challenge. It can also be described as a sort of 'anthropological exodus' from the dominant configurations of the human (Hardt and Negri, 2000, p. 215) – a colossal hybridization of the species which topples the anthropocentric Human from the sovereign position it has enjoyed for so long. This standard is posited in a universal mode as Man, but this pseudo-universal has been widely criticized (Lloyd, 1985) precisely because of its partiality. Universal Man, in fact, is implicitly assumed to be masculine, white, urbanized, speaking a standard language, heterosexually inscribed in a reproductive unit and a full citizen of a recognized polity. Massumi refers to this phenomenon as 'Ex-Man', 'a genetic matrix embedded in the materiality of the human' and as such undergoing significant mutations: 'species integrity is lost in a bio-chemical mode expressing the mutability of human matter' (Massumi, 1998, p. 60). Haraway puts it most lucidly: 'This is Man the taxonomic type become Man the brand' (1997, p. 74). Post-human times force us to confront the challenges of the post-anthropocentric turn and the different degrees of inhumanity it encompasses. What emerges from the post-humanist convergence with post-anthropocentrism is the vital politics of life, which in turn raises the question of the possible modes of critique of advanced, globalized capitalism.

The bio-genetic structure of advanced capitalism is such that it is not only geno-centric (Fausto-Sterling, 2000, p. 235), but also ruthlessly and structurally unjust. Deleuze and Guattari (1992) analyzed this in terms of capitalism as a conflict between, on the one hand, the rising demands for subjective singularities and, on the other hand, the conservative re-territorialization of desires for the purpose of commercial profit. This achieves the doubly disastrous effect of re-asserting liberal individualism as the unquestionable standard for subject formation, while reducing it to consumerism. Furthermore, as Keith Ansell Pearson argued, some grand narratives have come back into fashion through 'the dynamics of contemporary hyper-colonialist capitalism' (Ansell Pearson, 1997, p. 303). They tend to be deterministic and evolutionary in a naïve and oddly old-fashioned way: 'A new mythology of the machine is emerging and finds expression in current claims that technology is simply the pursuit of life by means other than life' (Ansell Pearson, 1997, p. 202). This simplistic and reductive reading of the transformations currently at work in our global system reveal a conceptual poverty that most critical thinkers have complained about. A hierarchical fantasy of vertical perfectibility, a technologically mediated quest for immortality and for disciplined and acquiescent subjects, has gained widespread currency, which betrays the nomadic potential of contemporary science (Stengers, 1997). In opposition to this master narrative, which corresponds to what Donna Haraway calls 'the informatics of domination', feminist matter-realist philosophers stress the relevance of materialist, vital and complex philosophies of becoming, as an alternative conceptual framework, in the service of a sustainable future.

The epistemological analysis intersects with the political one: because the self-replicating vitality of living matter is targeted for consumption and commercial exploitation of bio-genetic culture, environmentally-based political struggles have evolved into a new global alliance for sustainable futures. Haraway recognizes this trend and pays tribute to the martyrized body of onco-mouse (Haraway, 1997) as the farming ground for the new genetic revolution and manufacturer of spare parts for other species.

Vandana Shiva (1997) stresses the extent to which the bodies of the empirical subjects who signify difference (woman/native/earth or natural others) have become the disposable bodies of the global economy. Contemporary capitalism is 'bio-political' in that it aims at controlling all that lives: it has already turned into a form of bio-piracy in that it aims at exploiting the generative powers of women, animals, plants, genes and cells. This means that human and anthropomorphic others are relocated in a continuum with non-anthropomorphic or 'earth' others. The categorical distinction that separated the Human from his naturalized others has shifted, as a result of the enormous advances introduced by our own scientific and technological developments.

A further methodological issue arises as a result: the advanced, bio-genetic structure of capitalism as a schizophrenic global economy does not function in a linear manner, but is web-like, scattered and poly-centred. It is not monolithic, but an internally contradictory process, the effects of which are differentiated geopolitically and along gender and ethnicity lines, to name only the main ones. This creates a few methodological difficulties for the social critic, because it translates into a heteroglossia of data which makes both classical and modernist social theories inadequate to cope with the complexities. We need to adopt non-linearity as a major principle and to develop cartographies of power that account for the paradoxes and contradictions of the era of globalization, and which do not take shortcuts through its complexities. This call for new 'figurations' of the subjects we are in the process of becoming, and resonates positively with the radical feminist call for the elaboration of empowering alternatives to the dominant vision of the subject.

Feminist politics, as outlined in the previous section, is pragmatic: we need schemes of thought and figurations that enable us to account in empowering and positive terms for the changes and transformations currently on the way. We already live in emancipated (post-feminist), multi-ethnic societies with high degrees of technological intervention. These are neither simple nor linear events, but rather multi-layered and internally contradictory phenomena.

They combine elements of ultra-modernity with splinters of neo-archaism: high tech advances and neo-primitivism, which defy the logic of the excluded middle. Contemporary culture and institutional philosophy are unable to represent these realities adequately. The unitary vision of the subject cannot provide an effective antidote to the processes of fragmentation, flows and mutations which mark our era. As Deleuze predicted, we need to learn to think differently about ourselves, starting with adequate cartographies of our embedded and embodied positions.

One of the areas in which contemporary feminist philosophy is attempting to actualize this political project is social theory and globalization studies. The consensual discursive strategy attempts to account for the speed and simultaneity of the contradictory social effects induced by advanced capitalism, including the structural inequalities that emerge in the age of globalization – also known as 'scattered hegemonies' (Grewal and Kaplan, 1994) – and stresses the need to safeguard women's interests, dignity and well-being amidst the dissemination of hybrid and fast-changing ethnic, racial, national and religious identities. Others follow on from classical deconstructivist methodologies in attempting to map out processes of knowledge transfer and by adopting dynamic and non-linear methods of analysis. The field known as 'travelling theories' is significant (Hemmings, 2006). Feminist social theory tries to do justice to both complexity and processes of change as operational concepts in the constitution of social subjects. It stresses the productive aspects of the dislocation and recasting of identities under advanced capitalism, in either a conservative mode of rational and moral universalism (Nussbaum, 2006; MacKinnon, 2006) or in more innovative ways.

The theoretical advantage of this monistic and vital approach is the ability to account for the fluid workings of power in advanced capitalism by grounding them in immanent relations, and hence to resist them by the same means. This philosophical position is exemplified by the notion of non-hierarchical or horizontal transcendence (Irigaray, 1984) and by the idea of radical immanence in Deleuzian feminism (Braidotti, 1991; Colebrook, 2000, 2004; Grosz, 2004).

Third-wave feminism (Henry, 2004; Tuin, 2008) has embraced non-linearity by voicing anti-Oedipal philosophical and methodological claims about feminist time-lines that redesign possible futures in affirmative ways. This transversal convergence between philosophical anti-foundationalism and feminist epistemology results in a post-human wave that radicalizes the premises of science studies beyond anything envisaged by classical postmodernist feminism (Wilson, 1998; Bryld and Lykke, 1999; Franklin et al., 2000). Interest in Darwin and evolutionary theory has grown considerably (Grosz, 2004), as have feminist interests in non-teleological and anti-deterministic evolutionary theory. Feminist cultural studies of science attempt to disengage biology from the structural functionalism of DNA-driven linearity and to move it towards more creative patterns of evolutionary development (Halberstam and Livingston, 1995). The result is a non-essentialist brand of vital neo-holistic thought that points explicitly to a spiritual evolutionary dimension, best exemplified by the growing number of references to Bergson (Fraser et al., 2005; Grosz, 2004).

Post-human Feminism

This position stresses the extent to which the management of life in a post-human mode has taken centre stage in the political economy of advanced capitalism. This includes the proliferation of practices, both scientific and social, which go beyond human life. Contemporary genetics and bio-technologies are central to this shift towards post-human ideas of 'Life' or 'Zoe', the non-human. The mutual interdependence of bodies and technologies creates a new symbiotic relationship between them. This inaugurates an eco-philosophical approach to subjectivity and hence also new ecologies of belonging. It also marks a radical critique of anthropocentrism in favour of the recognition of the entanglement of material, bio-cultural and symbolic forces in the making of the subject.

In other words, what 'returns' with the return of life and of 'real bodies' at the end of postmodernism, under the impact of advanced technologies, is not only the others of the classical subject of modernity: woman/native/nature. What returns now is the 'other' of the living body in its humanistic definition: the other face of *bios*, that is to say *Zoe*, the generative vitality of non-or pre-human or animal life (Braidotti, 2006).

Zoe stands for the mindless vitality of life carrying on independently, regardless of rational control. This is the dubious privilege attributed to non-humans and to all the 'others' of Man, whereas *bios* refers to the specific social nexus of humans. That these two competing notions of 'life' coincide on the human body turns the issue of embodiment into a contested space and a political arena. Mind-body dualism has historically functioned as a shortcut through the complexities of this question by introducing a criterion of hier-archical distinction which is sexualized, racialized and naturalized. Given that this concept of 'the human' was colonized by phallogocentrism, it has come to be identified with male, white, heterosexual, Christian, property-owning, standard language speaking citizens. *Zoe* marks the outside of this vision of the subject, in spite of the efforts of evolutionary theory to strike a new relationship to the non-human. Contemporary scientific practices have forced us to touch the bottom of some inhumanity that connects to the human precisely in the immanence of its bodily materialism. With the genetic revolution, we can speak of a generalized 'becoming infrahuman' of *bios*. The category of 'Life' has accordingly cracked under the strain.

The emergence of vitalist politics causes a considerable amount of epistemological disarray. This is due to the redistribution of the self–other relation along a rhizomatic or multi-layered axis, in contrast to a binary or dualistic axis of opposition. As a result of the eruption of complexity at the heart of what used to be dialectics, the Other has lost its metaphysical substantial presence and the magical aura that surrounded it. By extension, it has ceased to be one of the privileged terms that index the European subject's relationship to subjectivity. The classical dialectics of otherness in fact displayed varying degrees of familiarity between the centre and the margins, that is to say an intimate and inner-looking relationship, which was framed nonetheless by the dominant human masculine habit of taking for granted free access to and the consumption of the bodies of others. This mode of relation is currently being restructured. A bio-egalitarian turn is taking place that encourages us to engage in a radically other relationship with others. I want to argue that the challenge today is how to deterritorialize or nomadize the human-other interaction, so as to bypass the metaphysics of substance and its corollary, the dialectics of otherness, secularizing accordingly the concept of human nature and the life which animates it.

The three dialectical axes of constitution of otherness according to the unitary subject of classical humanism – sexualization/racialization/naturalization – and the hierarchical scale of pejorative differences which they uphold, have shifted. They no longer correspond to a dialectical model of opposition, but rather follow a more dynamic, non-linear and hence less predictable pattern, that composes a zigzagging line of internally contradictory options. The 'others' are not merely the markers of exclusion or marginality, but also the sites of powerful and alternative subject-positions. Thus, the bodies of others become simultaneously disposable commodities and also decisive agents for political and ethical transformation (Braidotti, 2002). This relocation of otherness along a rhizomatic web, however, seems to leave miraculously unscathed the centuries-old forms of sexism, racism and anthropocentric arrogance that have marked our culture. The transformation of the axes of sexualized, racialized and naturalized difference form intersecting patterns of becoming. They compose a new political economy of otherness and are therefore of great ethical and political relevance.

The challenge post-human vital thought throws to feminism is that whereas the dislocation of sexualized and racialized differences can be accommodated into the critique of advanced capitalism, as they are integral to it, the transposition of nature poses a number of conceptual, methodological and practical complications linked to the critique of anthropocentrism. This is due to the pragmatic fact that, as embodied and embedded entities, we are all part of nature, even though philosophy continues to claim transcendental grounds for human consciousness. As a brand of 'enchanted materialism', philosophical nomadism contests the arrogance of anthropocentrism and strikes an alliance with the productive force of *Zoe* – or life in its inhuman aspects.

Thus, affinity for *Zoe* is a good starting point for what may constitute the last act of the critique of dominant subject positions, namely the return of animal or earth life in all its potency. The breakdown of species distinction (human/non-human) and the explosion of *Zoe* power, therefore, shifts the grounds of the problem of the breakdown of categories of individuation (gender and sexuality; ethnicity and race). This introduces the issue of becoming into a planetary or worldwide dimension, the earth being not one element among others, but rather that which brings them all together.

Social theory since poststructuralism has emphasized the materially grounded transformative processes of becoming, re-appraised the relevance of complexity in network societies, and shifted political analyses from bio-power to vital politics. Classical vitalism is a problematic notion, considering its dramatic history of holism and complicity with fascism. Contemporary neo-vitalism as a philosophy of flows of complex information systems and flux of data in the continuum of 'timeless time' (Castells, 1996), however, presupposes and benefits from the philosophical monism that is central to a materialist and non-unitary vision of subjectivity.

The Post-Secular Turn

Vitalist philosophies of matter-realism include a re-appraisal of spirituality. Such a claim needs to be qualified critically, considering the popularity of neo-eschatological visions of catastrophe and redemption that circulate nowadays. The call is emerging for a post-secular approach to feminism, in keeping with or as an answer to the acknowledgment of the return of the different facets of a religiously-driven vision of female agency (Mahmood, 2005). The new agenda includes straightforward religious matters; questions of neo-vital politics; environmental holism and deep ecology; the bio-political management of life and the quest for suitable resistance in the era of bio-genetic capitalism or what ethical values best suit the respect for ethnic and cultural diversity. A neo-vitalist notion of radical immanence also expresses the residual spiritual values of great intimacy and a sense of belonging to the world as process of perpetual becoming (Bataille, 1988). The resurgence of 'new age' spiritual practices is also a salient feature of the contemporary landscape. Because of these social phenomena, the issue of spirituality needs to be rethought from within the post-Enlightenment tradition of secularity. This is not the residual mysticism of a notion of life as pure becoming, empty of meaning, but rather a concrete plan for embedding and embodying new formations of living subjects. Not an evolutionary tale, but a qualitative leap of values.

The need for a new cosmopolitan or pan-human ethical project that would integrate a renewed interest in corporeality or bodily materialism with a serious critique of the limitations of the linguistic turn within postmodernism has been voiced by several feminist philosophers. Bio-ethics as an area has grown in importance of late (Diprose, 1994). Some humanistic philosophers like Martha Nussbaum (2006) point to the need for a return to Aristotelian principles of moral virtue; others like Benhabib (2002) argue for the unavoidable confrontation with Kantian morality. In a more creative vein, Gatens and Lloyd (1999) revisit Spinozist ethics with Gilles Deleuze so as to provide a robust new ethical standpoint. Noteworthy in this context is the interest in the philosophical work of Gilles Deleuze (Buchanan and Colebrook, 2000) and its applications to feminist philosophy (Braidotti, 2002; 2006).

An important reason for needing a new grounded, embodied and embedded subject has to do with the second half of that crucial sentence: 'we' are in *this* together. What *this* refers to is the cluster of interconnected problems that touches the structure of subjectivity and the very possibility of the future as a sustainable option. 'We' are in *this* together, in fact, enlarges the sense of collectively bound subjectivity to non-human agents, from our genetic neighbours the animals, to the earth as the biosphere as a whole. 'We', therefore, is a non-anthropocentric construct, which refers to a commonly shared territory or habitat (*this*). How to do justice to this relatively simple yet highly problematic reality requires a shift of perspective. As Haraway suggests, we need to work towards 'a new techno-scientific democracy' (1997, p. 95). *This* is indeed a totality, finite and confined.

Central to the fast convergence between post-humanist and post-anthropocentric positions are the new forms of cosmopolitan or pan-human interconnections devised by race theory. Edward Said, in his influential work on orientalism (1978), first alerted critical theorists in the West to the need to develop a reasoned and secular account of Enlightenment-based humanism by taking into account the 'postcolonial' condition. Postcolonial theory argued for and documented the extent to which the Enlightenment ideals of reason, secular tolerance, equality under the law and democratic rule, need not be and indeed historically have not been mutually exclusive with European practices of violent domination, exclusion and the systematic and instrumental use of terror. This has a number of significant implications: one concerns the theoretical priority granted to sexuality and the other concerns the sex/gender distinction.

Sexuality Beyond Gender

The matter-realist turn has important implications for the discussion of sexuality and gender, which has been central to feminist philosophy since the change of paradigm towards queer theory, introduced by de Lauretis (1990) and developed by Butler in the 1990s. As I have argued elsewhere (Braidotti, 2002), Butler's claim to undo gender (2004) is flatly contradicted by the binary structure of queer thinking, which locates the heterosexual matrix at the core of its analyses and opposes it to queer melancholia. The related criticism is that queer theory has avoided the main lesson of psychoanalysis about the polymorphous and perverse structure of human sexuality. It has accordingly narrowed down the scope of the original loss of unity of the subject, placing all the emphasis on the loss of the homosexual component. By contrast, Deleuze and Guattari broaden the scope of the discussion by stressing the theft of the complexity, polymorphousness and perversity of sexuality and its reduction through the capture of a majoritarian scheme of sexuality that privileges heterosexual reproductive sex.

Irigaray shifts the emphasis on the original and foundational act that is the theft of the little girl's sexuality – according to the sacrificial ontology of a phallocentric system that requires the exchange of women to fuel its socio-symbolic structures. The emphasis thus falls on the specificity of women's own sexual economy. It is in this spirit that Irigaray praises the specific instance of feminine homosexuality as a moment of high symbolic significance in confirming a woman's sense of self-worth. This primary narcissism, this love of oneself as reflected in the eyes of another who is morphologically 'the same,' is, according to the early Irigaray, a necessary pre-condition of the affirmation of a positive difference that repairs the symbolic damage suffered by women in a phallogocentric system. This is no essentialism but rather a molecular, transversal space of formation of collectively sustained micro-singularities.

Both Irigaray and Deleuze challenge queer theory's reductive rendition of the original foreclosure of the first love object – the mother – and of the sexual complexity that marks the polymorphous and perverse structure of human sexuality. Both engage, in different but powerful ways, with the unconscious or trans-historical and trans-personal carnal elements that are involved in the process of capture or theft of the primordial sexual body. What is emerging more clearly in current discussions about sexuality is that, whereas queer theory is solidly ensconced in social constructivist methods and political strategies, matter-realist thinkers affirm and explore the ontological aspects of sexuality and sexual difference and not only its constructed elements.

As a consequence, matter-realist or vitalist feminism, resting on a dynamic monistic political ontology, shifts the focus away from the sex/gender distinction, bringing sexuality as process into full focus. The first concerns the irrelevance of the category 'same sex' to account for the complex and multiple affects generated in the relation between two beings. The redundancy of the sex/gender distinction for feminist philosophies of the subject had been noted by English-speaking feminists working in continental philosophy, like Gatens (1991), Grosz (1999) and Braidotti (1991; 1994), before it was recast in a new paradigm by Butler's performative turn (1991). Contemporary feminist philosophers argue the same case on different grounds. For instance, Patricia MacCormack (2008) draws attention to the need to return to sexuality as a polymorphous and complex force and to disengage it from both identity issues and all dualistic oppositions. She looks for subversion not in counter-identity formations, but rather in pure dislocations of identities via perversion of standardized patterns of interaction.

MacCormack's emphasis on visceral subjects rests on Deleuze and Guattari's idea of radical empiricism and on Irigaray's emphasis on the sensible transcendental, to stress that becomings or transformations are open-ended and not necessarily contained by socio-symbolic forms, such as phallogocentrism or categories, such as the anthropocentric idea of the human. The ethics of becoming is rather an ethology of the forces that propel the subject to overcome both forms and categories, deterritorializing all identities on its line of flight. This means by extension that sexuality is a force or constitutive element, that is capable of deterritorializing gender identity and institutions.

A renewed emphasis on sexuality, as opposed to classical or queer theories of sex and gender, emerges from the shift of perspective introduced by matter-realist feminism. In a recent contribution to this debate, Benjamin Noys (2008) argues forcefully for the need to reconsider the by now canonical reception of Foucault's theses on sexuality. Emphasizing Foucault's earlier work, Noys re-appraises the radical critique Foucault developed of the over-emphasis our culture places on sex-gender as an indicator of identities and inner truths about ourselves. As an operator of power, a conveyor of major social regulations and a tool for consumerism, sex is a trap from which we need to liberate ourselves. Foucault's notorious criticism of feminist theories of sexual liberation, in the first volume of his history of sexuality, reiterates the point that there is no possible liberation through but only from sex-gender. By extension, the idea that sexual liberation is central to a political project of liberation or emancipation – which is constitutive of Western feminism and central to its secular bias – paradoxically reiterates the Christian notion that desire is central to the constitution of subjectivity.

Foucault's project challenges this bias by proclaiming the 'end of the monarchy of sex', as being in congruence with the deregulation of sexual repression and the commercial exploitation of marginal or dissident sexualities. The only credible subversive move, according to Foucault, is the refusal of all identities based on sex-gender and not only of a dominant heterosexual model or of its binary homosexual counterpart. Even more crucial is the effort to undertake serious experimentation with alternative modes of relation that are not mediated via sex and therefore escape both commercial commodification and the social normativity that accompanies it. This experimental sexual pragmatics also accomplishes the creative task of returning sexuality to its original complexity as a force of intensity, intimacy and relationality. The centrality of desire is accordingly displaced by experimenting with modes of ethical subjectivity (for the later Foucault) and transversal collective assemblages (for Deleuze and Guattari), that free the subject from the dictatorship of sex as a term that indexes access to identity formations and their respective power entitlements. Neo-asceticism (Braidotti, 2006) emerges as a resource, with renewed emphasis on a political spirituality that labours to free the subject from constituted identities and experiment with new modes of relation.

This element is crucial to the post-secular turn I mentioned above. Both Irigaray and Deleuze embody and embed the universal, according to the principle of carnal materialism. They also conceptualize the space of the relation, the interconnection among forces and entities. The universal therefore is located transversally, in the specific singularity of immanent interrelations among subjects collectively engaged in the expression and actualization of *potentia*. The inter-subjective space is a laboratory of becoming. Deleuze's anti-essentialist, high-tech vitalism echoes the ideas of Irigaray about the subject as a bodily human entity, sensitive flesh framed by the skin. Irigaray turns to non-Christian religions, notably Judaism and Buddhism, and the philosophy of Levinas. The model of alternative ethics proposed by philosophies of nomadism implies a non-hierarchical idea of transcendence and a non-binary model of interrelation. They propose immanent concepts of the subject as dynamic becoming, where the bodily self is analyzed according to the concrete forces or material variables that compose it and sustain it.

Sexual Difference Revisited

The ontological status of sexuality in contemporary matter-realist discussions combines realism about essences with vitalism in ethical interrelations. Relationality and affirmative experimentations with other modes of ethical interaction are the rule. They imply that sexual difference is the starting point for transformative practice: a robust and essential starting point, not a burden to be cast away at the earliest opportunity.

All the Deleuzian radical empiricists share this point and stress the ontological dimension of both sexuality and sexual difference. Other voices, however, are emerging in the discussion, arguing that sexual difference is simply not a problem at all. This statement can be construed in several different ways and the lines of differentiation are quite significant. For instance, in what could be described as a classical exposition of Deleuzian feminism, Gatens and Lloyd (1999) argue that the political ontology of monism, which Deleuze adapts from Spinoza, offers some relevant opportunities for feminist theory. Mind–body parallelism, as opposed to Cartesian dualism, can be rendered in terms of simultaneous effects. These entail the embodiment of mind as much as the 'embrainment of matter', to use an expression coined by John Marks. There is only one substance: an intelligent flesh-mind-matter compound. This implies that bodily differences are both a banality and a cornerstone in the process of differentiation of variation. The resonances between this feminist project and Deleuze's nomadism are many and many-fold.

Lloyd argues that the parallelism between mind and body and the intrinsically affective or conatus-driven vision of the subject implies that different bodies have different degrees and levels of power and force of understanding. This has clear implications for sexual difference. Given that, on a Spinozist account, the mind is nothing more than the actual idea of the body, sexual difference can reach into the mind as the mind is not independent of the body in which it is situated. If bodies are differently sexed, so are minds. Lloyd emphasizes the extent to which Spinoza recognizes that there are distinctive powers and pleasures associated with different kinds of bodies, which then are enacted in different minds. Thus, a female body cannot fail to affect a female mind. Spinoza's mind is not neutral and this, according to Lloyd, has great potential for a feminist theory of female subjectivity that aims at avoiding the essentialist trap of a genuine female nature, while rejecting the idea of the neutrality of the mind. Although Spinoza gives in to the traditionally subordinate vision of women of his times, and thus excludes women from the polity, Lloyd is careful in pointing out the liberatory potential of Spinoza's monistic vision of the embodied nature of the mind. Its worth can be measured most effectively in comparison with the Cartesian dualistic vision of the mind–body dichotomy, which historically proved more damaging for women than his idea of the sex-neutrality of the mind. What a female nature is, must consequently be determined in each case and cannot be spelled out *a priori*, because each embodied compound has its own specificity. This is due to the fact that, in a neo-Spinozist perspective, embodied subjects are constituted by encounters with other forces in patterns of affinity or dissonance that gives them very clear configurations which cannot be known in advance.

In a monistic perspective, difference need not be rendered in essentialist terms, be it biological, psychic or any other type. The fact that for Spinoza the body is intelligent matter and the mind is embodied sensibility has the advantage of bypassing the pitfalls of essentialism altogether. This offers a way out of the essentialism-constructivism impasse. Accordingly, Lloyd, even more than Gatens, contemplates a non-psychoanalytic theory of sexual difference which rests on Spinoza's monism and reaches out for what I have called the 'enchanted materialism' of immanence.

Lloyd (1994) stresses the continuing relevance of sexual difference, against the theoretical illusions of an infinitely malleable, free-floating gender. Grounded and situated, sexual difference as a mode of embodied and embedded actualization of difference shapes the space-time continuum of nomadic subjectivity. Lloyd and Gatens explicitly take aim at the dualism of the sex-gender distinction, which posits a transcendent gender as the matrix that formats sex. By extension, they also expose the absurdity of any political project that would aim at 'undoing gender' (Butler, 2004). To undo gender would mean to unmake bodies and much as this aspiration fits in with the consumerist logic of advanced bio-capitalism, it makes very little sense politically.

Thus, Lloyd argues that sexually differentiated bodies mark sexually differentiated spatio-temporal segments of subjectivity. In other words, sexual difference speaks through or is expressed in every cognitive, moral, political or other activity of the subject. Whereas Irigaray and the feminism of sexual difference attribute a (positive) normative value to this statement, Lloyd keeps it neutral. It is a factual statement: it is just the way things are. What does become important for both Lloyd and Gatens, however, is the extent to which this monistic vision of the subject, and its in-built assertion of sexual difference, allows for an enlargement of both the notion of moral agency and that of political subjectivity and more particularly of citizenship. Insofar as all subjects partake of the same essence, and are therefore part of nature, their common features can be located precisely in this shared capacity for affecting and being affected. This transversality lays the grounds for a post-individualistic understanding of the subject and a radical redefinition of common humanity. The latter is an embedded and embodied collection of singularities that are endowed with common features: qualitative complexities, not quantitative pluralities.

If for Lloyd and Gatens sexual difference is not a problematic issue, in that it remains of great relevance, for Claire Colebrook it is no longer a problem, because the political and theoretical terms of the feminist debate have shifted since the days of high, or early, feminist poststructuralism. Colebrook (2000) suggests that a younger feminist wave is looking at the question of sexual difference as not only or primarily a question that concerns the subject or the subject's body. She is very vocal in wanting to move beyond the phenomenological legacy of feminist theory and enlists Deleuze's philosophy in the attempt to bypass the quasi-transcendentalist mode of feminist theory. Colebrook stresses that for Irigaray sexual difference is clearly a metaphysical question, but in the foundational sense that it determines metaphysics as such. Sexual difference poses the question of the conditions of possibility for thought as a self-originating system of representation of itself as the ultimate presence. Thus, sexual difference produces subjectivity in general. The conceptual tool by which Irigaray shows up this peculiar logic is the notion of 'the sensible transcendental'. By showing that what is erased in the process of erection of the transcendental subject are the maternal grounds of origin, Irigaray simultaneously demystifies the vertical transcendence of the subject and calls for an alternative metaphysics. Irigaray's transcendental is sensible and grounded in the very particular fact that all human life is, for the time being, still 'of woman born' (Rich, 1976).

According to Colebrook, Deleuze's emphasis on the productive and positive force of difference is troublesome for feminist theory in so far as it challenges the foundational value of sexual difference. For Irigaray, the metaphysical question of sexual difference is the horizon of feminist theory; for Grosz (1994) it is its pre-condition; for Butler (1993) it is the limit of the discourse of embodiment; for Braidotti (1994) it is a negotiable, transversal, affective space. The advantage of a Deleuzian approach is that the emphasis shifts from the metaphysics to the ethics of sexual difference. Deleuze's brand of philosophical pragmatism questions whether sexual difference demands metaphysics at all. This for Colebrook translates into a crucial question: 'is feminism a critical inhabitation of metaphysical closure, or the task of thinking a new metaphysics?' (Colebrook, 2000, p. 112). Following Deleuze's empiricism, Colebrook wants to shift the grounds of the debate away from metaphysical foundations to a philosophy of immanence that stresses the need to create new concepts. This creative gesture is a way of responding to the given, to experience, and is thus linked to the notion of the event. The creation of concepts is itself experience or experimentation. There is a double implication here: firstly that philosophy need not be seen as the master discourse or the unavoidable horizon of thought: artistic and scientific practices have their role to play as well. Secondly, given that ethical questions do not require metaphysics, the feminist engagement with concepts need not be critical but can be inventive and creative. In other words, experimenting with thinking is what we all need to learn.

Colebrook struggles with the idea of what kind of problem sexual difference could be, if it were not defined as a question of truth, recognition, self-representation or radical anteriority. She does not come to a convincing conclusion, but this does not detract from the relevance of her project. In order to answer the question of sexual difference, one would simply have to redefine the function or status of philosophy altogether. This is a classical radical feminist statement, which situates Colebrook's third-wave feminism in a continuum with previous generations. Feminist theory does indeed challenge what we have come to recognize as thinking. Calling for an embodied philosophy of radical immanence marks the start of a bodily philosophy of relations. The body is for Colebrook an incorporeal complex assemblage of virtualities:

> The body is a relation to what is not itself, a movement or an activity from a point of difference to other points of difference. And so difference is neither an imposed scheme, nor an otherwise uniform substance, nor is difference the relation between already differentiated self-identical entities. What something is, is given through the activity of differentiation. (Colebrook, 2000, p. 87)

This is the basic meaning of the positivity of difference and it is linked to corporeality through the notion of virtual becomings. Loyal to her Deleuzian premises, Colebrook defines the ethics of sexual difference 'not as the telos of some universal law, but as the responsibility and recognition of the self-formation of the body' (Colebrook, 2000, p. 88). In other words, as the becoming of bodies occurs within a single substance, the question is no longer; 'how are the sexes differentiated?' but rather: 'how are different modalities of sexual differentiation due to the specificity of different bodies?' (Colebrook, 2000, p. 90). Once this question is raised, the whole issue of essentialism simply collapses.

The point of consensus among these different positions is that sexual difference is not a problem that needs to be explained in relation to an epistemological paradigm that assumes *a priori* sameness and a dialectical frame of pejorative difference. It is rather the case that sexual difference is just an embodied and embedded point of departure that signals simultaneously the ontological priority of difference and its self-organizing and self-transforming force. The ontology of becoming allows difference to emerge as radical immanence, i.e: as creative evolution. Chrysanthi Nigianni (2008) argues that this position moves political thought beyond both emancipationist historicism and liberal progressivism, allowing instead for a politics of becomings that posits transversal subjectivity as machinic assemblages that embrace the openness but also the materiality of the virtual (Massumi, 2002).

Conclusion

I have argued in the previous section that, in a feminist matter-realist perspective, sexuality deterritorializes the actual gender of the people it involves in the process of becoming. An important question that can be raised here is: what happens to gender if sexuality is not based on oppositional terms? What happens when there is sexuality without the possibility of heterosexual or homosexual union? (MacCormack, 2008). What happens is vitalist erotics, which includes intensive deterritorializations, unhealthy alliances, hybrid cross-fertilizations, productive anomalies and generative encounters.

Let me pursue this discussion with an example taken from the legendary relationship between Virginia Woolf and Vita Sackville-West – as a complex, multi-layered and highly sexualized encounter that produces effects, relations and texts of all sorts. Virginia and Vita propose an ethical model where the play of sameness-difference is not modelled on the dialectics of masculinity and femininity; it is rather an active space of becoming that is productive of new meanings and definitions. In other words: here is sexuality beyond gender (Braidotti, 2008).

This cuts two ways: firstly, the homophobic assumption that same-sex relationships cause fusion and confusion, in so far as they fail to establish sufficiently strong boundaries of alterity is flatly rejected by the experience of high-singularity and intense definition, which emerges from the encounter of Virginia with Vita. The fact that Virginia and Vita meet within this category of sexual 'sameness' encourages them to look beyond the delusional aspects of the identity ('women'), which they supposedly share. This proliferation of differences between women and within each one of them is evident in the outcomes and the products of their relationship, be it in the literature which Virginia and Vita produced, or in the many social, cultural and political projects they were engaged in. These included marriages, motherhood and child-rearing, political activism, socializing, campaigning, publishing and working as a publisher, gardening and the pursuit of friendships, pleasures and hard work.

Secondly, the assemblage composed by Virginia & Vita as blocks of becoming is post-gender but not beyond sex – it is actually deeply embedded in sexuality and can be best understood in relation to non-unitary subjectivity and neo-vital politics. The disappearance of firm boundaries between self and other, in the love encounter, in intense friendship, in the spiritual experience and in more everyday interpersonal connections, is the necessary premise to the enlargement of one's fields of perception and capacity to experience. In pleasure as in pain, in a secular, spiritual, erotic mode that combines at once elements from all these, the decentring and opening-up of the individual ego coincides not only with communication with other fellow human beings, but also with a heightening of the intensity of such communication. This shows the advantages of a non-unitary vision of the subject. A depersonalization of the self, in a gesture of everyday transcendence of the ego, is a connecting force, a binding force that links the self to larger internal and external relations. An isolated vision of the individual is a hindrance to such a process.

It is also important to stress the extent to which sets of interconnections or encounters constitute a project, which requires active involvement and work.

Desire is never a given. Rather, like a long shadow projected from the past, it is a forward-moving horizon that lies ahead and towards which one moves. Between the no longer and the not yet, desire traces the possible patterns of becoming. These intersect with and mobilize sexuality, but never stop there as they construct space and time and thus design possible worlds by allowing the unfolding of ever intensified affects. Desire sketches the conditions for the future by bringing into focus the present, through the unavoidable accident of an encounter, a flush (Woolf, 1993), a sudden acceleration that marks a point of no return. Call it falling in love, if you wish, but only if you can rescue the notion from the sentimental banality into which it has sunk in commercial culture. Moreover, if falling in love it is, it is disengaged from the human subject that is wrongly held responsible for the event. Here, love is an intensive encounter that mobilizes the sheer quality of the light and the shape of the landscape. Deleuze's remark on the grasshoppers flying in at 5:00 p.m. on the back of the evening wind also evokes non-human cosmic elements in the creation of a space of becoming. This indicates that desire designs a whole territory and thus it cannot be restricted to the mere human *persona* that enacts it. We need a post-anthropocentric theory of both desire and love in order to do justice to the complexity of subjects of becoming.

11 Philosophies of Life

Dorothea Olkowski

A Philosophy of Life?

The modern idea of a philosophy of life seems to have come about in conjunction with the rise in the importance of human reason (Klein, 1964, p. 216). The rise of modern science and its influence over all areas of experience produced a radical shift not only in science and philosophy, but in society, in the understanding of life. By the seventeenth century, among natural philosophers, mathematical reasoning applied to nature came to be regarded as the 'purest, deepest, and most efficacious form of all thought' such that not only science but 'philosophy, religion, politics, economics, ethics and aesthetics were to be recast, each in accordance with the natural laws of its field' (Klein, 1964, pp. 238–9). From this came a new type of 'man.' This new 'man' seemed to emerge from the state of nature fully clothed. That is, nature was postulated as a place of perfect freedom to order one's actions and possessions within the bounds of the newly discovered natural laws. As Hannah Arendt has commented, lacking any more solid basis for the establishment of private property, for taking it out of the commons, Locke founded it on the body, the property of one's own person (Arendt, 1998, p. 111). As such, property could be understood to be the result of a natural process that follows its own laws, and whose functioning cannot be checked (Arendt, 1998, p. 111). Thus the idea of life became a source of value and the glorification of life processes followed from their central role in the philosophies of the seventeenth and eighteenth centuries.

Eternal Return and the Affirmation of Life

The philosophy of Friedrich Nietzsche may stand as the original expression of the recently emerging philosophy of nature and life, a philosophy that has its roots in the natural sciences, but which often far exceeds the boundary of the scientific method. Nietzsche wanted to examine causality, reason, logic, the ego and morality, all of which he took to be creations of consciousness, and all of which, he argued, fail to provide us with either knowledge or truth. Instead, Nietzsche took the position that these faculties are falsifications of

188

reality insofar as the Newtonian view of nature as capable of being predicted with certainty no longer held; for nature, in Nietzsche's time, was already understood to be the realm of probabilities. Nietzsche proposed, therefore, to free consciousness from knowledge, from the bonds of logic, reason and moral evaluations, in order to follow life. This decision produces a new sort of understanding that is neither stable nor rational, but requires guesses and momentary insights, the labour of a complex of forces that affirms itself and the world as ceaseless becoming without aim or purpose; indeed, this is the meaning of eternal return.

Physicists characterize eternal return as the 'evolutions of systems that come back again and again to near the same state at a later time' (Ruelle, 1991, p. 86). Typically, this actually occurs in moderately complicated systems, but not in systems that are extremely complicated, because 'if a system is sufficiently complicated, the time it takes to return near a state already visited is huge,' making eternal return, at best, an idealization (Ruelle, 1991, p. 87).[1] Nevertheless, it is an idealization that Nietzsche clings to in the manner of Ludwig Boltzmann's formulation for atoms of helium in a one-litre container. For such an *isolated* system, over the course of time, 'the system would visit all energetically possible configurations . . . all configurations of positions and velocities of the particles that have the right total energy would be realized' (Ruelle, 1991, p. 111).[2] In simpler terms, if you wait long enough, a layer of hot and a layer of cold water that mix to luke-warm will eventually return to two layers, hot and cold. The question that arises for us, therefore, is how does Nietzsche translate this physical system into a philosophy of life?

Nietzsche understands conscious thought to be a series of relations among instincts, the reconciliation of drives and desires that often remain unconscious and even unfelt (Nietzsche, 1974, p. 333). Consciousness, he argues, is merely the last and latest development of the body. In this, it is not essentially different from other instincts and drives; it is a function that developed in society to facilitate communication and a tool of labourers for the sake of their preservation (Nietzsche, 1974, p. 354). Although the instincts and drives of the body are the tools of our animal functions, they are organized and adapted into will, idea or sensation to serve the body's chief function, which is to 'spin on the chain of life,' to increase power (Nietzsche, 1968b, §526, §674). Individual drives are simply blind activity, endlessly seeking power with no end in sight, except that of becoming stronger. Negative attitudes towards instincts and drives must change if 'man' is to overcome himself, to overcome his situation as cut off from himself and from life, all of which weakens him. Men must now recognize that instincts, not reason, are at bottom what guide the drive for knowledge in every form, such that decisions, categories and evaluations are all guided by instincts (Nietzsche, 1968a, §3). From this point of view, passions and drives are real and thought is, as sceptical philosophers have declared, merely the relation between them. If reason is and ought to be the slave of the passions, then the healthy body does not think or speak 'I' but performs 'I' (Nietzsche, 1969, §262). For Nietzsche, we can and must learn to be faithful to life. The world seems unintelligible because it changes continuously and what changes continuously, what is merely probable, seems to be unknowable. We try to give the world stable forms that make sense to us, but life has neither regularity nor goals; it is neither logical nor rational and so defies our categories. So to be faithful to life is to be first faithful to the body, to its necessities, as the same drives coalesce around both the body and life. This is why the affirmation of life requires supreme physical strength.

Nevertheless, human beings place a high value on consciousness, on what is logical, rational and distinct, because the most simplified and clearest thoughts are the easiest to understand and use. For the same reason, what is profound but uncertain, what leaves many questions *open* is thought to be obscure and in need of rational organization. Yet, for Nietzsche, the errors of consciousness are our greatest mistake because they are the least in contact with the body and with instincts, they are least faithful to the life. Life defies our rational organization and its inexhaustible forms, manifestations of will to power can be disordered, terrible and fear-inspiring. But like that other modern force, gravity, will to power is itself invisible and manifest only in its symptoms. The most highly developed consciousness is then the one that is closest to life, the one that is most symptomatic of the force of will to power. According to Nietzsche, in its innocence, it is the child that is in closest contact with the body and so is the most highly developed consciousness and the most intense form of will to power. This is revealed in the child's self-affirmation, such that the strongest and most dangerous instincts exist in the greatest possible quantity, yet in harmony, in full co-ordination (Stambaugh, 1972, pp. 80–1). The child seems to be commensurate with the Classical type, the so-called life-artist who lives the eternal return, who has acquired knowledge of life because 'he' has given up what is said to be knowledge, over and over again, in order to experiment anew with life's inexhaustible forms (Nietzsche, 1974, p. 343; 1968b, §500). In other words, like Boltzmann's particles, all possible configurations of life may well be realized, thus the Classical type must be prepared to meet any of these possible situations. The life-artist must be strong and wise enough experimentally to put the most terrible instincts to use or he will perish from it. This is the meaning, for Nietzsche, of being faithful to life and of being able to think the eternal return of the same.

Creative Evolution[3]

Although it is not immediately obvious, the philosophy of life of Henri Bergson arose precisely as a reaction to the conception of life formulated in the concept of eternal return. It has not gone unnoticed among physicists that 'Bergson saw a great opposition between "matter" and "life", and a related one between intellect and intuition' (Bricmont, 1996, p. 24).[4] To this end, Bergson distinguished between measured time, time as science conceptualizes it, and *duration*, which exists for *us*. In other words, unlike Nietzsche's eternal return, whose probability is guaranteed by the deterministic framework of classical physics, for Bergson 'duration is a deeply personal experience that affirms individuality and ensures the possibility of freedom' (Tasić, 2001, p. 37). The book *Creative Evolution* is one of Bergson's most difficult and notorious efforts, one that earned him intense criticism from largely conservative forces in France (Bergson, 1983). There, he proposes an original account of nature and of evolution that challenges the deterministic and positivistic approaches to science that dominated his era, but which also provides no support for factions seeking to justify the idea that there are final causes in nature, for it is a text that makes its own strong scientific claims and proposes its own original idea of creation. In that text Bergson argues that the classical, scientific view, derived from René Descartes's notion of matter as extended substance and Isaac Newton's laws of motion, is useful insofar as it makes possible the objective repetition of identical material parts and, therefore, the prediction of the motions of bodies, but that it is not an adequate model for the evolution of life. For matter, in the classical view, change is the displacement of parts that do not themselves change. As Descartes argues, they may be split into smaller and smaller parts, but in accordance with Newton's laws of motion, once any part has left its position, it can always return. In principle, any state of the group of material parts may be repeated as often as desired. The group then has no history; it is therefore said to be time-reversible, and, as Bergson points out, in this structure, nothing new is or can be created. What any group of material parts will be is already there in what it is, and what it is may well include all the points of the universe with which it is related (Bergson, 1983, p. 7; Depew and Weber, 1995, p. 25).

Moreover, for classical science, the tendency of matter is to constitute isolable systems that can be treated as closed mechanisms. However, as Bergson argues, in a startlingly original way, the isolation is never complete. Even a so-called isolated (closed) system generally remains subject to external influences, binding that system to another more extensive one and so on, until they reach the solar system, which is presumably the most objectively isolated and independent system aomng all. But even here (and this is perhaps the most precocious statement Bergson makes), there is no absolute isolation, meaning matter does not exist in a closed system. For our sun radiates heat and light beyond even the farthest planet, connecting our solar system by a tenuous thread to the rest of the universe which goes on infinitely. And along this thread, Bergson will argue, *something is transmitted to even the smallest particle*, something that does not conform to the universal laws of motion insofar as it is not repeatable, not atomistic, not isolated and not time-reversible. In short, it is not eternal return. This something is what he calls the duration immanent to the whole universe. This is, he maintains, how the universe endures as a whole, meaning this is how it *creates* forms and elaborates the absolutely new. (Bergson, 1983, pp. 7–11).

How such duration might occur is the subject of *Creative Evolution*. Indeed, for what became the science of non-equilibrium thermodynamics, Bergson's claims may well be standard. Non-equilibrium thermodynamics supports the idea that energy flows through structures and organizes them to be more complex than their surroundings. Organized and structured patterns appear out of seemingly random collisions of atoms. Non-equilibrium thermo-dynamics studies structures that increase in complexity and increase their capacity to do work insofar as they are *open* systems through which matter and energy flow. On the scale of living *bodies*, matter enters as food, drink, air, then it is transformed and then excreted. On the sub-atomic scale, life's basic process is to take the low-entropy, long-wavelength photons of visible and ultra-violet light from the sun and re-radiate them as shorter-wavelength infrared radiation. This is the conversion of light into living matter and heat; this is the tenuous thread along which heat and light are radiated from our own sun and from the multitude of suns in the universe releasing the low-entropy, long-wavelength photons of visible and ultraviolet light which are then re-radiated as shorter-wavelength infrared radiation: living matter, heat (Margulis and Sagan, 1997, pp. 28, 32, 37).

Strictly speaking, there is, in Bergson's formulation of a 'tenuous thread,' no notion of an original life force, no underlying will to power; for there is nothing at the beginning of evolution beyond the molecules of matter and heat, which have, however, physical and chemical forces of their own. And life, as it exists, arises from these molecules of matter and heat. The basic operation of life is to trap, store and convert starlight into energy through processes like photosynthesis whereby photons are incorporated, building up bodies and food. Photons (a quantum of electromagnetic radiation), there-fore, are the principle energy source for sex and eating (Margulis and Sagan, 1997, p. 16). Given this view of origins, it seems to make sense for Bergson to argue that

the resistance of [apparently] inert matter was the obstacle that had first to be overcome. Life seems to have succeeded . . . by making itself very small . . . bending to physical and chemical forces. . . . Of phenomena in the simplest forms of life, it is hard to say whether they are still physical and chemical or whether they are already vital. (Bergson, 1983, pp. 98–9)

Although the first animate forms were extremely simple, Bergson maintains that evolution does not follow a single line from these organisms but that it moves in bursts, breaking up the way a shell explodes into fragments; and in the evolutionary process, each fragment also bursts apart, and so on and so forth. This motion is an effect of two tendencies that, he argues, generate evolution: instinct and intelligence. As tendencies, they are not opposites and not contradictory; the presence of one does not signal the complete absence or negation of the other. Nor does the evolutionary process move along a continuous line from instinct to intelligence, so that they differ only in degree of complexity; intelligence is not conceived of as a higher degree or development of instinctual processes. Rather, they coexist and often intertwine insofar as they are defined, by Bergson, as differences in nature or kind. In other words, given instinct and intelligence, one is turned towards life, the processes Bergson calls duration, the thread of light that *creates* forms and elaborates them; and the other is turned towards matter, whose tendency, we have noted, is to be repeatable, to separate into homogeneous, independent units. Both stand out from a background of consciousness in general which is co-extensive with universal life; nevertheless, there is no continuity between them. Rather than differing in degree, instinct and intellect differ with respect to structure, function and orientation. Instinct grasps differences in kind, heterogeneities and what endures, whereas intelligence grasps differences of degree, homogeneities, binding like to like, and so only repeatable facts that are entirely adaptable to intellectual conceptions (Bergson, 1983, p. 186).

This is why instinct is not merely a diminished form of intelligence: it is not intelligence at all but has a completely different structure from that of intelligence, and this is what makes it possible for instinct to operate alongside intelligence. If we accept the argument that in its receptive and perceptive elements and in its viscera, every organism is a sum of contractions, retentions and protentions in virtue of its lived present, its cellular heredity and its actions in its environment, then pure duration can be understood as the temporalization of affective (receptive) states, the orientation of instinct. For human beings, it is 'the form which the succession of our conscious states assumes when our ego lets itself *live*, when it refrains from separating its present state from its former states,' thus allowing each state to be what it is, as when we listen to music and the notes, though qualitatively heterogeneous with respect to tone, nevertheless follow one another, constitute a duration, a tenuous thread, a temporalization, without ever losing their discreteness (Bergson, 1963, p. 67). Bergson argues that heterogeneous, affective states accompany all our perceptions, although our awareness of them may be overshadowed by external perceptions, which are always oriented towards our interests and actions in the world. That is, perceptions are external relations to other bodies, objects or phenomena, but there is one, the 'perception' of one's own body, that is not actually a perception insofar as it is not an external relation but is given from 'within'. The non-perception of one's own body alerts us to the existence of a relation that is not external, not extended as matter. It alerts us to affections that are situated precisely at the interval between the multiplicity of perceptual excitations received from without and the movements about to be executed in response to those perceptions.

In lower organisms, it is difficult to distinguish the perception that is oriented by action and is an external relation, from affective, temporal life, this tenuous thread between the organism and the world, because survival requires that the interval between perception and action is infinitesimal. Active perception, receptive feeling and active response must be simultaneous. In higher animals, perception, affective sensibility and action are, however, distinguishable. Philosophers like Merleau-Ponty, who prefer not to differentiate them, have tended to equate sensation with physiology and perception with psychology, and to focus almost entirely on auditory or visual perceptions. From this point of view, the distinction between sensory discrimination and perceptual discrimination is theoretical but not factual; it is thought to be impossible to dissociate the two elements because bare sensation is presumed not to exist but rather always to be included in the complex of perception. This follows from the Gestaltist idea that a stimulus associated with a context acquires a meaning and that an adequate behavioural response to a stimulus carries a meaning that may modify perception. Moreover, since 'hearing and sight are the main channels of communication; stimuli reaching the mind via these gates are therefore the most prone to bear a context-related message' (Cabanac, 1995, pp. 400–3). However, as some contemporary physiologists maintain, other sensory inputs exist in addition to the five senses, such that any of the various *afferent neuron pathways* discovered by physiologists is potentially a source of sensation (Cabanac, 1995, p. 404). Thus, the affective, sensible opening to the outside world as well as the mechanisms for transporting information from the outside world, to the body's sensitive receptors, are well defined. Additionally, afferent neurons convey a 'vast amount of information about the physiological state of the *milieu interieur*' (Cabanac, 1995, p. 404). Such internal nervous sensors, meagre as they are, sensing physical and chemical variations in the body, nevertheless contribute to the argument for the existence of sensations independently of perceptions. Insofar as most of these afferent pathways are limited to a bundle of only a few neurons, the contrast between this tenuous thread and the large avenues of the classical senses (especially sight and hearing) may explain how the latter have dominated not only psychology, but also philosophy (Cabanac, 1995, p. 404).

Perceptions, Bergson argues, are largely chosen on the basis of the organism's interests, thus they are decidedly narrow in their focus. Yet because the sensible affect, that is, the influence of the world on our bodies, cannot be chosen, it links us, sensibly, to the rest of the world on a far-reaching scale. In order to choose an appropriate response to each perceptual situation, higher organisms maintain a zone of indetermination that allows for an interval between each perception and their response to it. Such an interval, a zone of indetermination, makes possible the emergence of receptive, felt, sensible, affective images from the ontological unconscious, images that constitute what Bergson calls creative memory (as opposed to habitual or learned memory which remains the same in every similar situation). The movements of such organisms, following perception, are an effect of the tendency towards intelligence that is associated with the movement of the organism in the direction of action and matter. It is the tendency to act in the world on the basis of one's interests. But duration and action, like duration and perception, are differences in nature or kind and not merely differences of degree. This is because the 'moments' of heterogeneous, temporal duration are differentiated qualitatively. Qualitative differentiations, we have noted, are heard in music as differentiations of tone but also of modulation, loudness or softness; or beyond sound, they are felt. Such sensitivities, 'the capacity of an afferent neuron to detect a physical or chemical change occurring at its endings and to transmit this information to the nervous centers', have been described by physiologists as 'sensation' (Cabanac, 1995, p. 404). And while cautious physiologists recognize that 'the brain possesses properties that can no more be explained by its neuronal constituents than life can be explained by the atomic or molecular properties of the constituents of the living cell' and that what is called consciousness is one such property, nevertheless, insofar as consciousness may be defined as the border between those neuronal constitutents and the world, then perhaps 'sensation can be defined as the emergence of sensitivity into consciousness' (Cabanac, 1995, p. 404).

Thus, what for Bergson are affective sensitivities may now arise in the form of what we may call sensitive images, sensations emerging into a present perception, thereby *affecting one's self* and filling perception with their qualitative colouring – whether this is the shock of a painful fall or the pleasure of the sun's warmth against the skin. As we have argued, it appears that afferent neurons convey a vast amount of information concerning the outside world and the physiological state of the *milieu interieur*. And this transmission of qualitatively heterogeneous information is to be differentiated from the movements of material entities through space, movements that are continuous and homogeneous, movements that are intellectualized quantitatively in terms that can be measured and compared. Repetition, along with habitual perceptions and actions, dominate intelligence because they order the world in terms of causality, contiguity and identity. But affective sensibility, arising as the sensitive and felt component alongside perception, may be said to constitute a unique type of memory. This so-called ontological memory is constituted in relation to the sensation, the affective image, the *body's own influence on itself* resulting in the pleasure and pain that often arises with perception but does not merge with perception insofar as it is receptive rather than active and narrowly focused. These qualitative affects, these sensitivities, tend to become conscious only in relation to a new present. They emerge into perception precisely in the interval between perception and action. In the interval the organism pauses; in this pause, this slow-down, it ceases to pursue its interested actions, thereby allowing affective sensitivities to enter into perception, to provide an absolutely new interpretation of the present perception. Perhaps, viewed in this way, we can see how, for Bergson, every affective image emerging into perception is a point of view on the whole of affective life. Just as in the universe, our sun radiates heat and light beyond even the farthest planet many light years away, connecting our solar system by a tenuous thread to the rest of the universe, so along this thread, *something is transmitted to even the smallest particle*. By this means, light from the past time of the universe is converted into living matter and heat in our own bodies. So we are, all of us, constructed out of the memories of the universe itself. As such, when we are not acting merely out of habit, our perceptual life and the choices we make concerning when and how to act come from interpretations informed by such virtual, memory images when they are called forth by perceptual consciousness in an interval of attentive reflection (Olkowski, 1999, ch. 4; Bergson, 1988, p. 102).

Just as duration and action constitute differences in kind – although they are often found together in our conscious states and our actions – so too will instinct and intelligence. By instinct, Bergson means simply a tendency to connect with whatever an organism finds at hand using 'inborn' organized instruments, even if these instruments have to be constructed. For example, the inborn capacity of a baby to suck the breast is an instance of instinct because the mouth, a definite object, seeks another definite object, yet the two function as a single process. Instinct functions directly, constituting immediate connections, which are singularities (Bergson, 1983, p. 140). The most obvious instinctive connections that come to mind exist between animals and their world. If an amoeba is touched in any part by a foreign body, every part of the amoeba immediately retracts. 'Perception and movement being here blended in a single property – contractility' (Bergson, 1988, p. 55). What this implies, however, is that this tendency is just as well manifested in complex organisms, including humans, as when the eye is pulled by the motion of a thigh moving under clothing or the arm flings out to cushion a fall. The eye and the body's movement, the ground and the arm's trajectory are singularities, one thing not two. Instinct acts without the interposition of any distance, thus it acts 'sympathetically', but only as a singular connection in which there is no distinction between the perception, the emerging sensation and the action. The other tendency in evolution is intelligence, which extends itself in the direction of matter so as to induce matter to act on matter. It operates by extending, thus breaking the sympathetic singularity of the instinct into parts that are structurally independent of one another. By separating the elements of instinct into different parts, intelligence makes these parts into objects or tools that can function effectively for a wide variety of uses and actions. Intelligence often transfers functions from one object or tool to another, relating an object to another object, a part to a part, by means of reasoning processes that connect like to like, cause to effect and attribute to subject (Bergson, 1983, p. 147). Thus, fascinated by objects and action, intelligence externalizes itself in space and quickly constitutes the world in terms of immobile and independent objects.

The Bergsonian conception of tendencies that do not differ merely by degree but are really different in nature denies the prevalent view that takes instinct and intelligence to be merely successive degrees of the same development and opens up the possibility that they may co-exist in one act insofar as they are of different natures, thus their functioning and orientation in any realm are not the same. Other animal and plant characteristics, such as sex and gender, may turn out to be structured similarly. That is, sexes and genders, in accordance with a theory of sexual difference, would be able to be differentiated as differences in kind and not as differences in degree. Thus, there would be no original 'human nature', out of which 'male' and 'female' each represent degrees on a continuum, moving perhaps in opposite directions, to opposing extremes, along a continuum of homogeneous steps. Rather, 'female' and 'male' might be understood as truly heterogeneous, a relation of differences in quality. Bergson insists that the double form consciousness enacts arises because the 'real', the world, has this double form, so there is always a material basis for instinct and intelligence; they are structured by and in relation to the natural and social environment, but also, as we have argued, in relation to the matter and energy of the universe. In spite of Bergson's considerable originality, philosophers who followed him seem to have rejected Bergson's view of life in favour of a Nietzschean conception of eternal return. The implications of this have been far reaching and so we will now turn to an examination of the effects of this move.

Poststructuralist Scepticism

Poststructuralist/postmodernist philosophy initially took its cues from the Nietzschean critique of consciousness and the demand for faithfulness to life. This was read as a critique of Kantian and Hegelian signification systems in which one determines something by setting up a system or theory, a program or project, to then synthesize it into a higher good (Kant) or a final good (Hegel) (Lyotard, 1984, p. 37). For Jean-François Lyotard, it is precisely a rejection of the Kantian and Hegelian unifying signification systems that has splintered and fragmented the former so-called totality of life into social, cultural and linguistic units that bear little relation to one another. This dispersion and fragmentation of stabilizing factors leads to the general feeling that the 'progressive' movement towards an increase in knowledge and an expansion of democratic or socialist principles has veered off course. In the face of this perceived failure of modernism, new philosophies of life have emerged which do not follow the Bergsonian model. Our task, according to Lyotard, is to invent concepts that are unpresentable, categories free of good forms and judgements lacking in taste. Postmodernism, as a philosophy of life, is the continual state of what is being born, the perpetuity of what can never be presented to sensibility but can only be conceived (Lyotard, 1984, pp. 79–81). The only alternative Lyotard can envision would necessitate a return to the unity of thought and presentation as articulated by Kant and Hegel, which would return thought to absolutes.

Martin Heidegger can be said to have already articulated this problem in *Being and Time* as well as throughout his oeuvre. The meaning of the word being was to have been found in the wilful representing of an object as standing opposed to man within the transcendental horizon, but, for Heidegger, it cannot be found there (Heidegger, 1966, p. 74). In his account of language, Heidegger attributes this conception to the dominance of scientific rationality in the form of calculative thinking. Decrying reference, representation and expression, Heidegger claims that words signify by showing 'something as abiding into the range of its expressibility' so that in thinking, we may move freely in the realm of words and not be pinned down to categorical signification (1966, pp. 69, 71, 72). For this reason, Heidegger states that in the region of the word 'everything is in the best order only if it has been no one's doing' and human beings, insofar as they think meditatively, are appropriated to that-which-regions and released into the openness of that-which-regions (1966, p. 71). Elsewhere, Heidegger argues that this Nietzschean move is accomplished in the realm of the beautiful when we let what is beautiful come before us in its own stature and worth and freely grant it its way to be (Heidegger, 1979, p. 109). Following Nietzsche, Heidegger calls this an interest of the highest kind, 'the thrill of being in our world now, of getting rid of our anxiety in the face of things foreign' (1979, p. 112). When the beautiful is disclosed in this way, it transports us beyond ourselves and corresponds to what we take ourselves to be and what we demand of ourselves (Heidegger, 1979, pp. 112–3). The beautiful is no longer an object standing opposed to a subject, but an aesthetic state, an event that releases us into life, into the openness of that-which-regions, the event of appropriation (*Ereignis*), that realm through which man and Being reach one another and achieve their active nature (Heidegger, 1969, p. 37). Here language shows something as abiding into the range of its expressibility, but not as an actually existing object, a subjective expression or a categorical signification. The coming together of man and Being in appropriation is an event of language, one with the voice of conscience of *Being and Time*, the voice that calls and constitutes the Being of *Da* as disclosure, but says absolutely nothing about which one could actually speak (Agamben, 1991, p. 58, citing Heidegger, 1962, §54–62). As Georgio Agamben points out, the event of appropriation is first revealed to Dasein when the 'acoustics of the soul' (*Stimmung*), the mood known as anxiety, reveals that the place of language is a non-place, a negative experience revealing that between language and voice there is no link, not even a negation (Agamben, 1991, pp. 56–7). It is precisely this which Agamben opposes in so-called philosophies of life whose ontology he, along with other contemporary philosophers, would alter, in order to put life back into philosophy.

The Ethics of Speech and Action

Agamben points out that in the *Politics*, Aristotle had already collapsed the distinction between the unpresentable and unspeakable and what Agamben calls experience, where it is an aspect of bringing the household into the *polis* so that the *polis* comes to be located within the sphere of what formerly belonged to the necessity of the *private* life (Agamben, 1978, p. 6, citing Aristotle, 1962, pp. 28–9). Speech, according to Aristotle, indicates what is useful and harmful, right and wrong, and only humans, of all animals, have the perception of good and evil, right and wrong, just and unjust. 'And it is the sharing of a common view in these matters that makes a household (*oikia*) or a city (*polis*)' (Agamben, 1978, p. 7, quoting Aristotle, 1962, pp. 28–9). In other words, the division between the private and the public is something that has already been overcome. This division can be expressed as the separation between human language and the transcendental mathematics of modernism, between the historical and the structural, the human and the linguistic divine. This is what is metaphysical in Heidegger's conception of life. Like the Kantian and Hegelian systems that take nature to be a totality, Heidegger posits

> a pure intention to signify without any concrete advent of signification;
> a pure meaning that says nothing. . . . Having reached the limit, in its
> anxiety, of the experience of its being thrown, without a voice in the place
> of language, *Dasein* finds another Voice, even if this is a Voice that calls only
> in the mode of silence. (Agamben, 1991, p. 59)

Agamben's solution to this gap between the transcendental and what he refers to as experience, is the notion of infancy, a concept that follows from Arendt's positing of natality. Due to infancy, human beings do not speak from the start but must break into language, transforming pure language, the semiotic, into discourse, the semantic and thereby both being constituted as a subject in language and radically transforming the system of signs (Agamben, 1991, p. 55). The semiotic, rather than a pure transcendental limit, is the pre-babble language of nature, the semiotic sea in which humans swim in order to speak and into which their discourse, once uttered, falls back. This is, says Agamben, the very definition of human, the passage from pure language to discourse (1991, pp. 56–7).

This may be why, in *The Logic of Sense*, Gilles Deleuze asserts that linguistics operates like a system in equilibrium, a simple machine like an incline or a pulley, an object of modernist science whose variations arise only in expression (Deleuze, 1969). By contrast, he claims, writers of literature know that language can be a system in perpetual imbalance, a system affected by the forces of life, so that literature is on a par with or superior to linguistics, and only literature and not linguistics is adequate to the needs of philosophers (Lecercle, 2002, pp. 65, 78–9).[5] Scientific rationality in the linguistic proposition rests first on the relation of designation or reference, second on the expressivity of an inner subjectivity in the face of the outer world, and third on signification, the act of placing a particular under a category (Deleuze, 1969, pp. 22–4). Deleuze's logic of sense introduces a fourth dimension into the proposition, the pure sense-event, the verb that insists or subsists in the proposition and is an attribute of a thing or state of affairs. As such, the verb is a logical attribute and not a physical state of affairs; it is a quality or a relation, meaning not a being but a process, a living, changing process (Deleuze, 1969, pp. 23–4). Clearly, Deleuze is attempting to establish a new model of scientific rationality, one that accounts for Nietzsche's notion of the probability of eternal return and Agamben's notion of infancy. And Deleuze, most famously, attempts to bring Bergson into this model as well. His view of duration is that it is blocs of space time, divided into sets or closed systems and the movement of translation between these systems (Deleuze, 1986, pp. 10–11).[6] But the problem, for Bergson, a problem that Deleuze evades, is that modern science, which is the science of matter, follows from the tendencies of intellect and not those of instinct.

Deleuze's conception of life eventually takes Deleuze, along with Félix Guattari, back into the realm of the political, where they generate the idea of the state as an abstract unity. This idea might still be considered to be an idea of reason insofar as it is a political idea that functions according to the rules of a mathematical schema. It is not, however, a transcendent law, not an Idea that dominates and sub-ordinates an otherwise fragmented field from outside that field. Rather, to preserve its life-like qualities, the state is and must be organized in accordance with an immanent law, a law which exercises its functions within a field of forces whose flows it co-ordinates (Deleuze and Guattari, 1987). The capitalist state operates inside a field of decoded flows of money, commodities and private property. Expressed in terms of the mathematics of probabilities, the immanent law produces a vector field that emerges out of a complete set of functions. A vector field is defined, by Deleuze, as the complete determination of a problem given in terms of the existence, number and distribution of points that are its condition. This corresponds to the more or less standard mathematical definition for which a vector field is defined as associating a vector to every point in the field space. Vector fields are used in physics to model observations such as the movement of a fluid, which includes a direction for each point of the observed space. The structures offered by differential relations and vector fields make it possible for Deleuze to create a structure based on the new science of life without slipping into the formation of another totalizing system.

Yet a problem that looms here is that capitalism is the only social machine that is constructed on the basis of decoded flows of life. Such codes correspond to Nietzsche's falsifications: causality, reason, logic, the ego and morality. We find capital 'substituting for those codes an axiomatic of abstract quantities in the form of money' (Deleuze and Guattari, 1987, p. 139). On this account, capitalism liberates the flows of desire, when desire is understood to be the immanent binary-linear sphere of differentiations, in other words, the trajectory of differential relations that are deterministically probabalistic. This takes place under social conditions that define the limit even as liberated desire is posited to be one with unlimited qualitative becoming. So we find that it is the manner in which desire is limited, the manner in which the unlimited becoming is associated, conjoined and distributed that determines whether it forms human subjects, works of art or social institutions (Deleuze, 1969, pp. 307–9).[7] In this view, the capitalist machine establishes itself by bringing distribution expressed as conjunction to the fore in the social machine distributing desire in a pattern of conjunction (Foucault, 1973, p. 16). If nature is distributive, every conjunction may be transformed by the power of nature, which is the power to break apart what has been connected, transforming every 'and . . . and . . . and' (of conjunction) into the 'or . . . or . . . or' of disjunctive distribution. This is because conjunction can be logically and ontologically reformulated, immanently, as the power of things to exist one by one without any possibility of them being gathered together in a unity, a whole (Deleuze and Guattari, 1987, p. 223).[8] Conjunction is the if . . . then that is so easily torn apart, separated into distinct events, each one a limit. In economic theory, the differential relation and differential calculus make it possible to characterize change and rates of change. The differential equation can also be utilized to express 'the fundamental capitalist phenomenon of the transformation of the surplus value of code into a surplus value of flux' (Deleuze and Guattari, 1987, p. 228). The over-coded flows of the despotic state have been deterritorialized by means of nothing more than the formal power of conjunction/disjunction to separate what has been connected. What is left is nothing other than pure form. In other words, these are formal changes and there is nothing concrete in them, as whatever is concrete is contingent, an effect of formal transformations.

Perhaps capitalism could only have arisen when flows of commercial capital and financial capital were recognized to be flows among the multitude of flows and industrial capital, the direct appropriation of production by capital, the 'tighter and tighter control over production' had overtaken all other flows (Devlin, 1994, p. 52).[9] But what is the direct appropriation of production by capital except the pure process of production? This is not the domain of freedom from despotic regimes, but the domain of difference.

> We are in the domain of . . . the differential relation as a conjunction that defines the immanent social field particular to capitalism . . . the differential relation Dy/Dx where Dy is derived from labor power and constitutes the fluctuation of variable capital, and where Dx derives from capital itself and constitutes the fluctuation of constant capital. (Deleuze and Guattari, 1987, pp. 227–8)

Thus, from the conjunction of decoded flows arises the distribution '$x + dx$' (Deleuze and Guattari, 1987, p. 246).[10] From the surplus-value of the original investment of 100 pounds is derived the surplus-value of 10 pounds. This means that the so-called limit defining differential relations is reproduced and extended. In other words, everything, every single thing, animal, vegetable, mineral, industrial, conceptual, everything is included in the field of nature as processes of production. When production as a process overtakes idealistic categories, when production is the immanent principle of desire, then nature is nothing but processes of production and philosophy describes life as organized by this understanding of nature. In other words, for Deleuze and Guattari, nature is a vector field and the rules of nature, connection, conjunction, disjunction are ontological. This makes capitalism one of the deterministically probable outcomes of the organization of nature. So perhaps it is not surprising that Deleuze turns to Stoicism in order to bear the effects of nature, but other contemporary philosophies propose alternative views of nature and so alternative solutions.

Life and the Human Condition

According to Hannah Arendt, Marx understood the idea of growing wealth to be a natural process following its own laws, a process whose functioning cannot be checked (Arendt, 1998, p. 111). Marx posits labour as a pure process of production, producing both itself and surplus labour. Thus, the revaluation of all values arises from the life process and glorification of the life process eliminates the idea that making, speech and action exist and are, in any manner, crucial to nature's activity (Arendt, 1998, p. 117). This, for Arendt, is what makes philosophies of life which take their cue from Nietzsche and Marx problematic. Nature is sublimely indifferent to human beings and to language. The growth of wealth for society as a whole appears as a natural process that follows its own laws and can, in principle, go on infinitely. And yet, these natural processes can still be challenged by the finitude of individuals (Arendt, 1998, p. 116). But ours is not an era of freedom. Liberated by man-made technologies from the pain and effort of physical labour, human beings are now free to produce and consume the entire world. Things that were once made by humans and durable, lasting beyond an individual life, are being used up, consumed, at a faster and faster rate and nothing is safe from human consumption (Arendt, 1998, p. 133). Lacking any distinction between the private realm of necessity and the public realm of the *vita activa*, of persuasion through speech, all private activities are now on public display, resulting in the near domination of mass culture (Arendt, 1998, p. 134). What is needed is the ability to make things and perform deeds that are independent of humans, things that stabilize human life by enduring.

Arendt finds this in a life of speech and action, without which life ceases to be human life. We have seen Agamben's claim that infancy is the living bridge between the transcendental and the human. Arendt, some years before this, went further. 'With word and deed we insert ourselves into the human world and this insertion is like a second birth' (Arendt, 1998, p. 176 [not included]). This is the meaning of natality, an insertion that does not arise out of the necessity of labour or the utility of work. To act is to begin, to set something in motion, something that can be completely unexpected and improbable, yet something humanly disclosed in words, such that 'in acting and speaking, men show who they are, reveal actively their unique personal identities, thus make their appearance in the human world' (Arendt, 1998, pp. 177–9). What makes action unique is the boundlessness of its consequences, that is, that every consequence is a process that will bring about new and unknown processes. Thus it is unpredictable: processes are started whose outcomes are unpredictable, making uncertainty decisive in human affairs (Arendt, 1998, pp. 190–1, 232). What philosophies of life do not openly acknowledge is that nature as a process of production is a human invention. By experimenting rather than merely observing, humans have opened up elemental processes, essentially '"making" nature ... creating "natural" processes which without men would never exist and which earthly nature by herself seems incapable of accomplishing' (Arendt, 1998, p. 231). Thus, if nature is the model for philosophies of life, but natural processes are the effect of human intervention, then it seems that it is the human ability to speak and act, to start 'new unprecedented processes whose outcome remains uncertain and unpredictable' that is the real source of nature understood as process (Arendt, 1998, pp. 231–2). Because we humans are capable of acting, of starting processes, we can conceive of nature as a process as well.

Given this situation, the question becomes: how can human life be rescued from itself, from the endless necessity of the life process to which it has condemned itself? Some philosophers suggest non-action, allowing the so-called life processes to produce and define humanity.[11] For Arendt, speech and action are the keys, but what is also needed is the realization that without others, without other human beings to witness and affirm our speech and action, we are nothing but labourers and consumers. Specifically, Arendt calls for differentiating labour and necessity from making and duration, speech and action. Speech about action is the natality capable of producing meaningful stories, narrations that reveal the uniqueness and distinctness of human actors to other human beings. But also, insofar as once actions are begun, they are unpredictable, irreversible and in principle, immortal, human beings must exercise their capacity to forgive. Forgiveness undoes deeds by releasing the doer from the unknowable consequences of her deeds and so from nature's unforgiving processes. Given the contradiction and uncertainty of human nature, humans must allow themselves to be bound to the fulfillment of promises in the public realm. Forgiveness and promises are neither solitary activities nor mere effects of nature's life processes. They depend entirely on the presence of others, for no one can either forgive herself or make a promise in solitude (Arendt, 1998, pp. 236–7). In the end, this is the manner in which the unpredictability of both nature and other humans can be dispelled. The force that brings and keeps people together is not the force of nature, but the force of forgiveness and promises in the presence of other human beings, the ability to undo what has been done and to rein in the processes we have set in motion. It is this *natality*, this birth of action and the promise of the birth of new human beings, which, as Arendt proposes, might ultimately save the world (Arendt, 1998, p. 247).

In the end, it seems that Bergson's philosophy of life at least left open the possibility of greater harmony between the natural and the human sciences. Bergson does seem to have made an impact on some philosophers and natural scientists, who recognize that the denial of lived experience and common sense on the part of physics significantly increased the rift between science and philosophy. To mend this rift, perhaps we can take our cue from philosopher Isabelle Stengers and chemist Ilya Prigogine who propose a structure that takes its orientation from the point of view of an observer 'who measures co-ordinates and momenta and studies their change in time', and so has been led to conceptualize unstable dynamic systems, intrinsic randomness and irreversibility, dissipative structures and therefore a time-oriented observer (Stengers and Prigogine, 1984, p. 300). The extent to which this attempt is successful is still open to debate, but minimally, it raises again the question brought forth originally by Arendt, the question of what we are to do about what she calls earth alienation, the view of terrestrial life as governed by cosmic forces far removed from earthly affairs. If the development of modern science has been understood to shift away from concrete experience towards abstraction, this is, Stengers and Prigogine believe, only a consequence of the limitations of the classical scientific view, its inability to give a coherent account of the relationship between humans and nature. If many important results were repressed or set aside because they failed to conform to the classical model, this may have been to the detriment of humanity (Stengers and Prigogine, 1984, pp. 19–22). So, perhaps we may conclude with the idea that in order to free themselves from traditional modes of comprehending nature, science and philosophies of life must confront the limits of their own methods. Perhaps one can look to Bergson for original and 'pioneering step[s] towards the understanding of the pluralism involved in physical laws' (Stengers and Prigogine, 1984, p. 303). Then science can also be characterized by problems that arise as the consequence of 'deliberate and lucid questions asked by scientists who know that the questions had both scientific and philosophical aspects', in other words, change may occur as a result of both the 'internal logic of science' and 'the cultural and social context of our time' (Stengers and Prigogine, 1984, p. 309).

12 Philosophies of Science

Andrew Aitken

To speak of philosophy of science within the discipline of continental philosophy almost immediately brings us to the central concern of certain interdisciplinary disputes, both conceptual and historical. It brings us to the beginnings of any notion of continental philosophy, as well as that of its parallel practice in the analytic tradition. Many presumptions lie behind any easy categorization in this history. At one extreme, we could follow Ernst Cassirer in avowing that any modern philosophy entails an implicit philosophy of science (Cassirer, 1953). Gary Gutting is perhaps the first in recent times to attempt to objectively map such a history in his 2005 edition of essays, *Continental Philosophy Of Science*, devoted to clear canonical figures in the field, while Joseph J. Kockelmans and Theodore J. Kisiel had in 1970 provided an important collection of essays and translations in *Phenomenology and the Natural Sciences*.

Gutting sets out three post-Kantian attitudes to scientific knowledge within what can be called continental philosophy of science. First, there is the positivist attitude which regards scientific knowledge as representative of any kind of meaningful human knowledge whatsoever. Second, there is the Kantian critical attitude, which sees scientific knowledge as first-order knowledge, while philosophy has its own domain of investigation into the conditions of the possibility of such scientific knowledge. There then remains, third, the ontological, metaphysical attitude claiming a more profound access to the truth of a different nature entirely from the parameters set by scientific enquiry. As Gutting suggests, analytic philosophy has unsurprisingly shown sympathy for the positivist approach, allying itself in different measures to the work of Pierre Duhem, Henri Poincaré and, in the case of Mary Tiles, Gaston Bachelard.

What much codification has tended to overemphasize is the degree to which analytic philosophy is allied to mathematics and science, and the extent to which continental philosophy is not. This is largely due to analytic philosophy's growth as a sub-discipline out of the privileging of mathematical logic in philosophy developed by Rudolf Carnap after Bertrand Russell and A. N. Whitehead's *Principia Mathematica* (Whitehead and Russell, 1962), while Henri Bergson and Martin Heidegger had independently come into open conflict with received scientific wisdom or, one could say, technocracy. Another key to the different philosophies of science may lie in the philosophical status of history within them, as evidenced by the character of Foucault's philosophical development and work, with history as his methodological principle (Foucault, 2002; Gutting, 1989). Such a methodology takes its cue from the programmatic work of Jean Cavaillès in *On the Logic and Theory of Science*, presented for an English-speaking public for the first time by Kockelmans and Kisiel (1970). Cavaillès here calls for an abandonment of a philosophy of the subject and a turn instead to a philosophy of the concept. But, critically, this is guided by his dissatisfaction with his contemporaries' methodological impoverishment in denying formal thought its radically innovative and necessary nature.

Continental philosophy is allied to science and mathematics not only in many overlooked philosophers of the tradition, from Oskar Becker to Cavaillès, but equally in the prominent cases of Bergson and Heidegger. What much recent scholarship has been at pains to illustrate is the degree to which these philosophers, sometimes seen to be rejecting science in favour of mysticism, were actually seeking a deeper conceptual engagement with science at a revolutionary level. This was something that the many mathematically trained philosophers in the discipline were well equipped to do and something that, to Russell's chagrin, Whitehead turned himself to in *Process and Reality* (1985). The prevailing current instead appears to be that of a systematic use of history as opposed to mathematical logic, which becomes of conceptual rather than foundational import. Indeed, Nietzsche, who has commonly been seen as a canonical philosopher of continental philosophy before the fact, remains conceptually intertwined with the intellectual history of Darwinism for instance, while the epistemological consequences of his thought for a philosophy of science have been explored by Babette Babich among others (Babich and Cohen, 1999). Certainly the area of continental philosophy of science is not just of massive proportions; it is also contentious and intellectually rich, where not only the positivist proponents, but also many among the critical and metaphysical strands of the subject, are equipped with the training of a scientist, those of primary import being Bachelard, Bergson and Edmund Husserl.

The importance of history as the lens through which to penetrate a particularly continental philosophy of science is demonstrated equally by the neglected philosophers of the German tradition in continental philosophy. As much as Léon Brunschvicg, Bachelard, Émile Boutroux, Cavaillès, Georges Canguilhem, Gilbert Simondon and Jules Lachelier remained neglected as exponents of what we might call an 'engaged' continental philosophy of science in France (rather than the metaphysical dismissal of the method of science as a means to enquire after material veracity), so lesser-known

German figures were equally 'engaged' in their preoccupation with a historical method of philosophy, many taking inspiration from the work of Friedrich Albert Lange. As they saw it, history provided them with the possibility of remedying some of the aporias of Kant's still necessary schema. They found additional sources in texts of specialist scientific enquiry such as Hermann Cohen's *The Principle of the Infinitesimal Method and its History* (Cohen, 1928).

The problematics of continental philosophy of science were framed from an engagement with the philosophy of Kant and the diverging schools of interpretation that emerged. Following Kant's philosophical lead, they turned to the degree to which his philosophy relied upon Euclidean geometry and absolute time. The Marburg school established a possibility for Kantian philosophy's independence from these strictures by rejecting Kant's distinction of epistemic form and matter as an abstraction from the concrete reality of the objects of knowledge that necessarily contained both. The Marburg school therefore developed along similar lines to the French neo-Kantians, due to their conception that empirical objects were constituted within the duration of the history of science as scientists drew closer to formulating the necessary structures for comprehending the nature of the world. History of science became the philosophical means of understanding this science.

The Marburg school can be seen to be at heart of philosophy of science, just like its French parallel. Cohen had sought to show mathematics to be central in avoiding the essentialism of 'being' or 'substance' that was damaging to any conception of experience. Cohen found in mathematics the necessary balance between materialism and a kind of absolute idealism. Plato's mathematical idealism had the advantage of being naturally wary of the easy intuition of the senses. Calculus became the model for a non-essentializing process to determine certain instants of experience with reference to their context. Each fact, object, or moment of experience, can be defined in a relation between the particular, or integral, and its horizon of possibility, or differential. It is only through such a method that the laws and rules governing any particular moment can be explained. The project aims, through a critique of knowledge, to set out the synthetic principles or foundations of knowledge upon which scientific validity depends. Cohen suggested that rather than being limited to mathematics, the principal process of the infinitesimal is central to all types of perception. Cassirer explains Cohen's thought in terms of reading natural science after understanding that thought and intuition are part of a functional relation (Cassirer, 1953). The mathematical and physical concept will remain elusive while a presentational correlate is sought in the given. As would also be the case for Bachelard, the concept is the expression of a pure relation. Upon this relation the unity of the manifold lies, much as with the materialist monist intentions of Gilbert Simondon. Cohen takes the concepts of calculus to transform Kant, who based his philosophy in Newton's positing of space and time as absolute. For all continental philosophers of science this is the primary point of departure and for many it necessitates a determined move away from a hylomorphically constructed philosophy. One could not but radically revise any Kantian philosophy, once these bases had been transformed, whether this involved a turn to history or materialism for its genetic force.

For Cohen this revision was very subtle, but most significant in its consequences. While space and time may rely upon transcendental rules, they are actually formally dependent upon the mode of knowledge that is responsible for their construction (Cohen, 1928). Cassirer reinforced this point by asserting the transcendental dialectic to be the real generator of the critical method (Cassirer, 1953). The cosmological antinomies prove most important to this reading, in rooting out the false notions of being that confuse any accurate rendering of experience. The infinitesimal was seen by Cassirer and Cohen as an 'instrument of thought' in order to apprehend true being, while being only a means of relation in itself. Calculus played the key role in dissolving substantial ontological conceptions, as scientific inspirations were for so many thinkers within the continental field. Noumena and phenomena could now be seen as ideal poles of a functional relation and objects could be seen in their natural state as becoming. The neo-Kantian schools of continental philosophy of science in both Germany and France moved to de-emphasize the *a priori* categories of understanding and the intuitions of time and space, and shifted their consideration of the necessary elements of the first *Critique* to the schematism and principles.

Once the systemic unity supplied by the veracity of Newton's immutable laws was removed, the philosophers of this tradition looked to mould a more malleable philosophy susceptible to advances in science. Henri Bergson stands out as one whose philosophy was contentious to many scientific and philosophical contemporaries but proved later to anticipate the theories of quantum physics, as attested to by Louis de Broglie among others (see Gunter, 1969). At the time it was perhaps only Herbert Dingle among physicists who attempted to make the special relativity theory of the time fit the philosophy of Bergson's he intuited to be correct (without much success, one might say, and certainly to the denigration of his colleagues; see Bergson, 1965, and Chang, 1993).

Rather than Hans Reichenbach's 'context of justification' (Reichenbach, 1938), the 'historical epistemologists' setting the trend for continental philosophy of science are guided by 'the context of discovery'. The historical moment of 1900, as Frédéric Worms has shown (Worms, 2004), is of great consequence in mapping the difference in style between any well-known analytic philosophy of science and the continental method. Significantly, as has become a commonplace assertion, it is not a matter of geography or even language. As pragmatism contested analytic paradigms, so it crossed methodologically with the continental style, in affirming the philosophical potential of technology in a largely instrumentalist epistemology that prioritizes practice over theory. Gilles Deleuze and Félix Guattari saw it as emblematic of the creation of concepts (Deleuze and Guattari, 1994). Meanwhile, phenomenology can be seen to have problems in common with its analytic counterpart, at the very least in its foundation and in its opposition to any hint of vitalism or *Lebensphilosophie*. Another incident occurring around 1900 has been typified by Jean Gayon as the eclipse of Darwinism, which he saw taking place in terms of internalism (Gayon, 1992). It was an internal crisis within Darwin's own thought in terms of natural selection.

Husserl was to follow the neo-Kantians in seeking to determine the necessary conditions of experience, but did not wish to base this upon an uncritical assumption of science's validity: like Bergson, he wished to call upon a more profound philosophical method of intuition. But within Husserl's work, both implicitly and explicitly, is a bold codification of the possibilities for science. However, this often requires a philosophical deepening of the kind that, one could argue, Bergson also suggested. For him, science was already secondary to lived experience, which provided the intuitive knowledge required for scientific application. Husserl's very first work was the *Philosophy of Arithmetic* (Husserl, 2003), where he proposed the science of arithmetic to be a formal abstraction from the everyday experience of sensory objects.

This formalism was starkly different from the scientific positivism of Bachelard (1985). Lived experience was very familiar to Bachelard as Husserl's ideas took hold among his contemporaries, but he steadfastly held to his philosophy of science, while using phenomenology fruitfully where he saw it to be most pertinent, namely in studying the imagination. Lived experience could for him only serve to corrupt scientific enquiry through human valourization. The world of science was that of a logicist epistemology, one that at all times struggled against personal reveries. The world of science was one of a collective mind, of discursive knowledge, that of imagination a solipsistic one. Clearly, for many later philosophers of science in the continental tradition such as Isabelle Stengers and Bruno Latour, this became a problematic epistemology. Stengers is enthusiastic to draw epistemological parallels with the pre-scientific world of myth and magic that Bachelard would not countenance.

However, Husserl's philosophy of science was not so simply dismissed as Bachelard might infer on occasion in his rebuttal of existentialist concerns. He called upon all philosophers to examine the foundations of the sciences, and cannot but be acknowledged as a major figure of this tradition. Arithmetic is built from high cognitive associations based upon perceptual acts. Husserl was quite evidently no mere materialist, as evinced by the entry of phenom-enological language into Bachelard's philosophy of science. Bachelard sought, as Cohen had, to keep the Kantian schematism and synthetic principles, while introducing the discoveries of wave and particle physics. In this, he attempted to explicate himself through the current ideas, speaking of a *noumenology*, as mathematics is not only the unseen means of science, but particle physics is its unseen material for study (Bachelard, 1951).

For Husserl, though, lived experience was always primary; phenomen-ology was the transcendental science, its aim to investigate the essence of the sciences. Husserl saw scientists as following the natural attitude, intellect or human habit. They saw science as a technical extension of man as *homo faber*. Bachelard, on the contrary, saw science as philosophy, as the pure removal from the world of everyday reverie. For Husserl, science was involved in a means–ends thinking which could not reveal the foundations of experi-ence that required philosophical consideration. But, for Bachelard, science had the best philosophical concepts, while philosophy remained populated mainly with classical notions underpinning its systems. Gilbert Simondon accentuated Bachelard's ideas here and, importantly, also answered many phenomenological objections (Simondon, 2005). He did this by extending Bachelard's notion of technological creation into its artistic and scientific consequences, with a monist intra-worldly philosophy of individuation, as Jacques Garelli has elaborated in his *Rythmes et Mondes* (1991).

Simondon's main philosophical influence was Bergson, though he seeks to use Bergsonian intuition more widely. Intuition takes us to the deepest interior of its object. Yet Simondon does not hold the clear distinction that Bergson made between intuition and intellect. Science for him is not a second order abstraction. He sees a dualism in Bergson between matter and spirit, the technological and the philosophical, that he cannot endorse (Simondon, 1995). Simondon follows the intuition of many whose approach to science can be called positivist – Bachelard, Cassirer, Cohen – in stating that relations are as important as being (rather than being secondary, as they were for Aristotle). Simondon followed Bergson in elaborating the creative movement of evolu-tion against the classical models of abstract representation. But for Simondon, intuition does not require its own domain of priority: there is no domain beyond science, as posited by Bergson and Husserl, because in physics and technology it is possible to use intuition in much the same way as Bachelard used the concept of a *noumenology*.

As quantum physics was emblematic for Bachelard, so crystallization was for Simondon. This process occurs in a metastable structure (which itself emerges at certain temperatures). A process of organizing matter is begun by an igniting factor, a germ or shock. Molecules then gather in geometrical order around this germ, forming a crystal, layer upon layer. This demonstrates the process of individuation. In his turn, however, Bergson did not consider the crystal to contain individuals, but to be an unorganized solid. Clearly this material model may have presented different philosophical possibilities if so analysed by him. But, for Bergson, matter as actual did not present the virtual and intensive possibilities of mind (Bergson, 1988). Simondon saw both processes existing within crystallization; although the crystal is actual, the spread and structure of it is also virtual. *Transduction* describes this virtual aspect. There is, therefore, a key ontological and methodological difference: with Bergson intuition is applied to life and the intellect to matter. His perspective on science is the consequence of an ontology that poses a realm both prior to and more profound than the mind's technical interaction with matter and this realm is that of life.

Husserl saw the lacunae that scientists could not operate *on* their own thinking, for the simple fact that they were clearly *within* it (Husserl, 1970). Consequently, the phenomenologist could complement scientific activity. For Husserl, following Leibniz, Bolzano and Lotze, logic could be the science of the sciences. Formal consistency must be established in order to proceed with scientific enquiry and logic focuses on this form. Mathematicians directed themselves towards objects within the remit of mathematical thought, but not upon judgements themselves. As such, this *a priori* logic concerns itself with ideal, rather than real meanings. At the base of any science, therefore, is an *a priori*, universal grammar formed out of judgements. For Husserl, the kind of abstractly conceived thesis that Bachelard sees in Mendeleev can indeed occur: for as long as the judgements are consistent in their set they can be confidently operated and there do not necessarily have to be corresponding intuitions. Each science contains its own objects and properties, and each science has its own meaning-intentions. Husserl offers mathematics and logic as examples of exact sciences in virtue of their nature as dealing with essences (Husserl, 1970). Among the inexact sciences, on the other hand, he counts the empirical sciences. Nonetheless, the empirical sciences still provide the grounds for phenomenology as they presuppose essential truths which form the *a priori* domain of a *regional* ontology. Here, one can see in Husserl the necessity of science for philosophy and vice versa. But the key difference between this and the interaction laid out by a positivist such as Bachelard, is that Bachelard actually wishes to use scientific concepts in philosophy, as he does not see a realm of epistemic truth inaccessible to science – such as the phenomenological life-world – from which scientific concepts are derived. Husserl saw, as did Bergson, science as abstracting from the qualitative features of experience to focus upon the quantitative domain.

Both Bergson and Husserl took significant inspiration from the mathematician Bernhard Riemann in their philosophies, as did Bachelard and Gilles Deleuze. Husserl saw non-Euclidian manifolds as arising out of the elaboration of the mathematical imagination upon the Euclidian manifold, originally conceived by a formalization of perceptual intuition. The manifold unites geometry and topology and is a central model for Deleuze's philosophy, for it enables an end to dialectics. The manifold provides the conception of a regional ontology, made up of an interlacing of local spaces. Each of these spaces is susceptible to mapping by a Cartesian, Euclidian map without necessitating a universal structure, except in the instance of a Euclidian, homogeneous space. Riemannian manifolds, for instance, are susceptible to metric definition between their points; algebra can then formalize such measurements and curved spaces can therefore be measured. Deleuze followed Albert Lautman in seeing Riemannian space as pure patchwork – it is amorphous, not homogeneous (Deleuze, 1994). The differential manifold defines Deleuze's topology, and makes global the non-Euclidian nature of the metric and its striation. Deleuze also moves into the fertile concepts of algebra in his account of *The Fold* (2006), concepts which, as Arkady Plotnitsky (2003) has noted, brings him close to Derrida. Perhaps not only with Derrida, but also with Michel Serres, the particular approach to science germane to continental philosophy is writ large. Derrida sees Leibniz's pioneering work on the algebraic system of calculus as in terms of writing the one possible form of the book (Derrida, 1974, pp. 6–26).

Indeed the Simondonian monist philosophy of creation and production, typified by his topology of *information*, suggests a typically continental dynamic interplay between the technologies of art and science. But Simondon proposes this on a specifically ontological level, an idea that Serres finds amenable (Serres, 1969). Indeed, Serres seeks to separate himself from the dogma of the two cultures of science and philosophy. The one is commonly seen as rigorous and technically perfected, the other imaginative and free roaming.

But perhaps more important than this bifurcation in continental philosophy of science is the one that lies in the formation of historical epistemology itself. Many have noted how this tradition was inspired by Husserl's concepts put forward in both his early work on mathematics and his final work *The Crisis of the European Sciences*, notably that of the historical *a priori*. Yet this tradition was largely formed in critique. Undoubtedly, Cavaillès's *On Logic and the Theory of Science* served almost as a manifesto for historical epistemology. This was articulated most clearly by Michel Foucault in his introduction to Georges Canguilhem's *The Normal and the Pathological* (Canguilhem, 1989) and published in a revised form in the *Revue de métaphysique et de morale*. It may also be said that the problematics put into play by this critique of transcendental, logicist approaches to science and the subsequent possible interpretations of the project of the philosophy of the concept, served to define the current Deleuzian trend. Certainly, this is demonstrated by Deleuze's account of Foucault's project in his monograph on him (Deleuze, 1988). Deleuze sees in Foucault's work a challenge to a certain empirical dogmatism in the relation between words and things. Foucault reveals the transcendental field governing both the formation of words, but also of the visible – only now it is language that plays the determining role upon the visible. This represents a mere modification of the Kantian problematic that Foucault escapes (according to Deleuze) through his concept of power and force relations.

Of course, Husserl puts forward a theory of scientific enquiry wherein the propositions holding scientific objects must be inter-subjective and invariant. But as this is in contradiction with subjective experience, formal systems must be constructed, systems which are in turn sedimented – their foundation is forgotten – as they become used in a purely technical way. The intentional acts which sedimented these systems are reawakened, however, through an archaeological method. In Husserl, there is only one domain of justification and evidence – consciousness: as such the basic property of science is that it surpasses its past and obliterates its grounds. He sees the *crisis* in the sciences as resolvable only through a reversal of the process of sedimentation to reveal the genuine grounds of science, in an archaeology of the sciences. Husserl sees the need for a historical epistemology of the sciences to reveal the life-world *beneath* the sedimented scientific concepts. He seeks a transcendental logic, but one founded on real experience, rather than by transposing the categories of the sciences into cognitive faculties.

In his turn, Cavaillès noted that transcendental philosophies in general support their method and logical norms by deriving them from foundational acts of consciousness (see Kockelmans and Kisiel, 1970). Against such logicism, Cavaillès proposed the philosophy of the concept, a philosophy that seeks to comprehend the sciences by analysing the history of concepts and the norms by which they are utilized. This method does not require the closure which a transcendental method requires: historical *a prioris* are not conditions of what could be thought; rather, they are the conditions of what could be said within the parameters of a particular science within its time of operation. What critically separates the phenomenology from this conceptual method is the prioritization of language and structure as grounds of analysis, rather than consciousness and its intentional acts. The presupposition that the meaning of a physical sign is always a mental event is also rejected. Indeed, by rooting their scientific ontology in reason and the structures of thought, Kant and Husserl did not allow for the possibility of epistemic revolutions. This was enabled in the philosophy of the concept, however, by basing these structures instead in language. If Husserl suggested that there were conscious intentional acts that assigned meanings to signs, Cavaillès problematized this position as not accounting for scientific change, for being tied to an eternal form of reason. Basing a philosophy of science in the unity of consciousness

ignores the complexity of scientific objects and their potential for paradigmatic change in what Bachelard, in turn, would call a *double intentionality*
(Bachelard, 1951 and 2004).

The question of time is prominent for nearly all philosophers in the continental tradition, even if it is more often than not motivated (*pace* Bergson)
by the search for a more profound temporality rather than a measured time.
Nevertheless, the reflection upon time itself necessitates a relationship with
science (albeit a critical one). In the case of Bergson and Husserl, it was to
be a reflection deeply informed by science; in fact, one intended to re-orient
the boundaries and relations between philosophy and science. For Husserl,
science needed phenomenology to reveal the sedimented structures of both
scientific meaning and meaning in general. But the self-identity of phenomenological consciousness in the present itself necessitated protention and
retention for an awareness of time. Moreover, for Husserl (as also for Bergson)
a greater understanding of science's task was needed to enlarge its own methodological inventiveness and the question of ecology would bring together
reflections on time alongside those on technology. One prominent philosopher who has conducted work at this intersection is Don Ihde. Ihde (1990)
argues that intentionality as such is always technologically mediated and he
specifies several possible forms of this mediation. One: technologies can be
embodied by their users, as when looking through glasses: the glasses are not
so much noticed as incorporated as extensions of the body. Two: technologies
can be the terminus of our experiences in an *alterity* relation where human
beings interact with a device, as in an interaction with a cash dispenser. Three:
Ihde speaks of a *hermeneutic* relation where technologies provide representations of reality necessitating interpretation. This refers to the type of interaction one might have with a measuring device such as a thermometer,
where data requires interpretation. An actual experience is not provided, but
a statistical representation is. His fourth distinction is the background relation, where technologies provide a context for our perception. In this case,
technologies merely form part of the background, such as mechanical noise in
everyday life. In sum, intentionality can work through technological artefacts,
it can be directed at them, or it can be set against their background.

By contrast with Ihde's work, for Jacques Garelli (1991) the matter of
importance is not the relationship between human beings and technological
artefacts, but a reorientation of the ontological principles of instrumentalist
thought. With the body, Being or life as a genetic philosophical principle, the
means of thinking creation returns to the ancient meaning of *techne*, described
by Heidegger as the bringing forth of an idea into the world (1993, pp. 318–9).
Garelli also shows how the notions of creation, production and technique
must be conceptually expanded in an ontology of rhythm, and in so doing he
naturally returns to Aristotle. In this context, the problematic of temporalized

individuation inscribed at the heart of rhythm is information, the *informing* of sense, the creating of forms.

As has often been stated, Heidegger's philosophy contextualizes technology within an enormous philosophy of historical revelation. But, arguably, Heidegger underestimated the integral nature of technology within the very concepts he used against it. Perhaps the most significant proponent of such an argument in the contemporary field is Bruno Latour. If Heidegger posed the problem of technology as that of mastery without a master, Latour (2002) suggests that it is less than easy to allocate to their proper places the notions of means and ends. Instead, he suggests that significant research has been done within the fields of palaeontology and history which indicates that the historical emergence of technology and humanity has been significantly miscalculated. Technical ability has been seen to *precede* the birth of language. Indeed, Gilbert Simondon and before him Etienne Souriau, asserted the ontological priority of technology over any other category that could be assigned as essentially human. Yet, the mode of technology within this ontology is not the instrumental one so often assigned to it. Latour specifically wishes to understand technology in terms of the *fold*. According to Latour, technology primarily opens up new worlds and this is achieved by their presence actually changing the actor, by enfolding places, times and agents (Latour, 2002). When the specialist is at work he or she performs a technique that very few can master. Technologies are never a matter of means here, but are illustrated instead by the simile of the black box, of which one only knows the inputs and outputs. Technological life is a detour, it is its own autonomous process of creation taking into itself inputs to produce something that could never be envisaged in its actuality by the actor.

Alain Badiou has sought to mobilize category-theory for a doctrine of appearance, in a philosophy critically schooled in a Marxist and Bachelardian tradition. His scientific commitments are established with his first work *The Concept of Model* (2007). Here he re-orients Cavaillès's assertion of formal ingenuity within a phenomenological schema, to place formal thought itself as the primary unmediated access to reality. Badiou sees much of such debate to be in thrall to the same empiricist dogma. He also takes a good deal from the school of Bachelard and Cavaillès, however. After Bachelard, for instance, Badiou finds in mathematics a rigorous ontological discipline in its practice of actual scientific production. He also follows Bachelard (or more importantly Louis Althusser's adaptation of Bachelard) in his attempt to purge certain empiricist concepts from science in favour of materialist categories more apt to its advancement. This is most clearly shown in *The Concept of Model* when Badiou isolates the mathematical concept of model from concepts tied to more empirical strictures. For Badiou, there is a principle within bourgeois epistemology that is presupposed but never given – an ideological presupposition that distracts philosophy and science from pursuing an appropriately materialist epistemology. There is an interaction between formalism and empiricism that is always based upon an undisclosed principle. The error lies in conceiving empirical facts as the basis for formal theories, once again misusing the intra-mathematical relation of system and structure. In Badiou's view, however, there is a purely intra-mathematical relation between arithmetical and set-theoretical material in the concept of model. The formal system is modelled towards its own transformation in general. Transformation within the system of mathematics is always *mathematical*. Badiou hereby reverses what he sees as the ideological implementation of the theory of modelling, the passage of scientific practice moving from structure to system, and from model to theory and back (and as in the Bachelardian model of scientific refinement). A model is not an experimental realization of a formal system, but on the contrary a structure carrying within it a conceptual demonstration, the experimental verification of which is enacted through its encoding in a formal syntax. Mathematical thought defines the infinitely stratified nature of scientific discourse for Badiou and in so doing eschews the stable subject-object schema of empiricism. Badiou emphasizes the very intrinsic nature of epistemic change against any schema of shifting paradigms: it is in itself constituted by the very nature of scientific production's inseparability from itself in an enmeshed network of proofs and refinements. Science's process is defined by its continuing separation from its ideological tetherings.

Badiou first came to prominence with his critique of Gilles Deleuze. As stated earlier, Deleuze's philosophy makes great use of scientific concepts and has provided fertile ground for many contemporary thinkers in continental philosophy of science, among them Isabelle Stengers. She has, however, chosen to enter a dialogue with perhaps the most problematic text for those in continental philosophy who appreciate the free exchange of scientific and philosophic concepts: Deleuze and Guattari's *What is Philosophy?* (Deleuze and Guattari, 1994; Stengers, 2005). This text gives a more cautious, seemingly classical picture of philosophy's relation to science whereby philosophy is clearly demarcated from science (the former creates concepts while the latter creates 'functions'). Deleuze and Guattari pose an important question in their late work, one which could be said to endanger many uses of Deleuze's philosophy in contemporary thought: what are the conditions under which an appropriate relation between science and philosophy can take place?

Here, as Stengers poses, philosophy and science are able to interact only in their full maturity (Stengers, 2005). Science 'made' is privileged over the usually favoured image of science 'in the making'. One can say that Deleuze derives his definition of truth from his understanding of scientific experimentation. It is an experimental truth. Science provides this notion of 'minor', wherein each minor enquiry contains its own internal principles of coherence. For Stengers, this conception of minority explains Deleuze and Guattari's final statement concerning the parallel lines of science and philosophy. In some ways this preserves the dignity of science against a mimetic relation between the two. Philosophy must not intervene in a science in the making but wait up to its maturity. While it is important to relate science, art and philosophy to an ontology of creation, as Simondon, Garelli and Deleuze have successfully shown, Stengers cautions against speaking of a world before the processes of industrialisation (Stengers, 2005).

In sum, the equal measure of fertility and complexity in the rubric of a continental philosophy of science can be clearly seen here. It is equally clear, moreover, that this fertility not only enhances that of philosophy more generally, but also can be seen as the very basis of its fecundity. For the philosophers we have discussed, it can be said that philosophy as such is created through its interaction with science. Yet there is also an ethical questioning essential to philosophy's call to thinking in science, one that is as true of the positivist philosophies as it is of the ontological critiques (the positivist heritage attests to this in a figure such as Latour). Furthermore, of equal import for this tradition is the pursuit of questions to their necessary ends and across disciplinary boundaries immanent to the sciences in action (rather than within a universal framework placed above this action). This is particularly the case with the archaeological method of Foucault, but it is similarly the case with Serres's enfolding of the history of science within a temporality guided by functional concepts that are his key to the history of ideas. Finally, philosophy of science within continental thought can still be seen to be defined by its manoeuvre out of Kantianism, that is, through a particularly regional and practically founded enquiry. Kantianism found its genesis in a scientific refutation, that of Euclidian and Newtonian space and time, and has found itself enmeshed ever since in the internal workings of science in action.

Philosophies of Art

Jonathan Lahey Dronsfield

Perhaps all the writers to be discussed here take as their point of departure an injunction from Martin Heidegger: the necessity of *overcoming* aesthetics. Aesthetics, according to Heidegger, is the culmination of the way in which metaphysics conceives beings as objectively representable. Indeed, the prevalence of art which is 'objectless' and 'non-representational' – 'productions no longer able to be works . . . for which the suitable word is lacking' (Heidegger, 1996, p. 34) – in museums, the culture industry, and in aesthetic discourse, is testimony to the fact that such works are no less objectifiable than are representational ones. Heidegger calls for 'a new content for the word "art" and for what it intends to name'. He sets about the task in two ways. First, by questioning the basic conceptual oppositions determining aesthetic discourse and analyzing the way in which art's materiality is in excess of use, function, and form (Heidegger, 1993); second, by re-establishing art's fundamental orientation towards truth (Heidegger, 2000, p. 140).

We will consider two sets of approaches by which recent continental philosophy of art has sought to overcome aesthetics: through a consideration of the ways in which art is the expression of sensation, the exposition of sense, or the partition of the sensible; and through a retrieval of how art can be said to be truth. There is no more influential a figure in contemporary continental philosophy of art than Gilles Deleuze, and we begin with him. We will examine his principal idea of sensation in the light of questions raised against it by three of his contemporaries: Jean-Luc Nancy, Jacques Derrida and Jacques Rancière, before looking at the work of Nancy (sense) and Rancière (the sensible) in more detail. Art's relation to truth as set out contrastingly by Alain Badiou and Giorgio Agamben will comprise the second part. Again Rancière will provide a counterpoint. Both parts of the essay confront the privilege of writing over the image, and the order of dependency between philosophy and art.[1]

Art and Sensation, Sense, and the Sensible

Art and Sensation

The work of art is a being of sensation and nothing else: it exists in itself. (Deleuze and Guattari, 1994, p. 164)

Sensation is what is painted. (Deleuze, 2003, p. 35)

Gilles Deleuze accords art a status equal to that of philosophy and science in revealing the world. Concerned to invert the order of dependency between identity and difference, and to show how subjectivity is constituted by a differential play of movements and forces, Deleuze contends that art is able to show these otherwise invisible movements and forces in their original unity and in the economy of their difference. His 1981 book on the painter Francis Bacon (Deleuze, 2003) sets out to describe the invisible forces made visible by painting in the form of pre-individual, pre-personal figures – but figures constituted by their de-figuration. What Bacon's figures make visible are forces and affections constituting the 'I' and of which the 'I' is a function, the differential flux of affective forces which come before the security (which Deleuze thinks is illusory) and fixity (an imposition) of stable identity. The figural – a notion Deleuze takes from Lyotard (Lyotard, 1971; Deleuze, 1996, p. 181, and 2003, p. 173) – is interruptive both of the conventions of representation and of established ways of seeing. By isolating figures within the frame, liberating them from background or ground, Bacon's paintings displace the body from the representational whole which would make sense of it. Thus figural painting is not to be confused with figurative painting, which is to represent something by or with the body, a story (narration) or meaning (symbolism), in any case something external to the painting. But figuration is not simply opposed to figurative painting, since figurative painting has always needed de-figuration to fulfil its very aims of going beyond realism, beyond a representation of the world in terms of what it looks like, for example to an immaterial 'beyond' of 'celestial sensation' which, according to Deleuze, classical Christian religious painting has always sought (Deleuze, 2003, p. 8f).[2]

The figure allows for a relation between a sensible form and sensation; it gives sensible form to sensation. Doubly genitival, at once both subject and object, it synthesizes the manifold of the different orders of sensation into one thing, pure expressive matter. The source of its synthesis is rhythm (Deleuze, 2003, p. 42). Rhythm is the vital power extending over all domains (visual, auditory, etc) of sensation. It allows for communication between the senses, an 'existential communication', 'the "pathic" (non-representative) moment of *the* sensation', *the* sensation because the senses are an 'original unity'. The figure makes visible the flowing and gathering of sensation as an original material unity, between form and sensation and between the senses, both giving and receiving the sensation (Deleuze, 2003, p. 35). Rhythm is the co-existence of these different movements of the figure both subject to and of the forces of sensation. The primary way in which Bacon shows these forces is to assemble blocks and fields of colour and line not simply to be seen, but in such a way as to allow for the feeling of their rhythm and the sensing of their intensities as one thing, an experience which is as much spiritual as it is visual. Thus, what we gain from looking at art is a question as to the certainty of ourselves in what we see – 'every sensation is a question, even if the only answer is silence' (Deleuze and Guattari, 1994, p. 196) – for Deleuze this is liberating, it is what art can do which nothing else can do.

The primary task of the painter is to render a problem Deleuze argues is *specific* to painting, that of arranging lines and blocks of colour. For the writer the *specific* problem is to produce blocks of sentences in which the line unfurls or breaks; for the filmmaker, blocks of movement-duration in which what is seen is disjunctive to what is heard (Deleuze, 2006, pp. 182, 314). In each case it is a question of freeing the sensation, liberating the affect (Deleuze and Guattari, 1994, p. 167). How a painter, writer or filmmaker does so is his style. As creative acts all such arrangements of blocks, be they colour, sentences or movement-duration, have as their limit – and it is what enables them to communicate with other creative acts, such as the invention of concepts (philosophy) or functions (science) – the formation of space-time (Deleuze, 2006, p. 315).

But in order to become forms of space-time, art must first undergo a catastrophe, the collapse of its visual coordinates (Deleuze, 2006, p. 183). The artist must make himself blind to what he is in receipt of historically and surrounded by institutionally (Deleuze and Guattari, 1994, p. 194). The painter does not begin with the blank canvas, he must instead first leave the frame to achieve the blank canvas (Deleuze and Guattari, 1994, p. 188), or the blank canvas is already an image to be painted over (Deleuze, 1999, p. 65). Only by first clearing away the clichés and conventions of painting, the habits of perception and the constraints of memory, the pre-established norms of judgement and the authority of a master or the avant-garde, can the artist return to the canvas anew. Art is first of all a subtraction from the probable in favour of the possible. And what enables a departure from all that has come before and a return to the canvas after subtraction are the chance marks an artist might make – not deliberate, intentional marks but involuntary, chance ones. In his earlier writings, Deleuze likens the process to a throw of the dice. The artist must extract these chance marks and make them into possibilities in the form of a 'diagram' worked back into the visual whole in such a way that it causes the work to vibrate, giving it rhythm (Deleuze, 2003, p. 101ff). Thus manually worked in, the diagram 'introduces a properly haptic world and gives the eye a haptic function' (Deleuze, 2003, p. 138). Sight discovers in itself 'a specific function of touch that is uniquely its own, distinct from its optical function' (Deleuze, 2003, p. 155), hence the relations between colours, for instance, being described by Deleuze in terms of 'expansion and contraction', 'hot and cold' (cf. Deleuze, 1999). In being sensible in this way the painting itself has *its* body, its own material structure. Deleuze names this the 'pictorial fact', the culmination of the 'great moment in the act of painting', the passage from the hand (the manual intrusion of the diagram) to the haptic eye and its haptic vision (Deleuze, 2003, p. 160). The fact comprises several forms in the one figure, a 'properly pictorial (or sculptural) ligature . . . which makes these apparently arbitrary elements coagulate in a single continuous flow'. Thus is a third term formed, the haptic, a 'third eye', which overcomes the tactile/optical dualism.

Artists *compose* – 'composition is the sole definition of art' (Deleuze and Guattari, 1994, p. 191) – but composition must be understood to imply not an organization but a putting together in the process of disintegrating (Deleuze, 2003, p. 129). In putting things together, blocks of colour, blocks of movement-duration, or in separating or breaking a line in a sentence, compositions capture the counterpoint or tension of this spatial-temporal moment. In the case of film, it is achieved through making disjunctive the relation of sound to image. This disjunction is constitutive of what Deleuze (following Malraux) calls its resistance (Deleuze, 2006, p. 323). Here, the work of art resists not by providing counter-information in the form of a certain content, but by having the sound move in a direction counter to what is seen, such that the two encounter each other in a space set up by the disjunction between them – it is a relation which is a non-relation, of which both elements are a part and apart. Resisting in this way, works of art have a fundamental affinity with the struggles of man – Deleuze characterizes the affinity as the 'most mysterious' thing (Deleuze, 2006, p. 324) – fundamentally it is an identification between the way both resist death.[3]

Things so assembled make new connections and enable new forms of mobility and migration, new forms of connectivity. These assemblages, or compositions, are planes rather than hierarchical structures, smooth planes of consistency, univocal planes. The plane of composition is neither a prior intention, nor an effect which comes after (Deleuze and Guattari, 1994, p. 196). The composite sensation and the plane of composition are co-existent, they come into being one through the other. But sensation undergoes a de-framing and de-figuration on the plane of composition, releasing it, opening it onto infinity: 'perhaps the peculiarity of art is to pass through the finite in order to rediscover, to restore the infinite' (Deleuze and Guattari, 1994, p. 197).

Deleuze and Guattari borrow from Antonin Artaud's 1947 radio play *To Have Done with the Judgment of God* the name they give the non-hierarchical plane of composition in Bacon's paintings: a 'body without organs' (Artaud, 1988, pp. 570–1), a body not so much without organs as no longer organized by them. It is not that organs are absent but that they are transitory (Deleuze and Guattari, 1983, p. 9ff, and 1988, p. 30; Deleuze, 2003, p. 44f), and the deformation wrought by the loss or suspension of its organization renders the body a smooth surface on and through which sensations are released to flow into forces and into each other, the movement of which Bacon shows through the variation of texture and colour of paint assembled disjunctively. In the slightly earlier *Mille Plateaux* such a body is described as a continuous field of desire, where the plane of composition is a continuum immanent to the body (Deleuze and Guattari, 1988, p. 154) – there is no mention of immanence in the Bacon book – and it is the movement of this the artist tries to capture: 'the artist turns his or her attention to the microscopic ... for movement, for nothing but immanent movement' (Deleuze and Guattari, 1988, p. 337).[4]

The blocks and affects assembled thus on the canvas of a painting are the 'infinite passage of chaos' (Deleuze and Guattari, 1994, p. 197). The more an artist seeks to close off this passage and prevent escape from planes of de-figuration and de-framing, either by seeking to erase the chance mark altogether, or (but this would be to deny chance also) by imposing the dia-gram as a whole rather than working it in as a modulator of the whole, the more he sets up what Deleuze calls lines of flight out of them. These lines of flight too are immanent (as are the work's failures (Deleuze and Guattari, 1994, p. 255), and they are virtual, and Deleuze looks for those elements in an artwork which reveals underlying lines of flight and actualizes them. Hence Deleuze's taste for writers and artists who elevate change and becoming over permanence.

For criticisms of Deleuze, we turn to three of his contemporaries, Jean-Luc Nancy, Jacques Derrida and Jacques Rancière. Nancy makes his intervention at the point where Deleuze argues for rhythm as the vital power extending over and synthesizing all domains of sensation, as the source of an 'existential communication' between the senses in a 'pathic' moment (Deleuze, 2003, p. 42f). The 'pathic' refers to phenomenology, and to Merleau-Ponty in par-ticular, who analyzes sensation, or rather 'sense experience', not just as it relates sensible qualities to an identifiable object (the figurative moment), 'but insofar as each quality constitutes a field that stands on its own without ceasing to interfere with the others (the "pathic moment")' (Deleuze, 2003, p. 178; cf. Merleau-Ponty, 1967, pp. 207–42). This would seem to imply on Deleuze's part a continuity between Merleau-Ponty's synaesthetic perception and his own 'existential communication'. If so, Nancy would disagree: 'if there is indeed a unity or synthesis in the two cases, they are not of the same order, and this difference can be deciphered in Deleuze himself' (Nancy,

1996a, p. 106). Deleuze's 'original unity of the senses', for Nancy, 'proves to be but the singular "unity" of a "between" the sensuous domains', 'existential communication' between the senses 'turns out to take place in the element of the outside-itself, of an exposition of existence', and rhythm has its moment 'only in the gap of the beat that makes it into a rhythm' (Nancy, 1996a, pp. 23–4). Or in other words, and contrary to Deleuze's assertion, it is not rhythm that is made visible by the artwork but 'the movement of coming and going of forms or presence in general', a movement of *mimesis/methexis* out of which forms and presences arise (Nancy, 1996a, p. 24). A form is a 'ground that withdraws' (here the limit to phenomenology of art); it appears not as a figure detached from a ground but as 'the force of a ground that sets apart and dislocates itself, in its syncopated rhythm' (Nancy, 1996a, pp. 31–2). Art dis-figures in the sense that it presents not the unity or consistency of presence but the multiplicity of unity, exposing unity to its plural existence. As we will see, Nancy characterizes the rhythm of such presentation and exposition in terms of *touch*.

Derrida calls into question the haptic in Deleuze on the basis of the values of 'proximity' and 'closeness' determining its concept. The appeal to such values is enabled by what Derrida calls Deleuze and Guattari's 'continuistic proposition', best exemplified by the 'body without organs'. It is a postulation because the continuous, for Derrida, is 'never given' (Derrida, 2005, p. 125). There is never any 'immediate experience' of closeness or proximity or indeed smoothness, 'there is never any "immediate" given', thus there can be no 'pure experience' of the body without organs. What is experienced is always a mixture, an impurity, a mixed given. The smooth/striated opposition turns out to be not so much a conceptual opposition as an 'idealized polarity', 'the tension of a *contradictory* desire' (Derrida, 2005, p. 125). But perhaps in the non-happening or not coming of the pure experience of the haptic or of the body without organs (dependent as they are on the smooth), we find the contingent fact, one which would constitute the 'very condition of desire' embodied by such a body, and which might perhaps rescue the smooth/striated opposition. But just as the opposition between the striated and the non-hierarchical smooth is itself hierarchized in Deleuze, so too is that between the *de facto* and the *de jure*. What Deleuze calls a 'fact' is less an empirically contingent one than 'an eidetic law of structure (and thus of stricture or striation)' governing the *de jure/de facto* distinction itself (Derrida, 2005, p. 126): 'the de facto mixes do not preclude a de jure, or abstract, distinction between the two spaces . . . it is the de jure distinction that determines the forms assumed by a given de facto mix and the direction or meaning of the mix' (Deleuze and Guattari, 1988, p. 475). Thus is a crucial distinction deconstructed: the *de jure* cannot be authoritative as on the one hand Deleuze links it to one of the two agencies it seeks to govern (the striated), and on the other 'from a purely juridical-phenomenological point of view, the recourse to experience shows that the sense of this mixing never delivers anything that might be, de facto or de jure, pure and free from the said mixture' (Derrida, 2005, p. 126). The conclusion: there is no immediate intuition of the haptical.

Perhaps the most forceful, and certainly the most thoroughgoing criticism of Deleuze's position is made by Rancière. Deleuze, for Rancière, is nothing less than the 'fulfilment' of 'the destiny of the aesthetic' (Rancière, 1998 and 2002). On the one hand Deleuze wants to break with representation in favour of a radical materiality and immanence. On the other, because immanence is tied to the involuntary or the unconscious, he must transform it into an allegory or a scenario, an irreducibly metaphysical one for Rancière, in which everything depends on the fictional or indeed historical character of the artwork (Rancière, 2000b, p. 28). What characterizes the figure in Deleuze is not pure sensation, it is the 'sensible marks of the insensible that produces sensation'. For example, the 'itself' of the 'cry itself' that, according to Deleuze, Bacon's *Innocent X* is a painting of (Deleuze, 2003, p. 60f), is nothing but 'another relation of the cry to its cause . . . precisely the "aesthetic" cause in general, the invisible that is inherent in sensible manifestation' (Rancière, 2000b, p. 27). In other words, in order to show immanence or to give it a figure, Deleuze needs to reintroduce representational traits. He wants everything on one plane of expressive matter, everything that once went by the names form and content, which means that any fictional or representational trait can be taken as one of material expression, but in fact in Deleuze it is the representational that makes sense of the material.

There is a further objection mounted by Rancière to the Deleuzian project, and it concerns the way in which Deleuze appears to assert the physical materiality of painting at the expense both of the discourse which constitutes it, and of the discursive space it helps to construct (Rancière, 2007a, p. 87). Insofar as they both 'readily assign art the task of creating presence under representation', Deleuze and phenomenology, for Rancière, are one: they reduce representation to signification (Rancière, 2007a, p. 79). To see presence and representation as opposed in this way is to miss how the immediacy of presence is configured through the working of words. If Deleuze argues for a new visibility made possible by sensation, Rancière sees this newness to be the outcome of a new relation between forms and words, 'the surface of exhibition of forms and the surface of inscription of words', of which sensation is but one plaiting, and representation another. Visibility of presence and the immediacy of sensation are always already mediated through words: 'The transformation . . . of the figurative into the figural is only possible through the highly specific labour of the writer's words' (Rancière, 2007a, p. 81). For it is through such writing that new regimes of visibility are brought about, by which Rancière means that we are enabled to see what works of art make visible only if words construct an equivalence with it. This does not entail the two co-existing; on the contrary, a solidarity between them is possible only on condition of their being temporally distant from each other. Writing on art is no less a labour of de-figuration than is the practice of artists, achieving a discursive space in which the transformative work of art can be seen both retrospectively and prospectively. So the 'real' medium of painting, for example, is not its material or physical support, not blocks of colour and line or the flatness of the canvas, but the surface of form-signs/words on which words too make themselves into images, or where speech becomes visible (Rancière, 2000b, pp. 22–3). Only in this way is Deleuze's 'theatre of de-figuration', for Rancière, 'a space of conversion where the relationship between words and visual forms anticipates visual de-figuration still to come' (Rancière, 2007a, pp. 87–8).

Nancy too argues that the conditions for an artwork's visibility are provided by a legibility not its alone, and that the demand for legibility in, for instance, painting is itself inscribed in and by painting. It is a matter of what is not pictorial within the pictorial (Nancy, 2006, p. 150f). There is, for Nancy, a non-pictorial, in the form of a 'writability', at the very heart of the pictorial: 'the point here is that painting itself writes about painting, thus making itself possible' (Nancy, 2006, p. 151). 'In truth, every image and every text is potentially, and respectively, text and image for itself' (Nancy, 2005, p. 69), where the relation between text and image is one of sense, each saying the sense of the other, while at the same time exposing its being non-identical to the other (Nancy, 2005, p. 76).

It should not be forgotten that the question of the privileging of writing (philosophy) over the visual (art) is a question running also throughout the work of Derrida from the start right through to later works: there is always text, 'a little discourse somewhere', in the visual arts (Derrida, 1994, p. 15); 'the drawing of men', he says (in a catalogue to an exhibition curated by him in 1990), 'never goes without being articulated with articulation, without the order being given with words' (Derrida, 1993a, p. 56). Derrida seeks to do two things: first, to understand how words could have imposed an authority over drawing, suggesting that what he calls 'the withdrawal of the line', which happens at the very moment that what the line draws appears as a drawing, is 'that which grants speech'; second, to make readable the 'graphics of invisible words' (Derrida, 1993a, p. 37), a 'certain literality of the matter that does not go beyond painting in its material' (Derrida and Thévenin, 1998, p. 99). For both Nancy and Derrida it is always a case of questioning the order of dependency which would privilege writing and discourse over the image and art, and *vice versa*.

Art and Sense

Nancy's point of departure – and it is Badiou's too, as we will see – is the question of the unity of art, or rather, the multiple origin of that unity, or the plurality at the heart of the essence of art, specifically 'the ontological question of the *singular plural*' (Nancy, 1996a, pp. 1–3). It is not a question that can be answered by aesthetics, which 'always risks covering over what is at stake, inasmuch as the singular of "art" is not without its own consistency, since it *consists* in its own plural' (Nancy, 1996a, p. 37). For Nancy, there are several arts, indeed they are innumerable. He confronts the identity and difference between them on the basis of a difference between the senses and on the basis of the unity of the senses. Questioning to what extent art can be said to be 'for the senses' at all, he concludes that neither the senses nor their unity can be the conditions or a model for the arts. Rather, it is the plurality of sense itself, and the heterogeneity of sense, to which we must look for the origin of art. And what art does, for Nancy, is touch sense, and touch with the heterogeneity of sense.

Now, because touch is the only sense which senses itself sensing, because it touches itself when it touches, because it is touched by what it touches and because it is touched because it touches, touch, for Nancy, presents 'the proper moment of sensuous exteriority' (Nancy, 1996a, p. 17). Moreover, and as Derrida has pointed out, this sense of itself that touch has is both self-touching and an interruption of itself, at the same time – and thus a loss of the proper at the very moment of touching it (Derrida, 1993b, p. 127). And this is what art touches; art touches both the self-touching of touch – what could be called the immanence of touch – and the interruption of touch – what could be called the transcendence of touch – at the same time. Art is transimmanence, 'it touches on the transimmanence of being-in-the-world' (Nancy, 1996a, p. 18). Art is 'the transcendence of immanence that does not go outside itself in transcending' (Nancy, 1996a, pp. 34–5). Transimmanence is the exteriority and the exposition of sense. Art takes place as transimmanence. It exposes – exposes, not represents – the relation of sense to self, which sense has with and to itself.

Artworks are always more than signification, they 'make sense' beyond signification. Art 'exceeds signs, but without revealing anything other than this excess'. The excess is what Nancy calls the sense of the world (Nancy, 2005, p. 26). Part of art's making sense is to bring each sense out to be itself, beyond what is signified, but not simply as a sense (for that would be signification): the visual becomes a pictorial world, the sonorous becomes a musical world. Whatever is signified in the artwork is touched by the sense of the world it produces, touched by the unity of the pictorial or musical world it presents, and in that touch signification is suspended and the relation between sense and signification interrupted.

At the same time, art is dependent on technique – it must be if art's product-
iveness is not to be conceived of as mythical or romantic (Nancy, 2000 and
1996a, p. 30). Technique is the matter of producing something that does not
produce itself by itself – for art the question more specifically being 'how to
produce the ground that does not produce itself . . . that would be its plurality
of origin', plural because the ground is not one, and must be produced from
out of a heterogenesis. Nancy calls this ground existence and refers it to
Badiou's 'infinite multiplicity' (Nancy, 1996a, p. 26). If romanticism – where
technique is reduced to genius – is to be overcome then we must rethink the
finite, plural and heterogeneous constitution of the infinite, such that finitude
becomes the 'infinite affirmation' of another sense of existence and another
sense of technique (Nancy, 1996a, p. 37). That the unity of the world is multiple in origin leads Nancy, as with Badiou and Agamben, and Heidegger
before them,[5] to say that we are inexorably drawn to intelligible sense and
thus to poetry, but not in the form of the poem, or not necessarily: 'poetry,
before being the name of a particular art, is the generic name of art' (Nancy,
2000). If the sensuous and technical plurality of the arts is the unity of the one
world, then attempts to 'inter-express' the arts, and the demand to 'sense
sense sensing', will irresistibly involve the appeal to poetry and the 'permanent subsumption' of the arts under poetry. But this subsumption is itself
heterogeneous, it implies the plurality of all the arts, because poetry is also the
name, for Nancy, of a division at the heart of production through technique:
the sensuous dislocation of sense and the pure production of sense, the dissension of technical production and the production of this dissension as
essence. The tension between these two imperatives is untenable, which is
why all poetry touches upon 'the extremity of its own interruption', and has
this movement 'for its law and technique' (Nancy, 1996a, p. 28). At the same
time, technique, the technicity of art, 'dislodges art from its 'poetic' assurance,
if the poetic is understood as revelation or the emergence or birth of truth. If
technicity puts the work of art 'out of work', 'outside of itself, touching the
infinite' (Nancy, 1996a, p. 37), poetry would more properly name the moment
when art, any art, in touching its essence at the same time is touched by its
outside, its exteriority, by the sense of sense.

Art and the Sensible

We will not trace the trajectory of its emergence here, but Rancière argues that
an 'aesthetic revolution' took place around the turn of the nineteenth century:
the formation of an aesthetic regime, which he opposes to the ethical and
representational regimes (Rancière, 2004a, pp. 22–3), for which and in which
'everything is material for art, so that art is no longer governed by its subject,
by what it speaks of: art can show and speak of everything in the same
manner' (Rancière, 2003a, p. 205). There are two main consequences. First, the

equality of all subject matter in the aesthetic leads to the negation of any necessary relation between a form or content and a political effect (Rancière, 2004a, p. 14, and 2007b, p. 259). Second, art becomes absolutely singular in that its sensibility cannot be found elsewhere than in the aesthetic, but at the same time the aesthetic negates any criterion that might be utilized to distinguish what art is from what art is not. The second amounts to a paradox: at the very foundation of an autonomous aesthetic regime, art defines itself by its identity with non-art and has at its centre an irreducible and constitutive heterogeneous sensible (Rancière, 2003b, p. 10, and 2005, p. 20). All artworks, then, are identified by a 'sensible mode of being' specific to the aesthetic regime, a sensibility foreign and exterior to itself (Rancière, 2000a, p. 12; 2000b, p. 29; 2004a, p. 23). Extricated from the ordinary, art's sensibility is a power heterogeneous to it.

At the same time, artistic practices are but one form of doing and making, alongside the ordinary, the everyday and the general distribution of ways of doing and making; in other words, they are one form of the 'distribution of the sensible' by which society frames and re-frames the visibility of objects and situations, decides which are common and available for discussion and disagreement, divides and distributes identities, and determines who is visible and who is not visible, who is heard and who is not, who can speak and who cannot (Rancière, 2004a, p. 13). There is, then, an aesthetics at the core of politics, a 'primary aesthetics', and on this basis art practice can intervene in the partition of the sensible politically. Art is political not because of any content or 'message', but in virtue of the way in which it reconfigures or intervenes in the economy of the sensible. But it does so with a power which has become foreign to that sensibility, 'a difference of the sensible from itself' (Rancière, 2000b, p. 16), 'the invisible visibility of the visible' (Rancière, 2000b, p. 27). And because art makes this difference of the sensible to itself coincide with a difference of thought with respect to itself, it is contended that it is impossible to oppose the authentic practices of art to those which are proper to philosophy (Rancière, 2000b, p. 16). Art practice and the practice of aesthetics are two parts of a general regime of art, each a partitioning and distribution of the sensible in the forms of doing, making visible and speaking.

Those who seek to overcome aesthetics must confront the fact that the desire to oppose aesthetics is co-extensive with the very regime of aesthetics; or in other words, that the anti-aesthetic is internal to aesthetics and no less a proper part of aesthetics than is aesthetics itself: 'aesthetics is born as the refusal of its name' (Rancière, 2000b, p. 18). And if art is the place of an adequation between a sensible and a thought each different from itself, then the sensible is the presentation of an insensible. It is a regime in which *aisthesis* determines *poiesis* to the extent that the function of the latter becomes 'to produce a sensible element that verifies the power of thought immanent to the sensible' (Rancière, 2000b, p. 21). It is a realm wherein things are free of ordinary hierarchies and distinctions (in which, for instance, mute objects 'speak') and free of the will (which becomes co-extensive with its own abdication), and where the will is itself free (appearing in otherwise inanimate objects), or becomes nothing but the will to art (to produce whatever it wants, not something programmatic of art but anything as art) (Rancière, 2000a, p. 22, and 2000b, p. 31). It is a regime, then, where *aisthesis* doubles *poiesis*, which becomes both the power of artistic production and the will to art, 'the will to the manifestation of the equality of *aisthesis* with itself' (Rancière, 2000b, p. 30).

Art and Truth

We turn now to the second way in which our inheritance from Heidegger – the necessity of overcoming aesthetics – has been achieved: through a retrieval of art's relation to truth. We approach it through the work of Badiou and Agamben, specifically Badiou's departure from Heidegger, and Agamben's working through him. Badiou names his attempt to go beyond aesthetics *inaesthetics*: 'a relation of philosophy to art that, maintaining that art is itself a producer of truths, makes no claim to turn art into an object for philosophy'; instead, philosophy of art here is mere 'description' of 'strictly intraphilosophical effects produced by the independent existence of some works of art' (Badiou, 2005a, epigraph to the book). In rendering art to truth and demonstrating the destitution of objectivity as an ontological category, Heidegger founded a pertinent trait of modernity. His mistake, for Badiou, is to have misunderstood the true nature of the Platonic gesture of banishing poetry, which leads Heidegger to fail to invent a new relation between philosophy and poetry, and instead to restore the authority of the poetic utterance over the philosophical (Badiou, 2005b, p. 74). The Platonic gesture, for Badiou, consists in making recourse to the matheme, the literal univocity of mathematics, as a mode of interrupting the sacred authority vested in poetic narrative and the place or site from which it is uttered, an interruption which is the very possibility of philosophy in that it denaturalizes the idea and exposes it to the withdrawal of being. Plato seeks to control art because of its *immediacy*, its seduction of the senses. If art can imitate truth then the effect of truth perdures as charm (Badiou, 2005a, p. 2). Heidegger recognizes the impossibility and injustice of distancing poetry from philosophy through banishing it, and the need for philosophy to expose itself to poetry's challenge to the concept, but he succeeds only in entangling the two, allowing only the one truth to circulate through them: the withdrawal of being, a truth that thinking must endure (Badiou, 2005a, p. 7). 'What culminates with Heidegger is the anti-positivist and anti-Marxist effort to put philosophy in the hands of the poem' (Badiou, 1999, p. 66). Heidegger effectively reinstates the sacred authority of poetry through the romantic myth of the authenticity of the 'flesh of language' (Badiou, 1992, p. 74), a project Badiou claims is effectively continued in France by Blanchot, Derrida and Deleuze as a 'fetishism of literature', 'delegat[ing] the living flesh of thought to its artistic condition' (Badiou, 1999, p. 67).

Thus Deleuze too, for Badiou, remains trapped in the romantic schema, because by placing art on the side of sensation, in 'paradoxical continuity' with the Hegelian motif that art is the sensible form of the idea, he separates art from philosophy in such a way that the destination of art as a form of thought is left 'entirely unapparent': without the category of truth the plane of immanence from which the differentiation of art from philosophy proceeds cannot be established (Badiou, 2005a, p. 10). We have remarked on how the plane of composition for Deleuze de-frames sensation and opens it onto infinity, how art in the form of composite sensations 'wants to create the finite that restores the infinite', which would be its way of throwing a plane over chaos (Deleuze and Guattari, 1994, p. 197). Badiou's first thesis on contemporary art states the opposite: 'art is not the sublime descent of the infinite into the finite abjection of the body and sensuality. It is the production of an infinite subjective series through the finite means of a material subtraction' (Badiou, 2003). For Badiou, the passage of the finite into the infinite, as if art were the incarnation of the infinite-true, 'the power of infinity held within the tormented cohesion of form', is the very kernel of the romantic schema (Badiou, 2005a, p. 3).

Romanticism is but one of three possible schemata, for Badiou, of the link between philosophy and art, the other two being didacticism: that art is incapable of truth, but is the charm of its semblance (Plato), and classicism: that art is incapable of truth, but is innocent because its purpose is not in the least truth (Aristotle).[6] The twentieth century, its modernism, its avant-gardes: all are in fact syntheses of the didactic and romantic; and today, all of these schemata are saturated and their effects closed (Badiou, 2005a, p. 8). What Badiou seeks is a new relation of philosophy to poetry, a fourth modality of the link between philosophy and art, one which is demarcated in terms of presence: 'art is the process of a truth, and this truth is always the truth of the sensible or sensual' (Badiou, 2003, thesis 3), poetry is the 'truth of sensible presence' (Badiou, 2005b, p. 78), the 'thought of the presence of the present', whereas what is at stake for philosophy is 'the compossibility of time' (Badiou, 2005b, p. 75). To be sure, philosophy needs the literary, it needs literature in the form of narrative and fable to present and transmit to sense the way in which truth proves itself. But the point at which literature and the poem occur in philosophy is governed by philosophy, it is prescribed by philosophical argumentation. The literary, the poem – and for Badiou it is always 'more particularly a question of the literary act, whose kernel is the poem' (Badiou, 2005b, p. 78) – is a localized supplement, and never not subject to the law of rational argumentation. The truth of art is a 'hole', a 'void', in sense, and as such truth's relation to sense cannot be presented; it is unpresentable. The relation of truth to sense – which is always also an address to the senses – is thus for Badiou defective and it is this that philosophy needs to communicate and for which it needs the services of literature.

What all the above schemata rejected by Badiou have in common concerns the relation of art to truth. Only literature and art produce truths. Philosophy does not produce truths, it 'subtractively distributes them according to their proper regime of separation from sense' (Badiou, 2005b, p. 81). If art really is the immanent production of truths, as Badiou characterizes the romantic schema, then what is this unity named 'art'? For Badiou, a truth is what he calls an infinite multiplicity. Infinity is that property of a truth by which it subtracts itself from an identity with established forms of knowledge (Badiou, 2005a, p. 10). And for a truth to happen requires an event. A work of art on the other hand is finite, radically so in that it creates finitude, it is a finite multiplicity. This leads Badiou to conclude that if art is the production of truths then the singularity of the work of art is not the pertinent 'unit' of inquiry: 'it is impossible to say of the work *at one and the same time* that it is a truth and that it is the event whence this truth originates' (Badiou, 2005a, p. 11). If the event in Deleuze is always one of sense, then for Badiou this amounts to 'the aestheticization of everything' (Badiou, 2007, p. 40). Badiou shifts the emphasis onto the composition that a set of works is, which he calls a generic multiple or an artistic configuration. Works unfold a truth through their chance occurrences. A work of art is a local instance, a differential point of the truth unfolded by the configuration – it is the *subject* of the procedure initiated by the body of works. 'In the end, a truth is an artistic configuration initiated by an event . . . and unfolded through chance in the form of the works that serve as its subject points' (Badiou, 2005a, p. 12). The sequence or procedure or process initiated by an event is not a form, a genre, or a historical period. Rather, it is a 'virtually infinite complex of works' (including minor, ignored and redundant instances).

In a more recent paper, approaching the problem from the side of form, Badiou argues that the artistic configuration *is* a relation between sensibility and form, 'between chaotic disposition of sensibility in general . . . and what is a form', where the event of art is 'a change in the formula of the world' through the emergence of a 'new possibility of formalization', 'the becoming form of something which was not form', or vice versa, and the new artistic body thus created 'a new existence of the infinite' (Badiou, 2005c). That new existence of the infinite Badiou calls 'immanent infinity', in which the form is in direct relation to chaotic sensibility and the form itself infinite. It entails rethinking the notion of the infinite to take account of the new relation between a subject (the artwork) and its body (the artistic configuration, or body of works). The subject can neither be reduced to the body (immanent identity), nor separated from it (transcendent difference). Badiou proposes that the new relation be understood as immanent difference, the difference emerging through a subjective creative process, one which cuts through what he terms the 'contemporary war' between the subjective paradigms of enjoyment and sacrifice, where enjoyment would be the norm of identifying the subject with the becoming of its body (immanent identity), and sacrifice would be experimentation through the death of the body (transcendent difference).

It is philosophy that shows in what sense the artistic configuration 'lets itself be grasped' by the category of truth, philosophy and art coming together in the form of an 'effective process' within art seized by philosophy and shown by it. Badiou insists that this does not mean that philosophy thinks art; instead 'a configuration thinks itself in the works that compose it' (Badiou, 2005a, p. 14). On the one hand, then, philosophy seizes and describes the effects of art, effects which are themselves for the sake of art, yet 'intraphilosophical'; and on the other, only art produces the truths that philosophy describes. Stripped of its identity with any possible localized form of knowledge, liberated from the constraints of the site of its production, truth thus 'elaborated' is shown to be eternal. Philosophy turns time away from the specific place and moment of the artwork towards the eternity that is the truth of what art unfolds.

For a critique of Badiou we turn once again to Rancière, for whom Badiou's inaesthetics remains firmly ensconced within the tradition of modernism and its 'anti-aesthetic consensus', by which he means in broad terms those arguments which seek to distinguish art from non-art on the basis that what is proper to art can be defined in terms specific to art, outside of its articulation by philosophical discourse. However, Badiou's modernism, for Rancière, is not conventional; it is in an unholy alliance with Platonism. It is a twist on modernism in that it seeks to preserve the unitary and modern essence of art, the univocity of its concept, through an 'ultra-Platonism' expressed by the notion of a 'Platonism of the multiple' (Rancière, 2004b, p. 222). Anti-aesthetics, for Rancière perhaps the final phase of modernism, resists art's inclusion in what we have seen is for him a specifically aesthetic regime of art understood as a heteronomously constituted space. Badiou's work, it is argued, is part of the anti-aesthetic in that it steadfastly commits to the claim that the truth of art is proper to it and it alone, and to the existence of an inviolable border between art and discourses on it, especially philosophical discourses. What distinguishes Badiou from 'conventional modernism' is that he locates the specificity of art in the ideas that it produces rather than in its material specificity or its languages. His Platonism is modern in the sense that the eternity of the idea emerges *anti*-mimetically, in a form which is absolutely without semblance to it.

On Rancière's account, Badiou 'wants to highlight the Idea as pure abstraction, as the pure operation of the wholesale disappearance of the sensible', against 'every incarnation of the Idea which would engulf it in sensible matter' (Rancière, 2004b, p. 225). Yet at the same time Badiou needs to have the idea remain, and this is where philosophy comes in: philosophy reveals and describes the truths that art produces. Philosophy prevents the disappearance of the idea and confers upon its truth a consistency wrested from the inconsistency of the aesthetic site of its production. Hence a new form of Platonism, the 'pluralizing' of truth embodied in the one repeatable act, guaranteeing the inscription of truth beyond its emergence in the aesthetic moment. All of this is in the name of education for Rancière, since for the Platonist only ideas educate. But to preserve the educational value of the idea entails Badiou committing to aspects of modernism which are at odds with his rejection if it, namely that there is something irreducibly proper to art, that what is proper is independent of any discourse on art, and that that propriety is always the proper of a particular art. The act which subtracts the idea from its aesthetic site and form, for Rancière, is naming: 'there is art insofar as there is naming' (Rancière, 2004b, p. 225). And this is where we can locate Badiou's privileging of the poem; the poem names and thus preserves 'the passage of the infinite' (Rancière, 2004b, pp. 220, 223) through its embodiment in sensible form, preserves the disappearing over against what disappears. Philosophy discerns the truth subtracted by the poem. But such a naming, for Rancière, is the metaphorization and metamorphosis of the idea torn from its aesthetic regime, the very thing which constitutes the effectivity of the idea as it is embodied, appearing and disappearing, in the poem. It is as if the poem becomes, in philosophy's discerning and naming of its truth, an expression of the 'courage' of the thought which would withstand the ordeal the idea undergoes in the poem itself. But only because, in Badiou's hands, philosophy *pretends* to be surprised by what it finds in the poem, the poem only saying what philosophy 'needs it to say' (Rancière, 2004b, p. 228), needs it to say because said in the name of an ethical stance or a political programme achieved through the educative force of the idea.

The call to overcome aesthetics in the Heideggerian sense is made also by Agamben, and again it is uttered in the name of truth – but, contra Badiou, without at the same time overcoming Heidegger.[7] At the same time, Agamben is unsure whether now is the right time for a destruction of aesthetics, suggesting that it runs the risk of displacing any possible horizon for understanding art, instead facing man with an abyss and the task of working out how to leap over it. Then again, perhaps these latter are what is most needed today (Agamben, 1994, p. 6). But what is certain is that what we call our aesthetic enjoyment of a work of art is 'far from attaining the essential structure of the work, that is, the origin that gives itself in the work and remains preserved in it' (Agamben, 1994, p. 102). The artwork for Agamben is the gift of a site in which man may gain his 'original status in history and time', the gift of both his ecstatic dwelling on earth and the 'impetus towards shadow and ruin', of both freedom and alienation, of both historical consciousness and error. It is a site opened and maintained by rhythm (Agamben, 1994, p. 98), but rhythm understood not as sensation or as pure flow, but as implying a stop to flow, to the incessant flow of the instants of linear time, an 'atemporal dimension' in time. The artwork understood thus would be as much a with-holding as a giving, and the rhythm of the two a presencing. Agamben names the original site of this presencing, truth. We could compare this to Nancy, for whom art is the absenting of truth, 'by which it is the truth absolutely' (Nancy, 2005, p. 13). For Nancy, though, it is not that art makes truth appear; it is that truth makes art, by being what he calls the 'sense of sense', or the 'patency' of the world, by which is meant both the appearing of the non-apparent, and an appearance that does not simply appear or even appear at all (Nancy, 1996a, p. 33).

Art, for Agamben, is an origin which reveals itself essentially in the poetic act. But it is an origin now obscured. Art in our time is 'in crisis', and the crisis is 'in reality, a crisis of poetry' (Agamben, 1994, p. 59). Art, for Agamben as for Heidegger, is at the extreme point of its metaphysical destiny: nihilism (Agamben, 1994, p. 102). Alternatively, it is the fulfilment of aesthetics in being available in the form of pure potentiality ('availability-towards-nothingness') at the expense of its work character (Agamben, 1994, pp. 66–7). In any case, man has become alienated from his present moment, alienated from the proper place of the origin of his alienation, the present space between past and future in which the conflict between the old and the new can be resolved both individually and collectively. Aesthetics is the destiny of art in the sense that it has interrupted this relation to the past, has destroyed the transmissibility of the past and put in its place the transmission of the impossibility of transmitting the past; man is denied the appropriation of his own historicity in favour of a negative recuperation of his past. This is not merely one problem among others facing our culture, it is a matter of 'the very survival of culture' (Agamben, 1994, p. 111). One of the casualties of our failing to think art more originally is criticism. The critical judgement as to 'the logos of art and its shadow', otherwise known as the aesthetic judgement, is a space made superfluous – that is, no longer criticism's own – by art's having bridged the gap with criticism and itself become critical reflection on art, or in other words art (Agamben, 1994, p. 50). This loss of propriety has come

235

about, argues Agamben, through art having received within itself its own negation by identifying itself at least since Duchamp with the non-artistic product.

It is this last point which brings us to a fundamental difference between continental philosophy of art and analytical philosophical aesthetics (exceptions notwithstanding): its willingness to philosophize about, and along with, works of art contemporary with its own practice of doing philosophy. It also brings us to a difference internal to continental philosophy: its unwillingness to confront the ways in which contemporary art practice has taken on the role and function of theorizing and philosophizing about art, even as it frequently appeals to and enters into dialogue with continental philosophy of art in the process. Leaving aside Agamben, all the philosophers discussed here develop their philosophies of art through an encounter with contemporary art practice. Nonetheless, contemporary art practice often, and sometimes explicitly, claims for itself the wherewithal to philosophize about what art, or philosophy of art, is. Furthermore, it is common for it either to reject the theory/practice distinction in practical terms or even to become a practice that involves the performance of philosophy as art. This could well be a practice which would deserve the word-sign ~~art~~. But it would be no less art for that. ~~Art~~ has always been constitutive of art. And indeed, such art has always been the subject both of philosophical concerns over the loss of disciplinary propriety, and the charge that the thought immanent to the sensible is improper or impure in philosophical terms. But it is not as if philosophy has not recognized the philosophical worth of risking itself against performative, or more obviously performative, practices. For an example we could take the setting up of the Collège International de Philosophie (CIPh) in Paris in 1983. Part of the promise of this 'counter-institution' was to allow for the performativity of art practice to interrupt the teaching of philosophy, both by posing questions about philosophy and to provoke philosophy in the teaching of philosophy. In a newspaper interview prior to the inauguration of CIPh, Derrida, its founding director, states:

> more philosophy is still necessary, in less hierarchically organized spaces that are more exposed to the most irruptive provocations of the 'sciences,' of 'technologies,' of the 'arts' (whether one is talking about the discourse on art or 'practical,' performative operations) . . . openness to technical and artistic performances. (Derrida, 1992, pp. 110–11)

Two years into the life of that institution he says 'I would emphasize the fact that in the college we would like not only to study these arts in the traditional discursive mode . . . but also to *perform*' (Derrida, 1986, p. 67). Derrida's thought here, it would appear, is that the practice of a philosophy that is in touching distance of the doing of art might show us something essential about philosophy that philosophy 'itself' or alone could not. Consequently, it could be argued that it is precisely in these aspects of a possible (or impossible) practice of philosophy that the chance of overcoming aesthetics is now to be found.

14 Philosophy, Literature and Interpretation

Douglas Burnham and Melanie Ebdon

Is it a duty of philosophy to reflect upon its situation? If so then such reflection reveals, just down the corridor or perhaps in the next building, an army. This is an army of professional literary scholars, occupying departments of literature and languages at universities across the world, and outnumbering philosophers by five to one, perhaps more. Their assigned tasks are attentively to understand (in the broadest sense of the word) literary texts and the history of their reception, and of course to train an even larger army. The army and its huge college of cadets include a large proportion of contemporary writers, providing in addition to its numerical superiority a *systemic* advantage. Moreover, as a group, they are also the largest and most partisan consumers of continental philosophy. As philosophers with some type of interest in literature, then, our situation is rather like being on the slow, grubby local train and seeing the TGV (*train à grande vitesse*, 'high-speed train') whoosh past on its own line. Of course, philosophers have different interests in literature than the historical, critical or interpretative interest. However, it is the conclusion of a possible argument, and not an uncontested premise, that the two interests are entirely unrelated; it follows that philosophers ought to pay some attention to what is going on down the corridor.

The history of the study of literature over the past hundred years is often related as a story of '-isms': 'new' criticism, Freudianism, structuralism, feminism, post-colonialism, 'new' historicism and so forth. These movements arise because of social, political or intellectual contexts and because of a perceived exhaustion of the previous way of doing business. The movements always designate both a subject matter (what is focused on in a text, and which texts are favoured as in some way exemplary [the canon]) and a method. The latest hot topic in literary studies is 'ecocriticism', and not just in English-language criticism, although that will be our initial focus here. Now, philosophy knows and welcomes environmental thought, to be sure; but the relation to literature and particularly to a practice of criticism has not yet received extensive philosophical analysis. It is of interest for two main reasons. First, the practices of ecocriticism are philosophically suggestive and second, it appears to be different from other '-isms' in philosophically interesting ways. We will begin by sketching ecocriticism *on its own terms*, that is to say, as it is practised and theorized down the corridor.[1]

Ecocriticism

As with many critical approaches to literature, there is no common agreement over when, where and how ecocriticism began. Greg Garrard places its conception in 1962 with the publication of Rachel Carson's popular ecological text *Silent Spring* (Garrard, 2004, p. 1). While this text is foundational to a serious consideration of ecology within the humanities, a sense of ecocriticism as a notable literary critical 'movement' is not fully apparent until the 1980s in the USA and the 1990s in the UK (Barry, 2002, p. 248). The key thing to note about this relatively new movement in literary studies is that it is concerned with a mode of reading rather than a type of writing or a way of organizing literary history. Ecocriticism avoids positing something like a specifically ecocritical text and there is no 'green' canon. Terry Gifford notes that its interdisciplinarity and the range of texts covered 'is its distinctive strength, prevent[ing] the establishment of a monolithic methodology' (Gifford, 2008, p. 23). The emphasis is on diversity of focus and there is an implicit consensus among ecocritics that canonization of certain fictions should be resisted at all costs, lest the practice become constricted, in opposition to its inclusive ethos.

Two broad phases of ecocritical development can be identified:

> If first wave ecocriticism took the form of nature writing's seemingly metaphorical (but actually not quite) listening to the 'voice' of nature, second wave ecocriticism [. . .] has endeavoured to take scientific and technological development seriously because it bears so grievously upon our future and the future of our planetary home. (Wheeler and Dunkerley, 2008, p. 8)

In the United States, this first phase is aligned nicely with a long-standing tradition of nature-writing by the likes of Ralph Waldo Emerson (1803–82) and Henry David Thoreau (1817–62). In the UK (and, indeed, the rest of Europe), this practice of 'listening to the voice of nature' grafts on to the Romantic tradition; Raymond Williams's *The Country and the City* (1973) is seen as a text which makes an early crossover from studying nature in literature to performing ecocritical analysis (although this term is not used by Williams there). Both these traditions can ultimately be seen as belonging to the pastoral tradition which has been so fundamental to Western art and consciousness since ancient times. The second phase, then, turns its attention away from the spiritual, inspirational, epiphanic interactions with nature conceived as segregated 'otherness' and moves instead towards a revaluation of the concept of nature itself, one which takes its leads from ecological science and aims to revise the boundaries between what we consider natural and human.

There are, of course, texts which seem to have green issues more explicitly developed within them and such texts are obvious choices for ecocritical attention, particularly within pedagogic or proselytizing settings. For example, analysis of the poetry of John Clare (1793–1864) and William Wordsworth (1770–1850) features in the work of leading ecocritics such as Jonathan Bate and Greg Garrard. Yet the analytical practice yields many interesting results when applied to literature which does not engage so explicitly with 'obvious' aspects of nature, literature which may be set, for instance, primarily in urban environments. Such work engenders a radical questioning concerning what constitutes nature; is the human animal, with all its machines, factories and motorways – and indeed also its publishing and education institutions – fundamentally part of nature? Viewing the human species in this way is sometimes deemed deeply problematic as it would seem to excuse our worst excesses by reference to biological determinism; yet to fail to view humans in this way runs the risk of maintaining the fallacy of the human/nature distinction which itself may have contributed to ecological degradation. Ecocritical debate is abundant with such questions.

Of course, a depiction of the city as an ecological entity is not an endorsement of the city. However, it is crucial to perceive of the urban as implicated within an ecological framework simply because it *is*, and for most of us they are a larger part of our daily lived experience than savannahs or forests. To fail to integrate representations of the city in ecocritical debate is to insinuate that a large portion of humanity cannot really connect with ecological issues as it has limited contact with real nature. Yet, many ecologists and with them ecocritics argue that the city is part of our biological state. Only by recognizing it as integral to us as a species (as opposed to an imperious Self which alienates nature as the Other, a mode of existence which is imposed upon us, or a space which traps us against our will) can we have the opportunity of redirecting its effects, its waste products and its impact on the wider ecosystem within which it necessarily resides.

The polemic highlighted above marks out the spectrum of ecocriticism which ranges from deep ecology to 'shallow' environmentalism. Deep ecology has its foundations in the work of Arne Naess and harbours some of the most radical elements of ecological thought, some of which could be interpreted as misanthropic. In 1984, Warwick Fox published a paper on deep ecology in *The Ecologist* stating:

the world simply is not divided up into independently existing subjects and objects, nor is there any bifurcation in reality between the human and non-human realms. Rather all entities are constituted by their relationships. To the extent that we perceive boundaries, we fall short of a deep ecological consciousness. (Fox, 1984, p. 196)

This remains the founding principle of deep ecology, the darkest green shade in the ecocritical palette. At the opposite end of the spectrum is 'shallow' environmentalism, entrenched in a mechanistic view of the world which sees humans as fundamentally split off from nature: at best, they are nature's stewards (there is a relation here to Christian orthodoxy). This enables humans to feel that they act in nature's best interests, 'on nature's behalf', as it were. This stance maintains the human/nature distinction which might be considered regressive.

It is clear that ecocriticism rests on philosophical and/or scientific accounts of nature and the relationship between human beings and their environment. What is less clear is that it possesses a theory of literature, writing or criticism. One feature of the most recent phase is an acknowledgement that it is worth thinking about ecocriticism's relationship to the 'poststructuralist' or 'post-modern' thought that has been the staple of literary criticism for a couple of decades. Michael Bennett writes of the need for ecocriticism to find a way of integrating such theory with ecocritical practice in order that ecocriticism can develop a way of reading urban ecology. He writes, 'There is no unmediated way of existing in harmony with nature, and there never has been. Once we make human decisions on how to exist in our surroundings, we are already involved in sociocultural (and again, theoretical) modes of thought' (Bennett, 2003, p. 300). Ecocriticism will remain a 'relatively pale and undertheorized field unless and until it more freely ventures into urban environments' (Bennett, 2003, p. 304), for which purpose an interaction with more con-ventional theory is required. For example, Fredric Jameson's analysis of postmodern capitalism and Jean Baudrillard's account of the loss of the real are ideas which *should* be fruitful for urban ecocritics thinking about the atti-tudes or experiences of the city-dweller as cut off from that which is usually considered natural. A clear comprehension of the hyperreal and capitalist culture would seem to be good starting points for the urban ecocritic as such studies offer insight into the worldview of most of the Westernized world.[2] Despite calls such as Bennett's to bridge the gap between postmodern theory and ecocriticism, this will run against the latter's tendency to perceive itself as an all-encompassing paradigm, dragging in its wake many '-ism's which have been central to literary studies in successive waves throughout the latter part of the twentieth century, such as feminism, Marxism and postcolonial criticism. For instance, whereas these forms of study raised awareness among literary critics of a particular section of society or a historically recurring theme, ecocriticism attempts to show global and historical interconnection: nothing exists in isolation.

Ecocritical discourse is not homogeneous, partly because the scientific or theoretical discourses upon which it is built are not, and also because of the existing interests of critics. As well as having different phases of development and two broadly opposed ends of a green spectrum (environmentalism and ecology), there are hybrid forms within it which have sprung from grafting established areas of critical or theoretical discourse onto this new 'green stock', most notably ecofeminism and postcolonial ecocritcism. Lawrence Buell describes ecofeminism as a label for 'a range of theoretical and practical positions that share the view that the "twin dominations of women and nature" are artefacts of patriarchal culture instituted in antiquity and ... intensified by the epistemological dualism and rational instrumentalism of the scientific and technological revolutions' (Buell, 2005, p. 139). Postcolonial ecocriticism gives an interesting new insight into a well-established mode of literary study, taking as its premise the idea that colonization has typically been fuelled by the desire to control natural resources (e.g. climates amenable to the production of high-value crops, the labour of human beings). Postcolonial ecocriticism equips the traditional postcolonial critic with a valuable new vocabulary with which to investigate a curiously under-explored yet screamingly obvious area of the field (the eagerly awaited *Postcolonial Ecocriticism* by Helen Tiffin will help to consolidate this developing area). If decolonization is, in part, a process of realigning oneself with one's land and rethinking the connection between land and national identity then postcolonial ecocriticism explores issues such as the tension created between a sense of connection to one's land and the fact of living in a modern, globalized world (an issue which has long been prevalent in diaspora literatures). While the theme of a personal or communal connection to land (e.g. one's home territory) is typically thought of as a noble human feature (riddled with nostalgia as it may be), this polemic is problematized by a study of the Nazi *Blut und Boden* (blood and soil) ideology which is a case of this perceived connection to land taken to its most horrific extreme.[3] In this instance, a 'sense' of personal/communal connection to land is literalized into an exchange between humans and the earth upon which they depend, and the desire to preserve this link in an 'uncontaminated' form.

The relationship between ecocriticism and the chameleon that is postmodern theory is a fraught one which greatly depends on which strand of 'postmodern' is being used. In one sense, ecocriticism tracks beyond the way in which deconstruction was absorbed into literary theory. If postmodern discourse deconstructs, ecocritical discourse *re*constructs anew, with the emphasis being on pattern and an egalitarian interconnectivity, as opposed to structures concerned only with hierarchy, power and domination. Seen this way, ecocriticism can operate what Jonathan Coope amusingly terms a kind of 'ecological outreach work to postmodernism' (Coope, 2008, p. 78) which steps into what it sees as a mess of pessimism or nihilism made possible through this process of deconstruction and offers a new direction for constructive action. Deconstruction is seen as a necessary stage of development, preparing the ground for this new critical and philosophical paradigm. However, in another sense of the term, ecocritics see themselves as truly postmodern (i.e. being beyond the modern era) in espousing an integrated worldview which breaks away from the modern mechanistic one, which in nostalgia experiences itself as fragmented.

Ecocriticism offers not simply a consciousness-raising about issues presented in works of literature, and thereby also about ecological themes more generally, but an alteration in the very way we perceive our consciousness. Consciousness does not float God-like above the world, able to see all of its flaws and lies, but is a material part of this world and has a significant role to play within it. Therefore, the questions raised by ecocriticism, its key debates, are about restructuring the links between world, writer, text and reader: this comes full circle with the recognition that the reader exists within the world too. The author-text-reader relation – including the professional practice of criticism which in turn feeds back into new writing – is seen as an integrated sub-system of a larger ecological relation.

There is no specifically ecocritical text (no canon), but there are texts that explicitly mark their ecological engagement. What strategies of writing might best serve this aim? Or, expressed differently: as ecocriticism (or ecological awareness more generally) feeds back into practices of writing, might a tradition of ecoliterature be emerging, and what new possibilities of the literary can be envisaged for it? The reading of Jon McGregor's *If Nobody Speaks of Remarkable Things* below will suggest interesting ways of thinking about character, voice, setting and above all poetic style. A return to poetic language is, perhaps, indicative of a return to literature's ancient roots and its framing concept of humankind as part of a natural order, rather than superior to it. Jonathan Bate makes a related point in *The Song of the Earth*:

> The poet's way of articulating the relationship between humankind and environment, person and place, is peculiar because it is experiential, not descriptive. Whereas the biologist, the geographer and the Green activist have *narratives* of dwelling, a poem may be a *revelation* of dwelling. (Bate, 2000, p. 266)

The distinction Bate makes between description (or narrative) and experience (or revelation) is a version of the inside/outside distinction, as applied to the relation of author or reader not only to the text but to the world that grounds that text. If taken as part of a response to ecological debates it is very difficult to see ecocriticism as merely an ethereal, intellectual product, the latest issue from the ivory towers of academia; it becomes, instead, a way of reading and debating which is focused not just on the real world (the ecocritic pointedly leaves out the now-customary scare quotes), but, more particularly, on the *more-than-human world*. Arguably, this is the single characteristic which distinguishes ecocriticism significantly from previous 'isms'. Let us add this, then, to the list of key characteristics of this literary critical movement, in order to take them forward into readings and philosophical reflection. First, ecocriticism sees author, text and writer as an integrated material system, itself part of the more-than-human world. Second, ecocriticism is a practice of reading, and consciously avoids those processes such as canonization which tend to emerge, with greater or lesser insistence, from other literary critical movements. Third, ecocriticism – at least at its most philanthropic, deep ecology end – refuses to permit the human/nature distinction to be absolute at any level and thus reads industrial, technological and urban literary settings and themes in terms of a broader and richer conception of ecology. Fourth, it follows that ecocriticism does not and could not comprise a theory of literature, writing or language *per se*; it involves an identification of the *place* of literature within a wider system – as the moment when the ecosystem represents itself back to itself without ever leaving the system – rather than literature's inner nature.

First Reading

It is pressing that ecocriticism encompass literature which is centred upon urban environments, if the aim of a comprehensive revision of the human/ nature distinction is to be reached. *If Nobody Speaks of Remarkable Things* (2002) is the very well-received first novel by Jon McGregor. The action of this narrative remains tightly focused on life in one British street, closely resembling the streets of McGregor's home town, Nottingham. This text has the events of one day as its centre of consciousness, in particular a fatal traffic accident. The novel delivers a nexus of interconnected characters who touch on one another's lives without necessarily being aware of this. The narrative is a combination of first- and third-person narration, with few names used to identify characters and a lack of speech marks around dialogue, giving the effect of blurred or indistinguishable borders among characters, and between characters and narrator. *Remarkable Things* offers a model of urban life which centres upon the city as an inherently organic being. On the human level, the novel reflects especially multiculturalism: the city as a site of global integration without homogenization. The form of this novel is reflective of the way it portrays the status of nature in relation to the city: *Remarkable Things* dances from one first-person narrative to another and back again, with interjected third-person passages throughout. Characters are shown to be linked (neighbours, friends, family, people who pass each other in daily/weekly patterns). This ethos is evident from page one which delivers a striking account of a city in 'song' in a way that amends the focus on nature writing which characterized first-wave ecocritics' listening to the 'voice' of nature:

> If you listen, you can hear it.
> The city, it sings.
> If you stand quietly, at the foot of the garden, in the middle of the street,
>   on the roof of a house.
> It's clearest at night, when the sound cuts more sharply across the
>   surface of things, when the song reaches out to a place inside you.
>   (McGregor, 2002, p. 1)

The use of line endings here is indicative of the poetic prose throughout the novel. This raises the issue of the relation of form and content. Bate's idea, discussed above, of a poetic revelation of dwelling is certainly a helpful way to think of *Remarkable Things*, as we begin with this singing city and are then taken through the wide variety of 'notes' which make up this song: air-conditioners, traffic on tarmac, road-menders, jack-hammers and pneumatic pumps, alarms, sirens, fighting cats, 'the hobbled clip-clop of a slow walk home' (McGregor, 2002, p. 3). After a few pages of such description, building up a rich symphony of this urban mass, we are told that the actual starting point of the story is in the gap between one day and another, at a point when all the noise has just stopped and is about to begin again, a period of time which lasts as long as 'the falter between heartbeats, like the darkness between blinks [. . .]. We are in that moment now, there is silence and the whole city is still' (McGregor, 2002, pp. 3–4). This direct address of the reader in the present tense, at this exquisite point of entry to the novel, gives the hitherto disembodied narrator the identity of the story-teller, weaving the reader into the action so that this palpitating, blinking, singing city-mass becomes our dwelling place too.

Halfway through the novel, we follow a young girl (unnamed) in her exploration of a disused house. This section foregrounds the presence of aspects more typically labelled 'natural' in a degraded domestic setting. The present tense is used again as the house's interior is described as:

> hidden, furred over, concealed by a slow slather of wet growth, mould and
> moss and crusted lichen creeping over it all like a lascivious tongue,
> muffling the hard edges, crawling across the floor, climbing up walls,

clinging from ceilings, thickening and flowering and spraying out spores to breed in any untouched corners. (McGregor, 2002, p. 135)

This is excessive, carnivalesque language, a celebration of fecundity as the lichen seduces the interior, followed by a torrent of verbs which show its active reclamation of the domestic space. In this scene, we are made aware that urban space is temporarily borrowed from that which is typically conceived of as natural/wild, which lurks within it to reclaim it at the first opportunity. This unnerves as much as it excites the girl who is eventually startled from the house by a noise. However, the third-person narrative eye tells us what the girl would have seen had she continued up to the top floor of the house where the roof has partly fallen in on the attic room: '[m]ice, making tiny nests from scraps of magazines and bedding . . . Bats, hanging in wardrobes like tiny folded umbrellas. Pigeons, clustered in the corner of another room . . .' (McGregor, 2002, p. 135). Eventually, on reaching the exposed attic room we happen upon what is one of the most startling images of the novel:

> . . . she would have found the one room left open to the light, she would
> have stood, breathless, picking cobwebs from her fingers and her face,
> staring at a whole meadow of wildflowers and grasses, poppies and oxeyes
> and flowering coriander, all flourishing in bird droppings and all lunging
> pointedly towards the one square foot of available sky. (McGregor, 2002,
> p. 135)

So ends the chapter. This section moves from carnivalesque excess to a sublime moment of revelation which only the narrator and reader are privy to and which the character, crucially, misses: a remarkable thing that nobody will speak of within the frame of the story itself. The geometrical description given to the gap in the roof is at odds with the abundant over-spilling of wildlife throughout the house, and the lack of 'available sky' indicates that the opportunity for plant and non-human animal life to exist in an urban space *is* limited. However, the flowers 'lunging pointedly' suggests something like a conscious will on the part of the flowers to claim their place in this urban, domestic setting. An ecosystem in miniature is hinted at here too, as the 'bird droppings' (presumably the work of the cluster of pigeons) are the fertilizing soil for these plants. McGregor's work here can be read as a note on the often unacknowledged parallel existence of other species in the urban. Placing them in a recently abandoned domestic space, McGregor brings the human and the more-than-human spheres together, showing their necessary contiguity within an urban ecology.

From Ecological Thought to Aesthetics

It is one of the peculiarities of continental philosophy that everyone deals with literature. Few continental philosophers have not written about literary texts or the literary. Trying to understand how the phenomenon of ecocriticism might impact upon philosophy's relation to literature cannot begin with existing conceptions of that relation – for there are just too many. Instead, we shall start with those much rarer places where the issue of literature happily triangulates with a conception of system at least analogous to ecology. Now, concepts of natural systems are not new in philosophy or science. However, it is unusual to find such analysis put into explicit relation with aesthetic phenomena generally, and literature particularly. However, there are at least two traditions that do so: first, that Kantian thought which reaches a certain pinnacle with Nietzsche,[4] and second, the Heideggerian tradition. We will look briefly at the second of these later under the heading of eco-phenomenology. Our search for the philosophical resources needed to explore the significance of ecocritical practices can begin with Kant.

In the second part of the *Critique of Judgement*, the Critique of Teleological Judgement, Kant proposes a multi-faceted analysis of the transcendentally conditioning roles of teleology. One particularly curious way in which teleology is employed is his treatment of the basic object of biological sciences: the living organism. Kant's critical target here is the broadly mechanistic or naturalized view of the living body. According to this view, a living body (whether plant or animal) is an aggregate of parts or organs, each of which contributes something to making up the whole. Similarly, systems of organisms are understood as aggregates, and the notion of *interrelations* among organisms for example is a *subsequent* feature of such systems.

Kant contrasts this picture with a modified teleological conception. Something is understood teleologically if its existence or activity is conceived as coordinated by and oriented towards some purpose. Now, for Kant (following Aristotle), there is a distinction between two types of real purpose: first, an 'extrinsic' purpose which is the role a thing may play in being a means to some end, and second, an 'intrinsic' purpose in which a thing embodies its own purpose. These latter are what Kant calls 'natural purposes' (also translated as 'physical ends'), and the key examples are living organisms (Kant, 1987, §65). Such an organism is made up of parts, to be sure – individual organs, and below that, individual cells. Each has its function, but is also 'organized'. That is, the parts seem to be determined to be the parts that they are according to the form or 'purpose' which is the whole creature. That is to say, in contrast to the 'mechanistic' picture described above, the organs of the body must be conceived as in some way subsequent to the whole body. The teleological concept is extended in §75 to the whole of natural systems: what

247

today we would call ecosystems. Individual living beings cannot properly be understood as intrinsic entities, but rather reciprocally producing and produced by the system (organic and inorganic) of which they are a 'part'. (A similar point is made in Kant's *Opus Postumum*, 1995, 21:211.) The parts reciprocally produce and are produced by the form of the whole; everywhere is both system and part. Moreover, this reciprocity is repeated at the level of organ and cell, and at the level of ecosystem. (The parallel with the worlds within worlds of Leibniz's *Monadology* is striking.) In order to come near the concept of life, we need to assume a teleological causation, such that the form of the whole organism (the purpose or *telos* of the organs) is represented as the cause of the organs and their operation, which then collectively make up and maintain the whole. In summary, 'An organized product of nature is one in which everything is a purpose and reciprocally also a means' (Kant, 1987, §66).

Kant is very careful to distance himself from the rationalist position on teleology. This, he claims, takes teleology as a *constitutive* principle of knowledge. Kant claims that such a teleological causation is *utterly alien* to any natural causation as our understanding is able to conceive it. Even calling it 'causation' is quite peculiar. The thoroughgoing reciprocity is not 'exhibited'. Teleological judgement judges *through* but never entirely *with* available empirical laws governing the workings of the organism's parts. In order to satisfy reason's demand for self-consistency and completion, we are given 'permission' to apply reflectively the idea of causation according to purposes – a 'remote analogy' which necessarily brings with it the idea of purposive action, of something like 'an artist (a rational being) apart from nature' (Kant, 1987, First Introduction VI). If nature is defined as an object of determinate cognition, the organ, organism and system is 'in' nature and yet also 'escapes' it. Teleological organization is what we might call 'immanently transcendent'.

Now, much could be made of how this analysis – from the second half of Kant's *Critique of Judgement* – relates to the better-known studies of aesthetic judgement in the first half. For example, what should we make of the fact that Kant describes how the form of the beautiful 'enlivens' the structure of indeterminate cognition such that it is self-organizing and self-sustaining, having an inner 'purposive' causality (1987, §12; see Burnham, 2004)? Let us first look briefly at Nietzsche's incorporation of these ecosystemic ideas, and their relation to the project of literature. We will then have occasion to return to Kant; not to the judgement of the beautiful, but rather the *sublime*.

In the late 1860s, Nietzsche began writing a thesis on Kant's account of teleology (translation in Smith, 2005); the *Critique of Judgement* is thus the one Kantian text we can be sure he knew very well. We contend that the account of life and its relationship to cognition he encountered there reappears, albeit in modified form, in later works. There has been considerable discussion in the literature concerning the extent to which Nietzsche's thought can be appropriated for a philosophical engagement with ecological themes.[5] A plausible line of thought would argue that Nietzsche's conception of life is ecosystemic. To stress Nietzsche's concerns and his originality, 'life' here will be replaced by 'cultural life'. One of Nietzsche's key concerns is to show how culture is neither independent of, nor an epiphenomenon of, the underlying biological/physiological human animal, but has become a chief mode in which human life happens. The argument connecting Nietzsche to ecosystemic thought might proceed as follows. Cultural life is:

- materially naturalized without simply being reductive or entailing a transcendent view from outside incorporation (as Nietzsche often argues, the spiritual must be understood through the physiological. However, Nietzsche also presents his own version of Kant's critique of the limits of scientific cognition which culminates in the account of perspective.)
- reciprocally integrated (the will to power is multiple and originally relational; even a will to power that is not reactive could never be in- and from-itself, for it belongs to its fate.)
- comprised of a diversity of types (thus for example the task of a *Typenlehre* of morals in *Beyond Good and Evil* (Nietzsche, 2001, p. 186))
- involving spheres of embeddedness; that is, a dialectic of closedness *qua* system but historically contingent openness to adjacent systems (Nietzsche talks about different nations' relationships with landscape and climate (e.g. 2001, p. 255), as well as the vast reservoirs of history and culture, all as forming the account of national types; and yet these national systems also affect each other across Europe and are sometimes susceptible to external factors such as 'the Orient')
- a dynamic but self-regulating system (e.g. 'Art saves him and through art life saves him – for itself' (*Birth of Tragedy*, Nietzsche, 1999, p. 7), a theme that reappears in varying guises throughout Nietzsche's work; e.g. *Genealogy of Morality* (Nietzsche, 1998, Third treatise, para. 28).

However, in accordance with our theme, what is especially interesting about Nietzsche's thought here is the connection with art, as a key cultural domain. As a writer, Nietzsche is in constant pursuit of a literary mode that would not only be in some way adequate to this conception of cultural life, but which, through this 'adequacy', could intervene in a system that has become unhealthy, so as to bring about a form of human life that could affirm and love this system from within. The former corresponds to the problem of 'ecoliterature' discussed above; the latter to the moral and political vocation of ecocriticism. In other words, in Nietzsche, the ecological problem is also a problem of the nature and the function of literature.

Now, the most conspicuous of Nietzsche's attempts to theoretically describe and enact such a literature is in the Dionysiac dithyrahm, which preoccupies him from *The Birth of Tragedy* to his last poetic works. In the terms of the former, early work, the artistic project of the dithyrahm involves a revolution in the conception of literature (or, if one prefers, a repetition, suitably tailored for us moderns, of the Greek concept of literature as found in early Greek tragedy). Oversimplifying greatly, what this involves is a three-fold revolution. First, a correction of the position of the audience of tragedy (or *mutatis mutandis* of music or literary texts) from being mere spectators, essentially distanced and who can only be affected, to a position of coextensivity with the chorus. Second, a collapse of the position of poet as sovereign master, and the corresponding location of the poetic act within the 'work' itself (see Nietzsche, 1999, p. 8). Third, the rescue of the *symbolic* from its appropriation by intellectualist conceptions of both language and world, restoring to it the Dionysiac power of embodying metaphysical truth (see Burnham and Jesinghausen, 2009).

The first and second of these involves rethinking the nature of producing or receiving the literary (or musical) work such that the act of creation or reception is a *reciprocating part of the literary system*, with the system understood on the model of an ecosystem. This clearly resonates with the ecocritical theme of the writing-reading-criticism process as an ecological sub-system.

Such a conception of the work finds a more contemporary if partial echo in Alain Badiou. Or rather, it *should* do. Let us say that Badiou's ontology commences with the pure multiple; the situation is the multiple consistently presented. For example, at any point, the domain of what is taken or known to be art is a situation. One problem might be how something new (an event) comes to happen 'within' this situation. For Badiou, as for Nietzsche, this question is incalculable and the real issue is: 'what *now*?' That is, after the event, what subjectivities emerge as the carrying forward of the truth procedure faithful to that event? The truth of art is immanent (that is, the truth of art is identical with the function of art; the truth of art does not represent or reveal) and singular (its truth belongs to it alone, and is irreducible to science, philosophy or politics). Insofar as we think of ecocriticism as positing as normative an ecocritical text which would represent the 'truth' of ecological science, then to be sure our account of a certain literature fails both tests. However, ecocriticism does not posit such a canon or a normative ideal of representation. Instead, it reads in solidarity with texts. Accordingly, we might want to think ecocriticism as an element in a truth procedure whereby a literature inquires into the truth of the *systematicity of its own production*, these inquiries make up what above we rather poorly described as 'new possibilities' for literature. The truth of this literature (not itself finite) is 'across' works, writers, readers, critics and publishers.

Badiou, however, both makes this possible, and also forbids it. The artistic truth is an infinite generic multiple and is a series of works termed an 'artistic configuration' (Badiou, 2005, p. 2). Badiou, helpfully, feels compelled to 'imperfectly' name a few examples: classical tragedy, 'classical style' from Haydn to Beethoven, the narrative novel up to Joyce. 'Infinite' insofar as there is no principle of its completion; 'generic' insofar as it is and remains invisible with respect to the 'encyclopaedia' of the situation of art. The configuration is 'unfolded through chance in the form of works' (Badiou, 2005, p. 12). The work is the subject here, not the author (the name 'Aeschylus' is 'really the index of a central void in the previous situation of choral poetry' (Badiou, 2005, p. 13)) and *especially* not the reader. The revocation of the rights and position of mastery of the author is completely in alignment with our discussion of Nietzsche above; what is missing is Nietzsche's collapse of these elements (poet and audience) into *moments of* the re-understood work (Dionysiac chorus). '[T]he work of art is the only finite thing that exists', Badiou 'happily' argues (Badiou, 2005, p. 11). Almost all of Badiou's encounters with literature deal with isolated works. This position is . . . well, *endearing*, but not terribly convincing. It becomes impossible to reflect upon the practices of writing, publishing, criticism and education as elements of the truth procedures that enable the tenacity of the configuration. The truth procedures of science or politics are both conceived of as an 'inseparable unity of a theory and practice' (Badiou, 2003, p. 79); only in the case of art is the practice removed, leaving what may well be its culmination, but which evades it as a thinking. Much more recently, however, Badiou's work has come to speak of a 'materialist dialectics' in association with *Logiques des Mondes* and its analysis of location and relation.[6] It remains unclear whether this new work will enable us to employ Badiou's formidable philosophy to help us understand the Nietzschean problem of a 'collapsed' literature, a task made all the more timely by the phenomenon of ecocriticism.

We will turn to the idea of the literary system shortly. Let us first pursue the third 'recovery' (the rescue of the symbolic) with a reading.

Second Reading

William Faulkner is not commonly regarded as a novelist for whom 'nature' or 'environment' in itself is of the highest importance. Landscape and natural phenomena are more usually subordinated to *place*, locale, region. Or, they are employed symbolically – merely standing in for properly *human* isolation, strength, decay, fecundity, purity, 'animality', etc.

In 'The Old People' and especially in 'The Bear', two stories collected together in his 1942 *Go Down, Moses* (Faulkner, 1973), something different is encountered. 'The Bear' is a short novel with two intertwined plots. In the first, Ike McCaslin as a boy participates in the annual hunt for Old Ben, an enormous and legendary bear, in an untouched area of forest. In the second, Ike as a young man searches through the plantation accounting records and discovers inter-racial adultery and incest; the narrative continues with his mannered response to this discovery.

To be sure, the primeval forest and its sovereign lord, Old Ben, appear to be linked to the human characters by just such a symbolic link. The forest is the proper native land of the 'old people'; linked in history and in blood, it is the *proper site* of their nobility. In addition, the forest is the *spiritual father* to an ancient race and also, by the end, to Ike McCaslin: 'It seemed to him at the age of ten that he was witnessing his own birth' (Faulkner, 1973, p. 195). The forest merely concretizes a fecund wisdom, and an ancestry without chronograph which properly belongs to the human ('You mean he already knows me, that I aint never been to the big bottom before . . . It was me he was watching' (Faulkner, 1973, p. 201); and again: 'It was quite familiar, until he remembered: this was the way he had used to dream about it.'). As a meaningful entity, the novel *seems* to proceed through the natural, but always understood as a symbolic gesture that is *on the way to* the human.

The forest and Old Ben are evoked by Faulkner as sublime. The relevant account of the sublime here (the account which deals not just with experiential excess and fear, as for example Burke's, but also with transcendence) is Kant's, in the *Critique of Judgment*. 'Transcendence' here means: belonging to a distinct ontological region, especially one that is represented or thought as *prior*, or surpassing in value, originality or power. Kant seems to fall into line with this reduction of the natural to symbol. To be sure, Kant's account is that the sublime experience *begins* with an object or event (e.g. a mountain or storm) which overwhelms the imagination's ability to grasp, or the will's ability to master. However, Kant argues, this excess of the presented object *should* cause pain or fear. But the sublime, however, is if anything a *pleasurable* feeling. It follows, Kant argues, that some mental event or capacity must mediate between the breakdown of imagination or will and the subsequent pleasure. Kant's solution is that one feels pleasure in the sublime insofar as one's noumenal self (as opposed to one's phenomenal, bodily self) comes to display itself as that which *nonetheless* demands the *absolute* grasp, or *nonetheless* demands an absolute mastery by the will (which Kant defines as its freedom from natural conditions). Thus, according to Kant, the sublime proper has nothing to do with quantitative size, complexity or power, but is rather a question of reason's qualitative otherness to sensible cognition. Natural objects are called 'sublime' only through a mistake – or rather, by a 'subreption', a kind of hidden theft. Thus, again, as in the traditional readings of Faulkner sketched above, the natural (forest, bear) is the occasion for the human to reflect upon its own essential properties.

Such is the force Faulkner gives to the forest and the bear, however, that the merely associative links we discussed above buckle under the load. That is, at least at times the forest and Old Ben become *the* characters, *the* theme, *the* setting.

> ... [T]he wilderness, the big woods, bigger and older than any recorded document: – of white man fatuous enough to believe he had bought any fragment of it, of Indian ruthless enough to pretend that any fragment of it had been his to convey. (Faulkner, 1973, p. 191)

And Old Ben: '... not as big as he had dreamed it but as big as he had expected, bigger, dimensionless against the dappled obscurity, looking at him' (Faulkner, 1973, p. 209). The stream-of-consciousness movement from 'not as big' to 'as big' to 'bigger' and finally 'dimensionless' is revealing. Size, force, time become impossible, unexperienceable. Forest and bear lose their symbolic transparency, not because the narrative ceases to demand it of them, but because as sublime they transcend the *significative gaze* (of the characters, and by extension, the reader) which would make of them mere vehicles of narrative theme. As in Kant's account of the sublime, however, the real object remains human, and there seems to be a symbolic transfer of the 'excess' of the natural to the 'excess' of the human: the mysterious inscrutability of Sam Fathers, even in death; the mythic qualities of certain ancestors; the transcendent endurance of the black Southerners that Ike and his cousin debate; and the unintelligibility (to everyone around him, and perhaps even to himself) of Ike's adjuration of his family and history.

But this anthropocentric reading (which reads Faulkner as if just a sophisticated version of *Bambi*) is not the only reading possible, and not the one ultimately demanded by the text. In the following sequence, for example, the Kantian story (as given above) is decisively undone:

> Now he knew what he had heard in the hounds' voices in the woods that morning and what he had smelled when he peered under the kitchen where they huddled. It was in him too, a little different because they were brute beasts and he was not, but only a little different – an eagerness, passive; an abjectness, a sense of his own fragility and impotence against the timeless woods, yet without doubt or dread. (Faulkner, 1973, p. 200)

> But: he knew only that for the first time he realised that the bear which had run in his listening and loomed in his dreams since before he could remember and which therefore must have existed in the listening the dreams of his cousin and Major de Spain and even old General Compson before they began to remember in their turn, was a mortal animal. (Faulkner, 1973, pp. 200–1)

In these passages it is clear that this is no Kantian subreption, wherein the natural object is called sublime by a kind of mistake. Symbol and symbolized positions seem to hesitate, perhaps oscillate. The forest and the bear transcend the specificity of the human as given in the novel; they are the all but lost origin and the now all but impossible destination of the human. Thus the *most* we can say is that if nature signifies, then it signifies the no longer or the not yet of the human. The direction of the symbolism can reverse, and the human characters *can* become concrete symbols of the degraded possibilities that arise within the forest.

The narrator asserts that the bear had 'earned for himself a name, a definite designation like a living man' (Faulkner, 1973, p. 193) and again compares Old Ben to Priam (p. 194); similarly, Sam Fathers claims that the bear is 'the head bear. He's the man' (p. 198). In their heavy-handedness these anthropomorphisms act against themselves: in this novel, to compare Old Ben to a man is deprecation. The wilderness transcends and engulfs both nature and the human, understood as an opposition: nature as mere life and brute animality, the human with its tainting guns and compasses and its 'thin, clear, quenchless lucidity' (Faulkner, 1973, p. 207) (this should be compared to the unextended moment of quiet in McGregor's novel). In turn, we must reject a reading according to which the two (man and nature) can be separated, a direction or hierarchy established – that they do not *belong together from the beginning*.

However, a very similar constitutive ambiguity haunts Kant's account of the sublime. Three issues mount up to complicate that ordinary reading of Kant's text:

(i) As we saw, the sublime 'should' be painful, but instead is a kind of pleasure. In fact, however, it is *both*. '[T]he feeling of the sublime is a pleasure that only arises *indirectly*, being brought about by the feeling of a momentary check to the vital forces *followed* at once by a discharge all the more powerful' (Kant, 1987, §23, our emphasis). This is a real moment, not an anachronistic distinction arising within philosophical analysis. Does this first moment of pain, of the humiliation of sense, carry significance?

(ii) This painful experience is certainly not teleological with respect to reason – it does not contain within itself a reference or anticipation of its subsequent overthrow. The empirical faculties of the human feel themselves as not even abandoned but rather profoundly alone. Thus, humans without moral culture, Kant argues, are incapable of moving beyond this first moment (Kant, 1987, §29).

(iii) The subreption is not once and for all over – and thus the sublime proper cannot consist in any 'once and for all'. For the judgement remains stubbornly aesthetic, locked into our empirical senses, bodies and wills. Reason does not and cannot simply restore calm. So, between the 'outrage' against the empirical self, and the unanticipated redemption by reason, there is a 'vibration', a 'rapidly alternating repulsion and attraction produced by one and the same object' (Kant, 1987, §27). Thus, what we called the 'first' moment above constantly returns, reasserting its validity as the *equi-primordial* sublime otherness of nature. Thus, Kant must also admit that natural objects which in ordinary language we call sublime are, in themselves, greeted with a 'kind of respect' (1987, §25) without explaining what this term (so key in the ethical writings) might mean here. It is left to us to explore the implications.

This reveals a *double subreption* (cf. Burnham, 2004). If a storm – or the literary evocation of a storm – is judged sublime, then it is not the storm which is properly made into a negative presentation of my distinctively human and sovereign sublimity. Instead, or at least as much, it is my full humanity which becomes a symbol of the sublimity proper to the system that *includes the storm and the human*. The symbol refuses to unambiguously gesture in one direction; it encloses both. Thus the compelling ground of a 'kind of respect' mentioned above for natural objects in themselves; that is, a moral force.

Here, we have unearthed a sublimity which does not necessarily refer back to *human* spirituality and transcendence, but refers precisely to the immanent transcendence (which carries a moral demand) of the *inhuman* towards the eco-systematic. That is to say, a sublime nature which is irreducible to any account of nature that begins by excluding some aspect of the human, and at the same time cannot be read as an idealist projection of the human onto nature. What is sublime, then, is 'being in'. The oscillation of the sublime relation reveals the original inseparability of the *relata*.

With this new conception in mind, we can attempt a re-reading of the appearance of the sublimity of nature in Faulkner's novel. In a novel that appears to be about specifically *human* obligation and guilt, and where the inhuman (the forest, the bear) seems a mere allegorical vehicle, an ambiguity is observed that carries the text beyond its nominal humanist ambitions.

As Faulkner understands it here, the experience of this sublimity is the condition of possibility of a proper, respectful and thus ethical relation between human and forest as primeval nature and even, it is suggested, *among* humans. *Proper humanity begins in the recognition of the inhuman system.* This is the link between the two narratives which make up the novel. Ike's childhood experiences of entering a respectful and proper relation with the wilderness only through the deliberate abnegation of all the impurities of civilization (gun, watch, compass) seems to become the 'model' for his (morally charged but nevertheless pointless, theatrical, absurd) rejection of his inheritance, family and history. But importantly, it is not just a model, because the wilderness experience is transforming experience (i.e. unique and necessary) and not merely educational (i.e. exemplary and contingent).

Here, 'nature' is opposed to mere surface (law-governedness, available resources, matter). The map, the compass, the charter, the treaty, the straight locomotive line, the accounting register of the slaves, geometrically arranged concrete marker posts, are all metaphors for this surface. Entered on horseback, or on foot, the forest rather *encloses*. The novel too presents a surface, that of a literary fiction that circulates among anyone who can read. The text's ecological theme lies between the two directions of symbolic transference. Is it the forest as a symbol of human possibilities, or the human characters as symbols of degraded nature? The literary text as an internal system for the construction of meanings has broken down because of this ambiguity. Faced with the pages of the novel, we are no long anyone who can read, but instead are in the same situation as Ike faced with the pages of the accounting records: 'what to do?'.[7]

Other Paths for Research

Let us count the above as a concrete contribution to eco-phenomenology[8] and hermeneutics. Eco-phenomenology is a relatively new endeavour within the tradition of Husserlian thought, very broadly conceived, which seeks methods appropriate to the study of the ties that bind human subjectivity to nature. Husserl famously rejects naturalism, insofar as he thought it essentially incapable of incorporating the central insight of phenomenology, which is the intentional nature of all conscious acts. And yet, the eco-phenomenologists argue, this does not necessarily rule out the possibility of a constitutional analysis of the intentional bond itself that begins with the mutual enfoldedness, perhaps even essentially moral in character, of self and world. Conceiving this mutual enfoldedness need not exclude, but is also not reducible to, the cognitive or environmental sciences. Historically, of course, the key figures here are Martin Heidegger and Maurice Merleau-Ponty. Merleau-Ponty certainly accepts Heidegger's replacement of the classic account of intentionality with the notion of a projective and ultimately ecstatic being-in, but he then addresses this being-in through embodiment.

For Merleau-Ponty (as for many others) art is a privileged site in which the ecstatic being of the existing subject is revealed. Thus, in association with this new field of phenomenological enquiry, one might posit an 'ecohermeneutics'[9] particularly with respect to art and still more narrowly to literature. The task of an ecohermeneutics would be to complement ecocriticism with a philosophical discourse concerning the role of the latter (conceived of not as an academic topic or school of thought, but as a practice of reading and writing) in the constitution of meanings and experiences that unfold for us the pre- or proto-intentional bond with nature. So the invisible and thus unspoken 'encounter' with urban ecologies in McGregor's novel above. Or, again, in the above reading of Faulkner, the evocation of the sublime in such a way as to demand a new interrogation of it as a philosophical and indeed ethical category. Here, the discussion of Nietzsche comes into play with the positing of a poetic literature that could be in some way faithful to Dionysus.

One contributor to such an ecohermeneutics might be Paul Ricoeur, in at least two ways. First, in discussing Nietzsche and then Faulkner, it became clear that the category of the symbolic as normally understood needed to be rethought. We suggest that a plausible place to begin is Ricoeur's interpret-ation of *mimesis* in Aristotle's *Poetics* at the beginning of *La métaphore vivre* (Ricoeur, 1981). Second, the tenth study of *Oneself as Another* (Ricoeur, 1992) arrives at a brisk set of ontological sketches which amount to a programme of work Ricoeur recommends to himself and his readers. One of these is to take up the problem of 'flesh' (*Leib*) in Husserl's *Cartesian Meditations* – in itself an obvious enough move and one often made in ecophenomenology – and then to employ it as an alternative vision of the passivity of thrownness (Ricoeur acknowledges Michel Henry's importance here (Ricoeur, 1992, pp. 322–9)). Ricoeur's ontological analysis looks like it could be straightforwardly taken up into eco-phenomenology, and to some extent no doubt it can. However, what is important to remember is that this is not a sketch of a fundamental ontology, but a *hermeneutic* ontology. It is this that captures our attention here. The resources through which thought must pass are inevitably conditioned by available tools of thought and, ultimately, historical contingency in the discourses, methods and attitudes that fall to us. (There is an interesting struc-tural analogy to reason's partial and fragmentary employment of the concepts of mechanism and teleology in addressing itself to the phenomenon of life.) In this, Ricoeur explicitly includes 'voices of nonphilosophy' such as Greek tragedy as reappropriated by first Hegel and then Nussbaum (Ricoeur, 1992, pp. 241ff). Thus also Ricoeur's decision to give exemplary readings of canon-ical modernist texts in *Time and Narrative*. We should include among these 'voices', perhaps, the practices of contemporary criticism. Accordingly, the unity of the various paths of ontology is at best an 'analogical' unity (Ricoeur, 1992, p. 20n).[10]

Gadamer's hermeneutics takes a quite different route during the same period. The 'applied hermeneutics' he pursues often appears to take sides *against* a specialized technology of practices (Gadamer, 1992a and 1992b). We contrast this with Ricoeur, who is more likely to pursue an open dialogue; or with Vattimo, positively embracing the possibilities opened up by the nihil-ism of modernity.[11] I suspect this in part stems from the particular way the conception's 'situation' and 'horizon', so important in the early work, are defined. As visual and specifically geometric metaphors, they imply a homogeneous underlying space within which historical effects are understood primarily as 'near' or 'far'. Accordingly, a horizon cannot be closed (Gadamer, 2004, p. 303), because there is no 'geography' that could form an island. This 'mobility' of horizons is important, to be sure, but it permits Gadamer too easily to separate the questions that arise for historically effected consciousness and the methods a particular discipline of the humanities might employ to pursue these questions. He can thus conclude that disciplines, practices and discourses do not alter the underlying topology of the situation and that 'the really important things precede any application of historical methods' (Gadamer, 2004, p. 334). Hermeneutics reveals the systemic quality of the production and reception of literature but only if we follow insights such as those in Ricoeur or Vattimo regarding the radical embeddedness of the hermeneutical situation, and the 'localness' of the topology of its horizon. Since we have seen Nietzsche arrive at a similar conception of 'cultural life', it is not surprising that such a hermeneutics takes Nietzsche as a key departure point.

Down the corridor, in the next building, the disciplines of the study of literature are pursuing new tasks and employing new practices. A conception of literature is emerging as an integrated sub-system of what, in connection with Nietzsche, we called cultural *life*. This conception has consequences for how they understand literary production and consumption, the construction and valuing of literary histories, the basic arsenal of literary composition (e.g. symbol, character, point-of-view, etc.) and the role of criticism. What we have seen is that this new conception can lead to fertile avenues of research in philosophy and literature: for example, having to reappraise Nietzsche's ontology as an *essentially* literary phenomenon; reconsidering the apparently arbitrary constraints on the truth-procedures of literature as understood by Badiou and expanding the notion of situation in hermeneutics so as to encompass the full range of this sub-system and perhaps thereby realize an 'ecohermeneutics'. More generally, we offer a plea that interdisciplinary work in philosophy should take its name seriously, and inquire after not just the subject matter but *the ways of working* encountered in other disciplines. In short, we should get out more.

15 The Future of Continental Philosophy

John Mullarkey

Opening up the Future

Each of the volumes in the *Bloomsbury Companion* series to which the *BCCP* belongs concludes with a chapter tackling the future prospects for its subject. But to ask after the future with regard to continental philosophy is no simple matter. In fact, given how much the future, in both its possibility and impossibility, has been central to its thought, it is a task fraught with danger. From Nietzsche's philosophy of the future, through the future death that spells out the capital possibility for *Dasein* according to Heidegger, to the theories of the Event in Lyotard, Deleuze or Badiou, the future to-come, *l'avenir*, has been ever-present in much French and German thought of the last century. So what possible hubris could allow one to add the last word on the matter of this future, as if the clairvoyance needed to chart these prospects was already present to hand? Another dimension to this impropriety concerns the extremely unpredictable nature of much continental philosophy. There are more epistemic breaks between Bergsonism and phenomenology, or between phenomenology and structuralism, than there is incremental development. Revolution rules over evolution. Ironically, however, such revolutionary impetus raises the question of the future again in terms of its very predictability. Radicality is a byword for much that has proclaimed itself to be philosophical practice in France and Germany in the era we are tackling. So what would a future radicality entail? Simply more radicality again? But how predictable and, indeed, stereotypical would *that* be? How can one, *any longer*, out-rebel the rebels? Yet continental philosophy has often played the role of a rebellious thought, to wit, one adopting various forms of anti-establishment, iconoclastic and extreme positions as regards mainstream philosophy. Yet the general concept of a singular *avant-garde* is increasingly moribund given the implausibility of there (ever) being any one single philosophical tradition for it to transgress. If radicality, rebellion or transgression are to remain features of continental philosophy then they will, in future, have to mean something else than the conceptual equivalent of raising two fingers to common sense. One cannot 'out-future' the 'future-philosophy' anymore.

Of course, one could simply adopt a nominalist approach that dubs whatever is practised by those we choose to *call* German and French philosophers, 'continental philosophy'. The future will purely be . . . *whatever 'they' do.* But then we must return to the question of what differentiates continental philosophy from its Anglo-American equivalent given that geo-cultural properties invariably prove insufficient. For some, like Simon Glendinning, 'continental philosophy' is an Anglo-American invention with no substantive, internal unity at all (so that the question of what 'its' future might entail is an empty one):

> efforts to find an internal unity to the Continental collection [of philosophies] will always either underpredict or overpredict because the only perfect predictor is one that acknowledges that the set comprises the distinctive *'not-part'* part of analytic philosophy: it is a unity of exclusion, not a unity of inclusion. (Glendinning, 2006, p. 116)

'Philosophically' speaking, of course, Glendinning is correct: there is no such thing as 'continental philosophy' *per se* – this is both a sham geo-cultural distinction and a category error.[1] There is not one philosophical theme that is exclusive to the European continent, nor any outside the continent that is confined to 'Anglo-American' philosophy. The use of the term 'continental' also brings to mind its other ill-coined associate, 'analytic philosophy'; but no methodological barrier exists between the two traditions either. In fact, it is extremely difficult to make any distinction stand up under historical, methodological or philosophical scrutiny. The presence or absence of a host of actual properties, philosophical and non-philosophical, has been cited as a decisive causal factor in the origin and maintenance of the current partition in our discipline, some of them rather obvious, some less so. Among the more obvious we have national character, political history, geographical proximity, institutional procedure, the language barrier, methodology or different philosophical interests; among the more subtle candidates are a difference in style or mood, different philosophical lineages (most often spawned by Frege and Husserl), the supposed fact that analytic thought is uniquely objectivist, individualist and scientistic, or the supposed fact that continental thought is uniquely subjectivist, collectivist and historicist. But most commentators agree, nevertheless, that this segregation neither fully succeeds nor fully fails to map clearly onto any geographical, historical, methodological or philosophical difference. These factors are, at best, tendencies, directions more or less followed by both.

Nonetheless, even were one to accept Glendinning's own premise of continental philosophy's insubstantial content, its relational or differential meaning does have significance *for us* in the Anglophone world (both analytic *and* 'continental'), even if only to mark continental thought as what is always 'to come', that is, what is always to come over 'here'. As such, it would be what marks *our* future (*l'avenir*), a future that is always both filling itself out and receding from us (the further away, it seems, the more significant it gets). In addition, continental philosophy could be taken, in part, to signify what always recedes, about endings and deaths (Heidegger's, Sartre's, Foucault's, Deleuze's, Derrida's) as well as the significance, *to us*, of new beginnings and new philosophical lives – Badiou, Rancière, Balibar. Moreover, that the name of continental philosophy continues in the present to be used, and continues to have at least some intuitive appeal, must surely indicate some basis, if not in fact then at least in perception. The difference, then, is in how philosophers see things: it concerns the perceived differences between philosophies; or, in other words, a certain self-awareness or group-consciousness, that, misplaced or not, has actually engendered the difference between continental and analytic philosophy (for there clearly is a division between departments, books and book publishers, journals, conferences and personnel). Or, to put it another way, the analytic-continental distinction is philosophically erroneous but meta-philosophically accurate: it has less to do with what philosophers think about when they philosophize than *where* they philosophize, with *whom* they talk about their philosophical work, and *what* they say about it to each other.

As regards the previous, past futures of continental philosophy, furthermore, the perceptions of analytic thought have also been ever-changing: by the 1950s, for example, the work of Immanuel Kant had finally entered into the analytic fold and away from its previous position (according to some in the Vienna Circle) at the cusp of the philosophical rift; while Hegel, once the paradigm of non-sense for many in the Frege-Russell-Carnap school, is now a figure with whom analytic thought can do business without causing any controversy.[2] In fifty years' time, perhaps Derrida and Deleuze will have entered into the canon of acceptable philosophy just as some other foreign thinker will be deemed the paradigmatic outside(r) to (proper) thought. In this version of the 'relational' definition of continental philosophy, therefore, French and German thought becomes a receding tide whose waters, though inviting, should never be swum too far from shore.

A Closer Look at the Continent

Clearly, the *reception* of European thought in the Anglophone world (as 'continental philosophy') is not the same as European thought itself.[3] European interests over the last century (for instance, Personalism, neo-Thomism, neo-Kantianism, Bergsonism, French Epistemology, analytic philosophy) have rarely mapped well onto continental interests (Derrida, Irigaray, Lyotard, Foucault and so on). But that need not lead us into being sceptical about whether there is any such thing as European philosophy, *in itself*, and so whether or not it has a future. An alternative strategy might firstly be to look *harder* at what European philosophers do. Some recent Anglophone scholarship has tried to undo the filtered reception of European philosophy by taking just such a harder look. Alan Schrift's work on twentieth-century French philosophy, for example, comes across as a very grown-up assessment of the field of thought that has provided continental philosophy with most of its bells, whistles and sheer hyperbole for the last hundred years (Schrift, 2006). Its stated ambition is to shift attention away from the discourse of mastery, novelty and genius that has sparked much of the Anglophone reception of French philosophy since the 1950s and towards the institutional forces that have framed even the most seemingly radical and unprecedented thought. By showing how the French system of philosophical training, patronage and pupilage works – namely in an incredibly conservative, insular and hierarchical fashion – the outside reader will realize that Derrida, Deleuze and Foucault did not emerge *ex nihilo*. If they saw further than others (or at least were themselves more visible to the foreign eye), then it is because they stood on the shoulders of lesser known giants like Trân Duc Thao, Jean Wahl, Jean Hyppolite and Georges Canguilhem. The incommensurability between, for example, the status of Derrida's thought in France and the United States is noteworthy when compared with the exact opposite bearing of, say, Michel Serres's career. Where Derrida was an institutionally marginalized figure in France (he never taught in the French university system), he was a pillar of the anti-establishment establishment in the US, while Serres, who is only the tenth philosopher to be elected to the *Academie Française* since 1900, is mostly ignored in America. It is this background of social *habitus* and intellectual lineage – glaringly omitted in too many commentaries on French philosophy according to Schrift – that he wishes to fill in for the Anglophone reader.

Schrift's thesis also appears to be that the Anglophone image of French philosophy should be demystified and brought closer to the domestic and domesticated model of Anglo-American thought: emphasizing the institutional heritage and intellectual lineage standing behind every supposedly singular thought exposes its collaborative and traditional grounding. Derrida and Deleuze are not *causa sui*, but tips of an iceberg. Yet this strong reading is not wholly borne out by Schrift's own potted history of French thought in the first part of the text, for it follows a conventional narrative structured around personalities rather than positions, names rather than ideas (Bergson, Sartre, Lévi-Strauss, Foucault . . .) with less emphasis on the role institutional forces played in this intellectual itinerary, *qua set of ideas*, than one would imagine from what the rest of his study tells us. Names and nominalism again.

One Possible Future: Continental Naturalism

Nominalism or relationalism isn't the only way of hollowing out any substantive content to continental philosophy. If one were to allow the anglophone mind at least *some* facility to think about continental philosophy as the continentals 'themselves' do, then even here questions arise over its future. For Alain Badiou, for example, there are no events in philosophy, and so it has no future. Philosophy is atemporal, timeless, even though its role is to capture the truths generated by its conditions, in what he calls the 'measuring [of] our time' (Badiou, 1994). While there are events, and so a future, in the *conditions* of philosophy (for Badiou, these being love, art, politics and science), there are no events in philosophy itself: its space of thought is also the time of thought – the eternal – as first expressed by Plato and being for ever after Platonic.

According to Badiou, Platonism is philosophy's past, eternally renewed. Yet isn't this renewal, its phenomenological appearing and re-appearing in different 'times', real as well (to take only the very real formal differences between Plato and Badiou, for example)? Contra Badiou, I recently forwarded the thesis that continental philosophy was undergoing something like an event that could be seen in its new or newly recognized kinship with science and naturalism (see Mullarkey, 2006). This could be seen in the awakened interest in the empiricisms of Bergson and Deleuze, Michel Serres and Isabelle Stengers, in the re-estimations of lesser-known thinkers like Simondon, Cavaillès and Bachelard, or in the recent naturalizations of Hegel, Nietzsche, Husserl, Sartre and Merleau-Ponty. My own study ventured the possibility that a 'Post-Continental' thought might be found in the work of four figures in particular – Deleuze, Badiou, Michel Henry and François Laruelle – who each represent a real change in the intellectual current, one that both retains and abandons parts of what previously went under the rubric of 'continental philosophy'. This has nothing to do with the supposed 'death' of continental philosophy, but rather its evental transformation. Through their different forms of naturalism, the figures treated each mounts a challenge to previous Franco-German thought by embracing the value of absolute immanence over transcendence rather than making immanence supervene on transcendence. Rejecting both the phenomenological tradition of transcendence (of consciousness, the ego, being or alterity), as well as the poststructuralist valourization of language, they instead take the immanent categories of biology (Deleuze), mathematics (Badiou), affectivity (Henry), and science (Laruelle) as focal points for a renewal of philosophy. Whether any or all of this warrants the name of 'Post-Continental' or some other title is irrelevant: the primary wager made is that, *pace* Badiou's own *inert* metaphilosophy, an event is indeed unfolding in philosophical thought that amounts to a rekindled faith in the possibility of philosophy as a worldly and materialist thinking. Each of these thinkers is very different of course, so it was not my argument that these thinkers *together* embody a coherent approach to naturalism in their respective positions, but rather that they all radicalize our understanding of immanence and transcendence in order to rethink naturalism and science in philosophical terms, and therewith, the science and value of philosophy itself.

It is not insignificant, then, that many of the contributors to the *BCCP* also thematize the immanence-transcendence distinction: without wanting to say that this 'confirms' the view that immanence and transcendence represents the major axis in continental philosophy today, it does indicate that the turn to naturalism (in various forms) may well constitute the philosophical event of our day. However, nobody (not least I) could seriously say that this transformation has already happened, something that has actually occurred, an objective, completed event. This event is something that is unfolding, an event in the making. The 'Post-' in 'Post-Continental' was not intended as an accurate description of what is, but a prescription for what may be, what may come next. However, irrespective of whether or not there is already a general movement towards immanence (and some form of naturalism) afoot in continental philosophy that would 'radically' transform it, it is undoubted that the previous centrality of phenomenology – and with it its valourization of transcendence – has been rejected by much current continental thought. As the title of Eric Alliez's review of contemporary French philosophy denotes, the *Impossibility of Phenomenology* has become the question marking philosophy in France since the late 1980s (Alliez, 1995). Certainly, it was once true that phenomenology had been 'the single most important force driving French philosophy' up until that time (Prusak, 2000, p. 108), and it is equally true that Heidegger in particular formed 'the horizon of contemporary French philosophy' for a good deal of that period (Rockmore, 1995, p. 2). This has all changed in the last twenty years. Phenomenology has either transformed itself into something completely unrecognizable as phenomenology (which Dominique Janicaud labels its 'theological turn'), or it has been entirely sidelined by the huge French interest in the anti-phenomenologies of Deleuze and Badiou. Significantly, the Heideggerian position that linked the 'end of philosophy' to the triumph of science now causes special concern: for Badiou, Deleuze and Laruelle in particular, the errancy of previous French philosophy lay in following phenomenology too closely and establishing *so* a great respect for philosophy as an autonomous resource for *Wesensschau* or *Seinsdenken* that it forgot how to engage in an open manner with such matters as the relationship between mathematics and thought, culture and biology, or human and non-human animals.

Then again (and notwithstanding Heidegger's unique status), phenomenology as a whole need not be the incurable case it seems to be for any new turn towards naturalism in continental philosophy. Len Lawlor, for instance, has described two possible fates for continental thought: Deleuze's redemptive naturalism and Merleau-Ponty's post-phenomenological thought (see Lawlor, 1999). Both, he argues, turn to ontology to escape the subjectivism of classical phenomenology, and both invoke a form of naturalism at the core of that ontology. But, where Deleuze's metaphysics results in a newfound epistemology of the creation of concepts, Merleau-Ponty's ends in religion, according to Lawlor. Knowledge or faith. With regard to Merleau-Ponty's own theological turn, though, it is further arguable that a material remainder is still palpable. Renaud Barbaras' understanding of Merleau-Ponty as a figure at the limit of phenomenology tempers Lawlor's formulation: Merleau-Ponty does indeed transform phenomenology, but into a cosmology that does not go beyond experience; his cosmology is always of the visible world (see Barbaras, 1998). In addition to this, it is not just work on Merleau-Ponty that can be seen to mark a turn in current phenomenological thinking towards naturalism: the perceived need to naturalize phenomenology *in toto*, Husserl included, is equally evident in the studies of Francisco Varela, Dan Zahavi and Natalie Depraz, for instance.

Alternatively, the trajectory of French phenomenology that does head towards theology could be deemed inevitable in terms of French philosophy's strong institutional relations with religion as well as Heidegger's *Kehre*, without which, it is said, 'there would be no theological turn' (Janicaud, 2000, p. 31). Of course, the equation of metaphysics with 'onto-theology' was once an accepted term of abuse used by anyone working in the post-Heideggerian tradition, but in the current situation it has been put to a new, positive use. The 'new phenomenology' of the so-called 'theological turn' takes the old metaphysics of presence (as enframing, as control, as simple presence) out of purportedly conservative theology while also reforming presence as donation and metaphysics as creative. In the case of Michel Henry, the first of these divine phenomenologists, his thought remains Spinozistic and materialistic throughout. His is a heterodox thought of God, a radical empiricism, rather than a 'radical orthodoxy', whose world is a strange reality of affective processes and vital experiences. He does not focus on the phenomenology of the phenomena, on the given or donation (*données*) as a gift from a transcendent God (as, for instance, in the phenomenological theology of Jean-Luc Marion), but on *our* inhuman experience of already being divine, on immanent affectivity (see Henry, 2003, p. 50).

Nominalism or Essentialism? Becoming Continental

To return, then, to the question of nominalism, I, like almost every other continental philosopher, would never say that there is *just one essential dividing line* in contemporary philosophy, that between the continental and the analytic. That is a caricature, to be sure. There are myriad lines on both sides, some thicker, some thinner, all more or less porous. Take just method, for example. As we saw from James Burton's essay in this volume, there is a plurality of methods within what we dub continental philosophy, a plurality that is itself methodologically interesting. What each philosophy counts differently as method – be it the problematics of Deleuzian thought, or the descriptivism of phenomenology – is individually interesting at a meta-level. The plurality is interesting given that the methodologies belong to thoughts that are, nonetheless, gathered together *as one* in as much as they are all regarded by those outside mainland Europe as philosophies *of some kind*. Pure nominalism, in other words, is a non-starter. It begs the question in assuming that minimal concept or essence, whatever it may be, that allows certain names to be gathered together. We need at least some conceptual grounds, even if they are only based on impressions, should we wish to begin our dispute. We can take naturalism as one new emerging line, but this would still not make it an essential one. It would only be an emergent, futural one. I said above that the difference between continental and analytic is meta-philosophical rather than philosophical. This could be taken to approximate Simon Critchley's *de facto/de jure* distinction in his take on the divide (Critchley, 2001, p. 3), but the meta-philosophy I have in mind here should not be seen as a higher-order representation of (all) philosophy, nor identified with it as being just (more) philosophy. Rather, meta-philosophy should be understood as the immanent becoming-philosophical of subject-matter, what Laruelle and Badiou would call the 'non-philosophical' conditions that are in transition from an outside to an inside of something that will call itself 'philosophy'. Hence, there is no substantial philosophic-content difference between continental and analytic (you can take any theme and find a point of indiscernibility in the treatment it gets by either side), but a moving meta-philosophical difference – the processes, the manners, the forms of *how* continental and analytic philosophers do their thing.

In other words, from the perspective of its *process*, what might appear to other points of view as either a substantial or nominal difference can also be seen in terms of a 'process difference' – a difference which is in becoming. I prefer to the use the term 'meta-philosophical' for this process over that of it being a *de facto/de jure* distinction, given that the latter dualism begs questions concerning the *a priori*. Meta-philosophy is becoming-philosophy (the 'meta' is always a movement) – the dynamic and porous outlines which show that what may begin on the outside (as the broader paradigm of 'non-philosophy') may eventually be incorporated under philosophy's semi-permeable skin. The distinction between continental and analytic, being no less meta-philosophical to the (processual) view, is also always moving (from Kant, to Hegel, and then onwards): indeed it is a movement that is irreducible to all static forms, be they of methodology, or history, psychology, sociology or whatever else.

Primary or Secondary? From Philosophy to Non-Philosophy and Back Again

A continued complaint amongst some recent voices in Anglophone continental philosophy is that what we do remains, in numerous ways, a secondary philosophical form (see Critchley 2001, p. 125). Unlike our Anglo-American neighbours, we are definitionally incapable of generating primary philosophy, of going beyond producing commentaries, no matter how skilled or original, upon our French- and German-born primary matter. Where Anglo-American philosophy can be *both* primary and secondary, continental philosophy, at least as presently constituted (that is, as the Anglophone reception of European mainland thought), must always be secondary, that is, a reception. To purport any primariness to what we do in this part of the world, in this language, would be impudent. We work in the names of others who make philosophy, rather than in philosophical themes of our own making. Of course, Derrida was also a commentator on Husserl and Heidegger, as Deleuze was on Bergson and Nietzsche. But each of these names provided a 'violent' reading that eventually allowed him to find his own voice in grammatology and transcendental empiricism. Can we in the Anglophone world find our own voice too, or must we remain secondary thinkers, by definition? Can we only ever endorse the usual master-disciple relationship?

What makes us special, purportedly, is our history, our names. But the historicizing of our history and naming of our names may help us to do something else than repeat the old *avant-garde* gestures of transgression, of radicality and so on. Paradoxically, perhaps, we might create something newer than simply more newness. How might this work? To begin with, by raising critique to a new level, by *thematizing* the relation of continental and European *as* secondary to primary, and so, by implication of this thematization, going beyond the usual status of commentary and critique to one of first philosophy; a genuine Anglophone (but not analytic) *primary* thought that says things about reality directly, even though that reality has philosophical names immanent to it. French and German thought becomes 'our' primary object, our prime matter that we work over as a sub-routine of what François Laruelle describes as the essential task of 'non-philosophy' (in his philosophical materialism): to take the thoughts of philosophy as its raw material. The 'non-' in 'non-philosophy' here does not negate but *incorporates* its material within a broader paradigm. In some ways, this can be seen as one of the outcomes of the *BCCP*: if something does hold together the work within these pages, it could well be that the contemporary glance it provides – be they ones that extract their theory more from historical material (the essays of Aitken, Banham, Martin, May, Smith and Olkowski), or ones that are more explicitly engaged with the *actualités* (Kollias, Williams, Burnham and Ebdon, Dronsfield, Protevi, and Braidotti) – also allows us a glimpse of certain possible futures, one of which may be of a primary continental philosophy all its own. By the very act of summation that the *BCCP* embodies, we also glimpse a possible *non*-continental philosophy, that is, one whose status as primary is not in doubt. Douglas Burnham and Melanie Ebdon's work, in particular, gives us an outline of such a broader paradigm, one that incorporates recognizable philosophy with what before remained its other, its outside as non-philosophy (in the standard, *negative* use of this term).

The interest in non-philosophy is a perfectly respectable, and recognizable, dimension of orthodox continental philosophy (often made seemingly harmless as 'interdisciplinarity'). Long before Deleuze, Badiou or Laruelle prioritized the conditions of philosophy – the question of what conditions philosophy (if anything at all) or whether continental philosophy can be separated from non-philosophy – figures like Merleau-Ponty called for philosophy to engage with the non-philosophy of literature, painting, music and psychoanalysis (Merleau-Ponty, 1964, p. 16). Significantly, though, each of these figures is interested in the non-philosophical with respect to the renewal and future of philosophy, each of them offering us (different) strategies for new thinking and thinking about the new. But we must be wary here. More often than not, when a philosopher (of any hue) says that art or science, say, is its 'philosophical' condition, or even that it is practising philosophy directly in its 'own way', this is often on account of his or her own particular philosophical perspective finding something he or she calls philosophy in a subject-matter that was previously deemed 'non-philosophy'. Irrespective of whether philosophy is regarded as a recognizable list of names or a recognizable list of problems and methods, both strategies see philosophy as exhaustively, transcendentally, identifiable and definable.

But what if the opposite were the case? What if there is no *a priori* of what philosophy can be (or become): instead, there is only an *a posteriori* conditioning of the *a priori* – an experience which is itself dynamic, experience as already moving in to 'philosophy' – from the 'outside' to the 'inside' of the university. The issue of whether art, for example (or any other subject-matter), isn't always already philosophical, and *in its own way*, would remain moot. For what does it mean to *think* philosophically anyway? As we saw in

Rosi Braidotti's essay, for instance, feminist theory has long challenged what we mean by rational thinking (as supposedly disembodied, specular, transcendent): can't the same decentring be performed on philosophical thinking as such? Turning back to Laruelle, we might well ask after the nature of a non-philosophical thinking, be it in art, science or anywhere else. Laruelle himself doesn't offer any conceptual definitions. He does say, however, that thought is ubiquitous. Whereas (orthodox) philosophy is 'intrinsically anti-democratic' and judgemental, his non-philosophy denies nothing and affirms all: it seeks a 'democracy between philosophies, and between philosophy and the sciences, arts, ethics, etc . . .' (Laruelle, 1996, p. 54).

The principle of our post-Heideggerian age, on the other hand, has more often been to ask continually for true thought and real thinking. This is because, supposedly, the most thought-provoking thing in our thought-provoking time is that 'we are still not thinking' (Heidegger, 1968, p. 4). From the position articulated here, however, the opposite is the case. Thinking is everywhere. For some, this will be unacceptable. For some, the true philosophical horror is not that we are not (yet) thinking, but that we have *always* been thinking. Given the view that philosophy must have an essence and so an exclusivity, then what is (philosophically) unthinkable is that thinking might be found all about us. As F. H. Bradley quaintly put it in his *Aphorisms*: 'it is not true that Mr. X never thinks. On the contrary, he is always thinking – about something else' (Bradley, 1993, no. 79). In other words, one can't privilege any one form of thinking other than by sheer *fiat* – 'I hereby name *this* activity "thinking".' Outside of such baptisms, however, there are always so many counter-examples: thinking descriptively, poetically, mathematically, affectively, embodiedly, analogically, syllogistically, fuzzily, para-consistently; thinking through a method of questions, of problems, of dialogue, of dialectic, of genealogy, of historicism, of deconstruction. . . . As such, all definitions are exposed as question-begging because they privilege certain examples over others. For instance, when thinking is restricted to the articulation of language, then it is based normatively on human speech (be it as internal 'mentalese' or public behaviour). If it was restricted to information processing, then it would essentially be the same as the cognitivist view of perception and representation. The same goes for definitions in terms of complexity of response, which essentializes the question in terms of supposedly identifiable, extant and (normally) human behaviour. Even if thinking is given a privileged, special relationship with Being (rather than human being), then it would still be exhausted in the *ontology* of that relation. Or if it were seen in a creative encounter with an outside force, then it would be exhausted in the *concept* of that creativity.[4]

And so on. Each of these *exemplary* cases restricts the idea of thinking in a presumptive manner: each philosophy of (philosophical) thinking presupposes what it wishes to prove through the examples it chooses. That is, if thinking is ever described in terms of any exemplary activity, then it is confined to the implementations of that activity – be it the examples on which the definition has been based, or those which have 'based' themselves on the definition (either empiricist or rationalist rendering will suffice). If, alternatively, we reject this move, then we are left with either a dogmatic assertion from one amongst the contending definitions and examples (that will always involve a question-begging presupposition that selects just the right examples to support the dogma), or an openly axiomatic choice from the same set. Either covert or overt question-begging.

So, in coming back to the question, 'what is (philosophical) thinking?', perhaps we should stop begging for these questions of definition altogether. In his *Essays on the Blurring of Art and Life*, Allan Kaprow writes of the process of 'un-arting' or the taking of 'art out of art', which he describes as that 'act or thought whose identity as art must forever remain unknown' (Kaprow, 2003, p. xxix). Art's identity comes through not being self-identical. Can't we say the same for philosophy? To de-philosophize or un-philosophize, to embrace the insult of being 'unphilosophical' as one's own, because the alternative of being recognized as 'proper' comes at the cost of also being a *cliché*. This is not to romanticize a reflex negation of *all* philosophy following Wittgenstein or Rorty, but the necessary change of orientation that is the only way to enact a new philosophy. According to Badiou, remember, there are no events in philosophy, not real ones anyway: but what if there were? Just as a political event redefines what we mean by the political (a view he shares with Rancière), so too a philosophical event would redraw the map of philosophy and non-philosophy. Socratic unknowing, or the methodological agnosticism practiced in Laruelle's non-philosophy, is not about weaving exotic mysteries just for the sake of failing, for the sheer lack of it, but to create something new in the name of what *could* become 'philosophy'. If philosophy has always appeared most clearly when tackling insoluble problems (and hence 'mysteries'), it is not for reasons of representation (that either fails or succeeds to correspond with the whole), but because philosophy itself *is* the gap between part and whole, the mereological glimpse of an indefinite whole.

As regards its future status, then, perhaps all we can be sure of is that (continental) philosophy will continue to struggle with its own definition, with its own identity. Certainly, going by its track record, it has proven itself historically to be a subject perpetually in search of its content, and perpetually falling far short of success. Though many have tried and continue to try to give it an essence – in the *a priori*, or logical analysis, or concept creation, or intention, or fundamental questioning, or simply in being 'Heideggerian', 'Husserlian', 'Hegelian' – the sheer number and diversity of these attempts only recalls us to the fact that its identity has always been contested. No less than nominalism begged the question of essences, so the essentialist response to nominalism begs its own question too, in that it forms a circle with nominalism by presuming the primacy of *genera*, even though *genera* are formed first of all by an act of abstraction from certain *privileged* names. Of course, there are those who still hold out against this track record, who do believe that finally now, this time, we have made real advances in metaphysics, philosophy of mind, or epistemology on account of this or that scientific or conceptual breakthough. Hope springs eternal.

Given this circle of subjective nominalism and objective essentialism, however, there is an alternative path that weaves something positive out of it, namely in the *relation* between subject and object. Suddenly, then, philosophy's lack of inherent content becomes a positive rather than negative property: philosophy as symbiant, as inherently relational or evental. The philosophical is the moment or event when 'another' discipline, like politics or literature, or another object, like a film or a painting, finds itself in a state of transformation, with its own identity crisis.[5] Or rather, it is when such matters find subjects whose relationship with them is mutually transformative. It is the *relationship* between those subjects (the audience, the practitioners) and the subject-matter that *becomes* philosophical. That, at least, is the optimal case whereby the philosophical status of art, say, concerns what we mean by philosophy as much as what we mean by art (as Jonathan Lahey Dronsfield also remarks in his essay in this volume with respect to art practice). It is not that it is impossible to say anything genuinely new in philosophy anymore (that the 'philosophemes' have been exhausted), nor that we must still await the breakthrough that will end philosophy's perpetual dissensus, but that this dissensus, this ongoing (disputed) relationship between subject and object is generative of novelty, and is what makes philosophy definitively indefinite. There is no philosophy with a top-down, intensional essence (that may eventually complete or end itself), but always a set of philosophical studies, where materials admit themselves, bottom up, extensionally. There is, therefore, no definition of continental philosophy nor of its future, other than through its renewability and ongoing indefinite non-nature.

Back to the Future: The Return of Politics and Metaphysics

I could, of course, ignore all this and tell you what continental philosophy is going to be. I could simply set out the newer trends of the day in order to extrapolate certain futures where there will be more of this or more of that. Nonetheless, the comparison of today's philosophical work with that of the past as an indicator of an intellectual vector ensures very little, for emergent phenomena are, *qua* emergent, also ephemeral: there are always more hopeful monsters emerging at any one time than successful new species. Certainly, at

271

the close of this new century's first decade, there appears to be a much stronger emphasis on politics than there was in the two previous decades' work. The interest in Deleuze and the growing interest in Badiou, for instance, are partly related to their positive engagement with both the sciences and radical politics, something less obvious in Heidegger or Derrida, for instance. Philosophers, like most others no doubt, like to feel that they are relevant, that they have a role in the world. And it is doubtless reassuring to see philosophy thinking with embryology *and* political resistance movements, or set theory *and* militant insurgency. Philosophy has seemingly come back down to earth from the inconsequential heavens of transcendence.

Significantly, the political edge of *early*, post-war continental philosophy was founded on the political fluxes experienced in its homelands of France, Germany and, latterly, Italy. With the failure of 'May 1968' in France, and the apparent deconstruction of politics consequent upon it, however, these earlier *engagements* may well have seemed naïve subsequently. Yet, in contrast with the relative stasis of politics in western Europe, continental philosophers have turned to eastern Europe, the Middle East, South America and China, to gain a new political edge for their thought. Increasingly, continental philosophies must prove their mettle through their political relevance, their ability to engage with 'this world' (as if we are all agreed on what *this* world includes, as if an indexical like 'this' is not prone to deconstruction).[6] Hence, a continental philosophy must firstly show its stuff politically. Hence also, the recent priority of political ontology or even an unapologetically politicized ontology. Through the work of Badiou and Žižek in particular, but also Rancière and Balibar, Maoist and Marxist thought are back in vogue, and with them also the philosophical baggage of Althusser and Lacan.[7]

Another trend one could highlight is a renewed interest in classical metaphysics, philosophers now being happy to engage with traditional problems within metaphysics (rather than deconstructing them in the name of some post-metaphysical thought), and thereby renew classical philosophy rather than 'end' it. Again, Badiou and Deleuze are the primary figures here: the possibility of philosophy *qua* metaphysics is no longer decided in the negative and at length: philosophy is not dead, now let's get on with it. It is indeed notable that half the papers in the *BCCP* are Deleuzian – practising a kind of post-Kantian metaphysics – while the other half note the emergence of Badiou as a neo-classicist. Yet one must wonder at the new ease with which some are now able to practise classical metaphysics as if many of its categories (quality and quantity, mind and matter, finite and infinite) hadn't been deconstructed, as if Heidegger's and Derrida's work had never been written.

Acting Out a 'New' Future

An interesting case in point is the recent interest in Quentin Meillassoux's book, *After Finitude* (Meillassoux, 2008). Its opening move is to re-establish the importance of the traditional question of primary and secondary qualities in order to 'prove' the necessity of material contingency and the insufficiency of any correlationist thinking, that is, any thinking (especially that of a phenomenological or vitalist provenance) that secretes some form of consciousness (or supposed analogues of consciousness like spirit, will or life) into material nature (primary quantity/matter being always and merely a correlate to a privileged secondary quality/consciousness). Contra Derrida's post-metaphysical thinking, Meillassoux takes (certain) metaphysical issues seriously, even though making quality and quantity *the* problem already begs the question of the indiscernibility and/or undecidability, *between* quality and quantity. After all, how can we differentiate qualitative difference from quantitative difference? It is impossible to say what *type* of difference, of degree or of kind, differentiates the set of all differences in kind from the set of all differences of degree. To attempt an answer to this puzzle is to cite a difference that must fall into one of the two sets rather than a third that separates them. Hence, if one is to privilege the one over the other, one must state *by fiat* that either quality or quantity alone is fundamental. Phenomenology, according to Meillassoux, privileges qualitative difference (consciousness). But, following on from the mathematicism of his own mentor, Badiou, Meillassoux takes the opposite strategy of privileging quantity.

Significantly, in all of this there is an active forgetting, not only of the deconstructability of quantity and quality (or primary and secondary qualities), but also of any possible plurality of quantities and qualities. *Which* primary and which secondary qualities does Meillassoux have in mind? Do primary and secondary form such a simple either/or dichotomy? Is quantity truly dissociable from quality? A good deal of ink has been spilt by both phenomenologists and vitalists in discussing exactly these questions. The answers they, and Meillassoux, arrive at strongly depend on their meta-mathematical views, that is, on their view of quantity. But Meillassoux simply follows Badiou's Platonist leaning as to the sovereignty of quantity, no questions asked (see Meillassoux, 2008, p. 117). It is not that he is unaware of the history of these matters (far from it), but that he must actively neglect this history in order to get his own project started. This neglect of both alternative and prefigurative answers would become pernicious, however, were Meillassoux's work received in the Anglophone world as something 'radically' new. It is not. In fact, as Bill Martin's essay in this volume reminds us, its own avowed message of contingency in nature goes straight back to Althusser:

> That is the first point which . . . I would like to bring out: *the existence of an almost completely unknown materialist tradition in the history of philosophy: the 'materialism'* (we shall have to have some word to distinguish it as a tendency) *of the rain, the swerve, the encounter, the take* [prise]. . . . Let us say, for now, a *materialism of the encounter*, and therefore of the aleatory and of contingency. (Althusser, 2006, pp. 167–8).

What's more, such a philosophy of contingency also goes back, ironically, even further to the philosophy of Emile Boutroux, whose *De la Contingence des Lois de la Nature* (1874) argues for the same contingency as Meillassoux, only then in the interest of spiritualism (at that time meaning anti-reductionism), rather than materialism. Derrida would laugh.

This is not at all to dismiss the interest in classical questions, nor the turn to materialism, as seen also in enterprises – such as the 'Speculative Realist' group and the research associated with the journal *Collapse* – that neighbour both Badiou's materialism and the continental naturalism discussed earlier. It is simply to remind ourselves that this interest also involves a forgetfulness of the fact that these questions are old, and that many of their solutions have already been tested. Moreover, the type of continental neo-materialism that might pretend to eliminate all questions of consciousness by aping an out-dated Anglo-American form of cognitivism and neuro-philosophy does little service to anyone: it is neither rigorous nor contemporary with current Anglo-American positions (many of which are now actually open to *panpsychist* views),[8] but simply operates an uncritical scientism that lacks engagement with the best that analytic philosophy of science has to offer on questions concerning inter-theoretical reduction, identity statements, supervenience and much more. Indeed, one suspects that this new continental philosophy is still working in the tradition of *belles lettres* – argument by verbal analogy (often based on words like 'science' and 'matter') in order to generate dra-matic, zealous worldviews – rather than any real bridge-building with the long and highly undramatic labours of analytic philosophy of mind and science.

But such criticism is ultimately churlish, for every generation of new thinkers must forget something if they are to get started at all. Each new generation needs its heroes, be they from the present, like Badiou (as now), the future, like Meillassoux, or a reclaimed past that skips over the preceding generation to a more distant and malleable past (the names of Maimon, Lavelle, Ravaisson and Maritain are all now reappearing on the continental scene, for example). Or the heroes can come from an 'outside', from an ana-lytic philosophy or even a non-philosophy. Any new movement always acts as if it has a *real* novelty, and this 'as if' involves an act of forgetting (of the past) and fabulation (of the future) that creates its own starting point in an act of fidelity with this future and infidelity with this past. The same is true of every new movement: Derrida could only decentre the Sartrean subject by forgetting that Sartrean consciousness was already self-differentiated, just as Sartre forgot, in his early anti-Bergsonism, that Bergson understood movement to mean that there was no-thing in consciousness too. . . . And this youthful fundamentalism (even if only the fundamentalism of being a relativist), this desire for polemic, and this taste for certainty and political relevance, needs its sacrificial others, needs to pretend that these others got it wrong or simply never existed. How, otherwise, could it ever get started?

Indeed, the circle formed between the nominalist position that I outlined above and the opposing essentialist one as regards the definition of philosophy can only be broken by action, by *naming* something anew and in the name of continental philosophy. Only a performative philosophy can act its way out of the aporia of the past. This is a way of acknowledging the likes of Derrida *and* returning to metaphysics, but a metaphysics that uses the aporia (or history of failures) that make up philosophy as its raw material. Badiou is fond of reciting the end of Samuel Beckett's *Unnameable* with respect to the paradox of eventful action (pursuing an action whose justification *must be* a self-fulfilling prophecy): 'You must go on, I can't go on, I'll go on' (Badiou, 2004, p. 133). In order to act at all, one must stop representing the past (which will always bring one to a halt) and start acting out the future.

Part II

Resources

16 A–Z Glossary

Adorno

A critical theorist, essayist, philosopher, musicologist and social critic, Theodor Wiesengrund Adorno (Frankfurt am Main 1903 – Visp 1969) is best known as a leading member of the **Frankfurt School**. Following the submission of his doctoral thesis on **Husserl** he studied composition and sought a career in music. Though by the end of the 1920s his essays on music had become more popular, Adorno's early work as a composer and music critic was not well received and he came to devote more energy to philosophy, beginning his association with the Institute for Social Research in 1928.

For Adorno, thought generally misrepresents reality by making it conform to the instrumental human interests which dominate under capitalist modernity. Under Adorno's analysis, modern society falsely understands the world as a totality of facts, when it can never be fully described or cognized in general terms. He was deeply critical of what he saw as the political conservativism of scientific positivism, and argued for dialectical method in philosophical research. Rejecting the idea that philosophy provides access to a direct or unmediated set of truths, Adorno suggests that only dialectics can escape 'identity thinking': thought distorted by relations of social power which attempts to make objects conform to inadequate concepts. It is therefore in the anomalous – or 'non-identical' – that Adorno finds the strongest indictments of the poverty of the present state of things. Dialectics is 'the consistent consciousness of nonidentity', he writes in *Negative Dialectics* (1966).

Though heavily indebted to **Marx**, Adorno remained sceptical about the revolutionary potential of the working class, preferring to speak of the way in which late capitalism permeates all levels of society with its own instrumental logic. Adorno thought that the manipulation of popular opinion through mass media supported capitalism by distorting actual needs, and his work is characterized by an emphasis on art, literature and music. He argues that the bourgeois 'culture industry' attacks the reflexive autonomy of art, which requires us to transcend our impulses and identify with the experience of freedom. Nonetheless, art – rather than philosophical argumentation – remained Adorno's enduring hope for a humane counterpoint to the world that produced the horrors of Auschwitz, since it retains the ability to illuminate the shortcomings of the context from which it arises.

Adorno's work is difficult and often obscure. This has in no small measure hindered appreciation of his work in analytic philosophical circles, though he is widely considered to be one of the most important continental philosophers of the twentieth century. The unrelenting critical tone of his writing is an attempt to defy philosophical convention while remaining true to its most fundamental moral impulses. The pessimistic, despairing, and often misanthropic tenor of his composition belies the sense of hope and utopian promise that is essential for understanding his thought. Nonetheless, the criticism most routinely levelled at Adorno is that his philosophy is incapable of accommodating any adequate idea of progress or improvement in human fortune.

Robert Farrow

Althusser

The philosophy of Louis Althusser (Algiers 1918 – Paris 1990), though shaped by many influences and concepts, is concerned largely with **Marx's** thought and its application. A key concept of his work on Marx derives from Gaston **Bachelard**, that is the 'epistemological break' or rupture. Althusser applied this to Marx's oeuvre as a way of radically separating his early humanist work, characterized by the philosophy of the subject in Feuerbach, from the historical materialist philosophy that followed. Althusser's philosophy elaborates a materialist epistemology, and designates the grounds outside of this area as bourgeois ideology. His philosophy seeks, concept by concept, to separate the ideological from the real.

For Althusser, Marx himself is emblematic of an epistemological rupture. The concepts of the forces and relations of production enabled social and economic thought to comprehend society not simply as a collection of individual subjects, but as a complex multiplicity of processes. Althusser's interpretation struck a chord at a time when **structuralism** sought to found philosophy in the structures of language as opposed to subjective human agency. In much of his work, Althusser seeks to intervene in the cultural products of the establishment, to separate that which provides knowledge (science) from that which does not (ideology). On this basis, and influenced by Jacques **Lacan's** concept of *méconnaissance*, Althusser developed his most influential work on ideology. Ideology suffers a misrecognition of historical reality, but this misrecognition speaks of a desire underlying it. Perhaps his best-known text, his 1969 essay 'Ideology and Ideological State Apparatuses', was on this subject (*Lenin and Philosophy and other Essays*, 1971). His first approach to the subject, however, was in his 1963 essay 'Marxism and Humanism' (*For Marx*, 1965), where humanism is typified as an ideology.

Marx reveals for Althusser the fallacy of interpreting a society's products as unveiling a singular truth about it other than the nature of its economic base. Althusser was profoundly influenced by **psychoanalysis**, the basis for his 'symptomatic' readings of Marx in which he seeks to bring out the unconscious structures of a text. Althusser's friend Pierre Macherey was to set out these concepts influentially in *A Theory of Literary Production* in 1966. Macherey clarifies the multiple social determinations and resulting meanings behind any literary production, in opposition to searching for a singular unified interpretation of one mind's clear intention in a text. In contemporary philosophy, Althusser's materialist epistemology has had its most prominent influence on Alain Badiou.

Andrew Aitken

Arendt

Hannah Arendt (Hanover 1906 – New York 1975), celebrated philosopher and political theorist, influenced both academic and non-academic audiences through her diverse publications and lectures. Her first major work, *The Origins of Totalitarianism* (1951), reflected upon the traumatic and horrific upheavals in Germany and Russia under Nazism and Stalinism respectively. Modern forms of totalitarianism, she argues, coalesce around a central governing idea or principle such as race, nation or class ('ideology') and are characterized by the institutionalized but extra-judicial use of violence ('terror'). The way had been prepared for the rise of totalitarianism in Europe by the steady erosion of institutions of social belonging and the restriction of politics to administrative and coercive functions at the expense of its proper function as a space for citizens to engage in deliberation and collective action ('power').

Arendt's mature philosophical contributions can be considered under the headings of the *vita activa* and the *vita contemplativa*. While the Western intellectual tradition has typically privileged the life of contemplation which aims to transcend the realm of action and appearance, Arendt claimed that the life of action is the higher form of human existence. In *The Human Condition* (1958), she distinguishes three dimensions of the *vita activa*: labour, work and action. 'Labour' denotes the activity required to sustain bare life; at this level humanity is slave to biological necessity. 'Work' involves the fabrication of durable objects and institutions, giving rise to a human world of culture mediating our relation to nature. 'Action' refers to such things as speech, remembrance, argument and judgement – activities that take place at an interpersonal level. It is only in the dimension of action that human beings are truly able to realize their freedom. Modernity has been marked by 'the rise of the social', i.e. the increasing preoccupation in the sphere of politics with the organization and regulation of economic matters. But in fact politics

281

ought to be above all a domain of action and thus enable citizens to realize meaningful and free lives. According to *On Revolution* (1963), what we see expressed in the history of revolutionary politics, albeit imperfectly and with varied results, is the desire to reclaim such a public space of political action and hence freedom.

The Life of the Mind (1978) was intended to provide the analysis of the *vita contemplativa* missing from the earlier work. The analysis divides 'the life of the mind' into the faculties of thinking, willing and judging. Although the final volume of the project, on judgement, remained unwritten at the time of her death, Arendt's theory of judgement has nonetheless come to prominence through her posthumously published *Lectures on Kant's Political Philosophy* (1982). Drawing on **Kant's** idea of 'reflective judgement', she presents judgement as the use of one's imagination to arrive at a universal and impartial perspective on novel states of affairs or events. Through thinking from the standpoint of others, one is able to arrive at valid judgements even when there are no established rules or norms to apply.

Matheson Russell

Bachelard

The philosophy of Gaston Bachelard (Bar-sur-Aube 1884 – Paris 1962) can largely be described as positivist in relation to science. He saw science, specifically the advances of quantum physics, as having the greatest purchase on the structures of reality. Quantum physics suggested a material dimension that was unseen and yet rationally engaged through increasingly accurate mathematical approximation. This suggested that empiricism was a flawed philosophical premise tied to specifically human valourizations. This directly influenced Badiou in his separation of the ideological premises of logical empiricism from a properly materialist epistemology of mathematics (*The Concept of Model*, 1969).

Bachelard believed the laws of the human mind could be known only indirectly through its exercise in the laboratory, where its successes and failures could be materially followed through the history of science. He saw the philosophy and history of science as indistinguishable, and of equal import to the scientist himself, who relied upon science's history while simultaneously rewriting it through changing the significance of its concepts in what Bachelard termed a movement of historical recurrence.

Bachelard set out a thesis of science making fundamental epistemological breaks with each great advancement by means of a psychoanalysis of objective knowledge in *The Formation of the Scientific Mind* (1938). Here the archetypal human valourizations of matter, such as those manifested in a naïve empiricism, were purged to the benefit of scientific method and achievement.

Science is intersubjective, discursive, mathematical and historical, in that it can be temporally traced through its advancements. Meanwhile poetics exhibits the other dimension of man's relation to the world. This is ahistorical, as it represents man's unchanging primordial psyche, in an elemental reverie of matter. Here Bachelard takes direct inspiration from Jung. He sets out this thesis in his four works on the elemental imagination of the 1940s.

Foucault singled out Bachelard, alongside Canguilhem, Cavaillès and Koyré as typifying the alternate philosophical lineage in French philosophy to that of the philosophy of the subject prevalent in **phenomenology**. He represented them under the rubric of a philosophy of the concept, methodologically defined as a historical analysis of concepts alongside a philosophical analysis of the norms which govern them. Critically these thinkers avoided the necessary closure of a transcendental subject that could not account for the radical developments and shifts within the history of science and mathematics. This was significant to both **structuralism** and **poststructuralism** as they sought to detach philosophy from the unity of a transcendental consciousness.

Andrew Aitken

Bataille

Georges Bataille (Billom 1897 – Paris 1962) was never employed as a philosopher. While working as a librarian at the Bibliothèque Nationale in Paris, he engaged in close study of various philosophers, attending Kojève's lectures on **Hegel** and writing a book on **Nietzsche**. He was further influenced by the sociological works of Durkheim and Mauss, the surrealist movement, and the writings of mystics such as Böhme and Eckhart.

Bataille wrote in a variety of forms and on a wide range of subjects. He is best known for his erotic novels and short stories, such as *Story of the Eye* (1928) and *Madame Edwarda* (1937), his studies in philosophy, sociology and economics, including *Inner Experience* (1943) and *The Accursed Share* (1949), and his writings on art and literature such as *Literature and Evil* (1957).

The idea of the *sacred* plays a fundamental role in Bataille's thought. Following Durkheim, Bataille takes the distinction between the sacred and the profane to be absolute (admitting of no degrees, thus requiring a transformation to pass from one to the other), and views the sacred as the primary unifying force of society, without which society could not exist. The sacred, however, lies at the forbidden margins of society, where work, project and taboo are replaced (or transcended) by free play, transgression, squander and loss. From this Bataille distinguishes the 'restricted economy' from the 'general economy'. Capitalist society, an instance of a restricted economy, is driven by a scarcity of resources, and the need to accumulate and protect these precious resources by means of wealth production. The general economy, by contrast, is driven by a 'non-productive expenditure' that is excessive, serves no useful purpose and has no expectation of returns or profits. The highest form of expenditure, where a pure loss is consecrated, is 'sacrifice', though other examples include eroticism, poetry, laughter, war and potlatch ceremonies. In such activities we approach the state of 'sovereignty', another important notion in Bataille's writings. Sovereignty represents life lived freely and beyond utility – life at its most intense – where the contingency of the moment is unconditionally accepted in a pure revolt unmotivated by any end. The avenue to sovereignty lies in the exploration of 'inner experience', an attempt to reach outside one's self (in a moment of ecstasy or rapture) that brings intense pleasure but also anguish and 'non-knowledge', furnishing no insight or revelation.

Bataille extended and applied these notions in his writings on literature and art, showing for example in *The Tears of Eros* (1961) how art, especially violent and erotically charged images, can function as an expression of sovereignty and the general economy. Bataille exerted great influence on subsequent **poststructuralist** theory, particularly on **Foucault**, **Derrida**, **Kristeva** and Baudrillard.

Nick Trakakis

Benjamin

Walter Benjamin (Berlin 1892 – Portbou 1940) was a philosopher, literary and social critic, and a prominent member of the **Frankfurt School**. Since his youth Benjamin was fascinated with the notion of experience. He tried to give a richer account of it working with two conceptions: a pre-modern, lived experience (*Erfahrung*) and a modern, fragmented and discontinuous one (*Erlebnis*). In his *On the Program of the Coming Philosophy* (1918) he asserts that the Enlightenment's notion of experience is reduced to that of the natural sciences and becomes fragmented, disembodied, mechanistic and ultimately non-shareable; later he calls it 'shock experience' and attaches it to the emergence of the modern notion of the 'crowd'. Benjamin wants to give back the metaphysical weight of experience, dissolving the dualism between the subject and object of knowledge, and transcending the philosophy of consciousness. The place to start is, for him, transcendental aesthetics and the philosophy of language. This early period is his 'idealist and metaphysical period'.

A first elaboration of Benjamin's theory of language is found in his *On Language as Such and on the Language of Man* (1916). His theory of translation (1923), inextricably linked to language, is identified as an act of ontological significance. In *The Origin of German Tragic Drama* (1925) he tries to explicate language itself as the truth content of everything that exists. He subsequently attempts to retrieve certain idealist or theological elements and to reformulate his theory from a more materialist basis. Language is presented beyond its instrumental and arbitrary use as a transcendental surface for the manifestation of an immanent absolute. Benjamin moves from 'naming' to translation and then mimesis. Naming designates rather than signifies; translation and mimesis are not simple acts of imitation, but the discovery of non-sensuous similarities between the word and the signified. In translation as in naming, we 'open ourselves' to what is not familiar rather than affirm what is the same.

Rather than subjective consciousness, it is the major reworking of receptivity and its relation to the immanent absolute that are the major theoretical preoccupations of Benjamin's later aesthetic works. In *The Storyteller* (1936), he talks about mental relaxation, boredom and self-forgetting; in *On Some Motifs in Baudelaire* (1939), he considers the *flaneur*, who aimlessly strolls through the crowds as opposed to the hurried, purposeful activity of the modern subject. This is linked to a special kind of involuntary memory (Proust) that secretly keeps the trace of the past, which is nevertheless present on some material object. This is unveiled not as recollection, but as re-actualization. 'The true picture of the past *flits* by', says Benjamin in *Theses on the Philosophy of History* (1940), and the angel of history looks at nothing but the expanse of the ruins of the past as a way of redeeming it. Benjamin conceives history without invoking the ideas of a future, a linear time or human development.

Kostas Koukouzelis

Bergson

Perhaps Henri Bergson's (Paris 1859–1941) most original contribution to philosophy is his concept of duration, which conflates time and life in a philosophy of process and 'unforeseeable novelty'. He describes this in *Time and Free Will* (1889), illustrating the contradictions present in any spatial presentation of time, contradictions explored in the ancient paradox of Zeno, where measured time can be endlessly divided into infinitesimal instants, and exemplified in **Kant's** Transcendental Aesthetic. Duration can be described as the true, natural process of life underlying the representations in which life is organized by the means–ends logic of the intellect. Duration, by contrast, is received in intuition, where we comprehend the interior of the object in a philosophical attitude of sympathy. Spatialized thought fixes snapshots in the flux, a model of perception Bergson likens to the fixed images which run together in cinematic film, but give only an appearance of reality. Duration is defined as a qualitative multiplicity: it is intensive, not extensive, and it cannot be quantitatively divided. For example, a temperature of 2°C is not double 1°C; rather, 1°C is wrapped up in 2°C. Bergson's concept of duration, alongside his critique of negation and dialectics, made his philosophy one of the most important influences on that of Gilles **Deleuze**.

Bergson's lectures at the Collège de France were so popular that they attracted many important intellectual figures of the day. Both **Freud** and Proust attended his lectures on memory (later published as *Matter and Memory*, 1896). Bergson describes two kinds of memory: habit memory is contained in the brain and nervous system, whereas involuntary memory, containing our entire past, is not. A third kind of memory, concrete memory, is called upon when a correspondence between the two is needed, in object recognition for instance. The important consequence of this, for Bergson, is the degree to which we are not just physically located but also in-the-world, such as with 'pure perception', the conceptual antecedent of intuition. In *Creative Evolution* (1907), his best-received book at the time, Bergson draws on the concept of the *élan vital*, or vital impetus, to answer queries of a causal nature in his philosophy of vital processes. With this he hoped to avoid the teleological philosophy that he saw as deeply flawed.

Bergson believed his concept of duration had clear implications for science. But unfortunately, with *Duration and Simultaneity* (1922), a publication aimed at uniting his philosophy with the science of Einstein, his eminent reputation suffered a blow. A seemingly physicalist critique of Einstein's understanding of the twin-clock paradox in special relativity was not received well by the physicists of the time, and it took until the advent of quantum physics for Bergson's ideas to gain credence among scientists again.

Andrew Aitken

Beauvoir

Simone de Beauvoir (Paris 1908–1986) was a writer of both literature and philosophy, prominent in the French **existentialist** circle, with her writing drawing notably on **Hegel**, **Marx** and **Heidegger**. While often – but quite unfairly – portrayed as a mouthpiece of **Sartre's** philosophy, Beauvoir's thinking gave key ideas to existentialist ethics, and in *The Second Sex* (1949) provided **feminist philosophy** with a work of lasting significance and controversy.

The Second Sex opens with a one word question – 'Woman?' – and the book details not just the depth and scope of such a question, but also the inherent difficulty of even asking the 'question of woman' without pre-figuring the answer in patriarchal terms. Beginning with the Hegelian idea that humanity develops through a struggle for recognition, Beauvoir argues that woman is consistently conceptualized outside of this dialectic as an 'inessential Other', and thus not recognized as a subject in her own right. Narrating woman's oppression through a broad picture of myth, literature and history, Beauvoir argues that woman is defined as 'not man'. Thus, while man is human, woman is 'female': she is defined in terms of her biology, and remains as such an 'immanent' subject. Man can achieve transcendence over the situation of his body, but woman remains always–already identified as her body. Woman cannot affirm her power through her body because it is not 'active', but operates in repetitious cycles of reproduction: she is not 'being', but 'becoming'. Thus, patriarchy places women in an existential 'bad faith': lacking full subjectivity, they do not feel responsible for their freedom. Correspondingly, man finds his own subjectivity in the objectification of woman as 'Other', and her subjectivity remains unrecognized.

This issue of recognition reflects Beauvoir's concern with reconciling existentialism with ethics, and her appropriation of Sartre's account of intersubjectivity from one of conflict to one of mutual recognition and affirmation, or 'reciprocity'. Beauvoir uses Heidegger's term *Mitsein* to affirm the interdependence of subjects, and that an individual's freedom is only realized in terms of the freedom of others. But to understand this, one must recognize the body – a contextualized, sexed phenomenon – as the site in which we experience such freedom. If, as existentialism argues, 'existence precedes essence', then Beauvoir argues that one is not born a woman, but rather becomes one. Woman retains her existential freedom by recognizing that the ideal of femininity is not inherent but cultural. While sex may be determined anatomically, gender is socially produced and self created within a social and historical context. Beauvoir thus describes a distinction between sex and gender which has remained at the centre of debates in feminist philosophy. The notion that the body is not a defining essence but a site of interpretative and performative possibility has been hugely influential on second wave feminist theorists such as Friedan, Millett and Greer; in work by the likes of Judith Butler it retained an influence on the **poststructural** critiques of traditional feminist identity categories.

Tom Grimwood

CRITICAL THEORY – See FRANKFURT SCHOOL

Deconstruction

'Deconstruction' signifies a diverse range of modes of philosophical, literary and cultural analysis. In philosophy, deconstruction came to prominence through Jacques **Derrida**, who argued that prior to the question of being there is a question of difference. Nothing for Derrida is in itself, but is always dependent on a prior difference. This refers to signification, language, meaning and symbols as much as phenomena themselves. Deconstruction, as it became more influential, applied Derrida's findings in an effort to demonstrate how pre-established symbolic orders are always internally contradicted.

Following on from Derrida, deconstruction has become a form of critique which is conscientious of the ways texts, structures and institutions systematize meaning while inherently marginalizing alternate identities and cultures. Deconstruction aims at re-constructing such institutions in order to give wider expression to the demands of justice. For example, in his 'Force of Law' essay (1989), Derrida argues that deconstruction is justice. What initially began as a radicalization of philosophical themes soon had major resonance outside of philosophy. From the late 1960s to the late 1980s deconstruction influenced many theorists in literary criticism, some of the most notable being Paul de Man, Harold Bloom and J. Hillis Miller.

Literary criticism utilizes deconstruction as a textual strategy to disclose how literary texts are not constructed out of univocal meaning but instead are inherently multiple and discrete. Not only does this strategy attempt to show how texts are plural, it also seeks to unmask underlying ideological presuppositions and subtexts of different forms of writing. Deconstruction has also been influential on **feminist** thinkers such as Judith Butler, Julia Kristeva and Hélène Cixous. Butler, in *Gender Trouble* (1990), argues that gender is socially constructed and by deconstructing our comprehension of it, we may consider new forms of equality not restricted to traditional meanings attributed to masculine or feminine gender functions.

In this register of political thought, deconstruction has had direct impact on identity politics and postcolonialism. Postcolonialism aims to uncover how the discourse of the colonial oppressor undermines people's identity in its own interests, but equally seeks to express how hybridity and displacement escape colonial subordination. Deconstruction and the work of Derrida continue to have an immense influence on contemporary thought. Major thinkers who have been influenced by deconstruction include Ernesto Laclau, Chantal Mouffe, Jean-Luc Nancy, Philippe Lacoue-Labarthe, Bernard Stiegler and Homi K. Bhabha.

Patrick O'Connor

Deleuze

The philosophical career of Gilles Deleuze (Paris 1925–1995) began with a monograph on Hume (1953), followed by studies of **Nietzsche** (1962), **Kant** (1963), **Bergson** (1966), and Spinoza (1968). These were followed by his two most important solo productions, *Difference and Repetition* (1968) and *The Logic of Sense* (1969). In the wake of the events of May 1968, Deleuze teamed up with radical psychoanalyst Félix Guattari in the 1970s and together they produced *Anti-Oedipus* (1972) and *A Thousand Plateaus* (1980), as well as a study of Kafka (1975). In the 1980s Deleuze's work ranged widely, including volumes on cinema (1983, 1985), painting (1984), and his close friend Michel **Foucault**

(1986), as well as a volume on Leibniz (1988). In 1991 he reprised his collaboration with Guattari to produce *What is Philosophy?*.

Deleuze's theoretical philosophy is materialist, nominalist and empiricist. Following Nietzsche he presents it as a reversal of Platonism. Its central tenet, echoing Duns Scotus and Spinoza, is the univocity of being, namely that all entities exist at the same ontological level. There are no transcendent entities above or behind the empirical world, nor any substance dualism, only a unified plane of immanence. This monistic conception of reality is combined with a commitment to a process ontology, in which the processes that constitute the world are by their nature productive. Each moment or point within this process is unique, defined in terms of its difference. This dynamic naturalism rejects the existence of abstract concepts, adopting Whitehead's definition of empiricism: the abstract does not explain anything but must itself be explained. Defending Hume against post-Kantian **German Idealism**, Deleuze proposes a 'transcendental empiricism', namely an empiricism that insists on the existence of what is given to the subject as a condition of possibility for experience. The subject, rather than being a transcendental condition, is instead the contingent product of the processes of production of nature. Thus, Deleuze shares little with the **phenomenological** tradition and his closest philosophical allies are Michel Foucault and the other French anti-humanists.

Like Foucault, Deleuze rejects all notions of normative morality but does hold on to a conception of ethics as a process of self-fashioning. Given his view that the self is both contingent and often restrictive, having been shaped by external repressive forces, the principal ethical task becomes the careful dismantling of the self in an attempt to open up its creative powers of production, which are nothing more than another expression of the creative powers of nature. The same applies at the larger, political level, with Deleuze rejecting the conventional state in favour of a deterritorialized nomadic cosmopolitanism. The only ethical principle Deleuze offers is that we should not be unworthy of what happens to us, echoing both Nietzsche's *amor fati* and the philosophy of the ancient Stoics.

Deleuze is widely known in the English-speaking world for his writings on art, literature and cinema. However, he offers no real aesthetic theory or philosophy of art. Instead he likes to read artists and writers as if they were philosophers, extracting philosophical ideas from unexpected sources. It has been in disciplines such as film studies, fine art and literature that Deleuze's work has proved to be most influential in the English-speaking world.

John Sellars

Derrida

Algerian-born French philosopher Jacques Derrida (El Briar 1930 – Paris 2004) is widely regarded as the founder of **deconstruction**. Derrida radicalized the fundamental tenets of **phenomenology** and **structuralism**, the broadest articulation being his *Of Grammatology* in 1967. In particular, Derrida develops **Heidegger's** concept of 'destruction'. In thinking ontology and the history of Western metaphysics, Heidegger saw that every philosophical construction of being is entwined with a concomitant destruction. Derrida's text *Voice and Phenomenon* (1967) advances this position with regard to questions of voice and difference. For Derrida Western thought, in order to guarantee truth and certainty, has without fail founded itself on the *logos* or voice: an unmediated presence of consciousness and thought.

Derrida contests this description in his analysis of language in Rousseau, Plato, **Husserl** and Condillac by arguing that the self-presence of voice is always open to alteration. This operation is what Derrida calls 'arche-writing' which defines how any identity is dependent on the trace of other identities. No conscious experience is pure and sufficient unto itself; all intuition depends on what is non-present to itself. Derrida labels this dependence 'trace' where identity always holds a trace of difference and division. Every event is necessarily generated by an experience of delay (time: nothing can be at the same time) and deferral (space: nothing can be in the same place). Hence difference itself, or what Derrida coined *différance*, is necessarily constitutive of any possible experience. Différance radicalizes the classical question of ontology: nothing can *be* in itself; whatever *is* is divisible and rigorously dependent on what it is not, i.e. its difference.

These key insights formulate deconstruction, as developed in *Of Grammatology* (1967), *Margins of Philosophy* (1972) and *Dissemination* (1972). These texts contain meditations on Heidegger, Plato, de Saussure, **Hegel** and Rousseau, and question what Derrida considers the homogenous metaphysical history (metaphysics of presence) of philosophy: a history which fails to think the radical differential structure of thought which deconstruction expresses. This is why deconstruction resists strict formal definition. To think deconstruction, philosophically, one must paradoxically negotiate the affectation of what *is* with what is *not*. For instance, *Of Grammatology* deconstructs de Saussure's opposition between signifier and signified. Derrida suggests that signification never signifies only itself. This is precisely how an originary linguistics or arche-writing generates meaning through continual deferral and delay.

In later writings Derrida investigates the ethical and political inflection of deconstruction. *Spectres of Marx* (1993), *The Gift of Death* (1999), *The Politics of Friendship* (1994) and *Rogues* (2003) describe ethics and politics as reliant on an irreducible undecidablility. Investigating justice, responsibility, hospitality and democracy, he argues that responsibility and justice remain essentially compromised and mediated. Philosophically pure concepts of ethics and politics are impossible. Efforts to assert absolute justice are undesirable and hence deconstructible. Derrida has powerfully influenced a wide range of discourse, from **psychoanalysis**, literature and art, to architecture and political theory, and has influenced major European philosophers such as Giorgio Agamben, Jean-Luc Nancy, Philippe Lacoue-Labarthe, Judith Butler and Bernard Stiegler.

Patrick O'Connor

Existentialism

Existentialism is a key movement in philosophy that can be traced back to the work of Søren **Kierkegaard**. Against **Hegel's** systematic philosophy, Kierkegaard argued that the lived experience of the 'singular individual' formed a special mode of being that resisted capture by scientific or essentialist claims about human nature. It is this emphasis on the primacy of first-person experience that characterizes existentialism, in both its literary and philosophical manifestations.

Although Kierkegaard was primarily interested in the difficulties involved in the relationship between individual experience and Christian faith, the majority of the existentialists that followed him were atheists. Jean-Paul **Sartre**, the most famous exponent of existentialism, begins from the idea that without God, man's existence is 'absurd'. Although Sartre was heavily influenced by **Heidegger's** claims about *Dasein* ('being-there') in *Being and Time* (1927), Heidegger was himself critical of the term existentialism, believing it to be a popularized form of his more serious **phenomenological** ideas.

As set out in Sartre's *Being and Nothingness* (1943), existential philosophy takes its starting point from the idea that 'existence precedes essence' and that the meaning given to human life cannot be accepted from outside sources (religion, morality or science), but can only be chosen by the individual, if it is to be lived authentically. In his earlier novel, *Nausea* (1938), Sartre vividly describes the vertiginous experience of existence: 'Existence, liberated, detached, floods over me. I exist.' Sartre's radical existentialism was later tempered by claims about the role gender plays in restricting freedom, a theme investigated by Simone de **Beauvoir** in *The Second Sex* (1949). Beauvoir also took existentialism in an ethical direction with *The Ethics of Ambiguity* (1947).

Existentialism was extremely influential in the post-war period, making Sartre an international intellectual celebrity, particularly with the publication of *Existentialism is a Humanism* (1945), a somewhat condensed version of the ideas explored in *Being and Nothingness*. The radical uncertainty brought about by World War Two was expressed in existentialism's emphasis on ambiguity, decision and commitment. Although he was critical of the term, the writer Albert Camus is generally regarded as an existentialist for his emphasis on categories of existence such as 'absurdity'. The German thinker Karl Jaspers pursued the existentialist idea of the radical freedom of individual choice in works such as *Philosophy of Existence* (1938). Existentialism fell out of favour with the rise of **structuralism**, which explicitly attacked the naivety of existential ideas about freedom and consciousness. Nevertheless, existentialism is often one of the first forms of continental philosophy encountered by readers, and it sheds light on many other philosophical traditions, in particular phenomenology and **psychoanalysis**, with their emphasis on questions of meaning and the structure of consciousness.

Nina Power

Feminist Philosophy

Feminist philosophy on the continent can be divided into four strands. The first strand is phenomenological and existentialist, as exemplified by Simone de **Beauvoir** in *The Second Sex* (1949). The remaining three strands followed in Beauvoir's wake: the **psychoanalytic** and **poststructuralist** strand, known best through the work of Luce **Irigaray**, Julia **Kristeva**, Hélène Cixous and Sarah Kofman; the materialist strand, of which the best known representatives are Monique Wittig and Christine Delphy; and thirdly the work of Judith Butler. Continental feminist philosophy refers to a hybrid of **Hegel**, **Nietzsche**, **Freud**, **Derrida**, **Deleuze**, **Marxism**, **Foucault** and **Lacan** as its critical starting point, often in order to give due attention to difference and to question notions of identity. The debates about identity and difference started by feminist philosophy have found their way into other disciplines such as sociology, anthropology, politics and cultural studies. Feminist philosophy has also inaugurated feminist epistemology, which challenges commonly held assumptions about knowledge.

Irigaray, in *Speculum of the Other Woman* (1974) and *This Sex Which Is Not One* (1977), and Kristeva, in 'Women's Time' (1979), both influenced by Freudian and Lacanian psychoanalytic theories, stress the role that language plays in the formation of gendered subjectivity and the maintenance of gender categories. They engage in a critique of psychoanalysis for being 'phallocentric' and for ignoring the specificity of the woman's body. Cixous and Kofman offer **deconstructions** of women and femininity. Influenced by Nietzsche, Freud, and Derrida, Kofman's works include *Nietzsche and Metaphor* (1972) and *The Enigma of Woman: Woman in Freud's Writings* (1980). Cixous is renowned as the author of 'The Laugh of the Medusa' (1975) which considers a specifically feminine mode of writing or 'écriture feminine'.

Wittig and Delphy focus on arguments that sexual difference is not a natural phenomenon, but a social construction. They argue that gender inequalities are a consequence of material social conditions rather than discursive constructions of 'the feminine'. In 'One Is Not Born a Woman' (1981), Wittig claims that lesbians are not women because they do not occupy the social role within the family that women do. Both Wittig and Delphy consider psychological differences between men and women to be the result of material social inequalities, rather than viewing psychosexual difference as producing such social inequalities.

Butler is in the generation following the feminist philosophers outlined above and is critical of her predecessors. She questions the sex/gender distinction and deconstruction of the category of woman. In *Gender Trouble* (1990) and *Bodies That Matter* (1993), Butler argues that the coherence of the categories of sex, gender and sexuality is socio-culturally constructed through the repetition of certain bodily acts which establish the appearance of an essential and ontological core gender. The performance of gender is not a voluntary choice. Butler locates the construction of the gendered subject within discourses.

Thus, feminist philosophy has taken many existing perspectives and opened up possibilities for reconsidering dualistic ways of seeing ourselves.

Minae Inahara

Foucault

Michel Foucault (Poitiers 1926 – Paris 1984) was a political philosopher, a philosopher of history and a historian of thought, whose work continues to have a considerable impact throughout the humanities and social sciences. His work on power as a productive system of relations operating at a microscopic level, in connection with his work on prisons such as Bentham's panopticon, continues to be an important source for political theorists, sociologists and human geographers, while his work on aesthetics and literature, particularly his challenge to traditional accounts of 'the author', informs debates in literary theory and cross-disciplinary analysis.

Foucault's position in the history of philosophy is pivotal in that his work embodies the transition from **structuralism** to **poststructuralism**. While his early work draws on **Marxism** and **phenomenology** he went on to unseat subjectivity, dominant since **Kant**, as a starting point for enquiry. His later genealogies draw on **Nietzsche** and disallow totalizing narratives or explanatory schemes, such as Marxism and **psychoanalysis**. His book *The Order of Things* is structuralist insofar as it uncovers the 'epistemes' or fundamental epistemological fields that underlie and act as the condition of the possibility of knowledge. Here Foucault develops an 'archaeological method' that reveals the conditions of forms of knowledge and the discontinuities constitutive of various epistemic discourses. He adopts a historical perspective that implies the inability of structuralism to give an account of transitions between various systems of thought. Such a perspective prepared the way for his later genealogical studies of power and sexuality. These later works are generally regarded as paradigms of poststructuralist analysis.

There is no single methodological principle or theoretical position that characterizes Foucault's work as a whole. Rather, his writings are directed at specific problems or questions: the history of madness (*Madness and Civilization*, 1961); the archaeological method (*The Order of Things*, 1966, *The Archaeology of Knowledge*, 1969); genealogy (*Discipline and Punish*, 1975), sexuality and ethics (*History of Sexuality*, 1976–84). In *Madness and Civilization* for example, Foucault discloses three separate 'epistemes' in connection with madness: in the 'Renaissance episteme' madness is construed as disorder; in the 'Classical episteme' madness is construed as unreason; in the 'Modern episteme' madness is construed as mental illness.

Foucault's genealogies favour an analysis of systems of thought as essentially contingent products of a multiplicity of unrelated causes. His genealogies aim to 'account for the constitution of knowledges, discourses, domains of objects, etc., without having to make reference to a subject which is either transcendental in relation to the field of events or runs in its empty sameness throughout the course of history' ('Truth and Power', 1980). Foucault's genealogies insist that there is an essential connection between bodies of knowledge and power. His discussion of the relationship between knowledge and power is extensive and while knowledge is not reducible to systems of social control, bodies of knowledge are nevertheless bound to such systems.

Philip Tonner

Frankfurt School

The Frankfurt School (*Institut für Sozialforschung*) was founded in 1923 and operated as a relatively autonomous department affiliated to the University of Frankfurt. It was originally conceived as a place where the resources of a number of socialist academics could be pooled in the name of a scientific **Marxism**, and produced a number of studies examining the cultural developments of capitalism under modernity. However, under Max Horkheimer's leadership the Institute deviated from the orthodox economic determinism of the time in favour of more speculative, dialectical approaches. Thus, one unifying theme of the sometimes disparate output of the Frankfurt School is the critique of its own dominant influence: Hegelian Marxism.

The developments of the twentieth century provoked doubts about the end of capitalism predicted by Marx, and the drive behind the institute's research programme became the examination of the collapse of Western culture signified by the rise of European fascism and industrial rationalization. The resulting commodification of cultural life was explored in a number of studies into the family, popular culture, science, literature, television, art, technology and politics. Though interdisciplinary research – synthesizing work by economists, psychoanalysts, sociologists, psychologists and political scientists, among others – is central to the Frankfurt approach, it is the German tradition from **Kant** to **Freud** via **Hegel, Marx** and **Nietzsche** that provided its central orientation. Those works of the first generation of the school enduringly considered most important are primarily philosophical, and include Horkheimer and **Adorno's** jointly authored *Dialectic of Enlightenment* (1944) and Herbert Marcuse's *One Dimensional Man* (1964), both of which present the characteristic Frankfurt critique of false needs, failed autonomy and social pathology.

As a result of Nazi persecution, the Institute was disrupted between 1933 and 1950. Both during and after this time its members were disparate, and their research output was limited. The Frankfurt School underwent a renaissance in the 1960s, thanks to a resurgence of Marxist thought, but remained at something of an impasse until it was reinvigorated by a second generation of critical theorists. Principal among these was Jürgen **Habermas**, who argued that critical theory needed to address the issue of its own normative foundations (which he attempts to provide in the form of communicative rationality).

The foremost representative of the third generation of Frankfurt theorists is perhaps Axel Honneth, whose attempts to provide a normative theory of recognition have been prominent in recent debates about multiculturalism and the politics of recognition. Critical theory remains a vibrant part of the philosophical topography. However, it is too diffuse to be considered the unified research project it once was. Given the diversity of those referring to themselves as 'critical theorists', there is no one set of systematic assumptions shared by all. Rather, it is the commitment to the theoretical analysis of social reality and 'immanent' critique of the self-understanding of 'dominated' social actors that is characteristic of critical theory. Under this definition, many schools of thought – including **feminism**, race and gender studies, literary studies and political science – might also reasonably lay claim to the epithet 'critical', though the term remains closely associated with the interdisciplinarity of the Frankfurt School.

Robert Farrow

Freud and Psychoanalysis

Sigmund Freud (Příbor 1856 – London 1939) and the psychoanalytic method he developed have had a vast influence on a range of disciplines, including psychotherapy, art theory, film theory, philosophy, feminist theory and literary theory. Freud's most influential ideas include his view of the mind as a heterogeneous structure which is partly unconscious and characterized by conflict, his emphasis on sexuality, and the significance he attributed to language and its analysis.

Psychoanalysis aims to free people from psychological suffering and uncover unconscious conflict as a way of furthering self-knowledge. This broad framework has been adopted in many disciplines as an emancipatory principle and methodology.

Freud's most noted contribution to our view of the mind is the idea that most of the mind is unconscious, or unavailable to conscious introspection. This view of the mind – likened to an iceberg mostly submerged underwater with only its tip visible – was initially received with much hostility, although nowadays it is considered uncontroversial and is corroborated by recent findings in neuroscience. This 'decentralization of the self' has had a vast influence on philosophical approaches to the self and theories of subjectivity and Freud himself likened it to a third Copernican revolution, further destabilizing our view of man as the centre of the world and as transparent to himself. Freud's second topography – the division of the psyche into 'id' (the seat of the drives), 'ego' (the self) and 'superego' (the critical agency) – is less widely accepted, although his general view of the drives as motivational forces and of the human being as an organism operating under the same biological laws and evolutionary pressures as other species is now heralded as apt and empirically supported.

Within continental philosophy, many if not most twentieth-century thinkers engaged with Freud. Together with **Marx** and Weber, Freud had a decisive influence on the **Frankfurt School** and critical theory. More recently, Jean-François **Lyotard's** 'libidinal philosophy' is heavily based on Freud's notion of libido (*Libidinal Economy*, 1974). Others have engaged with Freud more critically, including Jacques **Derrida** (*The Post Card*, 1980), *Resistances of Psychoanalysis*, 1996) and Gilles **Deleuze** and Felix Guattari (*Anti-Oedipus*, 1972; *A Thousand Plateaus*, 1980). **Feminist philosophers** such as Julia **Kristeva**, Luce **Irigaray** and Hélène Cixous have developed a 'psychoanalytic feminism', which explores the structuring of female identity, the body and the effects of language on subjectivity. In film theory, Laura Mulvey and others have taken up Lacanian psychoanalysis and used the notion of 'the gaze' as a central analytic tool. Jonathan Lear, Philippe van Haute (who are also practising psychoanalysts), John Forrester and Slavoj Žižek have all commented extensively on psychoanalysis as well as relying on it heavily in their philosophical work. In philosophy of science, Karl Popper (*Conjectures and Refutations*, 1963), Adolph Grünbaum (*The Foundations of Psychoanalysis*, 1984) and Patricia Kitcher (*Freud's Dream*, 1992) have asked whether psychoanalysis counts as a genuine scientific enterprise; the view that it does not have this status has now become common.

Other than Freud, Jacques **Lacan** and Melanie Klein are probably the best-known psychoanalytic figures within philosophy. Lacan's thought has markedly influenced the work of the 'psychoanalytic' feminists and of Žižek. Lacan's 'return to Freud' aroused the interest of many French philosophers working in the second half of the twentieth century, notably Derrida and Lyotard. Freud was also an important literary critic, and a psychoanalytic interpretation of literature, focusing on unconscious or covert content and privileging psychic context, has influenced other branches of literary theory, including **deconstruction** and **poststructuralism**.

Havi Carel

Gadamer

A student of **Heidegger**, Hans-Georg Gadamer (Marburg 1900 – Heidelberg 2002) builds on his mentor's early 'hermeneutic' approach to being. In attempting to theorize the phenomenon of understanding and its correct interpretation, Gadamer develops a philosophical **hermeneutics** which moves well beyond the romantic framework of the German hermeneutic tradition in Heidegger's work. Gadamer develops the Heideggerian concept of 'effective-historical consciousness', whereby thinking begins not from an abstract point but always–already within a specific culture. Such a situatedness provides us with a 'horizon' for understanding; a fluctuating frame of reference which is shaped and changed by the limits of our historical situation and knowledge. For Gadamer, we do not simply arrive at an object of interpretation – be it a text, person, painting, etc. – from nowhere. Rather, we are bound to a 'tradition' of understanding which enables interpretation to begin. Gadamer employs the term 'prejudice' to describe this situatedness. One of the central theses of his most influential work, *Truth and Method* (1960), is to re-assert the notion of 'prejudice' as a condition of understanding, removing its post-Enlightenment negative connotations. This turns away significantly from the hermeneutic tradition of Schleiermacher and Dilthey, for whom understanding the meaning of a text or event involved reconstructing the original author's understanding. As such, the traditional hermeneutic task was to rid interpretation of prejudice. Gadamer argues, contrarily, that understanding constitutes an event in the present, and carries with it a historicity which conditions the meaning of the text. Gadamer reformulates understanding as *verstehen*, rather than **Kant's** *verstand*, in order to theorize a non-objectifying concept of understanding which recognizes the life and movement of the thing being understood. Gadamer thus enlarges the hermeneutic project precisely by limiting its claims to absolute knowledge: hermeneutics is an ontological task, not a methodological one.

For Gadamer, it is our prejudices which enable understanding, because we are always–already historically situated; yet, in understanding, we are able to adapt and develop these prejudices in terms of the object of understanding. He sees interpretation following the structure of a dialogue which runs back and forth between the interpreter, situated within the horizon of contemporary culture, and the text, situated within the horizon of its writing. The task of hermeneutics is not to appropriate an object into one's horizon, but to open oneself to the object as one does in dialogue, and thus 'fuse' the different horizons of interpreter and interpreted. Gadamer's hermeneutics is thus neither intentionalist (aimed at purely reconstructing the author's original meaning without regard for the reader's position), nor relativist (remaining within the reader's horizon and disregarding the original meaning). It depends, rather, on the cohesion of dialogue as the formation of speculative understanding.

Tom Grimwood

German Idealism

The age of German idealism, roughly 1770–1840, is often considered the golden age of German philosophy. Schematically, we can distinguish between the 'critical' or 'transcendental' idealism of **Kant** and the 'absolute idealism' of the three best-known philosophers who came after him, namely Fichte, Schelling and **Hegel**. German idealism grew out of the Enlightenment's own crisis. The Enlightenment was the age of reason, and was fundamentally based on the principles of rational criticism and scientific naturalism. But taken to their extremes these principles can lead to either scepticism or materialism, the former undermining the belief in the reality of the external world, the latter undermining the possibility of freedom. Though German idealism takes very different, sometimes quite incompatible forms, it can be evaluated as trying to save Enlightenment principles from these two extreme positions.

Accordingly, Immanuel Kant would insist that only his 'transcendental idealism' could provide a satisfactory answer. Instead of defining truth as the conformity of our representations to objects, Kant proposed that what we can know is limited to the conformity of objects with our concepts. Truth is the agreement of our perceptions with universal and necessary, that is, *a priori*, concepts that determine the form or structure of experience. Therefore, we know things only as they appear to us and not as things in themselves. With this move Kant thinks he defeats scepticism, because, on the one hand, reality's existence can still be defended and, on the other, reason becomes autonomous.

Fichte was convinced that the critical philosophy ends in a scepticism worse than Hume's and sought to reconstruct it on a new foundation. Thus he manages to bridge the problematic dualisms of Kant's philosophy and unifies them under a single source: the absolute ego, which is only a regulative idea. The finite ego, by contrast, is a constant striving to make nature conform to the demands of its rational activity, that is, our moral ideals. Fichte's philosophy can best be described as 'ethical idealism' because of the priority given to the activity of will in the production of knowledge.

The beginnings of 'absolute idealism' can be traced in the writings of the Romantics who claimed that the Fichtean ego does not escape scepticism. The solution to this problem comes with the development of a new philosophy of nature, *Naturphilosophie*. Schelling argued that it is nature as an organic whole that embraces spirit and dissolves the dualisms by defending a system of identity between nature as implicit rationality and mind as explicit rationality. Hegel accused both Fichte and Schelling of foundationalism, and doubted Kant's dualisms, claiming that the forms of thought arise historically through the interaction of subject and world. The form and matter of thought cannot be separate. Absolute idealism does not understand the ideal in terms of subjectivity or consciousness, but as the underlying purposiveness and rationality of nature itself.

German idealism had a significant impact on the great philosophers that followed its era including Feuerbach, **Marx**, and **Kierkegaard**.

Kostas Koukouzelis

Habermas

As a leading public intellectual and the foremost representative of critical theory, Jürgen Habermas (Düsseldorf 1929–) is perhaps the most influential living German philosopher. He is acknowledged as the leading 'second-generation' critical theorist and known for his theory of rational communication which attempts to reclaim the Enlightenment project of rational modernity from sceptical assault. In developing and defending his theory, Habermas has synthesized elements from a wide range of scientific and theoretical sources, engaging in extensive debates with thinkers from both the continental and analytic traditions. However, he has been consistently critical of what he sees as the neo-conservativism and superficiality of (neo-**Nietzschean** and neo-**Heideggerian**) postmodernists, whom he accuses of being unable to justify their sceptical positions.

Much in Habermas's philosophical and political project can be traced back to his experience of growing up under the moral catastrophe of National Socialism. Shocked by Heidegger's refusal to fully recant his support for Nazism, the young Habermas searched for the conceptual resources that could explain the failed aspirations of German philosophy, finding inspiration in the liberal democratic tradition. The persistent normative core of his work first emerged in 1962 in his *Habilitationsschrift, The Structural Transformation of the Public Sphere*, which analyzes the legitimating function of public debate in bourgeois liberal democracy. Twentieth-century European modernity, he argued, has instead been characterized by institutionalized media and the manipulation of popular opinion. As such, it has failed to realize its own ideals of inclusive, rational communication and political autonomy.

His subsequent early work explored the epistemological foundations of self-understanding, interaction, socialization and the reproduction of society, culminating in *Knowledge and Human Interests* (1968) which attempted to provide an anthropological basis for critique as a distinctive form of emancipatory human reflection. Habermas came to consider this work to be hampered by the 'philosophy of consciousness' and, during the 1970s, he embarked on a series of studies with the aim of stripping the **Hegelian** and metaphysical residues from his theory, leading him to something of a 'linguistic turn'. Habermas's thought found its mature expression in 1981 with the publication of the complex *Theory of Communicative Action* where Habermas provides a philosophical and sociological justification for his theory of communicative rationality. Speech acts, he contends, raise transcendental–pragmatic claims to validity that can only be ratified intersubjectively. These validity claims to truth, sincerity and normative rightness are inherently linked to social acceptability and therefore present social norms to rational scrutiny, indicating the possibility of consensual – rather than instrumental or strategic – social action. Under Habermas's analysis, the complex global structure of modern society leads to the authoritarian and technocratic organization of market and administrative structures though non-linguistic rationality. The theory attempts to show that such forms of rationality are parasitic upon communicative action, and so can be criticized in the public sphere. In his expansive later work, Habermas expands the communicative paradigm by developing a deontological discourse ethics and exploring its implications for law, politics and, more recently, naturalized religion.

Robert Farrow

Hegel

The most prominent of the **German idealists**, Georg Wilhelm Friedrich Hegel (Stuttgart 1770 – Berlin 1831) developed a philosophy of 'absolute mind' or 'spirit' (*Geist*) in response to Kant's delimitation of the mind's faculties. Hegel argues that to think a limit is already to be beyond it, with thought emerging in his work as the perpetual transcendence of its own apparent limits. This identification of thought and being at the same time gestures towards a materialism informing much later continental thought, from **Marxism** to **existentialism, psychoanalysis**, the **Frankfurt School, post-structuralism**, the twentieth-century 'linguistic turn' and the emergence of 'cultural studies'.

Hegel's contradictory legacy reflects his own appreciation of contradiction as productive rather than destructive of thought. For example, his first major theoretical work, the *Phenomenology of Spirit* (1807), describes each apparent 'shape' of the mind as pushing beyond itself due to an internal 'negativity'. Even simple sense-experience, or the certainty that I 'now' sense daylight – is both (1) made uncertain or 'negated' by the constant disappearance of the 'now' into the 'then', and (2) 'mediated' by the universality of the word 'now', whose consistency recuperates or 'negates the first negation' and makes possible the very *relation* of a perduring 'mind' to the sensory world. 'Sense-certainty', that is, turns out to be 'in truth' the more complex mental shape of 'perception', which approaches distinct 'things' as simultaneously both empirical *and* conceptual. This 'dialectical progression' from a naïve, implicitly contradictory shape of knowing, to one that resolves or 'sublates' the contradiction, continues until the mind 'finds itself' liberated in 'absolute knowing' or 'science'.

Hegel's *Science of Logic* (1812, 1813, 1816) accordingly leaves behind the 'existential' focus of the *Phenomenology* (intended as the 'introduction' to a forthcoming 'scientific system') for the realm of 'pure thought'. At stake, however, is more than a shift from psychology to ontology: the dialectical method results in a 'speculative' logic that, through contradiction, should 'produce its own content', transcend mere formalism, and account for the workings of nature and history as much as thought.

In the *Encyclopedia of the Philosophical Sciences in Outline* (1817, 1827, 1830), Hegel presents the entire 'system' implied by his two prior texts. The placement of a condensed (supposedly introductory) 'phenomenology of spirit' in 'part three' of this 'outline', however, exemplifies the difficulty of systematizing *all* mental resolutions of *all* actual contradictions. De Man, **Derrida** and Žižek have interpreted Hegel's struggles with systematization as indicative of his 'rigorous' and 'radical' undermining of the German idealist project. His 1820s lecture courses on aesthetics, religion, world history and the history of philosophy display a Euro-centrism suggesting that both systematization and 'mediation' are as much cultural as 'conceptual' processes.

Hegel's final major work, the *Elements of the Philosophy of Right* (1821), describes the mediation of 'the individual' by the dialectics of the family, the market or 'civil society', the state and 'world history'. Its critique of social-contract theory and analysis of the complexity of legal 'right' in the modern world have influenced political theorists from Marx to Nancy.

Patience Moll

Heidegger

Arguably the most important philosopher of the twentieth century, Martin Heidegger (Messkirch 1887 – Freiburg 1976) has been influential in many fields, including ontology, **hermeneutics**, theology, philosophy of language, aesthetics and ecology. His influence is particularly evident in the French philosophical movements of **existentialism** and **deconstruction**.

His principal work *Being and Time* (1927) poses the question of the meaning of being as a transformation of an ancient question: Plato and Aristotle question the being of beings without apprehending the *meaning* of being as a problem. Heidegger argues that the meaning of being has been taken for granted as 'presence' throughout the history of philosophy: traditionally 'to be' means 'to be present', but this fails to do justice to, first of all, the particularity of human being. In delimiting a 'vulgar' understanding of time as a series of now-points, which is first expressed in the work of Aristotle, Heidegger seeks to show that the human being is not something present, and that it is rather always and already stretched out beyond and behind itself according to what is termed its 'ecstatic temporality'.

Heidegger's elaboration of the specificity of human existence – which is termed *Dasein*, a being-the-there – is informed by readings of post-**Hegelian** thinkers such as Søren **Kierkegaard** and Friedrich **Nietzsche**. As his lecture courses of the 1920s show, it is also informed by readings of Aristotle, Leibniz and **Kant**, and by secularizing interpretations of St Paul and Luther. From Edmund **Husserl**, his teacher, Heidegger develops his own historically oriented version of **phenomenology** as a philosophical method, but the divergence in their views, particularly Heidegger's refusal of Husserl's transcendental idealism, meant that collaboration became impossible for them by the early 1930s.

Heidegger's reputation is overshadowed by his appointment as Rector of Freiburg University in 1933 under the nascent National Socialist regime. He resigned from this post after ten months, and later described his political intervention as the greatest stupidity of his life. His continuing membership of the Nazi party, and reluctance to address the atrocities of the Nazi regime, have led to severe criticism by later thinkers. Heidegger always maintained, however, that his aims as Rector were consistent with his philosophical orientation: his principal concern was to save German culture, and thus German *Dasein* itself, by defending the idea of a philosophically-grounded university from those who would transform it into disparate technical and vocational institutes.

From the 1930s, Heidegger's work is governed by questions of technology, art and language, and by a radicalized historical questioning of being. In early Greek thinking, he argues, being or *phusis* (nature) was thought not as presence but as a presencing or coming-to-presence. With Plato, however, philosophy falls away from this primary truth by means of a veiled attempt to master and dominate beings, the sense and consequences of which become manifest in our modern techno-scientific age. Understood as governed by a particular manifestation of being, the modern techno-sciences represent the completion of philosophy or metaphysics, and the task remains for us to think being in a different way, according to a 'new beginning'. For Heidegger, this can be accomplished only by means of a step backwards to the origins of Greek thought and through reflection on art as revelatory of truth.

Mark Sinclair

Hermeneutics

Taken in a non-philosophical sense the term 'hermeneutics' covers a range of disciplines that share a common problem: how is one to interpret a given expression, passage, text, etc.? Thus, law, theology and classical philology each represents a 'special hermeneutics', which addresses this problem by developing its own rules for the interpretation of texts. However, when taken in a philosophical sense the term refers to a theory of the operations of the understanding, which are said to underlie this first order interpretation of texts.

Friedrich Schleiermacher (1768–1834) was the first to propose a theory of this type. Inspired both by **Kant** and by Schlegel, his work is characterized by two antithetical tendencies: (1) a critical aspiration to determine the universally valid principles of the understanding; and (2) a Romantic appeal to a dynamic relationship with the creative process. This dual tendency can be found throughout the tradition of philosophical hermeneutics. Wilhelm Dilthey (1833–1911) continued the process of the 'de-regionalization' of hermeneutics that Schleiermacher had initiated, extending hermeneutics' field of operation beyond that of written texts to incorporate the entire range of historical expressions, including actions. Because Dilthey was deeply committed to a historicist view of understanding he sought to re-fashion hermeneutics along the lines of a 'critique of historical reason' that was arguably even more ambitious than Kant's *Critique of Pure Reason*. It is generally agreed that a deep-rooted conflict between an irrationalist philosophy of life and a rationalist philosophy of meaning is evident throughout this ultimately unfinished critique.

Martin **Heidegger** (1889–1976) further contributed to the development of a distinctly philosophical hermeneutics, but where Schleiermacher and Dilthey had seen this development in terms of a 'de-regionalization' of hermeneutics he saw it in terms of a 'radicalization' of the problem of understanding. 'Radicalizing' the problem of understanding meant re-casting it in terms which could be shown to be more 'original' and so arguably, more philosophical than those of epistemology. Thus, Heidegger moved the analysis onto the plane of a 'fundamental ontology' that jettisoned all references to mental faculties, re-interpreting understanding as the way of being of human beings. He then re-fashioned the problem of understanding as a failure to meet the criterion of 'authenticity', suggesting that the solution lay in 'a dismantling [*Abbau*]' of the traditional concepts that have been passed down to us. Hence, for Heidegger, 'hermeneutics is **deconstruction** [*Destruktion*]'.

Paul **Ricoeur** (1913–2005) criticized Heidegger for crafting hermeneutics in such a way that it 'is wholly engaged in *going back to the [ontological] foundations*' of a Kantian epistemological inquiry into the conditions of possibility of the ordinary sciences. He argued that Heidegger's interdiction on any movement of return from the level of ontological structures made it impossible to justify the claim that 'exegetico-historical critique' is 'derivative'. Taking a first step on the return journey to epistemological questioning, Heidegger's disciple Hans-Georg **Gadamer** (1900–2002) gave hermeneutics a dialogical character, whilst Ricoeur ultimately favoured a translation model that would allow hermeneutics to practice an 'ethics of hospitality'.

Eileen Brennan

Husserl

Founder of the **phenomenological** movement, Edmund Husserl (Moravia 1859 – Freiburg 1938) renewed the methods and orientation of philosophy in a manner that was pivotal for much of twentieth-century European thought. The philosophers he influenced include Max Scheler, **Heidegger** and Eugen Fink in Germany, and **Ricoeur**, **Sartre**, **Merleau-Ponty**, **Levinas** and **Derrida** in France.

Husserl's first work, *Philosophy of Arithmetic* (1891), offered an account of the foundations of mathematics that was influenced by the empirical psychology of the time. The *Logical Investigations* of 1900, however, are offered as an antidote to the dangers and contradictions of psychologism: logical and mathematical laws are not empirical generalizations describing how minds work here are now, but are rather *a priori* and objective truths intuited by the thinking subject. In developing the distinction of subjective mental act and apprehended objective content with regard to the manifold forms of linguistic expression and consciousness, the *Logical Investigations* develops Franz Brentano's idea of intentionality, according to which consciousness is always consciousness of something. For Husserl, the preparatory task of philosophy becomes that of studying the different modes of consciousness – perceiving, imagining, judging or reasoning mathematically, for example – and the essential structures of the objects of those modes, which structures can be grasped by a process of imaginative variation: the impossibility of, say, imagining a perceived object without spatial form shows that space is an essential invariant of all perceived objects. Husserl's concern for propositional sense led to important conceptions of language as 'expression' and of truth as 'fulfilment', which challenge traditional theories of language as a mere physical sign of thought and correspondence accounts of truth.

In *The Idea of Phenomenology* (1907), *Philosophy as a Rigorous Science* (1910) and *Ideas Pertaining to a Pure Phenomenology and to a Phenomenological Philosophy* Vol. 1 (1913), Husserl develops his conception of phenomenology as a presuppositionless science that is the necessary propaedeutic to all others. Phenomenology proceeds by a series of reductions, the first of which is the *epochē*, according to which all common sense, scientific and metaphysical claims concerning objects are bracketed or suspended so that we are better able to study phenomena and the modes of their apprehension. In the *Ideas*, however, further reductions ultimately lead to the discovery of a transcendental, sense-giving, 'constitutive' consciousness. On this basis Husserl offers influential accounts of our experience of others, and of our consciousness of time.

Husserl opposes all forms of naturalism and scientism, and in the late, unfinished work *The Crisis of the European Sciences and Transcendental Phenomenology* he argues that the spiritual and cultural problems of Europe can be resolved only by retrieving the primary and pre-theoretical life-world of the transcendental ego in which the natural sciences are rooted. Husserl envisaged the task of phenomenological philosophy as a communal one, but few of his students adopted his thought without qualification. The complexity of his thought, however, and the manifold ways in which other twentieth-century philosophers are indebted to it, has been underscored by the posthumous and still ongoing publication of his manuscripts.

Mark Sinclair

Irigaray

Luce Irigaray (Belgium 1932–) is a French **feminist philosopher**, linguist, **psychoanalyst**, **poststructuralist** and cultural theorist. She argues that sexual difference is foundational and remains one of the most controversial and significant subjects of philosophical discussion. Irigaray's philosophy is influenced by **Freudian** and **Lacanian** psychoanalytic theories, **Levinas's** philosophy and **Derrida's deconstruction**. Irigaray sees Western philosophical traditions as phallogocentric (male-centred) and challenges this in her own work. She criticizes the exclusion of women from philosophy, psychoanalytic theory and linguistics. Her aim is to create two equally positive and autonomous terms, 'woman' and 'man', to acknowledge two sexes, not only one.

Irigaray is one of the most important figures of psychoanalytically influenced French feminist philosophy, alongside **Kristeva** and Cixous.

Irigaray considers the existence of sexual difference as an ontological truth and asserts that it requires acknowledgement. She argues that, rather than trying to do away with differences between men and women, feminism ought to acknowledge the reality of difference and take it as the centre of both theory and practice. She seeks to reveal the absence of a female subject position, the demotion of all things feminine to the body and nature, and the absence of 'real' sexual difference in Western culture. She argues that both men and women should be equally able to attain the position of the subject. In the Western philosophical tradition, 'men' are considered the standard of the 'human'. The human has been defined in terms of characteristics associated specifically with men. Women have also been defined by men, as bearing those characteristics which men do not wish for in themselves. In Irigaray's view, men are the subject, self-conscious, the (main) One, and women are the 'Other' of the subject (the object, the supporting one). She claims that women should be the source of the definition of 'woman'. Irigaray believes that real social transformation will take place only if society changes its view of the body and nature, and by association of woman as the 'Other' of a thinking male subject, to be subjugated and restricted. Thus, her philosophy opens up new possibilities for theorizing embodied subjectivity and maintains that both men and women must see themselves as embodied subjects that belong to nature (the body) and culture (the mind). Irigaray's philosophy can be considered not as a fixed theoretical framework, but as a starting point to the opening up of possibilities of accepting diversity and living together in communities marked by difference.

Irigaray's work has moved through several phases. She discusses sexual difference in *Speculum of the Other Woman* (1974) and *This Sex Which Is Not One* (1977). She provides readings of classical philosophers such as Spinoza and **Heidegger** in *Elemental Passions* (1982) and *The Forgetting of Air in Martin Heidegger* (1983). She returns to the notion of sexual difference in her more recent work such as *To Be Two* (1997) and *The Way of Love* (2002).

Minae Inahara

Kant

Immanuel Kant (Königsberg 1724–1804), perhaps the most important philosopher of modern times, has had a decisive influence on virtually every aspect of continental philosophy.

Kant's first major work, The *Critique of Pure Reason* (1781, 1787), inaugurates what he called the 'Copernican revolution' in philosophy. This is a revolution towards the subject as the productive source of knowledge. Kant argues that knowledge arises from the collaboration of a faculty of intuition, which passively 'receives' what is given in the world, and a faculty of understanding that spontaneously gives it its form. With this thesis, Kant seeks to overcome the impasse between continental rationalism (which prioritizes understanding as the main source of knowledge) and British empiricism (which holds that the senses alone provide us with knowledge of external reality). It also, Kant believes, provides the only possible grounding for 'synthetic *a priori* knowledge': universal propositions (such as 'every event has a cause') that necessarily apply to, but do not arise from, experience.

Kant's 'transcendental idealism' aims to demonstrate these conditions of possibility of knowledge. Space and time are shown to be *a priori* forms of sensibility that necessarily structure all our intuitions. Twelve categories – including, for example, substantiality, causality and actuality – are the 'pure concepts' or *a priori* forms of understanding that necessarily structure every experience. Human knowledge is limited to those objects that 'appear' to us in space and time, which Kant calls appearances or *phenomena*. Other kinds of objects – 'things in themselves' or *noumena* – can only be *thought* by us. God, the soul and freedom are therefore only ideas of reason, of which we have no theoretical knowledge. These ideas may be used to regulate our understanding: we may entertain their possibility in order to make sense of our experience as a coherent and systematic whole, but we must never assume their actuality as constitutive of experience. Kant believed that most of the problems of rationalism and empiricism arose from their belief in knowledge of things in themselves. Transcendental idealism instead holds that knowledge applies only to appearances, and thereby overcomes the 'antinomies' of traditional metaphysics concerning the existence of God, the soul and freedom.

The necessity for us to assume our freedom, without having theoretical knowledge of it, is the guiding thread of Kant's moral philosophy. Autonomy, elaborated in Kant's *Critique of Practical Reason* (1788), is understood as the capacity of the will to legislate to itself, that is, to choose maxims for itself independently of sensuous inclinations. What kind of maxims should one choose to be morally good? This is the task ascribed to the categorical imperative, a command immanent to reason that requires us consistently to will that our own maxim become a universal law. Reason, grounded in freedom, commands us to act from moral duty, to treat all rational beings as ends in themselves, and to strive towards a society in which all rational beings are fully and equally autonomous.

Kant's third critique, the *Critique of Judgment* (1790), had an enormous impact on **German idealism** and Romanticism, and continues to be influential on continental aesthetics. Its purpose is to bridge the gap between nature with its causal laws, and freedom with its moral law, and to provide reflective judgement with a principle of its own. This is the regulative principle of the purposiveness of nature, which Kant examines through both aesthetic and teleological judgement. The book contains Kant's important doctrines of beauty and sublimity, along with much of his mature philosophy of nature, and his views on the relationship between teleology, theology, culture and morality.

Kant also wrote extensively on anthropology, natural science, history and politics. Kant's cosmopolitan political philosophy is based on the triad of 'freedom, equality, independence', and informs much of the contemporary liberal/republican tradition represented especially in the work of **Habermas**.

Kant's impact on German and continental philosophy in general is simply enormous, from Fichte to **Hegel** and Schopenhauer to the neo-Kantians, to **Husserl, Heidegger, Foucault** and **Deleuze**. The problems Kant raises in his three critiques continue to be addressed by both analytic and continental philosophers.

Kostas Koukouzelis

Kierkegaard

The Christian thinker and 'father of existentialism' Søren Kierkegaard (Copenhagen 1815–1855) was an extraordinarily prolific writer. His best-known works were published between 1843 and 1849, and during this period he produced eight significant philosophical works, written under various pseudonyms, as well as several volumes of explicitly religious 'edifying discourses' in his own name.

At the centre of Kierkegaard's thought lies the question of religious faith. For Kierkegaard, *being* a Christian can never be reduced to the knowledge that one has, or could have, of Christianity, but is rather a matter of the individual's personal relation to God. In *Concluding Unscientific Postscript* (1846) Kierkegaard distinguishes between the 'objective' and 'subjective' truth of Christianity – between truth as object of knowledge and truth as a way of living, an existential task – and insists on the priority of the latter.

Every aspect of Kierkegaard's writings is shaped by this one concern with the individual's existence, from his polemical criticisms of **Hegel** to his attack on the contemporary Danish church. His distinctive literary style is also in the service of this project: rather than presenting positive claims and theses, he used a method of 'indirect communication' which makes problematic the authorial voice and provokes the reader to an active interpretation of the text.

Kierkegaard's criticism of Hegel is present throughout nearly all of his work. He is critical of Hegel's subordination of both religion and individual, subjective existence within the framework of his philosophical system of absolute knowledge. This critique finds its most dramatic, condensed and renowned formulation in *Fear and Trembling* (1843), which meditates on Abraham's readiness to sacrifice his son Isaac at God's command. Kierkegaard argues that Abraham's actions remain incomprehensible even to one who is thoroughly schooled in the Hegelian system. In other words, faith – the subjective truth of religion which Abraham embodies – cannot be comprehended by thought. The significance of this critique goes beyond Hegel's philosophy, however: it demonstrates the impossibility of any systematic knowledge of existence, and protests against the reduction of existence to an object of knowledge. It is for this reason that Kierkegaard is widely considered the 'father' of **existentialism**.

This emphasis on the existing individual means that the major concepts of Kierkegaard's thought pertain to a person's manner of being, to *how* she is and not *what* she is. Of these, the most influential has been the concept of anxiety, which has been taken up and developed by both **Sartre** and **Heidegger**. In *The Concept of Anxiety* (1844) Kierkegaard, writing under the pseudonym Vigilius Haufniensis, suggests that anxiety arises in the face of our freedom, conceived existentially as a lack of fixity of being. The being of subjectivity is, then, a kind of nothingness, and this excites our anxiety, since we must consequently assume responsibility for our choices and actions.

As well as influencing existentialist philosophies, Kierkegaard's work has also shaped the thinking and writing of more recent philosophers within the continental tradition, such as Emmanuel **Levinas** and Jacques **Derrida**.

Keith Crome and Jonathan Hunt

Kristeva

Julia Kristeva (Silven 1941–) is a French **feminist philosopher**, literary critic and **psychoanalyst**. Kristeva is interested in notions of intertextuality, the semiotic, the process of identity formation and the role of abjection in that process, the limits of linguistic signification, embodied difference, and the risk of political solidarity. She provides critical theories of related thinkers including **Lacan**, **Foucault**, Barthes and **Derrida**. Kristeva makes an important contribution to the theoretical shift from **structuralist** to **poststructuralist** thinking. Like other French feminists, such as **Irigaray** and Cixous, Kristeva is known for advocating a domain of expression, distinct from language, which can capture 'the feminine'. However, Kristeva does not make gender the only site of political concern, nor does she accept sexual difference as fundamental. Rather, she seeks to deconstruct much Western feminist thought alongside male philosophies which manifest forms of essentialism.

While Kristeva's way of seeing the subject has many links with both **Freud** and Lacan, she denies any fixed position for the self, supporting the idea of a 'subject in process'. Kristeva contributes to the poststructuralist criticism of a fixed formation of identity, and maintains a logic of instability between what she terms 'symbolic identity' and the domain of the semiotic. For her, the semiotic is related to the infantile stage in both Freud and Lacan, prior to the emergence of language. In 'Women's Time' (1979), Kristeva discusses the possibility of a difference between the time of female subjectivity, which answers to the repetitions and sequences of bodily rhythms, and the time of masculine subjectivity, which is intelligible, hierarchical, patriarchal and teleological.

Kristeva is also renowned for her theories of abjection and intertextuality. Kristeva's work of the 1980s, such as *Tales of Love* (1983) and *The Black Sun: Depression and Melancholia* (1987) describe her experiences as an analyst. In *Powers of Horror: An Essay in Abjection* (1980) she describes a stage of development of the child's sense of self, which precedes Lacan's mirror stage. This stage is one where the child forms a sense of its own bodily boundaries by a process of abjection. Kristeva looks at how boundaries around the subject and objects emerge; those boundaries that allow one to experience oneself as detached from the maternal environment. The abject exists at the boundaries of the self, that which is neither subject nor object. Constituted by bodily fluids, materials that remind us that we have been derived from the maternal body, the abject has a compelling impact upon the body itself, often causing bodily reactions such as revulsion. Ultimately, it threatens the logic of the subject/object binary. In *Strangers to Ourselves* (1989) Kristeva elaborates on the concept of abjection in a socio-political context. She furnishes a new conception of abjection as a process of undoing or dismantling the 'Other', while recognizing otherness within ourselves.

Minae Inahara

Lacan

Jacques Lacan (Paris 1901–1981) attempts to show that **Freud's** psychoanalytic theory needs to be understood in terms of the triad of real, imaginary and symbolic. Lacan at first defines the real as the self-identical and later as uniqueness; the imaginary is the realm of images, and the symbolic comprises whatever is structured like a language. The human being is the region in which all three orders intersect.

As one becomes an individual, one is progressively alienated from what one really is. One moves from real singularity, to imaginary individuality (the ego, my conscious self-image), to symbolic generality (the characteristics I have that can be described in language). Each stage stifles the one before, but each stage is a necessary one. Humans are born without a sense of their own identity. The imaginary and the symbolic 'identifications' are needed in order to supplement this real deficiency.

My identity is formed by identifying with others, and as a result my identity will never truly be my own. I shall always be partly alienated from myself. As a consequence, I fantasize about acquiring the wholeness that I lack. This is the object of my desire, the *'objet petit a'*. This is something that is always possessed by the 'little other [*autre*]', an 'imaginary other' which is 'little' since it is not dissimilar to me, unlike the 'big Other' that is the symbolic order, which is radically unlike me.

In the symbolic order of signifiers, my individuality is repressed and this stirs in me the desire to express it. Signifiers are arbitrary in relation to that which is signified by them. Since culture is composed of elements that have significance, that which is desirable to us in our culture will be arbitrary, and so anything could take its place. Thus no one object will ever finally satisfy our desire. In contrast to animal need, desire is infinite. What is infinite cannot accede to finite consciousness, and so it remains unconscious. Consciousness makes sense of desire by assigning it to definite objects. It fails to understand that *no* object will ever satisfy desire, since desire really aims only at the destruction of definite objects. Desire is fundamentally a destructive 'death-drive'.

In Lacan's linguistic understanding of the unconscious, what is infinite is language itself, the number of different contexts in which a particular signifier can appear. If meaning is given by context, a signifier always has more than one meaning, and this 'overdetermination' allows a second, unintended context to show through in our conscious use of language. These revelations of the unconscious are 'symptoms' of repression. Traumatic events are pressing for an expression that is resisted by consciousness. These events have not been integrated into our ego because they occurred to us in such a way that we were unable to conceptualize or describe them, often during childhood when our conceptual and linguistic faculties were under-developed. In symptomatic behaviour, we use signifiers that are connected to an unintended context in which a traumatic event has taken up residence. The psychoanalyst must force the patient to recognize his symptom as bespeaking this traumatic event.

Among others, Lacan has influenced Badiou, Žižek, **Althusser, Kristeva** and Cixous. His work has been criticized by **Deleuze**, Guattari, **Lyotard** and **Derrida**.

Michael Lewis

Levinas

Emmanuel Levinas (Kaunas 1906 – Paris 1995) was one of the first people in France to appreciate the significance of the emerging **phenomenological** movement, having gone in 1928 to Freiburg to study with **Husserl** and

Heidegger. His first book, *The Theory of Intuition in Husserl's Phenomenology* (1930), was credited by **Sartre**, **Derrida** and others as the work which introduced them to phenomenology. Already in this early work, however, Levinas showed that what interested him about phenomenology was less its methodically rigorous reduction of the natural realist attitude to the correlates of consciousness than the way phenomenology led the thinker from abstract cognition to concrete life. This is evident in the ironic title, where Husserl's account of intuition is regarded as still too 'theoretical', and in the book's conclusion, where Heidegger is presented as the one who makes the breakthrough from a theory of intuition to analyses of concrete historical and social life.

However, the Holocaust (which claimed Levinas's parents and brothers) and Heidegger's sympathy for Nazism led Levinas to cultivate a distinctly ethical form of phenomenology. Indeed, the overriding theme of his first major work, *Totality and Infinity* (1961), is that Western philosophy, Husserlian and Heideggerian phenomenology included, has privileged 'ontology' at the expense of ethics by reducing the otherness of other people, which Levinas described in normative rather than physical terms, to the intellect's capacity to conceive objects (rare exceptions to this include Plato's good beyond being and Descartes's concept of infinity). To avoid this tendency to reduce the Other to the categories of the Same, Levinas emphasizes the transcendental status of 'the face of the other'. It is only by welcoming the Other – modelled on biblical injunctions such as 'do not murder' and 'look after the stranger' – that the original solipsism of thought is ruptured. Levinas thereby arrives at his signature notion of 'ethics as first philosophy', which points to the priority that respecting the 'alterity' and 'infinity' of the Other has over the epistemological accomplishments of philosophy.

Derrida's essay 'Violence and Metaphysics' (1964), the first substantial discussion of Levinas's philosophy, was to provoke a turning in Levinas's thought. Derrida argued that Levinas failed to acknowledge his dependence on the very language and concepts of the ontological tradition that he claimed to have left behind. In response, Levinas produced *Otherwise than Being or Beyond Essence* (1974). Here it is not a matter of trying to separate ethics from philosophy in order to privilege the former but of showing how ethics disturbs and unsettles ontology from the very outset of thinking. Levinas therefore describes thought as 'persecuted' by and 'hostage' to the Other, thus suggesting that the basic claims of ontology, especially the self-identity of the subject of thought, are fissured with responsibility for others. This exposure to the Other occurs in 'the Saying', the performative, ethical dimension of language where an interlocutor is invoked or addressed, in contrast to 'the Said', the realm of knowledge, thematization, calculation and planning.

Levinas also wrote several 'confessional' works (Talmudic readings and essays on Judaism) as well as commentaries on literature and art. In these essays it is usually a matter of highlighting the ethical basis of religion, language and representation. Levinas's 'obsession' with the ethics of the Other played a major role in determining the contours of modern European moral philosophy.

Nick Trakakis and Michael Fagenblat

Lyotard

Jean-François Lyotard (Versailles 1924 – Paris 1998) is widely known as one of the most influential theorists of the postmodern and a partisan of the artistic avant-garde. *The Postmodern Condition* (1979) defined the postmodern as the state of culture following the transformation of the epistemic, discursive and aesthetic rules of science, literature and the arts that occurred with the turning away from the 'grand narratives' of the Enlightenment in the latter part of the nineteenth century. Many have seen Lyotard's own work as part of the condition he penetratingly diagnosed, itself amounting to a series of disparate experimental (or postmodern) transformations of philosophical writing. Certainly, his works initially appear to be of a bewildering stylistic variety: ranging from his first conventional study of **phenomenology** (1954) through the highly performative, and perhaps unclassifiable, writing of *Libidinal Economy* (1974) to 'fictional' works and collaborations with artists (for example, *Récits tremblants*, 1977), and biography (*Signed Malraux*, 1996). However, informing the range of Lyotard's works is a concern to expose the limits of reason, and rather than reducing Lyotard's work to a series of examples of 'postmodern' philosophy, it is better to view his thinking about the postmodern as but one instance of his critique of reason.

Lyotard's first major work, *Discours, figure* (1971), is a contestation of the essentially Platonic opposition between the visible and the intellectual, the *figure* and thought, and the dominance of the latter over the former. Here, Lyotard discovers the inhabitation of the figural in thought, showing it to be a disruptive presence that thought cannot incorporate without being shaken. In this sense, thinking the figural transforms the way we picture thought itself. From a broadly phenomenological opening, Lyotard mobilizes the concepts of **Freudian psychoanalysis** in order to criticize his initial position. This turn informed Lyotard's next major work, *Libidinal Economy*. If the figural was a violence at work in thought and language, then libidinal energy is an affective force that inhabits and has the potential to disrupt all established structures and institutions.

After *Libidinal Economy*, Lyotard's interest shifted from a concern with libidinal energetics to a concern with language, and what, following Wittgenstein, he called 'language games'. The key work of this period is *The Differend* (1983). Lyotard defines a differend as a conflict between two or more parties that is impossible to resolve equitably for lack of a rule of judgement applicable to both. The differend is thus a concept indebted to **Kant's** description of the antinomies of reason in the *Critique of Pure Reason*. In this sense, Lyotard's engagement with Kant is a further attempt to critically disrupt the limits of reason.

Further works on Kant followed, including *Lessons on the Analytic of the Sublime* (1991). Lyotard's last works consisted of two studies of Malraux, *Signed Malraux* and *Soundproof Room* (1998), and a posthumously published (and unfinished) study of Augustine, *The Confession of Augustine* (1998). Lyotard's work has influenced many contemporary philosophers, and particularly through his concern with the postmodern, many contemporary cultural, literary and artistic theories.

Keith Crome and Jonathan Hunt

Marx and Marxism

Karl Marx (Trier 1818 – London 1883) conceived his project to be focused on a critique of political economy (*A Contribution to the Critique of Political Economy*, 1859; *Capital*, Vol. I, 1867; *Grundrisse*, 1939–1941). Informing this critique was his endorsement of the radicalism of the revolutionary proletariat in nineteenth-century Europe (with Engels, *Manifesto of the Communist Party*, 1848). He developed a materialist conception of history that argued that the prevailing manner in which material production is organized and implemented determines the political organization and intellectual output of a historical epoch (*The German Ideology*, 1932).

Hegel is a complex and central figure in Marx's intellectual development. Early on he developed his views in growing opposition to the subjective idealism of the Young Hegelians. In his *Critique of Hegel's Philosophy of Right* (1843) he criticizes Hegel's account of political institutions and structures for reading into these Hegelian metaphysics. He also criticizes Hegel for assuming that the state can resolve economic contradictions. For Marx, such an account misses the prior conditioning reality of 'civil society' from which the state originates and to which it remains subordinate.

Marx argued that the human 'species-being' is labour and correlatively, that to the extent to which labour is divided and carried out according to the dictates of the market, humanity is alienated. Only when labour becomes collective can human beings come to the realization that they are the true creators of history. Once achieved the necessity of characterizing the human essence in alien terms will be overcome. Another central notion in Marx's work is social class. Classes that can appropriate surplus freely are 'exploiting' classes whereas classes that produce more than they appropriate are 'exploited'. In capitalist societies, exploitation is characterized as a function of the private ownership of the means of production and by the fact that labour can be bought and sold like a commodity.

The term 'Marxism' has come to denote a vast amount of work that claims some inspiration from Marx's (and Engels's) writings. Generally, Marxism is a vast area that is divided into a variety of different theoretical and pragmatic tendencies, not all of which are in harmony. In Soviet Marxism, Plekhanov, Lenin and Trotsky are key figures. In Western Marxism, Lukács, Gramsci and **Althusser** have been influential. Soviet Marxism is characterized by the interplay of politics and theory and Western Marxism is characterized by posing epistemological, ethical and practical questions.

A figure who combines the theoretical and pragmatic dimensions of Marxism is Gramsci, who was elected to the Italian Parliament in 1924 and who, only two years later, was arrested and sentenced to over twenty years in prison. While in prison he wrote his *Prison Notebooks* and engaged in reflection on the political role of intellectuals. Most recently Alain Badiou and Slavoj Žižek have been influenced by Marxist thought. Žižek continues to explore the place of the 'critical intellectual', a notion associated with Marx and **Adorno**, while Badiou explores an ethic of truth that centres on the notion of fidelity to revolutionary events.

Philip Tonner

Merleau-Ponty

Described by Paul **Ricoeur** as the greatest of the French phenomenologists, Maurice Merleau-Ponty (Rochefort-sur-Mer 1908 – Paris 1961) took Edmund **Husserl's** work in a more embodied, historical and existential direction. He argued that **phenomenology** is essentially and necessarily **existential** philosophy, because any attempted reduction to the 'things themselves' will end up revealing the way in which experience is always permeated by the existential and social situation of which we are a part. In his own words, the 'most important lesson that the reduction teaches us is the impossibility of a complete reduction', in that its 'failure' reveals our ties to the world.

Although a consistent foil from which to present his own thoughts, Merleau-Ponty had a more far-reaching project in mind than merely contesting and reformulating Jean-Paul **Sartre's** more famous version of existentialism. In *Phenomenology of Perception* (1945), for example, he sets out to show the flaws of much of the history of Western philosophy and its tendency to bifurcate into either empiricism or 'intellectualism', both of which falsify the phenomenological evidence of perception, understanding it either in terms of sensation or judgement. These two tendencies have other theoretical failings, not the least of which is that, tacitly or otherwise, they both understand the body as an object, thereby perpetuating a mind-body dualism that Merleau-Ponty spent his career attempting to overcome by thematizing our ambiguous and paradoxical situation as embodied beings who are of the world but nonetheless are not reducible to it. Although he is often associated with the idea of the 'primacy of perception' (a thesis which is both ontological and epistemological), rather than rejecting scientific and analytic ways of knowing the world, Merleau-Ponty argued that such knowledge is always derivative in relation to the more practical aspects of the body's exposure to the world, notably our bodily intentionality that seeks equilibrium or 'maximum grip' with the world through the refinement of our 'body-schema' and the acquisition of flexible habits and skills. For him, these aspects of bodily motility and perception are the transcendental conditions that ensure that sensory experience has the form of a meaningful field rather than being a fragmented relation to raw sense data.

Merleau-Ponty was one of the first philosophers to bring **structuralism** and the linguistic emphasis of thinkers like Saussure into a relationship with phenomenology and existentialism, and an enduring cross-disciplinarity was a feature of his work throughout his career. His various essays on politics, history, biology, aesthetics, psychology, etc., are collated in several important books, including *Structure of Behaviour* (1942), *Humanism and Terror* (1947), *Sense and Nonsense* (1948), *Adventures of the Dialectic* (1955) and *Signs* (1960). Merleau-Ponty was the youngest ever Chair of Philosophy at the Collège de France when he was awarded this position in 1952. He fulfilled this role until his untimely death in 1961, leaving his major work of ontology, *The Visible and the Invisible*, uncompleted. It was subsequently published in 1964 and continues to stimulate much philosophical interest.

Jack Reynolds

Nietzsche

Friedrich Nietzsche (Röcken 1844 – Weimar 1900) is, perhaps above any other philosopher, defined by virtue of his legacy rather than his predecessors, and one 'Nietzsche' can differ drastically from another depending on the history of reception through which one arrives at his texts: receptions found in a wide range of art, literature, **psychoanalysis** and philosophy, such as surrealism, Kafka, Yeats, Bernard Shaw, **Freud**, Jung, **Bataille**, **Foucault**, **Heidegger**, **Deleuze**, **Derrida**, and **existentialism**.

The general theme of his work may be summarized with the title of a book which he never completed: the 're-valuation of all values'. Nietzsche applies a genealogical method to examine the origin of concepts, usually considered to be transcendent or universal, which underlie and structure our values. He uses this method to critique the dominant traditions of metaphysics, morality and 'truth' as symptoms of an 'ascetic ideal' which rejects the immediate world of phenomena as untrue or deceptive. Nietzsche argues that, even though belief in God has become unbelievable, society nevertheless retains the 'will to truth', whereby our lives are organized towards an unknowable metaphysics beyond our own immediate existence. This restrictive and ultimately destructive drive lies behind any kind of 'divine' truth – religious or scientific – and encourages us to be obedient and docile 'herd' animals rather than fulfil our potential as humans. Traditional moral values such as duty, justice, compassion and so on reflect a 'slave morality', motivated by the slavish man's *ressentiment* or desire for revenge on the strong or noble.

For Nietzsche, God is dead, as are the worn metaphors which form our idea of 'truth' as a universal or objective authority. While our language and grammar may mislead us into believing otherwise, Nietzsche proposes that the apparent order and value of this world is nothing but the imposition of certain perspectives over a Heraclitean flux. Our values are not motivated by any objective truth but rather the 'will to power'. It is through the creative expression of power that humans can rise above the slave morality of the herd. Thus, while knowledge and truth may only represent an individual's perspective on the world, not all perspectives are equal. Nietzsche looks to a number of figures whose elevated perspectives enable them to create new values and break from tradition. Perhaps the most famous of these is the 'Overman', or *Übermensch*, who Nietzsche claims will stand above man as man stands above the ape. Nietzsche insists that for these people, the overcoming of traditional values does not result in emptiness or nihilism, but rather ecstatic joy. This can be expressed in his notion of the 'eternal recurrence': Nietzsche asks how we would react to the thought that, rather than the world being justified by a teleology or purpose, instead each moment will repeat itself infinitely. While for most people this would be a distressing thought, those 'yes-sayers' who would will every moment to happen again (with all its pain, emptiness, triviality and so on), and joyfully embrace it, will be able to overcome the ascetic values and create new ones.

Tom Grimwood

Phenomenology

The term 'phenomenology' is occasionally used by philosophers of different persuasions in a broad sense to signify a description of experience, but it more specifically names the mode of thought central to twentieth-century European philosophy that was instituted by **Husserl**, and developed by **Heidegger**, **Sartre** and **Merleau-Ponty** amongst others. Husserl was not the first to use the term in a philosophical context: he seems to have borrowed it from Franz Brentano's lectures on philosophical psychology, and it is also prominent in the title of **Hegel's** *Phenomenology of Spirit* (1807).

The first methodical step of Husserl's phenomenology is the *epochē*, a suspension of all common-sense, scientific and metaphysical claims concerning the objects of experience. This does not commit Husserl to any traditional form of empiricism or idealism, since unprejudiced reflection on experience enables criticism of the notion that I encounter only 'ideas' or 'impressions' residing in a certain region of the world called 'mind'. Husserl will argue that phenomenology is genuine empiricism, and thus that the traditional forms of empiricism are not empirical enough. By means of a series of 'reductions', he comes to emphasize the meaning that is already present in experience prior to any act of judgement; and developing Brentano's idea of intentionality, he argues that modes of experience – perceiving, imagining, judging, for example – are given by means of an act of intending, a *noesis*, and a sense apprehended, a *noema*. For Husserl, analyzing experience in this way enables an apprehension of the *a priori* structures that are immanent to objects.

Husserl's most famous students develop these insights whilst refusing his attempts after the breakthrough text of 1900, *The Logical Investigations*, to ground the structures of experience in a transcendental ego. In *Being and Time* (1927) Heidegger conceives of phenomenology as a method for renewal of ontology, but he qualifies Husserl's conception of it as a presupposition-less science by conjoining phenomenological 'reduction' with a 'destruction' of the philosophical tradition, which uncovers the origins of the philosophical concepts that phenomenology has inevitably inherited in order better to understand them. Heidegger also moves beyond Husserl's conception of intentionality in arguing that prior to any particular *noetic* acts, a horizon of meaning – 'world' – has already been disclosed. In a comparable manner, Merleau-Ponty criticizes Husserl's 'intellectualism' and resort to a transcendental ego, and offers a phenomenology of embodiment. The posthumous publication of Husserl's manuscripts, however, has shown that Merleau-Ponty's analyses owe more to his work than previously suspected.

Jacques **Derrida's** critique of Husserl's phenomenological conceptions of time and language was pivotal in the formation of **deconstruction**. Derrida occasionally writes as if Husserl's work is co-extensive with phenomenology, but this seems to ignore Heidegger's remarks that he never left phenomenology behind, and that the possibility of phenomenology, as a movement of thought, is always higher than its actuality.

Mark Sinclair

Poststructuralism

While it is difficult precisely to define poststructuralism, it refers to those philosophers (especially those working in France like Michel **Foucault**, Gilles **Deleuze**, Jacques **Derrida** and Jean-François **Lyotard**) who contested and problematized the reigning orthodoxy in the humanities and social sciences in the early 1960s, which was **structuralism**. Structuralism sought to arrive at a stable and secure knowledge of a system or a structure by charting differences within that structure, and it sought to do so without any reference to subjectivity and consciousness. Poststructuralist philosophers share this wariness of philosophies that start from the basis of consciousness, but Foucault (at least in his middle and later work), Lyotard, Deleuze and Derrida, along with feminists like Luce **Irigaray** and Julia **Kristeva**, all challenge the 'centrist' assumption of structuralism that an understanding of one key element of the structure allows for an explanation of the entire system. These thinkers also question structuralism's rather strict determinism (cf. **Althusser**), instead insisting upon the role of unpredictable forces in the genesis of any structure, law or norm. Opposing structuralism's quasi-scientific claims to objectivity, rationality and intelligibility, they point to certain ruptures that disrupt any stable and secure sense of meaning and identity, ruptures that are argued to be the transcendental condition for the possibility of an 'event' (and genuine difference), rather than the mere repetition of the same. Their work consistently points to the limits of rationality, reason and knowledge, limits that are not merely peripheral but are envisaged as both constituting and problematizing any so-called 'core' (James Williams, *Understanding Poststructuralism*, 2005).

Many of the major poststructuralist texts were written during the period 1966–1969, including Derrida's *Speech and Phenomena*, *Of Grammatology*, and *Writing and Difference*, Deleuze's *Difference and Repetition* and *The Logic of Sense*, and Foucault's *The Order of Things* and *The Archaeology of Knowledge*. Without being able to summarize these rich and nuanced books here, suffice it to say that genealogical, archeological, dialectical and deconstructive analyses of the history of Western philosophy are important to all of the poststructuralists in their efforts to transform and make new. However, these engagements were never intended to constitute simple critiques of this tradition, but as sustained efforts to inhabit from within and to open up space for new possibilities. As such, an ongoing concern with marginality and a revaluation of difference characterize poststructuralism. This is arguably taken to its zenith in Deleuze's *Difference and Repetition*, where difference becomes the condition for identity, but we might also think of Derrida's famous neologism *différance* and Lyotard's *differend*, both of which point to a difference that is not susceptible to dialectical recuperation. Drawing on structuralism, **psychoanalysis**,

phenomenology (especially the work of **Heidegger**), and a **Kantian**-inspired preoccupation with transcendental arguments, poststructuralism remains arguably the major intellectual force in continental philosophy today, with the *nouveaux philosophes* failing to garner anything like the same attention.

Jack Reynolds

PSYCHOANALYSIS – See FREUD AND PSYCHOANALYSIS

Ricoeur

The work of Paul Ricoeur (Valence 1913 – Chatenay Malabry 2005) draws on three currents of European thought: French reflexive philosophy, **phenomenology** and **hermeneutics**. Ricoeur believed that the most fundamental issue for philosophy is the possibility of self-understanding. In holding to this belief throughout a long career he revealed a significant debt to French reflexive philosophy, notably to the work of Jean Nabert. Reflexive philosophy takes the Cartesian *cogito* as its starting point, exploring the theme in the light of **Kant** and Fichte. However, in the works of both Nabert and Ricoeur it came to represent a disavowal of the prevailing view that knowledge of the self is immediate, adequate and apodictic. Ricoeur's *Oneself as Another* (1995) provides an important illustration of this distinctive approach. There, in contrast with Descartes' understanding of *cogito*, Ricoeur describes the act of thinking as 'broken' (*cogito brisé*), a term that is meant to function on two levels: the epistemological and the ontological. For Ricoeur, the act of thinking is 'broken' insofar as it is deprived of the type of evidence that would support knowledge of the self. He holds that there is a similar 'lesion' within the subject's desire to be. As a solution to the epistemological problem, he proposes an 'attestation' whose degree of certainty can be compared to that of a witness. 'Attestation' thus occupies a place midway between knowledge and belief. As a solution to the ontological problem, he proposes what *The Conflict of Interpretations* (1974) had termed 'a re-appropriation' of the subject's desire to be; he suggests that this can be achieved by way of an engagement with works that testify to that desire.

When Ricoeur first established himself 'in the school of phenomenology' in the early 1950s, he did not see any connection between the use of the phenomenological method and interpretative or constructive understanding. However, from 1965 onwards he spoke of the need to 'graft' the hermeneutic thematic, discussed by **Heidegger** and **Gadamer**, onto **Husserl's** method. Significantly, he chose not to adopt Heidegger's version of hermeneutic phenomenology. Initially, Ricoeur based his own alternative hermeneutic phenomenology on 'the paradigm of the symbol'; then, in the early 1970s, he based it on 'the paradigm of the text', and from the mid-1980s onwards he based it on 'the paradigm of translation' (*On Translation*, 2006). This last paradigm shift signalled a growing conviction that hermeneutic phenomenology should be guided by ethical principles. In *Reflections on the Just* (2007), he insists that philosophy must learn to model the type of ethics that is 'at work' in the practice of translation. This so-called 'ethics of hospitality' is guided by a 'dialectical' conception of justice, i.e., a way of thinking that is pulled in two opposite directions: towards an Aristotelian 'justice as equality' and towards a Rawlsian 'justice as fairness' (*Lectures 1: Autour du politique*, 1991). Crucially, one of the motivations for this type of ethics is the desire to understand oneself. Thus, Ricoeur's 'grafting' of hermeneutics onto phenomenology is meant to realize his long-standing programme for a radicalized version of French reflexive philosophy.

Eileen Brennan

Sartre

Jean-Paul Sartre (Paris 1905–1980) was a French philosopher, novelist, playwright, critic and public intellectual. Along with his life-long companion, Simone de **Beauvoir**, Sartre's interventions into philosophical and political life dominated post-war thought to an extraordinary degree. Sartre's philosophy was eventually eclipsed by **structuralism** in the 1960s, and his later work famously dismissed by Michel **Foucault** as 'the effort of a nineteenth-century man to imagine the twentieth century'.

Sartre is best known for the existential ideas taken up in his early novel *Nausea* (1938), the 'Road to Freedom' novels (1945–1949), and *Being and Nothingness* (1943). Influenced by the **phenomenology** of **Husserl** and **Heidegger** as well as elements of **psychoanalysis**, Sartre fuses complex ideas of freedom and responsibility with concrete examples that give a literary depth to his philosophical insights. Sartre's **existentialism** is founded on a theory of consciousness that makes clear the difference between being-in-itself (characteristic of inanimate objects) and being-for-itself (characteristic of human beings and indicative of the primacy of existence over fixed essence). Sartre's influential idea of 'bad faith' described the way in which we try to pretend that our radical freedom is in some way determined, that in fact our existence is determined by our essence, and that we really are what we pretend to be. Sartre argued that we cannot take our conception of what it is to be human from ideas inherited from religion, culture or science, as to do so is to deny the essential choice at the heart of human existence. For Sartre, man is paradoxically 'condemned to be free'.

Criticized for his Cartesian emphasis on consciousness in *Being and Nothingness*, Sartre's later work takes a decidedly **Marxist** turn, particularly in his extremely long and unfinished two-volume *Critique of Dialectical Reason*

(1960). Here Sartre attempts to temper his earlier notion of freedom with conceptions of collective and historical praxis, describing the ways in which human beings sometimes come together through shared political projects, moving from a kind of selfish atomism (which he calls 'seriality') to a united organized body (termed 'group-in-fusion'). Sartre's last major work, a study of Flaubert, similarly attempted to situate human existence in terms of a new theory of the 'universal singular'. In this text, *The Family Idiot* (1971–1972), Sartre describes man's existence as 'universal by the singular universality of human history, singular by the universalizing singularity of his projects, he requires simultaneous examination from both ends'.

Sartre's wide-ranging work had an enormous impact on post-war philosophical, political and literary thought, and touches on almost every area of continental philosophy. Among the most important thinkers influenced by Sartre was Frantz Fanon, who used Sartre's early phenomenological ideas to explore questions of race, and his later political ideas to theorize resistance to colonialism. Sartre's preface to Fanon's *The Wretched of the Earth* (1961) and his continuing intervention into French and world affairs meant that Sartre remained a dominant force in intellectual life until his death in 1980.

Nina Power

Structuralism

Taken historically, the term structuralism is best thought of as signifying a multi-disciplinary movement that held sway over the intellectual scene in Europe (mainly France) in the mid-twentieth century. As a movement it reached its peak in the 1950s and 1960s when, in France, it unseated the hitherto dominant **existential phenomenology**. Since the 1970s, however, its popularity has declined. Generally, the term (and its cognate, structuralist) can be applied to any analysis whatsoever that places priority on structures and relations and that emphasizes the scientific and rigorous nature of enquiry. Structuralists also reject historical or 'diachronic' analyses in favour of 'synchronic' analysis. Such analysis seeks to comprehend the lawlike dynamics of a system at a particular point in time.

Structuralists have made significant contributions to virtually all of the disciplines in the humanities and social sciences, including linguistics, literary studies, anthropology, sociology, psychoanalysis, history, political science and philosophy, and include such figures as Ferdinand de Saussure (1857–1913), Roman Jakobson (1896–1982), Claude Lévi-Strauss (1908–), Louis **Althusser** (1918–1990), Jacques **Lacan** (1901–1981), Georges Dumézil (1857–1929) and Roland Barthes (1915–1980).

Although not uniform in their views, one thesis that unites later structuralists is that the concepts and methods characteristic of structural linguistics, particularly the linguistics of Ferdinand de Saussure, can be applied to the study of social and cultural phenomena generally. Saussure, generally regarded as the founder of structural linguistics, argued that what is primary is the underlying formal system of relations (*langue*) that can be combined to form sentences rather than the collection of words and statements characteristic of speech (*parole*) that might be collected empirically.

In the analysis of social and cultural phenomena, structuralism starts from the point of view that the 'object' under study is an object or event with meaning and that, given this fact, it is its signification that must be studied. Substituting an analysis that focuses primarily on the underlying structures that provide for the possibility of cultural objects and the internal structure of the object itself, structuralism rejects causal explanations and any attempt to deal with such cultural objects in isolation from the system that provides for their possibility. Structuralists consider that human culture and experience can be accounted for in terms of systems of signs, determined by laws that produce meaning in any particular context. Without appealing to subjectivity or consciousness as a starting point for philosophical enquiry, structuralists aim to provide a stable account of any structure, and therefore of human culture and experience, by way of an account of the oppositions or differences constitutive of that system. Their project is centrist in so far as it holds that an understanding of one central element of a structure provides for the possibility of an understanding of the totality of the structure, and deterministic in so far as the structure determines the limits of possible meaning and human experience within any given context.

Philip Tonner

A Contextual Timeline of Continental Philosophy: 1750–2008

James Burton

This timeline is intended to give a general indication of the major publications in continental philosophy within a wider historical and cultural context. Neither the list of philosophical publications nor the timelines of other cultural and historical events is (or could be) wholly comprehensive. The four divisions are intended as rough indicators; many works and events mentioned could easily appear in more than one category. Non-philosophical events have been selected on the basis of their importance for continental philosophy and their general cultural impact. Generally, the original year of publication of a work is given, along with the most common English title (even where English translations do not appear until much later).

Year	Continental Philosophy	Conflict and Crisis
1750		
1751	Diderot and d'Alembert (eds), *Encyclopedia* (35 vols, 1751–1777)	
1752		
1755	Rousseau, *Discourse on the Origin of Inequality*	Lisbon earthquake
1756		Seven Years' War begins (Prussia, Britain against France, Austria, Russia)
1757		Battle of Plassey (West Bengal) establishes British East India Company rule in India
1759	Hamann, *Socratic Memorabilia*	
1760		
1761	Rousseau, *Julie*	
1762	Rousseau, *Emile*	
1763		Seven Years' War ends
1764		
1766		
1769		
1770		
1771		
1772	Herder, *On the Origin of Language*	
1773		Boston Tea Party
1774		
1775		American Revolution begins

Science and Invention	Arts
Buffon, *Natural History* (36 vols, 1749–1778)	
B. Franklin demonstrates electrical nature of lightning	
	Birth of Mozart
Latent heat discovered (Black)	Scarlatti dies
	Fielding, *Tom Jones*
	Sterne, *Tristram Shandy* (1760–1767) Voltaire, *Candide*
Spinning Jenny invented (Hargreaves)	Walpole, *The Castle of Otranto*
Hydrogen isolated (Cavendish)	Goldsmith, *The Vicar of Wakefield*
First steam wagon (Cugnot) Water-frame spinning machine invented (Arkwright)	
First water-driven mill	Birth of Beethoven
	Smollett, *The Expedition of Humphrey Clinker*
	Goethe, *The Sorrows of Young Werther*

Year	Continental Philosophy	Conflict and Crisis
1776		US Declaration of Independence
1778		War of Bavarian Succession (Prussia against Austria)
1781	Kant, *Critique of Pure Reason* ('A' edition)	American Revolution ends with British surrender
1782		
1783	Kant, *Prologomena to any Future Metaphysics*	Russian government annexes Crimea US independence recognized (Treaty of Paris)
1784		First US representatives arrive in China and begin trading
1785	Kant, *Groundwork of the Metaphysics of Morals*	
1787	Kant, *Critique of Pure Reason* ('B' edition)	Adoption of US Constitution
1788	Kant, *Critique of Practical Reason*	First British convicts and settlers arrive in Australia
1789		French Revolution (storming of Paris Bastille, 14 July)
1790	Kant, *Critique of Judgement*	
1791		Haitian Revolution begins
1792	Fichte, *Attempt at a Critique of All Revelation* Wollstonecraft, *A Vindication of the Rights of Woman*	
1793		
1794	Fichte, *Foundations of the Entire Science of Knowledge* (1794–1795)	
1795	Schelling, *Philosophical Letters on Dogmatism and Criticism*	

Science and Invention	Arts
Watt steam engine Smith, *Wealth of Nations*	
	J. C. Bach dies Laclos, *Dangerous Liaisons*
First hot-air balloon passenger flight (Montgolfier brothers)	
Argand oil lamp	
Coulomb's law (electrostatic forces of attraction and repulsion)	
	Gluck dies
	C. P. E. Bach dies
Lavoisier, *Elements of Chemistry*	Blake, *Songs of Innocence*
Goethe, *Metamorphosis of Plants*	
	Mozart dies Sade, *Justine* Boswell, *The Life of Samuel Johnson*
	Birth of Rossini
First modern cotton gin (Whitney)	Blake, *Songs of Experience*
	Radcliffe, *The Mysteries of Udolpho*
Hutton, *Theory of the Earth*	

Year	Continental Philosophy	Conflict and Crisis
1796	Fichte, *Foundations of Natural Right*	
1797	Schelling, *Ideas for a Philosophy of Nature*	
1798	Fichte, *The System of Ethics*	Irish revolt against English rule (1798–1799)
1799		
1800	Fichte, *The Vocation of Man* Schelling, *System of Transcendental Idealism*	
1801		
1802	Schelling, *The Philosophy of Art* (1802–1803)	
1803		
1804		Napoleon becomes Emperor of France Haiti declared Free Republic
1805		Battle of Trafalgar and Battle of Austerlitz
1806		
1807	Hegel, *The Phenomenology of Spirit*	Britain abolishes slave trade
1808	Fichte, *Addresses to the German nation*	Beginning of Peninsular War in Spain
1809	Schelling, *Of Human Freedom*	
1810		
1811	Schelling, *The Ages of the World* (1811–1815)	
1812	Hegel, *Science of Logic* (1812–1816)	War between US and British Empire begins French invasion of Russia

Science and Invention	Arts
Scientific proof of vaccination (Jenner)	Matthew Lewis, *The Monk*
	Birth of Schubert
Malthus, *An Essay on the Principle of Population*	Wordsworth and Coleridge, *Lyrical Ballads*
Laplace, *Celestial Mechanics* (5 vols, 1799–1825) Discovery of Rosetta stone	
Electric cell invented (Volta)	
Jacquard's punch-card loom	
	Austen, *Northanger Abbey*
First oil lamp (Argand) First steam railway locomotive (Trevithick)	
Isolation of morphine from poppies (Sertürner)	
	Haydn dies
First use of term 'energy' in its modern sense (Young)	
	Goethe, *Faust* (Part One)
Gauss, *Theory of Celestial Movement* Lamarck, *Zoological Philosophy*	Birth of F. Mendelssohn
First tin cans for preserving food (Durand) Goethe, *Theory of Colours*	Birth of Chopin
Fourier series	Austen, *Sense and Sensibility* Austen, *Pride and Prejudice* Birth of Liszt

Year	Continental Philosophy	Conflict and Crisis
1813	Schopenhauer, *On the Fourfold Root of the Principle of Sufficient Reason*	
1814		Peninsular War ends War between US and British Empire ends (Treaty of Ghent)
1816		
1817	Hegel, *Encyclopedia of the Philosophical Sciences*	
1818		
1819	Schopenhauer, *The World as Will and Representation*	
1820		
1821	Hegel, *Elements of the Philosophy of Right*	Venezuela and Peru achieve independence from Spain
1822		Liberia founded by freed US slaves
1824		First Anglo-Burmese War begins
1825		Founding of Bolivia
1826		First Anglo-Burmese War ends
1827		
1828		Uruguay achieves independence
1829		
1830	Feuerbach, *Thoughts on Death and Immortality*	French invasion of Algeria
1831		
1832		

Science and Invention	Arts
	Birth of Wagner Birth of Verdi
Spectroscope invented (Fraunhofer)	
Stethoscope invented (Laennec)	
Dandy horse (early form of modern bicycle) invented (Drais)	
	Mary Shelley, *Frankenstein*
	Birth of Offenbach
Electromagnetism discovered (Oersted)	
Principles of electric motor demonstrated (Faraday)	De Quincey, *Confessions of an English Opium Eater*
Babbage begins work on 'difference engine' (early mechanical computer)	
Carnot, *Reflections on the Motive Power of Fire*	Birth of Bruckner
Electromagnet invented (Sturgeon)	Birth of J. Strauss
Olbers' paradox	
First photograph (Nièpce) Discovery of Brownian motion (Brown)	Beethoven dies
	Schubert dies
Stephenson's steam locomotive (the *Rocket*) First book in braille (Braille)	
First public railway opened (England, Liverpool-Manchester) Lyell, *Principles of Geology* (3 vols, 1830–1833)	Stendahl, *The Red and the Black* Balzac, *Sarrasine*
Darwin begins five-year Pacific voyage	Hugo, *The Hunchback of Notre Dame* Balzac, *La Peau de chagrin* [*The Magic Skin*]
	Goethe, *Faust* (Part Two) Sand, *Indiana*

Year	Continental Philosophy	Conflict and Crisis
1833	Schelling, *On the History of Modern Philosophy*	Britain abolishes slavery throughout Empire
1834		
1835		
1836		Texas achieves independence from Mexico Great Trek of Boers away from British Cape Colony (South Africa)
1838		Trail of Tears (forced relocation of indigenous North Americans)
1839		First Anglo-Afghan War begins First Opium War begins (Britain against China)
1840		
1841	Feuerbach, *The Essence of Christianity*	
1842		First Anglo-Afghan War ends First Opium War ends
1843	Feuerbach, *Principles of the Philosophy of the Future* Kierkegaard, *Either/Or* (2 vols) Kierkegaard, *Fear and Trembling* Kierkegaard, *Repetition* Marx, *Critique of Hegel's Philosophy of Right*	
1844	Kierkegaard, *The Concept of Dread* Kierkegaard, *Philosophical Fragments* Marx, *Economic and Philosophic Manuscripts* ('Paris Manuscripts')	
1845	Kierkegaard, *Stages on Life's Way* Marx, *Theses on Feuerbach*	

Science and Invention	Arts
Electromagnetic telegraph invented (Gauss/Weber) Coinage of term 'scientist' in modern sense (Whewell)	Birth of Brahms
Babbage designs first Turing-complete mechanical computer Ada Lovelace writes first computer program around this time	
Colt's revolver first produced	Balzac, *Father Goriot*
	Dickens, *Oliver Twist*
Daguerreotype process announced (Daguerre)	Birth of Mussorgsky
Introduction of postage stamps (Britain) Isolation of ozone (Schönbein) Joule's law discovered	Birth of Tchaikovsky
Thomas Cook's first package holiday (Britain)	Birth of Dvořák
	Gogol, *Dead Souls*
Fax machine patented (Bain)	Birth of Grieg
	Dumas, *The Three Musketeers*
	Dumas, *The Count of Monte Cristo* Poe, 'The Raven'

Year	Continental Philosophy	Conflict and Crisis
1846	Kierkegaard, *Concluding Unscientific Postscript* Marx and Engels, *The German Ideology*	
1847		Earthquake in Naples
1848	Marx, *Manifesto of the Communist Party*	Revolutions across Europe
1849	Kierkegaard, *The Sickness Unto Death*	California gold rush
1850		
1851		
1852	Marx, *The Eighteenth Brumaire of Louis Bonaparte*	Second Anglo-Burmese War
1853		Crimean War begins (Russia against Turkey, Britain, France, Sardinia)
1854		
1855		
1856		Crimean War ends Australian colonies become self-governing
1857	Marx, *Grundrisse* (1857–1858)	Indian Rebellion
1858		East India Company liquidated; British government assumes control of India
1859	Marx, *Critique of Political Economy*	

Science and Invention	Arts
Neptune discovered (Galle)	Balzac, *Cousin Bette*
Boole, *Mathematical Analysis of Logic* Helmholtz, *On the Conservation of Force*	Emily Brontë, *Wuthering Heights* Charlotte Brontë, *Jane Eyre* F. Mendelssohn dies
	Chopin dies
Clausius introduces concept of entropy	Hawthorne, *The Scarlet Letter*
Great Exhibition in London Singer patents sewing-machine Opthalmoscope invented (Helmholtz) Foucault pendulum shows rotation of the Earth (L. Foucault)	Melville, *Moby-Dick*
	Stowe, *Uncle Tom's Cabin*
	Dickens, *Bleak House* Nerval, *Sylvie*
Development of Riemannian geometry (Riemann)	
Paris Exhibition Florence Nightingale's nursing practices establish link between sanitation and health Cocaine alkaloid first isolated (Gaedcke)	
	Flaubert, *Madame Bovary* Baudelaire, *Les Fleurs du mal* Birth of Elgar
Möbius strip discovered (Möbius/Listing)	
Darwin, *On the Origin of Species* Invention of spectography (Bunsen)	

Year	Continental Philosophy	Conflict and Crisis
1860		
1861		American Civil War begins
1862		
1864		
1865		American Civil War ends with defeat of southern states Slavery outlawed in US (13th Amendment)
1866		
1867	Marx, *Capital* Vol. 1	
1868	E. Hartmann, *The Philosophy of the Unconscious*	
1869		
1871	Cohen, *Kant's Theory of Experience*	Paris Commune
1872	Nietzsche, *The Birth of Tragedy*	
1873		
1874	Brentano, *Psychology from an Empirical Standpoint* E. Hartmann, *The Religion of the Future*	

Science and Invention	Arts
	G. Eliot, *The Mill on the Floss* Birth of Mahler
Isolation of area of brain responsible for speech (Broca)	G. Eliot, *Silas Marner*
	Hugo, *Les Misérables* Birth of Debussy
Maxwell, *A Dynamical Theory of the Electromagnetic Field* Pasteur provides evidence for germ theory	Verne, *Journey to the Centre of the Earth* Birth of R. Strauss
First commercially sold typewriter (Hansen) Mendel presentes Laws of Inheritance	Carroll, *Alice's Adventures in Wonderland*
Completion of Transatlantic telegraph cable (Field) First self-propelled modern torpedo (Luppis/Whitehead)	Dostoevsky, *Crime and Punishment*
Paris Exhibition Dynamite first marketed (Nobel)	
	Alcott, *Little Women* Rossini dies
Suez canal completed First periodic table of elements (Mendeleev)	Tolstoy, *War and Peace* Flaubert, *L'education sentimentale* [*Sentimental Education*] Dostoevsky, *The Idiot* Lautréamont, *Les Chants de Maldoror* Baudelaire, *Paris Spleen*
Darwin, *The Descent of Man* Maxwell, *Theory of Heat* (including 'Maxwell's demon')	
	Monet, 'Impression, sunrise' (beginning of impressionism)
Maxwell, *A Treatise on Electricity and Magnetism*	Birth of Rachmaninoff Rimbaud, *A Season in Hell*
	Verlaine, *Romances sans paroles* Flaubert, *The Temptation of Saint Anthony*

Year	Continental Philosophy	Conflict and Crisis
1875		
1876	Nietzsche, *Untimely Meditations*	El Niño (ENSO) activity leads to famines in India, Brazil, China and many African countries over next three years
1877	Cohen, *Kant's Foundations of Ethics*	
1878	Nietzsche, *Human, All Too Human*	Second Anglo-Afghan War begins
1879		Anglo-Zulu War Second Anglo-Afghan War ends
1880		First Boer War begins (British Empire against Boers)
1881	Nietzsche, *Daybreak*	First Boer War ends
1882	Nietzsche, *The Gay Science*	
1883	Dilthey, *The Introduction to the Human Sciences* Nietzsche, *Thus Spoke Zarathustra* (1883–1885)	
1884		
1885	Marx, *Capital* Vol. 2	Third Anglo-Burmese War
1886	Nietzsche, *Beyond Good and Evil*	Britain annexes Burma
1887	Nietzsche, *On the Genealogy of Morals*	French Indochina established

Science and Invention	Arts
Coinage of 'biosphere' (Seuss)	
Telephone invented (Bell) First practical four-stroke internal combustion engine (Otto)	
Record-player invented (Edison) Report of channels (*canali*) on Mars (Schiaparelli)	
Paris Exhibition	
Berlin Exhibition Frege, *Begriffsschrift* (development of propositional calculus, basis for axiomatic predicative logic)	
	Dostoevsky, *The Brothers Karamazov* James, *The Portrait of a Lady* Zola, *Nana* Offenbach dies
	Mussorgsky dies Birth of Bartók
	Birth of Stravinsky
Light bulb invented (Edison) Maxim machine gun invented (Maxim) Galton advocates eugenics Mach, *The Science of Mechanics*	Wagner dies Maupassant, *Une Vie* [*A Woman's Life*]
	Abbott, *Flatland*
	Zola, *Germinal* Twain, *The Adventures of Huckleberry Finn* Birth of Berg Maupassant, *Bel-Ami*
Kraft-Ebbing, *Psychopathia Sexualis*	Stevenson, *Dr Jekyll and Mr Hyde* Tolstoy, *The Death of Ivan Ilych* Liszt dies
Michelson-Morley experiment refutes existence of luminiferous aether Hertz experiments with radio waves and photoelectric effect	Doyle, *A Study in Scarlet* (first appearance of Sherlock Holmes)

Year	Continental Philosophy	Conflict and Crisis
1888	Nietzsche, *Twilight of the Idols* Nietzsche, *The Anti-Christ* Nietzsche, *The Case of Wagner* Nietzsche, *Ecce Homo*	
1889	Cohen, *Kant's Foundations of Aesthetics* Bergson, *Time and Free Will*	
1890		
1891		Mino-Owari earthquake (Japan)
1892		
1893		New Zealand introduces women's right to vote
1894	Marx, *Capital* Vol. 3	
1895		
1896	Bergson, *Matter and Memory* Rickert, *The Limits of Concept Formation in Natural Science* (2 vols, 1896–1902)	
1897		
1898		
1899		Second Boer War begins
1900	Freud, *The Interpretation of Dreams* Bergson, *Laughter* Husserl, *Logical Investigations* (1900–1901)	Boxer Rebellion in China

Science and Invention	Arts
Alternating current patented (Tesla) Kodak handheld camera introduced (Eastman)	
	J. Strauss dies
James, *Principles of Psychology*	Ibsen, *Hedda Gabler* Zola, *La Bête humaine* [*The Beast Within*]
Discovery of *homo erectus* ('Java Man') (Dubois)	Hardy, *Tess of the d'Urbervilles* Wilde, *The Picture of Dorian Gray* Birth of Prokofiev
Poincaré, *New Methods of Celestial Dynamics* (3 vols, 1892–1899)	
	Tchaikovsky dies
First public demonstrations of wireless telegraphy (principles described by Tesla, 1893)	
First commercial demonstration of the Cinématographe (Lumière brothers) X-rays discovered (Röntgen) Coinage of 'Neo-Darwinism' (Romanes)	Wells, *The Time Machine* Art gallery *Maison de l'Art Nouveau* opens in Paris Hardy, *Jude the Obscure* Wilde, *The Importance of Being Earnest*
Discovery of radioactivity (Becquerel)	Housman, *A Shropshire Lad* Chekhov, *The Seagull* Bruckner dies Jarry, *Ubu Roi* [*King Ubu*]
Cathode ray tube invented (Braun)	Wells, *The Invisible Man* Stoker, *Dracula* Brahms dies
Discovery of radium and polonium, coinage of 'radioactive' (M. and P. Curie)	Wells, *The War of the Worlds* James, *The Turn of the Screw* Birth of Gershwin
	Conrad, *Heart of Darkness*
Gamma radiation discovered (Rutherford)	Baum, *The Wonderful Wizard of Oz* Conrad, *Lord Jim* Birth of Copland

Year	Continental Philosophy	Conflict and Crisis
1901	Nietzsche, *The Will to Power* (edited from the '*Nachlass*') Freud, *The Psychopathology of Everyday Life*	Theodore Roosevelt becomes US President Queen Victoria dies (Britain)
1902		Second Boer War ends Cuba becomes formally independent
1903	Du Bois, *The Souls of Black Folk*	
1904		Britain and France sign Entente Cordiale
1905	Weber, *The Protestant Ethic and the Spirit of Capitalism*	French law separates Churches and State Revolution in Russia
1906	Cassirer, *The Problem of Knowledge* (3 vols, 1906–1920)	San Francisco earthquake (US) Earthquake in Valparaíso (Chile)
1907	Bergson, *Creative Evolution*	
1908		Earthquakes in Italy
1909		
1910	Dilthey, *Hermeneutics and the Study of History*	Union of South Africa formed
1911	Brentano, *The Classification of Mental Phenomena*	British army massacre of civilians at Amritsar (India)

Science and Invention	Arts
First transatlantic radio transmission (Marconi)	Mann, *Buddenbrooks* Kipling, *Kim* Verdi dies
Blood types discovered (Landsteiner)	Gorky, *The Lower Depths* *A Trip to the Moon* (Méliès)
First flight in heavier-than-air machine (Wright brothers)	London, *The Call of the Wild* James, *The Ambassadors* Prix Goncourt established
Formulation of Lorentz transformations (Lorentz) Train travels above 100 mph for first time (Great Western Railway)	Conrad, *Nostromo* Dvořák dies
Special theory of relativity (Einstein)	Foundation of 'die Brücke' (expressionist art movement, Germany) Wharton, *The House of Mirth*
First *Dreadnought* warships launched (Britain) First description of Alzheimer's disease (Alzheimer)	Birth of Shostakovich
Einstein discovers equivalence of mass and energy (later described by the formula $E = mc^2$) Minkowski develops four dimensional space-time First piloted helicopter flights	Synge, *Playboy of the Western World* *Ben Hur* (Olcott) Grieg dies
First Model T car (Ford)	First cubist paintings by Picasso and Braque France, *Penguin Island*
	Marinetti, *The Futurist Manifesto*
Russell and Whitehead, *Principia Mathematica* (3 vols, 1910–1913)	*Manet and the Post-Impressionists* exhibition including works from mid-1880s onwards (Grafton Galleries, London) Forster, *Howard's End* *In Old California* (Griffith, first Hollywood film) Roussel, *Impressions of Africa*
Coinage of 'schizophrenia' (Bleuler) Rutherford's model of atom (positing existence of nucleus)	*Der Blaue Reiter* expressionist movement (Germany, 1911–1914) Chesterton, *The Innocence of Father Brown* Mahler dies

Year	Continental Philosophy	Conflict and Crisis
1912		Rebellion leads to founding of Republic of China Sinking of Titanic
1913	Freud, *Totem and Taboo* Husserl, *Ideas Pertaining to a Pure Phenomenology and to a Phenomenological Philosophy* Jaspers, *General Psychopathology*	
1914	Jaspers, *Psychologie der Weltanschauungen* [*Psychology of Worldviews*]	Assassination of heir to throne of Austro-Hungarian Empire: First World War begins
1915		First use of poison gas in warfare
1916	Saussure, *Course in General Linguistics* (reconstructed by students)	Easter Rising in Ireland against British government
1917		Russian Revolution US declares war on Germany
1918	Bloch, *Spirit of Utopia*	First World War armistice
1919	Bergson, *Mind–Energy*	Treaty of Versailles officially ends First World War, establishes League of Nations
1920	Freud, *Beyond the Pleasure Principle* Lukács, *The Theory of the Novel*	US prohibits sale of alchohol (lasts until 1933) Palestine becomes British Mandate Haiyuan earthquake (China)
1921	Benjamin, 'Critique of Violence'	Lenin introduces New Economic Policy in Russia
1922	Bergson, *Duration and Simultaneity*	Egypt gains independence from Britain

Science and Invention	Arts
Unified theory of continental drift (Wegener) Coinage of 'introvert' and 'extrovert' (Jung)	Mann, *Death in Venice* Birth of Cage
Bakelite (formica) invented (Baekeland) Bohr's atomic model (positing electron orbits)	Shaw, *Pygmalion* Lawrence, *Sons and Lovers* Proust, *Swann's Way* (*In Search of Lost Time* published in 7 vols, 1913–1927) *Raja Harishchandra* (Phalke, first Indian film director) Birth of Britten Alain-Fournier, *Le Grand Meaulnes* Apollinaire, *Alcools*
Completion of Panama Canal (begun 1881)	Joyce, *Dubliners* Roussel, *Locus Solus*
General theory of relativity (Einstein)	Kafka, *The Metamorphosis* Maugham, *Of Human Bondage* *The Birth of a Nation* (originally *The Clansman*) (Griffith)
First modern tanks used in warfare	Dada movement develops largely in protest against war (lasts until early 1920s) Joyce, *A Portrait of the Artist as a Young Man*
First deliberate splitting of the atomic nucleus (Rutherford, Cockcroft, Walton)	Duchamp, *Fountain* T. S. Eliot, *The Love Song of J. Alfred Prufrock* Valéry, *La Jeune Parque*
	Debussy dies
Discovery of proton (Rutherford) Wittgenstein, *Tractatus Logico-Philosophicus*	Bauhaus school and movement (Germany, 1919–1933)
	Wharton, *The Age of Innocence* *The Cabinet of Dr. Caligari* (Wiene)
Isolation of insulin (Best)	Čapek, *R.U.R.* (coinage of 'robot') *The Kid* (Chaplin) Pirandello, *Six Characters in Search of an Author*
	Joyce, *Ulysses* T. S. Eliot, *The Waste Land* Hesse, *Siddartha* *Nosferatu* (Murnau) Birth of Xenakis

Year	Continental Philosophy	Conflict and Crisis
1923	Cassirer, *The Philosophy of Symbolic Forms* (1923–1929) Buber, *I and Thou* Lukács, *History and Class Consciousness*	Great Kantō earthquake (Japan)
1924		Lenin dies
1925	Cassirer, *The Language of Myth*	
1926	Hartmann, N. *Ethics* (3 vols)	
1927	Heidegger, *Being and Time* Benjamin begins working on *Arcades Project*	
1928	Husserl, *The Phenomenology of Internal Time-Consciousness*	Women in United Kingdom get the vote on the same basis as men
1929	Husserl, *Formal and Transcendental Logic* Heidegger, 'What is Metaphysics?'	Wall Street Crash – US enters Great Depression
1930	Freud, *Civilisation and its Discontents* Levinas, *The Theory of Intuition in Husserl's Phenomenology*	
1931	Husserl, *Cartesian Meditations*	Statute of Westminster allows dominions of British Empire to have legislative independence
1932	Bergson, *The Two Sources of Morality and Religion* Jaspers, *Philosophy* (3 vols)	Franklin Roosevelt becomes US President BBC founds Empire Service (World Service)

Science and Invention	Arts
Morgan, *Emergent Evolution* Theory of electron waves (de Broglie)	
	Breton produces first *Surrealist Manifesto* Mann, *The Magic Mountain*
First working television (Baird) Hubble's observations demonstrate that other galaxies are distinct from the Milky Way Pauli's exclusion principle Development of matrix mechanics (Heisenberg)	*Exposition Internationale des Arts Décoratifs et Industriels Modernes* (Paris) inaugurates Art Deco movement (lasting until Second World War) Fitzgerald, *The Great Gatsby* Woolf, *Mrs Dalloway* Kafka, *The Trial* *The Battleship Potemkin* (Eisenstein)
Development of wave mechanics (Schrödinger) 'Primordial soup' theory of origins of life (Haldane, anticipated by Oparin, 1924)	
Heisenberg's uncertainty principle (and Bohr's Copenhagen interpretation)	Woolf, *To the Lighthouse* *Metropolis* (Lang)
Penicillin discovered (Fleming)	Bataille, *Story of the Eye* Lawrence, *Lady Chatterley's Lover* Brecht, *The Threepenny Opera* Remarque, *All Quiet on the Western Front* *Steamboat Willie* (Disney) Birth of Stockhausen
Hubble's law (describing expanding universe)	Faulkner, *The Sound and the Fury* *Un chien andalou* (Buñuel/Dalí) First Academy Awards (Oscars) *Blackmail* (Hitchcock)
Gödel publishes incompleteness theorems Pauling, *The Structure of the Chemical Bond*	*M* (Lang)
Positrons discovered (Anderson, predicted by Dirac, 1928)	Huxley, *Brave New World*

Year	Continental Philosophy	Conflict and Crisis
1933		Hitler becomes German chancellor; Nazis begin establishing camps that will later be used for imprisonment and extermination of Jews US Prohibition ends US 'New Deal' laws introduced
1934	Bergson, *The Creative Mind* Bachelard, *The New Scientific Spirit*	Long March of Chinese communists led by Mao Zedong
1935	Jaspers, *Reason and Existenz* Marcel, *Being and Having*	
1936	Benjamin, 'The Work of Art in the Age of Mechanical Reproduction' Sartre, *The Imagination* Sartre, *The Transcendence of the Ego* Bachelard, *Dialectic of Duration*	Spanish Civil War begins
1937		
1938	Sartre, *Nausea* Bachelard, *The Psychoanalysis of Fire*	Germany annexes Austria Coordinated Nazi attacks on Jews and Jewish businesses in Germany ('Kristallnacht', 9–10 November)
1939	Freud, *Moses and Monotheism* Sartre, *Sketch for a Theory of the Emotions*	Spanish Civil War ends Germany invades Poland: Second World War begins Erzincan earthquake (Turkey)
1940	N. Hartmann, *Der Aufbau der realen Welt* [*The Structure of the Real World*] Benjamin, 'On the Concept of History'	France surrenders to Germany
1941		Axis powers invade Soviet Union (Operation Barbarossa)
1942	Cassirer, *The Logic of the Humanities* Merleau-Ponty, *The Structure of Behaviour* Camus, *The Myth of Sisyphus*	Nazi extermination of Jews intensifies ('Operation Reinhard'): nearly six million killed by 1945

Science and Invention	Arts
Discovery of extraterrestrial radio waves announced (Jansky) First patent for a nuclear chain reaction (Szilard) First electron microscope (Ruska)	Malraux, *La condition humaine* *King Kong* (Cooper)
Nuclear fission Popper introduces 'falsifiability'	H. Miller, *Tropic of Cancer* Fitzgerald, *Tender is the Night* Elgar dies
	Triumph of the Will (Riefenstahl) Berg dies
Turing, 'On Computable Numbers' (proposes Turing machine)	
	Steinbeck, *Of Mice and Men* *Snow White and the Seven Dwarfs* (Disney) *La Grande Illusion* (Renoir) Gershwin dies
Nylon patented (Carrothers)	Welles' radio broadcast of 'War of the Worlds' H. Miller, *Tropic of Capricorn*
Operational radar developed in Britain ('Chain Home') and Germany ('Freya') First manufactured jet planes (Germany; Italy, 1940; Britain, 1941) First description of black holes (Oppenheimer/Snyder)	Joyce, *Finnegans Wake* Chandler, *The Big Sleep* *Gone With the Wind* (Fleming) *Mr Smith Goes to Washington* (Capra) *The Rules of the Game* (Renoir)
First production of plutonium (Seabord *et al.*)	Hemingway, *For Whom the Bell Tolls* Koestler, *Darkness at Noon* *The Great Dictator* (Chaplin) *Fantasia* (Disney)
Manhattan Project begins work to develop first nuclear weapon (US)	Blanchot, *Thomas the Obscure*
	Camus, *The Outsider* *Casablanca* (Curtiz)

Year	Continental Philosophy	Conflict and Crisis
1943	N. Hartmann, *New Ways of Ontology* Sartre, *Being and Nothingness* Canguilhem, *The Normal and the Pathological* (extended and re-published, 1966)	
1944		Allies invade Nazi-occupied France Women get the right to vote in France
1945	Marcel, *Homo Viator* Merleau-Ponty, *Phenomenology of Perception*	US drops atomic bombs on Japanese cities (Hiroshima and Nagasaki) Second World War ends with surrender of Germany and other Axis powers Founding of United Nations
1946	Cassirer, *The Myth of the State*	
1947	Buber, *Between Man and Man* Adorno and Horkheimer, *Dialectic of Enlightenment* Levinas, *Existence and Existents* Beauvoir, *The Ethics of Ambiguity* Merleau-Ponty, *Humanism and Terror*	Truman Doctrine (US offers support to countries resisting communism)
1948	Gramsci, *Prison Notebooks* (1948–1951) Levinas, *Time and the Other* Merleau-Ponty, *Sense and Nonsense*	Mohandas ('Mahatma') Gandhi assassinated State of Israel founded
1949	Heidegger, 'The Question Concerning Technology' Marcel, *The Mystery of Being* (2 vols, 1949–1950) Adorno, *Philosophy of Modern Music* Beauvoir, *The Second Sex* (2 vols) Lévi-Strauss, *The Elementary Structures of Kinship* Blanchot, *The Work of Fire* Bataille, *The Accursed Share*	North Atlantic Treaty Organization (NATO) formed by US and West European nations
1950	Heidegger, 'The Origin of the Work of Art'	

Science and Invention	Arts
McCulloch and Pitts compare brain to Turing machine	Sartre, *The Flies* Rachmaninoff dies
Von Neumann and Morgenstern, *Theory of Games and Economic Behaviour*	Sartre, *Huis clos* [*No Exit*]
Bush, 'As We May Think' (proposes 'Memex' machine, forerunner of hypertext systems) Schrödinger, *What is Life?*	Sartre, *The Age of Reason* American abstract expressionism begins to flourish *Spellbound* (Hitchcock) *Brief Encounter* (Lean) *Rome, Open City* (Rosselini) Bartók dies
	Isou begins Lettrist movement *It's a Wonderful Life* (Capra) *Notorious* (Hitchcock)
Holography invented (Gabor) Cellular mobile phones invented (Bell Labs/AT&T)	Sartre, *The Reprieve* Camus, *The Plague* Publication of Anne Frank's diary
Shannon, *A Mathematical Theory of Communication*	Sartre, *Dirty Hands* Blanchot, *Death Sentence* Mailer, *The Naked and the Dead* *The Bicycle Thieves* (de Sica)
Radiocarbon dating method developed (Libby *et al.*)	Sartre, *Troubled Sleep* Orwell, *Nineteen Eighty-Four* A. Miller, *Death of a Salesman* *The Third Man* (Reed) R. Strauss dies
Wiener, *The Human Use of Human Beings: Cybernetics and Society*	*Orpheus* (Cocteau) *Rashomon* (Kurosawa)

353

Year	Continental Philosophy	Conflict and Crisis
1951	Heidegger, 'What is Called Thinking?' (1951–1952) Adorno, *Minima Moralia* Arendt, *Origins of Totalitarianism* Camus, *The Rebel*	Libya declares independence
1952	Fanon, *Black Skin, White Masks*	
1953	Heidegger, *An Introduction to Metaphysics* Merleau-Ponty, *In Praise of Philosophy*	Stalin dies
1954	Husserl, *The Crisis of the European Sciences and Transcendental Phenomenology*	Algerian War of Independence begins
1955	Heidegger, *Identity and Difference* (1955–1957) Marcel, *The Decline of Wisdom* Marcuse, *Eros and Civilization* Merleau-Ponty, *Adventures of the Dialectic* Lévi-Strauss, *Tristes tropiques* Blanchot, *The Space of Literature*	European communist states sign Warsaw Pact
1956		Suez Crisis Morocco and Tunisia gain independence from France Sudan gains independence from Britain and Egypt

Science and Invention	Arts
First colour television broadcast (US) Monkeys sent into space (US)	Salinger, *The Catcher in the Rye* Beckett, *Molloy* Beckett, *Malone Dies*
First hydrogen bomb test (US/Marshall Islands)	Cage, *4'33"* Beckett, *Waiting for Godot* Hemingway, *The Old Man and the Sea* Pollock, *Blue Poles*
Discovery of structure of DNA (Crick, Watson, R. Franklin) Rapid eye movement linked to dreaming (Aserinsky/Kleitman) Summit of Mount Everest reached (Hillary/Tenzing)	Bradbury, *Fahrenheit 451* *The Robe* (Koster) Prokofiev dies Beckett, *The Unnameable*
First nuclear submarine built (US) First nuclear power plant (Soviet Union)	The *Independent Group* inaugurates 'pop art' in Britain, Johns and Rauschenberg simultaneously developing the movement in the US Golding, *Lord of the Flies* Tolkien, *The Lord of the Rings* (3 vols, 1954–1955) Beauvoir, *The Mandarins* *On the Waterfront* (Kazan) *Rear Window* (Hitchcock) *Seven Samurai* (Kurosawa)
	Nabokov, *Lolita*
First transatlantic telephone cable completed	Camus, *The Fall*

Year	Continental Philosophy	Conflict and Crisis
1957	Barthes, *Mythologies* Bataille, *Literature and Evil* Bataille, *Eroticism*	Treaty of Rome establishes European Economic Community (EEC) Ghana achieves independence from Britain
1958	Arendt, *The Human Condition* Bachelard, *The Poetics of Space*	Charles de Gaulle founds French Fifth Republic, becoming President French Community replaces French Union (Guinea elects not to join, becoming independent) Great Leap Forward (1958–1961) leads to mass starvation in China
1959	Bloch, *Principle of Hope* (3 vols) Blanchot, *The Book to Come*	Oil discovered in Libya (and other Gulf states soon after) Vietnam War begins
1960	Gadamer, *Truth and Method* Sartre, *Critique of Dialectical Reason*, Vol. 1 Merleau-Ponty, *Signs*	Most of remaining French colonies in Africa gain independence Most powerful earthquake on record in Chile (mag. 9.5) Agadir earthquake (Morocco)
1961	Levinas, *Totality and Infinity* Foucault, *Madness and Civilization* Fanon, *The Wretched of the Earth*	Berlin Wall installed Failed US invasion of Cuba ('Bay of Pigs') Tanzania and Sierra Leone gain independence from Britain
1962	Arendt, *On Revolution* Lévi-Strauss, *The Savage Mind* Deleuze, *Nietzsche and Philosophy* Derrida, *Edmund Husserl's Origin of Geometry: An Introduction*	Cuban Missile Crisis Algeria gains independence from France Uganda gains independence from Britain Rwanda and Burundi gain independence from Belgium
1963	Arendt, *Eichmann in Jerusalem* Deleuze, *Kant's Critical Philosophy* Foucault, *Birth of the Clinic* Habermas, *Theory and Practice*	Civil rights marches on Washington DC (US) US President Kennedy assassinated Kenya and Zanzibar gain independence from Britain

Science and Invention	Arts
Soviet Union launches first man-made satellites (Sputnik 1 and 2)	Bataille, *Blue of Noon* Founding of Situationist International (disbands 1972) Kerouac, *On the Road* Rand, *Atlas Shrugged* *The Seventh Seal* (Bergman) Beckett, *Endgame*
Formation of NASA (North American Space Agency) Integrated circuit invented (Kilby/Noyce)	*Touch of Evil* (Welles) Beckett, *Krapp's Last Tape* Sollers, *A Strange Solitude*
Van Allen belts disovered First photographs of far side of the moon (Luna III, Soviet Union)	Robbe-Grillet, *In the Labyrinth* Grass, *The Tin Drum* Burroughs, *Naked Lunch*
First laser (Maiman, term coined by Gould, 1959)	Lee, *To Kill a Mockingbird* *Breathless* (Godard) *Psycho* (Hitchcock) *L'avventura* (Antonioni) Beckett, *Happy Days*
First human in space (Yuri Gagarin, Soviet Union) Female oral contraceptives first become widely available First description of packet-switching (Baran)	Heller, *Catch-22* *Last Year at Marienbad* (Renais) Sollers, *The Park*
First communications satellite launched (Telstar 1) Kuhn, *The Structure of Scientific Revolutions*	Andy Warhol's first solo exhibition (Los Angeles) Borges, *Labyrinths* *La dolce vita* (Fellini) *La jetée* (Marker) *The Trial* (Welles)
	Pynchon, *V* Plath, *The Bell Jar* Jabès, *The Book of Questions* (7 vols, 1963–1973)

Year	Continental Philosophy	Conflict and Crisis
1964	Marcuse, *One-Dimensional Man* Adorno, *Jargon of Authenticity* Merleau-Ponty, *The Visible and the Invisible* Lévi-Strauss, *The Raw and the Cooked* Deleuze, *Proust and Signs*	Malawi and Zambia gain independence from Britain
1965	Ricoeur, *Freud and Philosophy* Althusser, *For Marx* Althusser et al, *Reading Capital* Barthes, *Elements of Semiology*	Gambia gains independence from Britain White regime in Rhodesia (now Zimbabwe) declares independence from Britain Malcolm X assassinated
1966	Lacan, *Ecrits I* and *II* Adorno, *Negative Dialectics* Deleuze, *Bergsonism* Foucault, *The Order of Things*	Lesotho and Botswana gain independence from Britain
1967	Horkheimer, *Critique of Instrumental Reason* Debord, *The Society of the Spectacle* Derrida, *Speech and Phenomena* Derrida, *Of Grammatology* Derrida, *Writing and Difference*	Six-Day War (Israel against Egypt, Jordan and Syria)
1968	Horkheimer, *Critical Theory* (2 vols) Deleuze, *Expressionism in Philosophy: Spinoza* Deleuze, *Difference and Repetition* Habermas, *Knowledge and Human Interests*	Student riots (Paris) and general strike in France Swaziland gains independence from Britain Nuclear Nonproliferation Treaty Martin Luther King assassinated
1969	Ricoeur, *The Conflict of Interpretations* Deleuze, *Logic of Sense* Kristeva, *Séméiôtiké* Serres, *Hermes I*	
1970	Barthes, *S/Z* Barthes, *Empire of Signs*	Severe droughts in northeastern Africa throughout 1970s and early 1980s Earthquake in Peru
1971		China joins United Nations

Science and Invention	Arts
Model of quark proposed (Gell-Mann/Zweig) First measles vaccine	*Dr Strangelove* (Kubrick)
First space walk (Leonov)	Bellow, *Herzog* *Alphaville* (Godard) Sollers, *Event*
Luna 9 sends first pictures from surface of moon (Soviet Union)	Bulgakov, *The Master and the Margarita* Capote, *In Cold Blood* Rhys, *Wide Sargasso Sea* Pynchon, *The Crying of Lot 49* *Blowup* (Antonioni) *The Battle of Algiers* (Pontecorvo)
First handheld calculator produced (Texas Instruments) First human-to-human heart transplant (Cape Town)	Márquez, *One Hundred Years of Solitude* *Ulysses* (Strick)
	Dick, *Do Androids Dream of Electric Sheep?* *2001: A Space Odyssey* (Kubrick) Sollers, *Nombres* [*Numbers*]
First transmission over ARPAnet (predecessor of Internet) First human walks on moon (Armstrong)	Fowles, *The French Lieutenant's Woman* Vonnegut, *Slaughterhouse-Five* Angelou, *I Know Why the Caged Bird Sings*
	Conceptual Art and Conceptual Aspects, first exhibition dedicated to conceptual art (New York Cultural Center) Fo, *Accidental Death of an Anarchist* *Zabriskie Point* (Antonioni)
First CAT scanning machine (Hounsfield)	*A Clockwork Orange* (Kubrick) Stravinsky dies

Year	Continental Philosophy	Conflict and Crisis
1972	Deleuze and Guattari, *Anti-Oedipus* Derrida, *Margins of Philosophy* Derrida, *Dissemination* Kofman, *Nietzsche and Metaphor*	'Bloody Sunday' in Northern Ireland Earthquake in Nicaragua
1973	Lacan, *The Four Fundamental Concepts of Psychoanalysis* Barthes, *The Pleasure of the Text*	Fourth Arab-Israeli War (Yom Kippur War) General Pinochet takes power in Chile
1974	Levinas, *Otherwise than Being* Lyotard, *Libidinal Economy* Derrida, *Glas* Irigaray, *Speculum of the Other Woman* Kristeva, *Revolution in Poetic Language*	Resignation of US President Nixon ('Watergate' scandal) Terracotta army discovered (China) India becomes sixth nuclear power (after US, Soviet Union, Britain, France and China)
1975	Ricoeur, *The Rule of Metaphor* Deleuze and Guattari, *Kafka: Toward a Minor Literature* Foucault, *Discipline and Punish*	US withdraws from Vietnam Khmer Rouge led by Pol Pot takes power in Cambodia
1976	Foucault, *The Will to Knowledge* (*History of Sexuality* Vol. 1)	Tangshan earthquake (255,000–655,000 fatalities, China) Mao Zedong dies; Deng Xiaoping emerges as leader of China
1977	Barthes, *Image-Music-Text* Irigaray, *This Sex Which is Not One* Canguilhem, *Ideology and Rationality in the History of the Life Sciences*	Andhra Pradesh cyclone (India)
1978	Arendt, *The Life of the Mind* (2 vols) Derrida, *Spurs: Nietzsche's Styles* Agamben, *Infancy and History*	Camp David Accords between Egypt and Israel signed in US Mass cult suicide in Jonestown, Guyana, led by Jim Jones
1979	Lyotard, *The Postmodern Condition* Lyotard, *Just Gaming* Derrida, *The Truth in Painting* Negri, *Marx Beyond Marx*	Margaret Thatcher becomes British Prime Minister Soviet Union invades Afghanistan

Science and Invention	Arts
First video games console produced (Magnavox Odyssey, Baer)	*Solaris* (Tarkovsky)
	Blanchot, *The Step Not Beyond* Pynchon, *Gravity's Rainbow* *Badlands* (Malick) Spiegelman, *Maus* (published serially 1973–1991) Picasso dies
Microsoft founded (Gates/Allen) Altair 8800 microcomputer produced	Borges, *The Book of Sand* Shostakovich dies
Dawkins, *The Selfish Gene* Apple Computer founded (Wozniak/Jobs)	Britten dies Haley, *Roots* Jabès, *The Book of Resemblances* (3 vols, 1976–1980)
Mandelbrot, *The Fractal Geometry of Nature* Last recorded case of naturally-occurring smallpox (Somalia)	Elvis Presley dies Charlie Chaplin dies *Star Wars* (Lucas)
First *in vitro* fertilization (IVF) baby born	Murdoch, *The Sea, the Sea* Irving, *The World According to Garp* McEwan, *The Cement Garden* *Days of Heaven* (Malick)
First cellular mobile phone network (Japan) First Sony Walkman on sale Lovelock, *Gaia*	

Year	Continental Philosophy	Conflict and Crisis
1980	Deleuze, *Empiricisim and Subjectivity* Derrida, *The Post Card* Irigaray, *Marine Lover of Friedrich Nietzsche* Kofman, *The Enigma of Woman* Kristeva, *Powers of Horror* Le Doeuff, *The Philosophical Imaginary* Serres, *The Parasite* Serres, *Hermes V* Blanchot, *The Writing of the Disaster* The 'Ends of Man' conference	Independent trade union Solidarity formed in Poland Zimbabwe gains independence from Britain President Tito dies (Yugoslavia) Iran-Iraq War begins
1981	Habermas, *The Theory of Communicative Action* Negri, *The Constitution of Time*	Reagan becomes President of US Mitterrand becomes President of France
1982	Levinas, *Ethics and Infinity* Barthes, *Camera Lucida* Derrida, *The Ear of the Other* Badiou, *Theory of the Subject* Serres, *Genèse* Agamben, *Language and Death*	Falklands War between Britain and Argentina
1983	Sartre, *Critique of Dialectical Reason* Vol. 2 (unfinished) Sartre, *Notebooks on Ethics* Ricoeur, *Time and Narrative* (3 vols, 1983–1985) Irigaray, *The Forgetting of Air in Martin Heidegger* Deleuze, *Cinema 1: The Movement-Image* Lyotard, *The Differend* Serres, *Rome* Nancy, *The Inoperative Community*	Terrorist bombing of US embassy in Lebanon
1984	Foucault, *The Use of Pleasure* (*History of Sexuality* Vol. 2) Foucault, *Care of the Self* (*History of Sexuality* Vol. 3) Irigaray, *An Ethics of Sexual Difference* Derrida, *Cinders*	Famines in Ethiopia (over 1 million fatalities) Industrial disaster in Bhopal (more than 18,000 fatalities) Indira Gandhi assassinated
1985	Deleuze, *Cinema 2: The Time-Image* Derrida, 'Before the Law' Habermas, *The Philosophical Discourse of Modernity*	Gorbachev becomes Soviet Union head of state Mexico City earthquake

Science and Invention	Arts
Prigogine, *From Being to Becoming* Voyager 1 passes Saturn	Eco, *The Name of the Rose*
First scientific description of Acquired Immune Deficiency Syndrome (AIDS) First mission of *Columbia* space shuttle First IBM Personal Computer produced (model 5150)	Rushdie, *Midnight's Children* Dick, *VALIS*
	Walker, *The Color Purple* Allende, *The House of the Spirits* *Blade Runner* (Scott)
	Nobel Prize for William Golding
GNU free software project begins (Stallman) First Apple Macintosh (128k) produced	Kundera, *The Unbearable Lightness of Being* DeLillo, *White Noise* First Turner Prize awarded
DNA profiling developed (Jeffreys) Human Genome Project begins Titanic wreck found (Michel/Ballard)	Márquez, *Love in the Time of Cholera*

Year	Continental Philosophy	Conflict and Crisis
1986		Chernobyl Nuclear Power Plant disaster (Ukraine) US bombs Tripoli (Libya) in response to terrorist attacks
1987	Derrida, *Of Spirit: Heidegger and the Question* Derrida, *Pysche: Inventions of the Other* Serres, *Statues*	Beginnings of First Intifada (resistance of Palestinians to Israeli occupation in Gaza and West Bank)
1988	Deleuze, *The Fold* Habermas, *Postmetaphysical Thinking* Lyotard, *The Inhuman* Badiou, *Being and Event* Nancy, *The Experience of Freedom*	Iran-Iraq War ends Spitak earthquake (Soviet Union)
1989	Badiou, *Manifesto for Philosophy* Le Doeuff, *Hipparchia's Choice* Žižek, *The Sublime Object of Ideology*	Berlin Wall dismantled George Bush becomes US President General Pinochet replaced by Aylwin (Chile) Velvet Revolution overthrows Communist government in Czechoslovakia Tiananmen Square protests and military response of government (China)
1990	Derrida, *Memoirs of the Blind* Irigaray, *Je, tu, nous: Towards a Culture of Difference* Serres, *The Natural Contract* Agamben, *The Coming Community*	Unification of East and West Germany Nelson Mandela freed in South Africa Namibia gains independence from South Africa Iraq invades Kuwait
1991	Derrida, *Given Time 1. Counterfeit Money* Serres, *The Troubadour of Knowledge*	Break-up of Soviet Union; Yeltsin replaces Gorbachev Secession of Slovenia from Yugoslavia begins ten years of conflict in Balkan states (Yugoslav Wars) Coalition led by US removes Iraqi forces from Kuwait Repeal of last apartheid laws in South Africa
1992	Derrida, *The Gift of Death*	NASA launches Search for Extra-terrestrial Intelligence (SETI) program Los Angeles riots in response to verdict of Rodney King trial Maastricht Treaty signed

Science and Invention	Arts
Mir space station launched (Soviet Union) Challenger space shuttle explosion	*Platoon* (Stone)
	Morrison, *Beloved* *The Dead* (Huston)
	Freeze exhibition launches careers of several Young British Artists Rushdie, *The Satanic Verses* (Ayatollah Khomeini pronounces death sentence upon Rushdie in 1989)
	Ishiguro, *Remains of the Day*
Hubble Space Telescope placed in orbit	Sebald, *Vertigo* Copland dies
World Wide Web released (Berners-Lee, CERN)	Cage dies

Year	Continental Philosophy	Conflict and Crisis
1993	Derrida, *Specters of Marx* Badiou, *Ethics* Žižek, *Tarrying with the Negative* Nancy, *The Sense of the World*	Bill Clinton becomes US President Waco Siege (US) European Union replaces EEC Oslo Accords between Israel and Palestine
1994	Derrida, 'Force of Law' Derrida, *Politics of Friendship* Agamben, *The Man Without Content*	First multi-racial election in South Africa: Nelson Mandela becomes president Genocide in Rwanda (500,000– 1,000,000 Tutsi killed by Hutu militia)
1995	Derrida, *Archive Fever* Agamben, *Homo Sacer*	Jacques Chirac elected President of France Prime Minister of Israel Yitzhak Rabin assassinated
1996	Derrida, *Monolingualism of the Other, or,* *The Prosthesis of Origin* Nancy, *Being Singular Plural*	Taliban takes power in Afghanistan First Congo War begins
1997	Derrida, *On Hospitality* Derrida, *Adieu to Emmanuel Levinas* Badiou, *Deleuze* Badiou, *Saint Paul*	Kyoto Protocol First Congo War ends Tony Blair becomes Prime Minister of Britain
1998	Badiou, *Handbook of Inaesthetics* Agamben, *Remnants of Auschwitz*	Second Congo War begins Good Friday Agreement between Britain and Northern Ireland
1999	Kristeva, *Female Genius* (3 vols, 1999– 2002) Žižek, *The Ticklish Subject*	World population exceeds 6 billion NATO bombing of Yugoslavia Izmit earthquake (Turkey)
2000	Derrida, *On Touching – Jean-Luc Nancy* Žižek, *The Fragile Absolute* Hardt and Negri, *Empire* Negri, *Kairòs, Alma Venus, Multitudo*	Vladimir Putin becomes President of Russia
2001	Žižek, *Did Somebody Say Totalitarianism?*	Gujarat earthquake George W. Bush becomes President of US 9/11 terrorist attacks in US US invades Afghanistan
2002	Irigaray, *The Way of Love* Agamben, *The Open*	
2003	Habermas, *The Future of Human Nature* Derrida, *Rogues* Žižek, *The Puppet and the Dwarf* Nancy, *Noli Me Tangere* Agamben, *State of Exception*	Columbia space shuttle disaster US and allies invade Iraq Second Congo War officially ends (fighting continues) Earthquake in Iran

Science and Invention	Arts
	Sebald, *The Emigrants* *Wittgenstein* (Jarman) *Schindler's List* (Spielberg)
Opening of Channel Tunnel (between Britain and mainland Europe)	Blanchot, *The Instant of My Death*
Microsoft launches Windows 95	Sebald, *The Rings of Saturn*
First mammal cloned from an adult cell (Dolly the Sheep)	
Sokal and Bricmont, *Intellectual Impostures* Deep Blue chess-playing computer defeats Gary Kasparov (world champion)	Rowling, *Harry Potter and the Philosopher's Stone*
	The Thin Red Line (Malick)
	The Matrix (Wachowski and Wachowski) *Magnolia* (Anderson)
	Klein, *No Logo*
Apple introduces the iPod First successful fully artificial heart implants (AbioCor)	Sebald, *Austerlitz* *Waking Life* (Linklater) *Memento* (Nolan) Xenakis dies
First Chinese manned space flight Near-completion of Human Genome Project announced	*Dogville* (von Trier) Brown, *The Da Vinci Code*

Year	Continental Philosophy	Conflict and Crisis
2004	Hardt and Negri, *Multitude*	Indian Ocean earthquake and tsunami (230,000+ fatalities) Forced evacuations in Darfur, Sudan (more than 1 million people)
2005	Badiou, *The Century*	Hurricane Katrina (US)
2006	Badiou, *Logics of Worlds. Being and Event* Vol. 2	Montenegro declares independence from Serbia
2007		
2008		Earthquake in China Global financial crisis leads to partial nationalization of many major finance insitutions in US and Europe US elects first African American President, Barack Obama

Science and Invention	Arts
Pluto reclassified as dwarf planet	
	Stockhausen dies
Large Hadron Collider begins experiments (Switzerland, CERN)	

Research Resources in Continental Philosophy

The following is a list of journals, websites and societies through which Anglophone research in continental philosophy can be pursued. Some of these resources, the online ones especially, offer general information with sections on continental thought; others have content that is entirely dedicated to it. These lists are not, of course, exhaustive, and are meant to be starting points rather than comprehensive directories.

Journals

Angelaki
Collapse
Continental Philosophy Review
Deleuze Studies
Graduate Faculty Philosophy Journal
Heidegger Studies / Heidegger Studien / Etudes Heideggeriennes
Husserl Studies
Hypatia: A Journal of Feminist Philosophy
International Journal of Philosophical Studies
Journal of Nietzsche Studies
Journal of the British Society for Phenomenology
Kant-Studien (multilingual)
Nietzsche-Studien (multilingual)
The Owl of Minerva
Parrhesia: A Journal of Critical Philosophy
Philosophy & Social Criticism
Philosophy Today (DePaul University)
Radical Philosophy
Revue internationale de philosophie (multilingual)
Southern Journal of Philosophy
SubStance
Symposium
Theory, Culture and Society

Websites

Les classiques des sciences sociales: http://classiques.uqac.ca/index.html (huge collection of classic texts on-line)
Continental Philosophy: http://pegasus.cc.ucf.edu/~janzb/continental
Continental Philosophy: www.continental-philosophy.org
Epistemelinks: www.epistemelinks.org
Guide to Philosophy on the Internet: www.earlham.edu/~peters/philinks.htm#topics
Organisation Non-Philosophique Internationale: www.onphi.net
Stanford Encyclopedia of Philosophy: http://plato.stanford.edu

Continental Philosophy Societies and Associations

Australian Society for Continental Philosophy
British Society for Phenomenology
Collegium Phaenomenologicum
Forum for European Philosophy
Foucault Circle
Friedrich Nietzsche Society
The Hegel Society of America
The Hegel Society of Great Britain
International Institute for Hermeneutics
Luce Irigaray Circle
Merleau-Ponty Circle
Nietzsche Society
Heidegger Circle
International Association for Philosophy & Literature
North American Sartre Society
North American Society for Philosophical Hermeneutics
Society for Continental Philosophy and Theology
Society for European Philosophy
Society for German Idealism
Society for Phenomenology and Existential Philosophy
Society for Women in Philosophy

Notes

Chapter 2

1 For a brief account of the entry of the term 'continental philosophy' into common usage see Critchley (2001, pp. 38–40). For an extended examination of the emergence and continuing status of continental philosophy in relation to the analytic tradition, taking into account both continental and analytic perspectives, see Glendinning (2006).

2 This sense of the ending of traditional philosophy could be abbreviated by pairing Whitehead's famous description of philosophy as 'a series of footnotes to Plato' (1985, p. 39) with Badiou's statement that 'The [twentieth] century – till now – has been anti-Platonic' (1989, p. 98).

3 It is not a pure coincidence that each of these declarations and explorations of the impossibility of traditional ontology leads to an ethical set of questions around notions of justice and communality. On the one hand, this can be regarded as a further sign of the sense of philosophy's ethical impossibility or unacceptability in the wake of the institutionalized genocide of Nazi Germany. On the other hand, this question of justice and the just decision (judgement) can be said to be one of the most traditional problems of Western philosophy – that which causes Plato to develop the figure of the philosopher-king in *The Republic* and which occupies Kant in the *Critique of Judgement* in a manner that is decisive for subsequent philosophy. If there is a general shift in the way such questions are addressed following the Second World War by thinkers like Lyotard and Derrida, who suggests that deconstruction has done nothing but address the question of justice (1992, p. 10), it is in the greater emphasis that is placed on the (im)possibility of justice and judgement. This is further reflected in Nancy's recent short text, *Juste impossible* (2007).

4 Cutrofello notes that Kant regarded his antinomies as having both the great positive effect of inspiring or provoking the search, through reason, for a resolution to the most difficult of human problems, and at the same time the great danger of leading to depression or despair: antinomy 'has the character of what Plato refers to in the *Phaedrus* as a *pharmakon*, something that can either poison or cure' (Cutrofello, 2005, p. 402). This comparison is not accidental, the *pharmakon* being the focus of Derrida's influential 1968 essay 'Plato's Pharmacy', later published as part of *Dissemination* (1972). Cutrofello's reference to the *pharmakon* is not only a further indication of the Derridean character of his approach to continental philosophy, but also implicitly reinforces Cutrofello's claim that this is really a meta-philosophical issue – in that the apparent contradiction (antinomy, paradox, aporia) itself gives way to another concerning what one takes to be the feasible responses to contradiction: where Russell must force the *pharmakon* to resolve itself into *either*

one path *or* the other – must open the box and either kill or not kill Schroedinger's cat – Derrida will allow the *pharmakon* to retain its duality – is happy to let the box remain closed.

5 An example may be found in Mullarkey's reading of the use of the diagram among French philosophers of immanence, and his attempt to develop a schema for 'Thinking in Diagrams' (2006, pp. 157–86): by doing philosophical work in a non-linguistic mode the diagram circumvents the difficulties of self-reference that Mullarkey sees as undermining other attempts to produce a philosophy of immanence (and which, as we have seen, Badiou attempts to deal with through set theory).

6 Paul Patton and John Protevi, in inaugurating the project of the critical comparison of Derrida and Deleuze, emphasize that 'the necessity of developing a non-Hegelian "philosophy of difference" was deeply felt by both' (Patton and Protevi, 2003, p. 4). Fabien Tarby begins his comparison of Deleuze and Badiou by identifying their shared principles that '[a] thought for our time is the thought of the multiple' and that '[o]ne can and one must elaborate an ontology of multiplicity' (2005, p. 23; my translation).

7 'Nietzsche substitutes the pathos of *difference* or distance (the differential element) for both the Kantian principle of universality and the principle of resemblance so dear to the utilitarians' (Deleuze, 2006, p. 2).

8 See Deleuze's 'Bergson 1859–1941' and 'Bergson's Conception of Difference' in *Desert Islands* (2004), both written in 1956, and *Bergsonism* (1990).

9 For Deleuze, this primacy of movement is also found in Spinoza – though in a way that would be difficult to discern (compared to Bergson, for example) without Deleuze's own unconventional reading: 'Spinoza's ethics has nothing to do with a morality; he conceives it as an ethology, that is, as a composition of fast and slow speeds, of capacities for affecting and being affected on the plane of immanence' (1988, p. 125).

10 Cf. 'every language, whether elaborated or crude, leaves many more things to be understood than it is able to express. Essentially discontinuous, since it proceeds by juxtaposing words, speech can only indicate by a few guide-posts placed here and there the chief stages in the movement of thought' (Bergson, 1988, p. 125).

11 The same would apply to the third category, where Irigaray's creativity and for example her psychoanalysis of psychoanalysis in *Speculum of the Other Woman* (1985) could be said to parallel Deleuze and Guattari's collaborations, yet perhaps leading ultimately in the direction of a new form of subjectivity that from the perspective of *Anti-Oedipus* would seem essentialist (even if such essentialism should in fact be seen as 'strategic', to the same degree as Deleuze and Guattari's anti-essentialism).

Chapter 3

1 The basis of Lyotard's reading of the Kantian work in a way that is resistant to system runs through the text that, in his own account, is the most given to systematic presentation, the *Critique of Judgment*. The ground of the argument is as follows: 'The reading that I advocate . . . consequently admits that if the third *Critique* fulfills its mission of unifying the field of philosophy, it does so, not primarily by introducing the theme of the regulative Idea of an objective finality of nature, but by making manifest, in the name of the aesthetic, the reflexive manner of thinking that is at work in the critical text as a whole' (Lyotard, 1994, p. 8).

2 The importance of this connection between time and space as stated at A99 is difficult to overestimate. Attention to it should dispel the view that the doctrine of

the second edition 'Refutation of Idealism' is, in its connection of time and space, entirely new.

3 This is through Heidegger's notion of 'transcendence' as a way of speaking of the presentation of something as standing-against: see his *Kant and the Problem of Metaphysics* (1990, pp. 65–77).

4 This element of Heidegger's reading brings him close to the Neo-Kantian view that he is otherwise opposed to and prevents a presentation on his part of the basis of Kantian dynamics.

5 Kant gives this argument in the *Inaugural Dissertation* (1992, Ak. 2:399) and is also using it in the transcendental exposition of time in the *Critique* in order to show how a science of motion requires time (2007, B48–9).

6 From this it also follows that the 'subject' is essentially in theoretical philosophy dissolved into the constant motion of auto-affection so that the original time is motile.

7 Nor is this all that could be said about the transcendental schematism itself since all the discussion we have set out here has been highly general while the real significance of the doctrine is given in application, that is, in the Analytic of Principles. For an extensive account of this see Banham (2006), chapters 6 and 7.

8 For further accounts of the role of schematism in Kant's practical philosophy see Banham (2003), especially chapter 5, and also Banham (2007b).

9 For the 'lingering' that emerges from the beautiful see Kant (1987) Ak. 5: 222 and for the infinite reflection involved in the mathematical sublime see §26 of the *Critique of Judgment* (Kant, 1987).

10 I say this is where Kojève's account would *appear* to leave us, since I am aware of the decisive question that *reading* Kojève poses problems of a speculative order and hence that the manifest apparent sense of his propositions is one that will mislead us in the understanding of his work. For the classic statement of his reading see Kojève (1969). The English translation is unfortunately a very incomplete rendition of Kojève's original text and the need for a full translation in order for a serious discussion in English of twentieth century – and particularly French – readings of Hegel is clear. For a further assessment of Kojève's view of Hegel it would be necessary to place alongside an account of these lectures the posthumously published work on the philosophy of right. See Kojève (2008).

11 See Fukuyama (1993), and for a trenchant response to this work, Derrida (1994).

12 This hypothesis of the need for resistance to Hegelian dialectics for new thought to have a chance is at the centre of one of the most influential discussions of French philosophy: see Descombes (1980). In relation to German philosophy the situation is perhaps less clear-cut but here the example of Adorno in particular suggests that the legacy of the post-war Frankfurt School was certainly bound up with a reaction as much to Hegel as to Marx.

13 This work is a rendition of Heidegger's lectures on Hegel's *Phenomenology of Spirit* from winter semester 1930–1931.

14 This citation is cited in a modified translation in Malabou's book as: 'The singular individual is, on its own terms, the transition of the category from its concept into external reality; it is the pure schema (*das reine Schema*) itself' (2005, p. 18). While these translations are quite different and the difference between them is surely important, I will not here attempt to decide between them but simply follow Miller.

15 Here she clarifies also in the process some problems with Heidegger's reading of Hegel.

16 For different, if partially parallel reasons for thinking this, see Banham (2007a).

17 In this respect the question that seems of real interest is the relationship between the account of Hegel Malabou gives and the work of Jean-Luc Nancy, not least in the account the latter is attempting of the 'deconstruction of Christianity'. See Nancy (2008a, 2008b).

18 This is due to the process of simplification of the past through the formation of culture. Malabou describes this simplification eloquently in Chapter 10 of *The Future of Hegel*.

19 For an engaging discussion of the essential nature of comedy in Hegel's view see Rose (1994).

20 This claim is made in Heidegger's 1930s lecture course on Nietzsche in the context of an argument for separating Nietzsche from biologism and so is, to say the least, an ambiguous verdict. See the translations of these courses in Heidegger (1991). For a distinctly different emphasis, see Heidegger (1977).

21 A celebrated account of the relationship between will to power and eternal return is given in Müller-Lauter (1999).

22 For a scintillating account of Nietzsche's view of ecstasy and a placing of it in a tradition of excessive thought, see Marsden (2002).

23 'What one has no access to through experience one has no ear for. Now let us imagine an extreme case: that a book speaks of nothing but events which lie outside the possibility of general or even of rare experience – that it is the *first* language for a new range of experiences. In this case simply nothing will be heard, with the acoustical illusion that where nothing is heard there *is* nothing. . . . This is in fact my average experience and, if you like, the *originality* of my experience' (Nietzsche, 1979, 'Why I Write Such Excellent Books', §1).

Chapter 4

1 Kaufmann translates *Hinterwelter* as 'afterworldly', meaning it to be a literal translation of 'metaphysics'; see Nietzsche (1954), p. 117.

2 This is one of the primary themes of Adorno's *Metaphysics*; see Adorno (2000), esp. pp. 17–18.

3 Other philosophers have proposed their own lists of 'categories', such as Charles Sanders Peirce and Alfred North Whitehead, but such notions do not have the same status as Aristotle's or Kant's categories.

4 See the great passage in the *Critique of Pure Reason* where Kant explains and defends his appropriation of Plato's notion of an Idea, while modifying its use (1929, A312–20/B368–77, pp. 309–14).

5 See Kant (1929) A295–6/B352, pp. 298–9: 'We shall entitle the principles whose application is confined entirely within the limits of possible experience, *immanent*; and those, on the other hand, which profess to pass beyond these limits, *transcendent*'. It should be noted that the terms 'transcendent' and 'transcendental' are not identical terms, and in fact are opposed to each other. The aim of Kant's *transcendental* or critical project is to discover criteria immanent to the understanding that are capable of distinguishing between legitimate (immanent) and illegitimate (transcendent) uses of the syntheses of consciousness. In this sense, transcendental philosophy is a philosophy of immanence, and implies a ruthless critique of transcendence.

6 See Derrida (1992), p. 30: 'The effort of thinking or rethinking a sort of transcendental illusion of the gift should not be seen as a simple reproduction of Kant's critical machinery. . . . But neither is it a question of rejecting that machinery as old fashioned'.

7 See Kant (1929), B3, p. 43: '*A priori* modes of knowledge are entitled pure when there is no admixture of anything empirical'. And A20/B34, p. 66: 'I term all

representations *pure* (in the transcendental sense) in which there is nothing that belongs to sensation'.

8 See also Derrida (1995), p. 84, where Derrida is still hesitating between the two terms: 'The concept of responsibility [would be] paralyzed by what can be called an aporia or an antinomy'.

9 See Badiou (2005), p. 1: 'Heidegger is the last universally recognized philosopher'.

10 See Heidegger (1975), p. 275: 'Metaphysics represents the beingness of beings in a twofold manner: in the first place, the totality of beings as such with an eye to their most universal traits (*ta kathalon, koinon*), but at the same time also the totality of beings as such in the sense of the highest and there divine being, or God (onto-theology)'.

11 See Heidegger (1975), pp. 268–9: 'From its beginning to its completion, the propositions of metaphysics have been strangely involved in a persistent confusion of beings and Being'.

12 See Heidegger (1962a), p. 274: 'To lay bare the horizon within which something like Being in general becomes intelligible is tantamount to clarifying the possibility of having any understanding of Being at all – an understanding which itself belongs to the constitution of the entity called *Dasein*'.

13 See Heidegger (1975), pp. 268–9: 'The thinking which is posited by beings as such, and therefore representational must be supplanted by a different kind of thinking which is brought to pass by Being itself'.

14 See Heidegger (1962a), p. 44: 'We are to *destroy* this traditional content of ancient ontology until we arrive at those primordial experiences in which we achieved our first ways of determining the nature of Being'.

15 See also Derrida (1981), p. 10: one must 'borrow the syntaxic and lexical resources of the language of metaphysics ... at the very moment one deconstructs this language'.

16 '*Différance*, the disappearance of any originary presence, is *at once* the condition of possibility *and* the condition of impossibility of truth' (Derrida, 1983, p. 168). For further discussion, see May's chapter on 'Philosophies of Difference' in this volume.

17 See Villani (1999), p. 130: 'I feel myself to be a pure metaphysician. Bergson says that modern science hasn't found its metaphysics, the metaphysics it would need. It is this metaphysics that interests me'.

18 For Deleuze's summary of his criticisms of Aristotle, see Deleuze (1994), pp. 269–70, and p. 303: 'The only common sense of Being is distributive, and the only individual difference is general'.

19 It would nonetheless be an error to suggest that Spinoza's *Ethics begins* with substance: in the order of definitions in Book One of the *Ethics*, God is not reached until Definition Six; and in the order of demonstrations, God is not reached until Propositions Nine and Ten. Strictly speaking, Spinoza's ontology has a beginning that is distinct from Being (something which 'is not'), but in Spinoza this 'something' is not the transcendence of the One beyond Being, but rather the immanence of the attributes as the source and origin of substance or Nature, its constitutive elements. See Deleuze (2004), pp. 146–55.

20 See Deleuze (1994), p. 38: Aristotle 'retains in the particular only that which conforms to the general (matter and form), and seeks the principle of individuation in this or that element of fully constituted individuals'.

21 See Deleuze (1994), pp. 284–5: 'None of this amounts to a list of categories. It is pointless to claim that a list of categories can be open in principle: it can be in fact but not in principle. For categories belong to the world of representation, where they constitute forms of distribution according to which Being is distributed among beings following the rules of sedentary proportionality. That is why philosophy

had often been tempted to oppose notions of a quite different kind to categories, notions which are really open and which betray an empirical and pluralist sense of Ideas: "existential" as against essential, percepts as against concepts, or indeed the list of empirico-ideal notions that we find in Whitehead, which makes *Process and Reality* one of the greatest books of modern philosophy'.

22 For further discussion of the distinction between ethics and morality in relation to ethico-political philosophy, see Williams' chapter on 'Ethics and Politics' in this volume.

23 See Hallward (2003), p. 90: 'Consistency is the attribute of *a* coherent presentation of such inconsistent multiplicity as *a* multiplicity, that is, as a coherent collecting of multiplicity into unity, or one'. Hallward's book is the best study of Badiou's thought available: it is both comprehensive and critical, although it was published before the 2006 appearance of the second volume of *Being and Event*.

24 Badiou (2005), p. 5: 'The essence of the famous problem of the continuum was that in it one touched upon an obstacle *intrinsic* to mathematical thought, in which the very impossibility which founds the latter's domain is said'.

Chapter 5

1 There is an archaic sense of the English word 'sense' meaning 'direction', as in 'the sense of the river'. This sense is still present in French, as in, among other uses, the expression *sens unique* for 'one-way street' (Protevi, 1994 and 1998).

Chapter 6

1 The term *différance* is not always the one Derrida uses, and his different terms sometimes reflect differences in the particular philosopher he is treating. Nevertheless, in reflecting on deconstruction, he writes, 'The word "deconstruction", like all other words, acquires its value only from its inscription in a chain of possible substitutions, in what is too blithely called a "context". For, me, for what I have tried and still try to write, the word has interest only within a certain context, where it replaces and lets itself be determined by such other words as *"écriture"*, "trace", *"différance"*, "supplement", "hymen", "pharmakon", "marge", "entame", "parergon", etc.' (Derrida, 1985).

Chapter 8

1 While I do not think there is a 'political turn' in Derrida's works, as represented by *Specters of Marx*, there is an issue that is very much worth investigating, namely that in the later work, Derrida argues that justice, like deconstruction itself, cannot be deconstructed – therefore *deconstruction is justice* and vice-versa – whereas, in *Of Grammatology*, Derrida says that deconstruction must submit to its own critique.

2 Again we might remark upon the resources for historical materialism that come through the Western monotheistic traditions and texts, and we might therefore raise some historical materialist questions concerning the preoccupation with the figure of St Paul in the work of Badiou, Žižek, Agamben and others. In the readings of Badiou and Žižek, Paul is singular, and in his singularity and indeed atemporality/ahistoricity he founds Christianity. Perhaps this ought to be called the 'dialectical materialist' view of the matter (Badiou and Žižek say as much), while a historical materialist reading of the New Testament would see an Early Christian Movement that was multivocal – even after the process of canonization had removed many other accounts of Jesus of Nazareth and his movement. We get to dialectical materialism by removing the rock, as it were – Peter.

3 For what it is worth, I count myself among those who were never comfortable talking of 'being', even in the case where one is decidedly on the side of the ontic, as with Sartre, or where there is no sense in which being is 'one', as with Badiou. There are simply too many theological resonances to the term and, if what we really want to do is to talk about God, well, let's just bite the bullet and do that.

Chapter 9

1 All translations from this volume are my own.
2 For detailed discussions of what Rancière means by the 'aesthetic regime', and by the 'regime of representation' (sometimes also called 'poetic regime'), the reader is referred to Rancière's *La parole muette* [*Mute speech*] (1998) in the first instance. For the most intricate discussion of these issues, central to Rancière's philosophical enterprise as whole, a reading of this not yet translated text is still indispensable.
3 It is worth noting that it was the reaction to this seminar that began another series of long and arduous debates within feminism. See Mitchell and Rose (1982).
4 For an extremely lucid discussion of the *après coup*, the use of which is also very important for an understanding of Žižek's often odd re-readings of philosophical texts through Lacanian lenses, see Kay (2003).

Chapter 11

1 Ruelle gives the example of 100 fleas on a checkerboard.
2 The proper name for this thesis is the *ergodic hypothesis*, 'in its motion through phase space, the point representing our system spends in each region a fraction of time proportional to the volume of the region'.
3 This section is reprinted from Olkowski (2006).
4 Bricmont is a theoretical physicist in Belgium who claims that ergodicity is a much stronger concept than what is needed to explain the equilibrium values of macroscopic variables (1996, p. 21). He also appears to claim that Bergson is unscientific insofar as he distinguishes between matter and life.
5 See also Olkowski, 'The Linguistic Signifier and the Ontology of Change', pp. 211–34 in Olkowski (1999), especially pp. 217–19. See 'Conditions for Equilibrium', http://hyperphysics.phy-astr.gsu.edu/hbase/torq.html#equi
6 This other dimension will be called the 'time-image', but it is beyond the scope of this essay to investigate the relation between Deleuze's concept of time-image and Bergson's concept of duration.
7 The hypothetical may be conceived of as the spatial manifold out of which things are determined to exist through the mutual determination of their position.
8 See also Freud (1966), pp. 64–78. Inertial states refers to the first law of motion in physics, that a body in uniform motion or rest continues in that state unless it is changed by an external force.
9 Devlin cites Bertrand Russell: 'Pure mathematics consists entirely of such asservations as that, if such and such a proposition is true of *anything*, then such and such another proposition is true of that thing. It is essential not to discuss whether the first proposition is really true, and not to mention what the anything is of which it is supposed to be true. . . . If our hypothesis is about *anything* and not about some one or more particular things, then our deductions constitute mathematics' (Devlin, 1994, p. 53).
10 Translation altered. Once the system is established what may have been contingent may become axiomatic. When flows are bounded by capitalism, it serves as a limit in a mathematical dynamical system, in other words, flows will cycle around it endlessly.

11 This, I would argue, is Deleuze's solution which he finds in Stoicism. Thus, 'no political program will be elaborated within the framework of schizoanalysis', the *miso-philosophe* does not mix 'himself' up in politics but commits to a mechanical view of the real, doing away with fear of the gods, who do not exist, as well as fear of punishment in the afterlife, which is a dream, practising cheerfulness, moderation, temperance and simplicity, in order to live as pleasantly as possible, without illusion, in a world whose continuous production of expression (prospects, functives, percepts, affects, concepts) makes it interesting enough to live in, but whose violent axiomatic makes it ultimately, a world from which one willingly departs (Deleuze and Guattari, 1987, p. 380). See my *The Universal (In the Realm of the Sensible)* (Olkowski, 2007), p. 84.

Chapter 13

1 None of these philosophers write primarily in English, but we are fortunate in that all their major texts on art have been translated into English, in large part or in whole. In order therefore to facilitate access to the work of these philosophers for an English-speaking audience we will in the main discuss texts published in English translation.

2 Cf. Nancy, in whose examination of Christian painting the 'being-there of the beyond' of Christianity is the form of the stripping away of its religious character and thus the point of departure for its deconstruction (Nancy, 2005, p. 124).

3 Cf. Badiou, for whom the task of contemporary art is to found a new paradigm, one which opposes what he sees as the choice today between two forms of the power of death: experimentation with the limits of pleasure, and sacrifice for an idea (Badiou, 2005c).

4 Cf. the unconscious, which for Deleuze and Guattari is also a constructed plane: 'the unconscious as such is given in microperceptions; desire directly invests the field of perception, where the imperceptible appears as the perceived object of desire itself, "the nonfigurative of desire" ' (Deleuze and Guattari, 1988, p. 284).

5 But not Deleuze, in whose work, as Nancy points out, we do not see 'the great, intimate debate between philosophy and poetry' – why? because Deleuze's philosophy, one of nomination rather than discourse, itself 'behaves, altogether naturally, as another poetry' (Nancy, 1996b, p. 111).

6 In his earlier *Conditions* (1992) Badiou specifies the three relations of philosophy to poetry as the Parmenidian, the Platonic and the Aristotelian; where the Romantic/ Heideggerian would fall under the Parmenidian (Badiou, 2005b, p. 72).

7 A clue to Agamben's distance from Badiou is given by his asserting that Badiou 'still conceives of the subject on the basis of a contingent encounter with truth' (Agamben, 1999, p. 221).

Chapter 14

1 The objection immediately arises that down the corridor is not and never was very far. First, as we have already pointed out, literary theory is saturated with continental philosophy, especially the Frankfurt School, hermeneutics, Derrida and Foucault. Second, one might argue (in one of various ways) that the modern conception of literature originated from within a philosophical problem (e.g. Lacoue-Labarthe and Nancy, 1988). Third, both are coordinated in advance as part of a university system with its traditions, aims, methods, systems and standards. There are other reasons. But all of these divide as much as they unite; and however much abstract convergence and overlap one may find, the *ways of working* are surprisingly (and interestingly) diverse.

2 See Jameson's *Postmodernism, or the Cultural Logic of Late Capitalism* (1991) and Baudrillard's *Simulacra and Simulation* (1994). Baudrillard has been dismissed by some ecocritics as bearing 'cynical complicity' with the despoliation of nature (Coupe, 2000, p. 7); however, this account of Baudrillard indicates a refusal to engage with urban, image and technology-dominated attitudes, thus risking precisely the kind of separatist viewpoint which the majority of ecocritics hope to avoid.

3 See Bramwell (1985) and Coffey (2007). See the work on bioregionalism by Lawrence Buell (2005) as a possible way of theorizing connection to land without reverting to the exclusivist mentality of Nazism.

4 And then splits: the logical and epistemological problems devolved to Derrida, the ontology of life and immanence to Deleuze, the conception of history (and thus of a genealogy of discursive practices) to Foucault. Lear's three daughters and not a Cordelia in sight.

5 A representative selection: Hallman (1991); Acampora (2004); Drenthen (2005); Parkes (2005); Zimmerman (2005); Del Caro (2004); Reinhart (2004).

6 See the 2008 collection of papers (ed. J. Ayerza) at the website of the journal *Lacan Ink*: www.lacan.com.

7 This state of affairs seems to invite an analysis inspired by Blanchot. There is a kind of intrinsic and troubling impossibility to the claims of meaning made by poetic or fictional language. As here, the symbol promises, it even *demands*, more than the text *qua* literature can provide; and both the promise and its impossibility are constitutive of the literary as such. For such an analysis, the work necessarily closes in on itself, and the work of interpretation keeps having to fold itself back into the text. The ecocritical reading responds insofar as it points to the material conditions of literary production and analysis itself (strategies of writing; social or political contexts; publishing, critical and educational industries, etc.). The symbol can only promise insofar as it already belongs to a system within which the literary text rests. These conditions ensure that the promised return of symbol to existence is impossible in an absolute sense, but necessary as fragment or equivocal gesture.

8 Toadvine and Brown (2003); Foltz and Frodeman (2004); Cataldi and Hamrick (2007).

9 The term has been used before but not, to my knowledge, as designating a general project.

10 This is of course an explicit reference to Aristotle.

11 For example, in Vattimo (1997). However, for a counter-appropriation of Gadamer see the special edition of *Poetics Today: Gadamer and the Mechanics of Culture* (Knapp and Pence, 2003).

Chapter 15

1 Though just what 'philosophical speaking' entails is contentious for a future philosophy too, as we will see later.

2 In his *The Rise of Scientific Philosophy*, Hans Reichenbach pointed out that it was probably Kant who was the last philosopher who did or could produce a philosophical system that was 'expressive of the science of ... [his] time' (Reichenbach, 1951, p. 122).

3 The reception of philosophers into 'continental' awareness may well be thought of in terms of stages:

- pioneers – early advocates (often translators or philosophically inclined staff

from foreign language departments) who stake a claim on a lesser known European author;
- general zeal/advocacy – much exposition, much interpretation, much application by all and sundry, but little critique;
- some first positive critiques (usually comparative – 'hey, x is like y');
- more general, negative critiques, either of the type 'x is just like y, so nothing new here' or 'x is plain wrong/not as good as y';
- general disinterest (though always with the possibility of resurrection/rehabilitation by later generations).

4 The allusion here, of course, is to Deleuze: 'To think is to create – there is no other creation – but to create is first of all to engender "thinking" in thought' (Deleuze, 1994, p. 147).
5 For a fuller discussion of the philosophical thinking proper to cinema, for example, that would, if acknowledged, radically transform what we mean by philosophy, see Mullarkey, (2009).
6 One is reminded of the conclusion of Derrida's at the end of 'Signature, Event, Context': '(*Remark:* the – written – text of this – oral – communication was to have been addressed to the *Association of French Speaking Societies of Philosophy* before the meeting. Such a missive therefore had to be signed. Which I did, and counterfeit here. Where? There. J. D)' (Derrida, 1982, p. 330).
7 It must have come as a shock to many theorists when, just as they thought that they had seen the back of the last Lacanian, suddenly, and seemingly from nowhere, its most ardent and prolific champion appeared in the figure of Žižek.
8 See Strawson, (2008).

Bibliography

Chapter 2

Badiou, A. (1999), *Manifesto for Philosophy: Followed by Two Essays: 'the (Re)Turn of Philosophy Itself' and 'Definition of Philosophy'*, trans. N. Madarasz. New York: SUNY Press.

Badiou, A. (2005), *Being and Event*, trans. O. Feltham. London: Continuum.

Bergson, H. (1988), *Matter and Memory*, trans. N. M. Paul and W. S. Palmer. New York: Zone Books.

Colebrook, C. (2002), *Gilles Deleuze*. London: Routledge.

Critchley, S. (2001), *Continental Philosophy: A Very Short Introduction*. Oxford: Oxford University Press.

Cutrofello, A. (2005), *Continental Philosophy: A Contemporary Introduction*. London: Routledge.

Deleuze, G. (1990), *Bergsonism*, trans. H. Tomlinson and B. Habberjam. London: Zone Books.

Deleuze, G. (1994), *Difference and Repetition*, trans. P. Patton. London: Continuum.

Deleuze, G. (2001), *Pure Immanence: Essays on a Life*, trans. A. Boyman. New York: Zone Books.

Deleuze, G. (2004), *Desert Islands and Other Texts, 1953–1974*, ed. D. Lapoujade, trans. M. Taormina et al. London and New York: Semiotext(e)/MIT Press.

Deleuze, G. (2006), *Nietzsche and Philosophy*, trans. H. Tomlinson. London: Continuum.

Deleuze, G. and Guattari, F. (1983), *Anti-Oedipus: Capitalism and Schizophrenia*, trans. R. Hurley et al. London: Continuum.

Deleuze, G. and Guattari, F. (1988), *A Thousand Plateaus: Capitalism and Schizophrenia*, trans. B. Massumi. London: Athlone.

Deleuze, G. and Guattari, F. (1994), *What is Philosophy?*, trans. H. Tomlinson and G. Burchill. London: Verso.

Derrida, J. (1973), *Speech and Phenomena and Other Essays on Husserl's Theory of Signs*, trans. D. B. Allison.

Derrida, J. (1981), *Dissemination*, trans. B. Johnson. Chicago: Chicago University Press.

Derrida, J. (1982), *Margins of Philosophy*, trans. A. Bass. London: Prentice Hall.

Derrida, J. (1992), 'Force of Law: the "Mystical Foundation of Authority" ', in *Deconstruction and the Possibility of Justice*, ed. D. Cornell et al. London: Routledge, pp. 3–67.

Derrida, J. (2005), *Paper Machine*. Stanford: Stanford University Press.

Glendinning, S. (2006), *The Idea of Continental Philosophy*. Edinburgh: Edinburgh University Press.

Goodchild, P. (1996), *Deleuze and Guattari: An Introduction to the Politics of Desire*. London: Sage.

Hallward, P. (2003), *Badiou: A Subject to Truth*. Minneapolis: University of Minnesota Press.

Heidegger, M. (1962), *Being and Time*, trans. J. Macquarrie and E. Robinson. Oxford: Blackwell.

Heidegger, M. (1977a), 'The Question Concerning Technology', trans. W. Lovitt and D. Farrell Krell, in *Basic Writings*. London: Routledge, pp. 311–41.

Heidegger, M. (1977b), 'The End of Philosophy and the Task of Thinking', trans. J. Stambaugh and D. Farrell Krell, in *Basic Writings*. London: Routledge, pp. 431–49.

Heidegger, M. (1982), *The Basic Problems of Phenomenology*, trans. A. Hofstadter. Bloomington: Indiana University Press.

Irigaray, L. (1985), *Speculum of the Other Woman*, trans. G. C. Gill. Ithaca, NY: Cornell University Press.

Irigaray, L. (1991), 'The Bodily Encounter with the Mother', trans. D. Macey, in *The Irigaray Reader*, ed. M. Whitford. Oxford: Blackwell, pp. 34–46.

Kearney, R. (ed.) (1994), *Twentieth-Century Continental Philosophy*. London: Routledge.

Khalfa, J. (ed.) (2003), *Introduction to the Philosophy of Gilles Deleuze*. London: Continuum.

Levinas, E. (1985), *Ethics and Infinity*. Pittsburgh: Duquesne University Press.

Lyotard, J.-F. (1988), *The Differend: Phrases in Dispute*, trans. G. van den Abbeele. Minneapolis: University of Minnesota Press.

Lyotard, J.-F. (1992), *The Postmodern Explained to Children. Correspondence 1982–1985*, trans. Barry et al. London: Turnaround.

Maldonado-Torres, N. (2006), 'Post-continental Philosophy: Its Definition, Contours, and Fundamental Sources', *Worlds and Knowledges Otherwise*, Fall 2006, 1–22.

Mark, J. (1998), *Gilles Deleuze. Vitalism and Multiplicity*. London: Pluto Press.

Massumi, B. (1992), *A User's Guide to Capitalism and Schizophrenia. Deviations from Deleuze and Guattari*. Cambridge, MA: The MIT Press.

Mullarkey, J. (2006), *Post-Continental Philosophy*. London: Continuum.

Nancy, J.-L. (1991), *The Inoperative Community*, trans. P. Connor et al. Minneapolis: University of Minnesota Press.

Nancy, J.-L. (2000), *Being Singular Plural*, trans. R. Richardson et al. Stanford: Stanford University Press.

Nancy, J.-L. (2007), *Juste Impossible*. Paris: Bayard Centurion.

Patton, P. and Protevi, J. (2003), *Between Deleuze and Derrida*. London: Continuum.

Riera, G. (ed.) (2005), *Alain Badiou: Philosophy and its Conditions*. New York: SUNY Press.

Schroeder, W. R. (2005), *Continental Philosophy. A Critical Introduction*. London: Blackwell.

Serres, M. (2007), *The Parasite*. Minneapolis: University of Minnesota Press.

Serres, M., and Latour, B. (1995), *Conversations on Science, Culture and Time*, trans. R. Lapidus. Ann Arbor: University of Michigan Press.

Spivak, G. C. (1988), 'Can the Subaltern Speak?' in *Marxism and the Interpretation of Culture*, ed. C. Nelson and L. Grossberg. Urbana: University of Illinois Press, pp. 271–313.

Stengers, I. (1997), *Power and Invention: Situating Science*. Minneapolis: University of Minnesota Press.

Stengers, I. (2000), *The Invention of Modern Science*, trans. D. W. Smith. Minneapolis: University of Minnesota Press.

Stengers, I. and Prigogine, I. (1984), *Order Out of Chaos: Man's New Dialogue with Nature*. London: Heinemann.

Tarby, F. (2005), *Matérialismes d'aujourd'hui. De Deleuze à Badiou*. Paris: L'Harmattan.

West, D. (1996), *An Introduction to Continental Philosophy*. Cambridge: Polity.

Whitehead, A. N. (1985), *Process and Reality*. New York: Free Press.

Whitford, M. (1991), *Luce Irigaray. Philosophy in the Feminine*. London: Routledge.

Chapter 3

Banham, G. (2003), *Kant's Practical Philosophy: From Critique to Doctrine*. London: Palgrave Macmillan.

Banham, G. (2006), *Kant's Transcendental Imagination*. London: Palgrave Macmillan.

Banham, G. (2007a), 'Introduction: Cosmopolitics and Modernity', in *Cosmopolitics and the Emergence of A Future*, ed. D. Morgan and G. Banham. London: Palgrave Macmillan.

Banham, G. (2007b), 'Practical Schematism, Teleology and the Unity of the Metaphysics of Morals', in *Kant: Making Reason Intuitive*, eds K. Goudeli, P. Kontos and I. Patellis. London: Palgrave Macmillan.

Derrida, J. (1994), *Specters of Marx: the State of the Debt, the Work of Mourning, and the New International*, trans. P. Kamuf. London: Routledge.

Descombes, V. (1980), *Modern French Philosophy*, trans. L. Scott-Fox and J. M. Harding. Cambridge: Cambridge University Press.

Fukuyama, F. (1993), *The End of History and the Last Man*. Harmondsworth: Penguin.

Hegel, G. W. F. (1977), *The Phenomenology of Spirit*, trans. A. V. Miller. Oxford: Oxford University Press.

Heidegger, M. (1977), 'Who is Nietzsche's *Zarathustra*?' in *The Question Concerning Technology and Other Essays*, ed. and trans. W. Lovitt. New York: Harper & Row.

Heidegger, M. (1988), *Hegel's Phenomenology of Spirit*, trans. P. Emad and K. Maly. Bloomington: Indiana University Press.

Heidegger, M. (1990), *Kant and the Problem of Metaphysics*, trans. R. Taft. Bloomington: Indiana University Press.

Heidegger, M. (1991), *Nietzsche*, Vol. 1, *The Will to Power As Art*, and Vol. 2, *The Eternal Return of the Same*, trans. D. Farrell Krell. San Francisco: Harper.

Kant, I. (1987), *Critique of Judgment*, trans. W. S. Pluhar. Indianapolis: Hackett.

Kant, I. (1992), 'Inaugural Dissertation', in *Theoretical Philosophy 1755–1770*, ed. and trans. D. Walford and R. Meerbote. Cambridge: Cambridge University Press.

Kant, I. (1996a), *Critique of Practical Reason*, trans. M. Gregor, in *Practical Philosophy*, ed. M. Gregor. Cambridge: Cambridge University Press.

Kant, I. (1996b), 'Groundwork of the Metaphysics of Morals', trans. M. Gregor, in *Practical Philosophy*, ed. M. Gregor. Cambridge: Cambridge University Press.

Kant, I. (1996c), 'Religion within the Limits of Reason Alone', trans. G. di Giovanni, in *Religion and Rational Theology*, ed. A. W. Wood and G. di Giovanni. Cambridge: Cambridge University Press.

Kant, I. (2007), *Critique of Pure Reason*, trans. N. Kemp Smith. Basingstoke: Palgrave Macmillan.

Klossowski, P. (1997), *Nietzsche and the Vicious Circle*, trans. D. W. Smith. London: Continuum.

Kojève, A. (1969), *Introduction to the Reading of Hegel*, trans. J. H. Nicols, ed. A. Bloom. New York: Basic Books.

Kojève, A. (2008), *Outlines of A Phenomenology of Right*, trans. R. Howse, P. P. Frost and D. Goulet. Rowman & Littlefield.

Lyotard, J.-F. (1994), *Lessons on the Analytic of the Sublime*, trans. E. Rottenburg. Stanford: Stanford University Press.

Malabou, C. (2005), *The Future of Hegel: Plasticity, Temporality and Dialectic*, trans. L. During. London: Routledge.

Marsden, J. (2002), *After Nietzsche: Notes Towards A Philosophy of Ecstasy*. London: Palgrave Macmillan.

Müller-Lauter, W. (1999), *Nietzsche: His Philosophy of Contradictions and the Contradictions of His Philosophy*, trans. D. Parent. University of Illinois Press.

Nancy, J.-L. (2008a), *Dis-Enclosure: The Deconstruction of Christianity*, trans. B. Bergo, G. Malenfant and M. B. Smith. New York: Fordham University Press.

Nancy, J.-L. (2008b), *Noli me tangere: On the Raising of the Body*, trans. S. Clift, P.-A. Brault and M. Naas. New York: Fordham University Press.

Nietzsche, F. (1968), *The Anti-Christ*, trans. R.J. Hollingdale. Harmondsworth: Penguin.

Nietzsche, F. (1969a), *The Genealogy of Morals*, trans. W. Kaufmann. New York: Vintage.

Nietzsche, F. (1969b), *Thus Spoke Zarathustra*, trans. R. J. Hollingdale. Harmondsworth: Penguin.

Nietzsche, F. (1972), *Beyond Good and Evil: Prelude to a Philosophy of the Future*, trans. R. J. Hollingdale. Harmondsworth: Penguin.

Nietzsche, F. (1979), *Ecce Homo Or How One Becomes What One Is*, trans. R. J. Hollingdale. Harmondsworth: Penguin.

Rose, G. (1994), 'The Comedy of Hegel and the Trauerspiel of Modern Philosophy', *Bulletin of the Hegel Society of Great Britain*, 29.

Chapter 4

Adorno, T. W. (2000), *Metaphysics: Concepts and Problems*, ed. R. Tiedmann, trans. E. Jephcott. Stanford: Stanford University Press.

Badiou, A. (2002), 'On the Truth-Process', http://www.egs.edu/faculty/badiou/badiou-truth-process-2002.html.

Badiou, A. (2005), *Being and Event*, trans. O. Feltham. London: Continuum.

Badiou, A. (2006), 'The Question of Being Today', in *Theoretical Writings*, trans. R. Brassier and A. Toscano. London: Continuum.

Deleuze, G. (1994), *Difference and Repetition*, trans. P. Patton. New York: Columbia University Press.

Deleuze, G. (1995), *Negotiations*, trans. M. Joughin. New York: Columbia University Press.

Deleuze, G. (2004), 'Gueroult's General Method for Spinoza', in *Desert Islands*, ed. D. Lapoujade, trans. M. Taormina. New York: Semiotext(e).

Derrida, J. (1980), *Writing and Difference*, trans. A. Bass. Chicago: University of Chicago Press.

Derrida, J. (1981), *Positions*, trans. A. Bass. Chicago: University of Chicago Press.

Derrida, J. (1983), *Dissemination*, trans. B. Johnson. Chicago: University of Chicago Press.

Derrida, J. (1984), 'Ousia and Gramme', in *Margins of Philosophy*, trans. A. Bass. Chicago: University of Chicago Press.

Derrida, J. (1992), *Given Time: Counterfeit Money*, trans. P. Kamuf. Chicago: University of Chicago Press.

Derrida, J. (1993), *Aporias*, trans. T. Dutoit. Stanford: Stanford University Press.

Derrida, J. (1995), *The Gift of Death*, trans. D. Wills. Chicago: University of Chicago Press.

Descartes, R. (1985), *Principles of Philosophy*, in *The Philosophical Writings of Descartes*, trans. J. Cottingham, R. Stoothoff and D. Murdoch. Cambridge: Cambridge University Press.

Hallward, P. (2003), *Badiou: A Subject to Truth*. Minneapolis: University of Minnesota Press.

Heidegger, M. (1962a), *Being and Time*, trans. J. Macquarrie and E. Robinson. New York: Harper & Row.

Heidegger, M. (1962b), *Kant and the Problem of Metaphysics*, trans. J. S. Churchill. Bloomington: Indiana University Press.

Heidegger, M. (1975), 'The Way Back to the Ground of Metaphysics', in *Existentialism from Dostoyevsky to Sartre*, ed. W. Kaufman. New York: New American Library.

Heidegger, M. (1977), 'The Question Concerning Technology', in *The Question Concerning Technology and Other Essays*, trans. W. Lovitt. New York: Harper & Row.

Heidegger, M. (1988), *Hegel's Phenomenology of Spirit*, trans. P. Emad and K. Maly. Bloomington: Indiana University Press.

Heidegger, M. (1998), 'Introduction to "What is Metaphysics?"', trans. W. Kaufmann, in *Pathmarks*, ed. W. McNeill. Cambridge: Cambridge University Press.

van Inwagen, P. (2002), *Metaphysics*. Boulder: Westview Press.

Kant, I. (1929), *Critique of Pure Reason*, trans. N. Kemp Smith. London: Macmillan.

Kant, I. (1987), *Critique of Judgment*, trans. W. S. Pluhar. Indianapolis: Hackett.

Levinas, E. (1969), *Totality and Infinity: An Essay in Exteriority*, trans. A. Lingis. Pittsburgh: Duquesne University Press.

Levinas, E. (1985), *Ethics and Infinity: Conversations with Philippe Nemo*, trans. R. A. Cohen. Pittsburgh: Duquesne University Press.

Lumsden, S. (2008), 'The Rise of the Non-Metaphysical Hegel', *Philosophy Compass* 3(1), 51–65.

Lyotard, J.-F. (1984), 'Answering the Question: What is Postmodernism?' in

The Postmodern Condition: A Report on Knowledge, trans. G. Bennington and B. Massumi. Minneapolis: University of Minnesota Press.

Lyotard, J.-F. (1994), *Lessons on the Analytic of the Sublime*, trans. E. Rottenburg. Stanford: Stanford University Press.

Nietzsche, F. (1954), *Thus Spoke Zarathustra*, in *The Portable Nietzsche*, trans. W. Kaufmann. New York: Penguin.

Robinson, R. (1953), *Plato's Earlier Dialectic*, 2nd edn. Oxford: Clarendon Press.

Villani, A. (1999), *La guêpe et l'orchidée: Essai sur Gilles Deleuze*. Paris: Belin.

Whitehead, A. N. (1979), *Process and Reality*. New York: Free Press.

Chapter 5

Barnes, J. (ed.) (1984), *The Complete Works of Aristotle*. 2 Vols. Princeton, NJ: Princeton University Press.

Bernet, R. (1999), 'Christianity and Philosophy', *Continental Philosophy Review* 32, pp. 325–42.

Calcagno, A. (2008), 'Michel Henry's Non-Intentionality Thesis and Husserlian Phenomenology', *Journal of the British Society for Phenomenology* 39 (2), pp. 117–29.

Chalmers, D. (1995), 'Facing up to the Problem of Consciousness', *Journal of Consciousness Studies* 2 (3), 200–19.

Clark, A. (1997), *Being There: Putting Brain, Body and World Together Again*. Cambridge, MA: MIT Press.

Colombetti, G. and Thompson, E. (2007), 'The Feeling Body: Toward an Enactive Approach to Emotion', in *Developmental Aspects of Embodiment and Consciousness (Jean Piaget Symposia)*, ed. W. F. Overton, U. Mueller and J. Newman. Hillsdale, NJ: Lawrence Erlbaum, pp. 45–68.

Decety, J. and Lamm, C. (2006), 'Human Empathy through the Lens of Social Neuroscience', *The Scientific World Journal* 6, pp. 1146–63.

Depraz, N., Varela, F. J. and Vermersch, P. (2003), *On Becoming Aware: A Pragmatics of Experiencing*. Amsterdam: John Benjamins.

Derrida, J. (2005), *On Touching – Jean-Luc Nancy*, trans. C. Irizarry. Stanford: Stanford University Press.

Dreyfus, H. (1992), *What Computers Still Can't Do: A Critique of Artificial Reason*. Cambridge, MA: MIT Press.

Dreyfus, H. (2007), 'Why Heideggerian AI Failed and How Fixing It Would Require Making It More Heideggerian', *Philosophical Psychology* 20 (2), pp. 247–68.

Freeman, W. J. (2000), *How Brains Make Up Their Minds*. New York: Columbia University Press.

Gallagher, S. (2005), *How the Body Shapes the Mind*. New York: Oxford University Press.

Gallese, V. (2001), 'The "Shared Manifold" Hypothesis: from Mirror Neurons to Empathy'. *Journal of Consciousness Studies* 8.5–7, pp. 33–50.

Gallese, V. and Goldman, A. (1998), 'Mirror Neurons and the Simulation Theory of Mind-Reading', *Trends in Cognitive Sciences* 2, pp. 493–501.

Gallese, V., Keysers, C. and Rizzolatti, G. (2004), 'A Unifying View of the Basis of Social Cognition', *Trends in Cognitive Sciences* 8 (9), pp. 396–403.

Gatens, M. and Lloyd, G. (1999), *Collective Imaginings: Spinoza, Past and Present*. New York: Routledge.

Gould, S. J. (1988), 'Kropotkin Was No Crackpot'. *Natural History* 97 (7), pp. 12–18.

Henry, M. (2003), *I Am the Truth: Toward a Philosophy of Christianity*, trans. S. Emmanuel. Stanford: Stanford University Press.

Henry, M. (2008), *Material Phenomenology*, trans. S. Davidson. New York: Fordham University Press.

Jonas, H. (2000), *The Phenomenon of Life: Toward a Philosophical Biology*. Evanston: Northwestern University Press.

Joyce, R. (2007), *The Evolution of Morality*. Cambridge, MA: MIT Press.

Kropotkin, P. (2007), *Mutual Aid: A Factor of Evolution*. London: Dodo Press.

Lawlor, L. (2006), *The Implications of Immanence: Toward a New Concept of Life*. New York: Fordham University Press.

Lewis, M. (2000), 'Emotional Self-Organization at Three Time Scales', in *Emotion, Development and Self-Organization: Dynamic Systems Approaches to Emotional Development*, ed. M. Lewis and I. Granic. New York: Cambridge University Press.

Lewis, M. (2005), 'Bridging Emotion Theory and Neurobiology through Dynamic Systems Modeling', *Behavioral and Brain Science* 28, pp. 169–245.

Manning, E. (2006), *The Politics of Touch: Sense, Movement, Sovereignty*. Minneapolis: University of Minnesota Press.

Massumi, B. (2002), *Parables for the Virtual: Movement, Affect, Sensation*. Durham, NC: Duke University Press.

Maturana, H. and Varela, F. J. (1980), *Autopoiesis and Cognition: The Realization of the Living*. Boston: Riedel.

Meltzoff, A. and Moore, M. K. (1977), 'Imitation of Facial and Manual Gestures by Human Neonates', *Science* 198 (4312), pp. 75–78.

Mullarkey, J. (2006), *Post-Continental Philosophy: An Outline*. London: Continuum.

Noë, A. (2004), *Action in Perception*. Cambridge, MA: MIT Press.

Petitot, J., Varela, F. J., Pachoud, B. and Roy, J.-M. (eds.) (1999), *Naturalizing Phenomenology: Issues in Contemporary Phenomenology and Cognitive Science*. Stanford: Stanford University Press.

Protevi, J. (1993), 'The Economy of Exteriority in Derrida's *Speech and Phenomena*', *Man and World* 26 (4), pp. 373–88.

Protevi, J. (1994), *Time and Exteriority: Aristotle, Heidegger, Derrida*. Lewisburg: Bucknell University Press.

Protevi, J. (1998), 'The "Sense" of "Sight": Heidegger and Merleau-Ponty on the Meaning of Bodily and Existential Sight', *Research in Phenomenology* 28, pp. 211–23.

Protevi, J. (2009), *Political Physiology: Imbrications of the Social and the Somatic*. Minneapolis: University of Minnesota Press.

Ratcliffe, M. (2007), *Rethinking Commonsense Psychology: A Critique of Folk Psychology, Theory of Mind and Simulation*. London: Palgrave Macmillan.

Robbins, S. (2006). 'Bergson and the Holographic Theory of Mind', *Phenomenology and the Cognitive Sciences* 5 (3–4), pp. 365–94.

Schusterman, R. (2008), *Body Consciousness: A Philosophy of Mindfulness and Somaesthetics*. Cambridge: Cambridge University Press.

Sheets-Johnstone, M. (1999), *The Primacy of Movement*. Amsterdam: John Benjamins.

Sheets-Johnstone, M. (2007), 'Essential Clarifications of "Self-Affection" and Husserl's "Sphere of Ownness": First Steps toward a Pure Phenomenology of (Human) Nature', *Continental Philosophy Review* 39, pp. 361–91.

Singer, P. (1999), *A Darwinian Left: Politics, Evolution and Cooperation*. New Haven: Yale University Press.

Singer, T., Seymour, B., O'Doherty, J., Kaube, H., Dolan, R. J. and Frith, C. (2004), 'Empathy for Pain Involves the Affective but Not Sensory Components of Pain', *Science* 303, pp. 1157–62.

Smith, D. (1996), 'Deleuze's Theory of Sensation: Overcoming the Kantian Duality', in *Deleuze: A Critical Reader*, ed. P. Patton. Oxford: Blackwell, pp. 29–56.

Smith, D. (2007), 'The Conditions of the New', *Deleuze Studies* 1 (1), pp. 1–21.

Stueber, K. (2006), *Rediscovering Empathy: Agency, Folk Psychology and the Human Sciences*. Cambridge, MA: MIT Press.

Thompson, E. (2001), 'Empathy and Consciousness', *Journal of Consciousness Studies* 8 (5–7), pp. 1–32.

Thompson, E. (2007), *Mind in Life: Biology, Phenomenology, and the Sciences of Mind*. Cambridge, MA: Harvard University Press.

Varela, F. J. (1991), 'Organism: A Meshwork of Selfless Selves', in *Organism and the Origins of Self*, ed. A. I. Tauber. The Hague: Kluwer, pp. 79–107.

Varela, F. J. (1995), 'Resonant Cell Assemblies: A New Approach to Cognitive Functions and Neuronal Synchrony', *Biological Research* 28, pp. 81–95.

Varela, F. J. (1996), 'Neurophenomenology: A Methodological Remedy for the Hard Problem', *Journal of Consciousness Studies* 3 (4), pp. 330–49.

Varela, F. J. (1999), 'The Specious Present: A Neurophenomenology of Time Consciousness', in *Naturalizing Phenomenology: Issues in Contemporary Phenomenology and Cognitive Science*, ed. J. Petitot et al. Stanford: Stanford University Press, pp. 266–314.

Varela, F. J. (2001), 'Intimate Distances: Fragments for a Phenomenology of Organ Transplantation', *Journal of Consciousness Studies* 8 (5–7), pp. 259–71.

Varela, F. J. and Depraz, N. (2005), 'At the Source of Time: Valence and the Constitutional Dynamics of Affect', *Journal of Consciousness Studies* 12 (8–10), pp. 61–81.

Varela, F. J., Thompson, E. and Rosch, E. (1991), *The Embodied Mind*. Cambridge, MA: MIT Press.

de Waal, F. (2006), *Primates and Philosophers*. Princeton: Princeton University Press.

Wheeler, M. (1997), 'Cognition's Coming Home: The Reunion of Mind and Life', in *Proceedings of the Fourth European Conference on Artificial Life*, ed. P. Husbands and I. Harvey. Cambridge, MA: MIT Press, pp. 10–19.

Wheeler, M. (2005), *Reconstructing the Cognitive World*. Cambridge MA: MIT Press.

Zahavi, D. (1999a), *Self-Awareness and Alterity: A Phenomenological Investigation*. Evanston: Northwestern University Press.

Zahavi, D. (1999b), 'Michel Henry and the Phenomenology of the Invisible', *Continental Philosophy Review* 32, pp. 223–40.

Zahavi, D. (2003), 'Inner Time-consciousness and Pre-reflective Self-awareness', in *The New Husserl: A Critical Reader*, ed. D. Welton. Bloomington: Indiana University Press, pp. 157–80.

Zahavi, D. (2005), *Subjectivity and Selfhood: Investigating the First-Person Perspective*. Cambridge MA: MIT Press.

Zahavi, D. (2007), 'Subjectivity and Immanence in Michel Henry', in *Subjectivity and Transcendence*, ed. A. Grøn, I. Damgaard and S. Overgaard. Tübingen: Morh Siebeck, pp. 133–47.

Chapter 6

Deleuze, G. (1983), *Nietzsche and Philosophy*, trans. H. Tomlinson. New York: Columbia University Press.

Deleuze, G. (1990), *Expressionism in Philosophy: Spinoza*, trans. M. Joughin. New York: Zone Books.

Deleuze, G. (1994), *Difference and Repetition*, trans. P. Patton. New York: Columbia University Press.

Derrida, J. (1973), *Speech and Phenomena and Other Essays on Husserl's Theory of Signs*, trans. D. B. Allison. Evanston: Northwestern University Press.

Derrida, J. (1978), 'Violence and Metaphysics', in *Writing and Difference*, trans. A. Bass. Chicago: University of Chicago Press.

Derrida, J. (1981), *Positions*, trans. A. Bass. Chicago: University of Chicago Press.

Derrida, J. (1985), 'Letter to a Japanese friend', in *Derrida and Difference*, ed. D. Wood and R. Bernasconi. Warwick: Parousia Press, pp. 1–5.

Foucault, M. (1972), *Histoire de la folie à l'âge classique*. Paris: Gallimard.

Heidegger, M. (1992), '*Being and Time*: Introduction', in *Basic Writings*, ed. D. Farrell Krell. San Francisco: HarperCollins.

Levinas, E. (1969), *Totality and Infinity*, trans. A. Lingis. Pittsburgh: Duquesne University Press.

Levinas, E. (1981), *Otherwise Than Being, or Beyond Essence*, trans. A. Lingis. The Hague: Nijhoff.

Nietzsche, F. (1966), *Beyond Good and Evil: Prelude to a Philosophy of the Future*. New York: Random House.

Chapter 7

Agamben, G. (1998), *Homo Sacer: Sovereign Power and Bare Life*. Stanford: Stanford University Press.

Agamben, G. (1999), 'Absolute immanence', in *Potentialities: Collected Essays in Philosophy*, trans. D. Heller-Roazen. Stanford: Stanford University Press.

Althusser L. (2003), 'The Philosophical Conjuncture and Marxist Theoretical Research', in *The Humanist Controversy and Other Writings*, ed. F. Matheron. London: Verso.

Badiou, A. (2000), *Gilles Deleuze: The Clamor of Being*, trans. L. Burchill. Minneapolis: University of Minnesota Press.

Badiou, A. (2001), *Ethics: An Essay on the Understanding of Evil*, trans. P. Hallward. London: Verso.

Badiou, A. (2005), *Metapolitics*, trans. J. Barker. London: Verso.

Badiou, A. (2008), 'Comments on Critchley's *Infinitely Demanding*', in *Symposium: Canadian Journal of Continental Philosophy* 12.

Balibar, E. (1997), 'Spinoza: from Individuality to Transindividuality', in *Mededelingen vanwege het Spinozahuis*. Delft: Eburon.

Balibar, E. (1998), *Spinoza and Politics*, trans. P. Snowdon. London: Verso.

Barrodori, G. (2003), *Philosophy in a Time of Terror: Dialogues with Jürgen Habermas and Jacques Derrida*. Chicago: University of Chicago Press.

Beardsworth, R. (1996), *Derrida and the Political*. London: Routledge.

Bensaïd, D. (2002), *Marx For Our Times: Adventures and Misadventures of a Critique*, trans. G. Elliott. London: Verso.

Butler, J. (2000), 'Ethical ambivalence', in *The Turn to Ethics*, ed. M. Garber, B. Hansen and R. Walkovitz. London: Routledge.

Butler, J. (2002), 'What is Critique: on Foucault's Virtue', in *The Political*, ed. D. Ingram. London: Blackwell.

Butler, J. (2004), *Precarious Life: The Powers of Mourning and Violence*. London: Verso.

Butler, J. (2005), *Giving an Account of Oneself*. New York: Fordham University Press.

Butler, J. (2006), 'The Desire to Live: Spinoza's *Ethics* Under Pressure', in *Politics and the Passions 1500–1850*, eds V. Cahn, N. Saccamano and D. Coli. Princeton: Princeton University Press.

Connolly, W. (1999), *Why I am Not a Secularist*. Minneapolis: Minnesota University Press.

Connolly, W. (2000), 'Politics, Power and Ethics: A Discussion between Judith Butler and William Connolly', *Theory and Event* 4 (2).

Connolly, W. (2005), *Pluralism*. Durham: Duke University Press.

Critchley, S. (1999), *The Ethics of Deconstruction: Derrida and Levinas*. Oxford: Blackwell.

Critchley, S. (2000), 'Remarks on Derrida and Habermas', *Constellations* 7 (4), 455–65.

Critchley, S. (2007), *Infinitely Demanding: Ethics of Commitment, Politics of Resistance*. London: Verso.

Deleuze, G. (1988a), *Foucault*, trans. S. Hand. London: Continuum.

Deleuze, G. (1988b), *Spinoza: Practical Philosophy*, trans. R. Hurley. San Francisco: City Lights.

Deleuze, G. (2001), *Pure Immanence: Essays on a Life*, trans. A. Boyman. New York: Zone Books.

Deleuze, G. and Guattari, F. (1984), *Anti-Oedipus: Capitalism and Schizophrenia*. London: Athlone.

Deleuze, G. and Guattari, F. (1994), *What is Philosophy?*, trans. G. Burchell and H. Tomlinson. London: Verso.

Derrida, J. (1992), 'Force of Law: The "Mystical Foundation of Authority"', in *Deconstruction and the Possibility of Justice*, ed. D. Cornell et al. New York: Routledge.

Derrida, J. (1997), *Politics of Friendship*. London: Verso.

Derrida, J. (1999), *Adieu*, trans. P.-A. Brault and M. Naas. Stanford: Stanford University Press.

Derrida, J. (2000), *Of Hospitality*, trans. R. Bowlby. Stanford: Stanford University Press.

Derrida, J. (2002), 'Ethics and Politics Today', in *Negotiations: Interventions and Interviews 1971–2001*, trans. L. Rottenberg. Stanford: Stanford University Press.

Derrida, J. (2005), *Rogues: Two Essays on Reason*, trans. P.-A. Brault and M. Naas. Stanford: Stanford University Press.

Derrida, J. (2006), 'Hostipitality', in *The Derrida-Habermas Reader*, ed. L. Thomassen. Edinburgh: Edinburgh University Press.

Habermas, J. (2006), *The Divided West*, trans. C. Cronin. Cambridge: Polity Press.

Hallward, P. (2001), *Badiou: A Subject to Truth*. Minneapolis: Minnesota University Press.

Hallward, P. (ed.) (2004), *Think Again: Alain Badiou and the Future of Philosophy*. London: Continuum.

Harasym, S. (ed.) (1998), *Levinas and Lacan: The Missed Encounter*. New York: SUNY Press.

Laclau, E. (2004), 'An Ethics of Militant Engagement', in *Think Again: Alain Badiou and the Future of Philosophy*, ed. P. Hallward. London: Continuum.

Lacoue-Labarthe, P. and Nancy, J.-L. (1997), *Retreating the Political*, ed. S. Sparks. London: Routledge.

Levinas, E. (1973), *Otherwise than Being or Beyond Essence*, trans. A. Lingis. Dordrecht: Kluwer.

Lloyd, M. (2007), *Judith Butler: From Norms to Politics*. Oxford: Polity.

Loizidou, E. (2007), *Judith Butler: Ethics, Law, Politics*. Oxford: Routledge-Cavendish.

Macherey, P. (1998), 'Foucault: Ethics and Subjectivity', in *In a Materialist Way*, trans. T. Stolze. London: Verso.

Marchart, O. (2007), *Post-Foundational Political Thought: Political Difference in Nancy, Lefort, Badiou and Laclau*. Edinburgh: Edinburgh University Press.

Massumi, B. (2002), *Parables for the Virtual: Movement, Sense, Affect*. Durham: Duke University Press.

Matuštík, M. B. (2006), 'Between Hope and Terror: Habermas and Derrida Plead for the Im/possible', in *The Derrida-Habermas Reader*, ed. L. Thomassen. Edinburgh: Edinburgh University Press.

Montag, W. (2005), 'Who's Afraid of the Multitude? Between the Individual and the State', *South Atlantic Quarterly* 104 (4), pp. 655–73.

Negri, A. (1991), *The Savage Anomaly: The Power of Spinoza's Metaphysics and Politics*, trans. M. Hardt. Minneapolis: Minnesota University Press.

Negri, A. (2004), *Subversive Spinoza: (Un)contemporary Variations*, ed. T. S. Murphy. Manchester: Manchester University Press.

O'Leary, T. (2002), *Foucault and the Art of Ethics*. London: Continuum.

Rajchman, J. (2000), *The Deleuze Connections*. Cambridge, MA: MIT Press.

Rancière, J. (1999), *Disagreement*, trans. J. Rose. Minneapolis: University of Minnesota Press.

Smith, D. W. (2003), 'Deleuze and Derrida, Immanence and Transcendence: Two Directions in Recent French Thought', in *Between Deleuze and Derrida*, ed. P. Patton and J. Protevi. London: Continuum.

Thomassen, L. (ed.) (2006), *The Derrida-Habermas Reader*. Edinburgh: Edinburgh University Press.

White, S. K. (2000), *Sustaining Affirmation: The Strengths of Weak Ontology in Political Theory*. Princeton: Princeton University Press.

Žižek, S. (2008), *In Defense of Lost Causes*. London: Verso.

Zupančič, A. (2000), *Ethics of the Real*. London: Verso.

Chapter 8

Althusser, L. (1971), *Lenin and Philosophy and Other Essays*, trans. B. Brewster. New York: Monthly Review Press.

Althusser, L. (2003), *The Humanist Controversy and Other Writings*, ed. F. Matheron, trans. G. M. Goshgarian. London: Verso.

Althusser, L. (2006), *Philosophy of the Encounter. Later Writings, 1978–1987*, ed. F. Matheron and O. Corpet, trans. G. M. Goshgarian. London: Verso.

Althusser, L., and Balibar, E. (1977), *Reading Capital*, trans. B. Brewster. London: New Left Books.

Anderson, K. (1996), *Lenin, Hegel, and Western Marxism: A Critical Study*. Urbana: University of Illinois Press.

Badiou, A. (1999), *Deleuze: The Clamor of Being*, trans. L. Burchill. Minneapolis: University of Minnesota Press.

Badiou, A. (2006a), 'Matters of Appearance: an Interview with Alain Badiou', by L. Sedofsky. *Artforum*, November, pp. 246–53.

Badiou, A. (2006b), *Meta-Politics*, trans. J. Barker. London: Verso.

Badiou, A. (2008a), 'The Communist Hypothesis', *New Left Review* 49.

Badiou, A. (2008b), *Logics of Worlds*, trans. A. Toscano. London: Continuum.

Benton, T. (1993), *Natural Relations: Ecology, Animal Rights, and Social Justice*. London: Verso.

Callinicos, A. (2006), *The Resources of Critique*. Cambridge: Polity Press.

Cutrofello, A. (2005), *Continental Philosophy: A Contemporary Introduction*. London: Routledge.

Derrida, J. (1974), *Of Grammatology*, trans. G. C. Spivak. Baltimore: Johns Hopkins University Press.

Derrida, J. (1985), 'Différance', in *Margins of Philosophy*, trans. A. Bass. Chicago: University of Chicago Press.

Derrida, J. (1994), *Specters of Marx: The State of the Debt, the Work of Mourning, and the New International*, trans. P. Kamuf. London: Routledge.

Derrida, J. (1997), *Politics of Friendship*, trans. G. Collins. London: Verso.

Feltham, O. (2008), *Alain Badiou: Live Theory*. London: Continuum.

Jameson, F. (1971), *Marxism and Form: Twentieth-Century Dialectical Theories of Literature*. Princeton: Princeton University Press.

Jameson, F. (1981), *The Political Unconscious: Narrative as a Socially Symbolic Act*. Ithaca: Cornell University Press.

Jameson, F. (1991), *Postmodernism; or, The Cultural Logic of Late Capitalism*. Durham, NC: Duke University Press.

Jameson, F. (1994), *The Seeds of Time*. New York: Columbia University Press.

Jameson, F. (1998), *The Cultural Turn: Selected Writings on Postmodernism, 1983–1998*. London: Verso.

Jameson, F. (2009), 'Marx's Purloined Letter', *New Left Review* Jan./Feb. 2009, pp. 75–109.

Martin, B. (2000), *The Radical Project: Sartrean Investigations*. Lanham, MD: Rowman and Littlefield.

Martin, B. (2008), *Ethical Marxism: The Categorical Imperative of Liberation*. Chicago: Open Court.

Negri, A., and Hardt, M. (1994), *Labor of Dionysus: A Critique of the State-Form*. Minneapolis: University of Minnesota Press.

Negri, A., and Hardt, M. (2000), *Empire*. Cambridge, MA: Harvard University Press.

Negri, A., and Hardt, M. (2005), *Multitude: War and Democracy in the Age of Empire*. New York: Penguin.

O'Connor, J. (1997), *Natural Causes: Essays in Ecological Marxism*. Boulder: Guilford Press.

Quine, W. V. (2008), *Quine in Dialogue*, ed. D. Follesdal and D. B. Quine. Cambridge, MA: Harvard University Press.

Rockmore, T. (2006), *In Kant's Wake: Philosophy in the Twentieth Century*. Oxford: Blackwell.

Sartre, J.-P. (1968), *Search for a Method*, trans. H. E. Barnes. New York: Vintage.

Sartre, J.-P. (1982), *Critique of Dialectical Reason. Vol. 1, Theory of Practical Ensembles*, ed. J. Ree, trans. A. Sheridan-Smith. London: Verso.

Sartre, J.-P. (1991), *Critique of Dialectical Reason. Vol. 2, The Intelligibility of History*, trans. Q. Hoare. London: Verso.

Spivak, G. C. (1980), 'Revolutions that as yet have no model: Derrida's "Limited Inc." ', *Diacritics* 10 (4), pp. 29–49.

Chapter 9

Althusser, L. (2008), *On Ideology*. London: Verso.

Bowman, P. and Stamp, R. (eds.) (2007), *The Truth of Žižek*. London: Continuum.

Butler, J. (1990), *Gender Trouble: Feminism and the Subversion of Identity*. London: Routledge.

Butler, J. (1993), *Bodies that Matter: On the Discursive Limits of 'Sex'*. London: Routledge.

Butler, J. (1997), *The Psychic Life of Power: Theories in Subjection*. Stanford: Stanford University Press.

Butler, J., Laclau, E., and Žižek, S. (2000), *Contingency, Hegemony, Universality: Contemporary Dialogues on the Left*. London: Verso.

Copjec, J. (1994), *Read my Desire: Lacan against the Historicists*. Boston: MIT Press.

Critchley, S. (2002), *On Humour*. London: Routledge.

Critchley, S. (2007), *Infinitely Demanding: Ethics of Commitment, Politics of Resistance*. London: Verso.

Dean, J. (2006), *Žižek's Politics*. London: Routledge.

Dean, T. (2000), *Beyond Sexuality*. Chicago: University of Chicago Press.

Dean, T. (2003), 'Lacan and Queer Theory' in *The Cambridge Companion to Lacan*, ed. J.-M. Rabaté. Cambridge: Cambridge University Press.

Dean, T., and Lane, C. (2001), *Homosexuality and Psychoanalysis*. Chicago: University of Chicago Press.

Edelman, L. (1994), *Homographesis: Essays in Gay Literary and Cultural Theory*. London: Routledge.

Edelman, L. (2004), *No Future: Queer Theory and the Death Drive*. Durham: Duke University Press.

Freud, S. (1913), *Totem and Taboo*, in *Standard Edition*, Vol. 13. London: Hogarth Press.

Freud, S. (1916), *Introductory Lectures in Psychoanalysis*, in *Standard Edition*, Vol. 15. London: Hogarth Press.

Freud, S. (1917), *Mourning and Melancholia*, in *Standard Edition*, Vol. 17. London: Hogarth Press.

Freud, S. (1920), *Beyond the Pleasure Principle*, in *Standard Edition*, Vol. 18. London: Hogarth Press.

Freud, S. (1930), *Civilization and its Discontents*, in *Standard Edition*, Vol. 21. London: Hogarth Press.

Freud, S. (1939), *Moses and Monotheism*, in *Standard Edition*, Vol. 23. London: Hogarth Press.

Hallward, P. (2003), *Badiou: A Subject to Truth*. Minneapolis: University of Minnesota Press.

Henry, M. (1993), *The Genealogy of Psychoanalysis*, trans. D. Brick. Stanford: Stanford University Press.

Henry, M. (2008), *Material Phenomenology*, trans. S. Davidson. Fordham: Fordham University Press.

Kay, S. (2003), *Žižek: A Critical Introduction*. Cambridge: Polity.

Lacan, J. (1972), *The Seminar on the Purloined Letter*, trans. J. Mehlman, *Yale French Studies* 48, pp. 268–338.

Lacan, J. (1992), *Seminar VII: The Ethics of Psychoanalysis*, trans. D. Potter. New York: Norton.

Lacan, J. (1995), 'Position of the unconscious', trans. B. Fink, in *Reading Seminar XI: Lacan's Four Fundamental Concepts of Psychoanalysis*, ed. R. Feldstein, B. Fink, and M. Jaanus. New York: SUNY Press.

Lacan, J. (1998), *Seminar XX: Encore – On Feminine Sexuality, the Limits of Love Knowledge*, trans. B. Fink. New York: Norton.

Lacan, J. (2007), *Écrits: The First Complete Edition in English*, ed. B. Fink. New York: Norton.

Lardreau, G. (1993), *La Veracité*. Lagrasse: Verdier.

Mitchell, K., and Rose, J. (1982), *Feminine Sexuality: Jacques Lacan and the École Freudienne*. London: Palgrave Macmillan.

Rancière, J. (1998), *La parole muette*. Paris: Hachette.

Rancière, J. (2001), *L'inconscient esthétique*. Paris: Galilée.

Rancière, J. (2004), *The Politics of Aesthetics*, trans. G. Rockhill. London: Continuum.

Shepherdson, C. (2000), *Vital Signs: Nature, Culture, Psychoanalysis*. London: Routledge.

Shepherdson, C. (2007), *Lacan and the Limits of Language*. Fordham: Fordham University Press.

Stavrakakis, Y. (1999), *Lacan and the Political*. London: Routledge.

Stavrakakis, Y. (2007), *The Lacanian Left*. Edinburgh: Edinburgh University Press.

Žižek, S. (1989), *The Sublime Object of Ideology*. London: Verso.

Žižek, S. (1991), *For They Know Not What They Do: Enjoyment as a Political Factor*. London: Verso.

Žižek, S. (1992), *Enjoy your Symptom! Jacques Lacan in Hollywood and Out*. London: Routledge.
Žižek, S. (1993), *Tarrying with the Negative: Kant, Hegel, and the Critique of Ideology*. Durham: Duke University Press.
Žižek, S. (1997), *The Plague of Fantasies*. London: Verso.
Žižek, S. (1999), *The Ticklish Subject: The Absent Centre of Political Ontology*. London: Verso.
Žižek, S. (2001a), *On Belief*. London: Routledge.
Žižek, S. (2001b), *Did Somebody Say Totalitarianism? Five Interventions in the (Mis)use of a Notion*. London: Verso.
Žižek, S. (2002), *Welcome to the Desert of the Real*. London: Verso.
Zupančič, A. (2000), *Ethics of the Real: Kant, Lacan*. London: Verso.

Chapter 10

Alcoff, L. (2000), 'Philosophy Matters: a Review of Recent Work in Feminist Philosophy', *Signs* 25 (3), pp. 841–82.
Ansell Pearson, K. (1997), *Viroid Life: Perspectives on Nietzsche and the Transhuman Condition*. London: Routledge.
Barad, K. (2003), 'Posthumanist Performativity toward an Understanding of how Matter comes to Matter', *Signs* 28 (3), pp. 801–31.
Barad, K. (2007), *Meeting the Universe Half Way*. Durham: Duke University Press.
Bataille, G. (1988), *The Accursed Share*. New York: Zone Books.
Bauman, Z. (1998), *Globalization: The Human Consequences*. Cambridge: Polity Press.
Beck, U. (1999), *World Risk Society*. Cambridge: Polity Press.
Beer, G. (2000), *Darwin's Plots*. Cambridge: Cambridge University Press.
Benhabib, S. (2002), *The Claims of Culture. Equality and Diversity in the Global Era*. Princeton: Princeton University Press.
Bhabha, H. K. (1996), 'Unpacking my library . . . again', in *The Post-Colonial Question. Common Skies, Divided Horizons*, ed. I. Chamber and L. Curti. London: Routledge.
Bhabha, H. K. (2004), *The Location of Culture*. London: Routledge.
Brah, A. (1996), *Cartographies of Diaspora – Contesting Identities*. London: Routledge.
Braidotti, R. (1991), *Patterns of Dissonance*. Cambridge: Polity Press.
Braidotti, R. (1994), *Nomadic Subjects. Embodiment and Sexual Difference in Contemporary Feminist Theory*. New York: Columbia University Press.
Braidotti, R. (2002), *Metamorphoses. Towards a Materialist Theory of Becoming*. Cambridge: Polity Press.
Braidotti, R. (2006), *Transpositions. On Nomadic Ethics*. Cambridge: Polity Press.
Braidotti, R. (2008), 'Intensive Genre and the Demise of Gender', *Angelaki* 13 (2), pp. 45–58.
Bryld, M. and Lykke, N. (1999), *Cosmodolphins: Feminist Cultural Studies of Technologies, Animals and the Sacred*. London: Zed Books.
Buchanan, I. and Colebrook, C. (eds.) (2000), *Deleuze and Feminist Theory*. Edinburgh: Edinburgh University Press.
Butler, J. (1992), 'Contingent Foundations: Feminism and the Question of Postmodernism', in *Feminists Theorize the Political*, eds J. Butler and J. Scott. London: Routledge.

Butler, J. (1993), *Bodies that Matter: on the Discursive Limits of 'Sex'*. London: Routledge.

Butler, J. (2004a), *Precarious Life*. London: Verso.

Butler, J. (2004b), *Undoing Gender*. London: Routledge.

Butler, J. and Scott, J. W. (eds.) (1992), *Feminists Theorize the Political*. London: Routledge.

Castells, M. (1996), *The Rise of the Network Society*. Oxford: Blackwell.

Colebrook, C. (2000), 'Is Sexual Difference a Problem?' in *Deleuze and Feminist Theory*, ed. I. Buchanan and C. Colebrook. Edinburgh: Edinburgh University Press, pp. 110–27.

Colebrook, C. (2004), 'Postmodernism is a Humanism. Deleuze and Equivocity', in *Women: a Cultural Review* 15 (3), pp. 283–307.

Cornell, D. (2002), The Ubuntu Project with Stellenbosch University, www.fehe.org/index.php?id=281. Consulted on 2 January 2007.

Crenshaw, K. (1995), 'Intersectionality and Identity Politics: Learning from Violence against Women of Colour', in *Critical Race Theory*, ed. K. Crenshaw, N. Gotanda, G. Peller, and K. Thomas. New York: The New Press, pp. 178–93.

Delanda, M. (2002), *Intensive Science and Virtual Philosophy*. London: Continuum.

Deleuze, G. (1953), *Empirisme et subjectivité*. Paris: Presses Universitaires de France.

Deleuze, G. (1962), *Nietzsche et la philosophie*. Paris: Presses Universitaires de France.

Deleuze, G. (1966), *Le Bergsonisme*. Paris: Presses Universitaires de France.

Deleuze, G. (1968), *Spinoza et le problème de l'expression*. Paris: Minuit.

Deleuze, G. (1969), *Logique du sens*. Paris: Minuit.

Deleuze, G. (1995), 'L'immanence: une vie . . .', *Philosophie* 47, pp. 3–7.

Deleuze, G. and Guattari, F. (1972), *L'anti-Oedipe. Capitalisme et schizophrénie I*. Paris; Minuit.

Deleuze, G. and Guattari, F. (1980), *Mille plateaux. Capitalisme et schizophrénie II*. Paris: Minuit.

Deleuze, G. and Guattari, F. (1991), *Qu'est-ce que la philosophie?* Paris: Minuit.

Diprose, R. (1994), *The Bodies of Women: Ethics, Embodiment and Sexual Difference*. London: Routledge.

Fausto-Sterling, A. (2000), *Sexing the Body. Gender Politics and the Construction of Sexuality*. New York: Basic Books.

Foucault, M. (1963), *Naissance de la clinique*. Paris: PUF.

Foucault, M. (1966), *Les mots et les choses*. Paris: Gallimard.

Foucault, M. (1976), *Histoire de la sexualité I. La volonté de savoir*. Paris: Gallimard.

Foucault, M. (1984a), *Histoire de la sexualité II: L'usage des plaisirs*. Paris: Gallimard.

Foucault, M. (1984b), *Histoire de la sexualité III: Le souci de soi*. Paris: Gallimard.

Franklin, S., Lury, C., and Stacey, J. (2000), *Global Nature, Global Culture*. London: Sage.

Fraser, M. (2002), 'What is the Matter of Feminist Criticism?', *Economy and Society* 31 (4), pp. 606–25.

Fraser, M., Kember, S., and Lury, C. (2005), 'Inventive Life: Approaches to the New Vitalism', *Theory, Culture & Society* 22 (1), pp. 1–14.

Fukuyama, F. (2002), *Our Posthuman Future: Consequences of the BioTechnological Revolution*. London: Profile Books.

Gatens, M. (1991), *Feminism and Philosophy: Perspectives in Difference and Equality*. Bloomington: Indiana University Press.

Gatens, M. and Lloyd, G. (1999), *Collective Imaginings: Spinoza, Past and Present*. London: Routledge.

Gilroy, P. (2000), *Against Race: Imaging Political Culture Beyond the Colour Line*. Cambridge, MA: Harvard University Press.

Grewal, I. and Kaplan, C. (eds.) (1994), *Scattered Hegemonies: Postmodernity and Transnational Feminist Practices*. Minneapolis: University of Minnesota Press.

Grosz, E. (1994), *Volatile Bodies*. Bloomington: Indiana University Press.

Grosz, E. (2004), *The Nick of Time*. Durham: Duke University Press.

Grosz, E. (ed.) (1999), *Becomings. Explorations in Time, Memory and Futures*. Ithaca: Cornell University Press.

Guattari, F. (1992), *Chaosmose*. Paris: Galilée.

Guattari, F. (2000), *The Three Ecologies*. London: Athlone.

Habermas, J. (2003), *The Future of Human Nature*. Cambridge: Polity.

Halberstam, J. and Livingston, I. (eds.) (1995), *Posthuman Bodies*. Bloomington: Indiana University Press.

Haraway, D. (1985), 'A Manifesto for Cyborgs: Science, Technology, and Socialist Feminism in the 1980s', *Socialist Review* 5 (2).

Haraway, D. (1988), 'Situated Knowledges: the Science Question in Feminism as a Site of Discourse on the Privilege of Partial Perspective', *Feminist Studies* 14 (3), pp. 575–99.

Haraway, D. (1992a), 'Ecce Homo, ain't (ar'n't) I a Woman and Inappropriate/d Others: the Human in a Post-humanist Landscape', in *Feminists Theorize the Political*, ed. J. Butler and J. Scott. London: Routledge.

Haraway, D. (1992b), 'The Promises of Monsters: a Regenerative Politics for Inappropriate/d Others', in *Cultural Studies*, ed. L. Grossberg, C. Nelson and A. Treichler. London: Routledge.

Haraway, D. (1997), *Modest_Witness@Second_Millennium.FemaleMan©_Meets_ Oncomouse™*. London: Routledge.

Haraway, D. (2003), *The Companion Species Manifesto. Dogs, People and Significant Otherness*. Chicago: Prickly Paradigm Press.

Harding, S. (1991), *Whose Science? Whose Knowledge?* Ithaca: Cornell University Press.

Harding, S. (1993), *The 'Racial' Economy of Science*. Bloomington: Indiana University Press.

Hardt, M. and Negri, A. (2000), *Empire*. Cambridge, MA: Harvard University Press.

Hartsock, N. (1987), 'The Feminist Standpoint: Developing the Ground for a Specifically Feminist Historical Materialism', in *Feminism and Methodology*, ed. S. Harding. London: Open University Press.

Hayles, K. (1999), *How We Became Posthuman: Virtual Bodies in Cybernetics, Literature and Informatics*. Chicago: University of Chicago Press.

Hemmings, C. (2006), *Travelling Concepts in Feminist Pedagogy: European Perspectives*. York: Raw Nerve Press.

Henry, A. (2004), *Not My Mother's Sister: Generational Conflict and Third-Wave Feminism*. Bloomington: Indiana University Press.

Hill Collins, P. (1991), *Black Feminist Thought. Knowledge, Consciousness and the Politics of Empowerment*. London: Routledge.

Irigaray, L. (1974), *Spéculum. De l'autre femme*. Paris: Minuit.

Irigaray, L. (1977), *Ce sexe qui n'en est pas un*. Paris: Minuit.

Irigaray, L. (1984), *L'éthique de la différence sexuelle*. Paris: Minuit.

Irigaray, L. (1992), *J'aime à toi. Esquisse d'une felicite dans l'histoire*. Paris: Grasset.

Kelly, J. (1979), 'The Double-Edged Vision of Feminist Theory', *Feminist Studies* 5 (1), pp. 216–27.

Lauretis, T. de (1990), 'Eccentric Subjects: Feminist Theory and Historical Consciousness', *Feminist Studies* 16 (1), pp. 115–50.

Lloyd, G. (1985), *The Man of Reason: Male and Female in Western Philosophy*. London: Methuen.

Lloyd, G. (1994), *Part of Nature: Self-knowledge in Spinoza's Ethics*. Ithaca: Cornell University Press.

Lloyd, G. (1996), *Spinoza and the Ethics*. London: Routledge.

MacCormack, P. (2004), 'Parabolic Philosophies. Analogue and Affect', *Theory, Culture & Society* 21 (6), pp. 179–87.

MacCormack, P. (2008), *Cinesexuality (Queer Interventions)*. Hampshire: Ashgate.

MacKinnon, B. (2006), *Ethics: Theory and Contemporary Issues*, Fifth Edition. Belmont: Wadsworth Publishing.

Mahmood, S. (2005), *Politics of Piety. The Islamic Revival and the Feminist Subject*. Princeton: Princeton University Press.

Margulis, L. and Sagan, D. (1995), *What is Life?*. Berkeley: University of California Press.

Massumi, B. (1988), 'Requiem for Our Perceived Dead: Toward a Participatory Critique of Capitalist Power', in *Deleuze and Guattari: New Mappings in Politics, Philosophy and Culture*, ed. E. Kaufman and K. J. Heller. Minneapolis: University of Minnesota Press, pp. 40–64.

Massumi, B. (2002), *Parables for the Virtual. Movement, Affect, Sensation*. Durham: Duke University Press.

Nigianni, C. (2008), *Re-thinking Queer: a Film Philosophy Project*. PhD Dissertation defended at the University of East London, December 12, 2008.

Noys, B. (2008), ' "The end of the monarchy of sex". Sexuality and Contemporary Nihilism', *Theory, Culture & Society*, 25 (5), pp. 104–22.

Nussbaum, M. (1999), *Cultivating Humanity: a Classical Defense of Reform in Liberal Education*. Cambridge, MA: Harvard University Press.

Nussbaum, M. (2006), *Frontiers of Justice. Disability, Nationality, Species Membership*. Cambridge: Harvard University Press.

Parisi, L. (2004), *Abstract Sex. Philosophy, Bio-Technology, and the Mutation of Desire*. London: Continuum Press.

Rich, A. (1976), *Of Woman Born*. New York: W. W. Norton.

Rich, A. (1985), *Blood, Bread and Poetry*. New York: W. W. Norton.

Rose, N. (2001), 'The Politics of Life Itself', *Theory, Culture & Society* 18 (6), pp. 1–30.

Said, E. (1978), *Orientalism*. London: Penguin.

Shiva, V. (1997), *Biopiracy. The Plunder of Nature and Knowledge*. Boston: South End Press.

Spivak, G. (1988), 'Can the Subaltern Speak?', in *Marxism and the Interpretation of*

Culture, ed. C. Nelson and L. Grossberg. Urbana: University of Illinois Press, pp. 271–313.

Spivak, G. C. (1999), *A Critique of Postcolonial Reason. Toward a History of the Vanishing Present*. Cambridge, MA: Harvard University Press.

Stengers, I. (1997), *Power and Invention: Situating Science*. Minneapolis: University of Minnesota Press.

van der Tuin, I. (2008), 'Deflationary Logic: Response to Sara Ahmed's "Imaginary prohibitions: some preliminary remarks on the founding gestures of the 'new materialism' " ', *European Journal of Women's Studies* 15 (4), pp. 411–16.

Ware, V. (1992), *Beyond the Pale. White Women, Racism and History*. London: Verso.

Wiegman, R. (2002), *Women's Studies on Its Own*. Durham: Duke University Press.

Wilson, E. (1998), *Neural Geographies. Feminism and the Microstructure of Cognition*. London: Routledge.

Woolf, V. (1993), *Flush*. London: Penguin Books.

Chapter 11

Agamben, G. (1978), *Infancy and History*, trans. L. Heron. London Verso.

Agamben, G. (1991), *Language and Death*, trans. K. E. Pinkus with M. Hardt. Minneapolis: University of Minnesota Press.

Arendt, H. (1998), *The Human Condition*. Chicago: University of Chicago Press.

Aristotle (1962), *The Politics*, trans. J. Sinclair. Harmondsworth: Penguin.

Bergson, H. (1963), *Oeuvres*. Paris: Presses Universitaires de France.

Bergson, H. (1983), *Creative Evolution*, trans. A. Mitchell. New York: University Press of America.

Bergson, H. (1988), *Matter and Memory*, trans. N. M. Paul and W. S. Palmer. New York: Zone Books.

Bricmont, J. (1996), 'Science of Chaos or Chaos in Science?' *Physicalia Magazine* www.fyma.ucl.ac.be/reche/1996/UCL-IPT-96-03.ps.gz

Cabanac, M. (1995), 'What is Sensation? *Gnoti se auton*,' in *Biological Perspectives on Motivated Activities*, ed. R. Wong. Northwood, NJ: Ablex, pp. 399–417.

Deleuze, G. (1969), *Logique du sens*. Paris: Les Editions de Minuit.

Deleuze, G. (1986), *Cinema One: The Movement-Image*, trans. H. Tomlinson and B. Habberjam. Minneapolis: University of Minnesota Press.

Deleuze, G. (1990), *The Logic of Sense*, trans. M. Lester with C. Stivale and C. Boundas. New York: Columbia University Press.

Deleuze, G. and Guattari, F. (1987), *Anti-Oedipus*, trans. R. Hurley, M. Seem, and H. R. Lane. Minneapolis: University of Minnesota Press.

Depew, D. J., and Weber, B. H. (1995), *Darwinism Evolving: Systems Dynamics and the Genealogy of Natural Selection*. Cambridge, MA: MIT Press.

Devlin, K. (1994), *Mathematics, The Science of Patterns: The Search for Order in Life, Mind and the Universe*, New York: Scientific American Library.

Foucault, M. (1973), *The Order of Things: An Archaeology of the Human Sciences*. New York: Vintage.

Freud, S. (1966), *Beyond the Pleasure Principle*, trans. J. Strachey. New York: W.W. Norton.

Heidegger, M. (1962), *Being and Time*, trans. J. Macquarrie and E. Robinson. New York: Harper & Row.

Heidegger, M. (1966), 'Conversations on a Country Path,' in *Discourse on Thinking*, trans. J. M. Anderson and E. H. Freund. New York: Harper and Row.

Heidegger, M. (1969), *Identity and Difference*, trans. J. Stambaugh. New York: Harper and Row.

Heidegger, M. (1979), *Nietzsche: The Will to Power as Art*, trans. D. Farrell Krell. New York: Harper and Row.

Klein, M. (1964), *Mathematics in Western Culture*. New York: Galaxy Books.

Lecercle, J.-J. (2002), *Deleuze and Language*. London: Palgrave.

Lyotard, J.-F. (1984), 'The Sublime and the Avant-garde,' trans. L. Liebman, *Artforum* April 1984.

Margulis, L. and Sagan, D. (1997), 'A Universe in Heat,' in *What is Sex?* New York: Simon & Schuster.

Nietzsche, F. (1968a), *Beyond Good and Evil*, trans. W. Kaufmann. New York: Vintage.

Nietzsche, F. (1968b), *The Will to Power*, trans. W. Kaufmann and R. J. Hollingdale. New York: Vintage.

Nietzsche, F. (1969), *Thus Spoke Zarathustra*, trans. R. J. Hollingdale. New York: Penguin.

Nietzsche, F. (1974), *The Gay Science*, trans. W. Kaufmann. New York: Vintage.

Olkowski, D. (1999), *Gilles Deleuze and the Ruin of Representation*. Berkeley: University of California Press.

Olkowski, D. (2006), 'Merleau-Ponty, Intertwining and Objectification', *Phaenex, The Journal of Existential and Phenomenological Theory and Culture*, 1 (1), pp. 113–39.

Olkowski, D. (2007), *The Universal (In the Realm of the Sensible)*. New York: Columbia University Press.

Ruelle, D. (1991), *Chance and Chaos*. Princeton: Princeton University Press.

Stambaugh, J. (1972), *Nietzsche's Thought of Eternal Return*. Baltimore: Johns Hopkins University Press.

Stengers, I., and Prigogine, I. (1984), *Order Out of Chaos, Man's New Dialogue with Nature*. New York: Bantam Books.

Tasić, V. (2001), *Mathematics and the Roots of Postmodern Thought*. Oxford: Oxford University Press.

Chapter 12

Aitken, A. (2005), 'Continental Philosophy and the Sciences: the French Tradition', *Angelaki* 10 (2) (special issue: *Continental Philosophy and the Sciences: The French Tradition*), pp. 1–12.

Babich, B. and Cohen, R. S. (1999), *Nietzsche, Epistemology, and Philosophy of Science: Nietzsche and the Sciences II*. Dordrecht: Kluwer.

Bachelard, G. (1951), *L'activité rationaliste de la physique contemporaine*. Paris: PUF.

Bachelard, G. (1985), *The New Scientific Spirit*, trans. A. Goldhammer. Boston: Beacon Press.

Bachelard, G. (2004), *Le rationalisme appliqué*. Paris: PUF.

Badiou, A. (2007), *The Concept of Model: An Introduction to the Materialist Epistemology of Mathematics*, trans. Z. L. Fraser and T. Tho. Melbourne: re.press.

Bergson, H. (1965), *Duration and Simultaneity: with Reference to Einstein's Theory*, trans. L. Jacobson (introduction by H. Dingle). Indianapolis: Bobbs-Merrill.

Bergson, H. (1988), *Matter and Memory*, trans. N. M. Paul and W. S. Palmer. New York: Zone Books.

Canguilhem, G. (1989), *The Normal and the Pathological*, trans. C. R. Fawcett and R. S. Cohen. New York: Zone Books.

Cassirer, E. (1953), *Substance and Function and Einstein's Theory of Relativity*, trans. W. C. Swabey and M. Collins Swabey. New York: Dover.

Chang, H. (1993), 'A misunderstood rebellion. The twin-paradox controversy and Herbert Dingle's vision of science', *Studies in the History and Philosophy of Science* 24 (5).

Cohen, H. (1928), *Das Prinzip der Infinitesimalmethode und seine Geschichte*. Berlin: Akademie.

Deleuze, G. (1988), *Foucault*, trans. S. Hand. Minnesota: University of Minnesota Press.

Deleuze, G. (1994), *Difference and Repetition*, trans. P. Patton. London: Continuum.

Deleuze, G. (2006), *The Fold*, trans. T. Conley. London: Continuum.

Deleuze, G. and Guattari, F. (1994), *What is Philosophy?*, trans. H. Tomlinson and G. Burchell. London: Verso.

Derrida, J. (1974), *Of Grammatology*, trans. G. C. Spivak. New York: Columbia University Press.

Foucault, M. (2002), *Archaeology of Knowledge*, trans. A. M. Sheridan Smith. London: Routledge.

Garelli, J. (1991), *Rythmes et Mondes: Au revers de l'identité et de l'altérité*. Grenoble: Jérôme Millon.

Gayon, J. (1992), *Darwin et l'après-Darwin: Une histoire de l'hypothèse de sélection naturelle*. Paris: Éditions Kimé.

Gunter, P. A. Y. (ed.) (1969), *Bergson and the Evolution of Physics*. Knoxville: University of Tennessee Press.

Gutting, G. (1989), *Michel Foucault's Archaeology of Scientific Reason: Science and the History of Reason*. Cambridge: Cambridge University Press.

Gutting, G. (2005), *Continental Philosophy of Science*. London: Blackwell.

Heidegger, M. (1993), *Basic Writings*, ed. D. Farrell Krell. London: Routledge.

Husserl, E. (1970), *The Crisis of European Sciences and Transcendental Phenomenology: An Introduction to Phenomenological Philosophy*, trans. D. Carr. Evanston: Northwestern University Press.

Husserl, E. (2003), *Philosophy of Arithmetic: Psychological and Logical Investigations with Supplementary Texts from 1887–1901*, trans. D. Willard. Dordrecht: Kluwer.

Ihde, D. (1990), *Technology and the Lifeworld*. Bloomington: Indiana University Press.

Kockelmans, J. J., and Kisiel, T. J. (1970), *Phenomenology and the Natural Sciences: Essays and Translations*. Evanston: Northwestern University Press.

Latour, B. (1987), *Science in Action: How to Follow Scientists and Engineers Through Society*. Cambridge, MA: Harvard University Press.

Latour, B. (2002), 'Morality and Technology: the End of the Means', trans. C. Venn, *Theory, Culture, and Society* 19 (5/6), pp. 247–60.

Plotnitsky, A. (2003), 'Algebras, Geometries and Topologies of the Fold: Deleuze,

Derrida and Quasi-mathematical Thinking (with Leibniz and Mallarmé)', in *Between Deleuze and Derrida*, ed. P. Patton and J. Protevi. London: Continuum.

Reichenbach, H. (1938), *Experience and Prediction: an Analysis of the Foundations and the Structure of Knowledge*. Chicago: University of Chicago Press.

Selinger, E. (2006), *Postphenomenology: A Critical Companion to Ihde*. Albany: SUNY Press.

Serres, M. (1969), *Hermès I. La communication*. Paris: Éditions Minuit.

Simondon, G. (1995), *L'individu et sa genèse physico-biologique (l'individuation à la lumière des notions de forme et d'information)*. Grenoble: Jérôme Millon.

Simondon, G. (2005), *L'individuation à la lumière des notions de forme et d'information*. Grenoble: Jérôme Millon.

Stengers, I. (2005), 'Deleuze and Guattari's last enigmatic message', *Angelaki* 10 (2) (special issue: *Continental Philosophy and the Sciences: The French Tradition*), pp. 151–69.

Whitehead, A. N. (1985), *Process and Reality: An Essay in Cosmology*. New York: Free Press.

Whitehead, A. N., and Russell, B. (1962), *Principia Mathematica*. Cambridge: Cambridge University Press.

Worms, F. (2004), *Le Moment 1900 en Philosophie*. Lille: Presse Universitaire de Septentrion.

Chapter 13

Agamben, G. (1994), *The Man Without Content*, trans. G. Albert. Stanford: Stanford University Press.

Agamben, G. (1999), *Potentialities: Collected Essays in Philosophy*, trans. D. Heller-Roazen. Stanford: Stanford University Press.

Artaud, A. (1988), *Selected Writings*, trans. H. Weaver. Berkeley: University of California Press.

Badiou, A. (1999), *Manifesto for Philosophy*, trans. N. Madarasz. Albany: State University of New York Press.

Badiou, A. (2003), 'Fifteen Theses on Contemporary Art', trans. P. Hallward. *Lacanian Ink*, 22. http://www.lacan.com/issue22.htm.

Badiou, A. (2005a), *Handbook of Inaesthetics*, trans. A. Toscano. Stanford: Stanford University Press.

Badiou, A. (2005b), *Infinite Thought: Truth and the Return to Philosophy*, trans. O. Feltham and J. Clemens. London: Continuum.

Badiou, A. (2005c), 'The Subject of Art'. *The Symptom*, 6. http://www.lacan.com/symptom6_articles/badiou.html

Badiou, A. (2007), 'The Event in Deleuze', trans. J. Joffe, *Parrhesia* 2, pp. 37–44.

Deleuze, G. (2003), *Francis Bacon: The Logic of Sensation*, trans. D. Smith. London: Continuum.

Deleuze, G. (2004), *Desert Islands and Other Texts (1953–1974)*, trans. M. Taormina. Los Angeles: Semiotext(e).

Deleuze, G. (2006), *Two Regimes of Madness: Texts and Interviews 1975–1995*, trans. A. Hodges and M. Taormina. Los Angeles: Semiotext(e).

Deleuze, G., and Foucault, M. (1999), *Gérard Fromanger: Photogenic Painting*, trans. D. Roberts. London: Black Dog Publishing Limited.

Deleuze, G., and Guattari, F. (1983), *Anti-Oedipus: Capitalism and Schizophrenia*, trans. R. Hurley, M. Seem, and H. Lane. Minneapolis: University of Minnesota Press.

Deleuze, G. and Guattari, F. (1988), *A Thousand Plateaus: Capitalism and Schizophrenia*, trans. B. Massumi. London: The Athlone Press.

Deleuze, G. and Guattari, F. (1994), *What is Philosophy?*, trans. H. Tomlinson and G. Burchill. London: Verso.

Derrida, J. (1986), 'On Colleges and Philosophy', in *Postmodernism: ICA Documents 4 and 5*, ed. L. Appignanesi. London: Institute of Contemporary Arts.

Derrida, J. (1992), 'Of a Certain Collège International Still to Come', trans. P. Kamuf, in *Points . . . Interviews 1974–1994*. Stanford: Stanford University Press.

Derrida, J. (1993a), *Memoirs of the Blind: The Self-Portrait and Other Ruins*, trans. P-A. Brault and M. Naas. Chicago: University of Chicago Press.

Derrida, J. (1993b), 'Le Toucher: Touch/to Touch him', trans. P. Kamuf. *Paragraph* 16 (2), pp. 122–57.

Derrida, J. (1994), 'The Spatial Arts: An Interview with Peter Brunette and David Wills', trans. L. Volpe, in *Deconstruction and the Visual Arts: Art, Media, Architecture*, ed. P. Brunette and D. Wills. Cambridge: Cambridge University Press, pp. 9–32.

Derrida, J. (2005), *On Touching – Jean-Luc Nancy*, trans. C. Irizarry. Stanford: Stanford University Press.

Derrida, J. and Thévenin, P. (1998), *The Secret Art of Antonin Artaud*, trans. M. A. Caws. Cambridge, MA: MIT Press.

Heidegger, M. (1971), 'The Origin of the Work of Art', in *Poetry, Language, Thought*, trans. A. Hofstadter. New York: Harper & Row, pp. 15–87.

Heidegger, M. (1996), *The Principle of Reason*, trans. R. Lilly. Bloomington: Indiana University Press.

Heidegger, M. (2000), *Introduction to Metaphysics*, trans. G. Fried and R. Polt. New Haven: Yale University Press.

Lyotard, J.-F. (1971), *Discours/Figure*. Paris: Klincksieck.

Merleau-Ponty, M. (1967), *Phenomenology of Perception*, trans. C. Smith. London: Routledge & Kegan Paul.

Nancy, J.-L. (1996a), *The Muses*, trans. P. Kamuf. Stanford: Stanford University Press.

Nancy, J.-L. (1996b), 'The Deleuzian Fold of Thought', trans. T. Gibson and A. Uhlmann, in *Deleuze: A Critical Reader*, ed. P. Patton. Oxford: Blackwell Publishers, pp. 107–13.

Nancy, J.-L. (2000), 'The Technique of the Present', trans. A Hartz. *Tympanum* 4. http://www.usc.edu/dept/comp-lit/tympanum/4/nancy.html

Nancy, J.-L. (2005), *The Ground of the Image*, trans. J. Fort. New York: Fordham University Press.

Nancy, J.-L. (2006), *Multiple Arts: The Muses II*, trans. L. Hill et al. Stanford: Stanford University Press.

Rancière, J. (1998), 'Existe-t-il une esthétique deleuzienne?', in *Gilles Deleuze: une vie philosophique*, ed. E. Alliez. Le Plessis-Robinson: Institut Synthélabo pour le progrès de la connaissance, pp. 523–36.

Rancière, J. (2000a), 'Literature, Politics, Aesthetics: Approaches to Democratic

Disagreement. Interview with Solange Guénoun and James H Kavanagh', trans. Roxanne Lapidu, *SubStance* 92, pp. 3–24.

Rancière, J. (2000b), 'What Aesthetics can Mean', trans. Brian Holmes, in *From An Aesthetic Point of View: Philosophy, Art and the Senses*, ed. P. Osborne. London: Serpentine Books, pp. 13–33.

Rancière, J. (2002), 'Deleuze accomplit le destin de l'esthétique', *Magazine Littéraire. Dossier: L'effet Deleuze*, 406, pp. 38–40.

Rancière, J. (2003a), 'Politics and Aesthetics: An interview', trans F. Morlock, *Angelaki* 8 (2), pp. 194–211.

Rancière, J. (2003b), 'The Thinking of Dissensus: Politics and Aesthetics', Goldsmiths College, London. http://homepages.gold.ac.uk/psrpsq/ranciere.doc

Rancière, J. (2004a), *The Politics of Aesthetics: The Distribution of the Sensible*, trans. G. Rockhill. London: Continuum.

Rancière, J. (2004b), 'Aesthetics, Inaesthetics, Anti-aesthetics', trans. R. Brassier. in *Think Again: Alain Badiou and the Future of Philosophy*, ed. P. Hallward. London: Continuum, pp. 218–31.

Rancière, J. (2005), 'From Politics to Aesthetics?', *Paragraph* 28 (1), pp. 13–25.

Rancière, J. (2007a), *The Future of the Image*, trans. G. Elliott. London: Verso.

Rancière, J. (2007b), 'Art of the Possible: In Conversation with Fulvia Carnevale and John Kelsey', *Artforum* XLV (7), pp. 256–59.

Chapter 14

Acampora, R. (2004), 'The Joyful Wisdom of Ecology', *New Nietzsche Studies* 5 (3&4) and 6 (1&2).

Ayerza, J. (ed.) (2008), *Lacan Ink* essay collection, www.lacan.com

Badiou, A. (2003), *Infinite Thought*. London: Continuum.

Badiou, A. (2005), *Handbook of Inaesthetics*, trans. A. Toscano. Stanford: Stanford University Press.

Badiou, A. (2008), *Logics of Worlds: Being and Event II*, trans. A. Toscano. London: Continuum.

Barry, P. (2002), *Beginning Theory: An Introduction to Literary and Cultural Theory*. Second edition. Manchester: Manchester University Press.

Bate, J. (2000), *The Song of the Earth*. London: Picador.

Baudrillard, J. (1994), *Simulacra and Simulation*, trans. S. Glasser. University of Michigan Press.

Bennett, M. (2003), 'From Wide Open Space to Metropolitan Places: the Urban Challenge to Ecocritcism' in *The ISLE Reader: Ecocritcism 1993–2003*, ed. M. P. Branch and S. Slovic. Athens: University of Georgia Press.

Bramwell, A. (1985), *Blood and Soil: Walther Darré and Hitler's Green Party*. Bourne End: Kensal.

Buell, L. (2005), *The Future of Environmental Criticism: Environmental Crisis and Literary Imagination*. Malden, MA: Blackwell.

Burnham, D. (2004), *Kant's Philosophies of Judgement*. Edinburgh: Edinburgh University Press.

Burnham, D. and Jesinghausen, M. (2009), *Nietzsche's Birth of Tragedy*. London: Continuum.

Cataldi, S. L. and Hamrick, W. S. (eds.) (2007), *Merleau-Ponty and Environmental Philosophy*. Albany: SUNY Press.

Coffey, D. (2007), 'Blood and Soil in Anne Michaels's *Fugitive Pieces*: the Pastoral in Holocaust Literature', *Modern Fiction Studies* 53 (1), pp. 27–49.

Coope, J. (2008), 'The Ecological Blind Spot in Postmodernism', *New Formations* 64 (*Special Edition: Earthographies: Ecocritcism and Culture*), pp. 78–89.

Coupe, L. (2000), *The Green Studies Reader*. London: Routledge.

Del Caro, A. (2004), *Grounding the Nietzsche Rhetoric on Earth*. Berlin: De Gruyter.

Drenthen, M. (2005), 'Wilderness as a Critical Border Concept', *Environmental Values* 14.

Dunkerley, H. and Wheeler, W. (2008), 'Introduction' to *New Formations* 64 (*Special Edition: Earthographies: Ecocritcism and Culture*), pp. 7–14.

Faulkner, W. (1973), *Go Down, Moses*. New York: Vintage Books.

Foltz, B. V. and Frodeman, R. (eds.) (2004), *Rethinking Nature: Essays in Environmental Philosophy*. Bloomington: Indiana University Press.

Fox, W. (1984), 'Deep Ecology: a New Philosophy of our Time?' *The Ecologist* 14 (5–6).

Gadamer, H.-G. (1992a), *Education, Poetry and History: Applied Hermeneutic* ed. D. Misgeld and G. Nicholson, trans. L. Schmidt and M. Reuss. Alban SUNY Press.

Gadamer, H.-G. (1992b), *The Enigma of Health*, trans. J. Gaiger and N. Wall Cambridge: Polity.

Gadamer, H.-G. (2004), *Truth and Method*, trans. J. Weinsheimer and D Marshall. London: Continuum.

Garrard, G. (2004), *Ecocritcism*. London: Routledge.

Gifford, T. (2008), 'Recent Critiques of Ecocriticism' *New Formations* 64 (*S Edition: Earthographies: Ecocritcism and Culture*), pp. 15–24.

Hallman, M. (1991), 'Nietzsche's Environmental Ethics', *Environmental* 13.

Jameson, F. (1991), *Postmodernism, or the Cultural Logic of Late Capitalism.*] Verso.

Kant, I. (1987), *Critique of Judgment*, trans. W. Pluhar. Indianapolis: Hacke

Kant, I. (1995), *Opus Postumum*, trans. E. Förster and M. Rosen, ed. F Cambridge: Cambridge University Press.

Knapp, J. A. and Pence, J. (eds.) (2003), *Poetics Today* 24 (4), specia *Gadamer and the Mechanics of Culture*.

Lacoue-Labarthe, P. and Nancy, J.-L. (1988), *The Literary Absolute*, trans and C. Lester. Albany: SUNY Press.

McGregor, J. (2002), *If Nobody Speaks of Remarkable Things*. London: Blc

Nietzsche, F. (1998), *On the Genealogy of Morality: A Polemic*, trans.] A. Swensen. Indianapolis: Hackett.

Nietzsche, F. (1999), *The Birth of Tragedy and Other Writings*, tra ed. R. Geuss and R. Speirs. Cambridge: Cambridge University Pr

Nietzsche, F. (2001), *Beyond Good and Evil: Prelude to a Philosophy of tl* J. Norman, ed. R.-P. Horstmann and J. Norman. Cambrid University Press.

Parkes, G. (2005), 'Nietzsche's Environmental Philosophy: a Perspective', *Environmental Ethics* 27.

Reinhart, M. (2004), 'Ecological Nietzsche? The Will to Power and the Love of Things', *New Nietzsche Studies* 5 (3&4), 6 (1&2).

Ricoeur, P. (1981), *The Rule of Metaphor*, trans. R. Czerny. London: Routledge.

Ricoeur, P. (1992), *Oneself as Another*, trans. K. Blamey. Chicago: University of Chicago Press.

Smith, P. (2005), *Becoming Nietzsche: Early Reflections on Democritus, Schopenhauer and Kant*. Lexington Books.

Toadvine, T. and Brown, C. S. (eds.) (2003), *Eco-Phenomenology: Back to the Earth Itself*. Albany: SUNY Press.

Vattimo, G. (1997), *Beyond Interpretation: The Meaning of Hermeneutics for Philosophy*, trans. D. Webb. Stanford: Stanford University Press.

Zimmerman, M. (2005), 'Nietzsche and Ecology' in *Reading Nietzsche at the Margins*, ed. S. V. Hicks and A. Rosenberg. Albany: SUNY Press.

Chapter 15

Alliez, E. (1995), *De l'impossibilité de Phenomenologie*. Paris: Vrin.

Althusser, L. (2006), *Philosophy of the Encounter. Later Writings, 1978–1987*, ed. F. Matheron and O. Corpet, trans. G. M. Goshgarian. London: Verso.

Badiou, A. (1994), 'Being by Numbers', *Artforum*, 33 (2), http://www.find articles.com/p/articles/mi_m0268/is_n2_v33/ai_16315394

Badiou, A. (2004), *Theoretical Writings*, ed. and trans. R. Brassier and A. Toscano. London: Continuum.

Barbaras, R. (1998), *Le tournant de l'experience: recherches sur la philosophie de Merleau-Ponty*. Paris: Vrin.

Bradley, F. H. (1993), *The Presuppositions of Critical History and Aphorisms*. London: Thoemmes Press.

Critchley, S. (2001), *Continental Philosophy: A Very Short Introduction*. Oxford: Oxford University Press.

Deleuze, G. (1994), *Difference and Repetition*, trans. P. Patton. London: Athlone.

Derrida, J. (1982), 'Signature, Event, Context', in *Margins of Philosophy*, trans. A. Bass. Chicago: University of Chicago Press, pp. 307–30.

Gendinning, S. (2006), *The Idea of Continental Philosophy: A Philosophical Chronicle*. Edinburgh: Edinburgh University Press.

Heidegger, M. (1968), *What is Called Thinking?*, trans. J. G. Gray and F. Wieck. New York: Harper and Row.

Henry, M. (2003), *I am the Truth: Toward a Philosophy of Christianity*, trans. Emanuel. Stanford: Stanford University Press.

Janicaud, D. (ed.) (2000), *Phenomenology and the 'Theological Turn': The French Debate*, trans. B. G. Prusak. New York: Fordham University Press.

Kaprow, A. (2003), *Essays on the Blurring of Art and Life*. California: University of California Press.

Laruelle, F. (1996), *Principes de la Non-Philosophie*. Paris: Presses Universitaires de France.

Lawlor, L. (1999), 'The End of Ontology: Interrogation in Merleau-Ponty and Deleuze', *Chiasmi International*, 1, pp. 233–51.

Meillassoux, Q. (2008), *After Finitude: an Essay on the Necessity of Contingency*, trans. Brassier. London: Continuum.

Merleau-Ponty, M. (1964), 'The Primacy of Perception and its Philosophical Consequences', trans. J. M. Edie, in *Primacy of Perception*. Evanston: Northwestern University Press, pp. 12–42.

Mullarkey, J. (2006), *Post-Continental Philosophy: An Outline*. London: Continuum.

Mullarkey, J. (2009), *Refractions of Reality: Philosophy of the Moving Image*. Basingstoke: Palgrave-Macmillan.

Prusak, B. (2000), 'Translator's Introduction', in *Phenomenology and the 'Theological Turn': The French Debate*, ed. D. Janicaud, trans. B. G. Prusak. New York: Fordham University Press.

Reichenbach, H. (1951), *The Rise of Scientific Philosophy*. Berkeley: University of California Press.

Rockmore, T. (1995), *Heidegger and French Philosophy: Humanism, Antihumanism, and Being*. London: Routledge.

Schrift A. D. (2006), *Twentieth-Century French Philosophy: Key Themes and Thinkers*. Oxford: Blackwell.

Strawson, G. (2008), *Real Materialism and Other Essays*. Oxford: Oxford University Press.

Index